INTERNATIONAL CORPORATE FINANCE

INTERNATIONAL CORPORATE FINANCE

Mark Eaker   Frank Fabozzi   Dwight Grant

The Dryden Press
Harcourt Brace College Publishers

Fort Worth   Philadelphia   San Diego   New York   Orlando   Austin   San Antonio
Toronto   Montreal   London   Sydney   Tokyo

Executive Editor	Mike Reynolds
Associate Editor	Shana Lum
Project Editor	Matt Ball
Art Director	Lora Knox
Production Manager	Ann Coburn
Product Manager	Craig Johnson
Art & Literary Rights Editor	Adele Krause

Copy Editor	JaNoel Lowe
Proofreader	Dee Salisbury
Indexer	Leoni McVey
Composition	ETP/Harrison
Text Type	10/12 Palatino
Cover objet d'art	Lora Knox

Requests for permission to make copies of any part of the work should be mailed to: Permissions Department, Harcourt Brace & Company, 6277 Sea Harbor Drive, Orlando, FL 32887-6777.

Address for Orders
The Dryden Press
6277 Sea Harbor Drive
Orlando, FL 32887
1-800-782-4479 or 1-800-433-0001 (in Florida)

Address for Editorial Correspondence
The Dryden Press
301 Commerce Street, Suite 3700
Fort Worth, TX 76102

ISBN: 0-03-069306-3

Library of Congress Catalog Card Number: 95-70062

Printed in the United States of America

5 6 7 8 9 0 1 2 3 4   016   9 8 7 6 5 4 3 2 1

The Dryden Press
Harcourt Brace College Publishers

To Lynn Eaker, Alfonso Fabozzi, and Mary Yoder.

THE DRYDEN PRESS SERIES IN FINANCE

Amling and Droms
Investment Fundamentals

Berry and Young
Managing Investments: A Case Approach

Bertisch
Personal Finance

Brigham
Fundamentals of Financial Management
Seventh Edition

Brigham, Aberwald, and Gapenski
Finance with Lotus 1-2-3
Second Edition

Brigham and Gapenski
Cases in Financial Management: Dryden Request

Brigham and Gapenski
Cases in Financial Management: Module A

Brigham and Gapenski
Cases in Financial Management: Module C

Brigham and Gapenski
Financial Management: Theory and Practice
Seventh Edition

Brigham and Gapenski
Intermediate Financial Management
Fifth Edition

Brigham and Houston
Fundamentals of Financial Management: The Concise Edition

Chance
An Introduction to Derivatives
Third Edition

Clark, Gerlach, and Olson
Restructuring Corporate America

Cooley
Advances in Business Financial Management: A Collection of Readings
Second Edition

Cooley
Business Financial Management
Third Edition

Dickerson, Campsey, and Brigham
Introduction to Financial Management
Fourth Edition

Eaker, Fabozzi, and Grant
International Corporate Finance

Evans
International Finance: A Markets Approach

Fama and Miller
The Theory of Finance

Gardner and Mills
Managing Financial Institutions: An Asset/Liability Approach
Third Edition

Gitman and Joehnk
Personal Financial Planning
Seventh Edition

Greenbaum and Thakor
Contemporary Financial Intermediation

Harrington and Eades
Case Studies in Financial Decision Making
Third Edition

Hayes and Meerschwam
Financial Institutions: Contemporary Cases in the Financial Services Industry

Hearth and Zaima
Contemporary Investments: Security and Portfolio Analysis

Johnson
Issues and Readings in Managerial Finance
Fourth Edition

Kidwell, Peterson, Blackwell
Financial Institutions, Money, and Markets
Fifth Edition

Koch
Bank Management
Third Edition

Leahigh
Pocket Guide to Finance

Maisel
Real Estate Finance
Second Edition

Martin, Cox, and MacMinn
The Theory of Finance: Evidence and Applications

Mayes and Shank
Financial Analysis with Lotus for Windows

Mayes and Shank
Financial Analysis with Microsoft Excel

Mayo
Financial Institutions, Investments, and Management: An Introduction
Fifth Edition

Mayo
Investments: An Introduction
Fourth Edition

Pettijohn
PROFIT+

Reilly
Investment Analysis and Portfolio Management
Fourth Edition
Reilly and Norton
Investments
Fourth Edition

Sears and Trennepohl
Investment Management

Seitz and Ellison
Capital Budgeting and Long-Term Financing Decisions
Second Edition

Siegel and Siegel
Futures Markets

Smith and Spudeck
Interest Rates: Principles and Applications

Stickney
Financial Reporting and Statement Analysis: A Strategic Perspective
Third Edition

Weston, Besley, and Brigham
Essentials of Managerial Finance
Eleventh Edition

THE HB COLLEGE OUTLINE SERIES

Baker
Financial Management

PREFACE

There is no doubt that the business world is now international. Advances in information exchange have created one global economy, accessible to all investors, both personal and corporate. This exponentially increases the number and complexity of financial decisions managers must make to be successful.

We wrote *International Corporate Finance* because we felt that students needed a textbook that presents financial concepts in a decision-making framework. The result is a unique approach that combines both cases and traditional text chapters. The cases are provided not as an additional feature of the book, but as a crucial part of the learning and application process of international finance concepts.

INTEGRATING THE CASE APPROACH

Although there are different ways to achieve applied knowledge of a subject, we believe that the use of case studies is the most effective. We have written this book around a series of real-life, current, and decision-oriented cases.

Using the cases as the focus of either class discussions or written assignments puts the student at the center of the learning process. The cases deal with an event or decision that challenges the student to develop a thorough understanding of the situation and to propose a solution. Each case provides the institutional background and data necessary to analyze a variety of alternatives and to determine the trade-offs represented by choosing among them.

However, this is not just a case book. The text chapters are fully developed and contain extensive problems and end-of-chapter material that can be used separately from the cases. The chapters and problems also emphasize analysis, so the chapters contain many examples and are rich sources of data.

This textbook is organized to allow for a great deal of flexibility in how it can be used. The book is for both undergraduate- and graduate-level courses, full semester and quarter courses, courses with a heavy case component, and courses where cases are used as supplements. Instructors of undergraduate courses will probably rely heavily on the problem sets and not assign all of the cases. That approach gives more structure to the student. The actual choice of a course design also depends on how much casework students have had in their curriculum. The more experience students have with cases, the more the instructor should rely on cases for this course.

For full semester graduate courses that meet 30 times over 15 weeks, the entire book has a natural fit. We suggest, as a basic model, assigning a chapter for the first session of the week and then using the related case for the second class. Some instructors will want to spend more time on some chapters and less on others. The basic model utilizes essentially all the material in the book. For shorter courses and for undergraduate courses where the cases might be used more as supplements, the instructor needs to choose which cases to include. We have experimented with a variety of combinations and offer the following graduate and undergraduate schedules as possible choices.

Session	Graduate Twenty Sessions (all cases)	Session	Undergraduate Fifteen Sessions (text and cases)
1	ABB Asea Brown Boveri (A): The Merger	1	Chapters 1 and 2
2	Mexico—1982	2	Mexico—1982
3	Dollar Disequilibrium in 1990	3	Chapter 3, Dollar Disequilibrium in 1990
4	The Mexican Peso: 1995	4	Chapter 4
5	Dozier Industries (A) and (B)	5	Chapter 5
6	Video Systems, Inc.	6	Dozier Industries (A) and (B)
7	Dow Europe	7	Chapter 6, Video Systems, Inc.
8	Western Mining	8	Chapter 7
9	International Paper: The Aussedat-Rey Acquisition	9	Western Mining
10	First Wachovia Corporation	10	Chapter 8
11	Grand Metropolitan PLC	11	International Paper: The Aussedat-Rey Acquisition
12-13	Olin Corporation	12	Chapter 9
14	A.P.S., S.A.	13	Olin Corporation
15	The Procter & Gamble Company: Mexico 1991	14	Chapter 10, The Procter & Gamble Company: Mexico 1991
16	Rodale Press in the Commonwealth of Independent States	15	Chapter 12, British Telecommunications, PLC
17	British Telecommunications, PLC		
18	The Travelers Corporation		
19	Japanese Yen Short-Term Note		
20	Sallie Mae Reverse Yen Perls Issue		

ORGANIZATION

We organized this book into four major parts, beginning with a macro view of the international environment and then focusing on exchange issues, international investing, and finally fund raising in global financial markets. All these topics are interrelated; consequently, our organization is flexible for any course structure.

As we discussed earlier, the main and distinguishing pedagogical element of this book are the cases. In addition, we feel strongly that learning about international corporate finance means understanding what types of decisions have to be made and how to make them. Each chapter concludes with "Implications for Managers," which is a refocusing of the chapter from a corporate manager's perspective. This discussion highlights the key concepts and explains how managers will apply them to decision making in the international arena.

Each chapter begins with a listing of the key elements and ends with questions and problems for the student to apply information from the chapter and test their understanding of the material. The questions and problems can be assigned as out-of-class preparation if the instructors choose to use the cases for class discussion.

The *Instructor's Manual* contains teaching notes to the cases, suggestions for integrating the cases with the chapter material, and solutions to all the questions and problems. The Dryden Press will provide complimentary supplements or supplement packages to those adopters qualified under our adoption policy. Please contact your sales representative to learn how you may qualify. If as an adopter or potential user you receive supplements you do not need, please return them to your sales representative or send them to:

Attn: Returns Department
Troy Warehouse
465 South Lincoln Drive
Troy, MO 63379

Most of the cases were written for this book and tested in class, but some cases were written by others who graciously allowed us to include them. The following people were either authors, co-authors, or research assistants of the cases, and we want to acknowledge their contributions.

Cases	Contributors
ABB Asea Brown Boveri (A): The Merger	Andrew Boynton, Eran Gartner
Mexico—1982	John Simms
Video Systems, Inc.	Robert Carraway
Dow Europe	John Pringle
Western Mining	Peter J. Maloney
International Paper: The Aussedat-Rey Acquisition	Robert Harris, Mark Mead
First Wachovia Corporation	Laura Connelly

Grand Metropolitan PLC

Robert Bruner, Philippe Demigne, Jean-Christophe Donck, Bertrand George, Michael Levy

A.P.S., S.A.

Ned Case

Procter & Gamble Company: Mexico 1991

Ken Eades, Peter Williams

Rodale Press in the Commonwealth of Independent States

Virginia Syers, Bonnie Matosich

British Telecommunications, PLC

Scott Mason, Sally Durdan

The Travelers Corporation

Leslie Schorr

Sallie Mae Reverse Yen Perls Issue

Troy Muniz

Others who have provided assistance on material in the book include Faith Rubenstein, George Collins, and Marie Payne. Debbie Quarles of the Darden School has been a pillar of strength and paragon of organization in helping prepare and assemble the manuscript.

Throughout the development of *International Corporate Finance,* many instructors have unselfishly given of their time and expertise to provide us with feedback on various drafts of the chapters. Their suggestions and comments were invaluable and we are grateful for their involvement with the book:

Fidelis S.E. Akagha, Johnson C. Smith University
George Anayiotos, University of Colorado at Boulder
Harvey Arbelaez, Pennsylvania State University—Harrisburg
Mohsen Bahmani-Oskooee, University of Wisconsin—Milwaukee
Hendrik van den Berg, University of Nebraska at Lincoln
Bharat Bhall, Fairfield University
Paul M. Bishop, University of Western Ontario
C. Callahan, Lehigh University
Pat Cantrell, University of Central Arkansas
Denis Carter, University of North Carolina at Wilmington
Charles R. Chittle, Bowling Green State University
Michael Claudon, Middlebury College
Joe B. Copeland, University of North Alabama
Andrea L. DeMaskey, University of Nevada—Reno
Charles N. Dennis, University of Southern Mississippi
Thomas F. Dernburg, American University
Asim Erdilek, Case Western Reserve University
Don Fleming, Central State University
Garry Fleming, Roanoke College
Bruce A. Forster, University of Wyoming
Fred R. Glahe, University of Colorado
Robert I. Goldberg, St. Francis College
Steven A. Greenlaw, Mary Washington College
Deborah W. Gregory, The University of Georgia
Thomas Grennes, North Carolina State University
Harrish C. Gupta, University of Nebraska
A.R. Gutowsky, California State University—Sacramento
Catherine A. Hofmann, University of Idaho
Jane Hughes, Brandeis University
Keith A. Johnson, University of Kentucky
Steven A. Johnson, The University of Texas at El Paso
Paul Kadjo, Millersville University of Pennsylvania

Rob Kamery, Christian Brother University
Hugo M. Kaufmann, Queens College
Michael Klein, Tufts University
G. Lamson, Carleton College
Judy McDonald, SUNY—Binghamton
Clair N. McRostie, Gustavus Adolphus College
David Martin, Bloomsburg University
F. John Mathis, Thunderbird American Graduate School of International Management
Ike Mathur, Southern Illinois University at Carbondale
Andreas G. Merikas, Mississippi State University
David Mira, Loyola University of Chicago
Shahruz Mohtadi, Suffolk University
Robert G. Murphy, Boston College
Michael R. Myler, Mount Union College
Donald A. Nast, Florida State University
Daniel E. Nolle, Middlebury College
A. Okokon, University of Wisconsin—River Falls
Heather O'Neill, Ursinus College
E. Phillips, Moorhead State University
Marlene Puffer, University of Toronto
Matiur Rahman, McNeese State University
J. Rinehart, Francis Marion College
Tom Rose
Don Schilling, University of Missouri at Columbia
John C. Shannon, Suffolk University
Michael Solt, San Jose State University
Deb Stevens, James Madison University
Roger C. Van Tassel, Clark University
David Townsend, Sam Houston State University
Emery Trahan, Northeastern University
R. Vaitheswaran, Coe College
Lori Warner, University of the Pacific
Alexander Zampieron, Bentley College
Allan H. Zeman, Robert Morris College

We encourage all instructors and students who examine *International Corporate Finance* to contact us or The Dryden Press with any comments for improving this book. We hope that your future explorations into the world of international finance are both interesting and rewarding.

Mark Eaker
Frank J. Fabozzi
Dwight Grant

September 1995

ABOUT THE AUTHORS

Mark R. Eaker is a professor of business administration at the Darden Graduate School of Business at the University of Virginia. Professor Eaker has published widely on topics related to foreign exchange, futures markets, and international portfolio diversification. He is also the co-author (with Jess Yawitz) of the textbook, *Macroeconomics*. Professor Eaker has an M.B.A., A.M., and Ph.D. from Stanford University. Prior to joining the faculty at Darden, he taught at Stanford, Duke, SMU, and the University of North Carolina. In 1991 he co-founded Sire Management Corporation, an investment management firm that has offices in New York City.

Frank Fabozzi is an adjunct professor of finance at Yale University's School of Management and editor of the *Journal of Portfolio Management*. From 1986 to 1992, he was a visiting professor of finance at MIT's Sloan School of Management. He is on the board of directors of the BlackRock complex of funds and the Guardian Life family of funds. He earned a doctorate in economics from the City University of New York in 1972 and in 1994 received an honorary doctorate of Humane Letters from Nova Southeastern University. He has written several textbooks in finance.

Dwight Grant is the Douglas M. Brown Professor of Finance at the University of New Mexico. He holds a B.A. in Economics from the University of Western Ontario, and an M.B.A. and Ph.D. from the Wharton School at the University of Pennsylvania. His recent research focuses on international investment and risk management.

CONTENTS

PART

THE INTERNATIONAL ECONOMIC FRAMEWORK

INTERNATIONAL FINANCE AND THE INTERNATIONAL CHALLENGE

1 CHAPTER

BALANCE OF PAYMENTS: A NATION'S INTERNATIONAL PROFILE

2 CHAPTER

INTERNATIONAL FINANCE AND THE INTERNATIONAL CHALLENGE

1

CHAPTER

KEY CONCEPTS

THE IMPORTANCE OF EXCHANGE RATE FLUCTUATIONS ▬

THE TYPES OF RISK INHERENT IN INTERNATIONAL FINANCE ▬

THE APPROACH TO LEARNING USED IN THIS BOOK ▬

INTRODUCTION

During the last 20 years, the jobs of the treasurer and senior financial officers of international corporations and banks have become increasingly challenging. Although many factors have contributed to the increasing complexity facing the corporate manager, one event stands out as being particularly significant.

That event was a decision made at the highest levels of the governments of the leading industrial countries. In 1973, in what has become known as the Smithsonian Agreement, the decision was made to abandon the fixed exchange rate system *established at Bretton Woods, New Hampshire, in 1944 and to allow currencies to float or fluctuate in value. The immediate consequence of that action was that managers could no longer make decisions about international business with the reasonable expectation that the value of the francs, dollars, or yen that they would receive or deliver when the transaction was complete would be the same as when they made the decision to enter into the transactions.* Exchange rate risk, *the uncertainty related to doing business in a currency other than one's own, increased dramatically. With fixed exchange rates, exchange risk was present but could safely be ignored except during infrequent crisis situations. Following the 1973 decision, it became a continual fact of business life requiring attention on a daily basis.*

A less immediate consequence of the Smithsonian Agreement was the increasing liberalization and deregulation of the international capital markets. Economic policy makers, freed from the constraint of maintaining fixed exchange rates, began a process of

*opening their borders to foreign competition and to the freer flow of capital. This liberal-
ization process set into motion an era of financial innovation that has continued to this day.
Included among the changes have been an increase in cross-border mergers, rapid growth
of international financial services, and a literal explosion of new financial products, many
of which are designed to help the international financial manager cope with the added
exchange risk related to floating rates.*

*The business opportunities and the new financial products that confront today's inter-
national manager are often very complex. The successful manager needs to be aware of what
financial products are available and how she can best utilize them to reduce the risk or enhance the returns to her firm. Understanding the risk and valuing the products requires a
combination of financial technique, institutional knowledge of capital markets, and economic analysis. In the broadest sense, those areas define the topic coverage of this book.*

*In the next section we extend our discussion of exchange rate risk and consider two other
important international sources of risk, economic risk and political risk.*

INTERNATIONAL RISK

EXCHANGE RATE RISK

It is one thing to state that exchange rate risk has increased, but how can we measure that increase and its impact on managers? One way to begin is to look at
macroeconomic measures of international activity and patterns of exchange rate
movements. They do not directly demonstrate the impact on individual firms, but
they do begin to indicate the dimension of exchange-related transactions and the
potential exposure to exchange rate fluctuation.

As firms expand their international activities, they begin to acquire assets outside their home countries. These assets might be financial assets, such as cash balances and receivables, or real property, such as land or manufacturing facilities. At
the end of 1993, U.S. *foreign direct investment* (FDI) was approximately $549 billion
on an historic cost basis.[1] FDI includes investments in businesses and other forms
of physical capital such as real estate. Figure 1.1 shows the geographic distribution
of those investments. It is part of the responsibility of the international treasurer or
financial manager to manage those investments and to reduce the impact of exchange risk on the parent firm's financial status.

To see what the potential effect on U.S. firms might be, take the case of their investment in Japan. By the end of 1993, U.S. firms' total foreign direct investment
was $499 billion, and 6 percent, or approximately $31 billion, of that was in Japan.
A 10 percent change in the value of the yen would lead to a $3.1 billion change in
the value of those investments. Changes of that magnitude have a significant impact on the financial performance of the firms holding the investments. Chapters
5, 6, and 7 discuss how to manage and account for that impact. *

---

[1] Sylvia E. Bargas and Jeffery H. Lowe, "Direct Investment Positions on a Historical-Cost Basis, 1993:
Country and Industry Detail," Department of Commerce *Survey of Current Business* (June 1994), p. 77.
The estimated market value of this investment is $993 billion. We note for comparison that foreign di-
rect investment in the United States at the end of 1993 was $445 billion on an historic cost basis and
$746 billion on a market value basis.

**1993 TOTAL U.S. FOREIGN DIRECT INVESTMENT AT
HISTORICAL COST $499 BILLION**

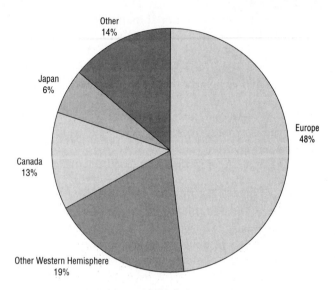

Other
14%

Japan
6%

Canada
13%

Europe
48%

Other Western Hemisphere
19%

SOURCE: Department of Commerce, *Survey of Current Business* (June 1994), p. 77.

We should point out that when we define specific measures of exchange risk exposure in subsequent chapters, we show that all of a company's overseas investment is not directly at risk. On the other hand, there are other risk exposures. When
a company invoices a transaction in a currency other than its own (in any trade
transaction that is true for at least one party), borrows funds in another currency,
or invests part of its capital in overseas equity or bond markets, it creates exposure.
Moreover, the size of those activities actually dwarfs the amount of foreign direct
investment. Total worldwide exports in 1991 exceeded $6 trillion and more than
$2 trillion of bonds and equities were held by investors outside of their own
countries.

These numbers are huge but as impressive as they are, they might obscure the
risk faced by individual firms. To bring home the point that firms experience significant risk, Table 1.1 lists the exchange rate losses of a number of institutions
around the world. It is a short list when in fact just about every *multinational corporation* (MNC) experiences some exchange gain or loss during every accounting
period. The list does include two enormous losses, those of Kashima Oil and Bank
Negara, which seem unbelievably large. Yet they occurred. Losses of that magnitude reflect a serious breach of responsibility and a breakdown in controls. However, the losses experienced by Abbott Laboratories and Quaker Oats are fairly
typical of those incurred by large multinationals in the course of their normal business activities and although undesirable, do not pose a threat to the solvency of
those firms.

A final point about Table 1.1 is that it displays only losses. Exchange rate fluctuations just as often lead to gains and another list could have easily been compiled with positive results. At this stage our concern is not with understanding the detail of how losses and gains are incurred but to demonstrate their importance as one of the challenges facing international managers.

A good question to ask now is whether a 10 percent change in the value of a currency is a frequent event or an unusual one. Before the Smithsonian Agreement, it was unusual. Since the agreement, changes of that magnitude have occurred frequently, often not over a period of a year but instead during a month or even a week. It is not unusual at all for the dollar value of the yen or German mark to change by 1 percent in a day. That would lead to an overnight gain or loss of $320 million on the Japanese investments alone, an amount that should demand a great deal of managerial attention.

Another way to appreciate the volatility of exchange rates is to examine a *trade-weighted index of exchange rates* over time. A trade-weighted exchange rate is a weighted average of a country's currency relative to that of each major trading partner; as such, it is not the exchange rate at which currencies are bought and sold but an overall measure of a currency's value. Because most companies do business in many countries and have multiple currency exposures, movement over time in the trade-weighted exchange rate is a good reflection of the net exposure or risk a company has faced.

Figures 1.2 and 1.3 trace the trade-weighted index for the United States dollar, British pound, Japanese yen, German mark, and French franc for the period since the Smithsonian Agreement. The figures illustrate two important points. First, currencies tend to have periods of weak or strong performance. They decline in value or gain value for several consecutive years. Second, the cumulative change in value over a number of years can be very dramatic. The yen has almost tripled in value, and the mark increased by two-thirds while the franc and pound have lost

■ TABLE 1.1

REPORTED FOREIGN EXCHANGE LOSSES

Company	Home Country	Loss in U.S. Dollars
Kashima Oil	Japan	$1,500,000,000 [a]
Abbott Laboratories	U.S.	41,298,000 [a]
Reader's Digest	U.S.	2,200,000 [b]
Telefonos de Mexico	Mexico	218,000,000 [c]
Bank Negara	Malaysia	2,100,000,000 [a]
Allied-Lyons	U.K.	219,000,000 [d]
Viking Star	Bahamas	31,400,000 [a]
Quaker Oats	U.S.	19,000,000 [b]

[a] Fiscal year 1993.
[b] Three-quarters fiscal year 1994.
[c] First-quarter fiscal year 1994.
[d] Fiscal year 1991.

■ **FIGURE 1.2**

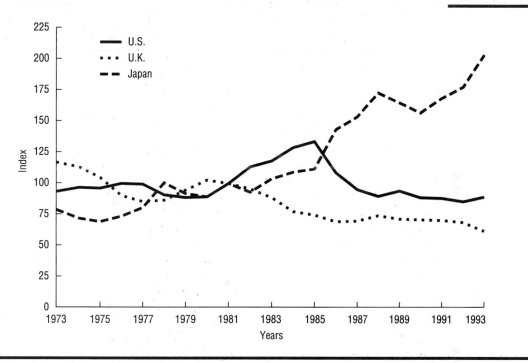

SOURCE: *International Financial Statistics*, various issues.

over one-third of their value. Financial managers must be prepared to deal with the problems and opportunities created by such substantial differences in the changes in values of the currencies of neighboring countries.

ECONOMIC RISK

Individual firms can restrict their activities to their home countries. If they choose to do so, we might think of them as subject to economic risks associated with the home country but immune to foreign economic risk. Such a view is incomplete. It is certainly true that a "strictly domestic firm" tends to prosper when the home economy performs well and tends to suffer when the home economy performs poorly. This is domestic economic risk. A domestic firm also does well or poorly, depending on its performance relative to its domestic rivals. Other factors, such as technological innovation in its industry, also influence its performance.

In many cases, the concept of a "strictly domestic firm" is an illusion. Many firms that appear to be strictly domestic confront foreign economic risk indirectly. They face foreign competitors or use foreign suppliers. Their domestic suppliers use

■ FIGURE 1.3

TRADE-WEIGHTED CURRENCY VALUES: 1981 = 100

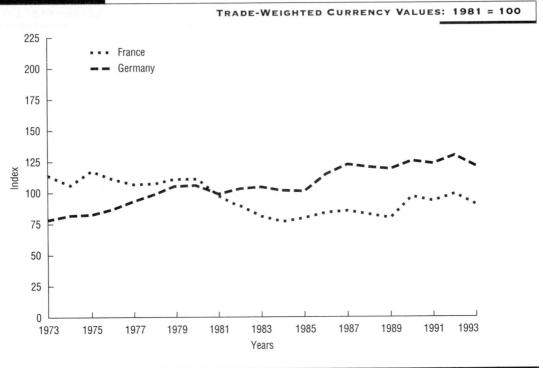

SOURCE: *International Financial Statistics,* various issues.

foreign suppliers or are subject to competition from foreign suppliers. A "strictly domestic firm" may have customers who work for foreign firms or for firms that compete against foreign firms. When the U.S. automobile companies performed poorly because of foreign competition, strictly local firms such as restaurants and food stores felt the effects of that competition. As this example illustrates, it is not an exaggeration to say that direct and indirect foreign economic risk is very common in our economy.

With increasing integration of the world economy, few firms are immune from the influence of foreign economic variations. Many firms have ambitiously embraced those risks and opportunities. For example, Table 1.2 lists the revenues, profits, and assets of five large U.S. MNCs that have accepted large foreign economic risks. Although we use the term *foreign economic risk,* a quick review of the data suggests that foreign economic opportunity is an equally accurate expression, especially for General Motors and Motorola. Clearly, General Motors earned a disproportionate share of its profit from its foreign sales. Foreign sales were 28 percent of the total sales, but foreign profits were 91 percent of the total profit. The same is true for Motorola, albeit to a lesser degree. Foreign sales were 44 percent of the total sales, but foreign profits were 85 percent of total profits. Both of these companies have enjoyed much more favorable results from their foreign opera-

■ TABLE 1.2

1993 REVENUES, PROFITS, AND ASSETS FOR FIVE U.S. COMPANIES

Company	Revenue			Profit			Assets		
	Foreign	Total	Foreign %	Foreign	Total	Foreign %	Foreign	Total	Foreign %
General Motors	$38,646	$138,220	28	$2,244	$2,466	91	$40,145	$188,034	21
Procter & Gamble	15,856	30,433	52	175	269	65	10,157	24,935	41
Hewlett Packard	10,671	20,317	53	675	1,177	57	7,508	16,736	45
Coca-Cola	9,351	13,957	67	1,484	2,188	68	5,844	12,021	49
Motorola	7,450	16,963	44	867	1,022	85	4,674	13,498	35

SOURCE: *Forbes*, July 18, 1994, pp. 276–277.

tions than from their U.S. operations. By contrast, Hewlett Packard and Coca-Cola experienced approximately proportionate foreign sales and profits. Whatever their individual experiences, all five of these companies have made substantial commitments to foreign investment and the profitability of that investment depends on the economic climate in the foreign countries in which they do business.

The phenomenon of MNCs is not restricted to U.S. based firms. Grand Metropolitan is a company based in the United Kingdom (U.K.). It owns 100 percent of Burger King, Pillsbury, and Perle Vision. Similarly, Bridgestone of Japan owns 100 percent of Bridgestone/Firestone, with U.S. sales of over $5 billion. Alcan Aluminum is a Canadian MNC with U.S. sales of $2.7 billion out of a total worldwide sales of $7.2 billion. To anyone unfamiliar with the extent of foreign investment in the United States the following list of foreign owned or controlled businesses is a surprise: Shell Oil, BP America, Citgo Petroleum, MCA, Giant Food Stores, Nestlé, Clorox, Fireman's Fund Insurance, and Hardee's Foods.

POLITICAL RISK ▬▬▬

Many types of political actions or events can influence the value of a firm's investment in a foreign country. These events can be catastrophic, for example, civil war such as that in the former Yugoslavia. These events can be quite subtle, for example restrictions on the acquisition of foreign exchange by all firms, caused by economic problems in the foreign country. Between these extremes are expropriation or nationalization of all firms in a specific industrial sector, or expropriation of all firms owned by foreigners. Each country in the world presents a different political profile and represents a unique source of political risk that firms must assess and manage when they make foreign investments. We discuss the nature of foreign political risk in more detail in Chapter 11. The case that accompanies that chapter relates the experience of a U.S. magazine publisher that introduces a magazine to the Commonwealth of Independent States (now Russia) and, in response to the imposed restrictions, ends up in the sausage business.

A FRAMEWORK FOR ANALYSIS AND LEARNING

Although this textbook is concerned with managerial issues, those issues must be examined in the context of the international economic environment. Accordingly, the first part of this book covers information similar to that in international economics courses. The coverage differs in two ways. First, it has a managerial orientation. The perspective is that of the treasurer of a large multinational corporation or a senior officer of an international bank. Little attempt is made to develop the nuances of the theoretical models or the historical evolution of the theory. The emphasis is on gaining insights into how economics can be applied to understanding government policies as they affect exchange rate movements, debt repayment, the performance of local firms, and other events of importance to managers.

Second, we give extensive treatment to many topics not covered at all in international economics courses. Those topics include exchange risk measurement and management, international aspects of capital budgeting, and trade financing. To allow time and space for managerial issues, the economics treatment is restricted to those tools and topics that most concern managers.

The presentation of material follows loosely the pattern of a firm's expanding international interests. The first step is an awareness and understanding of the world economy. It comes about as a firm begins to engage in export and import activities, either selling its own products or buying foreign inputs. Initial concern with international issues might also be motivated by the entrance of foreign competition into the firm's domestic market. Understanding the strategic consequences of foreign competition requires an appreciation of the economic factors, such as exchange rates and capital costs abroad, which affect the competing firm.

As importing and exporting activities expand, the firm requires more extensive knowledge of foreign exchange markets and exchange risk management. Moreover, the firm needs information about trade financing and import/export documentation. For the small firm, this stage often entails a reevaluation of banking relationships to determine whether they can handle the internationalization of the firm's activities.

Export activity leads many firms to make foreign investments as they establish service and distribution facilities to support foreign sales. Foreign investment opens a new range of concerns related to capital budgeting and management of working capital for foreign subsidiaries. If a firm's overseas investments expand to include production and/or sales outlets, the complexity of managerial problems increases and can involve raising capital abroad. Funding operations through foreign or international capital markets requires a knowledge of institutional arrangements as well as the economic underpinnings of those markets. The former leads to a discussion of Eurocurrencies, and the latter involves an application of the theory concerning interest rates and exchange rates.

The relationship between theory and practice is worth elaborating on because it represents the approach taken in this book. The focus here is on managerial decisions: What is the firm's exchange exposure? Should the exposure be altered? How can it be altered? Where should funds be raised? The major premise of the book is that managers' ability to make these decisions depends on a knowledge of economic and financial theory. The theory included here is restricted to that required for managerial concerns, but the important point remains that the theory introduced in the early chapters comes back in the later chapters when corporate financial topics are examined. This approach emphasizes the important lesson that theory, application, and institutional knowledge cannot be compartmentalized but are by necessity integrated.

Another way in which theory and practice are integrated and knowledge is built is through the use of case studies. Each chapter of text material is followed by one or two case studies. These case studies are not extended problem sets, nor are they fictitious. They utilize actual company information and market data, and most of them reveal the actual company. The cases describe decisions that managers have confronted.

The cases provide not only the data to analyze the problem and to develop a solution but also the context within which the manager made his or her decision. This is important because it adds to the institutional knowledge of the student, but, more critically, it emphasizes the point that business decisions are not just exercises in problem solving but complicated, often multifaceted, webs of issues that must be dealt with concurrently. When those issues are presented as a case study, it becomes essential for the student to put himself or herself in the shoes of the actual manager and confront all the ramifications of a decision.

IMPLICATIONS FOR MANAGERS

This chapter introduces the additional challenges facing managers who work in internationally oriented rather than purely domestic firms. A primary focus is the factors related to foreign exchange that create uncertainty in the valuation of foreign assets and cash flows. Managers must acquire the knowledge to evaluate that uncertainty and to determine methods to reduce it to acceptable levels. That knowledge requires an understanding of economic fundamentals and financial techniques. Subsequent chapters provide detail on the economic foundation of exchange rate determination and the methods available to measure and manage exchange risk, to value foreign investments, to assess economic and political risk in foreign countries, and to finance international activities. The text reinforces that information and those techniques through a series of case studies based on actual business situations.

QUESTIONS AND EXERCISES

1-1. What are three financial decisions affected by exchange rate fluctuations? What is a marketing, personnel, and manufacturing issue influenced by volatile exchange rates?

1-2. Coca-Cola and IBM are large U.S. firms. Do you believe that Coca-Cola is more or less international than IBM? Explain your answer.

1-3. What are five countries where relatively recent political events have affected the desirability of investing in those countries? Explain briefly the events and their effects of the desirability of investing in the countries.

1-4. Match the countries and their currencies. *The Wall Street Journal* is a convenient source of information because it provides price quotations on all of these currencies.

Australia	markka
Chile	escudo
Belgium	forint
China	renminbi
Ecuador	rupee
Finland	dollar
France	punt
Greece	shekel
Hungary	pound
India	guilder
Ireland	bolivar
Israel	dinar
Jordan	franc
Lebanon	dollar
Netherlands	baht
Peru	sucre
Portugal	peso
Taiwan	new sol
Thailand	franc
Venezuela	drachma

1-5. Listed below are 11 countries. The table below provides demographic and economic information on those 11 countries for 1991 but does not identify the countries by name. Try to match the countries with the data.

Brazil _____   France _____   Mexico _____   United Kingdom _____
Canada _____   India _____   Japan _____   United States _____
China _____   Italy _____   Korea _____

	A	B	C	D	E	F	G	H	I	J	K
Gross domestic product/per capita	$380	$20,320	$2,770	$20,510	$23,120	$6,790	$28,220	$310	$22,300	$3,470	$17,760
Consumer price index (1980 = 100)	213.3	187.8	659,535.0	266.9	165.3	201.4	126.3	262.3	189.9	18,470.0	199.7
Population density (per sq. km)	121.0	2.8	17.2	191.7	27.0	438.4	327.3	257.4	104.9	41.4	236.7
Birth rate (per 1000)	19.7	15.3	28.6	9.8	16.7	15.5	9.9	29.9	13.3	30.7	13.9
Unemployment rate	2.3%	10.3%	3.9%	11.0%	6.6%	2.3%	2.1%	—	9.3%	2.6%	8.1%
Wholesale prices (% change)	-2.6%	-1.0%	401.1%	6.4%	0.2%	5.4%	0.2%	13.9%	-1.3%	20.5%	5.6%
Current account balance (millions)	$13,765	-$25,529	-$3,788	-$21,451	-$92,123	-$2,172	$72,910	-$6,826	-$6,148	-$5,255	-$14,380
GDP (% change)	4.8%	-1.5%	-4.1%	1.6%	-0.7%	8.4%	4.5%	5.5%	1.3%	-3.6%	-2.1%
Investment (% GDP)	36.0%	20.4%	21.7%	20.3%	15.3%	39.1%	32.0%	24.0%	21.1%	18.5%	16.5%
Exports (% GDP)	18.5%	26.5%	8.5%	18.1%	10.7%	29.9%	10.2%	6.6%	23.0%	14.0%	23.3%
Illiteracy	0.3	0.0	0.2	0.0	0.0	0.0	0.0	0.5	0.0	0.1	0.0

continued on next page

	A	B	C	D	E	F	G	H	I	J	K
Female life expectancy	68.9	80.0	68.0	82.0	79.0	73.0	82.0	58.0	82.0	76.0	79.0
Infant mortality per 1,000 births	33	7	67	6	9	23	4	87	6	29	7

REFERENCES

Aliber, Robert Z., ed. *The Handbook of International Financial Management.* Homewood, Ill.: Dow Jones-Irwin, 1989.

Bargas, Sylvia E., and Jeffery H. Lowe. "Direct Investment Positions on a Historical-Cost Basis, 1993: Country and Industry Detail." Department of Commerce *Survey of Current Business,* June 1994, pp. 72–78.

Eaker, Mark R. "Teaching International Finance: An Economists Perspective." *Journal of Financial and Quantitative Analysis,* November 1977, pp. 607–608.

Folks, William. "Integrating International finance into a Unified Business Program." *Journal of Financial and Quantitative Analysis,* November, 1977, pp. 599–600.

Grabbe, Orlin. *International Financial Markets,* 2nd ed. New York: Elsevier Science Publishing, 1991.

Kolb, Robert W., ed. *The International Finance Reader,* 2nd ed. Miami: Kolb Publishing, 1993.

Levi, Maurice. *Financial Management and the International Economy.* New York: McGraw-Hill, 1983.

Shapiro, A. C. *Multinational Financial Management,* 3rd ed. Boston: Allyn and Bacon, 1989.

CASE 1.1

ABB ASEA BROWN BOVERI (A): THE MERGER

> I'm anxious to set an example. ABB will be a success story. We have no choice. There is no way back.[1]

While most families in Stockholm enjoyed the serenity of the Christmas season in December 1987, Percy Barnevik, age 46, prepared for his family's move to Zürich, where he would take charge of a new company to be born on January 5, 1988. The new company, ABB Asea Brown Boveri, was the result of a merger that Barnevik had engineered between Asea AB of Sweden, where he was chief executive officer, and BBC Brown Boveri Ltd. of Baden, Switzerland. The merged entity would constitute "the world's leading supplier in the $50 billion electric power industry, surpassing such household names as Westinghouse, General Electric, and Japan's Mitsubishi.... [ABB would control] as much as a third of Europe's business and more than 20 percent of the world market."[2]

The prospect of steering such a powerful entity into the 1990s was exciting for Barnevik. He intended ABB to join the elite club of successful cross-frontier mergers, including the Anglo-Dutch groups of Unilever (consumer products) and Shell (integrated oil). With the excitement, however, also came the responsibility for successful integration of 850 subsidiary companies and 180,000 employees operating in 140 countries. Barnevik believed that the popular phrase "think globally, act locally" would be his new corporate call to arms, and he relished the challenge of turning the slogan into profits.

BARNEVIK AT ASEA AB

Barnevik was born in 1941 in the western coastal town of Uddevalla, Sweden. He learned a disciplined work ethic that would guide his career as one of Sweden's most famous business leaders while working long hours in his father's printing shop.[3] He was educated in economics and computer science in Sweden and ultimately earned his MBA from the Gothenburg School of Economics. He later spent two years studying at Stanford University in California before entering Swedish industry with the specialty steelmaker Sandvik AB in 1969 as group controller.

Sandvik was one of several companies controlled by Swedish industrialist Peter Wallenberg and his family. Through a complicated web of leveraged cross-holdings, Wallenberg was thought to control an empire worth nearly 300 billion Swedish kronor (SKr) or U.S. $50 billion. After his position as group controller,

[1] Percy Barnevik, quoted in Jules Arbose, "ABB: The New Energy Powerhouse," *International Management*, June 1988, pp. 24–30.

[2] Jonathan Kapstein and Stanley Reed, "The Euro-Gospel According to Percy Barnevik," *Business Week*, July 23, 1990, pp. 64–66.

[3] Kapstein and Reed, "The Euro-Gospel," pp. 64–66.

Barnevik moved to run Sandvik's U.S. operations. Between 1975 and 1979, Barnevik rattled the underperforming North American subsidiary and tripled sales to $226 million. After his five years in the United States, Barnevik returned to Sweden as executive vice president of Sandvik AB.

Barnevik's decisive and determined style at Sandvik caught the attention of Asea's Chairman Curt Nicolin and Asea's largest shareholder—the Wallenbergs. In 1980, following success at Sandvik, Barnevik was asked to work a similar miracle at Asea AB, a sleepy industrial jewel of Sweden. Asea's business was broadly defined as "the generation and application of electric power." The company manufactured such diverse items as steam turbines for power plants and high-speed electric locomotives for passenger railroads.

In his first two years at Asea, Barnevik carved the amorphous company into rational divisions, each with clearly defined product and market responsibilities. Then he concentrated on focusing the company's resources on profitable lines of business in which the firm had some discernible technical or market advantages. At headquarters, Barnevik slashed staff from 2,500 to 100 in less than two years; he told those not retained to find a job in the operating companies or go home.

In a highly decentralized format, managers had direct accountability for annual budgets reported to headquarters and for complete balance sheets that reflected the health and profitability of their operating companies. Each unit, therefore, also had an opportunity to develop an identity beyond the parent company, which strengthened management and employee commitment.

In 1986, Asea announced the successful implementation of its Nordic strategy, an attempt to extend the firm's engineering and manufacturing operations beyond Sweden to gain economies of scale—both in manufacturing and in raising capital. The big step forward had been the acquisition in Finland of Strömberg AB with its 7,000 employees, which was followed in late 1987 by the acquisition of 63 percent of EB Corporation in Norway. By 1987, Barnevik had realized his plan, radically altering Asea "from a Swedish-centered into a pan-Nordic electrical multinational." The strategy worked wonders: revenues tripled, earnings grew fivefold, and market capitalization increased an incredible 15 times during Barnevik's tenure (see Exhibit 1.1).[4]

The experience with Asea had given Barnevik a thorough understanding of the electrical power equipment industry in Scandinavia and the rest of Europe. In particular, it gave him a sense of the dimension of change that the industry as a whole needed to undergo to match the impressive results Asea had achieved under new, lean management:

> When Europe in 1986 pledged to create a single, deregulated market, Barnevik knew he was hearing the death knell of the coddled European power industry.... Few industries nurture a cozier relationship with governments and state utilities than the equipment makers.[5]

As for Asea, Barnevik decided the company needed to look beyond Sweden's population of 8.5 million, and even beyond the Nordic countries, in order to continue realizing improvements in productivity and profit margins.

---

[4] "Asea-Brown Boveri: Power Play," *The Economist*, May 28, 1988, pp. 19–22.

[5] Kapstein and Reed, "The Euro-Gospel," pp. 64–66.

▪ EXHIBIT 1.1

ABB ASEA BROWN BOVERI (A)
▪ THE ASEA GROUP FIVE-YEAR REVIEW OF FINANCIAL POSITION
(SWEDISH KRONOR[2]; MILLIONS, EXCEPT AS NOTED)

	1983	1984	1985	1986	1987
Order bookings	KR27,255	KR35,635	KR39,358	KR47,438	KR56,165
Invoiced sales	30,589	36,600	41,625	46,601	52,271
Earnings after financial income and expense	1,970	2,337	2,413	2,425	2,724
Adjusted stockholders' equity	KR 6,593	KR 7,419	KR 8,635	KR10,532	KR11,570
Total capital	KR32,175	KR37,087	KR41,618	KR47,154	KR59,040
Capital expenditures for property, plant, and equipment	KR 1,077	KR 1,063	KR 1,427	KR 2,069	KR 2,097
Capital expenditures for acquisitions	358	260	1,009	2,137	2,111
Average number of employees	56,660	58,434	60,979	63,124	72,868
Operating earnings/invoiced sales, %	7.9	7.6	6.4	6.1	6.7
Return on capital employed, %	16.5	17.8	16.8	18.2	16.2
Return on equity, %	18.3	18.8	16.7	15.0	15.0
Debt/equity ratio	1.07	0.98	1.18	1.01	1.36
Interest coverage ratio	2.80	2.92	2.85	2.40	2.74
Net income per share (SKr, 50% tax)	16.00	18.90	19.60	19.60	22.10
Net income per share, fully diluted (SKr, 50% tax)	—	—	18.70	19.30	21.60
Dividend per share (Kr)	4.00	4.70	6.00	7.00	8.00

[2] Translation rate on December 31, 1987: $1.00 = KR 5.84.

SOURCE: Asea AB annual report, 1987, p. 4.

BBC BROWN BOVERI LTD.

While Barnevik's discipline had brought an admirable level of profitability to Asea by the late 1980s, the same was not true of other firms in the industry. Serious problems plagued Asea's fiercest European competitor, BBC Brown Boveri Ltd.

By the late 1980s, Brown Boveri had become one of Europe's most prestigious engineering firms, but engineering mastery had also become one of Brown Boveri's greatest liabilities. The company tended to respond more to the whims of its technical staff than to the requirements of the market. Rather than leverage experience from previous designs, Brown Boveri engineers were more inclined to build new and innovative solutions to suit customer specifications. The constant turnover of designs, and lack of shared components among them, led to reliability problems and high costs.

Dr. Fritz Leutwiler, appointed chairman in 1985 after a career in central banking, intended to redirect the company's energies toward the paying customer and to improve profit margins from their dismal levels (see Exhibits 1.2 and 1.3).[6] He outlined a series of "measures designed to pull the group out of its unsatisfactory profit position," including a new organizational structure, elimination of unprofitable businesses, and weaning the company of its excessive dependency on power generation.[7]

[6] "Asea/Brown Boveri: Closing the Generation Gap," *The Economist*, August 15, 1987, pp. 53–54.

[7] Fritz Leutwiler, "Chairman's Letter," *BBC Brown Boveri Annual Report*, 1986.

■ **EXHIBIT 1.2**

ABB ASEA BROWN BOVERI (A)
■ **BBC BROWN BOVERI LTD. FIVE-YEAR SUMMARY OF CONSOLIDATED BALANCE SHEETS[a]
(SWISS FRANCS; MILLIONS)**

	At December 31				
	1983	1984	1985	1986	1987
Assets					
Current assets					
Cash and marketable securities	FR1,999	FR2,722	FR3,048	FR3,133	FR3,275
Trade receivables	2,851	3,556	3,600	3,297	2,697
Other receivables, prepayments, and accrued income	764	938	970	760	571
Advances to suppliers	819	690	517	235	154
Inventories	7,833	8,786	7,217	4,421	4,238
Total current assets	FR14,266	FR16,692	FR15,352	FR11,846	FR10,935
Fixed assets and investments					
Property, plant, and equipment[b]					
At book value	FR1,685	FR1,903	FR1,786	FR1,773	FR1,740
Revaluation to current value	2,099	2,180	2,355	2,254	2,098
At current value	3,784	4,083	4,141	4,027	3,838
Investments and intangible assets	348	323	281	285	393
Total fixed assets and investments	FR4,132	FR4,406	FR4,422	FR4,312	FR4,231
Total assets	FR18,398	FR21,098	FR19,774	FR16,158	FR15,166
Liabilities and Equity					
Liabilities					
Short- and medium-term borrowings	FR1,363	FR1,468	FR1,400	FR1,233	FR1,230
Long-term debt	1,318	1,484	1,426	1,336	1,023
Accounts payable	1,471	1,639	1,867	1,900	1,334
Accrued expenses	878	1,281	1,673	1,829	1,694
Advances from customers	6,621	7,489	5,574	2,799	2,755
Total liabilities	FR11,651	FR13,361	FR11,940	FR9,097	FR8,037
Provisions and Adjustments	FR2,275	FR2,481	FR2,602	FR2,233	FR2,260
Equity					
Capital of BBC Baden	FR501	FR553	FR553	FR553	FR720
Reserves of BBC Baden	445	459	475	488	777
Retained profit of BBC Baden at beginning of year	3	5	5	12	24
Consolidation reserve	3,575	4,154	4,089	3,679	3,163
Net earnings/loss	(52)	85	109	96	186
Total equity	FR4,472	FR5,256	FR5,232	FR4,828	FR4,870
Total liabilities and equity	FR18,398	FR21,098	FR19,774	FR16,158	FR15,166
Equity attributable to minority shareholders	FR797	FR980	FR840	FR627	FR523
Contingent liabilities	FR311	FR406	FR565	FR491	FR365

[a] Balance sheet and income statement are reproduced here as presented in annual report.
[b] Insured value (at December 31): 1983—8,722; 1984—9,176; 1985—9,403; 1986—9,056; 1987—9,236.
SOURCE: BBC Brown Boveri Ltd. annual report, 1987, pp. 74—75.

■ EXHIBIT 1.3

ABB ASEA BROWN BOVERI (A)

■ BBC BROWN BOVERI LTD. FIVE-YEAR SUMMARY OF INCOME STATEMENTS[a]

(SWISS FRANCS; MILLIONS)

	1983	1984	1985	1986	1987
Orders Received	10,501	12,431	12,977	11,032	10,994
Income					
Sales	FR10,658	FR11,214	FR13,876	FR13,826	FR10,369
Changes in work in process and finished goods	615	916	(1,493)	(2,502)	127
Gross production income	FR11,273	FR12,130	FR12,383	FR11,324	FR10,496
Other operating income	377	395	402	409	378
Nonoperating income	234	487	436	321	334
Total income	FR11,884	FR13,012	FR13,221	FR12,054	FR11,208
Expenses					
Expenses for materials and goods	FR 4,958	FR 5,166	FR 5,251	FR 4,679	FR 4,131
Personnel expenses	4,152	4,421	4,590	4,515	4,371
Depreciation	516	565	521	537	495
Interest and other financial charges	418	424	336	202	169
Other expenses and taxes	1,892	2,351	2,414	2,025	1,856
Total expenses	FR11,936	FR12,927	FR13,112	FR11,958	FR11,022
Net earnings/loss	FR(52)	FR85	FR109	FR96	FR186
Net earnings/loss attributable to minority shareholders	13	18	17	16	18
Cash flow	FR464	FR650	FR630	FR633	FR681

[a] Balance sheet and income statement are reproduced here as presented in annual report.

SOURCE: BBC Brown Boveri Ltd. annual report, 1987, p. 76.

By 1986, Leutwiler was confident that "[t]oday's Brown Boveri Group has Business, Regional and Functional Divisions, standing shoulder to shoulder, each with clearly defined missions and responsibilities." These groupings paralleled the organizational lines Barnevik had drawn for Asea (see Exhibits 1.4 and 1.5).

By 1987, Leutwiler's next challenges were to overcome the independent directions pursued by the engineers, and the divergent course charted by Brown Boveri's German subsidiary. The Mannheim-based BBC Brown Boveri Aktiengesellschaft had, over the years, outgrown its parent company. Brown Boveri had followed the federalist model established when the Swiss cantons formed a federation of states in the 13th century. The states ceded no more authority to the collective central government than the powers needed for maintaining a common defense and facilitating trade among them. Brown Boveri had granted maximum independence to its foreign subsidiaries to encourage aggressive pursuit of local contracts and to develop relationships with governments, utilities, and suppliers. The proliferation of product variety in an industry with excess capacity had, however, taken its toll on Brown Boveri's cost structure. Most rebellious of the subsidiaries was the German affiliate, which Leutwiler intended carefully to rein in.

ABB ASEA BROWN BOVERI (A)
■ BBC BROWN BOVERI LTD. BUSINESS SEGMENTS, 1987

Business Segment	Divisions	Revenue (%)
Power supply	Power Plants	20.6
	Power Transmission	27.0
	Transformers	
	Medium Voltage Equipment	
	Power Systems Control	
	Power Lines	
Transportation	High-Energy Batteries	7.1
	Transportation Systems	
Standard products	Low Voltage Apparatus	10.4
	Supercharging	
Electronics	Factory Automation	9.1
	Measurement and Control	
	Information Technology	
	Electronics Components	
Installation	Installations	11.9
	District Heating Systems	
	Cable and Wire	
Industry	Mining and Metallurgical Industries	11.2
	Process Industries	
	Oil, Gas, and Marine Industries	
	Electrical Drives	
Other products and services		2.7

SOURCE: BBC Brown Boveri Ltd. annual report, 1987.

■ ELECTRICAL POWER: BRACING FOR DEREGULATION

Leutwiler's letter to the shareholders opened the BBC Brown Boveri annual report for 1987 with a gloomy forecast for his own company and the industry as a whole:

> The electrical market has essentially stopped growing, at least in the industrial countries. Demand remains high in the developing countries, but sales are hampered by financial problems and high debt. Overcapacities prevalent throughout the electrical manufacturing industry make retrenchment and restructuring measures inevitable.

In the coming years, Leutwiler predicted, the fragmented and localized industry would be exposed to extensive global competition, but electric power generation was simply too capital intensive to continue to support such a fragmented market. It would be forced into significant consolidation. By 1993, European Community (EC) governments were expected to open their national bidding policies to foreign-owned companies, which would force the weaker players to seek mergers or fail. In the United States, new plant construction had slowed considerably; nuclear orders had stopped altogether because of excessive litigation, the 1978 Three-Mile Island accident, and the specter of the meltdown at Chernobyl. In response, the

■ **EXHIBIT 1.5**

ABB ASEA BROWN BOVERI (A)
■ **ASEA AB BUSINESS SEGMENTS, 1987**

Business Segment	Divisions	Revenue (%)
Power plants	Hydropower Nuclear Power/Nuclear Fuel Thermal Power	5.3
Power transmission	Installations Protection Relays High Voltage Apparatus Transformers	13.4
Power distribution	Distribution of Electricity Cables Capacitors Copper and Aluminum Wire	9.5
Transportation	Railway Equipment All-Terrain Carriers[a] Hydraulics[a] Forklift Trucks[a]	7.0
Industrial equipment	Metallurgical Industry Process Control Motor Drives Electronic Components Industrial Robots Industrial/Shop Refrigeration	11.7
Financial services	Asset Management Stockbrokerage Insurance Trading and Countertrading Leasing	7.7
The Fläkt Group (environmental)	Air Pollution Control Industrial Processes Components Gadelius (Japan) Service Indoor Climate	22.6
Standard finished goods	Electrical Wholesale Business Household Appliances Low-Voltage Apparatus Electric Motors	10.0
Other operations	Industrial Plastics Power Utility Operations Service and Installation Castings Telecommunications	12.8

[a] Not included in Asea Brown Boveri merger.

SOURCE: Asea AB annual report, 1987.

century-old U.S. manufacturers, Westinghouse and GE, were busy diversifying away from the troubled power industry.

The situation facing electric power equipment makers was similar in related lines of business, most notably, car and locomotive manufacturing for electrified railroads. Unlike Americans, Europeans had not abandoned passenger rail services in favor of air travel. The rail infrastructure remained pervasive in the 1980s. Suppliers were fragmented. Twenty-four domestic manufacturers supplied Western Europe's national railroads with locomotives and cars built to custom specifications. Some manufacturers built only 10 or so locomotives annually.[8] With the introduction in 1981 of high-speed train service between Paris and Lyons, however, the industry changed forever. The race was on throughout the European continent to match the French TGV. European governments committed their national railways to high-speed projects whose construction would cost $200 billion through the year 2000. They were motivated not only by national pride but also economic necessity. To be left off the high-speed main line was to forgo the economic development that the new train routes promised to bring.

In this atmosphere, small rail equipment manufacturers could not match the resources of the big players (Alsthom, Siemens, GEC, BBC, and Asea). In rail equipment as in electric power generation, the smaller national companies would be forced to seek international partners with broad bases for capital investment in order to keep pace with the accelerating rate of technological development.

GLOBAL MARKETS

Harmonization among the 12 EC members had ramifications for the electric power industry beyond rationalization of capacity. The EC encompassed a total market of 345 million people generating a collective gross national product (GNP) in excess of $6 trillion and accounting for nearly 40 percent of world exports. The EC member countries had announced in 1987 their intent to complete legislation for integration of the European Common Market by the end of 1992 to allow the seamless flow of capital, goods, and people among the member states. Companies from nonmember countries could not know for certain whether the Common Market would bring new opportunities from the opening of national markets or shut the doors on existing businesses within a fortress Europe:

> National preference is such an ingrained habit that local favorites always have a definite and usually a decisive advantage everywhere—GEC and Northern Engineering in Britain, Siemens and AEG in West Germany, General Electric and Westinghouse in the United States, Hitachi in Japan, and so on.[9]

The fortress phenomenon was pronounced in Asia, where some of Asea's fiercest competitors—Hitachi, Mitsubishi, Toshiba, and Daewoo—dominated their protected home markets and used government export incentives to capture market

[8] William Taylor, "The Logic of Global Business: An Interview with ABB's Percy Barnevik," *Harvard Business Review,* March-April 1991, p. 92.

[9] "Asea-Brown Boveri: Power Play," pp. 19–22.

share from Western firms. In addition, in reaction to the growing regionalization of Europe and Asia, North American leaders had begun talking of a free trade zone encompassing Canada, the United States, and Mexico. These regional trading blocs could herald a new age of global trade or a new era of protectionism.

As a counterweight to the EC, neutral Sweden and Switzerland had joined the European Free Trade Association (EFTA), whose other members included Austria, Iceland, Finland, and Norway. To prevent being shut out of the more lucrative EC union, EFTA had opened negotiations to form a European economic area with the EC. Discussions on the form and operational details of such an association had so far failed to yield substantive results, and businesses within EFTA countries had begun to realize that presence in the EC countries would be the only way to guarantee access to EC markets. With respect to such investments within the EC, *The Economist* reported:

> Four factors help explain the sudden Swedish shopping spree: a tiny home market, an ailing domestic economy, the chance to tap new markets in the EC— and a rising fear of what is brewing in Brussels.... [Swedish firms] have already set up shop in as many countries as possible so that they can present themselves as local manufacturers.[10]

LOCAL PRESSURES

The domestic economy posed further problems for Swedish firms. The Swedish brand of socialism, which had enabled a period of growth and prosperity in the years since World War II, had recently soured. Government revenues consumed more than half of the GNP, a rate 50 percent higher than the EC average.[11] With a pervasive welfare system and extensive government employment, many Swedes lacked motivation to increase individual productivity. The local brand of social capitalism had muted employer-worker tensions and allowed uninterrupted national development, but it seemed in 1987 that Swedes would have to abandon some of their traditional social principles to maintain and improve the standard of living (as measured by worker productivity).

In Switzerland and Sweden, the small domestic markets had always created pressure on domestic firms to export in order to remain competitive. In 1987, Asea had reported that 70 percent of its business was carried on outside Sweden; Brown Boveri sold 95 percent of its turnover outside Switzerland (70 percent outside Switzerland and West Germany).

In addition to pressure to export, both firms felt the pressures of environmentalism years earlier than many of their competitors in other countries. Despite the cost of meeting such stringent regulations in the short term, this heightened consciousness could, however, become an advantage in the long term. When foreign markets adopted new environmental controls, competitors required years to gain the experience ABB engineers had accumulated in their home markets. In his annual report message, Leutwiler pointed out another silver lining in environmental and other pressures on the power generation business:

---

[10] "Swedish Firms Set Sail for Europe," *The Economist*, September 1, 1990, pp. 59–60.

[11] John Burton, "Fine-Tuning Reforms," *Financial Times*, October 23, 1991, p. 6, special survey on Sweden.

The brighter side of the [electrical power industry] picture is that new user needs and new technology are opening up new opportunities for future growth in the industry. The electrical industry is becoming an electronics industry. Energy-saving and nonpolluting technology is in demand, and so are better means of transportation and modern factory automation equipment. Exploitation of these growth opportunities requires a great deal of additional research and development expenditure coupled with first-rate manufacturing performance.

■ TRANSNATIONAL MERGER

Barnevik and Leutwiler intended their new company to be among the survivors of the industry shake-out. Asea and Brown Boveri were of roughly equivalent size in many respects (annual sales, net worth, number of employees) and had adopted similar lines of decentralized command. The companies also complemented each other in their geographical concentrations and in management strengths (see Exhibit 1.6). *The Economist* reacted to news of the merger by concluding that "the merger will combine Asea's reputation for tough management with Brown Boveri's technical know-how and marketing name."[12]

Leutwiler was confident that a marriage of equals with Asea would bring to bear the resources necessary to stay at the technological edge in the power industry:

The new Asea Brown Boveri Group has what it takes to meet these challenges successfully. It has the resources to finance research and development and can utilize production plants in many countries to make the most of the advantages of international specialization. No competitor has comparable omnipresence in the world's markets.

To Barnevik, upheavals in the electrical power equipment industry were a signal of potential rather than a cause for concern. In a market in which contracts would be won by managerial skill, low cost, and technological leadership,

■ EXHIBIT 1.6

ABB ASEA BROWN BOVERI (A)
■ SALES BY GEOGRAPHICAL MARKETS

Asea AB	%	BBC Brown Boveri Ltd.	%
Sweden	29.7	Switzerland	5.4
Nordic countries	20.6	West Germany	24.2
Western Europe	19.8	Rest of Europe	32.9
Eastern Europe	1.9	North America	8.8
North America	10.9	Latin America	6.3
Latin America	2.0	Australasia, Asia	17.2
Australasia, Asia	14.2	Africa	5.2
Africa	0.9		
SKr (millions) 52,271	100.0	SFr (millions) 10,369	100.0

[12] "Asea/Brown Boveri: Closing the Generation Gap," pp. 53–54.

Barnevik's lean and innovative company looked forward to significant order bookings:

> Mr. Barnevik observes with satisfaction that ABB's main competitors are fast diversifying into consumer electronics, defense equipment, even medical products to reduce their dependence on electrical-engineering in general and the power industry in particular... (for Mr. Barnevik the way to make money in manufacturing, as in the stock market, is to invest when everybody else is fleeing).[13]

QUESTIONS

As Barnevik prepared to leave Stockholm, he thought about how to apply the lessons he had learned in his years at Asea to the grander organization of which Asea was now a part. Barnevik believed that "ABB is on its way to becoming an entirely new breed of corporation, breaking ground for the post-multinational company of the 1990s."[14] Only the question of how to organize this new company remained. What would be his role at the center of the organization with respect to the operating companies around the world? How could he track the developments of ABB around the world in sufficient detail to make decisions without introducing delay, bureaucracy, and hierarchy? What would be the optimal organization for the diverse operations of ABB: along functional lines, product lines, or geography? His experience had taught him that decentralization was a powerful force in developing a high-performance organization, but which dimension of the organization was most important? What structure would allow adequate investment in basic research but also support quick commercialization of new technologies?

Finally and immediately, Barnevik was aware that the downfall of many mergers had been their inability to conduct business as usual during a prolonged merger process. He was eager to act quickly and decisively in structuring the new company to avoid any such paralysis.

---

[13] "Asea-Brown Boveri: Power Play," pp. 19–22.

[14] Kapstein and Reed, "The Euro-Gospel," pp. 64–66.

BALANCE OF PAYMENTS: A NATION'S INTERNATIONAL PROFILE

2

KEY CONCEPTS

THE ITEM(S) THAT THE BALANCE OF PAYMENTS ACCOUNTS MEASURE ▬

THE CONSTRUCTION OF BALANCE OF PAYMENTS ACCOUNTS ▬

THE SIMILARITY OF BALANCE OF PAYMENTS TO A CORPORATE SOURCES AND USES OF FUNDS STATEMENT ▬

THE DISTINCTION BETWEEN THE OVERALL BALANCE OF PAYMENTS AND PARTIAL OR COMPONENT BALANCES SUCH AS THE TRADE ACCOUNT BALANCE, THE CURRENT ACCOUNT BALANCE, AND THE CAPITAL ACCOUNT BALANCE ▬

INTERPRETATION OF THE VARIOUS MEASURES OF BALANCE ▬

THE RECENT HISTORY OF THE U.S. BALANCE OF PAYMENTS ▬

THE LINKAGE BETWEEN THE BALANCE OF PAYMENTS AND THE NATIONAL INCOME ACCOUNTS ▬

THE WAY TO CONDUCT A CASE STUDY OF BALANCE OF PAYMENTS FOR AN INDIVIDUAL COUNTRY ▬

INTRODUCTION

The United States, Canada, and Mexico signed the North American Free Trade Agreement, whose provisions began to take effect January 1, 1994. The treaty's objective is to create free trade in goods and services among the three countries. Because of the treaty, Mexican manufacturers can export cement to the United States, U.S. retailers can invest in Mexico, and Canadian manufacturers can export more telephone equipment to the United States. What impact will this important treaty have on each of these countries and how can a corporate manager analyze these important changes?

A recent report in the Wall Street Journal suggests that analyzing the countries' balance of payments *data is one way to determine the treaty's impact. The balance of payments data record and summarize all of the commercial transactions between countries. This includes transactions between private individuals, companies, and governments. The types of transactions include exports and imports, tourist expenditures, consulting fees, interest and dividend payments, transportation charges, and sales of real estate, businesses, and financial securities. A report in the June 22, 1994,* Wall Street Journal *indicates the importance of the balance of payments.*

> For the first four months of this year, exports to Mexico were higher than the same period last year—$15.65 billion, compared with $13.85 billion—but analysts said that the performance would have been even stronger if Mexico were healthier. The overall U.S. surplus with Mexico shrank to just $7 million, compared with $166 million the previous month.

With respect to Canada the Wall Street Journal *report continues:*

> Meanwhile, U.S.–Canadian trade rose to a record high in April, strengthening the outlook for Canada's trade-dependent economy. Canada's exports to the U.S. advanced 6 percent to a record 14.45 billion Canadian dollars (U.S. $10.39 billion) in April from C. $13.61 billion in March.
>
> The two countries, which trade more than any other pair of countries, have seen their trade flourish as they gradually dismantle trade barriers in accordance with the five-year-old U.S.–Canada Free Trade Agreement. In April, the U.S. took more than 83 percent of Canada's exports, and supplied more than 75 percent of Canada's imports.

This Wall Street Journal *report addresses important economic issues for the United States, Canada, and Mexico based on balance of payments data for these countries. A nation's balance of payments accounts summarize the international transactions of individuals, companies, financial organizations, and governments during a period of time, for example, a month, a quarter, or a year. The transactions involve the purchase and sale of goods and services and of real and financial assets as well as central bank transactions involving changes in the international reserve position of a nation. Individuals, businesses, and governments make these transactions, directly or indirectly. For example, when Exxon imports oil from Saudi Arabia, this export of oil appears in the Saudi balance of payments accounts as a source of funds and this import of oil appears in the U.S. balance of payments accounts as a use of funds. Likewise, when a Saudi company buys an office building in Philadelphia, this exportation of capital from Saudi Arabia appears as a use of funds in its balance of payments accounts and as a source of funds in the U.S. accounts.*

Besides providing an organized record of transactions, why are the balance of payments accounts important? When individuals, businesses, and governments demand goods and services from one another, the balance of payments traces the flows of those goods and services and the financial transactions that underlie them. Analyzing trends in the balance of payments can reveal, for example, whether nations are becoming more or less competitive in world markets and more or less dependent on other nations for goods and services. Further, one nation may invest in real and/or financial assets issued by businesses in another country. Analyzing trends in the balance of payments can reveal whether a "borrowing country" will be able to make the payments that "investing countries" expect. Because of links among the balance of payments position, domestic economic policies, and the exchange rate of a country, analysis of trends in one of these variables provides useful information about the other two. These interrelationships are particularly important for those responsible for managing companies' exchange rate exposures.

As a specific example, consider the position of a multinational bank that has lent money to Mexico. Beginning in August 1982, Mexico was unable to service its debts in a timely way. (In the last section of this chapter, we examine why this occurred.) Consequently, creditors have worked with Mexico to provide new financing and to restructure the existing debt to enhance the probability of eventual repayment. From the creditors' perspective, the critical question in these negotiations was "What economically and politically feasible actions by Mexico best meet the needs of the creditors?" From Mexico's standpoint, the question was "How much international financial support can Mexico generate to help us resolve this financial crisis?" To answer these questions, both parties must analyze Mexico's balance of payments. Specifically, they must forecast the components of Mexico's Current account, which we describe in detail in this chapter. For Mexico to be able to pay its interest obligations in foreign currency, it must earn that foreign exchange by selling more to other countries than it buys from them. Through negotiation and consultation, the creditors and Mexico identify performance targets that focus on Mexico's balance of payments accounts. If achieved, these targets will allow Mexico to produce the surplus in foreign exchange earnings necessary to make interest and principal payments.

Once Mexico identifies its performance targets, it must develop policies to achieve them. These policies might include domestic fiscal and monetary actions as well as direct intervention in the exchange markets. Regardless of their specific form, they are bound to have major consequences for both local and foreign firms operating in Mexico. For example, policies that influence the level of economic activity will affect firms' cash flows in the local currency; policies that influence the exchange rate will affect the value of those cash flows in foreign currencies. In addition, the local central bank might impose exchange controls that restrict firms' abilities to import raw materials, service existing debt, or pay dividends to foreign investors.

As indicated in Chapter 1, this book looks at ways to solve these problems; an important step in that task is the ability to anticipate them. Understanding the balance of payments is the first step in this process.

BALANCE OF PAYMENTS ACCOUNTING

It is useful in discussing balance of payments accounting to recognize its similarity to corporate financial accounting. Both use double-entry bookkeeping, in which each transaction has two accounting entries, a debit and a credit, describing it. As a consequence, a nation's balance of payments always balances because, by definition, the total debits must equal the total credits. This last statement may appear to contradict the very frequent discussions about international payments surpluses and deficits, but it does not. Surpluses and deficits refer to balances in components of the balance of payments accounts. We illustrate this with reference to three accounts formed by aggregating similar transactions in each account. The Current account balance is the summation of all transactions involving exports, imports, services, financial payments, and gifts. There is much discussion of the U.S. Current account deficit. This refers to the fact that the United States imports more in goods and services than it exports. The Capital account balance is the summation of all transactions involving the ownership of real or financial assets. The United States has a Capital account surplus, which means that foreigners have increased their ownership of U.S. assets. The third major account is the Official Reserves or Official Settlements balance, the measure of the extent to which the government has increased or decreased its official foreign reserves. It is typically quite a small account. Using these three balances, we can represent the balance of payments as

Current account balance + Capital account balance
+ Official Settlements balance = Balance of payments = 0.0

Deficits and surpluses refer to the fact that each of these three accounts is not typically 0.0, but their sum is 0.0. In the next section, we describe these and other accounts in more detail and examine their significance.

Textbooks and analysts compare the balance of payments to a corporate balance sheet or income statement; this analogy is incorrect. The balance of payments is a sources and uses of funds statement. It details those transactions that add to a nation's purchasing power (sources) and those that reduce its purchasing power (uses). Sources of funds are represented by credit entries and uses of funds are shown by debits. Whether a particular part of a transaction is a source or a use in balance of payments, accounting follows the same rules as in accounting for a firm. Decreases in assets and increases in liabilities lead to increases in purchasing power; they are sources of funds. Increases in assets and decreases in liabilities represent expenditures of purchasing power; they are uses of funds.

An example should help to clarify the details and provide a better understanding of what the balance of payments records reveal. Assume that a Canadian forest products company can trade C. $1,000,000 worth of lumber to a West German firm for DM 1,400,000 of sawmill machinery. (The effective exchange rate is 1.40 DM/C. $.) From Canada's standpoint, the lumber has been exported and the machinery imported. The sale of lumber represents a decrease in Canadian assets. It is a source of funds and is noted by a credit entry in the international books. (This book follows the international convention of listing credits on the left-hand side of the ledger and debits on the right-hand side.) How did Canada utilize its increased purchasing power? By importing the machinery, Canada's inventory of machinery, its assets, has increased. This is a use of funds by Canada and is reflected in a debit entry. The double-entry accounting that describes the transaction from the Canadian perspective follows:

	Credit	*Debit*
Canadian exports	C. $1,000,000	
Canadian imports		C. $1,000,000

This example is atypical because it involves trade of goods for goods. Such barter transactions do occur and for a variety of reasons have increased in importance, but they do not represent a major portion of international trade. Most trade involves the exchange of goods for a financial asset, either a currency or a receivable. The currency may be the exporter's currency, the importer's currency, or the currency of a third country.

In the example, assume that the Canadian exporter demands immediate payment and accepts DM 1,400,000 in the form of a check drawn on a German bank.

The Canadian exporter has acquired marks, which are a claim on German goods and services. Because the transaction results in an increase in a financial asset, it represents a use of funds. The appropriate entries for the transaction are as follows:

	Credit	*Debit*
Canadian exports	C. $1,000,000	
Private short-term assets		C. $1,000,000

It is unlikely that the exporter would hold the marks very long. After all, currency does not pay interest, so it is to the exporter's advantage to put the asset to work. One way would be to use the marks to buy a mark-denominated security such as a government note. As long as the maturity is less than one year (i.e., it is a short-term asset), its purchase would have no balance of payments impact because one short-term asset, marks, was exchanged for another short-term asset, government notes. If the maturity were larger than one year, a detailed balance of payments presentation would show a debit in private long-term assets. Information about changes in the maturity structure of a nation's foreign assets and liabilities is important in any analysis of that nation's creditworthiness.

Similarly, asset holdings and liabilities are usually disaggregated according to whether they are private or official. Official assets are those held by government agencies and official liabilities are obligations of public versus private debtors.

If the Canadian exporter had decided not to hold the marks but to sell them for Canadian dollars to the central bank of Canada, a private asset would have been exchanged for an official (government) asset. These entries would be made:

	Credit	*Debit*
Private short-term assets	C. $1,000,000	
Official short-term assets		C. $1,000,000

The Canadian government might then decide that it no longer wishes to hold the marks. It arranges with the German central bank, the Bundesbank, to exchange marks for Canadian dollars. Canada is decreasing an asset, represented by its 1,400,000 mark holding, so that part of the transaction is a credit entry. At the same time, Canada is receiving an equivalent amount of Canadian dollars held by the German government. The C. $1,000,000 is a liability for Canada, and decreasing it is a use of funds recorded as a debit.

	Credit	*Debit*
Official short-term assets	C. $1,000,000	
Canadian liabilities to foreign agencies		C. $1,000,000

At first, these examples might appear to be too detailed and too abstract to have much relevance for managers. After all, managers do not keep balance of payment books, nor do most discussions of balance of payments involve debits and credits. Despite that, the concept of the balance of payments as a sources and uses of funds statement is very important. By keeping in mind which transactions are uses (debits) and which sources (credits), a manager develops a better picture of a nation's international position, which is important for an MNC. As an example, consider Olin Corporation, which we study in a case at the end of Chapter 8.

Olin Corporation, a U.S. chemical company, is participating in a joint venture in Brazil. Olin expects to earn its return on investment in the form of dividends from its Brazilian venture, paid in U.S. dollars. The Brazilian government has in the past, and may in the future, restrict the right of Brazilian companies to pay such dividends. If Brazil's imports rise dramatically, might this cause the Brazilian government to restrict dividend payments and jeopardize the value of Olin's investment? For Olin's managers to answer that question, they must understand and analyze the implications of an increase in imports.

Brazilian imports are a use of funds for Brazil. They must be offset by some source of funds. Whether the increase in imports signals a potential problem for Olin depends on the source of funds that finances the imports. The imports might be financed by an increase in exports, a source of funds. This indicates a healthy, growing economy and suggests no need for the government to restrict dividend payments. On the other hand, private or governmental borrowing might finance the imports. Private borrowing to support increased imports may reflect companies' efforts to purchase machinery or raw materials to expand future exports. This would have a positive effect on the economy and suggests that there is no need to restrict dividends. Official borrowing, on the other hand, might reflect increased government subsidization of consumption. This increases Brazil's need for funds to pay interest in the future. The government may choose to increase the funds available to it by restricting the use of funds for activities such as paying dividends to foreigners. If Olin believes this is what will happen, it might choose to sell its business now and repatriate its investment before the Brazilian government imposes restrictions.

The next two sections continue the discussion of the balance of payments. The purpose is to illustrate the analysis of the balance of payments accounting that is essential if financial managers are to improve their operations through an understanding of international transactions.

MEASURES OF IMBALANCE

Most media and public discussions of the balance of payments emphasize the occurrence or continuation of payments imbalances, either deficits or surpluses. Sometimes the measure discussed is the balance of trade, sometimes the balance in goods and services, and sometimes the current account. The following quotation from the *Wall Street Journal*, June 22, 1994, concerning the U.S. goods and services balance is typical.

> The Commerce Department said the trade deficit in goods and services jumped to $8.4 billion from $6.7 billion in March. As is common, it was the imbalance in the trade in goods that hurt the U.S. trade performance: Exports of goods were $1.8 billion less in April than in the previous months and imports grew slightly to record levels. The service surplus actually improved a bit during the month.

Over the years, fashion has changed and different measures have taken center stage. The reason for the different emphasis has nothing to do with economic theory but with the nature of analysts' concerns with the world economy.

The balance of trade is a key measure when the concern is international competitiveness. Under a fixed exchange rate regime, nations are required to support their currencies' values. This makes the official settlements balance very important. And in recent years, when the concern has been with indebtedness and the ability to meet debt service obligations, the Current account balance has been the center of analysis.

The relationship among the balances is clearest in the context of the sources and uses of funds analogy. Sources and uses analysis identifies the balance sheet changes over a period of time, which determine a change in a residual account such as Cash, Working Capital, or Fixed Assets. In other words, if a firm's cash position changes by a positive $2,000,000, sources and uses of funds reveals what other activity led to the change in cash (i.e., earnings, sales of assets, increases in liabilities, or new equity). The choice of the residual account is left to the analyst; what is certain is that the changes in all other accounts will be equal in size but of the opposite sign, because we use double-entry bookkeeping.

The various measures of the balance of payments represent different choices of the residual account. Table 2.1, which is a simple presentation of the balance of payments, illustrates this. The table classifies international transactions in six categories: merchandise trade, services, unilateral transfers, private claims and longterm government claims, official claims and reserves, and discrepancies. Because accounting for international transactions is difficult to perform precisely, there is also a residual category called *discrepancies*. This "fudge" factor is necessary to adjust for accidental errors, such as those in measurement and reporting, and purposeful errors, such as smuggling.

Recall from previous discussion that an export is a source. Consequently, in Table 2.1, exports of goods or merchandise are sources of funds and the credit is represented by A. Imports are uses of funds and the debit is represented by A'. Likewise, a German family traveling in the United States purchases food and lodging that are the export of a service by the United States. It is recorded as a credit and represented by B. Dividends paid by U.S. firms to foreign shareholders are

▪ TABLE 2.1

		BALANCE OF PAYMENTS ACCOUNTS	
	Credits (Sources)	Debits (Uses)	Credits – Debits (Sources – Uses)
Merchandise trade	A	A'	$A - A'$
Services	B	B'	$B - B'$
Unilateral transfers	C	C'	$C - C'$
Private claims and long-term government	D	D'	$D - D'$
Official reserves	E	E'	$E - E'$
Discrepancies	F	F'	$F - F'$
Total	$A + B + C + D + E + F$	$A' + B' + C' + D' + E' + F'$	0

uses of funds or imports of services. They appear as debits represented by B'. An unrequited transfer occurs when a Swedish parent sends money to a child studying in the United States or a charitable agency in the United States sends aid to people in a foreign country. The former appears as a source of funds to the United States and is shown as a credit, C, in Table 2.1. The latter appears as a use of funds as a debit, C'.[1] A foreigner acquiring U.S. assets, real or financial, generates a source of funds recorded as a credit to private claims and long-term government claims. It is noted by D. Similar purchases abroad by Americans are uses of funds represented by D'. An increase in official claims or reserves is also a use and is included in E'.[2] Finally, the reporting process might omit transactions in any of these categories, and we allow for that by including a discrepancy account as either an omitted source F or an omitted use F'. There will be omissions of both types, but in practice we know only the net amount and so the entry must appear as either F or F'. Because of double-entry bookkeeping, the sum of all the sources of funds must equal the sum of all the uses of funds. $(A + B + C + D + E + F) = (A' + B' + C' + D' + E' + F')$. But there is no reason for various subtotals such as A and A' or $(A + B + C)$ and $(A' + B' + C')$ to be equal. The differences among the subtotals or partial balances are the surpluses and deficits that economists and other analysts discuss. The most important of these appear in Table 2.2. We define each of these balances in the following material and discuss their relevance for analysis. To make discussion of the measures more concrete, Tables 2.3 and 2.4 summarize the U.S. balance of payments for 1993 in the format of Tables 2.1 and 2.2.

TRADE BALANCE

One of the most frequently used balance of payments measures is the trade balance. It measures the difference between exports and imports of goods (merchandise). For 1993, U.S. merchandise imports exceeded exports by $132.5 billion; the United States had a merchandise trade deficit of that amount. The frequency with which the balance of trade is referred to is due in part to its availability. It is calculated and released monthly. In addition, there is some belief that jobs are most closely related to merchandise trade, meaning deficits are linked to jobs lost due to import competition. Trade deficits that occur during times of rising unemployment often provoke calls for protectionist measures such as tariffs and quotas.

Although there is a tendency to define trade deficits as undesirable, there are clear examples of a trade deficit making sound economic sense. Consider the case of a relatively poor country with many profitable investment opportunities. Ignoring international transactions, such a country would face the undesirable choice of either forgoing needed consumption (remember that this is a poor country and saving is difficult) in order to invest or postponing desirable investments in order

---

[1] When we examine the data, we find that the United States reports these data on a net basis with just one entry.

[2] As with transfers, the U.S. data appear on a net basis.

■ TABLE 2.2

BALANCE OF PAYMENTS BALANCES

Trade balance	$A - A'$
Services balance	$B - B'$
Goods and services balance	$(A - A') + (B - B')$
Current account balance	$(A - A') + (B - B') + (C - C')$
Capital account balance	$D - D'$
Official settlements balance	$E - E'$

---

to consume. With international transactions, that is not necessary. The country can import more than it exports in order to simultaneously invest in its future and maintain a reasonable level of consumption. As long as the new investment produces returns sufficient to more than repay their funding, this trade deficit is self-financing: The developing country can consume more now and more later. In this case, the trade deficit has very desirable features. Arguably, this is what is happening in some parts of the developing world. In 1993, foreign investors supported trade deficits in 12 Asian and Latin American countries by investing more than $120 billion in those economies.[3]

SERVICES BALANCE

In 1993 the United States had a net surplus in services of $55.7 billion. Services transactions include the purchase of insurance and transportation, expenditures by

---

■ TABLE 2.3

1993 U.S. BALANCE OF PAYMENTS (BILLIONS)

	Credits (Sources)	Debits (Uses)	Credits – Debits (Sources – Uses)
Merchandise trade	$456.8	$589.2	($132.5)
Services	$297.1	$241.4	$55.7
Unilateral transfers[a]	($32.5)		($32.5)
Private claims and long-term government	$226.4	$142.5	$83.9
Official reserves[a]	($1.4)		($1.4)
Discrepancies		($26.7)	$26.7
Total	$946.4	$946.4	$0.0

[a]Reported on a net basis
SOURCE: *Survey of Current Business*, March 1994, p. 67.

---

[3] "Coping with Capital," *The Economist*, October 29, 1994, p.86.

■ TABLE 2.4

1993 U.S. BALANCE OF PAYMENTS SUBBALANCES (BILLIONS)

Trade balance	($132.5)
Services balance	$55.7
Goods and services balance	($76.7)
Current account balance	($109.2)
Capital account balance	$83.9
Official settlements balance	($1.4)

tourists, and payment of royalties, license fees, dividends, and interest. A more detailed breakdown of the data is available in Table 2.5. It reveals, for example, that in 1993 the U.S. had surpluses in royalties and fees of $15.7 billion ($20.4 – $4.7) and in travel of $14.2 billion ($56.5 – $42.3).

GOODS AND SERVICES BALANCE

The goods and services balance expands the trade balance to include services transactions. It is a more comprehensive measure of a nation's international competitive position than is the balance on trade because it recognizes that some economies have comparative advantages in producing and delivering services rather than goods. The inclusion of services reduces the trade deficit to a goods and services deficit of $76.7 billion. (Please note that because of rounding, there may appear to be small errors in the arithmetic.)

CURRENT ACCOUNT BALANCE

The Current account balance adds to the goods and services balance one additional category of transactions, unilateral transfers. Unilateral transfers include foreign aid, disaster relief through organizations such as the Red Cross and other humanitarian groups, and gifts to family living in another country.

During 1993 the U.S. government and residents of the United States sent abroad a net amount of $32.5 billion. This meant that the Current account deficit was $32.5 billion larger than the balance on goods and services. Therefore, the Current account deficit was $109.2 billion. To place that in context, the United States had deficits ranging from a high of nearly $170 billion in 1987 to a low of $8 billion in 1991. But in 1981, the United States had a Current account surplus of $4.6 billion. The United States recorded Current account surpluses in 27 of 35 years between 1946 and 1981. Clearly, the U.S. relationship with the rest of the world as regards trade, services, and transfers changed dramatically in the 1980s. Even the low deficit in 1991 was an anomaly, because it included the unusual $42.5 billion unilateral transfers to the United States by its Gulf War coalition partners.[4]

---

[4] Department of Commerce, *Survey of Current Business*, June 1992, p. 98.

U.S. BALANCE OF PAYMENTS ACCOUNTS (NOMINAL VALUES)

	1982	1983	1984	1985	1986	1987	1988	1989	1990	1991	1992	1993
Merchandise exports	211.2	201.8	219.9	215.9	223.3	250.2	320.2	362.1	389.3	416.9	440.1	456.8
Military sales	12.6	12.5	10.0	8.7	8.5	11.1	9.3	8.6	9.7	10.5	11.0	11.3
Travel	12.4	10.9	17.2	17.8	20.4	23.6	29.4	36.3	43.0	48.3	53.9	56.5
Fares	3.2	3.6	4.1	4.4	5.6	7.0	9.0	10.6	15.3	15.9	17.4	17.8
Transportation	12.3	12.6	13.8	14.7	15.8	17.3	19.5	20.5	22.0	22.3	22.8	23.5
Royalties and fees	5.6	5.7	6.1	6.6	7.9	9.9	11.8	13.8	17.1	18.5	20.2	20.4
Other services	18.0	18.8	19.8	20.8	27.9	28.9	31.0	37.0	41.3	48.7	54.5	57.3
Direct investment income	23.9	26.5	30.6	29.6	30.9	38.1	50.4	55.4	59.2	49.8	49.9	55.8
Portfolio investment income	58.2	53.4	63.2	54.4	50.2	51.7	65.1	83.9	81.5	69.5	53.7	49.5
U.S. government receipts	4.1	4.8	5.2	5.5	6.4	5.3	6.7	5.7	10.5	8.0	7.0	5.0
Merchandise imports	-247.6	-268.9	-332.4	-338.1	-368.4	-409.8	-447.2	-477.4	-498.3	-490.7	-536.3	-589.2
Defense expenditures	-12.5	-13.1	-12.5	-13.1	-13.7	-14.9	-15.6	-15.3	-17.5	-16.4	-13.8	-12.3
Travel	-12.4	-13.1	-22.9	-24.6	-25.9	-29.3	-32.1	-33.4	-37.3	-35.3	-40.0	-42.3
Fares	-4.8	-6.0	-5.7	-6.4	-6.5	-7.3	-7.7	-8.2	-10.5	-10.0	-10.9	-11.3
Transportation	-11.7	-12.2	-14.8	-15.6	-16.7	-17.8	-19.5	-20.7	-23.4	-23.3	-23.5	-24.5
Royalties and fees	-0.8	-0.9	-1.2	-1.2	-1.4	-1.8	-2.6	-2.6	-3.2	-4.2	-5.0	-4.7
Other services	-9.6	-9.5	-10.5	-11.9	-15.6	-19.1	-20.3	-21.8	-25.7	-29.2	-30.3	-36.0
Direct investment income	-1.9	-4.2	-8.7	-7.2	-7.1	-7.4	-11.7	-6.5	-3.0	3.0	-1.6	-9.8
Portfolio investment income	-35.2	-30.5	-39.7	-38.0	-43.1	-53.8	-66.2	-85.2	-87.1	-75.6	-61.6	-58.5
U.S. government income	-19.3	-19.0	-21.2	-23.1	-24.6	-26.2	-31.7	-38.4	-40.8	-41.7	-41.2	-41.9
Remittances	-17.1	-17.7	-20.6	-23.0	-24.2	-23.1	-24.9	-26.1	-33.8	-32.5	-32.9	-32.5
U.S. official reserves	-5.0	-1.2	-3.1	-3.9	0.3	9.1	-3.9	-25.3	-2.2	5.8	3.9	-1.4
U.S. nonreserve assets	-6.1	-5.0	-5.5	-2.8	-2.0	1.0	3.0	1.3	2.3	2.9	-1.6	-0.1
Foreign direct investment	1.0	-4.9	-10.9	-13.4	-17.1	-27.2	-15.4	-36.8	-27.1	-29.1	-34.8	-50.2
Securities	-8.0	-6.8	-4.8	-7.5	-4.3	-5.3	-7.8	-22.1	-28.8	-44.7	-48.0	-125.4
Nonbank claims	6.8	-11.0	5.8	-5.8	-8.2	3.1	-13.2	11.8	-4.4	3.3	4.6	-1.6
Bank claims	-111.1	-29.9	-11.1	-1.3	-60.0	-42.1	-54.0	-58.2	16.0		24.9	34.6
Foreign official assets	3.6	5.8	3.1	-1.1	35.6	45.4	39.8	8.5	34.2	17.6	40.7	71.2
Foreign direct investment	12.5	10.5	24.7	20.0	35.6	58.2	57.3	67.7	48.0	24.0	2.4	31.5
U.S. treasury securities	7.0	8.7	23.0	20.4	3.8	-7.6	20.2	29.6	-2.5	18.8	36.9	24.3
Other securities	6.1	8.2	12.6	51.0	71.0	42.1	26.4	38.8	1.6	35.1	30.3	79.6
Nonbank claims	-2.4	-0.1	4.7	-0.4	-2.6	2.9	5.6	5.6	7.5	-0.7	0.7	7.5
Bank claims	65.6	50.3	33.8	41.0	79.8	89.0	70.2	63.4	16.4	-11.4	18.6	12.2
Discrepancy	41.4	19.8	28.0	27.6	18.3	-1.4	-0.9	17.4	30.8	-15.1	-12.2	26.7
Balances												
Trade balance	-36.4	-67.1	-112.5	-122.2	-145.1	-159.6	-127.0	-115.3	-109.0	-73.8	-96.2	-132.5
Services balance	42.1	40.3	32.8	21.4	1.9	15.3	24.8	39.7	51.1	58.8	62.5	55.7
Goods and services balance	5.7	-26.8	-79.7	-100.8	-126.1	-144.3	-102.2	-75.6	-57.9	-15.0	-33.7	-76.7
Current account balance	-11.4	-44.5	-100.3	-123.8	-150.3	-167.4	-127.1	-101.7	-91.7	-8.4	-66.6	-109.2
Capital account balance	-25	25.8	75.4	100.1	131.6	159.5	132.1	109.6	63.2	17.7	74.7	83.9
Official settlements balance	-5.0	-1.2	-3.1	-3.9	0.3	9.1	-3.9	-25.3	-2.2	5.8	3.9	-1.4

Current account balances represent net foreign expenditures and receipts. Any deficit on the Current account must be accommodated or financed by capital trans-actions. On the other hand, surpluses on the Current account generate offsetting capital outflows which add to a nation's portfolio of international assets. Changes occur in either private or public sector wealth or indebtedness. Interest and divi-dend flows from capital investments are a function of past Current account per-formance. In general, countries receiving net investment income have had cumu-lative Current account surpluses. Those with net payments have had deficits.[5]

To reduce their outstanding indebtedness, debtor countries must generate Current account surpluses. That is one reason that the Current account is a pivotal measure of balance of payments activity. It summarizes the relationship between total international receipts and expenditures and indicates changes in the asset po-sition of nations. It is also related to national income accounting in a way that is very revealing of macroeconomic policies and performance. This relationship will be developed in the next section.

CAPITAL ACCOUNT BALANCE

The Capital account includes short-term flows such as bank loans, overseas de-posits, and trade credit as well as long-term investments in foreign stocks and bonds. Most, but not all, Capital account transactions reflect private sector activi-ties. Long-term government loans, which are usually provided on a subsidized basis, are also included. During 1993 the United States acquired $142.5 billion of for-eign assets through lending and investment. At the same time, foreigners acquired $226.4 billion worth of U.S. real and financial assets through the purchase of man-ufacturing plants, real estate, and common stocks and bonds. The amount of the Capital account surplus was $83.9 billion, which was the net source of funds from capital transactions.

OFFICIAL SETTLEMENTS BALANCE

The Official Settlements account measures changes in reserve holdings and liabil-ities to foreign official agencies, including the International Monetary Fund. Reserves consist of gold, convertible currencies, and Special Drawing Rights (SDRs).[6] To finance a Current account deficit, nations can reduce their reserves (a source because an asset position is being lowered) or borrow from abroad. Private borrowing appears in the Capital account, while borrowing from official

---

[5] Investment income and payments are also determined by the interest rates. A country might have net investment outflows if the interest it pays is at a higher rate than it receives even if it had a cumulative Current account surplus.

[6] Special Drawing Rights (SDRs) are a form of international money or credit established by the International Monetary Fund. Its value changes every day based on a fixed combination of U.S. dol-lars, British pounds, French francs, German marks, and Japanese yen.

creditors by official debtors appears in official settlements. In 1993 the U.S. official settlements balance was –$1.4 billion, indicating that the United States acquired reserves with funds generated from other transactions.

DISCREPANCY

In 1993 the Current account was in deficit by $109.2 billion. The Capital account was in surplus by $83.9 billion, and the official reserves used $1.4 billion of funds. Together, they produce a net use of funds of $26.7 billion, but the international sources and uses statement must balance. Therefore, measurement and reporting errors equal a net of $26.7 billion in sources of funds. That is a fairly typical error figure. While both the sign and the size of the discrepancy account have varied over time, the tendency has been toward sources.

Although no one knows the exact reasons for discrepancies in any year, there are several possible explanations. Suppose that residents of the United States wanted to consume foreign-produced goods that are banned in the United States, for example, marijuana, heroin, or cocaine. Smugglers might bring those goods into the country and sell them. Suppose that the smugglers take their receipts out of the United States and use them to buy U.S. government bonds. The purchase of the bonds would be a source of funds to the United States, but the importation of the illegal good would not appear in the accounts. This creates a source of funds without an offsetting use of funds. One way to balance the books is to acknowledge that we are not able to identify all transactions and to include a discrepancy account to include adjustments for all mistakes. In this example, the inability to include the smuggled good in the regular accounts as an import requires that it be included as a use in the Discrepancy account.

Although we know that smuggling occurs, we note that its omission produces a uses entry in the discrepancy account. Thus, smuggling cannot explain the persistent sources entries recorded for the United States. There are other possible explanations. First, exporters may have an incentive to understate the value of their exports to reduce the tariffs they pay on them. Second, undocumented workers in the United States may be earning income and either returning with it to their home countries or sending it home. In either case, it is likely that they go out of their way to avoid official contacts and records. Third, a large volume of cross-border shopping by both Mexicans and Canadians may go unrecorded.[7]

The discrepancy balance serves as an excellent reminder that the balance of payments statistics represent a best effort to measure foreign transactions. They are based, in part at least, on samples of transactions and estimates of their values. Errors in estimates, as well as unrecorded transactions, inevitably produce discrepancies.

---

[7] For a more detailed discussion of these issues see John Evans, *International Finance* (Ft. Worth, Fla.: The Dryden Press, 1992), p. 99.

THE RECENT U.S. BALANCE OF PAYMENTS RECORD

Having reviewed the summary of U.S. international balances for 1993, now consider the same data for the 12 years, 1982 to 1993. Figures 2.1 to 2.9 provide graphical representations of the recent history of the balance of payment accounts detailed in Table 2.5. To reduce the effects of inflation, we express the values in terms of 1987 dollars.[8]

Figure 2.1 illustrates that U.S. merchandise exports did not increase at all from 1982 to 1987. Since 1987 they have increased by $100 billion in real terms. In contrast, merchandise imports increased steadily from 1982 until 1993. The total increase was $150 billion in real terms. The merchandise trade deficit reached its highest value in 1987, at $170 billion, declined until 1991, and then increased in 1992 and 1993. Certainly one of the important issues a financial manager should consider is the likelihood that the increases in 1992 and 1993 represent the beginning of a pattern, like that experienced in the early 1980s. If it does, then this suggests, as we discuss in more detail in Chapter 3, market pressure to reduce the value of the U.S. dollar and to increase U.S. interest rates. Managers adjust their plans in response to both possibilities.

■ FIGURE 2.1

U.S. MERCHANDISE TRADE (1987 PRICES)

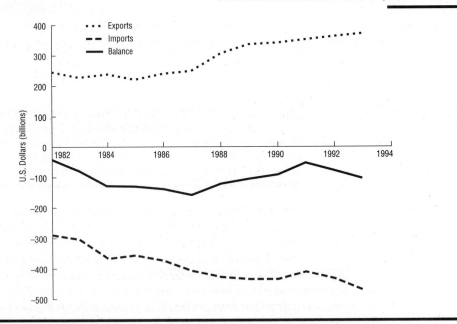

---

[8] The values have been adjusted by the gross national product deflator reported in the Department of Commerce, *Survey of Current Business*, September 1992, p. 44, and September 1994, p. 43.

The services accounts appear in Figure 2.2. The United States has traditionally earned more abroad in services than it has paid, although that varies by individual service account, as can be seen in the detailed accounts in Table 2.5. For a number of reasons, not the least of which is increasing payments to foreign holders of U.S. assets and debts, the services balance declined from approximately $50 billion in 1982 to slightly more than $15 billion in 1987. Since then, the gap again increased to a surplus of approximately $45 billion in 1993. (All values in 1987 prices.)

Figures 2.1 and 2.2 report the merchandise trade and the services balances. Figure 2.3 plots the history of their sum, the U.S. goods and services balance. Consistent with what we observed in the first two figures, this plots a steady decline in the goods and services balance from a small surplus in 1982 to a deficit of approximately $145 billion in 1987. The balance increased steadily from 1987 to a deficit of only $13 billion in 1991. As we discussed in the earlier section, since 1991 the balance has again declined substantially.

Figure 2.4 shows that the United States has, with one exception, consistently run a deficit in unilateral transfers or remittances. The three components of that deficit are foreign aid, government pensions, and private remittances. The year 1988 is typical. Government grants were $10.5 billion, and government pensions paid to people outside the United States were $2.5 billion. Private individuals sent abroad a net amount of $12.0 billion. The sole exception to this pattern is the Gulf War payments in 1991.

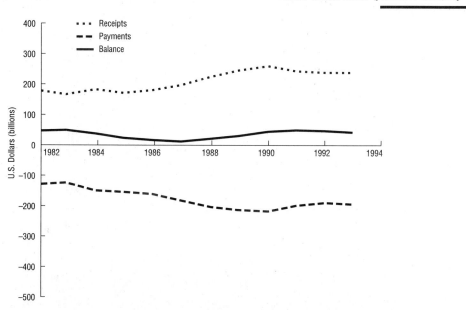

■ FIGURE 2.2

U.S. SERVICES (1987 PRICES)

■ FIGURE 2.3

U.S. GOODS AND SERVICES ACCOUNTS (1987 PRICES)

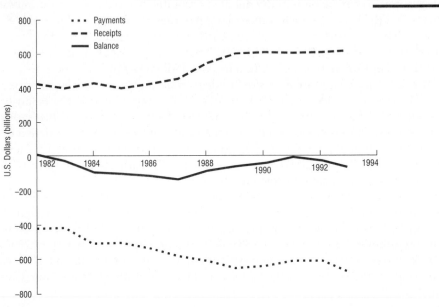

■ FIGURE 2.4

U.S. REMITTANCES (1987 PRICES)

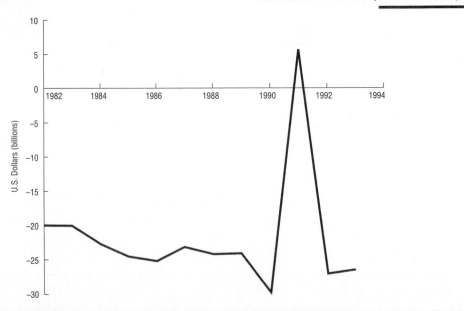

The Current account balance is the sum of the goods and services balance and the transfer payments. Figure 2.5 plots this value. It follows a pattern very similar to that of the goods and services balance. There was wide press coverage of the U.S. "international deficits" in the latter part of the 1980s when the Current account deficit reached its largest value of $170 billion. As we noted earlier, one of the issues raised was whether this deficit contributed to unemployment in the United States. Another question that received attention was "Why is the richest country in the world buying more from other countries than it is selling them?" This question reflects the concern that the rich should not need to import more than they export. We mentioned one possible explanation earlier. The United States might have many desirable investment opportunities and, therefore, have high levels of consumption and investment supported by an excess of imports over exports. The next section of this chapter demonstrates that this is not so. The United States did not undertake an especially large amount of investment but, instead, imported to consume and must repay this later by forgoing consumption. The accumulated value of the deficits, the amount that must be repaid, is $1,100 billion, in 1987 prices.

Figure 2.6 reports the inflows and outflows of capital. Recall that an outflow represents Americans' investment in other countries. An inflow represents an investment by foreigners in the United States. For more detail on the forms that these investments take, see Table 2.5, which identifies foreign direct investment,[9] and

■ FIGURE 2.5

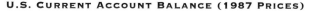

U.S. CURRENT ACCOUNT BALANCE (1987 PRICES)

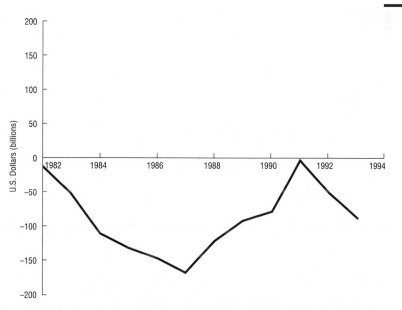

---

[9] This includes the purchase of physical assets such as real estate and plant and equipment.

■ FIGURE·2.6

U.S. CAPITAL ACCOUNT (1987 PRICES)

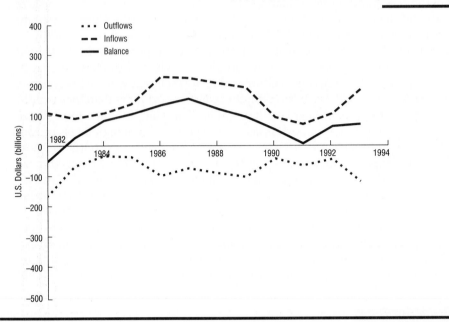

investment in various forms of financial assets, including bank deposits, government securities and nongovernment securities. U.S. investment abroad declined sharply from 1982 through 1984. Since 1984 investment has returned to approximately the level of 1979 (not shown). Foreign investment in the United States increased from 1981 through 1986, when it exceeded $200 billion. Since then it has declined considerably. The net effect of these patterns is that the United States switched from being a small foreign lender in 1982 to being a large-scale borrower. The cumulative borrowing is $900 billion in 1987 prices, approximately the same value as the cumulative Current account deficit.

The U.S. government holds reserves in the form of gold, balances at the International Monetary Fund, Special Drawing Rights, and other currencies. The government can use these funds to participate in currency markets when that is appropriate. Usually, that would mean selling reserves and buying dollars when the value of the dollar is "too low," and buying reserves and selling dollars when the value of the dollar is "too high." That would stabilize the value of the dollar and the government would also make speculative profits. Whether it does the former is hard to measure; there does not seem to be much evidence of the profits. Figure 2.7 indicates that the government has been a net seller of reserves only three times during these 12 years. With the exception of 1989, the quantity of reserves the government acquired has been relatively small.

The sixth account in the summary statement of international transactions is the Discrepancy account (Figure 2.8). Positive discrepancies occur in 8 of the 12 years.

■ FIGURE 2.7

U.S. OFFICIAL SETTLEMENTS (1987 PRICES)

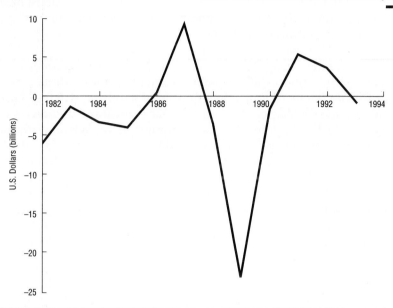

■ FIGURE 2.8

U.S. DISCREPANCY (1987 PRICES)

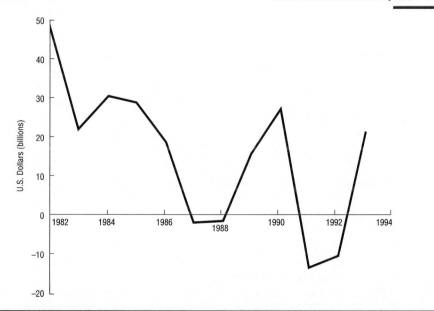

This is consistent with understating exports or overstating imports, understating capital outflows, or overstating capital inflows. In two years the discrepancies are approximately 0.0 and in two years they are negative. The most likely explanation for this pattern is a consistent undervaluing of exports, an understating of transfers, and cross-border shopping.

Figure 2.9 is the most interesting presentation of the international accounts. It incorporates the Current account deficit and the Capital account surplus. The symmetry of this graph should remind us that the sum of these two accounts is approximately zero. (It is precisely the sum of the changes in the Official Settlements account and the Discrepancy account. One is small and the other is an error in measurement.) Although they are the mirror images of each other, the relationship between the Current and Capital account balances is controversial. Some argue that an overvalued dollar, uncompetitive U.S. industry, and high U.S. consumption rates create a Current account deficit and the need to borrow abroad. Others argue that a highly favorable economic, political, and social environment make the United States an attractive place for foreigners to invest their savings, which produces a Capital account surplus. We will have more to say about this in Chapter 3. We know one thing for sure: It is hard to prove cause and effect for an accounting identity.

■ FIGURE 2.9

U.S. CURRENT AND CAPITAL ACCOUNTS (1987 PRICES)

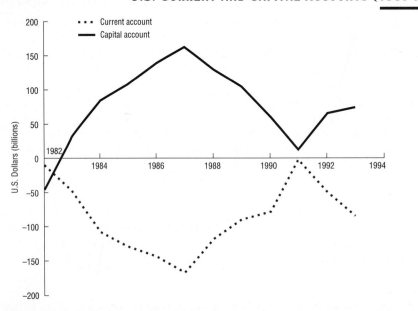

BALANCE OF PAYMENTS AND THE NATIONAL INCOME ACCOUNTS

DEFINING THE RELATIONSHIPS

Balance of payments activity reflects overall macroeconomic performance and policy. Accordingly, it is possible to relate the various international balances to the national income accounts and to analyze balance of payments performance in the context of the economy. [10] This section analyzes the relationship between international payments and macroeconomic performance with reference to the United States. The next section illustrates similar relationships for Mexico in the late 1970s and early 1980s. The case study at the end of the chapter analyzes these relationships for Mexico beginning in 1982.

The basic national income identity follows:

$$Y = C + I + G + (X - M) \tag{1}$$

where Y = gross national product (GNP)
C = private sector consumption
I = private sector domestic investment
G = government sector spending
X = exports of goods and services
M = imports of goods and services

Rearranging equation (1) yields a grouping that has a convenient conceptual interpretation:

$$Y - (C + I + G) = X - M \tag{2}$$

Y (or GNP) is a measure of the output of the economy whereas $(C + I + G)$ is a measure of total expenditure by the private and public sectors. $(X - M)$ is the balance on the Goods and Services account. When a nation has a goods and services surplus, its GNP or output is larger than its expenditures. When it experiences a deficit, the nation's total expenditures exceed its production. To absorb goods and services beyond what it has produced, a deficit nation must "borrow" goods and services from other nations.

We can interpret the Current account in a similar manner. We expand equation (1) and manipulate it to isolate the Current account. From each side we subtract net taxes, T (taxes less domestic transfer payments) and add international transfer payments, R. For the United States, the value of R that we add is negative in most years.

$$(Y + R - T) = (C + I) + (G - T) + (X + R - M) \tag{3}$$

The left side of equation (3), $(Y + R - T)$, is net disposable income. The right side consists of private expenditures $(C + I)$, net public expenditure $(G - T)$, and the Current account balance $(X + R - M)$. Noting that saving is defined as disposable income minus consumption, we can relate the Current account balance to private sector saving (S), investment, and the budget deficit.

---

[10] This section draws on the excellent exposition found in Rudiger Dornbusch, *Open Economy Macroeconomics* (New York: Basic Books, 1980).

$$(X + R - M) = (S - I) + (T - G) \tag{4}$$

The Current account surplus or deficit equals the excess of private sector saving over investment plus the public sector budget surplus or deficit. A nation has an external deficit when its investments and government spending exceed its saving and tax collection. A surplus nation saves and taxes more than it invests and consumes in government expenditures.

THE RECENT U.S. RECORD

These relationships will have more meaning if we place them in a real economic context. The 1993 *Economic Report of the President* provides a convenient data source for the United States. Table 2.6 contains the data for 1982–1993. In 1993 U.S. GNP was $6,374.0 billion. Private consumption was $4,390.6 billion, private investment was $892.0 billion, and government purchases of goods and services was $1,157.1 billion. The total of consumption, investment, and government purchases of goods and services is $5,981.5 billion. This value, subtracted from GNP, yields a difference of –$65.7 billion, which is the international balance on goods and services.[11] This discussion is a verbal presentation of equation (2). To emphasize that point, we reproduce equation (2) and its matching numerical values.

$$Y - (C + I + G) = X - M \tag{2}$$

$$\$6,374.0 - (\$4,390.6 + \$892.0 + \$1,157.1) = -\$65.7$$

Net taxes in 1993 were $933.4 billion, so the government sector ran a deficit of $223.7 billion. U.S. international transfers payments were a net deficit of $32.5 billion. Therefore, disposable income in the United States was $5,408.1 billion. In terms of equation (3), disposable income is equal to domestic private expenditures, plus the excess of government expenditures over taxes, plus the Current account balance.

$$(Y + R - T) = (C + I) + (G - T) + (X + R - M) \tag{3}$$

$$(\$6,374.0 - \$32.5 - \$933.4) = (\$5,282.6) + (\$223.7) + (-\$98.2)$$

Domestic saving in 1993 was $1,017.5 billion. Note that this is $125.5 billion more than domestic investment. When the private sector saves more than it invests domestically, it can use the difference two ways. It can invest abroad or lend the difference to the government. If it lends to the government, then, in effect, the government deficit absorbs the excess of private saving in excess of investment. In 1993 the government sector deficit was $223.7 billion, so the government deficit absorbed all of the surplus saving, plus another $98.2 billion. Therefore, the United

---

[11] This value differs from the number used earlier because the accounting rules for GNP calculations differ from those used for the Department of Commerce's international transactions reports. This difference should also serve as a reminder that all of these numbers are estimates with varying degrees of estimation error.

NATIONAL INCOME ACCOUNTS
(BILLIONS OF DOLLARS)

	1982	1983	1984	1985	1986	1987	1988	1989	1990	1991	1992	1993
GDP	$3,149.6	$3,405.0	$3,777.2	$4,038.7	$4,268.6	$4,539.9	$4,900.4	$5,244.0	$5,513.8	$5,671.8	$5,950.7	$6,374.0
C	2,059.2	2,257.5	2,460.3	2,667.4	2,850.6	3,052.2	3,296.1	3,517.9	3,742.6	3,886.8	4,095.8	4,390.6
I	503.4	546.7	718.9	714.5	717.6	749.3	793.6	837.6	802.6	725.3	770.4	892.0
G	607.6	652.3	700.8	772.3	833.0	881.5	918.7	971.4	1,042.9	1,086.9	1,114.9	1,157.1
GNP	3,179.8	3,434.4	3,801.5	4,053.6	4,277.7	4,544.5	4,908.2	5,248.2	5,524.5	5,687.3	5,961.9	6,374.0
X	379.9	372.5	410.5	399.3	415.2	469.0	572.9	650.3	698.2	704.9	765.1	660.1
M	-370.3	-394.6	-488.9	-500.0	-538.6	-607.6	-673.0	-729.0	-761.8	-716.6	-784.3	-725.8
R	-11.6	-12.5	-15.2	-16.9	-17.9	-16.0	-17.3	-17.3	-19.2	26.7	-30.8	-32.5
S	610.0	651.9	734.0	722.3	723.0	706.5	774.4	824.6	859.3	911.5	1,002.9	1,017.5
T	499.0	512.5	592.0	647.0	686.2	769.8	820.4	888.4	903.4	915.7	832.4	933.4
T − G	-108.6	-139.8	-108.8	-125.3	-146.8	-111.7	-98.3	-83.0	-139.5	-171.2	-282.5	-223.7
I − S	-114.1	-95.0	-24.2	-21.6	-4.2	18.0	-9.2	10.3	-48.7	-186.2	-198.4	-98.8
X + R + M	-2.0	-34.6	-93.6	-117.6	-141.3	-154.6	-117.4	-96.0	-82.8	15.0	-50.0	-98.2

States had a shortage of savings of $98.2 billion that it borrowed from abroad. The United States "imported savings" by running a Current account deficit.

$$(X + R - M) = (S - I) + (T - G) \tag{4}$$

$$(-\$98.2) = (\$1,017.5 - \$892.0) + (-\$223.7)$$

Figures 2.10, 2.11, and 2.12 provide graphical representations of some of these data over the last 12 years. Figure 2.10 plots the components of GNP, consumption, investment, and government purchases as proportions of GNP. Consumption increased from 64.8 percent to 69.1 percent of GNP over this 12-year period. Consumption in 1993 was $275 billion higher than it would have been if the proportion had not changed. Some analysts suggest that this increase in the U.S. rate of consumption is one reason the value of the U.S. dollar continues to decline. For example, "the dollar's persistent weakness is caused by America's bad habits, mainly its lack of savings and stubborn deficits."[12] Investment fell from 15.8 percent of GNP in 1982 to 14.0 percent of GNP in 1993. Again, analysts suggest that the United States is investing too little in recent years. Contrary to what might be the general impression, government spending declined slightly as a percentage of GNP. It began this 12-year period as 19.1 percent of GNP and ended it at 18.2 percent of GNP. Total expenditures, not shown, began this period just slightly less than

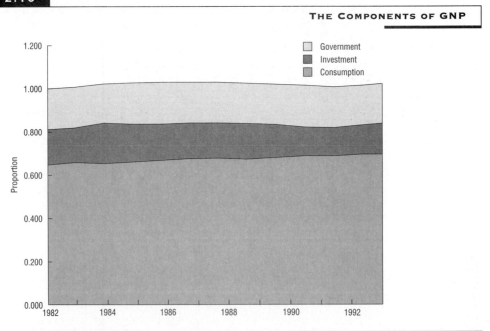

■ FIGURE 2.10

THE COMPONENTS OF GNP

[12] "The Dwindling Dollar," *The Economist*, October 29, 1994, p. 96.

■ FIGURE 2.11

THE CURRENT ACCOUNT, INVESTMENT, AND NET SAVING
AS PROPORTIONS OF GNP

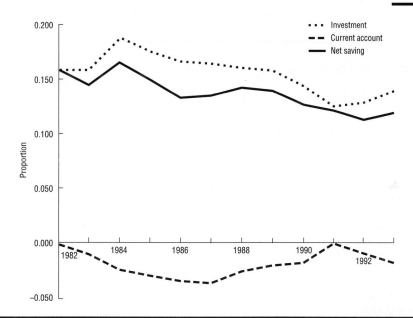

GNP and ended the period just slightly more than GNP. During the middle 1980s, however, total expenditures exceeded GNP by a considerable margin. In 1987, for example, total expenditures exceeded GNP by approximately $140 billion. This is consistent with our discussion in the first chapter, where we pointed out that the United States borrowed large amounts of money from foreigners during the 1980s.

It is not straightforward to identify relationships as desirable or undesirable. It is even more difficult to establish cause-and-effect relationships. We can attempt to arrange the data in a manner that indicates as clearly as possible what is happening. Figure 2.11 tries to do that by reporting the values of net domestic saving, $S + (T - G)$ (private saving plus government saving or borrowing), gross investment, and the Current account balance. Recall from equation (4) that the net domestic saving is equal to the sum of investment and the Current account balance. In 1982 net saving and investment were both approximately equal to 16 percent of GNP and the Current account balance was approximately 0. In 1991 the Current account balance was again approximately 0. The major difference is that by 1991 both saving and investment had declined by more than three percentage points and were about 12.5 percent of GNP. Saving declined more quickly than investment. In 1987 the gap between them was approximately three percentage points. As we saw above, that was when the Current account recorded its largest deficit. By the end of 1993, saving declined further to 12.1 percent of GNP and investment increased to 14.0 percent (see Table 2.6).

In Figure 2.12 we plot government deficits and capital inflows. It has been fashionable to claim that government deficits and the associated borrowing caused the capital inflows. During the various periods, they seem to be correlated, but at other times, they move in opposite directions. In 1991 the capital flow approached zero while the government deficit was large. In 1993 the capital inflows increased while the government deficit decreased. Clearly, the connection between these two variables is not simple.

To take this discussion one step further, we can analyze the relationship between the change in government deficits and the change in the capital account by plotting these changes in a graph. Figure 2.13 does that. We note that there is a mild positive relationship between the capital account balance and the government deficit. The positive slope of the linear regression line reflects that. The scatter of the observations around the line is very wide; the low value of R^2 reflects that. The relationship between the two variables is not statistically significant at the 95 percent confidence level. Therefore, we cannot accept as proven the contention that the capital account surplus is related to the government deficit.

Figures 2.12 and 2.13 suggest the care necessary in concluding that one variable causes another. Some economists engaged in policy debates examine data not unlike this and conclude that the "bad" government deficit is causing the "bad" Current account deficit. For various periods, this may have appeared to be the case.

■ FIGURE 2.12

**GOVERNMENT DEFICITS AND THE CAPITAL ACCOUNT
AS PROPORTIONS OF GNP**

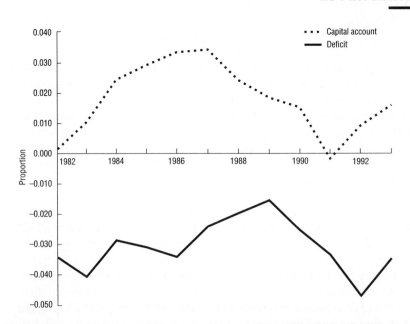

■ **FIGURE 2.13**

THE RELATIONSHIP BETWEEN THE CAPITAL ACCOUNT BALANCE AND THE GOVERNMENT DEFICIT

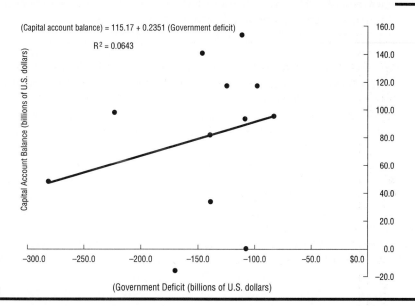

Recent results help us emphasize that causes and effects are usually much more complex than such simple relationships.

ECONOMIC PERFORMANCE IMPLICATIONS

We have already indicated that a nation with a Current account deficit must finance that deficit by increasing its obligations to other nations or reducing its claims on other nations. An equivalent way to describe the process is that deficit nations require net foreign investment inflows to support their spending. Surplus nations have an excess of saving, which is channeled overseas in the form of net foreign investment outflows.

Deficits are often considered indications of poor economic policies and performance; this conclusion is not correct. Deficits are neither per se bad, nor are surpluses per se good. Nations tend to run deficits at times when their need for investment exceeds their production and saving capacity. Therefore, they look to foreign investments to meet the shortfall. As long as the external borrowing is utilized to generate sufficient future production with which to repay the foreign debt and increase the borrower's standard of living, the deficit will have been good. If it is not well utilized, either creditors or citizens of the borrowing country will suffer.

Because investment usually has a long time horizon, it is not easy to evaluate its success or failure in a short period. What looks like a good investment might turn out to be a poor one if technological change occurs or raw material prices change dramatically. Some factors that influence the outcome are cyclical (dependent on economic conditions) and others change over time. An analyst should identify the factors and determine whether they are temporary or permanent before classifying a major expenditure as a loss or a gain.

A nation's balance of payments performance must also be evaluated over a period of time. It must be analyzed in the context of domestic policies. In the case of a deficit, the key issue is the use of the funds and their long-term impact on the nation's output. A crucial part of any effort to understand balance of payments performance is to identify trends and patterns and judge them in the context of domestic and international policies and events. In the final section of this chapter, we illustrate this analysis with reference to Mexico.

Before proceeding to that analysis, we should make one final point. Balance of payments data are ex post; that is, they are a record of the transactions that occurred during a period of time. Countries with Current account deficits are those that were able to arrange financing. Other nations might have much smaller deficits or even a balance. That does not mean that those nations had all the goods and services they needed or had sufficient savings to support all the investment they desired. Very poor nations have great needs but cannot find creditors, especially among private lenders. Those nations are forced to do without because without financing, they cannot support their deficits. If their prospects are such that potential creditors are wary of providing funds, their consumption will be limited to their production, and their goods and services and Current account balances will be close to zero. That is hardly a desirable situation.

BALANCE OF PAYMENTS ILLUSTRATION: MEXICO

This section reviews Mexico's balance of payments for the period 1977 to 1982. The purpose is not to provide a detailed or comprehensive analysis of Mexico's international position but to present an example of how to apply the basic concepts presented in this chapter. In fact, an analysis such as this one raises as many questions as it answers. More in-depth research would fill in the gaps, but by beginning this way we can identify the key areas of inquiry.

Table 2.7 summarizes Mexico's balance of payments performance during the period under study. It provides all of the partial measures of balance discussed in the earlier part of the chapter. Recall that the Current account is just a more comprehensive measure of transactions than the trade and goods and services balances. As such, it is the amount that needs to be financed (deficit) or is available as an addition to the wealth portfolio of the nation (surplus). Therefore, the total of the Current, Discrepancy, and Official Settlements accounts should equal the capital account balance.

For example, in 1977 the Current account had a $1,854 million deficit. At the same time, Mexico had an inflow of capital (including the $52 million Discrepancy account balance) of $2,524 million. Mexico used the excess source of funds to increase its international reserve position. Although Mexico had Current account

MEXICAN BALANCE OF PAYMENTS 1977 TO 1982
(MILLIONS OF U.S. DOLLARS)

	1977	1978	1979	1980	1981	1982
Trade balance	($1,021)	($1,745)	($2,830)	($2,830)	($4,099)	$6,885
Goods and services balance	(2,023)	(3,363)	(5,685)	(8,437)	(14,188)	(3,225)
Current account balance	(1,845)	(3,171)	(5,459)	(8,162)	(13,889)	(2,943)
Capital account balance	2,473	3,701	5,144	12,890	23,208	6,348
Discrepancy	52	(75)	597	(3,703)	(8,593)	(6,856)
Official settlements balance	(680)	(455)	(282)	(1,025)	(726)	3,451

SOURCE: International Monetary Fund, *International Financial Statistics* (1983).

deficits in every year for which information is provided, it also added to its reserve position in every year except the last one, 1982. That is a good example of the importance of not focusing on just one measure of the balance of payments. Considering only the changes in reserves would paint a rosy picture of Mexico's position and obscure more important changes in the nation's level of indebtedness.

It is not possible from the information to determine Mexico's total indebtedness, but during the six years, Mexico's external obligations grew by $54,034 million, the cumulative total of the capital account. That included direct foreign investment, but a look at detailed balance of payments data would reveal that almost all of it was debt. Almost 40 percent of that debt was incurred in 1981 when the Current account deficit rose to $13,889 million.

Focusing on the discrepancy leads to an interesting theory about the Mexican situation. Notice that beginning in 1980, the errors and omissions become very large and negative. In line with previous discussion, the most plausible explanation is that those outflows represent flight capital, money taken illegally out of Mexico. Flight capital responds to doubts about the economic conditions in a country and the fear of future exchange restrictions. The evidence in Table 2.7 suggests that Mexicans began to take capital out of the country before foreigners were aware of Mexico's financial difficulties. From 1980 through 1982, almost $19 billion left the country so that the net swing in the capital position was more than $70 billion, the flight capital outflows and the borrowed inflows. Capital that leaves Mexico illegally is unlikely to generate income that will be available for debt service. Instead, it remains overseas as insurance for the wealthy against a complete collapse of the domestic economy.

Related to the large capital inflows is the increase in debt service obligations. Interest and dividend payments are included in the service component. The large increases in the goods and services deficit not reflected in the trade balance are due to the rapidly increasing interest payments. The size of the payment burden is particularly evident in 1981 and 1982.

In 1982 the Mexican government took major steps to correct its balance of payments difficulties. The goal of these actions was to generate a surplus that would allow Mexico to resume timely debt service. The trade balance for 1982 gives some evidence of the progress made toward those goals. It was in surplus by $6.9 billion, an increase of $11 billion over the previous year and a reflection of major policies enacted by the Mexican government. As it turns out, almost all improvement came from reduced imports, not increased exports. Imports fell by $9.6 billion while exports rose by only $1.4 billion. This is an important piece of information because policies to reduce imports can be implemented and their effects felt more quickly than policies to stimulate exports. The positive trade balance might be sustained, but it is unlikely that the large increase can be repeated.

Despite the dramatic increase in the trade surplus, the Current account remained in deficit. The major explanatory factor was the interest obligation. Whatever the cause, there is a more important point to make. Even with the major restructuring of trade flows, Mexico was still deeper in debt at the end of 1982 than it had been at the beginning. The $11 billion swing in the trade balance was not sufficient to eliminate the need to borrow. Because the new debt must be serviced, Mexico required increasing trade surpluses. The Current account does not measure the full growth in new obligations. Because of capital flight and despite a large reduction in reserves, Mexico's Capital account surplus (its new obligations) grew more than $6 billion. This amount is much less than was borrowed in 1981; however, it still represents new borrowing for a country that in August 1982 announced that it could not service its debt.

The next stage in the analysis of Mexico's international position is to identify the domestic policies that led to the 1982 improvement and to make suggestions for future progress. Once we identify promising policies, we can assess their effectiveness and determine their impact. This part of the analysis requires an understanding of balance of payments adjustment and the factors that influence trade and capital transactions, topics that are the subject of the next chapter.

IMPLICATIONS FOR MANAGERS

Financial managers need international financial data to make important strategic decisions related to international business. The balance of payments is an important source of that data. A manager should understand the basic balance of payments concepts. He or she might never conduct the type of analysis discussed in this chapter but may read reports prepared by others. These reports typically refer to balance of payments data and contain analysis of trends over time and examine different measures of imbalance. We will close this chapter with illustrations of decisions that rely, in part at least, on an analysis of balance of payments data.

U.S. banks make many large loans to foreign countries and companies. These loans typically require dollar interest payments and repayment of principal in dollars. The borrowers can repay these loans only if they are able to acquire dollars. They can do that by earning dollars or other currencies convertible into dollars by exporting or by earning domestic currency that is convertible into dollars. The domestic currency is convertible only if the country earns, or has the prospect of earning in the future, a surplus of dollars or other convertible currency. What do we call this surplus? It is a Current account surplus. Therefore, assessing the feasibility of foreign lending requires analysis of the foreign country's balance of payments and, especially, its capacity to produce future Current account surpluses to finance debt payments.

Countries such as Brazil, Mexico, Malaysia, and Thailand have received large inflows of foreign capital in recent years. These countries have had large capital account surpluses. Some of this investment has been in plant and equipment; some has been in financial securities such as common stocks. Investors buying common stocks must ask how this inflow of capital is affecting the economy in which they are investing. If the countries receiving this capital have relatively high rates of investment, investors can anticipate that the foreign capital will stimulate the country's economy and help build a stock of investment capital that will provide the rate of return that the investors want to earn on their investment. Therefore, investors buying common stock in a foreign country examine the relationship between a country's capital account balance and its investment in plant and equipment.

Finally, MNCs make large commitments to plant and equipment investment in foreign countries. One reason they do so is to produce goods for export from the foreign country. The competitiveness of those goods depends, in part at least, on the value of the foreign currency. Complex interaction among many factors, including current and future balance of payments transactions and balances, determine the value of a currency over time. MNCs investing abroad must examine the balance of payments data to determine whether the competitive advantage that encourages investment today may be lost as the foreign currency changes value in the future. In the next chapter, we examine how the balance of payments transactions influence the values of currencies.

QUESTIONS AND EXERCISES

2-1. Using the following transactions, prepare a balance of payments account for the county in question. Organize the information in a table similar to Table 2.1. Be sure to include all the relevant measures of imbalance.

a. Residents receive $100,000 worth of dividends from overseas. They hold the dividends in the form of short-term bank accounts in foreign countries.

b. Foreign nationals purchase wheat valued at $450,000. They pay by drawing down balances at domestic banks.

c. The government provides refugee assistance in the form of wheat valued at $175,000.

d. Colossal Corporation establishes an overseas plant at a cost of $750,000. It sells bonds in the foreign country to finance the project.

e. The central bank of a foreign country sells $125,000 worth of U.S. T-bills and uses the proceeds to purchase an equivalent amount of its own currency in the foreign exchange market to support the price of its currency.

f. A trading company swaps $225,000 worth of maize for 20,000 barrels of oil.

g. Smugglers import cocaine and sell it to U.S. dealers who pay them in $500,000 cash. This money is smuggled out of the United States and then used to buy, on behalf of a Panamanian company, $500,000 worth of common stock on the New York Stock Exchange.

2-2. In Table 2.3, the credit and debit balances for services are $297.1 and $241.4, respectively. Use the data in Table 2.5 to separate each of those balances into its nine component parts.

2-3. The following tables summarize the balance of payments for 1982 and 1987. Compare them with each other and the data for 1993.

1982 U.S. BALANCE OF PAYMENTS (BILLIONS)

	Credits	Debits	Credits – Debits
	(Sources)	(Uses)	(Sources – Uses)
Merchandise trade	$211.2	$247.6	($36.4)
Services	150.3	108.2	42.1
Unilateral transfers[a]	(17.1)		(17.1)
Private claims and long-term government	92.4	117.4	(25.0)
Official reserves[a]	(5.0)		(5.0)
Discrepancies	0.0	(41.4)	41.4
Total	$431.8	$431.8	$ 0.0

[a] Reported on a net basis.

1987 U.S. BALANCE OF PAYMENTS (BILLIONS)

	Credits	Debits	Credits – Debits
	(Sources)	(Uses)	(Sources – Uses)
Merchandise trade	$250.2	$409.8	($159.6)
Services	192.9	177.6	15.3
Unilateral transfers[a]	(23.1)		(23.1)
Private claims and long-term government	230.0	70.5	159.5
Official reserves[a]	9.1		9.1
Discrepancies	0.0	1.2	(1.2)
Total	$659.1	$659.1	$ 0.0

[a] Reported on a net basis.

2-4. Why does Figure 2.9 with the U.S. Current and Capital account balances look symmetrical?

2-5. With only the information in Figure 2.7, explain whether the U.S. dollar was weak or strong at different times between 1982 and 1992.

2-6. Why do countries in which private and public sector saving exceed investment have positive Current account balances?

2-7. Economists and politicians have argued that the high U.S. government deficits have caused the high U.S. Current account deficits. Comment on that assertion.

2-8. Use the U.S. international transactions data from the *Survey for Current Business*, for the most recently available year to construct a table similar to Table 2.3. Compare your data to that for 1993.

2-9. Using data from Tables 2.5 and 2.6, calculate the aggregate value of the government deficit, $(T - G)$, and the Capital account surplus, $-(X + R + M)$, for the years 1982 to 1993. If we assume that the rate of return on both of these is 8%, calculate the dollar value of the return earned by both aggregate deficits. Express that dollar value as a percentage of the respective deficits in 1993.

2-10. For 1982 and 1993, express each of the components of Table 2.6 as a percentage of GNP. Compare your results.

REFERENCES

Alexander, Sidney S. "The Effects of a Devaluation on the Trade Balance." International Monetary Fund, *Staff Papers*, April 1952, pp. 263–278. Reprinted in Richard E. Caves and Harry G. Johnson, eds. *AEA Readings in International Economics*. Homewood, Ill.: Richard D. Irwin, 1968.

Baldwin, Robert E. "Determinants of Trade and Foreign Investment: Further Evidence." *Review of Economics and Statistics*, Fall 1979, pp. 40–48.

Bame, Jack J. "Analyzing U.S. International Transactions." *Columbia Journal of World Business*, Fall 1976, pp. 72–84.

"Coping with Capital." *The Economist*, October 29, 1994, p. 86.

Department of Commerce. *Survey of Current Business*, various issues.

Evans, John. *International Finance*. Orlando, Fla.: The Dryden Press, 1992.

Kravis, I. B., and R. E. Lipsey. Price Behavior in the Light of Balance of Payments Theory." *Journal of International Economics*, May 1978, pp. 193–246.

Meyer, Stephen A. "The U.S. as a Debtor Country: Causes, Prospects and Policy Implications." Federal Reserve Bank of Philadelphia, *Business Review*, March/April 1989, pp. 13–23.

Salop, Joanne, and Erich Spitaller. "Why Does the Current Account Matter?" International Monetary Fund, *Staff Papers*, March 1980, pp. 101–134.

"The Dwindling Dollar." *The Economist*, October 29, 1994, p. 96.

CASE 2.1
MEXICO—1982

On Sunday, December 5, 1982, Miguel de la Madrid had been president of Mexico for five days. He undoubtedly felt that the decisions immediately confronting him would determine his success as president and, more importantly, the future of Mexico. His country was facing an economic crisis with pressures being exerted from both within and without. Mr. de la Madrid's task was to choose a set of economic policies that would prevent the collapse of the Mexican economy.

Mr. de la Madrid had already committed himself to a path that was very different from that chosen by his immediate predecessor, Lopez Portillo. Mr. Portillo had followed the advice of those who urged Mexico toward economic isolation or independence. For Mr. Portillo, the causes of Mexico's problems were external—high U.S. interest rates, greedy international bankers, obdurate international bureaucrats, and a depressed market for oil, Mexico's major natural resource. Under Mr. Portillo, Mexico pursued a program designed to increase the Mexicanization and nationalization of the economy. The program included three initiatives: the requirement that Mexican companies be 51 percent owned by Mexican nationals, government ownership of banks, and policies to support the development of Mexican steel and automobile industries. Mr. de la Madrid had to determine whether the continuation of this policy was the proper course and, if it was not, what changes to implement.

THE MEXICAN ECONOMIC PICTURE

The economic situation in Mexico was grim. Under- and unemployment was estimated at 40 percent, while the work force was growing at some 600,000 to 700,000 persons annually. Exhibit 2.1 provides information about population growth in Mexico. Inflation, detailed in Exhibit 2.2, was approaching 100 percent annually, even with subsidized prices on necessities such as foodstuffs and with price and wage controls in place in many other sectors of the economy. Mexico's international debt totaled some $80 billion, including $24 billion in short-term obligations. Of this sum, $60 billion was public debt. Oil export earnings, the primary source of foreign exchange, had been crippled by the current weakness of oil prices worldwide and the glut of oil, which did not seem likely to abate soon. Mexico had herself increased production in an effort to earn additional foreign exchange. Mexico's current account deficit, combined with raging inflation, had led to a severe depreciation in the value of the peso, making the importation of essential goods and the repayment of debt even more difficult. The recent history of the peso is chronicled in Exhibit 2.3. The government budget deficit was almost one-fifth of gross domestic product (see Exhibit 2.4), and Mexico's international reserve position had deteriorated seriously over the past year (see Exhibit 2.5).

MEXICO—1982 POPULATION
(MILLIONS, MID-YEAR ESTIMATE)

1975	1976	1977	1978	1979	1980	1981
60.15	62.33	64.59	65.43	67.42	69.35	71.19

The options open to Mr. de la Madrid were equally unpleasant. Advocates of Mexican nationalism, including Carlos Tello, director of the central bank, and Fidel Velazquez, head of Mexico's unions under Mr. Portillo, favored exchange and import controls. Proponents of more conventional remedies, who were largely from the business community, would accept the usual package of International Monetary Fund conditions—currency depreciation, budget restraint, and monetary discipline—in return for funds to meet the country's external commitments. The former solution would tend to isolate Mexico and make servicing its external debts more difficult. Success would depend on increasing Mexican independence from foreign imports and investment by reliance on domestic production and on gains in exports of Mexico's manufactured goods and oil. The more conventional solution would require enduring more unemployment and slow growth while the peso depreciated further and the Mexican economy returned to international competitiveness.

MEXICO—1982 CONSUMER PRICES
(PERCENTAGE CHANGE OVER CORRESPONDING PERIOD PRIOR YEAR)

1978	1979	1980	1981	Jan. 1982	Feb. 1982	Mar. 1982	Apr. 1982	May 1982	Jun. 1982	Jul. 1982
17.4	18.2	26.4	27.9	32.8	44.30	34.7	38.9	44.5	49.4	54.4

Consumer Prices in Mexico and the United States (1975 = 100)

Year	Mexico	United States
1975	100.0	100.0
1976	115.8	105.8
1977	149.5	112.7
1978	175.4	121.2
1979	207.4	134.9
1980	262.1	153.1
1981	335.2	169.0
1982, January	407.7	175.6
1982, February	470.1	178.2
1982, July	518.9	181.3

■ EXHIBIT 2.3

MEXICO—1982 PESO EXCHANGE RATE
(PESOS PER DOLLAR)

	1975	1976	1977	1978	1979	1980	1981	Jan. 1982	Feb. 1982	Mar. 1982	Apr. 1982	May 1982	Jun. 1982	Jul. 1982	Aug. 1982
End of period	12.5	19.95	22.74	22.72	22.80	23.26	26.23	26.62	44.64	45.50	46.32	47.09	48.04	48.88	122.00
Period average	12.5	15.43	22.57	22.77	22.81	22.95	24.52	26.43	31.33	45.23	45.92	46.76	47.62	48.52	90.19

■ EXHIBIT 2.4

MEXICO—1982 GOVERNMENT DEFICIT
(BILLIONS OF PESOS, END OF YEAR)

1972	1973	1974	1975	1976	1977	1978	1979	1980
17.04	27.48	34.25	53.62	64.07	61.13	62.74	101.88	133.68

■ EXHIBIT 2.5

MEXICO—1982 INTERNATIONAL LIQUIDITY
(END OF PERIOD, $000,000)

	1975	1976	1977	1978	1979	1980	1981	Feb. 1982
Total Reserves Minus Gold	1,383	1,188	1,649	1,842	2,072	2,960	4,074	2,243
Gold	155	210	279	404	955	852	852	665

The Mexican economy historically had gone through boom and bust cycles. Until 1980 its future had looked relatively promising. During the middle to late 1970s, Mexico had embarked on a program of industrial development fueled by the discovery of oil and the earnings of the domestic oil industry. A large devaluation of the peso in 1976 had restored the competitiveness of Mexican goods, and a relatively stable period of growth followed. Exports of petroleum products and crude oil had provided the margin to absorb growing budget and current account deficits. International lenders had been happy to provide the funds necessary to carry out Mexican plans for industrialization on the basis of future oil earnings.

Imports of consumer, intermediate, and capital goods increased rapidly during 1979 and 1980. The industrial buildup in the petroleum industry and in other heavy industries such as steel and chemicals was in full swing. Exports of petroleum products doubled in 1979 and almost tripled in 1980. The future looked bright

EXHIBIT 2.6

MEXICO—1982 GROSS DOMESTIC PRODUCT AND TOTAL SPENDING
(MILLIONS OF 1970 PESOS)

	1970	1973	1974	1975	1976	1977	1978	1979	1980
Gross domestic product	418,700	499,730	529,374	551,820	559,916	578,270	616,436	671,915	728,356
Annual GDP growth (%)	5.4	7.6	5.9	4.2	1.7	3.2	6.6	9.0	8.4
Total domestic spending (TDS)	425,592	503,825	547,277	573,974	575,447	580,283	624,285	689,285	758,821
Annual growth of TDS (%)	4.8	7.8	7.7	4.9	0.3	0.8	7.6	10.4	10.1
Total consumption (TC)	335,392	389,978	412,070	446,317	448,420	458,210	489,272	531,349	577,045
Annual growth of TC (%)	4.9	5.6	5.3	3.9	0.5	2.2	6.8	8.6	8.6
Private consumption (PC)	302,817	348,667	362,802	388,871	381,202	388,169	405,923	439,615	476,982
Annual growth of PC (%)	4.5	5.4	4.4	2.2	-1.7	1.8	4.6	8.3	8.5
Share of PC in TDS (%)	71	69	66	68	66	67	65	64	63
General government consumption (GGC)	32,575	41,311	49,268	56,446	67,218	70,041	83,349	92,017	100,851
Annual growth of GGC (%)	8.9	6.9	12.5	16.6	15.2	4.2	19.0	10.4	9.6
Share of GGC in TDS (%)	8	8	8	10	12	12	13	13	13
Gross fixed investment (GFI)	82,200	104,221	117,628	127,657	115,516	109,278	127,309	151,625	176,795
Annual growth of GFI (%)	4.2	16.7	9.8	8.5	-10.0	-5.4	16.5	19.1	16.6
Share of GFI in TDS (%)	19	21	21	22	20	19	20	22	23

as Mexico anticipated continued growth in these sectors. Less emphasis on traditional exports, mostly agricultural products, was evidenced by a decline in the value of these exports in 1980. Information on Mexico's domestic economic performance, imports/exports, and balance of payments is contained in Exhibits 2.6, 2.7, 2.8, 2.9, and 2.10.

Weakness in the price of oil began to occur in 1981 as conservation and a worldwide recession slowed growth in the industrialized countries. Continued high production by OPEC and non–OPEC producers led to an oil glut and further weakness in prices, as shown in Exhibit 2.11. Mexico, which had never been a member of OPEC, depended heavily on its export earnings from oil and did not heed OPEC's call for reduced production. As the price of oil fell, Mexico was forced to increase production to try to maintain export earnings. It became apparent that the

▪ EXHIBIT 2.7

MEXICO—1982 PETROLEUM EXPORTS
(BILLIONS OF PESOS, TOTAL FOR PERIOD)

1975	1976	1977	1978	1979	1980	1981	Jan. 1982	Feb. 1982
5.75	8.40	23.23	41.42	89.32	225.67	338.35	105.67	168.36

▪ EXHIBIT 2.8

MEXICO—1982 EXPORTS AND IMPORTS: MAJOR COMPONENTS

	Exports of Goods FOB ($000,000)					
	1975	1976	1977	1978	1979	1980
Hydrocarbons	460	557	1,033	1,799	3,861	10,306
Main traditional exports	731	1,044	1,170	1,438	1,782	1,693
Main nontraditional exports	281	295	569	866	972	1,184
Others	1,387	1,420	1,679	2,209	2,671	2,968
Total	2,859	3,316	4,451	6,312	9,286	16,151
	Imports of Goods ($000,0000)					
Consumer	600	311	417	447	1,002	2,426
Intermediate goods	2,903	2,903	2,489	5,356	7,406	11,028
Capital goods	2,391	2,510	2,087	1,981	3,577	5,118
Other	686	503	848	208	152	52
Total	6,580	6,030	5,841	7,992	12,137	18,634
Public	2,498	2,155	2,199	2,841	4,028	6,790
Private	4,082	3,875	3,643	5,151	8,109	11,844

■ EXHIBIT 2.9

MEXICO—1982 PRINCIPAL TRADING PARTNERS

	General Iports ($000)		
Country	1978	1979	1980
USA–Puerto Rico	$4,867,165	$7,562,321	$12,175,976
Germany	568,045	778,951	971,955
Japan	586,088	726,573	988,811
France	312,035	500,239	516,325
United Kingdom	211,306	251,187	405,042
Canada	134,570	184,814	352,740
Italy	241,626	221,112	305,169
Switzerland	124,585	153,392	186,516
Brazil	135,416	273,422	419,031
Argentina	101,251	117,378	109,614
Other	770,918	1,733,237	3,085,780

	General Exports FOB ($000)		
USA–Puerto Rico	$4,509,610	$6,251,713	$9,688,077
Japan	174,635	248,150	563,166
Brazil	165,332	149,789	348,808
Germany	175,292	213,078	255,954
Venezuela	99,223	95,199	61,772
Italy	34,972	56,415	210,405
Canada	57,307	74,582	162,504
Switzerland	34,972	56,415	210,405
Israel	107,898	286,576	507,653
Spain	143,075	457,512	1,061,911
Other	798,335	908,816	2,237,725

Value a Percentage of World Total

General Imports				General Exports			
Country	1978	1979	1980	Country	1978	1979	1980
USA–PR	60.4	60.5	62.4	USA–PR	71.6	71.1	63.3
Germany	7.1	6.2	5.0	Japan	2.8	2.8	2.7
Japan	7.3	5.8	5.1	Brazil	2.6	1.7	2.3
France	3.9	4.0	2.6	Germany	2.8	2.4	1.7
UK	2.6	2.0	2.1	Venezuela	1.6	1.1	0.4
Canada	1.7	1.5	1.8	Italy	0.6	0.6	1.4
Italy	3.0	1.8	1.6	Canada	NA	NA	NA
Switzerland	1.5	1.2	1.0	Switzerland	NA	NA	NA
Brazil	1.7	2.2	2.1	Israel	1.7	3.3	3.3
Argentina	NA	NA	NA	Spain	2.3	5.2	6.9
Other	10.8	14.8	16.3	Other	14.0	11.8	18.0

▪ **EXHIBIT 2.10**

MEXICO—1982 MEXICO: BALANCE OF PAYMENTS (MILLIONS OF U.S. DOLLARS)

	1975	1976	1977	1978	1979	1980[a]
Exports of goods and services	$ 6,248	$ 7,081	$ 8,042	$11,431	$15,814	$24,310
Goods	3,009	3,476	4,604	6,443	9,416	18,380
Services	3,239	3,605	3,438	4,988	6,398	7,930
Transport and insurance	181	181	200	250	323	449
Travel	2,171	2,233	2,121	3,206	4,061	4,060
Imports of goods and services	8,025	8,429	7,850	11,441	16,724	25,060
Goods	6,292	5,773	5,620	7,786	11,632	17,860
Services	2,333	2,656	2,230	3,655	5,092	7,200
Transport and insurance	527	508	487	769	1,124	1,700
Travel	1,359	1,618	1,183	2,265	3,207	4,410
Trade balance	$-2,377	$-1,340	$ 192	$ -10	$ -910	$ -750
Profits and interest	$-1,818	$-2,216	$-2,210	$-2,784	$-3,655	$-5,380
Profits	-840	-666	-401	-479	-568	-800
Interest	-978	-1.552	-1.809	-2,305	-3,267	-4,580
Unrequited private transfer payments	114	129	152	182	205	250
Balance on current account	$-4,081	$-3,437	$-1,866	$-2,612	$-4,560	$-5,880
Unrequited official transfer payments	$ 27	$ 25	$ 16	$ 19	$ 15	
Long-term capital	4,716	4,997	4,588	4,569	4,381	
Direct investment	610	628	556	533	668	
Portfolio investment	153	431	1,338	755	-401	
Other long-term capital	3,953	3,938	2,694	3,281	4,114	
Official sector	362	1,089	1,060	349	-190	
Loans received	373	1,098	1,127	829	1,757	
Amortization payments	-11	-9	-67	-480	-1,947	
Commercial banks	1,753	1,851	697	860	1,274	
Loans received	2,114	2,399	2,269	3,194	3,454	
Amortization payments	-361	-548	-1,372	-2,334	-2,180	$ 6,795
Other sectors	1,838	998	737	2,072	3,030	
Loans received	2,297	1,746	1,784	3,754	5,768	
Amortization payments	-464	-701	-982	-1,665	-2,756	
Basic balance	$ 662	$ 1,585	$ 2,738	$ 1,976	$ -164	
Short-term capital	$ 766	$ 866	$-2,416	$-1,096	$ 501	
Official sector	-6	314	-295	-3	32	
Commercial banks	481	957	-464	-548	1,123	
Other sectors	291	-405	-1,657	-545	-654	
Errors and omissions	-1,250	-3,045	54	-450	-22	
Counterpart items	-1	-73	-41	-74	62	
Global balance	$ 177	$ -667	$ 335	$ 356	$ 376	$ 915
Total variation in reserves (− sign indicates an increase)	$ -177	$ 667	$ -335	$ -356	$ -376	$ -915
Monetary gold	—	83	-6	-6	-4	-4
Special drawing rights	52	98	-54	5	-141	51
IMF reserve position	—	113	—	—	—	-150
Foreign exchange assets	-260	-27	-337	-75	-26	
Other assets	31	32	-55	-42	-42	-698
Use made of IMF credit	—	388	117	-238	-163	-134

[a] Preliminary estimate based on incomplete data.

■ **EXHIBIT 2.11**

MEXICO—1982 WHOLESALE OIL PRICE
(U.S. $ PER BARREL)

	1977	1978	1979	1980	1981	January 1982	February 1982
Saudia Arabia	$12.40	$12.70	$16.79	$28.67	$32.50	$34.00	$33.29
Libya	13.87	13.71	21.06	35.87	39.83	36.50	35.15

■ **EXHIBIT 2.12**

MEXICO—1982 MONEY SUPPLY
(BILLIONS OF PESOS, END OF PERIOD)

1975	1976	1977	1978	1979	1980	1981	June 1982
122.4	158.0	208.2	270.2	360.9	477.2	635.0	672.0

oil prices were in for a continued decline and that an economy heavily dependent on oil would not be as robust as it would be just a year earlier. Lenders who had provided Mexico with funds on the basis of her oil capacity were now forced to look beyond oil to the essential soundness of the Mexican economy, and they did not like what they saw.

Government deficits, intended to promote economic growth, had fueled a continuing increase in the money supply, as shown in Exhibit 2.12, and inflation. The growth rates of these two indices were clearly too rapid for even a healthy economy. Of equal concern was the gradual deterioration of the value of the peso during 1981 and 1982. It had become obvious that the situation in Mexico was serious.

MEXICAN POLITICS

Mexico's political processes were dominated by one party, the Institutional Revolutionary Party (Partido Revolucionario Institucional, or PRI). Its control extended from the presidency and Congress to mayoralities and municipal councils. Opposition parties existed, but they had little influence on Mexican policies and represented no threat to the PRI.

As a result of its dominance, the PRI could select in its party caucuses the president of Mexico; the national election only confirmed what the PRI decided. In 1976, Lopez Portillo had received 98.7 percent of the vote.

Under the Mexican constitution, the president was limited to one six-year term of office. Effectively, the president had total power during his term. As a result, Mr. Portillo was able to enact rather dramatic policies in August and

September 1982, and three months later Mr. de la Madrid was in a position to reverse them.

Until 1982, the drift of the PRI's economic policies had been decidedly to the left of center. The 1976 election platform had called for increased government participation in the economy, and because Mr. Portillo's administration continued this policy, it was perceived as an extension of the Echeverria government that had preceded it. Initially, Mr. Portillo was considered more sensitive to the problems of the business community than Mr. Echeverria, but subsequent events and actions altered that view.

THE EVENTS OF 1982

By early 1982, it was apparent that the Mexican economy was a shambles. Declining oil prices had cut export earnings, other industrial sectors could not pick up the slack in a recession-wracked world economy, and inflation and unemployment were seemingly out of control. By February the international liquidity of Mexico had decreased to half its year-earlier level.

On February 18 the peso closed at P38:$1, down from P27.72:$1 on February 17, after the Mexican central bank said it would no longer intervene temporarily in foreign exchange markets to maintain a more gradual devaluation. Banks suspended new lending, and effective interest rates, already at 49 percent, were expected to increase another 5 to 6 percent. In late April Treasury Minister Silva Herzog announced a 17-point anti-inflation, economic recovery program. The three key points were (1) a planned decrease in the growth rate of foreign debt, (2) a reduction in government expenditures, and (3) an increase in bank reserve requirements.

In early August, the government announced a two-tiered exchange rate. Imports of consumer goods and luxury items as well as principal payments on debts denominated in foreign currencies were subject to a freely floating rate, while "priority imports" were given a preferential rate of P49.5:$1. The latter were items such as food, capital goods, private-firm interest payments, and interest and principal payments on the public debt. Many in the business community were skeptical, wondering where the government would obtain the funds to subsidize the preferential rate. IMF standby credit facilities were not available to countries employing two-tiered exchange systems.

On August 19, after the foreign exchange markets had been closed by the government for one week, the freely floating peso rate opened at P130:$1 and closed that day at P109:$1. In addition, the government suspended dollar withdrawals from Mexican banks. Withdrawals could be made only in pesos at the rate of P69.5:$1. Also in August, Mexico obtained a 90-day moratorium on repayment of debt principal so that a rescheduling of Mexico's external debt could be accomplished.

On September 1, President Portillo announced the nationalization of private banks and imposed additional exchange controls. The bank nationalization increased government ownership of Mexico's economy to 80 percent, up from 50 percent. In addition, the dollar would no longer be legal tender in Mexico and all dollar accounts were to be phased out. One week later, a new official financial rate for the peso of P70:$1 was instituted. Later in September, the government announced that banks would begin selling foreign exchange, but these sales never occurred except to tourists at airports. Firms were not able to obtain dollars with which to remit dividends or pay debt outside of Mexico.

Negotiations with the IMF for additional credits, which had begun in August, were moving slowly. President Portillo did not want to be the one to have to accept the stringent conditions certain to be required by the IMF. The slow pace of the IMF talks was holding up two-thirds of a $1.8 billion bridge loan available from the Bank for International Settlements. The United States had already provided $2 billion in credits for agricultural goods and as prepayment for oil. Cash-flow projections by Mexico's finance ministry called for a Current account deficit in 1983 of $2.7 billion, down from 1982's $5.9 billion. Imports would be reduced by 31 percent, from $23.1 billion to $15.9 billion. Net foreign borrowing in 1983 was projected at $7.0 billion to cover the Current account deficit and to meet obligations to multilateral financial institutions, trade-related liabilities, and bonds. These figures included the IMF funds being negotiated for at that time. The cash-flow projections were based on exports of $22.2 billion in 1983, an amount that would yield a trade surplus of $6.3 billion, up from a surplus of $1 to $2 billion in 1982.

In November, an IMF credit of $3.9 billion was arranged, but the conditions were strict. The letter of intent between Mexico and the IMF called for budget deficits to be no more than 8.5 percent of gross national product in 1983, down from 16.5 percent in 1982. In 1984 and 1985, the percentage was limited to 5.5 percent and 3.5 percent, respectively. The limit on increased net external borrowings in 1983 was to be $5 billion. The letter of intent also contained references to modified exchange controls, an apparent attempt to move Mexico toward a unified exchange rate. In a statement the day after the IMF letter of intent was released, Mr. Tello and Mr. Herzog asserted that the dual rates would continue and that exchange controls would be maintained for the time being. Finally, the debt repayment moratorium begun August 20 was extended for another 120 days, by which time a complete rescheduling agreement was to be finished.

THE POLITICAL DEBATE OVER THE OPTIONS

The situation facing Mr. de la Madrid was difficult, at best. Labor unrest was almost certain if wage boosts were not granted to compensate for the inflation still plaguing the economy. Interest rates in the 50 to 60 percent range were stifling investment. Uncertainty over government policy made foreign investors wary and unwilling to commit more capital in Mexico. The possibility of further exchange rate devaluation added to the already bleak situation. The IMF conditions would certainly contribute to slower growth in the economy, impeding any dramatic comeback.

The desire of some within the president's party to reduce economic dependence, particularly on the United States, fueled their support of the nationalistic solution. Exhibit 2.13 gives figures detailing the extent of U.S. claims on Mexico. The

■ **EXHIBIT 2.13**

MEXICO—1982 UNITED STATES–MEXICO CLAIMS/LIABILITIES (MILLIONS OF U.S. $, END OF PERIOD)

	1975	1976	1977	1978	1979	1980	1981	June 1982
U.S. liabilities to Mexico	$2,096	$2,893	$2,899	$3,430	$4,168	$ 4,590	$ 7,245	$ 9,119
U.S. claim on Mexico	3,784	4,830	4,923	5,654	9,290	12,942	22,947	29,930

strong nationalistic tendencies had been part of Mexico's heritage since the revolution of 1916. But, Mr. de la Madrid asked himself, was this the best way out of a difficult economic situation for his country? How isolated could Mexico afford to become? Could the Mexican economy generate sufficient growth on its own to provide for the needs of a growing, and increasingly restless, population? On the other hand, could the nation endure the painful process of recovery offered by the IMF and other international lenders who insisted on fiscal and monetary discipline as a condition for aid?

As the new president, Mr. de la Madrid would have to make hard choices in the days ahead. The IMF terms would require strict fiscal control, and the need to move toward a unified exchange rate would put further strain on the economy. Decisions made in the coming weeks would determine Mexico's fate for years to come. Mr. de la Madrid needed good counsel.

PART

UNDERSTANDING INTERNATIONAL CURRENCIES

INTERNATIONAL MONETARY ARRANGEMENTS AND ADJUSTMENT MECHANISMS

3

KEY CONCEPTS

THE EFFECT OF SUPPLY AND DEMAND FOR CURRENCIES IN DETERMINING EXCHANGE RATES ▬

THE ECONOMIC FACTORS THAT AFFECT EXCHANGE RATES ▬

THE RELATIONSHIP BETWEEN BALANCE OF PAYMENTS AND EXCHANGE RATES ▬

THE RECENT PERFORMANCE OF MAJOR CURRENCIES ▬

THE ADJUSTMENT OF EXCHANGE RATES UNDER DIFFERENT INTERNATIONAL MONETARY ARRANGEMENTS, INCLUDING THE GOLD STANDARD, ADJUSTABLE FIXED RATES, AND FLOATING RATES ▬

THE INTERACTION BETWEEN DOMESTIC ECONOMIC POLICIES AND EXCHANGE RATES ▬

INTRODUCTION

A Japanese manufacturer exporting a home entertainment system that sells for $1,000 in the United States received 270,000 yen in 1985, 140,000 yen in 1991, and only 100,000 yen in 1994. How do Japanese manufacturers respond to these dramatic changes in the yen value of their U.S. sales?

Electronics maker Toshiba Corp. is confident. "I'm not worried about the yen," says Nobuyuki Horiuchi, vice president of corporate planning. Mr. Horiuchi believes that the latest upswing is temporary. Just as important, he adds, is that Toshiba can cut its costs by about 5 percent a year, enough to offset the yen's gain in the past 12 months.[1]

---

[1] *Wall Street Journal,* June 22, 1994.

Mr. Horiuchi's confident comments have two dimensions. First, he predicts that the recent appreciation of the yen will be temporary. Second, he states that his company copes with an appreciating yen by increasing its productivity. Jack F. Welch, chairman and chief executive officer of General Electric, also addressed this aspect of international competitiveness.

> *Currency is a critical element in a country's competitiveness, and it is increasingly volatile and explosive in its effects. When Italy and Britain left the European monetary system in the summer of '92 and devalued their currencies against the franc and mark, Italy's export growth surged to more than 18 percent annually from 4.6 percent. Britain shot to a 14 percent growth in exports from 3.5 percent—in a year.[2]*

Exchange rates clearly influence operation, analysis, and planning at Toshiba and General Electric. These are, of course, large companies with obvious international involvement. The belief that exchange rates are not important to smaller companies with national orientations is a popular misconception. Exchange rates influence the revenues of exporters, their suppliers, and their competitors. Similarly, they influence the revenues of importers, their customers, and their competitors. If that does not suggest a pervasive influence, consider that exchange rates also have an important influence on the level of interest rates. In short, exchange rates are extremely important economic variables. But what are they?

Exchange rates are the prices of currencies in terms of each other. Like all prices, the supply of and demand for currencies determine these prices. Individuals, companies, financial institutions, and governments supply and demand currencies to conduct international commerce. When the factors affecting international commerce change or when the market's perception of them changes, exchange rates change. To explain (a hard task) and predict (a very hard task) exchange rate movements, it is necessary to explain the linkages between exchange rates and all the elements that influence their supply and demand. This chapter develops a framework for analyzing exchange rate behavior.

Using this framework, we can examine the different international monetary arrangements that have been utilized or proposed. This is important because exchange rates behave differently under each set of arrangements. National economic policies vary as well. Managers interested in evaluating the economic environment must understand the institutional arrangements in which policy is conducted. Those policies will, in turn, be determined largely by the constraints and commitments made by nations under different monetary systems or regimes.

Theories of exchange rate determination are broadly part of macroeconomics. Within that field, there is considerable disagreement, some would say confusion, about what causes changes in exchange rates. The approach taken in this chapter is eclectic. It is important to be aware of the various views and what they imply about exchange rate behavior. A manager who becomes wedded to a single view will likely be less responsive to changes in the environment of international business and less successful at adapting to changing conditions.

---

[2] John F. Welch, chairman and chief executive officer of General Electric, as reported in the *Wall Street Journal*, June 21, 1994.

A FRAMEWORK FOR ANALYZING EXCHANGE RATE DETERMINATION

In a free market, the factors that determine the supply and demand for currencies determine exchange rates. The transactions that make up a nation's balance of payments generate the supply and demand for currencies. We use this insight and our analysis of the balance of payments to produce a supply and demand framework for depicting and analyzing exchange rate determination. For simplicity, consider the supply and demand for British pounds in the bilateral relationship between Britain and the United States. Individuals, firms, and the government in Britain supply pounds in this bilateral foreign exchange market. They supply pounds to acquire dollars to use those dollars for balance of payments transactions. Examples include the purchase of U.S. exports and services, payments of dividends and interest in U.S. dollars, transfer payments in U.S. dollars, foreign investment in the United States, and any official reserve transactions. From the U.S. perspective, all of these transactions are credits, or sources of funds, in the balance of payments accounting. Individuals, firms, and the government in the United States demand pounds in this bilateral foreign exchange market. Examples include all of the balance of payments transactions that are debits, or uses of funds, in the balance of payments accounting. Understanding the balance of payments as discussed in Chapter 2 is, therefore, fundamental to understanding exchange rate determination. We indicate this connection in Figure 3.1A.

■ **FIGURE 3.1A**

EXCHANGE RATE DETERMINATION (DOLLAR/POUND)

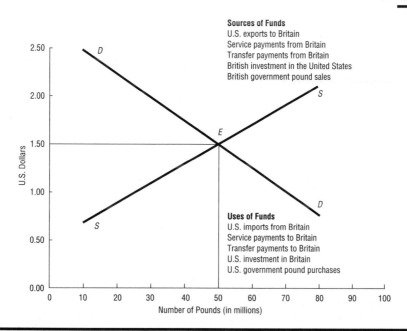

Sources of Funds
U.S. exports to Britain
Service payments from Britain
Transfer payments from Britain
British investment in the United States
British government pound sales

Uses of Funds
U.S. imports from Britain
Service payments to Britain
Transfer payments to Britain
U.S. investment in Britain
U.S. government pound purchases

U.S. Dollars

Number of Pounds (in millions)

In Figure 3.1A, we identify the supply curves as SS and the demand curves as DD. The commodity being priced is the pound; the unit of pricing is the dollar. The horizontal axis indicates the number of pounds and the vertical axis, the price of pounds in dollars. The supply and demand curves represent the supply of pounds and the demand for them. The equilibrium dollar price of the pound, E, is the price that clears the market. Everyone who is willing and able to buy pounds at that price or lower does so, and everyone who is willing and able to sell at that price or a higher price does so: For what purposes are they willing to buy and sell pounds? We indicate the purposes by identifying the types of balance and payments transactions that give rise to the supply and demand of pounds.

Because the exchange rate is the price of one currency in terms of another, there are two equivalent ways to quote it. A dollar price of the pound of 1.5 is identical to a pound price of the dollar of 0.67. The two prices are reciprocals. Both ways to express the exchange rate indicate that pounds can be exchanged for dollars at a ratio of 1:1.5. Consequently, if we label the axes of the supply and demand graph differently, we can provide the same information conveyed in Figure 3.1A, but in terms of the supply and demand for dollars. We do this in Figure 3.1B with the price expressed in pounds.[3]

■ **FIGURE 3.1B**

EXCHANGE RATE DETERMINATION (POUND/DOLLAR)

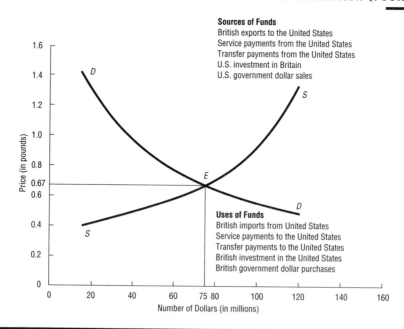

---

[3] For convenience, the supply and demand expressions in Figure 3.1A are linear. For consistency, we convert those same expressions to create the supply and demand curves in Figure 3.1B. The conversion changes supply and demand from linear to curved.

SHIFT IN THE DEMAND CURVE (DOLLAR/POUND)

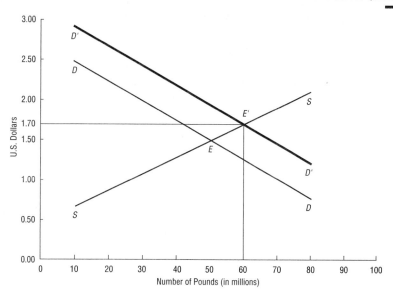

A simple mathematical relationship exists between Figures 3.1A and 3.1B; it is important to understand the conceptual connection between the two. An individual who buys pounds does so with dollars; an individual who sells pounds receives dollars. The demand curve for pounds in Figure 3.lA represents both the number of pounds the market desires to buy at every exchange rate *and* the number of dollars the market desires to sell at every exchange rate. Because of the construction of the graph, the number of pounds demanded can be read directly on the horizontal axis, whereas the number of dollars supplied is the product of the exchange rate and the number of pounds. In Figure 3.lB the converse is true. The number of dollars supplied at a particular price is shown directly on the horizontal axis, and the number of pounds is the product of the number of dollars and the pound per dollar exchange rate. Likewise, the specification of the types of balance of payments transactions that create the sources and uses of dollars changes in words. Both diagrams contain identical information, which implies we can use either representation to study the underlying economic relationships. For most of the discussion in this book, we discuss issues in terms of dollars per units of the non-dollar currency.

Before beginning to examine the economic factors that influence exchange rates, it is useful to look more closely at the mechanics of the supply and demand framework as applied to foreign exchange. In Figure 3.2A, the demand curve *D'D'* represents a shift to the right in demand. In comparison with the original demand curve, people are willing and able to buy more pounds at every price. This drives the equilibrium price of the pound up to $1.70. Using the appropriate terminology, the pound has *appreciated* in value relative to the dollar. It is now more expensive to buy pounds. Because it takes more dollars to buy a pound, the dollar has *depreciated* in value. It commands fewer pounds on the exchange market.

The movement of the supply curve in Figure 3.2B illustrates an opposite change in the equilibrium price. The supply of pounds has shifted to the right as represented by the new supply curve $S'S'$. In comparison with the original supply curve, people now desire to exchange more pounds for dollars at every exchange rate. The increase in the supply of pounds leads to a depreciation of the pound to $1.28, relative to the dollar, or, equivalently, an appreciation of the dollar. It requires fewer dollars to acquire a pound, or, conversely, more pounds to buy a dollar.

The factors that determine the positions of the supply and demand curves include everything that influences individuals, firms, and nations to acquire the currency of another nation. We have discussed this in terms of a bilateral relationship between Britain and the United States. In fact, the same logic applies to the multilateral relationships. Every U.S. balance of payments transaction recorded as a use of funds represents a supply of dollars and every transaction recorded as a source of funds represents a demand for dollars. For example, when a Brazilian firm buys machine parts from a U.S. manufacturer, the transaction represents a source of funds in the U.S. balance of payments accounts and creates a demand for dollars. When a U.S. company pays interest on money borrowed from Germans, the transaction represents a use of funds in the balance of payments accounts and creates a supply of dollars. It does not matter which of the types of transactions included in the balance of payments is examined; as long as the transaction is not barter, it creates a supply or demand for a currency. These factors are at work continuously

■ **FIGURE 3.2B**

SHIFT IN THE SUPPLY CURVE (DOLLAR/POUND)

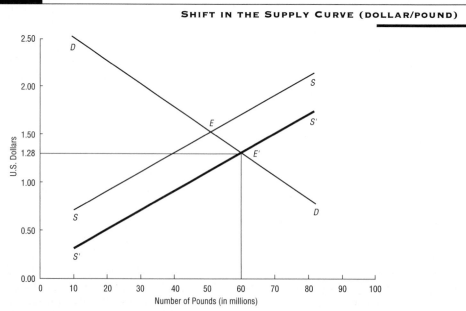

in the foreign exchange markets, creating simultaneous equilibrium in all of the bilateral foreign exchange markets.

It is convenient to use the balance of payments taxonomy—goods and services, capital, and official transactions—as a way to organize the discussion about exchange rates. Then, once we identify the component parts, we can analyze the whole system.

GOODS AND SERVICES TRANSACTIONS

The demand for foreign currency to acquire foreign goods and services is a function of relative prices, income, and tastes. In choosing to import a good, people compare the price of the domestic good to the price of a foreign good of comparable quality. If the foreign good is more expensive, they purchase the domestic good; if the foreign good is less expensive, they import it.

Foreign goods are usually priced in the currency of the manufacturing country, so the appropriate comparison must consider the prevailing exchange rate to permit comparison. For example, in the case of Japanese goods, we must compare the

Dollar price versus (Yen price)(Dollar per yen exchange rate)

Anything that causes the dollar price to increase, such as inflation in the United States or a specific cost increase in the production of the good in question, makes the domestic product less desirable and leads to an increase in imports. Relatively higher inflation in the foreign country makes imports less desirable. Changes in the exchange rate, as well as changes in the prices of goods, have the same impact. An appreciating dollar makes foreign goods relatively less expensive, which leads to an increase in imports whereas a depreciating dollar has the opposite effect.

As an example, assume that a turbine generator costs $2,000,000 or 250,000,000 yen (¥). If the dollar to yen exchange rate is $.008 per yen (¥125 per dollar), a U.S. purchaser is indifferent between the two on the basis of price considerations alone. A change in either the dollar price or the yen price alters that decision, as would a change in the exchange rate. If the yen were to become more expensive, $.009, the Japanese generator would cost $2,250,000 and Americans would import fewer of them. On the other hand, a depreciation of the yen to $.007 lowers the dollar price to $1,750,000 and makes imports more favorable.

Thus far, the discussion has centered on the decisions of U.S. purchasers, but it should be apparent that Japanese users of generators are also concerned about price. Changes in relative prices that induce Americans to import more Japanese equipment also lead to fewer Japanese imports of U.S. generators. That is true because the U.S.–made equipment is then more expensive. The same events that cause U.S. imports (Japanese exports) to increase cause Japanese imports (U.S. exports) to decrease. The trade balance between the two countries widens or narrows due to changes on both ends of the trade accounts, exports, and imports.

The same logic applied above explains the effects of price changes. Differences in inflation rates produce shifts in the supply and demand of currencies. When inflation in the U.S. is higher than inflation in Japan, the increase in U.S. demand for Japanese goods leads to an increase in the demand for yen. The decrease in the demand for U.S. goods leads to a smaller supply of yen. Both the increased demand for yen and the reduced supply of it induce appreciation of the yen. The new equilibrium exchange rate decreases the number of yen supplied and increases the number of yen demanded relative to the old exchange rate.

While considering this sequence of adjustments, notice that the exchange rate changes in response to relative price changes in the direction of equalizing the prices of goods in the two countries. Higher inflation in the United States made U.S. goods relatively more expensive than Japanese goods. Purchase responses reduce U.S. exports and increase Japanese exports. This produces an increased demand for yen and a decreased supply of yen. These changes lead to an appreciation of the yen, which makes Japanese goods more expensive to Americans and U.S. goods less expensive to the Japanese. This relationship between relative prices and exchange rates forms the basis of the purchasing power parity theory of foreign exchange, which we will discuss in Chapter 4.

The second major factor influencing the demand for imports and thereby the demand for foreign currency is the level of income in a nation. The income effect is a straightforward extension of the Keynesian theory of aggregate demand. An important concept in that theory is the propensity of individuals to increase their consumption as their incomes increase—the marginal propensity to consume. When individuals increase their consumption, they divide that consumption between goods and services produced domestically and those produced internationally. Therefore, there is a marginal propensity to import just as there is a marginal propensity to consume. As a nation earns an additional dollar of income, it increases its consumption. Some portion of the total goods demanded is supplied by foreign countries, so imports increase as income increases. The marginal propensity to import is the percentage of an increase in income that a nation spends on imports.

As a nation's economy and that of its major trading partners go through the business cycle, their imports and exports respond to the changes in income. These changes, in turn, are transmitted to the market for foreign exchange. An increase in income in the United States increases U.S. demand for Japanese goods. The increased demand for Japanese goods increases the demand for yen, causing the price of yen in terms of the dollar to rise.

This story is incomplete. An increased demand for Japanese goods stimulates Japan's economy and leads to a second-round effect of increased Japanese imports (U.S. exports) and an expanded supply of yen. The changes in economic activity might also lead to other changes. It is important to keep in mind these second-round effects because they emphasize the complexity of the analysis and the interdependence of the national economies. In this discussion, the emphasis is on the direct effects. However, the good analyst must consider the indirect effects on the exchange rates.

CAPITAL ACCOUNT TRANSACTIONS

The volume of Capital account transactions has grown dramatically in the last 20 years and likely now dominates trade-related flows in terms of their impact on exchange rates. There is considerable uncertainty about the size of the transactions because the numbers reported in the balance of payments accounts measure the change in capital position from one period to the next, not the total flow or adjustment that took place during the reporting period. For example, if the Saudi Arabian Monetary Authority (SAMA) begins the year with $150 billion in liquid assets overseas and ends the year with $151 billion, the net change is $1 billion. However, portfolio adjustments might have been many times that amount as the managers of the portfolio react to information about economic and political news. When SAMA moves funds from German bonds to Japanese certificates of deposit, a currency transaction affecting exchange rates occurs, even though it does not affect the size of SAMA's aggregate external holdings. Again, it is worth emphasizing that this is different from trade transactions for which the balance of payments accounts represent a cumulative total, not just the net change.

What motivates all these adjustments as well as the final amount of capital flows? It is the search for higher rates of return than can be earned elsewhere at comparable levels of risk. Money managers and corporate treasurers make their investment decisions on the basis of current interest rates, the state of the economy, political risk, and expectations about future exchange rates. How important each of these factors is depends in large part on the time horizon of the decision maker.

For example, direct foreign investment decisions are influenced more by the long-term economic outlook than by short-term interest rate considerations. When one nation's economy begins to grow more rapidly than others, it attracts both long- and short-term capital. Long-term investment occurs because there are increased opportunities and growing markets. Short-term capital flows in because expanding firms need financing, and their borrowing needs drive up the real rate of interest. The prospect of higher returns than are available at home lead decision makers to shift funds overseas. Foreign direct investment and lending cause an increase in demand for the currency of the recipient nation. This shifts the demand curve to the right and causes that country's currency to appreciate in value.

It is important to remember the role played by inflation and exchange rate expectations when discussing capital flows. An investor who moves money from one currency to another in response to differential rates or long-term strategic opportunities will be affected by future exchange movements. As an example, consider the case of a French investor who invests FR3,000 (French francs) worth ¥30,000 in Japanese bonds because the interest rate is 10 percent for yen bonds and only 5 percent for francs. At the end of the one-year holding period, the yen investment, principal, and interest will be worth ¥33,000. Its value in francs depends, however, on the exchange rate. If the exchange rate is still ¥10 = FR1, the rate of return on the yen is 10 percent. If the exchange rate has changed, the effective yield in francs is different. A depreciation of the yen relative to the franc lowers the rate of return; an appreciation raises it. Table 3.1 illustrates the point.

We discuss the relationships among exchange rates, interest rates, and expected inflation in more detail in Chapter 4. At the present time, it is sufficient to develop more fully the role of inflation expectations.

When expectations of inflation rise, the nominal rate of interest rises. That is the reason, in general, that high inflation countries also have high interest rates. Because high rates of inflation usually cause a country's currency to depreciate, the

■ **TABLE 3.1**

RATE OF RETURN EFFECTS OF EXCHANGE RATE CHANGES

Exchange rate (¥/FR)	8	9	10	11	12
Franc value	4,125.00	3,666.67	3,300.00	3000.00	2,750.00
Franc rate of return	37.5%	22.22%	10%	0%	–8.33%

nominal yield at the time of the investment is higher than the effective yield in terms of appreciating currencies. That is an important issue with respect to the previous franc/yen example. If investors expect the currency adjustment to offset the interest rate differential, then there is no incentive to move funds. For example, if investors expect the exchange rate at the end of the year to be 10.476 yen per franc, the expected rate of return for the French investor is 5 percent [(¥33,000)(10.467¥/FR) = FR1,050]. Consequently, if capital movements are going to influence exchange rates by virtue of interest differentials, investors must believe that the differentials will not be wiped out by exchange rate changes.

A final motive for capital flows is the avoidance of political risks. Countries frequently resort to capital controls in times of economic and political distress. Firms and individuals like to have the unrestricted use of their funds and, at times, fear expropriation. To avoid restrictions, investors often are willing to accept lower returns. Capital flight from nations experiencing political or economic upheaval is common and results in an increased supply of currency from the uncertain environment and an increased demand for the safe-haven currency. The Swiss franc and U.S. dollar are frequently given as examples of currencies benefiting from political instability in other nations.

OFFICIAL TRANSACTIONS

Government activities in the foreign exchange market cannot be measured completely on the basis of the balance of payments statistics such as the capital account transactions. The government also influences exchange rates through Official Reserve account transactions. Changes in the official reserve position represent the net change in the government's holdings of foreign exchange. Changes in reserve positions occur when governments alter the currency composition of their portfolio, use reserves to service outstanding obligations, or intervene in the exchange markets for the purpose of setting or controlling the exchange rate. Whatever the reason for the transaction, government activities in the exchange market have the same impact as individual or commercial transactions.

We illustrate the effect of government intervention in Figures 3.3A and 3.3B. These figures extend the illustrations in Figures 3.2A and 3.2B. In both cases, the initial equilibrium value of the pound is $1.50. In Figure 3.3A, we assume that there is a shift in the demand for pounds and ask whether the British government can do anything to stop the pound from increasing in value because of this shift in de-

■ **FIGURE 3.3A**

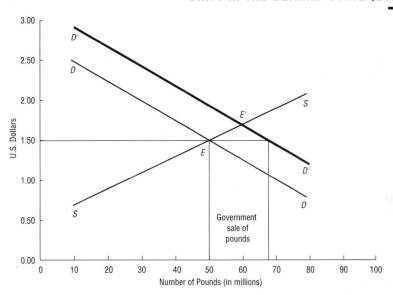

mand. The answer is yes. The government can intervene in the foreign exchange market by selling enough pounds to maintain the exchange rate of $1.50. In Figure 3.3A, the required sales would be approximately 18 million pounds. The government can certainly do that because it has access to an unlimited quantity of pounds through its right to print money. In Figure 3.3B, we assume that there is a shift in the supply of pounds. Without government intervention, the pound falls in value. If the government wants to avoid that result, it must again intervene in the market, but in this case it must buy almost 20 million pounds. Buying pounds is the same as selling dollars. The government can do this by decreasing its reserves by $30 million, as long as it has the dollar reserves to sell. In this case, the government's ability to support the pound is limited by the level of its foreign exchange reserves.[4]

PUTTING IT ALL TOGETHER

It should be apparent that explaining exchange rate movements is a complex task. A large number of factors are involved, and they operate on the exchange rate in conflicting ways. Identifying the influence of each factor is rarely straightforward. The complexity and the contradictions can be demonstrated easily by examining the case of the U.S. dollar from December 1978 to December 1985.

---

[4] Foreign exchange reserves of the 10 largest central banks exceed $500 billion. For a discussion of reserves and the activities of central banks see Simon Brady, "How Central Banks Play the Markets," *Euromoney,* September 1992, pp. 49–57.

■ FIGURE 3.3B

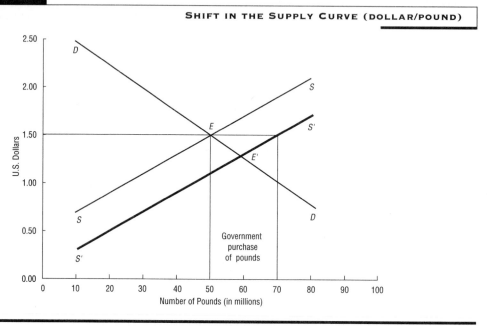

SHIFT IN THE SUPPLY CURVE (DOLLAR/POUND)

Figure 3.4 describes the movements of the dollar against three European currencies, the German mark, the Italian lira, and the U.K. pound. Figure 3.5 describes the movements of the dollar against two non-European currencies, the Canadian dollar and the Japanese yen. These figures plot index values of the price of the dollar in terms of units of the respective foreign currencies. Positive slopes mean that the dollar is increasing in value (appreciating); negative slopes mean that the dollar is decreasing in value (depreciating).

The most striking characteristic of Figure 3.4 is the similar pattern that the indices follow. Although the degree varies, the U.S. dollar appreciated in value against each of the other currencies from December 1978 to December 1984. The dollar appreciated most against the lira and approximately the same amount versus the mark and pound.

The plotting for the Canadian dollar and the Japanese yen in Figure 3.5 differs from those for the three European currencies in Figure 3.4 and from each other. The U.S. dollar appreciated steadily against the Canadian dollar but erratically against the yen. The movement of its value vis-à-vis the Canadian dollar was much smaller than that observed in Figure 3.4. The dollar did not appreciate as much or as steadily as it did against the European currencies, but it did appreciate more against the yen than the Canadian dollar.

What factors created the strength of the dollar from December 1978 to December 1985? One possible factor is the difference in inflation rates. If the U.S. inflation rates were lower than those in the other countries, this might account for the dollar appreciation. Figures 3.6 and 3.7 plot corresponding consumer price indices.

■ **FIGURE 3.4**

EXCHANGE RATE INDICES (FOREIGN CURRENCY/$; 1979 = 1.00)

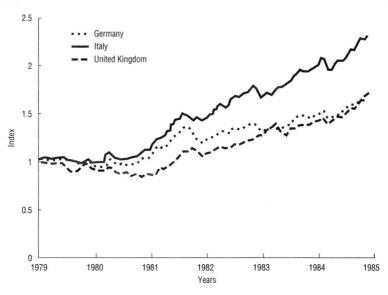

■ **FIGURE 3.5**

EXCHANGE RATE INDICES (FOREIGN CURRENCY/$; 1979 = 1.00)

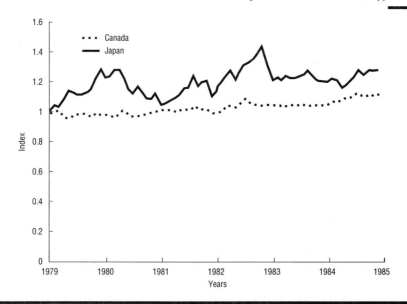

■ FIGURE 3.6

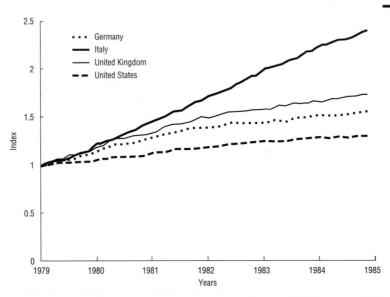

NATIONAL PRICE INDICES (1979 = 1.00)

■ FIGURE 3.7

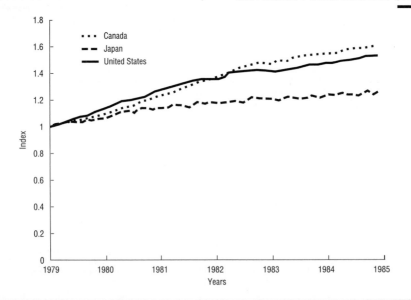

NATIONAL PRICE INDICES (1979 = 1.00)

The change that would explain the currency results does not appear to be consistently present. The U.S. inflation rate is much lower than the Italian rate, slightly lower than the U.K. rate, but higher than the German rate. Similarly, the Canadian rate was slightly higher than the U.S. rate, but the U.S. inflation rate was much higher than the Japanese rate.

Another possible factor is the Current account balance. Was the strength of the U.S. dollar related to a surplus in the Current account, reflecting an increased demand for dollars? The answer is no. Figures 3.8 and 3.9 provide information on the Current accounts for each of the countries during this period. The United States had small surpluses turn into large deficits during this time, whereas all of the other countries had consistently small deficits and surpluses. If anything, the other countries moved toward larger surpluses. This would support the idea expressed earlier that the transformations in the Current account were brought about by the strength of the dollar rather than the possibility that the Current account balances drove the exchange rates. Rather than continuing to look at each possible factor separately, we develop a scenario that explains much of the dollar's strength. It highlights the different impacts of trade and capital flows.

We have already observed that the United States moved from a small Current account surplus to a large deficit from 1980 to 1985. The Current account deficit was financed by capital flows that were attracted to the United States. We might ask why foreigners were willing to invest in the United States. This is an interesting

■ FIGURE 3.8

CURRENT ACCOUNT BALANCES (BILLIONS)

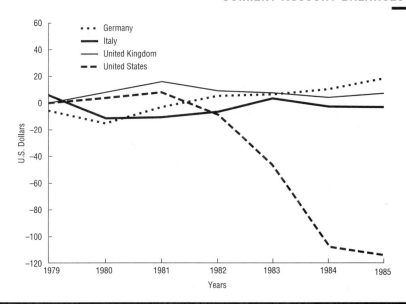

question because it may be that positive factors in the United States attracted the capital, which drove up the price of the U.S. dollar and generated Current account deficits.

One factor that influences the flow of capital internationally is the real rate of return available in a country. Higher real rates of interest (nominal interest minus inflation) in a country will attract capital from other countries. Figure 3.10 displays the average annual real rate of return on short-term government securities for the United States and the other five countries for the period 1979 to 1985. The difference between the U.S. rate of return and that of the other countries is the greatest for the United Kingdom and Germany, the countries where the currencies fell the most, and smallest for Japan and Canada, where currencies fell the least.

The higher real interest rates in the United States resulted from a combination of domestic monetary and fiscal policies. Foremost among them were the federal budget deficits, which competed with private users of funds and forced the United States to borrow from abroad. The competition for funds domestically and the need to attract foreign lending brought about an increase in the real rate. Once the United States economy began to grow in 1983, increased business opportunities contributed to the demand for funds and the appeal of dollar investments. That generated an increase in the demand for and an appreciation of the dollar.

The higher dollar and the growth in the United States beginning in 1983 caused U.S. exports to become less competitive and imports to be more desirable. As a result, the United States began to experience a decline in its Current account balance.

■ **FIGURE 3.9**

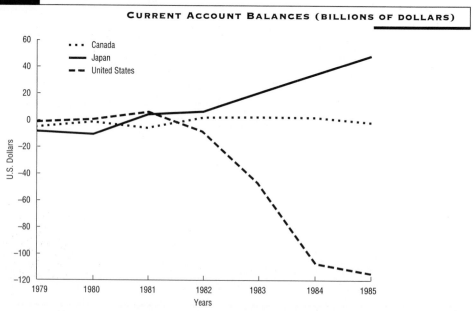

CURRENT ACCOUNT BALANCES (BILLIONS OF DOLLARS)

■ FIGURE 3.10

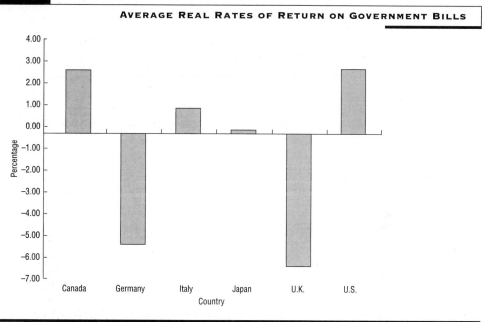

AVERAGE REAL RATES OF RETURN ON GOVERNMENT BILLS

INTERNATIONAL MONETARY ARRANGEMENTS

When people discuss international monetary arrangements or systems, they focus on the mechanism by which balance of payments imbalances among nations are either corrected or accommodated through financial flows. The method of correction and the need for accommodation are in large measure determined by the exchange rate system under which nations choose to operate. Accordingly, different time periods are often referred to by the exchange rate system predominating at the time: the gold standard era before World War I, the fixed rate or Bretton Woods period of 1946 to 1971, and the floating rate period since 1973. We will discuss each, in turn, using the balance of payments analysis to examine the adjustment process under the different exchange rate systems. This permits us to identify how international transactions affect domestic conditions and vice versa.

THE GOLD STANDARD

The pure gold standard dominated world currency transactions prior to World War I but has long since been relegated by textbook writers to discussions dealing with historical or theoretical issues of interest rather than practical importance. However, increased concern with inflation, problems of monetary policy, and government deficits have generated renewed interest in a gold standard on the part of conservative politicians. A return to a gold standard was implicit in the Republican party platform in 1980, and a special commission was established by the U.S. Congress in 1981 to study the past, present, and future role of gold in the U.S.

monetary system. Although the commission did not recommend a return to the gold standard or even an expanded role for gold, sufficient interest in the standard has been developed to warrant its restoration to the policy section of textbooks.

Under a gold standard, nations refrain from intervening in the foreign exchange markets and at the same time maintain a fixed or permanent rate of exchange. The two policies, nonintervention and a fixed rate, are made compatible because the government establishes the value of its money in terms of gold. Intervention in the gold market substitutes for exchange market intervention and brings about the requisite domestic adjustments to maintain the fixed rate of exchange. Understanding the gold standard requires a knowledge of the linkages among gold, money supply, prices, income, and foreign exchange. Money supply affects the economic system through its effect on prices and income. These economic variables influence the demand for foreign currency and serve as the links between money and foreign exchange rates. The gold standard has an automatic adjustment mechanism to address imbalances, while other systems allow influence through the monetary policies of central banks.

A nation on the gold standard establishes a gold value for its currency such as $300 per ounce. To maintain the value, the treasury must be prepared to buy and sell gold at the fixed rate of exchange for currency. In actual practice, there is a small difference between the buying and selling rates to cover the costs of minting. Because the treasury is obligated to exchange gold for currency at a fixed rate, the amount of currency in circulation is limited by the government's gold holdings. If a government issued more currency than it has gold to back it, there might be a run on the country's gold. Monetary policy is restricted under a gold standard essentially to buying and selling gold as the public chooses to increase or decrease its currency holdings. Growth in the money supply, measured by the public's gold holding and currency in circulation, is constrained under a pure gold standard to new discoveries of gold or the inflow of gold from abroad.

Fiscal policy is also limited under a gold standard. Because money supply growth is determined by the flow of gold, deficits cannot be *monetized* (financed by the monetary authority). If the government chooses to run a deficit, the deficit must be financed from previous surpluses or by borrowing from the public.

The relative price of gold in two nations establishes the exchange rate between their currencies. If the United States establishes a $300 per ounce gold price and the United Kingdom sets the price at £150, the exchange rate must be $2.00 per pound. What would happen if the exchange rate deviated from $2.00 to $1.50? Gold *arbitrage* would occur. (*Arbitrage* involves the simultaneous purchase and sale of identical items at different prices. Because it involves no time and requires no capital, arbitrage opportunities disappear rapidly as people exploit them.) At an exchange rate of $1.50/£, it would be profitable for individuals to take dollars to England, buy pounds in the exchange market, use the pounds to buy gold, transport the gold to the United States, and sell the gold for dollars.

The opportunity to profit from arbitrage increases the demand for pounds. As we have shown, this shifts the demand curve upward to the right and raises the price of pounds. The pound appreciates until arbitrage profits are no longer available, which occurs at an exchange rate of $2 per pound. (In practice, it will be slightly less than $2 to reflect the arbitrage-related transactions costs such as shipping and insurance. The prices at which gold flows between nations due to arbitrage are referred to as the *gold points*.)

Recall from the previous discussion of the foreign exchange market that changes in income, relative prices, or tastes can shift the supply and demand curves, disturbing the equilibrium. These shifts also generate arbitrage opportunities and induce the gold flows necessary to restore the old equilibrium. Using the gold prices given earlier, $300 and £150 per ounce, assume that incomes in the United States increase relative to those in the United Kingdom. U.S. imports rise due to the marginal propensity to import, and the demand for pounds shifts upward. When the pound appreciates above the gold point, say to $2.50 per pound, arbitrage is profitable and gold flows from the United States to the United Kingdom.

As gold leaves the United States, the U.S. money supply decreases. The reduction in the money supply acts as a brake on the economy and both prices and income. The decreases in prices and income lead to a reduction in imports and an increase in U.S. exports. At the same time, gold flowing into the United Kingdom stimulates that country's economy, leading to higher incomes and prices and higher imports and lower exports. The changing pattern of exports and imports shifts the supply and demand curves and restores the exchange rate to the parity value.

The major benefit of the gold standard is that as long as countries adhere to the rules of the game and keep their currencies convertible into gold at the established rate, the exchange rates are fixed between the gold points. Any significant movement from the fixed rate is automatically corrected by the flow of gold. By adhering to the gold standard, nations accept the domestic consequences of correcting external imbalances. For a deficit nation, that means accepting adjustments through unemployment and deflation; for a surplus nation, that means accepting adjustment through inflation.

As nations became increasingly concerned with unemployment during the 1920s and 1930s, they became less willing to accept the strong medicine prescribed by the gold standard. It was in this environment that the famous British economist J. M. Keynes developed his ideas about how nations could and should take steps to actively stabilize their economies. This meant abandoning the gold standard in favor of international monetary arrangements that allow more flexible monetary and fiscal policies. That is the system that evolved after World War II. In fact, Keynes played an important part in designing the agreement reached at Bretton Woods, New Hampshire.

Disappointment over the lack of success of those policies to eliminate inflation and unemployment in the 1970s certainly contributed to the renewed interest in the gold standard. The standard's advocates argue that the gold standard era was stable because government officials lacked discretionary authority over monetary and fiscal policy. They argue that returning to a gold standard will eliminate inflation, promote full employment, and reduce government deficits. Skeptics argue that the era of the gold standard was far from stable, that government intervention in the economy is not perverse, and that tying the supply of money to gold restricts the liquidity required to finance world trade.

ADJUSTABLE FIXED EXCHANGE RATES

The Bretton Woods agreement required governments to maintain fixed exchange rate relationships among their currencies. In addition, the United States agreed to convert dollars held by foreign governments to gold at $35 per ounce. Under the Bretton Woods agreement, the International Monetary Fund (IMF) became responsible for monitoring exchange rates and working with countries that experienced imbalances that threatened the value of the currency. The IMF could loan reserves, on either a short-term or long-term basis, to countries that were losing them. This would allow countries to support their currencies at the existing exchange rates. In more extreme cases, the IMF would support devaluation, typically counseling or requiring as a condition of loans domestic austerity measures that would also support the value of the currency. These periodic adjustments through devaluation are the reason this system was an adjustable fixed exchange rate system.

A government can commit itself, through treaties or a unilateral policy, to maintain its exchange rate at a specific value or par rate compared to another currency. That requires the government to enact necessary domestic policies or to intervene in the exchange markets to maintain the exchange rate at the target level. Intervention takes the form of a government selling its currency if the exchange rate is under pressure to appreciate or buying its currency if it is depreciating.

As an example, assume that the German government commits to an exchange rate of $0.65 per mark but that in the absence of any intervention, the equilibrium rate is $0.60. At any exchange rate above the equilibrium rate, the number of marks supplied exceeds the number demanded. The difference between supply and demand is the same as the difference between the uses and sources of funds, $(A + B + C + D) - (A' + B' + C' + D')$, considering only the transactions between the two countries. It is the total by which private uses of marks exceed private sources and represents a German balance of payments deficit. Germany has the deficit because with existing prices, interest rates, income levels, and preferences for consumption in the United States and Germany, any exchange rate above $.60 makes U.S. goods, services, and assets more attractive to the Germans than German goods, services, and assets are to Americans.

To support the $0.65 rate, the German central bank must absorb the excess marks. It does so by purchasing marks in the foreign exchange market. Germany can intervene only so long as it has sufficient dollars or other reserve assets. Under a fixed rate regime, the official settlements balance is closely watched as a barometer of future exchange rate crises. When a nation's reserves fall rapidly, that nation eventually reaches the point at which it must stop intervening and take other steps.

The most obvious alternative to intervention is for Germany to allow the exchange rate to depreciate to the equilibrium rate. Devaluation, which lowers the par or fixed value of the currency, is often referred to as an *external measure or external correction*. Devaluation increases the demand for marks because German goods cost Americans fewer dollars; devaluation decreases the supply of marks because U.S. goods cost Germans more marks. When the exchange rate declines from $0.65 to $0.60, German goods priced at DM 1,000 decline in price from $650 to $600. Conversely, U.S. goods priced at $650 increase in price from DM 1,000 to DM 1,083

[\$650/.60\$/DM = DM 1,083]. While a devaluation is an obvious solution to the problem of imbalance, devaluation is inconsistent with a policy of maintaining a fixed rate.

Once a nation decides not to devalue and can no longer intervene because its reserves have been depleted, it must use domestic policies to change the equilibrium. The required policies either decrease the supply of marks or increase the demand for them. The first represents a reduced demand for dollar purchases and the second, an increased demand for German goods, services, and assets.

Domestic policy measures available to the deficit country to alter the supply and demand curves are referred to as *internal measures or internal corrections*. There is a range of alternatives that can be categorized as expenditure-switching or expenditure-reducing policies.

Expenditure-switching remedies cause the pattern of expenditures to change. German residents reduce their demand for U.S. exports while Americans increase their demand for German exports. This category includes domestic policies that lower the rate of inflation in Germany relative to the United States. As the prices of German goods fall relative to U.S. products, both the Germans and Americans switch expenditures to the German goods. The process works in the same fashion as the effect of the devaluation except that internal prices have been altered instead of the external exchange rate.

Other expenditure-switching policies include tariffs and quotas imposed on imports, subsidies to stimulate exports, and exchange controls that restrict the amount of foreign currency available. Nations using these policies frequently impose harsher controls or higher tariffs on luxury items rather than necessities. This brings about a reduction in the demand for foreign currency without inhibiting the ability of the economy to acquire essential goods from overseas, especially those required in manufacturing or processing exports.

Expenditure-reducing policies decrease the demand for imports by reducing the level of national income and aggregate demand. Because the marginal propensity to import is more than zero, as a nation's income falls, so also will its demand for foreign goods and services. Restrictive monetary policies and a contraction in fiscal policies are the prescribed cures for deficit nations.

It should be evident by now why nations often resist taking domestic steps to correct a balance of payments problem even if that reluctance leads to a significant reduction in reserves. Strategies that switch or reduce expenditures involve austere economic policies that reduce prices and contract income and that can lead to more unemployment. Nations often face a conflict between external and internal objectives. Policies that address balance of payments problems can generate or exacerbate internal domestic difficulties and vice versa.

Figure 3.11 describes different positions a nation faces. This figure depicts four quadrants or zones. Two of the zones, I and III, are nonconflict areas. The necessary internal policies for achieving domestic goals are also the appropriate remedies for achieving external balance. However, in zones II and IV, policy makers are confronted with a difficult dilemma. Those policies suitable for combating domestic economic ills conflict with the policies needed to achieve balance in the international position.

POLICY TRADE-OFF DIAGRAM

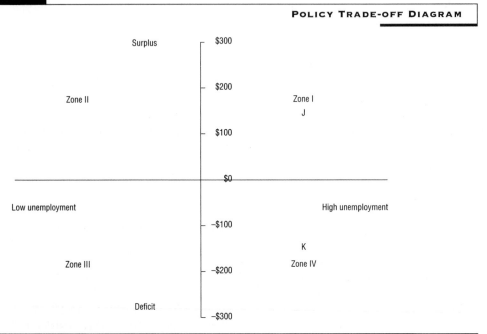

As an example, point *J* in Zone I describes an economy experiencing a balance of payments surplus and unemployment above the target or desired level as represented by the origin. The appropriate internal policies call for stimulating the economy to decrease the level of unemployment. This would also raise income and prices, generating expenditure switching and adjusting consistent with a reduction in the surplus. The United States during the Great Depression of the 1930s is an example of an economy in Zone I.

Point *K* in Zone IV is a less enviable position. Western Europe in the 1930s and the United States in the early 1960s are examples of Zone IV economies. At the same time that they had balance of payments deficits, they also experienced higher than desired unemployment. Restrictive fiscal policies such as tax increases or monetary restriction pursued to eliminate the deficits would have hindered the effort to reduce unemployment.

One of the major shortcomings related to the fixed rate system is that the burden of external imbalances is asymmetrically distributed between surplus and deficit nations. Most of the adjustment burden falls on the country experiencing the balance of payments deficit. A surplus nation has no constraint on its ability to ride out temporary imbalances before either revaluing its currency (establish a higher fixed value) or implementing appropriate domestic remedies. As long as it allows the imbalance to continue, it must accumulate reserves as it sells its currency in exchange for the deficit country's currency to hold down its exchange rate at the par value. On the other hand, deficit nations are constrained by the supply of reserves at their disposal. Once their reserves have been depleted, an alternative measure, other than intervention, must be pursued.

FLEXIBLE OR FLOATING EXCHANGE RATES

Beginning in 1973, much of the industrialized world adopted a floating exchange rate system. Strict adherence to this system allows exchange rates to fluctuate freely in response to market forces. It is exceedingly difficult for governments to stick to a hands-off policy with respect to currency values. Thus, governments do intervene, occasionally, even while they profess to follow a floating exchange rate system. Indeed, the major industrial countries occasionally intervene on a coordinated basis to support a specific currency. This type of intervention leads some to refer to this type of floating exchange rates as a *dirty float*. Exchange rate movements address the problem of external balance while the country pursues whatever domestic policies are appropriate for internal balance. As an example, the Zone IV economies (see Figure 3.11) can allow their exchange rates to depreciate while pursuing expansionary monetary and fiscal policies. The latter stimulate the economy and reduce unemployment. This would exacerbate the deficit problem except that the falling exchange rate corrects not only the initial deficit but also offsets the external effects of the expansionary domestic policies.

Flexible exchange rates offer a number of benefits. Adjustments are automatic and market driven rather than administered by the government. Rates are allowed to fluctuate in the exchange market, and nations have no obligation to intervene or determine the appropriate equilibrium rate. External adjustment is continuous as market demand and supply for the currency shift in line with changes in the demand for goods and services produced in that country as well as its demand for goods produced overseas. The exchange rate responds rapidly. This contrasts starkly with the exchange rate adjustments that occur under a fixed rate system. Those adjustments are generally large in size and occur at discrete intervals, frequently in an atmosphere of crisis. One of the major drawbacks of the fixed rate system is that countries are reluctant to devalue their currencies, turning to this action only when they have exhausted other policy options.

The major disadvantage associated with flexible rates is that they generate uncertainty about future rates. This adds to the complexities of international trade and business and is a possible barrier to international trade and the movement of international capital. Because international trade and investment allow countries to enjoy the benefits of comparative advantage, anything that depresses the volume of transactions is undesirable. A counterargument is that there are methods by which the risks created by flexible rates can be reduced; an example is the use of forward exchange contracts. (Forward contracts establish a price at which currencies will be exchanged in the future. See Chapter 4 for more detail.) Unfortunately, there are forward contracts in few currencies and for few delivery dates. As a consequence, forward contracts and other risk-reducing techniques are not perfect substitutes for stable exchange rates.

Flexible rates might also have an inflationary bias. Because they allow a country to pursue an independent domestic policy, a deficit nation is not forced to deflate its economy to correct a balance of payments deficit. Pressure to attack inflation must come entirely from domestic concerns. Moreover, flexible rates can make inflation worse. As the exchange rate falls, imported goods and services increase in price, raising the cost of living. This can lead to higher wage and price demands, pushing up costs further. Because wages and prices are more flexible in the upward direction than downward, there is no offsetting decline of prices in nations with surpluses. Globally, prices ratchet upward, resulting in an inflationary bias across all nations.

A final argument against flexible rates relates to the degree to which exchange rate variation corresponds to the fundamental problems underlying imbalances. It has been argued that under a flexible exchange rate system, when an exchange rate changes, it tends to change by too much—it overshoots the true sustainable equilibrium value. This means that an exchange rate tends to always be wrong. Sometimes it is too high, and sometimes to low. This adds instability to the international economy. Much of the discussion of this subject has been extremely technical. It has focused on the conditions under which exchange rate variation might be destablizing and motivated by speculation rather than changes in relative prices or income in the two countries. Because exchange rates influence trade and capital flows, when currency prices overshoot, they can induce economic inefficiency. As an example, an appreciation of a country's currency beyond its equilibrium level reduces that nation's exports and increases its imports. This idles resources in the country with the overvalued currency and stimulates the use of resources when the currency is correspondingly undervalued. Because the exchange rate does not reflect actual price or income differentials, the shift in resource utilization leads to less efficient production and trade patterns. The evidence, provided earlier in the discussion of the U.S. dollar's performance during the 1980s, is consistent with the overshooting hypothesis.

IMPLICATIONS FOR MANAGERS

Understanding exchange rates and the economic policies that influence them begins with knowledge about the exchange rate system. For example, countries that adhere to fixed exchange rates respond differently to economic conditions than countries whose exchange rates float freely. In the former, we might expect higher interest rates during a slow growth period; in the latter, we might observe lower interest rates but also higher inflation rates over time because there is not the external discipline of the fixed exchange rate. Also, countries with fixed exchange rates experience exchange rate stability as the norm but may also experience occasional exchange rate crises and extremely large revaluations. That is what happened when the British government took the pound out of the Exchange Rate Mechanism in Europe in the late summer of 1992. Conversely, countries with floating exchange rates experience daily volatility but are less likely to experience the dramatic changes associated with devaluations. A manager making investment or financing decisions needs to understand these relationships when making foreign commitments.

Recent changes in Latin America illustrate another important respect in which exchange rates are a fundamental determinant of the success of foreign business exposure. In these examples, exchange rate policy change has been a central component of dramatic economic changes creating economic opportunities. Argentina is one example of a country using exchange rate policy to help reshape its economy. Argentina's successful (so far) efforts to eliminate chronic high inflation from its economy and establish a stable currency fixed to the dollar have completely changed its economic climate and the opportunities for foreign businesses.

After years of economic stagnation and inflation as high as 5,000 percent per year,[5] in April 1991 Argentina implemented an aggressive plan to change its economy. A fixed exchange rate between its peso and the dollar was a key element of that plan. To achieve stability, Argentina limited its domestic money supply to the size of its foreign exchange reserves, outlawed central bank financing of government deficits, allowed unrestricted conversion of pesos to dollars, and even made the U.S. dollar legal tender. The government also made significant structural changes in the economy by selling government-owned enterprises, lowering tax rates, and establishing private pension plans.

One measure of the success of this program is the rate of wholesale inflation, down to 3 percent in 1992, and the stability of the peso, with no change in value relative to the U.S. dollar. How has this affected business? Motorola and Bell South have invested millions of dollars in cellular telephone systems. Houston Power and Light has invested in power distribution. Exports from the United States to Argentina grew by more than 20 percent in 1992.[6] In addition, European companies are active in both exports and foreign direct investment. All of these foreign companies have recognized an improvement in opportunities related to the change in economic policies, including exchange rate policy. For all of these opportunities, there is also an important risk that every company involved in Argentina must assess. Since 1989 the real value[7] of the peso has increased by approximately 60 percent. Every firm with commitments, or considering commitments, in Argentina must understand that this may not be a sustainable increase in value and a significant devaluation may occur in the future.

This observation is not hypothetical. In July 1992 there was a run on the peso. Large companies sold hundreds of millions of pesos in exchange for dollars. The managers of these firms thought that the peso was overvalued and that the government would be forced to devalue it. In that case, the government resisted the pressure to devalue and the peso has maintained its value, relative to the dollar, through December 1994.[8] Every financial manager of a firm doing business in Argentina had to analyze the risk of an immediate, substantial devaluation and adjust her firm's financial position accordingly. She must also consider the long-run stability of the peso. A thorough understanding of international monetary arrangements and adjustment mechanisms is essential to this process.

---

[5] One of the effects of this inflation was the effective substitution of the dollar for the Argentinean currency, or what has been referred to as the *dollarization of the economy*. For a discussion of currency substitution, see Federico A. Sturzenegger, "Hyperinflation with Currency Substitution: Introducing an Indexed Currency," *Journal of Money, Credit and Banking,* August 1994, pp. 377–395.

[6] Marita van Oldenborgh, *International Business,* May 1993, pp. 65–68.

[7] We discuss this concept in detail in Chapter 4. It refers to the purchasing power of a country's currency relative to other currencies. In this case, it means that the peso will buy 60 percent more in international markets than it did formerly. While that means that it is cheaper to buy foreign priced goods, it also means it is much harder to sell peso-priced goods.

[8] By the time you are reading this book, that may have changed. You might check the currency listings to see whether the peso is still worth $1. Also, keep in mind that during this period, the dollar has declined in value relative to most other major currencies. Therefore, the peso has also devalued relative to the currencies such as the mark and yen.

QUESTIONS AND EXERCISES

3-1. How would each of the following changes affect the dollar price of the French franc?

   a. A disastrous root fungus destroys the California wine industry and the United States imports much more French wine.

   b. Disney invests in a large theme park outside Paris.

   c. The French government sends thousands of students to the United States to study computer engineering.

   d. U.S. insurance companies experience large losses from floods in southern France.

   e. The French government decides to sell its U.S. dollar reserves to hold yen reserves instead.

3-2. For each of the prices of the Ecuadorian sucre in the following table, calculate the U.S. dollar rate of return on an Ecuadorian one-year bill that you buy for 8,000,000 sucre and redeem for 10,000,000 sucre, if the price of the sucre when you buy the bill is $0.0005.

Exchange rate ($/sucre)	0.000325	0.000375	0.000425	0.000475	0.000525
Dollar rate of return					

3-3. Assume that a party that advocates the separation of Quebec from the rest of Canada has unexpectedly won an election to form the government in the Province of Quebec. This increases the likelihood that Quebec will separate. What will happen to the value of the Canadian dollar when the foreign exchange markets open the day after the election?

3-4. The following table presents Current account supply and demand functions for pounds.

   a. Plot these functions in a graph.

   b. Assuming that there are no capital market transactions, what is the equilibrium price of the pound?

   c. If the U.S. government wants the price of the pound to be $1.50, what transaction is necessary to achieve this value?

Pound Market Current Account (in millions)

Price	Supply	Demand
$1.40	100	220
1.45	120	200
1.50	140	180
1.55	160	160
1.60	180	140

3-5. The following table presents the capital market supply and demand functions for pounds.

   a. Plot these functions in a graph.

   b. Assuming that there are no Current account market transactions, what is the equilibrium price of the pound?

   c. If the U.S. government wants the price of the pound to be $1.50, what transaction is necessary?

Capital Account (in millions)

Price	Supply	Demand
$1.40	140	180
1.45	160	160
1.50	180	140
1.55	200	120
1.60	220	100

3-6. In the following table, enter the values for the total supply and demand functions for pounds from questions 4 and 5 (the sum of the current account and capital account functions).

Pound Market Total (in millions)

Price	Supply	Demand
$1.40		
1.45		
1.50		
1.55		
1.60		

a. Plot these functions in a graph.

b. What is the equilibrium price of the pound?

c. If the U.S. government wants the price of the pound to be $1.55, what transaction is necessary to achieve this value?

d. If the U.S. government wants the price of the pound to be $1.45, what transaction is necessary to achieve this value?

e. If the U.K. government wants the price of the pound to be $1.45, what change in interest rate policy is necessary to achieve this value?

f. If the U.K. government wants the price of the pound to be $1.45, how else might it achieve this result?

3-7. Daily accounts in the business press often refer to a currency weakening in response to a decline in interest rates or strengthening in response to an increase. What is the economic rationale for these statements? What do they imply about inflation and inflation expectations? Is this consistent with the information in the exhibits in Chapter 3?

3-8. Facing a crisis of confidence in its currency, Sweden raised its overnight interest rate for bank lending from the central bank to 500 percent in October 1992. Why would it do that? Would that have been necessary if Sweden had been part of a gold standard system?

3-9. In response to international debt problems, the International Monetary Fund advises many debtor nations to pursue austerity policies. These include devaluation of their currencies and restrictive monetary and fiscal policies. Why does the IMF advocate these policies?

3-10. Countries can address internal problems with external solutions.

a. Why might a country in a severe recession consider devaluation of its currency attractive?

b. Why might a country experiencing high inflation consider appreciation of its currency attractive?

REFERENCES

Alexander, Sidney S. "The Effects of a Devaluation on the Trade Balance." International Monetary Fund, *Staff Papers*, April 1952, pp. 263–278. Reprinted in Richard E. Caves and Harry G. Johnson, eds. *AEA Readings in International Economics*. Homewood, Ill.: Richard D. Irwin, 1968.

Baldwin, Robert E. "Determinants of Trade and Foreign Investment: Further Evidence." *Review of Economics and Statistics*, Fall 1979, pp. 40–48.

Bame, Jack J. "Analyzing U.S. International Transactions." *Columbia Journal of World Business*, Fall 1976, pp. 72–84.

Brady, Simon. "How Central Banks Play the Markets." *Euromoney*, September 1992, pp. 49–57.

Corrigan, E. Gerald. "Coping with Globally Integrated Financial Markets," *Quarterly Review*, Federal Reserve Bank of New York, Winter 1987, pp. 1–5.

Dornbusch, Rudiger. "Exchange Rate Risk and the Macroeconomics of Exchange Rate Determination." *Research in International Business and Finance* 3, 1983, pp. 3–27.

Frankel, J. "On the Mark: A Theory of Floating Exchange Rates Based on Real Interest Differentials." *American Economic Review*, September 1979, pp. 610–622.

Friedman, Milton. "The Case for Flexible Exchange Rates." *Essays in Positive Economics* Chicago, Ill.: University of Chicago Press, 1953.

Giddy, Ian H. "An Integrated Theory of Exchange Rate Equilibrium." *Journal of Financial and Quantitative Analysis*, December 1976, pp. 883–892.

Kravis, I. B., and R. E. Lipsey. "Price Behavior in the Light of Balance of Payments Theory." *Journal of International Economics*, May 1978, pp. 193–246.

Krugman, Paul. "Vehicle Currencies *and* the Structure of International Exchange." *Journal of Money, Credit and Banking*, August 1980, pp. 513–526.

Levi, Maurice D. "Taxation and 'Abnormal' International Capital Flows." *Journal of Political Economy*, June 1977, pp. 635–646.

Salop, Joanne, and Erich Spitaller "Why Does the Current Account Matter?" International Monetary Fund, *Staff Papers*, March 1980, pp. 101–134.

Sturzenegger, Federico A. "Hyperinflation with Currency Substitution: Introducing an Indexed Currency." *Journal of Money, Credit and Banking*, August 1994, pp. 377–395.

van Oldenborgh, Marita. *International Business*, May 1993, p. 65–68.

Westerfield, Janice Moulton. "An Examination of Foreign Exchange Risk under Fixed and Floating Rate Regimes." *Journal of International Economics*, May 1977, pp. 181–200.

CASE 3.1

DOLLAR DISEQUILIBRIUM IN 1990

When the leaders of the G-7[1] nations met for their annual economic summit in Houston, Texas, in July 1990, the final communique was 17 pages long. It dealt with a range of issues related to international economic concerns, including Third World debt, agricultural subsidies, and trade and financial aid to China, and the rapidly changing economies of Eastern Europe. All of these topics were important and had been the subject of discussions and the source of disagreement among the G-7 countries. What was not mentioned in the communique but was perhaps of more immediate concern to businesspeople throughout the world was foreign exchange.

The absence of a section in the final statement addressing exchange rate levels was apparently a surprise to market observers. The yen had traded higher "since a French newspaper reported... that a draft communique said the yen's current [low] levels could have undesirable consequences for the process of global adjustment. [C]urrency market participants had been expecting a G-7 statement supporting the yen.[2]"

The anticipation of action or at least a statement by the G-7 leaders was a reflection of market concerns about exchange rate movements and an indication of the importance of governments' roles in the market. The quote itself highlights the dual nature of exchange rate concerns: the market responds to news or information, which leads to short-term changes such as the yen trading higher that day, but concerns also exist about the longer-term path of exchange rate movements and their impact on global adjustment, by which is meant changes in trade and investment flows throughout the world.

Economists and policy makers generally agreed that exchange rates have been more volatile than was anticipated when generalized floating rates were adopted in 1973. At that time, the widely held view was that rates would move in response to fundamental economic factors such as relative inflation rates, interest rates, or changes in growth or productivity. Although the economic performance measures vary, exchange rates have exhibited much greater volatility than the movements in the underlying fundamentals would seem to justify. This volatility is at least partially demonstrated by Exhibit 3.1, which plots monthly movement in the effective rate for the dollar since 1980.

Little agreement exists about the causes of the volatility or, for that matter, its effect. Republican administrations in the United States during the 1980s have been accused of pursuing a policy of benign neglect. The arguments in favor of such inaction have ranged from the inability of governments to intervene effectively in

---

[1] United States, Great Britain, France, Italy, Japan, Germany, and Canada.

[2] "Dollar Regains Some Ground, Aided by Profit Taking and Pounds Sell Off," *Wall Street Journal*, July 12, 1990.

■ EXHIBIT 3.1

DOLLAR DISEQUILIBRIUM IN 1990
■ U.S. REAL EFFECTIVE EXCHANGE RATE

U.S. REAL EFFECTIVE EXCHANGE RATE. The real value of the U.S. dollar appreciated sharply in the first half of the 1980s before depreciating and then stabilizing at lower levels.

NOTE: Data are monthly.
SOURCE: *Economic Report of the President*, 1990.

exchange markets to the view that the observed volatility in the markets is not unusual for the prices of financial assets being traded in a relatively free and efficient capital market. Those views are reflected in the 1990 *Economic Report of the President (ERP):*

> Although this fact is widely recognized, the problems associated with short-term volatility may be overstated. Exchange rates are the prices of assets.... Short-term interest rates and other asset prices, such as stock prices, are even more volatile than exchange rates. Furthermore, short-term volatility should not disrupt production decisions, such as where to purchase imported inputs, provided that longer term trends are predictable. Forward and futures markets can be used to hedge against short-run uncertainties.[3]

The *ERP* is more ambiguous about the role of intervention. It argues that any intervention is likely to be small in comparison with the daily $650 billion of transactions in the world's exchange markets; intervention that is coordinated, however, and used in combination with other policy actions might be successful:

> What has been the actual experience with intervention in foreign exchange markets? Most studies have concluded that sterilized intervention is unlikely to be an effective tool

---

[3] *Economic Report of the President*, 1990, Washington, D.C., p. 93.

for moving exchange rates in directions that are inconsistent with underlying fundamentals of policy and performance—except perhaps in the very short run. The effects are larger and more lasting if backed by other policy changes such as interest rate adjustments, which help to make the signal credible. Also, coordinated intervention by monetary authorities in more than one country seems to have a greater and more sustained effect on exchange rates than intervention by a single country alone.[4]

The current administration does acknowledge that medium-term disequilibrium might occur and that it may have an impact on production and investment decisions:

> Unlike short-term variance, medium-term misalignments can have a profound effect on the allocation of resources. Large changes in the value of the dollar relative to the Japanese yen, for example, have led to large changes in prices of Japanese goods. These large relative price movements, and uncertainty about how quickly they might be reversed, may complicate decision-making for both producers and consumers.
>
> An appreciation of more than 60 percent, such as the U.S. dollar experienced in the mid-1980s, can erode the international competitiveness of domestic exporters and import-competing firms, putting firms out of business and generating unemployment. At the same time, goods and services produced abroad become bargains to domestic consumers, helping foreign firms to capture a larger share of the home market. Even if the appreciation is fully reversed within a few years, domestic firms may find it difficult to recapture the market share they held before the exchange-rate cycle.[5]

WHAT IS EQUILIBRIUM?

The most difficult, perhaps intractable, issue is the determination of the equilibrium or "right" level of exchange rates. One of the oldest and most widely used theories of exchange-rate determination is the purchasing power parity (PPP) theory. It relates exchange rates to relative prices of goods in two countries. A country experiencing relatively high rates of inflation will have a depreciating currency, whereas a country with lower rates of inflation will see its currency appreciate. PPP appears to be more valid for some countries than others, and for longer time periods than for shorter ones. Exhibits 3.1 and 3.2 provide bilateral exchange rates for several countries and their inflation performances since 1973.

PPP is usually applied by using aggregate measures of price performance such as the GNP Deflator Consumer Price Index in Exhibit 3.3 or the Producer Price Index. Another way of looking at exchange rates is to compare the dollar cost of specific items in order to get a feel for the relative cost of living in different countries. What items should be included in the comparison is arbitrary. *The Economist,* somewhat whimsically, likes to report on the relative prices of Big Macs; *Fortune* recently produced a broader selection, reproduced in Exhibit 3.4.

An alternative view of exchange rate determination focuses on some measure of the balance of payments. Under this approach, the equilibrium exchange rate is

---

[4] *Economic Report of the President,* 1990, Washington, D.C., p. 94.

[5] *Economic Report of the President,* 1990, Washington, D.C., p. 93.

■ EXHIBIT 3.2

DOLLAR DISEQUILIBRIUM IN 1990
■ FOREIGN EXCHANGE RATES

Period		Canada (dollar)	France (franc)	Germany (mark)	Italy (lira)	Japan (yen)	United Kingdom (pound)
March 1973		0.9967	4.5063	2.8131	568.87	261.83	247.24
1973		1.0002	4.4534	2.6714	582.39	271.30	245.25
1974		.9780	4.8106	2.5867	650.80	291.84	234.03
1975		1.0175	4.2876	2.4613	653.09	296.78	222.16
1976		.9863	4.7824	2.5184	833.55	296.45	180.48
1977		1.0633	4.9160	2.3236	882.76	268.62	174.49
1978		1.1405	4.5090	2.0096	849.12	210.38	191.84
1979		1.1713	4.2567	1.8342	831.10	219.02	212.24
1980		1.1693	4.2250	1.8175	856.20	226.63	227.74
1981		1.1990	5.4396	2.2631	1138.58	220.63	202.43
1982		1.2344	6.5793	2.4280	1354.00	249.06	174.80
1983		1.2325	7.6203	2.5539	1519.32	237.55	151.59
1984		1.2963	8.7355	2.8454	1756.11	237.45	133.68
1985		1.3658	8.9799	2.9419	1908.88	238.47	129.74
1986		1.3896	6.9257	2.1705	1491.16	168.35	146.77
1987		1.3259	6.0122	1.7981	1297.03	144.60	163.98
1988		1.2306	5.9595	1.7570	1302.39	128.17	178.13
1989		1.1842	6.3802	1.8808	1372.28	138.07	163.82
1988	I.	1.2665	5.6679	1.6761	1236.27	127.95	179.91
	II.	1.2299	5.7811	1.7082	1269.03	125.74	184.05
	III.	1.2196	6.3262	1.8681	1386.78	133.71	169.51
	IV.	1.2066	6.0563	1.7737	1316.06	125.14	179.16
1989	I.	1.1921	6.2971	1.8524	1358.39	128.95	174.51
	II.	1.1934	6.5459	1.9335	1408.45	138.15	162.59
	III.	1.1823	6.5018	1.9226	1385.22	142.29	159.75
	IV.	1.1688	6.1688	1.8125	1335.69	143.13	158.53

SOURCE: *Economic Report of the President*, 1990.

the rate that accompanies or leads to a balanced current account. Countries with Current account deficits have overvalued currencies; those with surpluses have undervalued currencies. Because of its large deficits during the 1980s (Exhibit 3.5), the United States is seen by many as having an overvalued currency, despite the dollar's decline from its peak in 1985.

Among those holding the view that the dollar is overvalued is C. Fred Bergsten:

It seems clear, however, that the dollar run-up of 1988—as of early fall, about 5 percent above the dollar's average value in the fourth quarter of 1987, and 12 percent from its trough at the end of 1987—will need to be reversed. In addition, our model shows that a further dollar depreciation

• EXHIBIT 3.3

DOLLAR DISEQUILIBRIUM IN 1990
• CONSUMER PRICE INDICES (1982–1984 = 100)

Year of Quarter	United States	Canada	Japan	France	Germany	Italy	United Kingdom
1973	44.4	40.7	47.9	34.5	62.8	20.6	27.9
1974	49.3	45.2	59.0	39.3	67.2	24.6	32.3
1975	53.8	50.1	66.0	43.9	71.2	28.8	40.2
1976	56.9	53.8	72.1	48.1	74.2	33.6	46.8
1977	60.6	58.1	78.0	52.7	76.9	40.1	54.2
1978	65.2	63.3	81.3	57.5	79.0	45.1	58.7
1979	72.6	69.1	84.3	63.6	82.3	52.1	66.6
1980	82.4	76.1	90.9	72.2	86.8	63.2	78.5
1981	90.9	85.6	95.4	81.8	92.2	75.4	87.9
1982	96.5	94.9	98.0	91.7	97.0	87.7	95.4
1983	99.6	100.4	99.9	100.3	100.3	100.8	99.8
1984	103.9	104.8	102.1	108.0	102.7	111.5	104.8
1985	107.6	108.9	104.2	114.3	104.8	121.5	111.1
1986	109.6	113.4	104.9	117.2	104.7	128.5	114.9
1987	113.6	118.4	105.0	121.1	104.9	134.4	119.7
1988	118.3	123.2	105.7	124.3	106.3	141.1	125.6
1989	124.0	129.3	—	—	109.2	150.4	135.4
1988 I.	116.4	121.1	104.8	122.7	105.6	138.6	121.8
II.	117.7	122.6	105.6	123.9	106.2	140.0	124.8
III.	119.0	124.0	105.7	125.0	106.4	141.5	126.5
IV.	120.3	125.0	106.5	125.8	106.7	144.2	129.2
1989 I.	121.9	126.5	105.9	126.8	108.2	147.1	131.2
II.	123.8	128.7	108.4	128.4	109.3	149.6	135.0
III.	124.6	130.5	108.6	129.3	109.3	151.1	136.3
IV.	125.8	131.5	—	—	109.9	153.7	139.0

SOURCE: *Economic Report of the President*, 1990.

of about 15 percent in real terms, during the course of 1989, will be required to fully eliminate the current account deficit by 1992 if other industrial countries achieve the faster expansion recommended above. The dollar will thus probably need to fall by about 15–20 percent from its level in the early fall of 1988.[6]

At that time, the dollar was worth about 128 yen and about 1.82 deutsche marks.

Bergsten's comment refers to another important influence on the Current account balance, expansion or growth in gross national product. The reasoning

---

[6] Bergsten, C. Fred, *American in the World Economy: A Strategy for the 1990s*, p. 110, Institute for International Economics, Washington, D.C.

■ **EXHIBIT 3.4**

DOLLAR DISEQUILIBRIUM IN 1990
■ **SNAPSHOT OF PRICES AND PAY**

	Frankfurt	Hong Kong	London	New York	Paris	Mexico City	Manila	Singapore	Tokyo	Sydney
Costs										
Six-pack Coca-Cola	$ 2.89	$ 2.08	$ 2.07	$ 2.55	$ 3.61	$ 2.14	$ 2.85	$ 2.29	$ 5.01	$ 2.47
Chicken, per lb.	2.57	2.06	2.49	1.49	2.75	1.68	1.29	2.17	3.99	1.90
Hairdresser, Woman's	24.52	18.89	30.89	29.94	24.65	13.66	10.65	16.41	47.97	22.83
Man's shirt, Arrow	44.78	25.66	38.66	34.64	51.41	21.88	32.57	29.679	63.95	34.41
Tylenol, 100 tablets	15.94	5.69	8.52	5.93	11.71	4.59	13.56	6.48	22.16	7.41
VCR, VHS, internationally compatible	878.12	588.69	620.13	399.39	954.14	740.14	497.69	476.17	951.38	736.22
Tune-up, labor only	90.70	67.10	107.06	54.99	124.38	29.16	14.74	45.60	201.96	62.99
Paperback, recent best-seller	10.20	10.41	6.85	5.74	9.87	6.17	5.17	8.08	8.58	8.23
One golf ball	2.55	2.23	2.62	1.56	3.39	2.02	1.99	2.06	6.01	2.41
Johnnie Walker Red, 750cc	15.17	13.74	16.33	15.61	13.07	12.20	10.09	24.04	21.42	18.11
Premium gasoline 1 gallon	2.59	2.56	2.50	1.30	3.57	0.85	1.10	2.07	4.18	1.92

SOURCE: *Fortune*, July 30, 1990, p. 120.

■ **EXHIBIT 3.5**

DOLLAR DISEQUILIBRIUM IN 1990
■ **UNITED STATES CURRENT ACCOUNT (MILLIONS OF DOLLARS)**

	Balance on Current Account
1973	7,140
1974	1,962
1975	18,116
1976	4,207
1977	−14,511
1978	−15,427
1979	−991
1980	1,533
1981	8,163
1982	−6,997
1983	−44,286
1984	−104,186
1985	−122,682
1986	−133,249
1987	−143,700
1988	−126,548

SOURCE: *Economic Report of the President*, 1990.

behind the relationship between GNP growth and the balance is that, as an economy expands, it consumes more goods and services than previously—both domestically produced and imported items. The increase in imported items directly affects the Current account balance. The increase in domestic items consumed is more indirect and results from a smaller amount of the economy's output being available for export. Bergsten advocates more rapid growth in the economies of the U.S. major trading partners than in the United States itself in order to facilitate the correction in the U.S. Current account balance. The greater the growth differential, the smaller the currency depreciation necessary to bring about a given adjustment. GNP information for several countries is provided in Exhibit 3.6.

■ **EXHIBIT 3.6**

DOLLAR DISEQUILIBRIUM IN 1990
■ **INDUSTRIAL PRODUCTION (1977 = 100)**

Year of Quarter	United States	Canada	Japan	France	Germany	Italy	United Kingdom
1973	94.4	94.7	99.0	95	96.7	94.5	99.2
1974	93.0	97.7	96.7	98	96.7	98.3	97.3
1975	84.8	91.9	86.5	91	90.5	89.6	92.1
1976	92.6	97.5	96.1	98	98.7	100.0	95.1
1977	100.0	100.0	100.0	100	100.0	100.0	100.0
1978	106.5	103.5	106.3	102	102.7	101.9	102.8
1979	110.7	108.5	113.8	107	107.7	108.7	106.8
1980	108.6	104.8	119.0	107	108.0	114.8	99.8
1981	111.0	106.9	120.3	106	105.9	113.0	96.7
1982	103.1	96.5	120.7	105	102.7	109.5	98.7
1983	109.2	102.7	124.5	105	103.3	105.9	102.2
1984	121.4	115.2	136.1	106	106.2	109.5	102.4
1985	123.7	121.6	141.0	106	111.0	110.7	107.9
1986	125.1	121.5	140.8	107	113.2	114.7	110.1
1987	129.8	128.3	145.7	109	113.7	119.3	114.0
1988	137.2	136.3	159.2	114	117.8	126.4	118.1
1988 I.	134.5	134.4	156.6	112.4	115.7	125.0	116.3
II.	136.0	136.3	157.1	113.0	116.7	124.4	118.1
III.	138.4	137.6	160.2	115.9	119.0	126.2	119.3
IV.	139.9	136.7	163.1	115.6	120.0	129.6	118.9
1989 I.	140.7	137.1	167.7	117.4	121.2	128.4	118.1
II.	141.8	138.0	168.1	119.3	122.1	127.1	117.8
III.	142.2	137.4	168.8	120.6	125.0	129.5	119.4
IV.	142.3	—	—	—	—	—	—

SOURCE: *Economic Report of the President*, 1990.

WHAT POLICIES TO PURSUE?

As indicated previously in *The Economic Report of the President,* the current Council of Economic Advisors is wary of intervention for short-term management of exchange rates but might be in favor of combining that management with other policy actions to influence the medium- or longer-term direction of rates. How should the United States go about such management?

The answers are not as straightforward as they might appear. Monetary and fiscal policies designed to fight inflation or slow economic growth are not politically popular. They lead to increasing unemployment and possibly even recession. Moreover, the impact of interest rates (Exhibit 3.7) on exchange rates is not immediately apparent. Conventional wisdom seems to be that higher interest rates lead to stronger currencies, at least in the short run. However, those countries with the strongest currencies in the 1970s and 1980s have not had high interest rates. Conversely, those with relatively high interest rates have not had strong currencies.

Amidst all the uncertainty about what is the right rate, what policies influence exchange rates, and how best to implement those policies, perhaps an attitude of benign neglect is appropriate. Market forces will move rates and also motivate bankers and others to develop new instruments and approaches to managing exchange rate–related risks.

■ EXHIBIT 3.7

DOLLAR DISEQUILIBRIUM IN 1990
■ LONG-TERM GOVERNMENT BOND RATES

Year of Quarter	United States	Canada	Japan	France	Germany	Italy	United Kingdom
1973	7.35	7.70	7.79	8.03	8.48	7.57	11.39
1974	8.13	8.77	9.96	11.21	9.73	12.65	16.27
1975	8.05	9.49	9.01	10.18	8.73	11.37	13.71
1976	7.20	8.47	8.55	11.04	7.28	13.92	14.31
1977	7.97	8.77	6.12	11.07	5.52	10.82	10.53
1978	9.00	9.68	6.40	9.94	6.65	13.04	12.75
1979	10.20	11.32	8.63	12.59	7.91	14.00	13.83
1980	11.46	12.69	9.04	14.31	9.19	16.33	13.05
1981	14.33	15.27	8.32	16.44	9.71	21.39	15.02
1982	10.61	11.69	7.96	15.40	7.90	19.70	10.62
1983	12.00	12.02	7.45	13.96	8.38	17.69	9.94
1984	11.61	11.66	6.36	12.70	7.17	14.52	10.25
1985	9.49	9.61	5.92	10.47	6.57	11.84	10.51
1986	7.79	8.79	4.48	8.94	6.65	12.97	10.29
1987	8.95	10.02	4.88	9.99	6.51	10.45	9.51
1988	9.11	10.22	5.65	8.57	6.25	12.74	9.67

SOURCE: *World Financial Markets,* J.P. Morgan, various issues.

CURRENCY TRADING AND PARITY RELATIONSHIPS

4

CHAPTER

KEY CONCEPTS

FOREIGN EXCHANGE TRADING IN THE INTERBANK MARKET ▬

READING AND INTERPRETING FOREIGN EXCHANGE QUOTATIONS ▬

BID AND ASK QUOTATIONS USED IN THE EXCHANGE MARKET ▬

TRIANGULAR ARBITRAGE AND COVERED INTEREST ARBITRAGE ▬

THE DIFFERENCE BETWEEN SPOT AND FORWARD FOREIGN EXCHANGE TRANSACTIONS AND BETWEEN FORWARD AND FUTURES FOREIGN EXCHANGE TRANSACTIONS ▬

FOREIGN CURRENCY CONTRACTS ▬

THE EFFECT OF INFLATION ON CURRENCY VALUES ▬

ANALYSIS OF CHANGES IN CURRENCY VALUES AND CALCULATION OF REAL EXCHANGE RATES OVER TIME ▬

THE MEANING AND IMPORTANCE OF PURCHASING POWER PARITY ▬

INTEREST RATE PARITY AND THE RELATION OF SPOT AND FORWARD CURRENCY PRICES TO INTEREST RATES ▬

INTRODUCTION

Chapters 2 and 3 presented a framework for understanding the effects of international transactions, such as exports and the purchase of foreign financial securities, on the values of currencies. This chapter introduces the markets in which currencies trade: the spot market, the forward market, the futures market, and the options market. Financial managers responsible for international transactions trade currencies in at least some of these markets, and frequently they trade in all of them. Successful trading depends on a thorough understanding of each market and their interrelationships.

The same fundamental assets, currencies, trade in all of these markets and are differentiated in each market by contract terms. For example, the spot market for currencies requires immediate delivery of the currencies traded. The forward and futures markets call for delivery at a later date. Options markets have even more complicated terms that we will study in detail in Chapters 5 and 6.

The prices of currencies in these markets are interrelated because the currencies are the underlying asset or security in each market. Forward contracts, futures contracts, and options contracts are called derivative securities *because they derive their value from their relationships to currencies, the underlying security. After examining the markets, we explore two extremely important parity relationships.* Purchasing power parity *(PPP) links foreign exchange prices in the spot market through time with national inflation rates. Interest rate parity (IRP) links the spot market prices of currencies with forward market prices and with national interest rates.*

A great deal of change and innovation in foreign exchange markets has occurred over the last 15 years. First, the volume of transactions has grown rapidly in response to the increase in international trade and investment. Second, technological changes in communications and information processing now allow the linkage of markets around the world and the reality of 24-hour-a-day trading. Third, the volatility of exchange rates and the volume of international trade and invesment have stimulated the development of markets in derivative securities. As financial officers need more flexibility to manage their foreign exchange positions, these new securities have become important instruments in their tool kits.

Options and futures make the task of managing exchange risk more complex and impose an increased burden of technical competence on the manager. It is important for the manager to understand how the variety of exchange rate instruments can be utilized singularly or in combination, how they can be used to achieve different objectives, and the risks related to each alternative.

FOREIGN EXCHANGE SPOT AND FORWARD MARKET TRANSACTIONS

In terms of monetary volume, the foreign exchange market is the largest market in the world. The vast majority of the volume occurs in the *interbank market*, which is the wholesale market for foreign exchange transactions. The interbank market is not a formal market in the sense that the London and New York Stock Exchanges or the Chicago Mercantile Exchange are formal markets. It does not have a central trading floor, fixed hours, or a board of directors that establishes rules. Instead, the interbank market is an electronic market in which telephones, telexes, and television monitors displaying recent quotes link participating banks. The communications equipment links traders around the world who close trades over the telephone.

The United States has approximately 14,000 banks. Most of these banks do not trade directly in the interbank market. If a customer of one of these banks needs a large amount of foreign exchange, the bank refers the customer to a larger bank or makes arrangements through one of its major bank correspondents. Only the largest 50 or so banks trade in the interbank market. Even among these largest banks there is substantial variation in foreign exchange operations. The largest money center banks trade in a wide range of currencies and have trading rooms throughout the world. By having active traders in New York, San Francisco, Hong Kong, Kuwait, Frankfort, and London, the largest banks can trade 24 hours a day as trading follows the time zones around the globe. Such all-day trading allows them to constantly monitor and adjust their positions. Other banks limit themselves to a single trading operation and even limit their activity to a few major currencies or a currency of regional importance such as the Mexican peso for banks in the Southwest or the Canadian dollar for those in the upper Midwest. In countries other than the United States, the banking industries tend to be dominated by a small number of very large banks. Many of these banks participate actively in the interbank market, both for customers and for their own accounts. Interbank market transactions are typically for an aggregate value of $1 million or more. For smaller transactions there is a retail market for foreign exchange.

Broadly speaking, there are two types of transactions in the interbank market for foreign exchange: spot and forward. A *spot foreign exchange transaction* is a trade of one currency for another for "immediate delivery" at an agreed upon price. *Immediate* can mean the day of the agreement, or in a short time such as a day or two, depending on the custom in the market, the efficiency of communications, and the respective time zones of the trading parties. For example, Citibank has a customer that requires 10,000,000 French francs to pay for French wine. Citibank contacts Credit Lyonnais, a large French bank that trades currencies in the interbank market and agrees to pay $1,864,000 for FR10,000,000. This transaction prices the French franc at $0.1864. Citibank is trading to accommodate its customer and will make a profit on this transaction by charging the customer a slightly higher price than it pays, perhaps $1,865,000. Credit Lyonnais may also be trading to accommodate a French customer who needs dollars or may be trading to adjust its own trading portfolio.

A *forward foreign exchange transaction* is a trade of one currency for another for later delivery at an agreed upon price. In principle, later delivery can mean in 20, 35, 57, or 275 days, or whatever time two parties choose. In practice, the standard forward contracts in the interbank market are for delivery in 30, 90, and 180 days. Consider this example. Citibank has a customer that requires 10,000,000 French francs to pay for French wine when it arrives in 90 days. The customer wants to guarantee a fixed dollar cost for this wine. It can do so by buying the francs in the forward market today. To do so, Citibank contacts Credit Lyonnais and agrees to pay $1,866,000 for FR10,000,000 in 90 days. This transaction prices the French franc at $.1866, for delivery in 90 days. (We will subsequently examine why the immediate delivery price and the forward price differ. For now it is sufficient to note that they are different items, differentiated by the delivery date.) Again, Citibank is trading to accommodate its customer and will make a profit on this transaction by charging the customer a slightly higher price than it pays, perhaps $1,867,000.

Daily periodicals with an emphasis on business publish foreign exchange quotations from the interbank market. Tables 4.1A and 4.1B display the exchange rate presentations from the *Wall Street Journal* and the *London Financial Times* for trading on January 3, 1995. We have taken the French franc prices in the preceding examples from Table 4.1A. The two papers use different formats that reflect

■ TABLE 4.1A

WALL STREET JOURNAL FOREIGN EXCHANGE PRICE
QUOTATIONS FOR JANUARY 3, 1995

	Direct	Indirect	Foreign Currency[a]
			Premium (+) or or Discount (−)
Britain (pound)	1.5640	0.6394	
30-Day forward	1.5638	0.6395	−0.0015
90-Day forward	1.5638	0.6395	−0.0005
180-Day forward	1.5634	0.6396	−0.0008
Canada (dollar)	0.7114	1.4057	
30-Day forward	0.7114	1.4057	0.0000
90-Day forward	0.7121	1.4043	0.0039
180-Day forward	0.7106	1.4073	−0.0022
France (franc)	0.1864	5.3651	
30-Day forward	0.1864	5.3642	0.0019
90-Day forward	0.1866	5.3602	0.0036
180-Day forward	0.1868	5.3539	0.0042
Germany (mark)	0.6428	1.5557	
30-Day forward	0.6433	1.5545	0.0093
90-Day forward	0.6448	1.5509	0.0124
180-Day forward	0.6476	1.5442	0.0149
Japan (yen)	0.009932	100.68	
30-Day forward	0.009963	100.37	0.0375
90-Day forward	0.010033	99.67	0.0407
180-Day forward	0.01016	98.43	0.0459
Switzerland (franc)	0.7610	1.3141	
30-Day forward	0.7623	1.3118	0.0205
90-Day forward	0.7652	1.3068	0.0221
180-Day forward	0.7706	1.2977	0.0252

[a]This column does not appear in the *Wall Street Journal*.
NOTE: −0.0015 = ($1.5638 − $1.5640)(12/1)/$1.5640
SOURCE: *Wall Street Journal*, January 4, 1995.

alternative methods of quoting exchange rates. Before examining those differences and the information provided by the tables, it is important to note that the quotes are representative of exchange rates, but specific transactions trade at different prices as supply and demand conditions change with time. Exchange rates change constantly as trading moves from London to New York and around the world to London again. The New York closing exchange rates differ slightly from the London closing rates because supply and demand conditions differ at their different closing times.

Exchange rates can be quoted equivalently in terms of either currency, that is, dollars per French franc ($/FR) or French francs per dollar (FR/$). A quote in local currency per unit of foreign currency is a *direct quote*. A quote in foreign currency per unit of local currency is an *indirect quote*. The *Wall Street Journal* provides both direct and indirect quotes for spot and forward rates, and it is easy to see that the

■ TABLE 4.1B

SPOT—FORWARD AGAINST THE POUND

Jan 3	Closing midpoint	Bid/offer spread	One month		Three Months		One Year	
			Rate	%p.a.[a]	Rate	%p.a.[a]	Rate	%p.a.[a]
Canada	2.1928	920–935	2.193	–0.1	2.1946	–0.3	2.2054	–0.6
France	8.3728	703–753	8.3711	0.2	8.3649	0.4	8.3081	0.8
Germany	2.4284	273–294	2.4265	0.9	2.4204	1.3	2.3838	1.8
Japan	156.806	734–878	156.269	3.9	155.191	4.1	148.996	5.0
Switzerland	2.0511	500–522	2.0472	2.3	2.0395	2.3	1.9905	3.0
United States	1.5628	625–630	1.5629	–0.1	1.5625	0.1	1.5612	0.1
ECU[b]	1.2764	757–771	1.2764	0.0	1.2759	0.2	1.2684	0.6

Commercial rates taken toward the end of London trading.
[a]p.a. refers to per annum.
[b]European Currency Unit

SOURCE: Financial Times, January 4, 1995.

two price quotations are equivalent because they are reciprocals of each other. For example, if the price of a French franc is $0.1864 (0.1864 $/FR), then the price of a dollar is 5.3651 FR/$ [(1/0.1864 $/FR) = 5.3651 FR/$].

The exchange rate given in the *Wall Street Journal* is the *selling rate* or the *asking rate*, that is, it is the rate at which Bankers Trust, which provides the quotes, is offering to sell foreign currency. But what happens if a customer wants to sell currency to the bank rather than buy it? The *bid rate* is a different and lower rate at which the bank is willing to buy. (The *Wall Street Journal* does not provide Bankers Trust's bid rates.) The difference between the two rates—the bid rate and the ask rate—is the *bid-ask spread* and generates revenues for the bank's trading activities. The bid rate is always lower than the ask rate in line with the business maxim, buy low and sell high. The bank makes money if it simultaneously buys currency at a low price from one customer and sells it at a higher price to another customer.

The bid-ask spread in the interbank market is usually very small. The *London Financial Times* indirect quotations in Table 4.1b give the bid-ask rates at the close of the foreign exchange market in London. In Table 4.1b the closing quotations for the dollars per pound in the spot market are a midpoint of $1.56275 (rounded to $1.5628) and bid-ask prices of $1.5625 – $1.5630 (reported as 625–630). The spread of $0.0005 means that if a bank were to buy £1 million at the bid rate and sell £1 million at the ask rate, it would earn $.0005 per pound, or $500. That represents the bank's revenues from this transaction because there are no commissions in the interbank market. The $500 markup is only .032 percent of the price. Banks operate with slim bid-ask spreads because their volume is large. In addition, banks may plan on making money in their foreign exchange transactions through speculation.

■ **TABLE 4.2**

POTENTIAL PROFIT FROM TRIANGULAR ARBITRAGE

Transaction Number	Beginning Position	Exchange Rate	Ending Position
1	£5,000,000	2.4343 DM/£	DM 12,171,500
2	DM 12,171,500	0.6428 $/DM	$7,823,840
3	$7,823,840	1.5640 $/£	£5,002,455

The bid-ask spreads given in the *Financial Times* are for interbank transactions, which are trades between major banks. Corporate customers are quoted a lower bid rate and a higher ask rate. The wider spread for corporate transactions reflects costs and risks that are higher than those involved in an interbank transaction. The interbank transactions are analogous to a wholesale activity and the corporate transactions are analogous to retail activity.

The exchange rate quotes in Table 4.1a are in terms of dollars and another currency. What happens if someone wants to price British pounds (£) in terms of German marks (DM)? This is known as the *cross-rate*. The dollar price of marks and the dollar price of pounds establish the equilibrium mark price of the pound. The relationship between the exchange rates can be expressed as

$$DM/£ = (\$/£)/(\$/DM)$$

For example, if the price of a pound is $1.5640 (1.5640 $/£) and the price of a mark is $0.6428 (0.6428 $/DM), then the price of a pound in marks is

$$2.4331 \; DM/£ = (1.5640 \; \$/£)/(0.6428 \; \$/DM)$$

While this expression is appealing on the basis of arithmetic, market behavior enforces the relationship. If the mark/pound exchange rate deviates from 2.4331 DM/£, dealers engage in arbitrage transactions to earn riskless profits. For example, if the rate is 2.4343 DM/£, the pound is overpriced in terms of marks relative to its price implied in the $/DM and $/£ markets. It is profitable to sell pounds for marks in the DM/£ market and repurchase the pounds through the $/£ and $/DM markets. Specifically, a dealer sells pounds for marks, uses the marks to buy dollars, and uses the dollars to buy pounds. In this series of transactions, the dealer is, in effect, selling pounds for 2.4343 DM/£, repurchasing them for 2.4331 DM/£, and earning the difference without risk or investment. Table 4.2 shows the flow of funds from the set of transactions and the resulting profits, and Figure 4.1 represents it graphically. Starting with an arbitrary amount of £5 million, the dealer sells these for marks at the price $2.4343. This yields DM 12,171,500. The next step is to sell the marks for dollars at the price $0.6428. This yields $7,823,840. Selling these dollars for pounds at the price 1.5640 $/£ yields £5,002,455, a profit, without risk or effective investment, of £2,455, or approximately 0.05 percent of the initial transaction.

■ FIGURE 4.1

TRIANGULAR ARBITRAGE

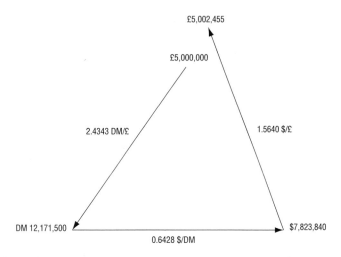

The three transactions that produce this arbitrage profit create changes in the supply and demand conditions for the currencies that lead to a higher dollar per pound rate, a higher mark per dollar rate, and a lower mark per pound rate, precisely the changes needed to bring the rates into equilibrium. Bank dealers conduct this activity, known as *triangular arbitrage*, whenever the cross-rates move out of equilibrium. Because the profits are riskless, even small deviations motivate the dealers, and deviations from equilibrium do not last long.

The profit in the arbitrage example is approximately .05 percent, and we have not considered transactions costs. Recall that the *Financial Times* quotations indicate a bid-ask spread for the $/£ market of 0.032 percent. Triangular arbitrage requires three transactions. The transactions costs are approximately 0.048 percent. (The bid-ask spread involves two transactions and triangular arbitrage involves three transactions. Therefore, the transactions costs for triangular arbitrage are 3/2 as large as the bid-ask spread.) If the example included transactions costs in the form of realistic bid-ask spreads, the triangular arbitrage would break even, approximately. Thus, 2.4343 DM/£ is approximately the largest deviation from the price implied by the other two exchange rates, before arbitrage is profitable.

It is apparent from the *Wall Street Journal* exchange rate quotations that the spot and forward rates differ. Later in this chapter we discuss the reasons for these differences. Using direct quotes, when a unit of foreign currency is more expensive for forward delivery than for spot delivery, the currency is at a *premium*. When the forward price is less than the spot price, the foreign currency is at a *discount*. For example, in Table 4.1a, the price of the spot yen is $0.009932 and the 30-day forward rate is $0.009963. The yen is at a premium of $0.000031 relative to the dollar. From the Japanese perspective, the dollar is at a discount to the yen. We see later in the chapter that this difference relates to differences in interest rates in the United

States and Japan. For that reason, it is conventional to express the difference as a percentage per year. In the case of the yen, the calculation is

$$[(\text{Forward} - \text{Spot})/\text{Spot}][12/(\text{Number of Months})] =$$
$$[(0.009963 - 0.009932)/0.009932](12/1) = 3.75\%$$

The *Financial Times* quotations are indirect. Therefore, the calculation for the premium (+) or discount (–) of the three-month forward yen to the pound is[1]

$$[(\text{Spot} - \text{Forward})/\text{Spot}][12/(\text{Number of Months})] =$$
$$[(156.806 - 155.191)/156.806](12/3) = 4.1\%$$

This corresponds to the *Financial Times* value. The yen is at a premium to the pound because the pound costs less in the forward market than the spot market.

The presentation of exchange rates is, in itself, not very important and at times discussions of the methods used have been too detailed for the purposes of most managers. However, presentation formats do vary and by being aware of alternatives, users of rate information can avoid confusion and errors. Throughout this book, we use direct quotes with the U.S. dollar as the home currency, and, except when they are essential to the issue being discussed, we ignore the bid-ask spread.

FOREIGN EXCHANGE FUTURES MARKET TRANSACTIONS

At the time of transaction, *futures contracts* in foreign currencies establish a price at which a currency will be traded in the future. In that fundamental respect, futures contracts are identical to forward contracts. The two types of contracts trade in different types of markets and differ in contractual details.

Currency futures contracts are relatively new instruments that trade in organized markets with a physical location.[2] For example, the International Monetary Market (IMM) of the Chicago Mercantile Exchange began trading currency futures in a building in Chicago on May 6, 1972. Trading activity increased rapidly, and there are currency futures markets at an increasing number of locations, including, for example, London and Singapore.

Table 4.3 summarizes five other important differences between futures and forward contracts. Futures contracts have standard sizes and delivery dates. Each contract involves a fixed amount of foreign currency whereas for interbank contracts, the amount is negotiable. Table 4.4 reports the standard contract sizes for the IMM futures. Futures contracts also have a standardized maturity date. IMM contracts have a single settlement date in each of four months, March, June, September, and December. The number of contracts that trade at any one time varies with the currencies and depends on the needs of market participants. Table 4.5 indicates that three yen contracts are active at one time. On that same date, only two Swiss franc contracts were active, but five Canadian dollar contracts traded. (Table 4.5 displays only the yen contracts; see the *Wall Street Journal* for the other examples.) These dif-

---

[1] Recognizing that indirect quotes are the inverse of direct quotes, this expression is identical in form to that used to calculate that the yen is at a premium to the dollar.

[2] In contrast, banks trade currency forward contracts over the telephone.

■ **TABLE 4.3**

FUTURES VS. FORWARD CONTRACTS

		Forward	Futures
1	Marketplace	Traders linked by telephone	All traders in one physical location
2	Size of contract	Negotiated, with large minimums	Standardized with small minimums
3	Delivery date	Negotiated with 90% settled by delivery	Standardized with less than 1% settled by delivery
4	Accessibility	Limited to large, highly creditworthy participants	Open to anyone with a small amount of capital
5	Settlement	At the end of the contract	Daily payment of gains or losses
6	Security deposit	Positions guaranteed by the credit of the parties	Small security deposit

SOURCE: International Monetary Market, *Understanding Futures in Foreign Exchange Futures*, pp. 6–7.

ferences reflect differences in the needs and interests of those trading in this currency futures market. Futures contracts are standardized to concentrate trading in a small number of contracts. This allows traders to buy or sell a large number of contracts quite quickly without affecting the price very much, that is, the market is very liquid. The disadvantage is that the contracts match individual preferences only approximately.

Standardized futures contracts are somewhat less desirable for firms that have access to forward contracts for hedging. For example, if on July 10 a firm wants to buy £720,000 for delivery on October 10, it can make those precise arrangements in the forward market. In the IMM, the closest the firm could match the size of its preferred position is by buying either 11 contracts worth £687,500 or 12 contracts worth £750,000. The nearest delivery date that provides coverage over the entire period is the December contract. If the firm traded in the futures market, on July 10 it would buy either 11 or 12 December futures contracts and on October 10, it would sell the chosen number of December futures contracts and buy £720,000 in the spot market. We will see later that the firm's gains or losses from waiting to purchase in the spot market equal approximately, but not exactly, its losses or gains on the

■ **TABLE 4.4**

CHICAGO MERCANTILE EXCHANGE CURRENCY FUTURES CONTRACT SIZE

Australian dollar	British pound	Canadian dollar	German mark	Japanese yen	Swiss franc
100,000	62,500	100,000	125,000	12.5 million	125,000
$80,000	$100,000	$70,000	$80,000	$125,000	$95,000

SOURCE: *Wall Street Journal*, January 4, 1995.

■ TABLE 4.5

FOREIGN EXCHANGE FUTURES PRICES

Japanese Yen (CME)—12.5 million yen; $ per yen (.00)

	Open	High	Low	Settle	Change	Lifetime High	Low	Open Interest
Mar	1.0060	1.0073	1.0006	1.0010	−0.0098	1.0560	0.9680	65,799
Jun	1.0180	1.0187	1.0140	1.0140	−0.0099	1.0670	0.9915	6,421
Sept	—	—	—	1.0276	−0.0099	1.0775	1.0200	328
Dec	1.0451	1.0451	1.043	1.0416	−0.0098	1.076	1.0415	130

Est vol 20,589; vol Fri 9,754; open interest 72,725, +223

SOURCE: *Wall Street Journal*, January 4, 1995.

futures contracts. The net gain or loss is small, but not zero, because neither the number of futures contracts nor the delivery date perfectly matched the firm's needs.

The currency futures market is much more accessible than the currency forward market. Anyone with a modest amount of capital can participate in the futures market. Because participation is wider, the futures market requires security deposits and also provides daily settlements of gains and losses. The security deposit and daily settlement protect the exchange against default. If a holder of a contract fails to make good on daily losses, the exchange closes the contract and uses the security deposit to cover the losses. The holder of a contract that appreciates can withdraw profits as they occur. Because participants in the interbank market all have high credit ratings, there is no security deposit, and gains and losses accrue at maturity.

Table 4.5 is an example of the futures prices that the *Wall Street Journal* reports daily. It reports the opening and closing (settle) yen futures prices as well as the high and low for the day and over the life of the contract. It also reports the volume of contracts traded that day and the number of contracts outstanding (open interest) at the close of business. The interbank spot and forward markets have the highest daily dollar volume of transactions of any market in the world. The futures market is much smaller, but note that it is still a very large market. Table 4.5 reports that the volume that day was approximately 20,589 contracts. Open interest, the number of contracts outstanding, is 72,725 contracts, an increase of 223 that day. Trading of 20,589 contracts translates to daily volume in the yen of approximately $2.5 billion [(20,589)($125,000)] and open interest of 72,725 contracts equals open interest of more than $9 billion [72,725)($125,000)]. Financial managers find that both the futures and the forward markets provide enough volume for excellent liquidity.

FOREIGN EXCHANGE OPTIONS TRANSACTIONS

The newest financial derivative that can be used to take a position in a foreign currency is a *currency option* contract. Option contracts give the holder of the contract the right to either buy or sell a currency at a preestablished price during some period in the future. Unlike a forward or futures contract, an option does not obligate the holder to buy or sell but makes the choice available, hence the name *option*.

Option contracts come in two forms, depending on whether they confer the right to buy or sell. A *call option* gives the owner the right to buy; a *put option* gives the right to sell. Individuals or firms can own or sell calls and own or sell puts or hold them in a variety of combinations, so that although there are only two types of options, they can be used to create a large number of different foreign currency positions.

Currency option contracts trade on a number of exchanges around the world, with London, Montreal, Amsterdam, Philadelphia, and Chicago being the foremost. The Chicago market, which is the newest, has the largest volume and differs slightly from the others. It trades options on currency futures contracts rather than options on the spot currency. The variation is not important for our purposes.[3]

In addition to these organized markets, there is also an *over-the-counter market* in options. In the over-the-counter market, major banks offer their customers tailored option contracts. The major advantage for the purchaser of options is the ability to purchase contracts that match specific needs. The major disadvantages are a lack of liquidity and a reliance on the bank, rather than the market, to set the price.

Table 4.6 displays the price quotations for the German mark contracts. The size of the German mark options contract on the Chicago Mercantile Exchange is 62,500 marks. Table 4.6 presents price quotations for three maturities or delivery dates, January, February, and March 1995. There are quotes for both calls and puts. Table 4.6 includes quotations for nine combinations of strike prices and expiration dates.

■ **TABLE 4.6**

FOREIGN EXCHANGE OPTION PRICES

62,500 German Mark-cents per unit				64.33	
Strike Price		Calls Volume	Last	Puts Volume	Last
62.0	January	—	—	225	0.02
62.5	February	10	1.97	—	—
63.5	January	—	—	1020	0.17
63.5	February	—	—	60	0.43
64.0	January	60	0.66	—	—
64.0	February	—	—	31	0.64
64.0	March	2	1.31	7	0.88
64.5	January	155	0.35	22	0.45
67.0	January	3	0.01	—	—

SOURCE: *Wall Street Journal*, January 4, 1995.

[3] The Chicago exchange made this change to facilitate settlement because the option contracts are traded on the same exchange as the currency futures.

The exact number of contracts traded and quoted varies over time. We illustrate how to interpret the quotations by discussing a specific example, the January expiration call option with a strike price of 64.5. The *strike price* is the price or exchange rate at which the holder of a call option has the right to buy and the holder of put option has the right to sell. A strike price of 64.5 means that the holder of a call option has the right to buy 62,500 marks at a price of $0.645 each. The spot price on that day was $0.6433. On January 3, 1995, 155 of these call contracts traded. The closing or last price for buying that option was $.0035 per mark, or $218.75 per contract [($0.0035)(62,500)].

Because it is profitable to buy low and sell high, call options with low strike prices are more valuable than those with high ones. For the same reason, as the strike price rises, put options become more valuable. Options also become more valuable as their maturity is extended because the longer the life of the option, the higher the probability that the price of the underlying asset will make exercise of the option profitable. We will discuss these and other value issues more thoroughly in Chapters 5 and 6.

EXCHANGE RATE RELATIONSHIPS

Chapter 3 presented an extensive discussion of the determinants of exchange rates, including theories of exchange rate determination based on the relationships among exchange rates, inflation rates, and interest rates. These relationships are important for two reasons. They provide a basis for modeling exchange rate behavior, which can be used to analyze policy alternatives and forecast exchange rates. These relationships also present a framework for analyzing a wide range of managerial decisions. This section elaborates on these relationships. In subsequent chapters, we frequently refer to the theoretical and empirical relationships described in this section.

PURCHASING POWER PARITY (PPP)

Purchasing power parity refers to the relationship between the exchange rate and the rates of inflation in two countries. In Chapter 3 we argued that a country experiencing a relatively high rate of inflation generally has a depreciating currency. PPP demonstrates that the rate of depreciation should be precisely the same as the disparity in inflation rates. A country that has a rate of inflation ten percent higher than another country has a currency that depreciates by 10 percent during that period, relative to the low inflation country's currency.

The basis for PPP is the relationship between the prices of goods in two countries. The *law of one price* states that the same commodity should sell for the same price, regardless of the currency of denomination. For example, suppose that the price of gold in the United States is $400 per ounce and the price in Germany is DM 645 per ounce. The ratio of these two prices

$$(400 \text{ \$/oz})/(645 \text{ DM/oz}) = 0.62 \text{ \$/DM}$$

creates an implied spot price for the mark. If this ratio does not equal the spot price in the foreign exchange market, there is a profit opportunity from triangular arbitrage with dollars, marks, and gold. These arbitrage transactions change prices until the law of one price prevails. For example, suppose that the price of the mark is $0.60. In that case, the mark is cheap in the currency market compared to its price in the gold market. Therefore, it is profitable to buy marks in the currency market and sell them in the gold market. For example, a trader with $387,000 can buy DM 645,000 [$387,000/(0.60$/DM) = DM 645,000]. With DM 645,000 the trader can buy 1,000 ounces of gold. The trader can sell 1,000 ounces of gold for $400,000, earning a $13,000 profit, ignoring transaction costs and transportation.[4] Such transactions tend to increase the price of the mark in the currency market, increase the price of gold in Germany, and decrease the price of gold in the United States. Together, these effects eliminate arbitrage opportunities and equate the price of marks in the currency and gold markets.

There are two limitations to the law of one price. First, transportation is expensive, and in the case of many goods and especially services, not even possible. This segments markets. Therefore, some deviations from the law of one price are likely because transportation barriers prohibit arbitrage. To earn the profits from the gold transactions discussed, arbitrageurs would incur commissions, shipping charges, and insurance fees. Unless the deviations are large enough to cover those costs, commodity arbitrage does not occur, and the price/exchange rate relationship is only close to that suggested by the law of one price. Consequently, what we might expect to observe is movement of the exchange rate and prices within a band determined by the size of transactions costs.

The law of one price does not hold between segmented markets, which is especially important in international business because segmented markets are very common. Segmented markets are separated by prohibitive transaction costs, cultural differences, regulations, tariffs, quotas, or taxes. Segmentation implies that goods do not flow between markets in such a way to equalize prices. As an examples of market segmentation, the United States restricts the importation of sugar, Japan restricts whiskey, and the European Community restricts dairy products. As a consequence, the prices of those goods in the restricted or segmented market are several times as high as in other countries. Clearly, the law of one price does not hold for those goods.

The second limitation of the law of one price concerns its applicability to nonstandardized goods. Bulk commodities such as cotton, wheat, and soybeans and metals such as gold and silver can be graded for standardization. Moreover, they are traded on organized exchanges, which ensures that they are competitively priced and that those prices respond to changes in supply and demand. Most manufactured goods and services do not trade in that way. Quality differentials exist, and long-term customer relationships are important, sometimes more important

---

[4] Transactions and transportation costs are quite low for gold. Therefore, the law of one price holds quite closely. You might go to a library and verify this by examining the exchange rate between two countries and the prices of gold as quoted in a newspapers of each country.

than price differences. In cases in which price information is hard to obtain or price considerations are of secondary importance, the law of one price will not hold as closely.

Even though the law of one price does not hold precisely for all goods, some people argue that it is a good approximation. When the pricing relationship is extended to all goods and services produced by an economy, it leads to what is known as *absolute purchasing power parity*:

$$\text{Prices}_{us} = \text{Prices}_{mex}(\$/\text{Peso}) \qquad (4.1)$$

Prices refers to a price index for all the goods and services produced in a country; the subscripts *us* and *mex* refer to the United States and Mexico, respectively. The absolute version of PPP asserts that at any point in time, the exchange rate equals the ratio of prices. Because we know that many goods (for example, houses) and many services (for example, hair cuts) cannot be traded and are not subject to the law of one price, absolute purchasing power parity is not likely to be a very accurate relationship.

A modified form of PPP is more useful than the absolute version. This form is known as *relative purchasing power parity*. This version of PPP asserts that over a period of time, exchange rate changes reflect relative price change differences (inflation differences) between two countries. We can illustrate the logic underlying this claim.

Suppose that Mexico and the United States are exclusive trading partners and their only transactions involve trade in goods. In 1993, for example, the United States demands goods from Mexico with a value of 30 billion pesos (P30 billion). In the same year, Mexico demands goods from the United States worth $10 billion. Both countries are satisfied with this exchange. If so, the equilibrium price of the peso is the value that equates the value of the goods exchanged.

$$P30 \text{ billion} = \$10 \text{ billion}$$
$$P1 = \$0.3333$$

The price of the peso is $0.3333 in 1993. Suppose that in 1994, nothing changes that affects the demand for U.S. goods by Mexicans or the demand for Mexican goods by the United States. This requires that real incomes, tastes, and relative prices remain unchanged. The only thing that changes is the price levels in both countries, that is, there is inflation in both countries. For example, assume that the inflation rates in Mexico and the United States are 15 percent and 5 percent, respectively. Therefore, the United States demands goods from Mexico priced at P34.5 billion [P30(1.15)], and Mexico demands United States goods priced at $10.5 billion [$10(1.05)]. In 1994, the equilibrium price of the peso is again established by the equality of the demands.

$$P34.5 \text{ billion} = \$10.5 \text{ billion}$$
$$P1 = \$0.3043$$

The peso has declined in value because Mexican inflation exceeded U.S. inflation. We can identify the relationship between currency prices over time and inflation rates by rewriting the preceding expression.

$$P34.5 \text{ billion} = \$10.5 \text{ billion}$$
$$P30(1.15) \text{ billion} = \$10(1.05) \text{ billion}$$
$$P1 = \$0.3043 = \$0.3333(1.05/1.15)$$

Expressed in general terms, this PPP relationship is

$$s_1^* = s_0(p_{1,us}/p_{0,us})/(p_{1,mex}/p_{0,mex}) \tag{4.2}$$

where s_1^* is the rate implied by PPP, p indicates a price index and its first subscript refers to time and its second subscript identifies the country. Therefore, $(p_{1,mex}/p_{0,mex})$ is 1 plus the rate of inflation in Mexico from time 0 to time 1. If we are to use this relationship effectively, we must recognize that its precise form depends on whether we express currency prices directly or indirectly. When the foreign country has high rates of inflation, we often express this indirectly to avoid having the value of the currency become very small. We illustrate this by repeating the derivation expressing the price of the dollar in terms of pesos.

$$\$10.5 \text{ billion} = P34.5 \text{ billion}$$
$$\$10(1.05) \text{ billion} = P30(1.15) \text{ billion}$$
$$\$1 = P3.2857 = P3.0000(1.15/1.05)$$

In this form, the Mexican inflation rate is in the numerator and the U.S. inflation rate is in the denominator.

One other concept, *real exchange rate,* is especially useful. When PPP holds perfectly, the real exchange rate is constant. When PPP does not hold perfectly, the real exchange rate changes to reflect the increased or decreased purchasing power of a currency. We can illustrate the concept by extending our example. Suppose that the value of the peso declines, in dollar terms, from \$0.3333 to only \$0.3200, not the PPP exchange rate of \$0.3043. We say that the real exchange rate has increased. The reason is that the same quantity of Mexican goods now buys more U.S. goods. The value of U.S. goods that can be purchased at the exchange rate of \$0.3200 is \$11.04 billion [(P30 billion)(1.15)(\$0.3200)]. That value of goods in 1994 is equivalent to \$10.51 billion in terms of 1993 prices [\$10.51 = \$11.04/1.05]. To be able to purchase this many U.S. goods in 1993, the price of the peso would have been \$0.3505 [\$0.3505 = \$10.51/30]. We refer to \$0.3505 as the real value of the peso in 1994, relative to 1993. These calculations lead to a general relationship.

$$\$0.3505 = \$10.51/30 = \$11.04/(30)(1.05)$$
$$= (P30)(1.15)(\$0.3200)/(30)(1.05)$$
$$= (\$0.3200)(1.15)/(1.05)$$

If we let $s_t^{\#}$ be the real value of currency relative to time 0, using direct quotations for the currency value, we can write:

$$s_t^{\#} = s_t \ (p_{t,mex}/p_{0,mex})/(p_{t,us}/p_{0,us}) \tag{4.3}$$

The real value of the peso in 1994, relative to its 1993 value, is its market price in 1994, adjusted upward for Mexican inflation and downward for U.S. inflation.

An understanding of relative PPP and the concept of real exchange rates allows a manager to determine whether exchange rates adjust in line with price level changes. If we assume that PPP is a long-term or equilibrium phenomenon, exchange rates should move to eliminate deviations from PPP. Currencies that are overvalued according to PPP calculations should tend to fall and those that are undervalued should tend to rise.

Many foreign exchange advisory services incorporate PPP in their forecasting models. When a currency is overvalued according to PPP, the forecast tilts toward depreciation, and when it is undervalued, the forecast tilts toward appreciation. However, the empirical evidence is strong that although comparative inflation is a factor, it is not the only factor that influences exchange rates. Currencies frequently diverge from PPP for substantial periods and by significant amounts.

There are three problems related to using PPP to develop exchange rate forecasts or for other empirical analysis. The most important problem is selecting appropriate price indices. There are a number of alternatives, consumer price indices, producer price indices, GNP deflation indices, and trade related indices. Because PPP appears to relate directly to tradable goods, indices based on such goods appear most appropriate. For some countries, however, services such as tourism are important, and the prices of tourism services should also appear in the indices. Anyone choosing indices must be aware of the relative influence of different commodities and services on exchange rates.

A second problem concerns the choice of the base year. The implicit assumption is that the exchange rate is in PPP equilibrium in the base year and that deviations occur from that point. However, if another base year were chosen or it were assumed that the currency was overvalued or undervalued in the base year, the measured deviations from PPP would be different. The choice of a base year for analysis is difficult and unavoidably subjective.

The final problem concerns the appropriate length of time to analyze. PPP requires an adjustment that cannot occur instantaneously. Should we expect it to occur in a month, a year, or five years? The record suggests that the longer the period of adjustment, the smaller the deviations, but within a 5- or 10-year period, large deviations can have severe repercussions for firms, industries, and countries.

We illustrate the relationship between price changes in two countries and the changes in their exchange rate by examining the data for Canada and the United States from December 1978 to December 1994. We have end-of-year values for the consumer price indices in the two countries and for the exchange rate between the Canadian and U.S. dollars. We report these in Table 4.7. The five columns A through E report the calculation that we use in this discussion.[5]

Column A measures the exchange rate relative to its value at the end of 1978, scaled so that value is 100. Column B produces a PPP forecast of the exchange rate at the end of each year based on the cumulative inflation that has occurred since

---

[5] To help with the interpretation of this table, we reproduce the calculations for 1980 for columns A to E.

  A: 99.27 = 100($0.8370/$0.8432)

  B: $0.8874 = $0.8432(126.40/100.00)/(120.10/100.00)

  C: −2.23% = ($0.8370−$0.8561)/$0.8561

  D: 3.09% = {[$0.8561(126.40/111.39)/(120.10/109.11)]−$0.8561}/$0.8561

  E: $0.7953 = $0.8370(120.10/100.00)/(126.40/100)

■ **TABLE 4.7**

PPP DATA FOR THE UNITED STATES AND CANADA

				A	B	C	D	E
	Market Exchange Rate	Canadian Price Index	U.S. Price Index	Currency Index	PPP Exchange Rate Forecast	Market Exchange Rate Change	PPP Exchange Rate Change	Real Exchange Rate
1978	$0.8432	100.00	100.00	100.00	$0.8432			$0.8432
1979	0.8561	109.11	111.39	101.53	0.8608	1.53%	2.09%	0.8386
1980	0.8370	120.10	126.40	99.27	0.8874	−2.23	3.09	0.7953
1981	0.8432	135.05	139.44	100.01	0.8706	0.74	−1.90	0.8167
1982	0.8134	149.66	148.02	96.47	0.8339	−3.54	−4.21	0.8224
1983	0.8036	158.42	152.81	95.31	0.8133	−1.21	−2.48	0.8331
1984	0.7568	165.29	159.41	89.75	0.8131	−5.83	−0.02	0.7847
1985	0.7156	171.82	165.02	84.87	0.8098	−5.45	−0.41	0.7451
1986	0.7244	179.04	168.15	85.91	0.7919	1.23	−2.21	0.7713
1987	0.7693	186.77	174.42	91.24	0.7874	6.21	−0.57	0.8238
1988	0.8384	194.33	181.35	99.44	0.7869	8.98	−0.07	0.8984
1989	0.8637	204.16	190.17	102.44	0.7854	3.01	−0.19	0.9273
1990	0.8618	213.78	200.39	102.21	0.7903	−0.22	0.63	0.9195
1991	0.8654	225.76	208.81	102.63	0.7799	0.41	−1.33	0.9356
1992	0.7867	229.18	215.22	93.31	0.7918	−9.09	1.53	0.8377
1993	0.7553	233.45	221.63	89.58	0.8005	−4.00	1.09	0.7956
1994	0.7130	239.29	229.39	84.56	0.8083	−5.60	0.98	0.7438

the end of 1978. Column C measures the percentage change in exchange rate each year. Column D measures the forecast percentage change in the exchange rate each year, based on the price index changes each year. Column E reports the real value of the exchange rate at the end of each year, measured relative to its 1978 value. We use these data in the comparisons that follow.

Figure 4.2 plots the values of the price indices and the exchange rate converted to an index. Note that the U.S. inflation rate exceeded the Canadian rate initially, but, on average, inflation was slightly higher in Canada over the entire period. The value of the Canadian dollar drifted downward until 1985, drifted up until 1990, and then drifted downward after 1990.

This graph does not indicate very clearly whether the inflation differences accounted for the changes in the values of the dollars, in part at least, because the inflation rates were quite similar. To gain further insight into that relationship, we examine the PPP forecast of the value of the Canadian dollar at the end of each year, calculated using a modified form of equation (4.2) and reported in column B.

$$s_t^* = (s_0)(p_{t,us}/p_{0,us})/(p_{t,c}/p_{0,c}) \qquad (4.4)$$

The PPP exchange rate at the end of each year, t, is the rate at the beginning of the period, s_0, multiplied by the ratio of the price indices, from time 0 to time t.

PRICE AND EXCHANGE RATE INDICES 1978 TO 1994

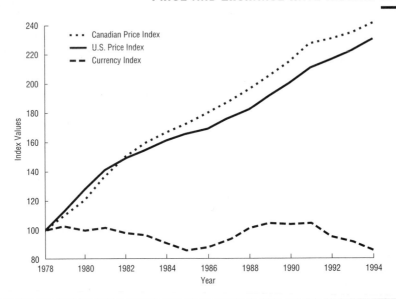

Figure 4.3 plots the actual exchange rate and the PPP exchange rate for the Canadian dollar in terms of the U.S. dollar from December 1978 to December 1994. Over the first six years the two rates are quite close together. Over the remainder of the period, the Canadian dollar falls below the PPP rate, rises above it, and then falls below it again.

To provide a statistical perspective on how well the PPP rate predicts the actual rate, we regress the actual rate against the PPP rate. The dependent variable (y) is the actual exchange rate and the PPP forecast s_t^* is the independent variable (x). Figure 4.4 summarizes the results. If the PPP rate were a perfect forecast, the x coefficient in the regression would be 1.0 and the R^2 would be 1.0. In fact, the PPP rate does not have any material predictive capacity. The x coefficient is 0.35, and the R^2, at 0.04, is very close to zero.

We have used the relative PPP relationship to forecast future exchange rates given an exchange rate at the beginning of the period. We can also use the relative PPP relationship to predict next year's exchange rate, given the current year's value:

$$(s_t^* - s_{t-1})/s_{t-1} = [s_{t-1}(p_{t,us}/p_{t-1,us})/(p_{t,c}/p_{t-1,c}) - s_{t-1}]/s_{t-1} \qquad (4.5)$$

We use this expression because we are interested in the accuracy of the forecast percentage change in the exchange rate. Gains or losses are determined by these changes.

Figure 4.5 summarizes the results of a regression of the actual percentage change in the exchange rate on the forecast percentage change. The actual change is the de-

■ FIGURE 4.3

**MARKET PRICE OF THE CANADIAN DOLLAR AND
PPP FORECASTS 1978 TO 1994**

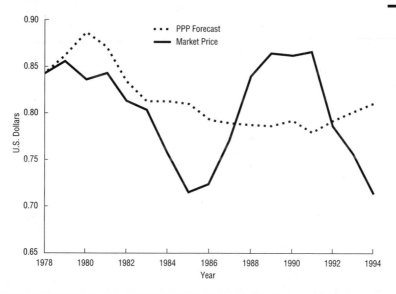

■ FIGURE 4.4

**PPP FORECASTS OF ANNUAL EXCHANGE
RATE LEVELS 1978 TO 1994**

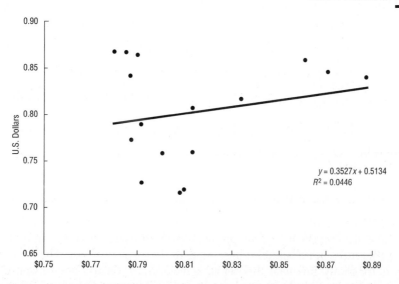

$y = 0.3527x + 0.5134$
$R^2 = 0.0446$

PPP FORECASTS OF ANNUAL EXCHANGE
RATE CHANGES 1978 TO 1994

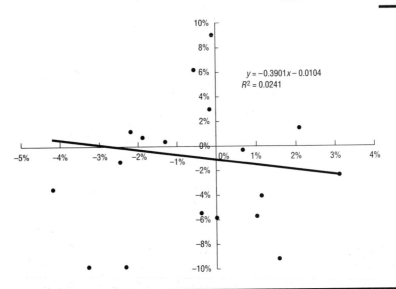

$y = -0.3901x - 0.0104$
$R^2 = 0.0241$

pendent variable (y) and $(s_t^* - s_{t-1})/s_{t-1}$ is the independent variable (x) in the regression equation. The PPP forecast of changes in the exchange rate has no predictive capacity. The estimated regression coefficient is less than zero and the R^2 is effectively zero. The realized inflation rates do not explain changes in the value of the Canadian dollar, at least over one-year intervals. Figure 4.6 confirms that result. This figure plots the actual change and the forecast change for each time period. The actual changes are more variable, and that variability appears unrelated to the forecast changes.

We close this section by plotting how the real value of the Canadian dollar changed over this period in Figure 4.7. For the first 7 years, the Canadian dollar depreciated in real terms, from $0.85 to $0.75. From 1985 to 1991, it apppreciated substantially, reaching a high of almost $0.95. Since then it has tumbled back to the low of approximately $0.75. With enormous investments in Canada, many U.S. firms must be asking themselves, "Are the wages of our Canadian employees going to remain almost 20 percent lower, in real terms than they were just three years ago?"

INTEREST RATE PARITY (IRP)

PPP links spot exchange rates through time to differences in inflation rates. IRP links differences between spot and forward exchange rates, at a point in time, to differences in nominal interest rates in the two countries. The foundation for IRP, as for many financial theorems, is a variation on the law of one price: assets of equal risk should offer the same rate of return, regardless of the currency of denomination.

■ FIGURE 4.6

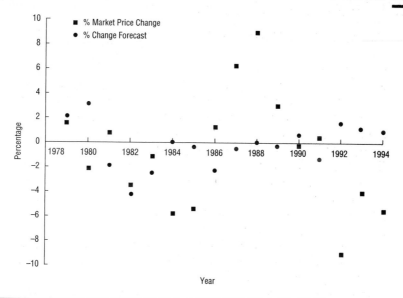

MARKET PRICE CHANGES AND PPP FORECAST
CHANGES 1978 TO 1994

■ FIGURE 4.7

REAL EXCHANGE RATE OF THE
CANADIAN DOLLAR 1978 TO 1994

A convenient way to derive the IRP relationship and to understand its implications is to think of an individual comparing investments in securities denominated in two currencies, the dollar and the pound. Both securities have a maturity of one year and are default-free government bonds that offer principal and interest payment at maturity.

At the end of one year, an investment of $1 in the U.S. bond generates $1(1 + r_{us})$, where r is the interest rate in the United States. To buy the British bond, an investor must convert the $1 to pounds, $1 = £1/s_0$, where s_0 is the price of pounds ($/£) at time zero. One dollar invested at the British interest rate produces £$(1/s_0)(1+r_{uk})$ pounds at maturity. This is worth $(1/s_0)(1+r_{uk})(s_1)$ at maturity, where s_1 is the price of the pound at maturity. The value of s_1 is unknown at the time of investment. Therefore, the two investment alternatives, investing in the United States and investing in Britain, are not equally risky. For an investor interested in dollar returns, the U.S. bond offers a certain rate of return, but the rate of return on the British bond varies with the exchange rate.

Investors can remove the exchange risk by entering into forward contracts at the time of the investment. For example, a U.S. investor who buys a British bond can sell the pounds in the forward market for delivery at the maturity of the bond. The forward price (f_0) is known at the time of the investment. Therefore, a $1 investment in British bonds provides $(1/s_0)(1 + r_{uk})(f_0)$ dollars at maturity if the investor sells £$(1/s_0)(1 + r_{uk})$ at the forward rate.

This transaction, converting dollars to pounds, investing in British government bonds, and simultaneously selling the proceeds from the British bonds in the forward market creates an investment with the same risk as an investment in a US government security. Two investments with the same risk must offer the same return. Therefore,

$$(1 + r_{us}) = (1/s_0)(1 + r_{uk})(f_0) \qquad (4.6)$$

This is the IRP expression. To understand why it holds, think about what would happen if it did not. Assume that annual interest rates in the United States and the United Kingdom are 10 percent and 12 percent, respectively, and that the spot and forward rates are equal, both at $2.00 ($s_0 = f_0 = 2.00). Investing in the dollar security produces $1.10 in one year, and investing in the British security while selling pounds forward produces $(1/2.00)(1.12)(2.00)$, or $1.12. All investors, including some who hold dollar bonds, would choose the British bonds over the U.S. bonds. As people adjusted their portfolios or made initial investment decisions, they would sell U.S. bonds, buy pounds spot, buy British bonds, and sell pounds forward. This leads to higher interest rates in the United States, lower interest rates in Britain, and an appreciating spot pound and a depreciating forward pound. All four of the rate adjustments tend to eliminate the difference in returns on the two investments, reestablishing IRP. Lenders seeking the highest possible rate of return and borrowers seeking the lowest possible cost of borrowing monitor foreign exchange markets carefully to identify deviations from IRP and profit from them. Consequently, such deviations are rare.

A more frequently used expression for interest parity is an arithmetic variation of equation (4.6).

$$(f_0 - s_0)/s_0 = (r_{us} - r_{uk})/(1 + r_{uk}) \qquad \textbf{(4.6a)}$$

IRP makes clear an important aspect of the exchange and interest rate relationship. Countries with relatively high nominal interest rates have currencies that trade at a forward discount relative to currencies of low interest rate economies. When a nation's interest rate changes, the spot and forward rates also adjust. If the interest rate falls relative to other countries, either the forward discount will shrink or the forward premium will increase. This is another illustration of linkage between internal characteristics (interest rates) and external characteristics (exchange rates) of economies.

Is IRP empirically valid? The answer is yes, but only when the closest attention is paid to its basic assumptions. It is more difficult than it first appears to identify equally risky assets. For example, because the British and U.S. governments issue default-free treasury bills, they appear to be suitable assets for examining whether IRP holds. The same is true for Canadian government bills, and those of several other major countries. The results of studies using treasury bills consistently identify deviations from IRP. The deviations persist and are frequently large, as much as 2 percent per annum. Several explanations for the deviations have been proposed. The three factors that appear to be the most important are taxes, controls, and liquidity concerns.

Taxes enter into the IRP calculations by altering the rate of return actually earned by investors. Because tax rates differ among nations, a before-tax combination of interest and exchange rates might indicate arbitrage opportunities that disappear on an after-tax basis. In addition, in some countries, foreign investors are subject to special withholding taxes that add to the cost of arbitrage.

Restrictions on capital flows and currency controls all have been suggested as causes of the deviations. They interfere with arbitrage even when the rate of return differential exists and is substantial. In some cases, individuals cannot hold certain assets; in others, currencies cannot move freely across borders. Earning a higher rate of return in marks than in pounds is of little value to an investor if the marks cannot be freely exchanged for pounds and transferred out of Germany. Many nations have imposed exchange or capital controls that have led to parity deviations. Moreover, even if existing controls do not hinder arbitrage, the threat of future controls might keep arbitrage from occurring. If funds are invested in England and controls are imposed, then those funds will be frozen or in some way restricted. A small arbitrage profit might not be sufficient to induce investors to bear the jurisdictional risk related to moving funds across borders.

Liquidity is the third possible factor creating deviations from IRP. Some traders use borrowed funds to arbitrage deviations from IRP. If the supply of funds is limited, traders must decide if the additional rate of return is worth the added risk of not having funds available. If the answer is no, such liquidity concerns restrict arbitrage activity and contribute to deviations from IRP.

The asset market in which these three factors play a minimum role is the *Eurocurrency market*. Without going into detail about Eurocurrencies, they are bank deposits denominated in a currency other than that of the country in which the bank is located. As an example, U.S. dollar and Swiss franc deposits at a London

COVERED INTEREST ARBITRAGE COMPARISONS

Country	Spot Rate	Three-Month Forward Rate	Three-Month Eurocurrency Interest Rate	Return on $1,000,000 Covered Interest Arbitrage
Canada	$0.7534	$0.7499	4.81%	$1,007,521
Germany	0.6165	0.6112	6.56	1,007,668
Japan	0.009551	0.009561	2.75	1,007,929
Switzerland	0.7018	0.6990	4.69	1,007,682
United States	—	—	3.13	1,007,813
United Kingdom	1.5274	1.5172	5.88	1,007,911

SOURCE: *Financial Times*, September 6, 1993.

bank are Eurocurrencies. Because the deposits are at the same bank in the same country, default risk, taxes, exchange controls, and liquidity problems are identical for all Eurocurrencies. When we test for IRP using Eurocurrencies, it holds within very narrow bounds that represent the transaction costs incurred in the arbitrage activity.

Table 4.8 reports three-month Eurocurrency interest rates and exchange rates, spot and forward, for September 3, 1993. To examine how closely IRP holds for these quotations, we calculate how much money an investor who invested $1,000,000 at the U.S. dollar Eurocurrency interest rate would have at the end of three months. We also calculate how much money the investor would have by converting $1,000,000 to each of the foreign currencies, investing it at that currency's Eurocurrency interest rate and selling the proceeds at the three-month forward currency rate. The value $1,000,000 represents the minimum size of transaction in these markets. The maximum deviation in the outcomes is $408, or .04 percent, an amount easily accounted for by transactions costs. Thus, these quoted rates are consistent with the assertion that IRP holds in the foreign exchange and Eurocurrency markets.

INTEGRATING RELATIVE PURCHASING POWER PARITY AND INTEREST RATE PARITY

Relative purchasing power parity relates a currency price today and one in the future to the relative inflation rates in the two countries. The interest parity relationship identifies an arbitrage relationship between the spot and forward rates and relative interest rates. We also know that inflation rates and interest rates are related. We expect that the future spot rate and the forward rate today are also related. We can identify the relationship explicitly by reexamining Equations (4.1) and (4.6). If we let i refer to the rate of inflation and consider the dollars per pound relationship, we can write equation (4.2) as

$$s_1^* = s_0(p_{1,us}/p_{0,us})/(p_{1,uk}/p_{0,uk}) \tag{4.2}$$

or

$$s_1^* = s_0(1 + i_{us})/(1 + i_{uk})$$ (4.2)

According to the theory of relative purchasing power parity, the expected value of the future spot rate depends on the expected value (E) of the relative inflation rates.

$$E(s_1^*) = s_0 E[(1 + i_{us})/(1 + i_{uk})]$$ (4.2a)

To connect purchasing power parity and interest rate parity, we must specify a relationship between interest rates and inflation rates. One well-known and highly regarded relationship is the Fisher effect; that is, the interest rate is equal to a real rate of interest, r^*, and an expected inflation adjustment.

$$(1 + r_{us}) = (1 + r^*)(1 + E(i_{us}))$$ (4.7)

If we assume that the real rates of interest are equal in the two countries, we can combine equations (4.7) and (4.6)

$$(1 + r_{us}) = (1/s_0)(1 + r_{uk})(f_0)$$ (4.6)

to form equation (4.8)

$$f_0 = (s_0)(1 + r^*)(1 + E(i_{us}))/(1 + r^*)(1 + E(i_{uk}))$$
$$f_0 = (s_0)(1 + E(i_{us}))/(1 + E(i_{uk}))$$ (4.8)

Although the expressions $E[(1 + i_{us})/(1 + i_{uk})]$ from (4.2a) and $(1 + E(i_{us}))/(1 + E(i_{uk}))$ from (4.8) are not identical, they are approximately equal. Therefore, combining equations (4.2a) and (4.8), we can write that the forward rate is approximately equal to the expected value of the PPP implied future spot rate:

$$f_0 = E(s_1^*)$$ (4.9)

Figure 4.8 presents the same relationships in a diagram. We close by emphasizing that these relationships depend on important assumptions about inflation, exchange rates, and interest rates. These assumptions are at least approximately

■ FIGURE 4.8

THE PARITY RELATIONSHIPS

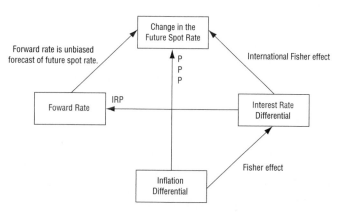

accurate in devloped and integrated economies; they are less likely to be valid for less developed countries where there are significant impediments to the free flow of capital.

IMPLICATIONS FOR MANAGERS

This chapter opened with an overview of the markets for foreign exchange. Any manager engaging in international business must be familiar with these markets. In most cases, international business requires transactions in the foreign exchange markets when a company converts the foreign exchange it has earned to domestic currency, or when it acquires foreign exchange to pay bills denominated in foreign currency. Even a manager who insists on dealing solely in home currency must be familiar with changes occurring in the foreign exchange markets because those changes affect the buying capacity of its foreign customers and the costs of its suppliers.

Familiarity with the markets and the mechanisms of foreign exchange trading is just one requirement. It is imperative that managers understand the potential effects of inflation on a currency's value in the foreign exchange markets. Events in Mexico, to which we refer in the case that accompanies this chapter, provide an excellent illustration. Through 1993 and 1994, the Mexican government bought and sold foreign exchange to maintain the peso/dollar exchange rate within a guaranteed band. Among the factors that influence the government's capacity to do this is the effect these actions have on the real value of the peso. These actions, given relative inflation in Mexico and the United States, may increase or decrease the real value of the peso. In the former case, this causes Mexican exports to become less attractive on world markets and to attract large imports to Mexico, producing a current account deficit. Of course, a current account deficit could also arise if investment opportunities in Mexico induce a large inflow of capital. A manager observing a managed exchange rate and a large current account deficit must ask whether the policy is sustainable. Understanding how the real value of the exchange rate has changed over time is crucial in answering that question.

Interest rate parity explains the premium or discount in the forward markets. There are rarely deviations from IRP in the public markets. Individual firms, however, may confront deviations from IRP in their private dealings with banks and other businesses. The parity relationship creates a benchmark against which to measure other contractual possibilities. Finally, in Figure 4.7 we have summarized the interrelationships of expected inflation, spot and forward exchange rates, and interest rates. This creates a framework around which a manager can build an understanding of foreign exchange prices, interest rates, and inflation that supports effective decision making.

QUESTIONS AND EXERCISES

4-1. The following prices of the U.S. dollar in terms of the Belgian franc, French franc, the Italian lira, and the Japanese yen the come from the *Wall Street Journal* for January 3, 1995.

Spot Rates

Belgium	France	Italy	Japan
31.83	5.3390	1622.25	99.60

a. How much, in U.S. dollars, would it cost to buy 1,000 lira?
b. How much, in U.S. dollars, would it cost to buy 100 yen?
c. What are the prices of the French franc in yen and the Italian lira in Belgian francs?

4-2. The *London Times* bid-ask price quotations for the Swiss franc are 2.1775–2.1875 SFr/£. The prices of gold in London and Zurich are, respectively, 233.75£/oz, and 508.85 SFr/oz. Are these prices consistent with the theory of absolute purchasing power parity? Explain your answer.

4-3. The price of the British pound at the end of 1994 was $1.5650. In 1995, I expect U.S. inflation to be 3.5 percent and British inflation to be 6 percent. What is an appropriate forecast for the price of the pound at the end of this year based on these expectations and the theory of relative purchasing power parity?

4-4. Suppose that the expected rates of inflation in Chile and the United States are 33.1 percent and 10 percent, respectively, and the spot price of the Chilean peso is $0.0025.
  a. What are the nominal interest rates necessary to produce expected real interest rates of 5 percent in each country?
  b. What expected value of the peso one year from now does the purchasing power parity theory imply?
  c. If someone offers to sell you pesos for delivery in one year, what will you be willing to pay?

4-5. The data in the table below report the foreign currency prices of the pound.
  a. Identify all currencies that are at a discount to the British pound and all currencies that are at a premium to the pound.
  b. Calculate the one-month, three-month and one-year premiums or discounts as percentages per annum.

Foreign Exchange Price Quotations

	Spot Closing Mid-point	Forward One-Month Rate*	Forward Three-Months Rate*	Forward One-Year Rate*
Canada	2.2500	2.2504	2.2512	2.2536
France	8.3502	8.3498	8.3490	8.3466
Germany	2.3610	2.3615	2.3625	2.3660
Japan	157.100	156.905	156.680	155.900

*percentage per annum

4-6. Does interest rate parity hold for Spain and Germany against the United Kingdom, given these spot and three-month forward exchange rates, in Spanish pesetas per British pound and German marks per British pound, respectively, and the three-month Eurocurrency interest rates?

	Spot	Three-Month Forward	Three-Month Eurocurrency Rate Percentage Per Annum
United Kingdom	—	—	5½
Spain	208.07	210.95	9¹⁄₁₆
Germany	2.893	2.8980	6³⁄₁₆

4-7. Using the information in Question 4-6, what differences in the rates of inflation would you predict for Britain and Germany, and for Germany and Spain, for the next 3 months?

4-8. Given the following data, calculate the implied one-year forward price of each currency in U.S. dollars.

Country	Spot Rate	One-Year Interest Rate	Implied One-Year Forward Rate
Canada	$0.7534	5.25%	
Germany	0.6165	6.00	
Japan	0.009551	2.69	
Switzerland	0.7018	4.38	
United Kingdom	1.5274	5.69	
United States		3.44	

4-9. Below are exchange rate and consumer price indices (CPI) data from the U.S. and Chile for the years 1975–1980.

	1975	1976	1977	1978	1979	1980
Peso/$	8.5	17.4	28.0	34.0	39.0	39.0
Chilean CPI	100.0	312.0	599.0	838.0	1,118.0	1,511.0
U.S. CPI	161.2	170.5	181.5	195.4	271.4	257.0

Based on these data, would you argue that the peso is over- or undervalued at the end of 1980?

REFERENCES

Adler, M., and B. Lehman. "Deviations from Purchasing Power Parity in the Long Run." *Journal of Finance*, December 1983, pp. 1471–1488.

Branson, William H. "The Minimum Covered Interest Differential Needed for International Arbitrage Activity." *Journal of Political Economy*, December 1969, pp. 1029–1034.

Clinton, Kevin. "Transaction Costs and Covered Interest Arbitrage: Theory and Evidence." *Journal of Political Economy*, April 1988, pp. 358–370.

Cumby, R. E., and M. Obstfeld. "A Note on Exchange Rate Expectations and Nominal Interest Differentials: A Test of the Fisher Hypothesis." *Journal of Finance*, June 1981, pp. 697–704.

Deardorff, Alan V. "One–Way Arbitrage and Its Implications for the Foreign Exchange Markets." *Journal of Political Economy*, April 1979, pp. 351–364.

Dooley, M. P., and P. Isard. "Capital Controls, Political Risk, and Deviations from Interest Rate Parity." *Journal of Political Economy*, April 1980, pp. 370–384.

Frenkel, Jacob A., and Richard M. Levich. "Covered Interest Arbitrage: Unexploited Profits?" *Journal of Political Economy*, April 1975, pp. 325–338.

———. "Transaction Costs and Interest Arbitrage: Tranquil Versus Turbulent Periods." *Journal of Political Economy*, November 1977, pp. 1209–1226.

Shapiro, Alan C., and D.P. Rutenberg. "What Does Purchasing Power Parity Mean?" *Journal of International Money and Finance*, December 1983, pp. 295–318.

Solnik, Bruno. "International Parity Conditions and Exchange Risk." *Journal of Banking and Finance*, August 1978, pp. 281–293.

Wyman, Harold E. "Analysis of Gains and Losses from Foreign Monetary Items: An Application of Purchasing Power Parity Concepts." *The Accounting Review*, July 1976, pp. 545–558.

CASE 4.1 ▬▬▬▬▬▬▬▬▬▬▬▬▬▬▬
THE MEXICAN PESO: 1995

January 4, 1995

Matamoras, Mexico

Dr. Dwight Grant
Anderson Schools of Management
University of New Mexico
Albuquerque NM 87131

Dear Dr. Grant:

Help!!!

      I arrived here yesterday and my world has turned upside down. As I told you at graduation last month, I am starting my new job as manager of a maquiladora producing dental products for export to the States. I figured that I had everything under control and was ready to roll. Then the Mexican government cut the peso loose. That changes things. I think that our business is okay, at least for now. My problem is that I do not really know what to expect in the future. I remember that we talked in class about the Mexican government fixing the peso to the dollar. You said you had some reservations about whether that was a feasible strategy in the long run. Well the long run didn't last very long.

      Like everybody else, I would like to know what happens now. What I would love to have is an accurate forecast of the future. I guess that is too much to hope for. What I really need is a sensible way to think about what just happened to the peso and how I should think about the future. I sure would appreciate any help you can give me.

Your former student,

Jim Greene

January 14, 1995

Mr. James Greene
Matamoras, Mexico

Dear Jim:

      It was good to hear from you. You are getting an opportunity to apply your international finance studies—maybe sooner than you hoped. The best advice I can give you relates to the material in Chapter 4 of your international finance notes. You should study the history of the peso with special attention to how its real value has changed over time. Of course, Current and capital account variations over time are important and related to the real value of the peso. If you prepare an analysis and send it to me, I will add whatever useful suggestions I might have.

You may not have access to all of the necessary data, so I have included some with this letter. I estimated the rate of inflation for Mexico for 1994, but I think that number is reasonably close. The peso/$ rate at the end of the year was 4.94. Two days ago it was 5.47. (For consistency, I have left the dollar exchange rate in the tables in terms of the old peso.) There is likely to be a good deal of volatility as the market searches for its equilibrium. Also, you should know that Mexico's Current account deficit for 1994 was approximately $26 or $27 billion. Mexico's foreign exchange reserves peaked in early 1994 at $30 billion. By June, they were down to $16 billion and in December they were as low as $6 billion, before the government let the peso float.

I look forward to receiving your analysis. Good luck with your new business!

Sincerely,

Dwight Grant

MEXICAN ECONOMIC DATA

	Market Exchange Rate (peso/$)	Mexican Price Index	U.S. Price Index	Merchandise Exports	Goods and Services	Mexican Merchandise Imports	Goods and Services	Transfers + Capital	Reserves Increases (−) Decreases (+)
1978	22.7	100.0	100.0	$6,246	$5,718	($7,992)	($6,797)	$3,234	($409)
1979	22.8	117.5	111.4	9,301	6,702	(12,131)	(9,556)	6,080	(396)
1980	23.3	147.6	126.4	15,511	6,483	(18,896)	(14,132)	12,113	(1,079)
1981	26.2	188.9	139.4	20,102	7,535	(23,948)	(20,053)	17,697	(1,333)
1982	96.5	301.6	148.0	21,230	6,290	(14,435)	(19,695)	3,068	3,542
1983	143.9	607.9	152.8	22,312	6,266	(8,550)	(14,927)	(2,918)	(2,183)
1984	192.6	1006.3	159.4	24,196	8,182	(11,255)	(17,339)	(1,429)	(2,355)
1985	371.7	1587.3	165.0	21,663	7,881	(13,212)	(16,202)	(3,102)	2,972
1986	923.5	2955.6	168.2	16,031	7,653	(11,432)	(14,389)	1,905	232
1987	2209.7	6852.4	174.4	20,655	11,944	(12,222)	(14,357)	766	(6,786)
1988	2281.0	14676.2	181.4	20,566	11,441	(18,898)	(16,119)	(4,137)	7,147
1989	2641.0	17620.4	190.2	22,765	13,204	(23,410)	(18,592)	6,440	(407)
1990	2945.4	22304.2	200.4	26,838	14,749	(31,271)	(20,896)	14,059	(3,479)
1991	3071.0	27367.3	208.8	26,855	16,442	(38,184)	(22,747)	25,468	(7,834)
1992	3115.4	31605.1	215.2	27,516	16,807	(48,193)	(23,957)	28,945	(1,118)
1993	3105.9	34683.1	221.6	30,033	17,469	(48,924)	(24,655)	32,206	(6,129)
1994	4940.0	38845.1	228.3						

CREATING AND ADJUSTING CURRENCY POSITIONS

5

CHAPTER

KEY CONCEPTS

HEDGING AND SPECULATING IN FOREIGN EXCHANGE ▬

ESTABLISHING LONG OR SHORT FOREIGN EXCHANGE POSITIONS ▬

TAKING SPECULATIVE POSITIONS ▬

MEASURING THE RISK RELATED TO AN EXPOSED POSITION ▬

SPECULATING ON PREMIUM OR DISCOUNT ▬

USING FORWARDS AND MONEY MARKET POSITIONS TO SPECULATE ▬

CONSTRUCTING SIMPLE HEDGES AND ALTERNATIVE HEDGING STRATEGIES ▬

CREATING FOREIGN EXCHANGE POSITIONS USING OPTIONS CONTRACTS AND PUTS AND CALLS ▬

DETERMINING OPTION VALUE ▬

INTRODUCTION

On September 8, 1992, the British pound traded at $2.00. On September 17, 1992, it traded at $1.78. On November 9, 1992, it traded at $1.54. The pound declined in value, relative to the dollar, by almost 25 percent in two months. You might ask, "Who cares?" Anyone who owned pounds or pound assets cared, because he took a beating relative to holding dollars or dollar assets. Anyone who owed pounds cared, because she made a killing relative to owing dollars. In short, most internationally oriented companies cared a great deal about this event.

Changing curency values present individual investors and corporate financial managers with an "opportunity," a "challenge," and, often, a "challenging opportunity." Consider the opportunity perspective first. Changing values create opportunities. Investors can create foreign currency positions specifically to take advantage of those opportunities. When they do so, they are speculating. That was the position, in September 1992, of George Soros, the famous money manager. Because he forecast a decline in the pound, Soros sold pounds short. This means that he sold pounds that he did not own, creating a negative position in pounds. He planned to buy these pounds later at the lower price that he forecast. Why did he do this? The answer is found in his income statement. When prices moved as he had predicted, the value of his speculative position increased by more than $1 billion in a matter of weeks.

Now consider the challenge perspective. Firms engaged in international business may own or owe assets denominated in a foreign currency. This can occur as an unavoidable aspect of their businesses. For example, a U.S. firm may sell goods to a British firm and extend accounts receivable financing as part of the customary business relationship. Until the British firm pays its account, the dollar value of the account receivable varies with the price of the pound. The U.S. firm faces the challenge of managing its exposure to fluctuations in the value of the pound. We describe this as a challenge because the firm did not seek the currency exposure as a positive business opportunity but accepted it as an unavoidable business requirement. If firms object to the foreign exchange risk, they can try to minimize it by employing risk management techniques: they can hedge their foreign currency exposure.

Between those speculators like Soros who seek out currency risk as part of their primary business activity and hedgers who want to eliminate risk, some people view currency risk as a challenging opportunity. This group recognizes that changing currency values can affect the risk and return of their firms. They recognize that the minimum level of risk does not always offer the most attractive risk/return combination. They also recognize that currency speculation is not their primary business. These firms try to meet the challenge of managing their currency risk by taking judicious advantage of profitable currency exposures that arise in the normal course of business. This calls for selective hedging. A firm that practices selective hedging will reduce its currency risk through hedging except when the opportunity to profit from the currency exposure is attractive.

In this chapter, we examine the issues associated with currency speculation and risk management. We begin with pure currency speculation, in which currency risk is viewed as an opportunity. Then we examine risk-minimizing hedging, in which currency risk is a challenge. We close by examining the challenging opportunity when firms with business exposures to currencies sometimes hedge to reduce their risks and sometimes do not hedge in order to increase their returns.

SPECULATION

SPECULATION ON CHANGES IN THE LEVELS OF CURRENCIES

People speculate in currencies when they create an exposed position in a currency with the expectation that changes in the currency's value will lead to profits. Most people, when thinking about taking a position in a currency, assume that holding marks, pounds, or yen as cash positions is a typical way to speculate. It is not. Speculators do not hold cash because it does not earn interest. Instead, they use other ways to speculate that provide greater leverage and often entail smaller transaction costs than trading in cash.

The easiest way to understand speculation is to work through a speculative transaction in a forward contract. Recall that a foreign currency forward contract is an agreement between two parties to exchange a specific amount of currency at a future time at a price agreed upon today. For example, assume that the current spot rate between the U.S. dollar and the German mark is $0.65 and the one-year forward rate is $0.67. The dollar is at a forward discount (the mark at a forward premium) because it is more expensive to buy marks with dollars for future exchange than for current exchange.

A speculator analyzes the economic conditions in the two countries and decides that future policies will lead to an appreciating mark. She wants to take advantage of her prediction, so she buys a 1 million mark, one-year forward contract. Using the jargon of international finance, the speculator creates a long position in marks. A *long position* means that the speculator holds a currency in cash or some other asset or has an obligation to receive that currency in the future. Because the speculator has bought marks forward, she has an obligation to receive marks in exchange for dollars, thus creating the long position. Had she expected a depreciation in the mark, she would have sold marks forward and incurred an obligation to deliver marks. In this case, the speculator would have had a *short position*.

Figure 5.1 summarizes the possible outcomes from this speculation in marks. Depending on the future value of the mark, the speculator might break even, lose

■ **FIGURE 5.1**

PAYOFFS TO LONG AND SHORT POSITIONS IN THE MARK

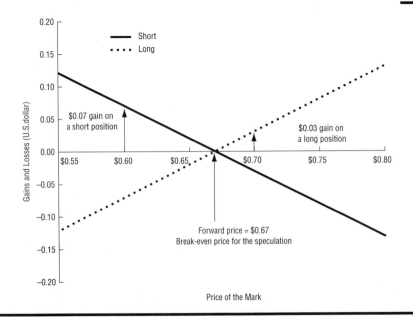

money, or make money. The key to whether the speculation is profitable is the relationship between the forward rate at which the speculator transacted and the spot rate when the forward contract matures. The speculator accepts delivery of the 1 million marks at the forward rate of $0.67. She will make or lose money based on the spot price at which she can sell the marks. If the spot price is $0.70, she will make $0.03 per mark, or $30,000. If the spot price is $0.64, she will lose $30,000. The break-even price is the forward rate, $0.67 in this example. If the spot rate turns out to be $0.67, she neither profits nor loses.

The following example illustrates an important point. Suppose that the value of the mark at the end of the year is $0.665. Notice that between the date of the speculation and the delivery date of the forward contract, the spot rate rose from $0.65 to $0.665 per mark. The mark appreciated against the dollar as the speculator predicted, but the long forward position led to a loss. Why? The answer is clear cut. The relationship between the forward rate and the future spot rate, not the spot rate and the future spot rate, generates profits and losses. Although the mark appreciated, it did not appreciate by as much as the premium at which it was selling at the time of the speculation. For the speculator's long position in marks to make sense, she must have predicted that the mark would appreciate by more than $0.02, the difference between the forward rate and the spot rate at the time of the purchase. Successful speculation requires predicting changes in exchange rates more accurately than the prediction implicit in the forward rate. It is not enough to correctly forecast just an appreciation or depreciation. You must forecast the magnitude of the change and whether it will exceed or fall short of the change "forecast" in the forward market. If the forward rate already anticipates the forecast change, there is no opportunity to profit.

How could the speculator have profited if she had predicted a smaller appreciation than the $0.02 represented by the forward rate? For example, if the speculator believed that the mark would appreciate to $0.66, she could create a short position by selling marks forward. A future spot rate less than $0.67 would generate profits, whereas any rate higher than $0.67 would lead to losses. The possible results of the short speculation are also summarized in Figure 5.1. Note that the payoffs to a short position are equal in size but opposite in sign to those for the long position. Forward markets are known as *zero-sum games*: what one party wins, some other party loses.

Both of these examples assumed that the speculator held the forward position until the delivery date. That does not have to be the case. It is possible for profits or losses to be realized prior to the delivery date by reversing or closing out the forward position. A long position is closed out with an offsetting forward sale and a short position is closed with a forward purchase. For example, the speculator might believe that the mark will rise above $0.67 in the next year. On that basis, she takes a long forward position. Two months later, events confirm her prediction, and the mark rises to $0.75 in the spot market. If the speculator now believes that the mark is correctly priced, she can eliminate her position by selling forward a 10-month mark forward contract, the contract that is identical to her one-year contract after two months pass. The price on that contract will be close to $0.75. The mark premium or discount at the time will determine the exact value.

ANNUALIZED STANDARD DEVIATIONS OF RETURN FOR 1979 TO 1994

	Canada	Germany	Japan	Switzerland	Britain
Currency risk	4%	12%	12%	13%	12%

It is important to be aware of the risk element in taking speculative positions. At the time that a firm or individual is comparing the forward rate to his prediction of the future spot rate, he also considers the whole distribution of possible outcomes. Generally, the wider the distribution or standard deviation of possible outcomes, the greater the risk and the less desirable the position. To provide some idea of the risk of currency positions, we have estimated the standard deviation of five currencies over the 16-year period 1979 to 1994 (Table 5.1). The most striking relationship is that between the Canadian and U.S. dollars. The currency of this closely related country, Canada, fluctuates much less relative to the U.S. dollar than do other currencies. From the U.S. perspective, the Canadian currency is much less risky than the other currencies.

Risk preferences and vulnerability also influence the willingness to speculate. Some individuals have a higher tolerance for risk and are more willing to bear it. Part of the explanation of differences in risk preference is related to investors' psychological characteristics. Another part is determined by default or bankruptcy risk. Speculators want to be able to continue to play the game. A speculator who might find a speculative transaction acceptable as a normal risk/return trade-off might find it unacceptable if it has the potential to bankrupt her.

Finally, this discussion used the forward contract to illustrate speculation. The discussion is essentially identical for futures contract speculation. (See Table 4.3 on the differences between futures and forward contracts.) The motivation for trading and the risks related to taking a position are the same as with the forward contract. One important difference is that the exchange requires a security deposit. When the value of the futures position increases, the speculator can withdraw cash, but when the value of the futures position decreases, the investor must add cash to the deposit. This difference and others do not affect the fundamental elements of the speculative decision.

SPECULATION ON THE PREMIUM AND DISCOUNT: SWAPS[1]

In the previous section, speculation involved a single forward position in a currency. In this section, we consider combinations of positions that reduce the risk related to speculation and alter the basis for the speculative decision. Specifically, this

---

[1] This type of swap should not be confused with interest rate swaps and foreign exchange swaps discussed in detail in Chapter 15.

section describes a swap transaction—a combination of long and short positions with different maturities. Swaps generate profits or losses on the basis of changes in the premium or discount on the currency. Depending on whether the speculator believes that the premium will widen or narrow, she structures the swap differently, going long in the distant maturity to benefit from a widening premium or long in the near maturity to benefit from a narrowing premium.

We illustrate a swap transaction with a numerical example. At the time the investor creates the swap position in the German mark, the spot price is $0.65, the 6-month forward price is $0.66, and the 12-month forward price is $0.67. In this swap illustration, the initial transactions involve a short position of DM 1 million in the 6-month forward and a DM 1 million long position in the 12-month forward. The investor holds the positions for six months. After six months, the short position matures and is closed out on the spot market. At that time, the long position has six months to maturity and is closed out by selling a 6-month forward contract at the prevailing rate. Table 5.2 illustrates three sets of possible price changes: I, a profitable swap; II, a break-even swap; and III, an unprofitable swap.

The profit or loss on the swap transaction is the sum of the profit or loss on the component parts. What determines whether a net profit or loss results is whether the premium widened, narrowed, or remained the same. The swap in this example involves forward contracts of 6- and 12-month maturity, which initially have a $0.01 premium ($0.67 – $0.66). After six months, when the positions were closed, neither profits nor losses accrued when the premium stays $0.01 ($0.71 – $0.70, case II). Profits accrue when the premium widens (case I); losses result when the premium narrows (case III). Note that after six months pass, the relevant premium is that between the six-month forward rate and the spot rate.

To emphasize that what matters is the spread not whether the price rises or falls, Table 5.3 illustrates the same swap profit and loss results but with quite different results on the long and short positions because the spot rate falls from $0.65 to $0.62 rather than rising to $0.70 as in Table 5.2. The swap results for each of the cases are the same because the spreads remain the same.

Two points concerning swaps are important. One is the basic point that speculating on changes in the premium or discount is possible. If someone observes an

■ TABLE 5.2

GAINS OR LOSSES ON A SWAP TRANSACTION

Prices at the End of Six Months	I Forward = $0.72 Spot = $0.70	II Forward = $0.71 Spot = $0.70	III Forward = $0.70 Spot = $0.70
Twelve months long	+$50,000	+$40,000	+$30,000
Six months short	–40,000	–40,000	–40,000
Swap	+10,000	0	–10,000

GAINS OR LOSSES ON A SWAP TRANSACTION

	I	II	III
	Forward = $0.64 Spot = $0.62	Forward = $0.63 Spot = $0.62	Forward = $0.62 Spot = $0.62
Twelve months long	−$30,000	−$40,000	−$50,000
Six months short	+40,000	+40,000	+40,000
Swap	+10,000	0	−10,000

unusually wide or narrow premium that he believes will not last, there is a way to speculate on those beliefs. The second point is that opposite positions of equal size but different maturities do not create a neutral or balanced position. A swap position is a speculative position that is exposed to gains or losses. When a firm establishes a control system to monitor its exposure, it must measure exposure on every maturity. A major U.S. bank failed to do this and suffered an $8,000,000 loss on what it thought was a riskless position.

MONEY MARKET POSITIONS

Using forward contracts is not the only way to speculate on foreign currency fluctuations. A forward contract creates an obligation to take or make delivery of a fixed amount of foreign currency at some future time. Any other method of establishing an equivalent position or obligation also leads to speculative gains or losses. Whether the size of those gains or losses is the same as those related to the forward speculation depends on whether the cost of acquiring the position is the same as the forward price. A speculator will examine the alternative ways to create a foreign exchange exposure and choose the least expensive one.

As an illustration, return to the example of the speculator taking a long position in German marks (DM). How else could she have created the obligation to receive DM 1 million in a year? The answer is that she could have invested or lent money in the German money market. To create an exposure of DM 1 million in one year, she would have had to invest the present value of DM 1 million. Assume that the interest rate on marks is 4.75 percent per annum and that the rate on dollars is 7.97 percent. The spot rate is $0.65 and the forward rate is $0.67. To have DM 1 million in a year, she must acquire and invest DM 954,654 [(DM 1 million/1.0475]. The value of this investment will be DM 1 million multiplied by the spot exchange rate at the end of the year. At the current spot rate, the DM 954,654 cost $620,525. As an alternative investment, the speculator could invest this money at 7.97 percent without exchange exposure. This would produce a value of $670,000 [($620,525)(1.0797) = $670,000]. The gain or loss from investing in marks is the difference between the value of DM 1 million marks converted to dollars at the future spot rate and $670,000.

For example, consider the case in which the future spot value of the mark is $0.70. This value produces a gain of $30,000, equal to a gain of $0.03 per mark of exposure. The amount, per mark exposure, by which the German investment exceeds or falls short of the alternative U.S. investment, is identical to the gains and losses on the long forward position shown in Figure 5.1. This is no mere coincidence; neither is it due to unusual or rigged numbers. The equivalence of the outcomes was determined by the use of rates consistent with interest rate parity. Whenever interest parity holds, speculating with forward contracts and money market instruments will yield the same result. If interest parity does not hold, there is an advantage to using one method of speculation over the other. Of course, if interest parity does not hold, there might also be arbitrage opportunities. Tax policies and capital controls might prevent profitable arbitrage while still allowing for speculation.

An advantage to using forward contracts over borrowing and lending as a means to speculate is that they are off-balance-sheet items. As a consequence, forward contracts do not alter any of the financial ratios that would be affected by borrowing and lending activity. Firms concerned with those ratios because of debt covenants or market perceptions favor the use of forwards. A disadvantage of forward contracts is that they are not available for all currencies and usually for maturities of only two years or less. Thus, using money market instruments is the only alternative for some currencies and offers a longer time horizon in others.

RISK-MINIMIZING HEDGING

WHAT IS HEDGING?

Currency hedging is the process of reducing the risk related to a currency position that exists as a result of other business activity. Generally, hedging involves creating an offsetting position in a currency, either a long position to reduce a short position, or a short position to reduce a long one. For example, if a German firm exports machine goods to a British company and accepts a six-month note for £2,000,000 pounds, it has a long pound exposure. The firm can reduce this risk exposure by creating a short position in pounds either by selling pounds in the forward or futures market or by borrowing pounds. If the original export transaction is denominated in marks so that the British firm has a short mark exposure, the British firm can hedge by either buying marks forward or investing marks to create offsetting long positions in marks.

Forward and futures contracts are available for only a limited number of currencies. For example, the *Wall Street Journal* reports daily spot price quotations for approximately 50 currencies but forward price quotations for only six currencies: the British pound, the Canadian dollar, the French franc, the German mark, the Japanese yen, and the Swiss franc. The currencies with active forward markets are the most important currencies for international finance, but there are other currencies in which firms generate exposures and for which forward contracts are unavailable. When other exposures need to be hedged, there are two ways to go about it. The most widely used is to create offsetting positions by appropriate borrowing and lending; this is exactly the same process as the money market speculation described earlier. When the firm has a long position in the currency, it hedges by creating an offsetting short position through borrowing. A short position in a currency is hedged by creating an offsetting long position by investing.

Assume that the German exporter with the £2,000,000 receivable could not sell the pounds in the forward market. To hedge, the exporter could create an obligation to deliver £2,000,000 on the same date that the receivable is due. That involves borrowing an amount that, with interest and principal, equals £2,000,000. When the receivable is collected, the funds are used to pay the debt obligation because both are for the same amount of pounds and the change in the exchange rate has no effect on the German firm. What does the firm receive in marks from the commercial transaction? It gets the borrowed pounds converted to marks at the spot exchange rate and invested at the going rate of interest in Germany. The amount that investment will be worth at maturity is known (if invested at fixed rates) and unaffected by movements in the mark/pound exchange rate. Table 5.4 shows the transactions underlying the hedge, assuming the spot exchange rate is DM 3.0 per pound and the six-month interest rates in Britain and Germany are 5 percent and 4 percent, respectively.

The forward and money market hedges are equivalent if interest rate parity holds. When it does, the hedging methods produce the same result. If parity does not hold, one method is preferable to the other. Because firms usually encounter a spread between their borrowing and lending rates or confront subsidized interest rates in less developed countries, interest parity may not hold for an individual firm, even when it is valid for the economy as a whole. In those cases, the treasurer should evaluate the alternatives to determine the best hedging choice. In the preceding example, interest rate parity holds if the forward exchange rate is DM 2.9714. Given the interest rates, it is advantageous to use the forward market hedge rather than the money market hedge if the forward rate is higher than DM 2.9714, and the money market hedge is preferable if the rate is lower than that.

■ **TABLE 5.4**

CALCULATING THE MONEY MARKET HEDGE

At the time of sale, the German company borrows the present value of £2 million.	£2 million/(1.05) = £1,904,762
The company converts this to marks at the spot rate and invests it.	(DM 3.0/£)(£1,904.762) = DM 5,714,286
Six months later, the company pays its borrowing plus interest with the £2 million.	£2 million − (£1,904,762)(1.05) = 0
The German company is left with the money it invested in Germany.	(DM 5,714,28)(1.04) = DM 5,942,857

The next section provides a more detailed analysis of the use of forward and futures contracts to achieve minimum risk exposure. That is the position a firm prefers when it perceives currency risk as a challenge and chooses to minimize it.

A GEOMETRIC EXAMINATION OF FORWARD HEDGING

Risk management concerns how firms deal with risks created by their basic business activities. There are many examples of firms accepting risks, even if they would prefer not to do so, as part of the price of competing for business. For example, a food service company might agree to a fixed price contract to provide food for a year to a school cafeteria. The price that the company will pay for food is uncertain and so the company's profit from the contract depends on the variations in price and is risky. An example more relevant to this book supposes that a U.S. firm sells goods to a Canadian company and agrees to accept payment in Canadian dollars (C$) in 30 days. The 30-day lag in payment reflects the time it takes to ship the goods to Canada and for the U.S. company to extend credit.

The U.S. company owns a Canadian dollar receivable, and the value of that receivable depends on the value of the Canadian dollar in 30 days. We say the firm has a foreign exchange exposure in Canadian dollars. An exposure means that the home currency value is uncertain and will be determined by factors outside the control of the firm, in this case the factors that determine the Canadian dollar exchange rate. If the Canadian dollar appreciates unexpectedly, the value of the receivable will be higher than expected. If the Canadian dollar depreciates unexpectedly, the Canadian dollar receivable will be worth less than expected.

Whether the exposure is a Canadian dollar receivable or payable does not affect the analysis. In this example we assume that it is a Canadian dollar receivable. In terms of the analysis to follow, we would indicate a payable by putting a negative sign in front of the value. If the exposure were a payable, the analysis is identical except for the signs, + and −, which are reversed.

We examine the case of the Canadian dollar receivable in detail, beginning with the geometry of hedging. The price in U.S. dollars of the risky asset, in this example, the Canadian dollar receivable, is S. The forward price today is known with certainty and is shown as f. The forward or futures price in the future is F. (Uppercase letters indicate that the value is currently uncertain but will be known at a later date. Lowercase letters indicate that the value is known with certainty at the time of the decision.)

For simplicity, Figure 5.2 and the graphs that follow illustrate the case for a receivable of a single Canadian dollar. Figure 5.2 graphs the value of owning the right to receive a single Canadian dollar for values of S. (We refer to this as a *long* position. The term *long* is synonymous with owning. That is, we own a Canadian dollar receivable. If we examined a Canadian dollar payable, we would refer to it as a *short* position because short is synonymous with owing.) This is a straight line tracing equal values on the two axes because the value of a Canadian dollar receivable is simply S. We start with Figure 5.2 as our business position. The position is risky because the value of our business position as plotted on the y-axis varies as the value of S varies. We now investigate how we can alter that variability.

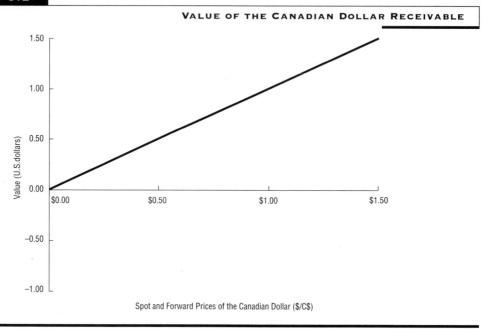

■ FIGURE 5.2

VALUE OF THE CANADIAN DOLLAR RECEIVABLE

Spot and Forward Prices of the Canadian Dollar ($/C$)

Figure 5.3 displays the relationship between a long position in a forward contract and S. For this example, we assume that f is $0.85. Note that because we are currently considering only forward contracts, the price of the forward contract and the spot price of the currency are equal when the forward contract matures, $F = S$. The line in Figure 5.3 is identical to that in Figure 5.2 except that it has shifted to the right by the amount f. Recall that a forward contract is essentially a bet on whether the value of the asset in the future, F, will be above or below the forward price now, f. Therefore, the revenue from a long forward contract is $(F - f)$. This follows because for a long position, we buy the forward contract $(-)$ at a price f today and sell $(+)$ it at the price F in the future.

Figure 5.3 is not very interesting in terms of reducing the risk of the business position as shown in Figure 5.2 because revenue varies directly with S in both cases. Figure 5.4 displays the payoffs from a short position in the forward contract. This is more promising because revenue in this figure varies inversely with S. Note that because forward contracts are zero-sum games, winners gain only at the expense of losers. Therefore Figure 5.4 plots a payoff to a short forward position, $-(F - f)$, which is the exact opposite of the payoff to the long forward position in Figure 5.3 $(F - f)$.

Figure 5.5 illustrates the potential for reducing the business risk of a long position in the Canadian dollar by taking a short position in the forward contract. Figure 5.5 combines Figure 5.4 and Figure 5.2. The new line is literally the sum of the receivable, Figure 5.2, and the short position in the forward contract, Figure 5.4. The revenue from the combination is the sum of the value of the receivable, S, and

■ FIGURE 5.3

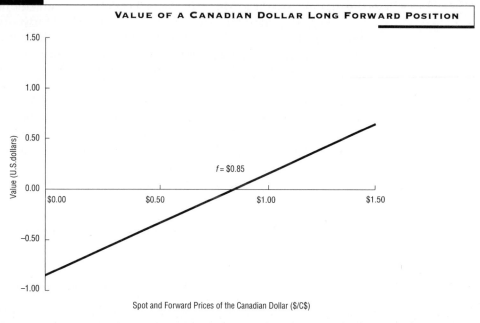

VALUE OF A CANADIAN DOLLAR LONG FORWARD POSITION

Spot and Forward Prices of the Canadian Dollar ($/C$)

■ FIGURE 5.4

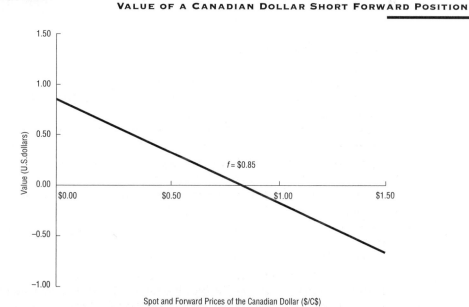

VALUE OF A CANADIAN DOLLAR SHORT FORWARD POSITION

Spot and Forward Prices of the Canadian Dollar ($/C$)

the short forward, $-(F - f)$. Recall that the value of the spot and forward are equal at the expiration of the forward contract. Therefore, $S = F$, and the revenue from the receivable and the short forward is $S - (F - f) = f$. The short forward position, added to the receivable position, has eliminated all of the variability in value. The short forward position has *hedged* the risk of the Canadian dollar receivable.

Although the result in Figure 5.5 is important, it is not the only possible position to take with respect to risk management. It is the position preferred by a firm that has decided that it does not want to bear foreign currency risk; it sees currency risk as a challenge, not an opportunity. This type of firm minimizes its currency risk; as we have seen, Figure 5.5 defines a zero risk position. (We see later that there are circumstances under which risk-minimizing hedging is best even for firms that view currency risk as a "challenging opportunity.") Figure 5.6 illustrates what happens if a firm chooses to sell forward only 0.5 Canadian dollars. Now the slope of the payoff on the forward contract is -0.5 as compared to -1.0 in Figure 5.4. When the forward position is added to the business exposure, the resulting revenue is $S - 0.5(F - f) = (0.5S + 0.5f)$. This revenue function has a minimum value of $(0.5)(f)$ and is half as variable as the original receivable position.

A NUMERICAL HEDGING ILLUSTRATION

Suppose that a U.S. firm sells goods to a Canadian company for C.$1,000,000 and receives payment one month later. The U.S. firm is exposed to currency risk for the

■ FIGURE 5.5

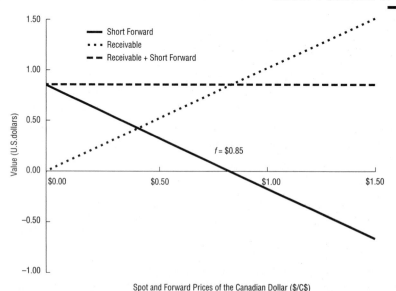

VALUE OF A CANADIAN DOLLAR RECEIVABLE PLUS A SHORT FORWARD OF EQUAL SIZE

▪ FIGURE 5.6

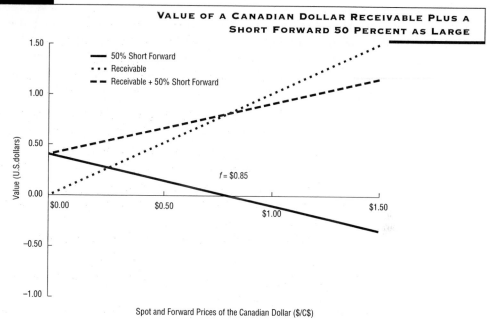

VALUE OF A CANADIAN DOLLAR RECEIVABLE PLUS A SHORT FORWARD 50 PERCENT AS LARGE

50% Short Forward
Receivable
Receivable + 50% Short Forward

$f = \$0.85$

Value (U.S. dollars)

Spot and Forward Prices of the Canadian Dollar ($/C$)

month between the time of sale and the time of payment. One way to investigate the currency risk and the effects of hedging is to see what would have happened over some time in the past. For this illustration, we examine a series of sales every month over the period from 1979 to 1994.

We illustrate the process by examining the first sale in detail. We assume that it occurred at the end of December 1978. At that time, the spot price of the Canadian dollar was $0.8432. The U.S. firm expects payment at the end of January. The forward price for delivery at the end of January was $0.8435.

If, at the time of the sale, the firm does nothing, it expects to receive between approximately $843,200 and $843,500 for the C.$1 million it receives at the end of January. We calculate these two values as C.$1 million times the spot and forward rates. We are inclined to think of the forward rate as the logical predictor of the future spot rate, but we will show in Chapter 6 that for countries with relatively low rates of inflation, the spot rate is at least as good a predictor of the future spot rate. Nevertheless, in this example, we assume that the best prediction is the forward price, or $843,500. The actual amount received is C.$1 million multiplied by S, the spot rate at the end of January, which will vary depending on what happens in the Canadian economy and the world economy. The firm's position is risky and if it does nothing, its actual receipt will depend on the value of the Canadian dollar.

Alternatively, the firm can place a 100 percent hedge by selling C.$1 million in the forward market for January delivery. The forward price, f, is $0.8435 per Canadian dollar. At the end of January, the firm receives payment and delivers the

Canadian dollars to the bank to close its forward contract. It receives $843,500 from the bank.

At the end of January 1979, the spot price of the Canadian dollar was $0.8330. If the firm did not hedge, it receives $833,000. This produces an unexpected loss of $10,500 because the hedged receipts would have been $843,500 [($0.8330 − $0.8434)(C.$1 million) = −$10,500]. In this period, the Canadian dollar depreciated unexpectedly, and hedging eliminated the loss that would have occurred. This example puts hedging in a very positive light because it eliminates an unexpected loss. Had the Canadian dollar appreciated unexpectedly, hedging would have eliminated that unexpected profit. This may appear less desirable, but it is not. Risk reduction is supposed to eliminate or reduce unexpectedly positive outcomes as well as unexpectedly negative outcomes.

To illustrate the effects of hedging and not hedging, we continue this example to cover the the 16-year period 1979 to 1994. This allows us to summarize some of these relierationships in meaningful statistical terms. We assume that at the end of each month, the firm makes a Canadian dollar sale and collects it at the end of the following month. The hedging alternative requires a short sale in the forward market for delivery at the end of the next month.

Figure 5.7 plots the unexpected gains and losses for each of the first 40 months, assuming that the firm did not hedge. (Space does not allow all 192 observations.) Note that the unhedged results range widely with both gains as large as $30,000

■ FIGURE 5.7

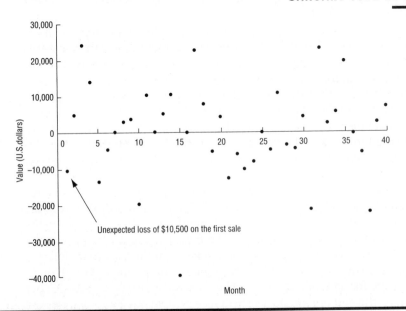

UNEXPECTED GAINS AND LOSSES IN THE VALUE OF THE SALE
JANUARY 1979 TO APRIL 1982

STANDARD DEVIATION OF U.S. DOLLAR RETURN WITH
SHORT FORWARD POSITIONS RANGING FROM
$0 TO $2 MILLION CANADIAN DOLLARS

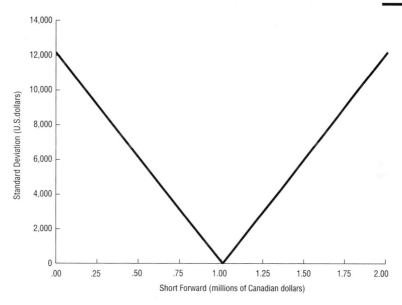

and losses as large as $40,000. Approximately 13 percent of all the cases involve losses of more than $10,000. We calculate the standard deviation of the unexpected earnings; it is $12,100.

Before leaving this topic, we should address one other question. How risky is the position if we consistently hedge less or more than C.$1 million? Figure 5.8 illustrates that the standard deviation of the cash flows produced by the Canadian receivable risk varies linearly with the size of the hedge, declining to zero as the hedge increases to C.$1 million and then increasing linearly if the hedge exceeds C.$1 million.

SELECTIVE HEDGING

There should be little doubt that forward hedging can materially reduce foreign exchange exposure. Before advocating it as a policy, however, we should ask one more question: What does it cost to hedge?

Hedging incurs two types of costs. The first is a transaction cost. Although it is relatively inexpensive to trade forwards, some modest cost exists. In addition, trading currencies involves managerial time. Companies with substantial international business already deal with foreign currencies, so the marginal cost of a currency hedging program is likely to be quite small. We focus on the second type of cost, the extent to which hedging decreases a firm's cash flow. Keep in mind that hedging can also increase receipts, in which case there is a benefit, not a cost, to hedging.

We can extend the preceding Canadian dollar example to illustrate the second type of hedging cost, the effect on the firm's cash flow. If the U.S. firm did not hedge its sales to its Canadian customer, it would have received an average of $804,100 per month over the 16-year period. The standard deviation of the unexpected receipt each month would have been approximately $12,100. If the firm hedged the full amount each month, it would reduce its standard deviation of unexpected receipts to $0.00. We did not ask earlier how hedging affects the average receipts. A check of the data reveals that receipts would average $803,000 per month. If we define the second cost of hedging in terms of the reduction in the average receipt, in this case hedging cost $1,100 per month.[2] If we forecast these values in advance, the choice is between not hedging and receiving sales of $804,100 on average with a standard deviation of $12,100 or hedging and receiving average sales of $803,000 with a standard deviation of $0.00. The choice between these two alternatives depends on how sensitive the decision maker is to risk. Hedging reduces risk but also reduces average income.

Recognizing that hedging affects both risk and return, some firms treat the challenge of risk management as an opportunity to increase their returns. These firms combine speculation with risk reduction. They attempt to forecast when hedging offers the opportunity to reduce risk while reducing return very little or actually increasing return. In those cases, the firm hedges. When it forecasts that reducing risk will also reduce return substantially, the firm may conclude that the cost of hedging is too expensive and decide not to hedge. Such selective hedging policies improve the firm's position to the extent that the firm bases its decisions on accurate forecasts.

We can illustrate the effects of a selective hedging strategy by combining a simple market-based forecasting technique with an all-or-nothing hedging strategy. The forecasting technique involves the spot and forward rates. The forecast for the future spot price is the spot price today. When the forward price is lower than the spot price, the forecast is for the forward price to rise; the firm expects to lose money by selling in the forward market. When the forward price is higher than the spot price, the forecast is for it to decline; the firm expects to make money selling in the forward market. In the example of sales to a Canadian firm, the U.S. firm will hedge by selling short Canadian dollars when the forward price is higher than or equal to the spot price. Otherwise, the firm does not sell forward. This forecasting rule and trading strategy for the period 1978 to 1994 increased average receipts to $804,500, $400 per month more than the no-hedging strategy produced and $1,500 more than hedging every month. This selective hedging strategy generated a standard deviation of unexpected receipts of $5,800. In this case, selective hedging dominates no hedging because it produces a higher return and lower risk. The selective hedge increased cash flow by $1,500 per month compared to a one-for-one hedge each month, but it also increased risk by $5,800. Thus, in this case, the choice between selective hedging and always hedging depends on risk tolerance.

---

[2] This value is not statistically different from zero. Therefore, we cannot reject the reasonable hypothesis that this cost of hedging Canadian dollars is zero. In addition, note that if the firm had been buying goods from Canada and hedging its payable, it would have reduced its cost of goods by hedging with a long position in the Canadian dollar.

The success of any selective hedging strategy depends fundamentally on the accuracy of price forecasts. In the next chapter, we discuss currency forecasting in detail. In this chapter, we continue our examination of speculating and hedging by examining another important class of financial instruments, currency options.

CURRENCY OPTIONS

UNDERSTANDING CURRENCY OPTIONS

Option contracts for foreign exchange offer opportunities for firms and individuals to manage their currency positions in different ways than are available by just using forward or futures contracts. Options provide a means to hedge or speculate in ways that limit the effects of price changes in either or both directions. Therefore, options are a potentially valuable tool for risk management. At the same time, they are complicated and involve costs, which means that their use requires a thorough understanding of the characteristics of options and the financial implications of trading them.

In Chapter 4 we identified two basic types of options contracts, calls and puts. Recall that a *call* gives the holder the right, but not the obligation, to buy an asset at a fixed price. This fixed price is called the *exercise price* or the *strike price*. A put gives the holder the right, but not the obligation, to sell an asset at an exercise price. In contrast with a forward or futures contract, the holder of an option contract does not have to transact at the strike price but has the choice, or option, to do so. There are European-style options and American-style options. The holder of a European option can exercise it only at the end of the option's life; the holder of an American option can exercise it any time during its life. The discussion in this chapter focuses on European options. In that case, the holder of an option exercises it at the end of its life if it is *in the money*, that is, if the option has a positive value.

An option can be written on any asset. There are organized markets in which option contracts on real assets, such as wheat, and financial assets, such as common stocks, trade. Foreign currency options also trade on exchanges. The important difference between foreign currency options and other options that trade on exchanges involves subtle differences in their pricing. The basic determinants of the value of an option before it expires are the market price of the asset underlying the option contract, the exercise price, the length of time the option is outstanding (its expiration date), the variability of the price of the underlying asset, and interest rates. In Chapter 6, we develop the pricing relationship before expiration in more detail. At this point, we focus on the value of the option at expiration.

When an option expires, its value is the difference between the exercise price and the prevailing market price of the currency. Calls have value when the exercise price is lower than the market price. In that case, the call holder can exercise the call and sell the underlying asset, receiving the difference between the exercise price and the market price of the asset. If the market price is below the exercise price, the call holder allows the option to expire. A put has value when the exercise price exceeds the value of the currency. The holder of the put can buy the currency at the lower market price and deliver it to satisfy the option and receive the higher exercise price. If the market price is higher than the strike price, the option expires unexercised because its value is zero.

Because there are two parties to an option contract, a buyer and a seller, for each transaction there is a winner and a loser. When the buyer of a call exercises the call, it is at the expense of the seller, who must deliver the currency at a price below market value. If the cost of doing so is higher than the original selling price of the call, the seller loses. Likewise, if the buyer of a put exercises the put, the seller loses if the difference in the prices is higher than the original sale price of the put.

Figure 5.9 illustrates the values of calls and puts at expiration as a function of the value of the currency at the expiration of the options. In these examples, the option is written on the Canadian dollar and the exercise price is $0.85. Note that both of these options have payoffs that are always greater than or equal to zero, at expiration. Therefore, before expiration, they must sell for some positive value.

Figure 5.10 extends this example to illustrate the net payoff to the options, assuming that they cost $0.05 each, several months prior to expiration. (Later in this chapter we discuss the basic determinants of options values; in the next chapter we consider that subject in more detail.) Given that the option buyer pays a price, we now see that she has a fixed potential loss and an unlimited potential gain on the call and a potential gain on the put equal to the value of the exercise price. This is a popular way to describe the payoffs, but it is misleading. The buyer's potential

■ **FIGURE 5.9**

VALUES OF A LONG CALL AND A LONG PUT AT THE EXPIRATION OF THE CONTRACTS

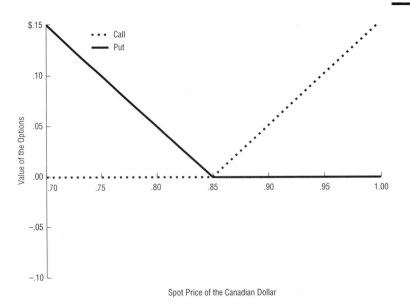

Spot Price of the Canadian Dollar

■ **FIGURE 5.10**

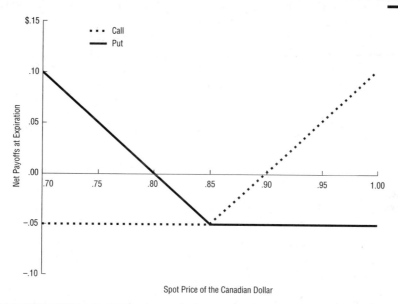

Spot Price of the Canadian Dollar

loss is 100 percent of her investment, an outcome that occurs quite frequently in option transactions.

Figure 5.11 plots the payoffs to the seller (*writer*) of the options, the party who is short the *options*. Because option transactions are zero-sum games, these payoffs mirror those of the buyers. We note that the writer of an option has a fixed maximum gain and an unlimited potential loss on a written call and a potential loss on a written put equal to the strike price. This is again an accurate statement, but it ignores the ability of the option writer to cover her position at any time by buying back the option she sold.

The relationship between the strike price and the market price determines the value of the option at expiration. For years, some of the best minds in economics and finance could not identify how to value options before expiration. A number of people noted certain regularities in option prices, but no one could identify a model that would explain them. In 1971 Fischer Black and Myron Scholes solved the puzzle. We refer to that solution as the *Black/Scholes option pricing model.*[3] You may have worked with it in other classes.

Most option pricing models in use are variants of the Black/Scholes formulation, which uses stochastic calculus to determine the value of an option. Option pricing formulas are quite complex and difficult to derive mathematically but are

[3] Fischer Black and Myron Scholes, "The Pricing of Options and Corporate Liabilities," *Journal of Political Economy,* May 1973, pp. 637–659.

■ **FIGURE 5.11**

NET PAYOFFS TO SHORT CALLS AND PUTS PRICED AT $0.05

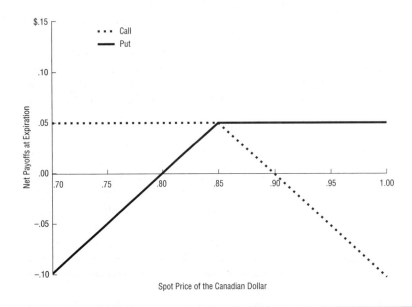

Spot Price of the Canadian Dollar

not particularly difficult to use. Table 5.5 summarizes the parameters that influence the options' prices and the direction of their impact.

We can explain most of these effects intuitively without reference to the Black/Scholes model. Because an option's value depends on the difference between the strike price and the market price, the value of a call varies directly with the asset price and inversely with the striking price; it is vice versa for a put. Option prices vary directly with both time to expiration and volatility because the longer

■ **TABLE 5.5**

OPTION PRICING PARAMETERS

Parameter	Call Price Effect	Put Price Effect
Currency price	Varies directly	Varies inversely
Exercise price	Varies inversely	Varies directly
Domestic interest rate	Varies directly	Varies directly
Foreign interest rate	Varies inversely	Varies inversely
Volatility	Varies directly	Varies directly
Time to expiration	Varies directly	Varies directly

the time to expiration and the more volatile the asset price, the higher the probability that the option will be exercised. The more time the option has before it expires, the higher the chance that market forces will move the exchange rate into the profitable range. Likewise, the more volatile the rate, the higher the probability that it will exceed the strike price to make a call valuable or fall below it for a put. The influence of the interest rates is not so obvious. Think of the option as a levered investment. For much less than the cost of the asset, the owner gets all of the action. In a sense, an option offers a levered investment without the cost of borrowing at the domestic interest rate. To adjust for this advantage, the price of the option varies directly with the domestic interest rate. On the other hand, the buyer of an option could invest in the foreign currency. By not doing so, the buyer is forgoing the foreign interest rate. Therefore, the price of the option varies inversely with the foreign interest rate.

Five of the parameters in Table 5.5 are known variables. The only one that is an unknown value is the volatility measure. Consequently, disagreements about option prices often stem from different predictions of the volatility of an exchange rate or a different model of option pricing. It is also possible for people to hold divergent views about the value of the currency and thus to value the option differently. Nevertheless, active trading in the currency markets guarantees that the market price of an option depends on the five known factors and a consensus view about the volatility of the currency.

The Black/Scholes solution of the option-pricing puzzle depends on the use of an arbitrage relationship between the asset and the option. Their solution is elegant and complex, but other researchers used their key idea to convey the essence of option pricing in a much simpler form. This simpler analysis depends on the assumption that the value of the underlying asset can assume only one of two alternative values on the expiration of the option contract. This is not a limiting assumption because it is not too difficult to extend the model to allow, in succession, 4, 8, 16, ... outcomes. We demonstrate the theory of option pricing using the simplifying assumption that the price of the asset either increases or decreases by a set amount by expiration. We use the principle that two portfolios that cost the same and are worth the same amount at the end of the period if the currency falls in value must also be worth the same amount at the end of the period if the currency rises in value.

Assume that the spot price of the British pound is $1.41. There is a call option on the currency with an exercise price of $1.40. The domestic interest rate is 0.5 percent per month and the British interest rate is 1.0 percent per month. What will the price of a call option be if the price of the currency will be either $0.05 higher, $1.46, or $0.05 lower, $1.36, at the end of the month?

To value the call, we create two portfolios that cost the same amount and are worth the same amount if the currency declines in value and include the option. One of these portfolios is the British pound. The other is a combination of calls on the British pound and lending in the United States. We begin by creating a long position in pounds. A long position in pounds costs $1.41 per pound and with interest is worth either (1.01)($1.46) or (1.01)($1.36) per pound at the end of one month, depending on whether the pound rises or falls.

■ TABLE 5.6

OPTION PRICING

Case	Domestic Interest Rate	Foreign Interest Rate	Currency Price	Currency Increase or Decrease	Exercise Price	Call Value	yc	y
1	0.50%	1.00%	$1.41	$0.05	$1.40	$0.0257	$0.0432	1.6833
2	**1.00**	1.00	1.41	0.05	1.40	0.0297	0.0500	1.6833
3	0.50	**0.50**	1.41	0.05	1.40	0.0299	0.0500	1.6750
4	0.50	1.50	**1.39**	0.05	1.40	0.0144	0.0367	2.5375
5	0.50	1.50	1.39	**0.07**	1.40	0.0240	0.0569	2.3683
6	0.50	1.00	1.41	0.05	**1.38**	0.0342	0.0432	1.2625

Next we create a portfolio of options and lending that costs the same as one pound. Let the option price be c. If we buy y calls, they will cost yc. We can lend the difference between the cost of the calls and $1.41 at the domestic rate of interest. This portfolio is worth either $(1.005)(\$1.41 - yc) + y(\$1.46 - \$1.40)$ or $(1.005)(\$1.41 - yc)$ at the end of the month, depending on whether the pound rises or falls.

Note that if $yc = \$1.41 - \$1.36(1.01/1.005)$, the investment in the pound and the investment in the call and the risk-free domestic interest rate have the same value when the pound declines in value. Both investments cost the same; therefore, they must be worth the same amount when the pound rises in value. This requires

$$(1.01)(\$1.46) = (1.005)(\$1.41 - yc) + y(\$1.46 - \$1.40)$$

Substituting,

$$yc = \$1.41 - \$1.36(1.01/1.005)$$

we find that

$$c = \$0.025683 \text{ and } y = 1.683333$$

For this example, there is no difference in either cost or return between buying £1 and investing it at the British interest rate and the alternative of buying 1.683333 calls at $0.29872 each and investing the difference between that cost and the cost of £1 at the U.S. interest rate.

Table 5.6 shows how the call option value in this example varies as each of the variables changes. The numbers in bold identify the variable that changes in each row.

USING CURRENCY OPTIONS FOR SPECULATING

Forward and futures contracts offer opportunities for investors to speculate on their forecasts of currency price changes. The same is true for options. An investor who forecasts a large increase in the value of a currency can buy calls on that currency. An investor who forecasts a large decline in the value of a currency can buy puts on the currency.

■ **TABLE 5.7**

£ OPTION PRICES AND EXCHANGE RATES

Spot Price	30-Day Forward	Exercise Prices	Calls October	Puts October
$1.9827	$1.9774	$1.950	5.10¢	0.73¢
1.9827	1.9774	2.025	1.60	4.35

To understand why an investor might choose to speculate by taking option positions, consider the market for the British pound available to George Soros on September 1, 1992, described in Table 5.7. The spot price of the pound was $1.9827, the 30-day forward price was $1.9774, and puts on the pound with maturities in October traded for $0.0073 and $0.0435 per pound for exercise prices of $1.95 and $2.025, respectively. Consider Mr. Soros' opportunities. He believes that the pound will decline by a relatively large amount in a relatively short time. He can buy puts, the right to sell the pound, at a fixed price. If he buys the right to sell at $1.95, he pays $0.0073 per pound, $7.30 per £1,000, and $7,300 per £1 million. For $7,300,000 Mr. Soros can buy puts on £1 billion. (To do so, he must transact in the over-the-counter market because there is insufficient volume on the options exchanges.) By the middle of September, the pound dropped to $1.78, or $0.17 below the exercise price. At that time the puts on a billion pounds were worth approximately $170,000,000, a profit of 2,300 percent. (As noted at the beginning of this chapter, Mr. Soros made approximately $1 billion with trades like this.) It is important to note that if the pound had simply stayed above $1.95, the put buyer would have lost 100 percent of his investment. On the other hand, options do limit the total possible loss. For example, had Mr. Soros sold forward £1 billion at $1.95 and the price of the pound rose to just $2.00, an increase of only $0.0226, the forward position would have lost $22,600,000. The high leverage and limited total possible loss inherent in options make them an attractive, but very risky, speculative asset.

USING CURRENCY OPTIONS FOR HEDGING

Consider the position of a business that has a C.$1,000,000, 30-day receivable. The officer responsible for currency management believes that the value of the Canadian dollar will increase, raising the U.S. dollar value of the receivable. At the same time, she recognizes that there is some probability the Canadian dollar will decrease in value and does not want that risk exposure. If she sells the Canadian dollar in the forward market, she eliminates the risk of depreciation but also eliminates the opportunity to gain from an appreciation in the value of the Canadian dollar. She can solve her problem by buying puts. If she trades on the Philadelphia Options Exchange, she can buy 80 contracts of 12,500 Canadian dollars each.[4]

---

[4] The Philadelphia Options Exchange trades options currency. The Chicago Mercantile Exchange trades options on currency futures, which are priced slightly differently, but are otherwise very similar. Banks also make a market in currency options.

In this case, buying puts is akin to buying insurance. It has the effect of placing a floor on the value of the account receivable plus the put at the time of maturity. We illustrate this in Figure 5.12, which, to make comparable with earlier figures, we present for a receivable of C.$1, assuming the purchase of a put on C.$1 with an exercise price of $0.85. The cost of the put is $0.05. That is like an insurance premium, if the Canadian dollar falls below $0.85, the insurance has value and limits the value of the receivable plus the put to a minimum of $0.80. This is $0.85 per Canadian dollar, less the $0.05 cost of the put. If the Canadian dollar increases in value above $0.85, the receivable plus the put is equal to the value of the Canadian dollar less the cost of the put. In this example, if the Canadian dollar increases to $0.95 by the time of payment, the value of the receivable less the cost of the put is $0.90.

A receivable, or asset, is one type of Canadian dollar exposure. The other type is a Canadian dollar payable or liability. Consider a firm that has a C.$1,000,000, 30-day payable. The currency manager is concerned that the value of the Canadian dollar may increase but wants to retain the potential advantage of a decrease in the value of the Canadian dollar. In this case the manager buys Canadian dollar calls. This creates a limit on the value of the Canadian dollar payable but leaves open the possibility that it will cost less. Figure 5.13 graphs outcomes for the payable, the call, and the combined position. In this example the manager purchases a call with an exercise price of $0.85 for $0.05. If the Canadian dollar increases above $0.85, the account payable costs $0.90, the exercise price of the call plus its cost. If the Canadian dollar decreases in value, the total cost below $0.80 is the value of the Canadian dollar plus the $0.05 cost of the call.

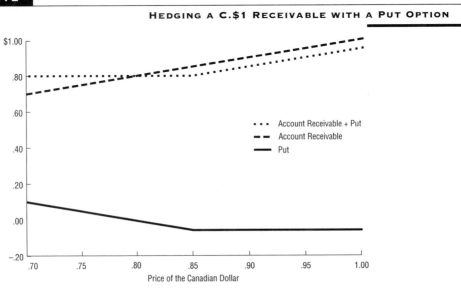

FIGURE 5.12

HEDGING A C.$1 RECEIVABLE WITH A PUT OPTION

- ... Account Receivable + Put
- -- Account Receivable
- — Put

Price of the Canadian Dollar

HEDGING A C.$1 PAYABLE WITH A CALL OPTION

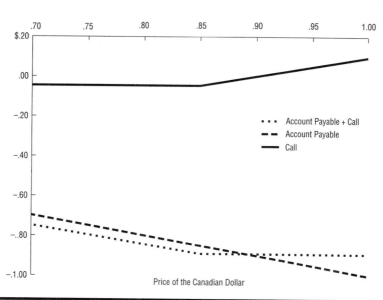

Price of the Canadian Dollar

- ···· Account Payable + Call
- – – Account Payable
- —— Call

IMPLICATIONS FOR MANAGERS

International business creates significant opportunities for firms to benefit from changing currency values but also exposes firms to significant risks from changing currency values. The most obvious effect of changing currency values is on the values of individual purchases and sales by firms. Currency changes also affect the value of the assets that firms hold in different countries and the value of liabilities denominated in different currencies. These changing values affect the profitability and values of firms.

It is important for international financial managers to understand both challenges and opportunities associated with currency fluctuations. As part of this understanding, it is important to understand the potential to manage those challenges and opportunities with appropriate financial market transactions. This chapter has described how forward contracts, futures contracts, and options can modify a firm's exposure to currency fluctuations. These derivative securities *allow international financial managers to adjust their exposures to currency fluctuations without having to disrupt their normal business operations. Such flexibility is invaluable in our dynamic international economy.*

To emphasize this reality, we close the chapter by examining a real-life example of a managerial decision that created currency exposure.[5] In mid-1985 Lufthansa German

---

[5] See "Lufthansa: Where Options Would Have Made a Difference," *Intermarket*, Supplement/November 1986, pp. 20–22.

Airlines decided to buy 20 Boeing 737 aircraft. The aircraft cost $500 million and were to be delivered and paid for in mid-1986. This meant that Lufthansa would, if it did nothing, have a $500 million currency exposure for one year. The spot price at the time of the contract was $0.3267 per mark and the one-year forward price was $0.3373. This was an interesting problem for Lufthansa because the mark was at an historic low, as indicated in Figure 5.14. If the mark continued to decline in value, the aircraft would cost even more in marks one year hence. If the mark recovered in value, the aircraft would cost less. What should Lufthansa do? One possibility was to avoid this risk by dealing with a German manufacturer. That was not possible, because there was no such manufacturer. There was a European consortium and buying its aircraft would have involved the lower risk of a European currency. Lufthansa must have decided that the Boeing aircraft were more appropriate on technical grounds or a better economic value. The second approach was to negotiate a price in German marks. The only thing that would have accomplished is shifting the currency risk to Boeing, which might then charge a higher price. If Lufthansa could not avoid this risk, how could it manage it?

We consider four possibilities: do nothing, hedge 100 percent, hedge 50 percent, and buy calls on the dollar. Calls on the U.S. dollar with an exercise price equal to the forward price cost DM 0.047 per dollar. If we let the price of the mark in mid-1986 be S, we can display these four choices in Table 5.8. These values are all expressed in terms of marks in mid-1986. That is the reason that the cost of the calls ($500 million)(DM 0.047) is mul-

■ **FIGURE 5.14**

**TIME SERIES OF THE GERMAN MARK SPOT PRICES
JANUARY 1976 TO JUNE 1985**

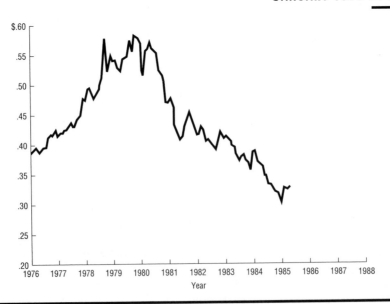

▪ TABLE 5.8

THE ANTICIPATED COST OF THE AIRCRAFT UNDER EACH ALTERNATIVE

Choice	Cost
Do nothing	$500 million/$S$
Hedge 100%	$500 million/$0.3373
Hedge 50%	($250 million/$S$) + ($250 million/$0.3373)
Buy $500 million calls	($500 million)(DM 0.047)(1.07) + $500 million/max($S$, $0.3373)

tiplied by the German interest rate of 7 percent. Clearly, once we know the value of the mark in mid-1986, we know which of these choices is best. That is like saying, "Once we know which horse won the race, we know how to bet." Lufthansa had to make its decision without knowing what the outcome would be.

In this case, Lufthansa believed that the dollar was likely to depreciate in value. The company was not willing to bet $500 million on that, so it chose to hedge 50 percent of its purchase price and leave 50 percent exposed. Lufthansa was correct. The actual value of the mark in mid-1986 was $0.4548. Table 5.9 presents the costs of each of the four alternatives. Because the dollar depreciated, doing nothing cost the least. Using options was next cheapest, and hedging 50 percent was third cheapest. Hedging 100 percent was the most expensive. This last sentence is factually accurate, but keep in mind it is equivalent to saying, "Not buying car insurance was a good idea in any year you didn't have an accident."

As a final note to this example, it is worth mentioning the reaction to Lufthansa's decision. The managers could have been praised for having the foresight to hedge only 50 percent and saving DM 91 million compared to hedging 100 percent. Instead, they were criticized for hedging 50 percent and losing DM 92 million as compared to doing nothing.

▪ TABLE 5.9

ACTUAL COST OF THE AIRCRAFT UNDER EACH ALTERNATIVE

Choice	Cost
Do nothing	DM 1.099 billion
Hedge 100%	DM 1.482 billion
Hedge 50%	DM 1.291 billion
Buy $500 million calls	DM 1.125 billion

QUESTIONS AND EXERCISES

5-1. The current spot rate of the British pound is $1.560 , the six-month forward rate is $1.550 , and the one-year forward rate is $1.540 . The U.S. six-month interest rate is 4.00 percent per year, and the one-year interest rate is 4.25 percent per year.

   a. What are the six-month and one-year British interest rates consistent with interest rate parity?

   b. A speculator expects that six months from now the British six-month interest rate will be 2 percentage points higher than the U.S. six-month interest rate. The speculator wants to take a £1,000,000 swap position to take advantage of this forecast. What position should the speculator take?

   c. If the speculator is correct about the spread in the interest rates, how much will she earn if, six months from now, the U.S. six-month interest rate is 4.25 percent and the British pound currency rate is $1.550? How much will she earn if the spot currency rate is $1.500? How much will she earn if the spot currency rate is $1.600?

5-2. Trinity Forge is a small company with little international experience. It has agreed to buy two forging machines from a manufacturer in Germany. The price is DM 2,000,000 with delivery and payment in 0.5 years. The spot price of the mark is $0.600. The 180-day forward price is $0.597. Trinity is currently earning 5.00 percent per year on its short-term deposits. Its banker has offered Trinity the opportunity to earn 6.50 percent per year on short-term mark deposits.

   a. If Trinity Forge wants to eliminate its mark exposure with a forward hedge, what transaction should it make?

   b. What is the dollar cost of the machines if Trinity Forge hedges its mark exposure in the forward market?

   c. If Trinity Forge wants to eliminate its mark exposure with a money market hedge, what transactions should it make?

   d. What is the dollar cost of the machines if Trinity Forge hedges its mark exposure with a money market hedge?

   e. Holding the other information unchanged, for what forward price would the two hedges yield identical costs for the machines?

5-3. With currency prices on the x-axis and dollar values on the y-axis, plot the value of Trinity Forge's account payable and money market hedge for a range of values of the spot price 0.5 years from now.

5-4. A firm has just begun to do business in Japan and the financial manager anticipates approximately ¥10,000,000 sales per month, outstanding for approximately one month. He has not decided whether to hedge your receivables or not. To help decide, he has collected a small sample of prices, reported in the following table. Interpret the table as follows: On January 15, the 30-day forward and the spot rates of the yen were 0.008778 and 0.08752, respectively. The actual spot rate on February 15 was 0.009654. Assuming sales of ¥10,000,000 each month, January 15 through May 15, collected one month later, what would the dollar receipts have been over this period with no hedge? What would they have been with a 100 percent forward hedge? How might these results influence the decision to hedge?

Dollar/Yen Exchange Rates

Time	Forward	Spot
January 15	$0.008778	$0.008752
February 15	0.009681	0.009654
March 15	0.008941	0.008912
April 15	0.009223	0.009191
May 15	0.008843	0.008815
June 15	—	0.009111

5-5. Assume that the spot price of the British pound is $1.41. There is a put option on the currency with an exercise price of $1.40. The domestic interest rate is 0.5 percent per month and the British interest rate is 1.0 percent per month. What will the price of a put option be if the price of the currency is either $0.05 higher, $1.46, or $0.05 lower, $1.36, at the end of the month?

5-6. Draw a graph of the payoff at maturity from a portfolio comprising of a long call and a short put with the same exercise price.

5-7. Calculate the values of both a put and a call for the example in Question 5-5 but with the exercise price equal to the one-month forward price implied by interest rate parity. What would it cost to buy one put and sell one call? Why?

REFERENCES

Biger, N., and J. Hull. "The Valuation of Currency Options." *Financial Management*, Spring 1983, pp. 24–28.

Black, Fischer, and Myron Scholes. "The Pricing of Options and Corporate Liabilities." *Journal of Political Economy*, May 1973, pp. 637–659.

Cox, J. C., Stephen A. Ross, and Mark Rubinstein. "Option Pricing: A Simplified Approach." *Journal of Financial Economics*, September 1979, pp. 229–263.

Garman, Mark B., and Steven W. Kohlhagen. "Foreign Currency Option Values." *Journal of International Money and Finance*, December 1983, pp. 231–237.

Giddy, Ian H. "Foreign Exchange Options." *The Journal of Futures Markets*, Summer 1983, pp. 143–166.

Grabbe, J. Orlin. "The Pricing of Call and Put Options on Foreign Exchange." *Journal of International Money and Finance*, December 1983, pp. 239–253.

Jacque, L. L. "Management of Foreign Exchange Risk: A Review Article." *Journal of International Business Studies*, Spring/Summer 1981, pp. 81–101.

Hull, John. *Options, Futures, and Other Derivative Securities, 2nd ed.* Englewood Cliffs, N.J.: Prentice-Hall, 1993.

Levi, Maurice. "Spot versus Forward Speculation and Hedging: A Diagrammatic Exposition," *Journal of International Money and Finance*, April 1984, pp. 105–109.

"Lufthansa: Where Options Would Have Made a Difference." *Intermarket*, Supplement/ November 1986, pp. 20–22.

Marshall, J. F., and K. R. Kapner. *Understanding Swap Finance*. Cincinnati: South-Western, 1990.

Perold, Andre F., and Evan C. Shulman. "The Free Lunch in Currency Hedging: Implications for Investment Policy and Performance Standards." *Financial Analysts Journal*, May-June 1988, pp. 45–50.

Smithson, Charles W. "A LEGO Approach to Financial Engineering: An Introduction to Forwards, Futures, Swaps, and Options." *Midland Corporate Finance Journal*, Winter 1987, pp. 16–28.

Stulz, Rene, and Clifford W. Smith. "The Determinants of Firms' Hedging Policies." *Journal of Financial and Quantitative Analysis*, December 1985, pp. 391–405.

CASE 5.1

DOZIER INDUSTRIES (A)

Richard Rothschild, the chief financial officer of Dozier Industries, returned to his office after the completion of his meeting with two officers of Southeastern National Bank. He had requested the meeting to discuss financial issues related to Dozier's first major international sales contract, which had been confirmed the previous day, January 13, 1986. Initially, Rothschild had contacted Robert Leigh, a vice president at the bank who had primary responsibilities for Dozier's business with Southeastern National. Leigh had in turn suggested that John Gunn of the bank's International Division be included in the meeting because Leigh felt that he lacked the international expertise to answer all the questions Rothschild might ask.

The meeting had focused on the exchange risk related to the new sales contract. Dozier's bid of £1,175,000 for the installation of an internal security system for a large manufacturing firm in the United Kingdom had been accepted. In accordance with the contract, the British firm had transferred by cable £117,500 (i.e., 10 percent of the contract amount) as a deposit on the contract, with the balance due at the time the system was completed. Dozier's production vice president, Mike Miles, had assured Rothschild that there would be no difficulty in completing the project within the 90-day period stipulated in the bid. As a result, Rothschild expected to receive £1,057,500 on April 14, 1986.

HISTORY OF THE COMPANY

Dozier Industries was a relatively young firm specializing in electronic security systems. It had been established in 1973 by Charles L. Dozier, who was still president and the owner of 78 percent of the stock. The remaining 22 percent of the stock was held by other members of management. Dozier had formerly been a design engineer for a large electronics firm. In 1973 he began his own company to market security systems and began by concentrating on military sales. The company experienced rapid growth for almost a decade. However, in 1982, as Dozier faced increased competition in this market, management attempted to branch out to design systems for the private sector, namely small firms and households. Dozier's inexperience in this market, combined with poor planning efforts, slowed sales growth and led to a severe reduction in profits (see Exhibit 5.1A). The company shifted its focus to larger corporations and met with better success. In 1985 the company showed a profit for the first time in three years, and management was confident that the company had turned the corner. Exhibit 5.1B contains the balance sheet at the end of 1985.

The company's management believed that sales to foreign corporations represented good prospects for future growth. Consequently, in the spring of 1985, Dozier had launched a marketing effort overseas. The selling effort had not met with much success until the confirmation of the contract discussed previously. The new sales contract, although large in itself, had the potential of being expanded in the future because the company involved was a large multinational firm with manufacturing facilities in many countries.

This case was written by Mark R. Eaker, professor of Business Administration. Copyright © 1986 by the University of Virginia Darden School Foundation, Charlottesville, Va. All rights reserved.

■ EXHIBIT 5.1A

DOZIER INDUSTRIES (A)
■ SALES AND INCOME SUMMARY

Year Ended December 31	Sales ($000)	Net Income ($000)
1973	$ 456	$ 41
1974	631	54
1975	890	73
1976	1,610	151
1977	3,860	324
1978	7,242	760
1979	11,338	1,162
1980	15,138	1,488
1981	20,371	1,925
1982	21,455	712
1983	22,501	(242)
1984	23,986	(36)
1985	25,462	309

■ EXHIBIT 5.1B

DOZIER INDUSTRIES (A)
■ BALANCE SHEET AS OF DECEMBER 31, 1985

Assets

Current assets

Cash and securities	$ 294,572
Accounts receivable	1,719,494
Inventories	2,227,066
Total current assets	$ 4,241,132

Properties, plants, and equipment

At cost	$ 8,429,812
Less: Accumulated depreciation	2,633,404
Net plant	$ 5,796,408

Other assets

Investments and loans	$ 450,000
Total assets	$10,487,540

Liabilities and Equity

Current liabilities Accounts payable	$ 934,582
Notes payable—bank	652,800
Total current liabilities	$ 1,587,382
Long-term liabilities Notes payable	$ 550,000

Common equity

Common stock	$ 2,253,410
Reserves	627,244
Retained earnings	5,469,504
Total equity	$ 8,350,158
Total liabilities and equity	$10,487,540

On January 13, the day the bid was accepted, the value of the pound was $1.4480. However, the pound had weakened over the past six weeks (see Exhibit 5.1c). Rothschild was concerned that the value of the pound might depreciate even further during the next 90 days, and this worry prompted his discussion at the bank. He wanted to find out what techniques were available to Dozier to reduce the exchange risk created by the outstanding pound receivable.

Gunn, the international specialist, had explained that Rothschild had several alternatives. First, of course, he could do nothing. This would leave Dozier vulnerable to pound fluctuations, which would entail losses if the pound depreciated,

■ **EXHIBIT 5.1c**

DOZIER INDUSTRIES (A)

■ **HISTORICAL SPOT AND FORWARD POUND RATES IN U.S. DOLLARS**

	Spot	Three-Month Forward Rate
7/9/85	1.3640	1.3490
7/16	1.3880	1.3744
7/23	1.4090	1.3963
7/30	1.4170	1.4067
8/6	1.3405	1.3296
8/13	1.3940	1.3828
8/20	1.3900	1.3784
8/27	1.3940	1.3817
9/4	1.3665	1.3553
9/10	1.3065	1.2960
9/17	1.3330	1.3226
9/24	1.4200	1.4089
10/1	1.4120	1.4005
10/8	1.4155	1.4039
10/15	1.4120	1.4007
10/22	1.4290	1.4171
10/29	1.4390	1.4270
11/5	1.4315	1.4194
11/12	1.4158	1.4037
11/19	1.4320	1.4200
11/26	1.4750	1.4628
12/3	1.4820	1.4704
12/10	1.4338	1.4214
12/17	1.4380	1.4249
12/23	1.4245	1.4114
12/30	1.4390	1.4260
1/7/86	1.4420	1.4284
1/14/86	1.4370	1.4198

SOURCE: *Chicago Mercantile Exchange Statistical Yearbook*, 1985 and 1986.

■ EXHIBIT 5.1ᴅ

DOZIER INDUSTRIES (A)
■ INTEREST AND EXCHANGE RATE COMPARISONS
JANUARY 14, 1986

	United States	United Kingdom
Three-month money[a]	7.65	13.41
Prime lending rate	9.50	13.50
Three-month deposits (large amounts)	8.00	12.90
Euro dollar three-month (LIBOR[b])		8.3
Euro pound three-month (Paris)	13.2	
Spot rate for the pound	1.4370	
Three-month forward pound	1.4198	

[a]Prime commercial paper in the United States; interbank rates in the United Kingdom.
[b]LIBOR is the London interbank offer rate.
SOURCE: *The Economist.*

or gains if it appreciated versus the dollar. On the other hand, Rothschild could choose to hedge his exchange risk.

Gunn explained that a hedge involved taking a position opposite to the one that was creating the foreign exchange exposure. This could be accomplished either by engaging in a forward contract or via a spot transaction. Because Dozier had an outstanding pound receivable, the appropriate hedging transactions would be to sell pounds forward 90 days or to secure a 90-day pound loan. By selling pounds forward, Dozier would incur an obligation to deliver pounds 90 days from now at the rate established today. This would ensure that Dozier would receive a set dollar value for its pound receivable, regardless of the spot rate that existed in the future.

The spot hedge works similarly in that it also creates a pound obligation 90 days hence. Dozier would borrow pounds and exchange the proceeds into dollars at the spot rate. On April 13, Dozier would use its pound receipts to repay the loan. Any gains or losses on the receivable due to a change in the value of the pound would be offset by equivalent losses or gains on the loan payment.

Leigh assured Rothschild that Southeastern National would be able to assist Dozier in implementing whatever decision Rothschild made. Dozier had a $3 million line of credit with Southeastern National. John Gunn indicated that there would be no difficulty for Southeastern to arrange the pound loan for Dozier through its correspondent bank in London. He believed that such a loan would be at 1.5 percent above the U.K. prime rate. To assist Rothschild in making his decision, Gunn provided him with information on interest rates, spot and forward exchange rates, and historical and forecasted information on the pound (see Exhibits 5.1c. 5.1ᴅ, and 5.1ᴇ).

DOZIER INDUSTRIES (A)
■ WHY STERLING WILL FALL AGAIN

Declining oil revenues and industrial uncompetitiveness will put pressure on sterling next year.

Sterling has been on the sidelines since the Group of Five meeting in September. With the yen/dollar rate being the main focus of attention, the Bank of England sterling index has been remarkably stable in the 79 to 81 range, a pleasant change from the volatile movements of earlier months. The Chancellor's autumn statement was designed to maintain market confidence with optimistic projections of United Kingdom (UK) economic growth and inflation. More important is the support sterling has received from the recent firmness in oil prices and the maintenance of high UK interest rates. Support will have lessened by next spring.

The mid-November $30 a barrel spot price for Brent crude, compared to a summer low of around $26, reflects a seasonal rise in oil demand at a time of low inventories. Renewed pressure on prices is widely expected as demand falls away after the winter. Pressures on Opec will be compounded by Saudi Arabia's aggressive moves to boost output. The stability of the market will depend on whether other Opec countries maintain discipline over production. While a collapse in prices is unlikely, the most probable outcome is a cut of around $2 a barrel. But uncertainty on prices can be expected to undermine optimism towards sterling.

The United Kingdom Government does not seem in any hurry to bring down interest rates. Memories of the sterling crisis earlier this year linger on. Monetary growth is way over target with the broad monetary aggregate sterling M3 up to 14.5 percent in the year to October. The high level of interest rates is a signal to the markets that government policy is maintaining its anti-inflation bias. An early reduction in rates would appear to be against the spirit of the Group of Five agreement to bring down the value of the dollar. This is especially true following the Bank of Japan's aggressive monetary tightening.

The hard line on interest rates will not be sustained for very long, given the government's hopes of strong economic growth and falling inflation. For example, it will be almost impossible to hit the 3¾ percent inflation target for the fourth quarter of 1986

without further significant cuts in mortgage costs. Lower interest rates will be needed to justify the treasury's optimistic projections of private capital expenditure. It is reasonable to expect United Kingdom base rates to move into single figures during the first half of 1986.

Lower interest rates leading to lower sterling would be welcomed by British industry. The latest Confederation of British Industry industrial survey showed falling export orders and a general loss of business confidence. This has been backed up by recent statistics which showed that manufacturing output fell 0.5 percent in the third quarter while non-oil export volume fell 3.5 percent. Against this background, the CBI is lobbying hard for interest rates to be brought down.

UK goods are clearly uncompetitive. Sterling's real effective index (as calculated by Morgan Guaranty) is around 4 percent higher than its 1983 average. The non-oil trade deficit has risen from £7.8 billion in 1983 to around £11 billion this year. Competitiveness has not been helped by the rapidly rising UK wage costs. The latest 7 percent year-on-year rise in UK manufacturing industry's unit labour costs compares to 2 percent in the US, 1 percent in Japan and no increase in Germany.

The decline in UK competitiveness will start to receive increasing attention now that oil production is in decline. Output of North Sea oil is expected to slip from 2.64mb/d in 1985 to 2.54mb/d next year. In its peak month, output reached 2.77mb/d. Since the sterling oil price has fallen sharply since the turn of the year, UK oil export revenues are declining steadily (see chart). It will become important to arrest the deterioration in non-oil trade to prevent an unacceptable rise in the trade deficit. In the absence of a sharp deceleration in wage growth (which is unlikely), UK competitiveness will have to be increased by a reduction in sterling.

Continued on next page

(CONTINUED)

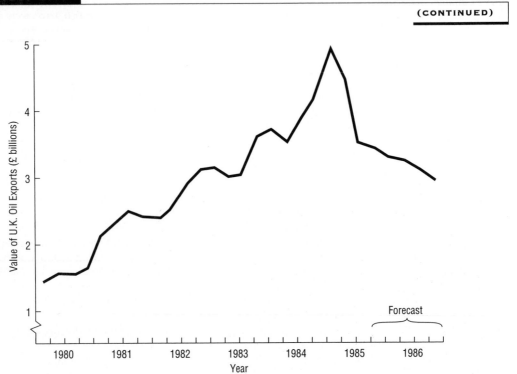

An analysis of sterling's overvaluation depends on the appropriate choices of base year and price indices. Using producer prices and a 1975 base year, purchasing power parity values would be 1.50 for the dollar/sterling rate and around 3.00 for the Deutschemark/ sterling rate. Such calculations take on a new importance given the speculation about membership of the European Monetary System. Even allowing for a generous margin of error, a DM/£ rate of over 3.50 would probably prove to be unsustainable even over one year.

By the second half of next year the foreign exchange market will start to look ahead to the next UK election. This will cause some jitters as another Conservative Party victory will by no means be certain. UK fund managers might feel it prudent to step up overseas investment if they fear a re-introduction of exchange controls. Sterling's effective index fell sharply ahead of the last election following Labour Party comments on the need for devaluation.

No such worries will undermine the yen or the Deutschemark. In contrast to the UK, both Japan and Germany are major beneficiaries of lower oil prices and already have large current account surpluses. Inflation is likely to average below 2 percent next year in the two countries and both monetary and fiscal policies are sound. On this basis, a significant decline of sterling against the yen and EMS bloc currencies seems almost inevitable over the next year. Fortunately for sterling, the dollar faces even greater weakness and this should moderate the decline in sterling's trade-weighted value.

SOURCE: *Euromoney*, December 1985. Martin Barnes is an international economist for Wood, Mackenzie and Company, Edinburgh.

■EXHIBIT 5.1F

DOZIER INDUSTRIES (A)
■ BID PREPARATION

Materials		$ 847,061
Direct labor		416,820
Shipping		70,000
Direct overhead[a]		208,410
Allocation of indirect overhead		100,492
Total cost		$1,642,783
Profit factor		98,567
Total		$1,741,350
Spot pound rate on December 3	1.4820	
Pound value of the bid	£1,175,000	

[a]Based on 50 percent of direct labor.

Rothschild was aware that in preparing the bid, Dozier had allowed for a profit margin of only 6 percent to increase the likelihood of winning the bid and, hence, developing an important foreign contact. The bid was submitted on December 3, 1985. In arriving at the bid, the company had estimated the cost of the project and added an amount as profit but kept in mind the highest bid that could conceivably win the contract. The calculations were made in dollars and then converted to pounds at the spot rate existing on December 3 (see Exhibit 5.1F) because the U.K. company had stipulated payment in pounds.

Rothschild realized that the amount involved in the contract was such that an adverse move in the pound exchange rate could put Dozier in a loss position for 1986 if the transactions were left unhedged. On the other hand, he also became aware of the fact that hedging had its own costs. Still, a decision had to be made. He knew that no action implied that an unhedged position was the best alternative for the company.

CASE 5.2

DOZIER INDUSTRIES (B)

Richard Rothschild, the chief financial officer of Dozier Industries, was still contemplating how best to manage the exchange risk related to the company's new sales contract. The £1,057,500 balance of the contract was due in three months on April 14, 1986, creating a long position in British pounds. Rothschild had spoken previously to John Gunn, an officer in the International Division of Southeastern National Bank, about hedging Dozier's long pound exposure. Gunn had explained two alternatives available to Dozer to reduce the exchange risk: a forward contract or a spot transaction. Either transaction would ensure that Dozier receive a set dollar value for its pound receivable, regardless of any change in the value of the pound. Given his previous analysis of the foreign exchange market, Rothschild was concerned that both of these hedging alternatives would "lock in" a profit margin below the 6 percent he had originally anticipated for the contract. He wondered if there were some way to get the upside potential without all the risk.

The pound had weakened since his bid submission date on December 3 (see Exhibit 5.2A), but he was not entirely convinced that it would continue to fall, or at least not as much as the forward rate indicated. If the future spot rate were higher than the current forward rate, an unhedged position could lead to a gain, whereas a hedged position would create an opportunity cost. Rothschild wondered if other alternatives were available, and he again called John Gunn at the bank for advice.

Gunn explained that Rothschild could also use currency options to hedge against his uncertain foreign exchange exposure. Options provide a means of hedging against volatility without taking a position on expected future rates. Gunn explained that there are two basic varieties of options contracts: puts and calls. A put gives the holder the right, but not the obligation, to sell foreign currency at a set exercise or "strike" price within a specified time period. A call gives the holder the right to buy foreign currency at a set price. In comparison with a forward or futures contract, the holder of an option does not have to transact at the agreed-upon price but has the choice or option to do so. Gunn told Rothschild that options are complicated and increase the front-end cost of hedging in comparison with a forward hedge. He said that Rothschild could find the prevailing option contract prices in the *The Wall Street Journal* (see Exhibit 5.2B).

It appeared to Rothschild that options contracts might provide some benefit. He wondered whether options contracts were the best alternative for Dozier right now. He also wondered whether he could have used options contracts when preparing his bid (see Exhibit 5.2C).

This case was written by Leslie Zanetti Schorr, MBA, under the supervision of Mark R. Eaker, professor of Business Administration. Copyright © 1987 by the University of Virginia Darden School Foundation, Charlottesville, Va. All rights reserved.

DOZIER INDUSTRIES (B)
■ HISTORICAL SPOT AND FORWARD POUND RATES IN U.S. DOLLARS

	Spot	Three-Month Forward Rate
7/9/85	1.3640	1.3490
7/16	1.3880	1.3744
7/23	1.4090	1.3963
7/30	1.4170	1.4067
8/6	1.3405	1.3296
8/13	1.3940	1.3828
8/20	1.3900	1.3784
8/27	1.3940	1.3817
9/4	1.3665	1.3553
9/10	1.3065	1.2960
9/17	1.3330	1.3226
9/24	1.4200	1.4089
10/1	1.4120	1.4005
10/8	1.4155	1.4039
10/15	1.4120	1.4007
10/22	1.4290	1.4171
10/29	1.4390	1.4270
11/5	1.4315	1.4194
11/12	1.4158	1.4037
11/19	1.4320	1.4200
11/26	1.4750	1.4628
12/3	1.4820	1.4704
12/10	1.4338	1.4214
12/17	1.4380	1.4249
12/23	1.4245	1.4114
12/30	1.4390	1.4260
1/7/86	1.4420	1.4284
1/14/86	1.4370	1.4198

SOURCE: *Chicago Mercantile Exchange Statistical Yearbook*, 1985 and 1986.

■ EXHIBIT 5.2ʙ

DOZIER INDUSTRIES (B)
■ FOREIGN CURRENCY OPTIONS ON JANUARY 14, 1986

Options and Underlying	Strike Price	Calls—Last			Puts—Last		
		January	February	March	January	February	March
12,500 British pounds—cents per unit							
B Pound	130	s	r	13.50	s	r	r
144.41	135	s	r	9.20	s	0.20	0.50
144.41	140	s	4.50	4.75	s	0.80	1.55
144.41	145	s	1.55	2.50	s	3.10	4.40
144.41	150	s	0.40	0.90	s	r	r

r—Not traded   s—No option offered
Last is premium (purchase price).

SOURCE: *The Wall Street Journal*, January 15, 1986. Foreign currency options listed on the Philadelphia Exchange.

■ EXHIBIT 5.2ᴄ

DOZIER INDUSTRIES (B)
■ FOREIGN CURRENCY OPTIONS ON DECEMBER 3, 1985

Options and Underlying	Strike Price	Calls—Last			Puts—Last		
		December	January	March	December	January	March
12,500 British pounds—cents per unit							
B Pound	120	29.00	s	28.95	r	s	r
148.86	130	19.10	r	r	r	r	r
148.86	135	13.80	r	14.60	0.05	r	r
148.86	140	8.80	r	10.00	0.05	r	s
148.86	145	4.00	4.50	5.70	0.20	1.05	3.20
148.86	150	0.65	1.65	3.35	r	r	5.60
148.86	155	r	0.50	1.70	r	r	r

r—Not traded   s—No option offered
Last is premium (purchase price).

SOURCE: *The Wall Street Journal*, December 4, 1985. Foreign currency options listed on the Philadelphia Exchange.

ADVANCED TOPICS IN FORECASTING, HEDGING, AND OPTIONS

6

CHAPTER

KEY CONCEPTS

THE VARIOUS TECHNIQUES USED TO FORECAST EXCHANGE RATES ▬

METHODS THAT MEASURE THE EFFECTIVENESS OF FORECASTING TECHNIQUES ▬

AN ALGEBRAIC APPROACH TO HEDGING ▬

THE USE OF RISK-MINIMIZING HEDGES ▬

THE ROLE AND EFFECTIVENESS OF CROSS-HEDGING ▬

THE BLACK-SCHOLES OPTION PRICING MODEL APPLIED TO FOREIGN EXCHANGE ▬

THE USE OF OPTIONS TO CONSTRUCT A DELTA HEDGE ▬

INTRODUCTION

Chapter 1 reported losses in foreign exchange by individual companies ranging from $50 million to $1 billion. These adverse experiences make a strong case for the need for managers to have a thorough understanding of currency price changes and methods for managing the risk associated with them. This chapter extends the reader's understanding by examining more advanced concepts concerning forecasting, risk management, and derivative securities trading. It begins with forecasting.

FORECASTING EXCHANGE RATES

Effective decisions about hedging and speculating require forecasts about future spot exchange rates. To make money by speculating, it is necessary to "outpredict" the forward rate; to evaluate hedging decisions, it is necessary to compare the firm's forecast with the forward rate. Forecasting exchange rates is fundamental to speculating and hedging. Therefore, it is natural to ask the question, "How do people forecast exchange rates and how well do they do?" This section addresses those questions. The subject of forecasting is important and complex. Therefore, this section should be viewed as no more than an introduction to forecasting.

FORECASTING TECHNIQUES

Forecasters use three general approaches or techniques to predict exchange rates: fundamental analysis, technical analysis, and market-based forecasts. Many forecasters combine these techniques, and almost every forecaster applies his or her own twist to the basic method. As a result, the approaches examined here are generic techniques rather than specific examples of the forecaster's art or science.

FUNDAMENTAL ANALYSIS Fundamental analysis forecasts are based on underlying economic models of exchange rate behavior. According to this approach, economic factors such as relative inflation rates, growth rates, and Current account balances determine exchange rates. To forecast exchange rates, it is necessary to predict the economic factors, such as inflation, growth rates, and Current account balances. This in turn requires an understanding of the relationship between economic policies and inflation, growth, and Current account balances.

Most forecasters using the fundamental analysis approach build large-scale econometric models. Those allow the forecaster to develop the linkages among the various sectors of the economy and their impact on exchange rates. Econometric models are information intensive and therefore relatively expensive to develop and maintain. Arriving at an exchange rate forecast involves several steps. The first step is modeling the relationship between economic policies and economic performance. The second is linking performance factors and the exchange rate. The third step is predicting the policy inputs. Because the exchange rate is influenced by events in two countries, it is not enough to analyze economic policies and performance in just one country. For example, most exchange rate models assume that a high rate of inflation causes a currency to depreciate. Whether inflation is high must be measured relative to the inflation in some other country. If inflation is 10 percent in France, will the franc fall relative to the mark? The answer depends on the rate of inflation in Germany. If it is lower than 10 percent, the answer is yes. If it is higher than 10 percent, the answer is no.

Because of the complexity and the information requirements for fundamental exchange rate forecasting, only large banks, large companies, and economic forecasting services develop fundamental forecasts. Smaller firms buy those forecasts because they cannot afford to develop their own.

TECHNICAL ANALYSIS Technical analysis relies on patterns of historic exchange rate movements and trading activities to forecast future rates. Also known as *charting* because of the graphs or charts that make up a major part of the methodology, technical analysis assumes that exchange rates follow recurring patterns. The keys to forecasting on the basis of technical analysis are to identify and measure the patterns or cycles and to spot them as they occur.

As many discernible patterns exist as there are forecasters using technical analysis. A major academic criticism of technical analysis is that it lacks any underlying theory to support the analyst's conclusions or predictions. Analysts respond that whatever forecasts well is a good method, or, in other words, success is the best argument in favor of any forecasting methodology.

An example of technical analysis is momentum analysis. It measures both the direction of recent exchange rate changes and changes in the rate of change. Many technical analysts believe that an appreciating currency is likely to continue to appreciate; that is particularly so if the rate of appreciation is increasing. Technical analysts plot the daily change or level of exchange rates to detect the trends or thresholds on which they base their forecasts.

Empirical studies of exchange rate behavior have shown that exchange rate changes are serially correlated; that is, today's change is related to or similar to yesterday's change. Because technical analysis is premised on the existence of serial correlation, it does well at predicting very short-term changes; however, there is less reason to believe that technical analysis is successful at predicting turning points or long-term exchange rates.

MARKET-BASED FORECASTS Market-based forecasts of exchange rates employ current market prices of exchange rates to forecast values of exchange rates in the future. The expectations theory hypothesizes that the current forward or futures price is a consensus forecast of the value of the exchange rate in the future. For example, today's 90-day German mark forward rate is a market forecast of the spot rate that will exist in 90 days.

The rationale for the expectations theory is that market participants, including currency traders, corporate treasurers, and money managers, buy and sell foreign exchange in the forward market based in large part on their expectations or forecasts of future exchange rates. That is true whether the motive for the transaction is hedging or speculating. If a trader believes that the forward price is higher than the expected future spot price, he or she has an incentive to sell forward. When the contract matures, if the spot price is lower than the forward price, the seller of the forward contracts earns a profit. The lure of expected profits keeps people selling until the forward price is driven down to the point at which it equals the expected future spot price and expected profits disappear. Similarly, when the expected future spot price is higher than the forward price, expected profits generate buying pressure, which forces the forward price up. Equilibrium occurs when the forward price and expected future spot price are equal.

Another way to describe the equilibrium is that the equilibrium forward price is the price that divides the bulls, those who believe it is undervalued, from the bears, those that believe it is overvalued. In competitive markets with continuous transacting, the price is always changing, so equilibrium is a temporary or short-lived phenomenon. Participants process new information, revise expectations, or alter their willingness to bear risk, which leads them to adjust their portfolios. At any given time, some participants' expectations will differ from the existing price, but that causes the market to be fluid (prices to change) and liquid (accommodating transactions).

The major criticism of the expectations theory is that it fails to adequately take into account risk aversion. The argument is as follows. Individuals are interested in both risk and return. To induce people to bear risk, the expected profit or return must be commensurate with the risk. It is possible, but unlikely, that the forward price will exactly divide those willing to take short and long positions in the forward market on the basis of the same expectation about future spot rates. More likely, there will an excess of either desired short or long positions. To induce people to transact, the forward price must differ from the expected future spot price by just enough to balance the demand and supply of forward contracts. The difference between the forward price and the expected future spot price is the risk premium. The existence of a risk premium causes the forward price to be a biased estimate of the future spot price. It is higher than the expected future spot price if it is necessary to attract short sellers to balance demand and supply. It is lower if it is necessary to attract buyers to balance supply and demand.

As an example, assume that the market consensus is that the pound sterling will be at $1.48 in 30 days. Although that is the consensus forecast, it still represents a range of opinion. Assume also that at that price, the quantity of pounds demanded in the forward market exceeds the quantity supplied. With excess demand, the forward price of the pound rises, causing it to diverge from the consensus forecast. This divergence creates expected profits from a short position, which lead some participants to increase the number of forward pounds they supply and others to decrease the number they demand. This process continues until supply equals demand, but at a forward price that differs from the expected future spot price.

Why was the initial price not an equilibrium? One possible scenario is that at $1.48, the amount of forward pounds demanded to hedge short positions exceeds the amount supplied to hedge long positions. This could be due to either differences in risk preferences of the firms on each side of the market or just an imbalance in the size of the two positions caused by differences in the relative sizes of exports and imports. Either way, the $1.48 is not an equilibrium even though it is the market forecast of the future spot price. The equilibrium price needs to be higher to bring the two sides of the market into balance.

The existence and size of the risk premium are controversial issues among economists and finance theorists. Without a way to measure expectations, there is no way to explicitly test the expectations theory or other theories related to the risk premium. Tests of the theory require some assumption about expectations and, therefore, are tests of both the risk premium theory and the model of expectations, leaving no clear-cut result or conclusion.

Before leaving this section, we examine how well the Canadian dollar futures prices predict future spot prices. We employ data from 1978 to 1993 to make non-overlapping three-month forecasts that we compare with actual outcomes. We have 59 futures prices that forecast the level of 59 subsequent spot prices. If we regress the spot price outcomes against the futures price forecasts, we can test whether the forecasts were unbiased and accurate. In the regression equation,

$$S_t = a + bF_{t-1} + e_t$$

the estimated regression intercept is zero if the forecasts are unbiased and the estimated slope coefficient, b, equals 1.0. The R^2 (correlation squared) measures the accuracy of the forecasts.

Figure 6.1 reports the results for this regression. Note that the intercept is close to 0.0 (0.04) and the slope coefficient is close to 1.0 (0.95). The forecasts explain 88 percent ($R^2 = 0.88$) of the variation in the spot prices. These results suggest that the futures price is a good forecast of the future spot price. The evidence is less strong than it may appear. Figure 6.2 reports the results of an identical regression, except that the independent variable, the predictor, is the current spot price, not the current futures price. The results are very similar. To the extent that there is a difference, the level of the current spot price is a better predictor than the level of the current futures price. The futures price tells us nothing more than the spot price.

We can confirm this result by testing whether the futures price predicts changes in the spot price. Instead of predicting levels of prices, we predict changes in prices. We can do this by estimating the following equation:

$$(S_t - S_{t-1}) = a + b(F_{t-1} - S_{t-1}) + e_t$$

This equation tests whether the difference between the current futures and spot prices is a good forecast of the change that will occur in the spot price. Figure 6.3 reports the estimation results for this equation using the same data. The predictive

▪ FIGURE 6.1

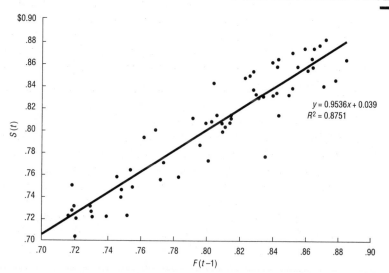

FORECAST OF THE SPOT PRICE BASED ON THE PREVIOUS FUTURES PRICE 1979–1994

$y = 0.9536x + 0.039$
$R^2 = 0.8751$

■ FIGURE 6.2

FORECAST OF THE SPOT PRICE BASED ON THE PREVIOUS SPOT PRICE 1978–1993

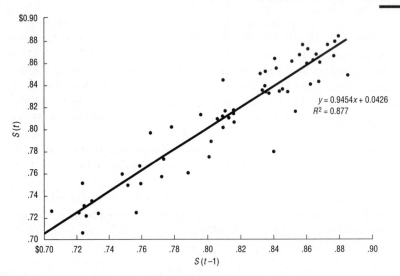

$y = 0.9454x + 0.0426$
$R^2 = 0.877$

■ FIGURE 6.3

FORECAST OF THE CHANGE IN THE SPOT PRICE BASED ON THE PREVIOUS DIFFERENCE BETWEEN THE FUTURES AND THE SPOT PRICE 1978–1993

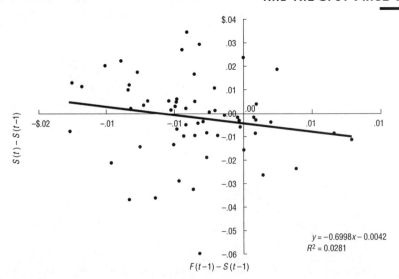

$y = -0.6998x - 0.0042$
$R^2 = 0.0281$

capacity is essentially zero ($R^2 = 0.03$). The slope coefficient has a negative sign but is not statistically different from zero. Figure 6.4 plots the forecasts and the actual changes as a time series, demonstrating that the forecast would be of no value in predicting the outcome.

FORECASTING EFFECTIVENESS Academics tend to be interested in theory and methodology, so the problems related to the risk premium controversy are part of its appeal. For them, the journey is as important as reaching the destination. Practitioners have a different perspective. The elegance and originality of a forecasting model do not matter to the corporate treasurer or banker; what counts is the model's forecasting effectiveness. If a technique works, it is valuable whether it conforms to some economist's theory or to the restrictions applied to statistical models. At the same time, however, it is reassuring to have an effective forecasting model that is consistent with reasonable views of how exchange rates are determined.

A large number of studies have analyzed the forecasting effectiveness of forward rates, foreign exchange advisory services, and economic models. Because of the currencies included and the time periods studied, the results of the research are not comparable and at times are inconsistent. Therefore, we do not attempt to summarize all of the studies. Instead, we report the results of two, one that focuses on the accuracy of various models versus the forward and spot rates, and the other that evaluates the accuracy of several forecasting services.

Meese and Rogoff evaluate the forecasting effectiveness of seven models using three currencies: the mark, yen, and pound for the period November 1976 to June

■ **FIGURE 6.4**

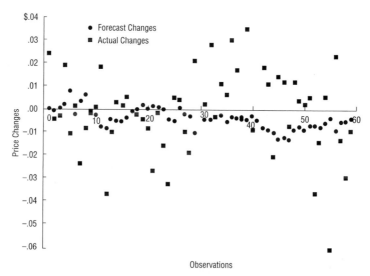

CHANGES IN THE CANADIAN DOLLAR 1978–1993

1981.[1] For each currency, they examine forecasting horizons of 1, 6, and 12 months. Included in the models that the authors evaluate are examples of what we have called *fundamental analysis, technical analysis,* and *market-based forecasts*. Meese and Rogoff chose the models to represent the state of the art in economic and statistical theory. The forecasts are those produced by a straight application of the model without any refinements based on a forecaster's intuition. Because most forecasters admit to some massaging of the output in line with gut feelings or hunches, Meese and Rogoff's results assess techniques rather than any specific forecaster's success.

To compare and rank the alternatives, Meese and Rogoff use as their primary measure the root mean square error, which measures the error of the forecasts. Table 6.1 reports their results. Each of the entries in the table represents the percentage error of the forecast over the period studied; the higher the number, the larger the error. Fundamental models 1 through 3 are based on the three most widely used exchange rate models in the economic journals. Technical analysis 1 and 2 represent statistical forecasting models that employ only past price data. Meese and Rogoff use both the spot price and the forward price as market-based forecasts.

■ **TABLE 6.1**

FORECASTING ACCURACY OF ALTERNATIVE MODELS

				Technical		Fundamental		
	Horizon	Spot	Forward	1	2	1	2	3
Dollar/Mark	1 month	3.72%	3.20%	3.51%	5.40%	3.17%	3.65%	3.50%
	6 months	8.71	9.03	12.40	11.83	9.64	12.03	9.95
	12 months	12.98	12.60	22.53	15.06	16.12	18.87	15.69
Dollar/Yen	1 month	3.68	3.72	4.46	7.76	4.11	4.40	4.20
	6 months	11.58	11.93	22.04	18.90	13.38	13.94	11.94
	12 months	18.31	18.95	52.18	22.98	18.55	20.41	19.20
Dollar/Pound	1 month	2.56	2.67	2.79	5.56	2.82	2.90	3.03
	6 months	6.45	7.23	7.27	12.97	8.90	8.88	9.08
	12 months	9.96	11.62	13.35	21.28	14.62	13.66	14.57
Trade-	1 month	1.99	NA	2.72	4.10	2.40	2.50	2.74
Weighted	6 months	6.09	NA	6.82	8.91	7.07	6.49	7.11
Dollar	12 months	8.65	14.24	11.14	10.96	11.40	9.80	10.35

NA: not available.

---

[1] R. A. Meese and K. Rogoff, "Empirical Exchange Rate Models in the Seventies: Do They Fit Out of Sample!" *Journal of International Economics*, February 1983, pp. 3–24.

■ **TABLE 6.2**

PERCENTAGE OF ACCURATE PREDICTIONS OF THE DIRECTION OF THE THREE-MONTH TREND

	Forecast Service						
	1	2	3	4	5	6	Forward Price
Canadian dollar	83%	53%	NA	30%	31%	NA	62%
French franc	63	43	30%	73	27	25%	37
German mark	57	77	60	73	45	63	67
Japanese yen	50	67	67	47	37	NA	54
U.K. pound	60	63	60	43	37	29	50

NA: not available.

Although there is some variation across currencies and time horizons, the implications of Meese and Rogoff's analysis are clear. The market forecasts predict more accurately than those based on both technical and fundamental analysis and, of the two market forecasts, the spot rate performs slightly better than the forward rate.

The second study we discuss by Stephen Goodman, assistant treasurer of The Singer Company, evaluates the record of specific forecasting services.[2] He examines their forecasts for a larger sample of currencies than those in Meese and Rogoff's study but for a shorter period of time, January to June 1978. Like Meese and Rogoff, Goodman uses the forward rate as one of his benchmarks and includes both fundamental and technical forecasts in his comparison set. Goodman concludes that the fundamental forecasts, those using econometric models, do worse than the forward rate at predicting the direction and size of changes but that technical forecasts can lead to profitable speculation.

Tables 6.2 and 6.3 summarize Goodman's results for the econometrically oriented services. Table 6.2 indicates success at predicting the direction of change by measuring the percentage of forecasts that correctly predicted the direction of change. Some of the services performed better than others, but on average they did not perform better than the forward rate, and no individual service appears to be more materially more accurate than the forward rate. Table 6.3 reports the percentage of times that the service forecasts of the future spot price were closer to the actual rate than the forward rate. Overall, the forecasting services do not do well in Goodman's study, and because they cost several thousand dollars, managers should carefully assess a service's performance before subscribing to it.

It is more difficult to summarize and evaluate the technical services. Rather than provide point estimates of some future rate, they tend to give trend assessments for the outlook for varying lengths of time. Goodman used the trend predictions as the

---

[2] Stephen H. Goodman, "Foreign Exchange Rate Forecasting Techniques: Implications for Business and Policy," *Journal of Finance*, May 1979, pp. 415–427.

PERCENTAGE OF PREDICTIONS OF THE SPOT PRICE MORE ACCURATE THAN THE FORWARD PRICE

	Forecast Service					
	1	2	3	4	5	6
Canadian dollar	60%	27%	NA	13%	37%	NA
French franc	57	33	48	40	38	57%
German mark	24	63	57	41	33	53
Japanese yen	37	60	62	30	20	NA
U.K. pound	70	33	47	47	40	48

NA: not available.

basis for buy and sell decisions at each point that a recommendation was published. He found those speculative transactions to be profitable, suggesting that the technical services do provide forecasts useful for successful speculation. Goodman's results are inconclusive because they cover only a short period, but they indicate that technical analysis might have something to offer a perspective purchaser of foreign exchange forecasts.

It is incorrect to use Goodman's results to conclude that the exchange markets do not reflect all available information and thus are inefficient. Goodman showed that a speculative position based on technical analysis yields a profit. Without identifying or measuring the risk, it is impossible to say whether the profit more than compensated for the risk of the speculative position. The currency markets are inefficient only if the profit is larger than that appropriate for the associated risk.

HEDGING

In the previous chapter we examined geometrically how hedging influences risk. In this chapter we examine some of the same material algebraically. This approach also allows us to investigate more specifically how exchange rate forecasts affect hedging decisions.

AN ALGEBRAIC EXAMINATION OF HEDGING

We continue with the example of a U.S. company that has sold goods to a Canadian firm and has accepted a 30-day Canadian dollar receivable in payment. We represent the size of the Canadian dollar receivable as q Canadian dollars. There are spot and forward markets in the Canadian dollar. The price of a Canadian dollar in 30 days is S dollars, a random variable. The price today of a Canadian dollar for delivery in 30 days is known with certainty, which we represent as f dollars. Because the firm trades in the forward market, the forward contract price in 30 days will be F (i.e., $F = S$).

If it does not trade in the forward market, the firm's revenue, R, is

$$R = qS \qquad (6.1)$$

The firm can alter its revenue stream by trading in the forward market. Let the size of the forward position be h (as in hedge). For a forward purchase of Canadian dollars, h is positive; it is negative for a forward sale. Including the possibility of a forward position, the firm's revenue is

$$R = (q + h)S - hf \qquad (6.2)$$

where h is the quantity sold in the forward market. $(q + h)$ is the amount not sold in the forward market and therefore the amount sold in the spot market. At the maturity of the forward contract, $S = F$. Therefore, the expression for the firm's revenue is also

$$R = qS + hF - hf \qquad (6.3)$$

This form is especially useful when we consider hedging in futures rather than forwards. The interpretation of this expression for the example of a U.S. firm that sells to a Canadian firm and wants to hedge, in the forward market, the Canadian dollar receivable it accepts in payment is the following. The firm owns an asset q, the Canadian dollar receivable. Its value in 30 days will be qS. At the time of the sale, the firm sells h Canadian dollars in the 30-day forward market as a hedge (h is negative). When the customer pays the receivable 30 days later, the firm buys h dollars in the 0-day forward market (the 30-day forward market 30 days later) and at the same time sells the Canadian dollars it receives in the spot market. The value the firm receives, in dollars, depends on the sizes of the variables in the equation above. The foreign exchange markets determine the size of three of these, S, F and f. The first two are random variables, that is, they can assume a range of values depending on what happens in the world over the 30 days. The value of f is known when the firm trades initially in the forward market. The firm's business operations determine the value of q. That leaves h as the only choice or decision variable. Therefore the question is, What size should the firm choose for h?

To choose a value for h, the firm must have an objective. For the moment, assume that its objective is to earn the highest possible expected return with the minimum risk, measured as the variance of return. This is not a complete description of the objective because we know that the firm makes trade-offs between expected return and risk. It is enough, however, to start, because it suggests that we calculate the expected value and the variance of revenue. Let E indicate expected value, var indicate variance, and cov indicate covariance.

$$E(R) = qE(S) + hE(F) - hf \qquad (6.4)$$

$$\mathrm{var}(R) = q^2\mathrm{var}(S) + h^2\mathrm{var}(F) + 2qh\mathrm{cov}(S,F) \qquad (6.5)$$

The firm is interested in how changes in h affect the expected value and variance of revenue. To identify these effects, take the derivative of these two expressions with respect to h.

$$dE(R)/dh = E(F) - f \qquad (6.6)$$

$$dvar(R)/d(h) = 2hvar(F) + 2qcov(S,F) \qquad (6.7)$$

The minimum risk case is of special interest. To find this equation, (6.7) is set equal to zero. In that case

$$h = -qcov(S,F)/var(F) \qquad (6.8)$$

It is often useful to refer to the hedge per unit of exposure. That value is the *hedge ratio*, h/q. Equation (6.8) indicates that the risk-minimizing hedge ratio is a short forward position equal to $cov(S,F)/var(F)$ Canadian dollars.

$$h/q = -cov(S,F)/var(F) \qquad (6.9)$$

This example assumes that the firm can enter into a contract for any amount of Canadian dollars to be delivered at exactly the same time the firm receives its Canadian dollar payment. In that case, S, the price of the Canadian dollars in the spot market, is identical to F, the price of the Canadian dollar in the forward market on the day of delivery. Therefore, $cov(S,F) = var(F)$. The variance-minimizing hedge ratio is

$$h/q = -var(F)/var(F) = -1.0 \qquad (6.10)$$

This means that the firm minimizes risk if it sells in the forward market exactly one Canadian dollar for every Canadian dollar of receivables exposure. This is called *squaring the position*, and this result corresponds to the analysis in Chapter 5.

When trading in the forward market does not affect the expected value of revenues, the firm prefers to minimize risk. This is true if

$$dE(R)/dh = E(F) - f = 0 \qquad (6.11)$$

If that is the case, the forward price is an unbiased estimate of the expected value of the future spot price because $S = F$. There is no risk premium earned by bearing risk, for example being long Canadian dollars in the forward market, and there is no cost paid for being short Canadian dollar forwards.

If $[E(F) - f]$ is negative, selling Canadian dollars in the forward market increases the firm's expected revenue. In that case, the firm sells more than the risk-minimizing number up to the point at which the value of the increase in expected revenues is just offset by the increase in the variance of revenues. If $[E(F) - f]$ is positive, the firm sells less than the risk-minimizing number because each Canadian dollar it sells reduces expected revenues as well as risk. At some point before it minimizes risk, the firm concludes that the reduction in risk is not worth the reduction in the expected value of revenues.

This discussion of hedging can be generalized to include hedging in contracts that call for delivery on a date other than the exact day the customer pays the receivable.[3] In this case, it is not necessarily true that $F = S$, although the two values

---

[3] Hedging in futures typically creates this situation. Recall that currency futures contracts call for delivery on only four dates per year. The probability of a contract delivery date exactly matching a payment date is approximately 1 in 90. We should also note, however, that perfect matching of the payment date and the forward contract date is often not possible. Experience indicates that 30-day receivables are rarely paid in exactly 30 days.

are usually closely related. The company repurchases its forward contract at the price F and sells its Canadian dollars in the spot market at price S. If F does not equal S, then cov(S,F) does not equal var(F), and the variance-minimizing hedge ratio is

$$h/q = -\text{cov}(S,F)/\text{var}(F) \tag{6.12}$$

Typically, cov(S,F) is somewhat smaller than var(F), so the variance-minimizing hedge is somewhat smaller than the size of the business exposure. There are two explanations for this, one statistical and one intuitive.

The statistical explanation is that S and F are sufficiently similar that they have approximately the same variance. They are not perfectly related, so the correlation between them is less than 1.0. Therefore,

$$\text{cov}(S,F)/\text{var}(F) = \rho_{S,F}\sigma(S)\sigma(F)/\text{var}(F) = \rho_{S,F}\sigma(S)/\sigma(F) \tag{6.13}$$

where $\rho_{S,F}$ indicates the correlation between S and F and σ indicates standard deviation. The correlation should be close to, but less than, 1.0 and $\sigma(S) \approx \sigma(F)$. Therefore, the variance-minimizing hedge of a receivable should be a short sale that is somewhat smaller than the size of the business position.

The intuitive explanation follows. If $S = F$, when the firm sells Canadian dollars in the forward market, it has two effects. First, because S and F are closely related, the sale of Canadian dollars reduces risk. If S is unexpectedly high, F will also be unexpectedly high and their effects will offset each other. This reduces risk. The same thing occurs if S is unexpectedly low. Second, because S and F are not exactly equal, selling Canadian dollars forward introduces risk associated with their difference. At some point before the hedge equals the business position, the reduction in risk achieved from the relationship between S and F is offset by the addition of risk associated with their difference. At that point, an increase in the size of the hedge increases, rather than decreases, risk.

Three elements influence the size of the preferred hedge ratio. One is the firm's attitude toward risk. The more risk averse the firm is, the greater the tendency to reduce risk, despite any cost of doing so. The second factor is the relationship between the spot and forward prices, cov$(S,F)/$var(F). The more closely related S and F are, the closer the hedge ratio will be to 1.0. The third influence is the relationship between the current forward price and the expected value of the future forward price, $[E(F) - f]$. When this value is zero, the firms prefer risk-minimizing hedges. When it is not zero, hedging increases or decreases expected revenues, in which case the absolute value of the hedge is larger or smaller, respectively.

Prior experience with the capital asset pricing model suggests how to estimate cov$(S,F)/$var(F). The capital asset pricing model derives an expression for the expected risk premium (the expected rate of return minus the risk-free rate of return) on any asset i, $E(r_i)$, in terms of the expected risk-premium on the market portfolio of assets, $E(r_m)$, and systematic relative risk, β_i. Specifically,

$$E(r_i) = \beta_i E(r_m) \tag{6.14}$$

Systematic relative risk, β_i, is a measure of the systematic risk of asset i's return, relative to the risk of the market return. The estimate of β_i is a line drawn through the points that plot the risk premiums on the asset and the market over time. The statistical approach to estimating β_i is to use time series observations of the risk premiums to calculate the ordinary least squares regression line

$$r_i = a_i + b_i r_m + e_i \qquad (6.15)$$

where b_i is the estimate of β_i, a_i is the intercept, and e_i is the random error term. Figure 6.5 illustrates that process.

The connection between estimating β_i and estimating the variance-minimizing hedge ratio becomes obvious if we write the definition of β_i, which is identical in structure to the definition of the variance-minimizing hedge ratio, h/q.

$$\beta_i = \mathrm{cov}(r_i, r_m)/\mathrm{var}(r_m) \qquad (6.15)$$

$$h/q = -\mathrm{cov}(S,F)/\mathrm{var}(F) \qquad (6.16)$$

S takes the place of r_i, and F takes the place of r_m. Therefore, at least to start, the variance-minimizing hedge can be estimated by regressing S as a dependent variable against F as the independent variable. The variance-minimizing hedge is the negative of the slope.

One issue remains. The ordinary least squares regression calculations assume that the observations on the variables (S and F) minus their respective averages is a measure of the deviations of the variables from their expected values. In other words, the means of the variables are the best estimates of their expected values at each time. With currencies, that is not a good assumption. It is clear that the expected value of a currency in the future varies over time as the value of the currency rises and falls.

■ FIGURE 6.5

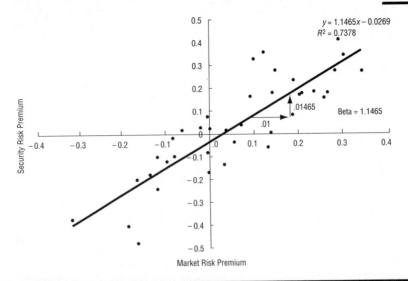

ESTIMATE OF A SECURITY BETA USING ANNUAL RATES OF RETURN

ESTIMATE OF THE CANADIAN DOLLAR HEDGE RATIO USING
MONTHLY PRICE CHANGES 1979–1994

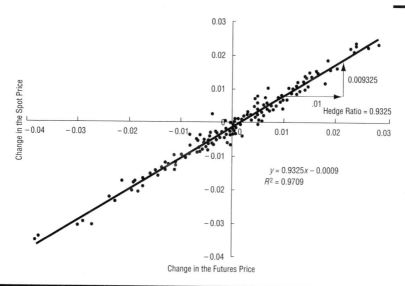

If the sample mean is not an acceptable estimate of the expected value over time, what is? There are two possibilities. The spot price today is a good approximation of the expected value of the future spot price. Alternatively, the futures value today is a good approximation of the expected value of the future spot rate.[4] For comparisons of pairs of countries with relatively low inflation rates, the choice of the expected value does not affect the empirical results, because the current spot rate and the current futures rate are approximately equal. The following illustration uses the current spot price as the estimate of the future expected spot price.

AN ILLUSTRATION OF ESTIMATING THE RISK-MINIMIZING HEDGE

This illustration expands the example considered in Chapter 5. A U.S. firm sells goods to a Canadian company for C.$1,000,000 and receives payment one month later. In Chapter 5, the firm eliminated all risk by hedging with a 30-day forward contract that perfectly matched the delivery date of the receivable. This illustration assumes that the firm hedges with futures. In this case, the delivery date cannot match perfectly the payment of the receivable. Figure 6.6 reports the variance-minimizing hedge estimate based on changes in the spot and futures prices from the end of one month to the next month for the period from 1979 to 1994.

[4] Figures 6.1 and 6.2 support this contention.

Figure 6.6 reports the results of regressing the changes in the value of the spot price from the time of sale as the dependent variable against the monthly changes in the futures prices as the independent variable. The variance-minimizing hedge ratio for a Canadian dollar receivable is the negative of the slope coefficient

$$-0.9325 = h/q = -\text{cov}(S,F)/\text{var}(F)$$

The U.S. firm minimizes its risk if it sells short $932,500 Canadian dollars at the time of sale of its product. Based on historical relationships, this eliminates 97.1 percent of all of the currency risk ($R^2 = 0.9709$).

Recall from Chapter 5 that the minimum risk hedge is a short position of C.$1 million and completely eliminates risk (Figure 5.8). Figure 6.7 reports the risk levels for short hedges ranging from C.$0 to C.$2 million. The minimum risk occurs for a short hedge of C.$0.9325 million. The corresponding standard deviation is $2,500. The reduction in the absolute size of the hedge from a short position of C.$1 million to C.$0.9325 million and the increase in the risk from zero to $2,500 occur because the spot and futures prices do not converge at the time of payment of the receivable ($S \neq F$).

CROSS-HEDGING

International financial managers confront the challenge of managing risk exposure to currency for which forward and futures contracts are unavailable. *Cross-hedging* is one way to deal with this challenge. Currency cross-hedging involves the use of a forward or futures contract in one currency to hedge an exposure in another

■ FIGURE 6.7

STANDARD DEVIATIONS OF C.$1 MILLION RECEIVABLE FOR HEDGES
RANGING FROM C.$0 TO SHORT C.$2 MILLION 1979–1994

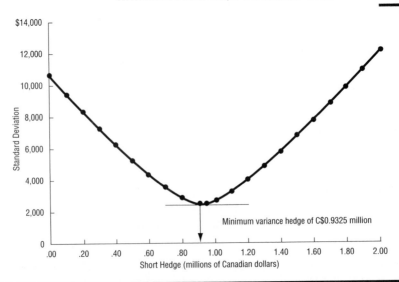

■ **TABLE 6.4**

ESTIMATES OF CROSS-HEDGES AND THEIR EFFECTIVENESS

Hedged Currency	Cross-Hedging Currency	Risk-Minimizing Hedge Ratio In Sample	Risk-Minimizing Hedge Ratio Out of Sample	Hedging Effectiveness
Italian lira	German mark	1.34	1.41	0.73
Greek drachma	German mark	0.82	1.00	0.34
Spanish peseta	German mark	1.06	0.94	0.30
South African rand	Yen	0.64	0.96	0.36

currency. As an example, a U.S. company with an Italian lira position might use British pounds or German marks to hedge it. The key to effective cross-hedging is to find currencies that are correlated in a meaningful and stable way. Empirical work suggests that the task of identifying good cross-hedges is difficult. Table 6.4 provides a summary of an empirical study that measures the effectiveness of a variety of cross-hedges.[5] This study reports the estimates of the risk-minimizing cross-hedges for a seven-year period, 1976 to 1983. The authors divided the period in half and estimated the hedges for each half separately to indicate the stability of the hedge over time. They used the hedge ratio estimated in the first half of the period (in sample) as a hedge in the second half of the period (out of sample). This provided evidence on how well the hedges performed after they were measured. A perfect hedge has an effectiveness measure of 1.0, and a completely ineffective hedge has an effectiveness measure of 0.0. Table 6.4 reports the results for the most effective cross-hedges of three European currencies and the South African rand.

The Italian lira was part of the exchange rate mechanism during this period. Consequently the German mark, the anchor of that system, was quite an effective cross-hedge, eliminating 73 percent of the lira/dollar risk. The mark was also the most effective cross-hedge for the drachma and the peseta, but its effectiveness was less than half that for the lira. The Japanese yen proved the most effective cross-hedge for the South African rand and was about as effective as the mark was with the drachma and the peseta. This evidence suggests that cross-hedging falls significantly short of perfection. If, however, it is the only alternative available, it may be better than doing nothing.

CURRENCY OPTIONS

In the previous chapter we examined the basic elements of option valuation and discussed the factors that influence option values. We now consider some of those issues in more detail.

---

[5] Mark R. Eaker and Dwight M. Grant, "Cross-Hedging Foreign Currency Risk," *Journal of International Money and Finance*, March 1987, pp. 85–105.

THE BLACK/SCHOLES VALUATION FORMULA

Fischer Black and Myron Scholes[6] recognized that the prices of a stock and an option written on it are perfectly positively correlated. Therefore, it is possible to create a portfolio of the two, for example a long position of one call and a short position of a fraction of a share of stock, that is riskless. This risk-free combination must earn the risk-free rate of return with certainty. This insight, combined with a knowledge of mathematics that is in common use in the physical sciences, allowed them to value the option as a function of the price of the stock, the exercise price, the stock's volatility, the term to maturity of the option, and the risk-free rate of interest. Subsequent research modified this result to apply to currency options. As we saw in Chapter 5, this modification considered the risk-free rate of interest in the country of the foreign currency. The modified Black/Scholes expression for the price of a European currency call is

$$Se^{-rf(T-t)}N(d_1) - Xe^{-r(T-t)}N(d_2)$$

S = the spot price of the foreign currency.

X = the exercise price of the call.

r = the risk-free domestic rate of interest.

rf = the risk-free foreign rate of interest.

$T-t$ = the amount of time before the expiration of the option.

$d_1 = [\ln(S/X) + (r - rf + \sigma^2/2)(T-t)]/[\sigma(T-t)^{1/2}]$

$d_2 = d_1 - \sigma(T-t)^{1/2}$

σ = the volatility of the option.

$N(x)$ = the area under a normal curve between $-\infty$ and x, for any value of x.

In the Chapter 6 Appendix on pages 203–204, we include a table of values for $N(x)$ and the valuation formulas for European puts.

Although this formula may seem quite complicated, it is actually easy to use. As an illustration, in Table 6.5 we report the values of the components of this expression, where $S = \$1.55$, $X = \$1.55$, $r = .03$, $rf = .05$, $T-t = .333$, $\sigma = .15$. In Table 6.6 we report the values of calls when all of the other parameters remain the same and S takes on a range of values. All of these calculations are easy to do with a calculator or a computer spreadsheet program.

When $S = X$, the value of the call, if exercised immediately, is zero. The actual value of the call shown in Table 6.5 is $\$0.0479$. This difference exists because the holder of the call has a levered investment, without an explicit payment of interest and because the holder of the call will benefit from appreciation in the currency, but will not suffer a loss, unless the call price is positive. As S increases, the difference between the exercise value and the price declines and the value of the call approaches its exercise value. Table 6.6 and Figure 6.8[7] illustrate this relationship.

---

[6] Fischer Black and Myron Scholes, "The Pricing of Options and Corporate Liabilities," *Journal of Political Economy,* May 1973, pp. 637–659.

[7] The value of the expression "Max(0,$S - X$)" in Figure 6.7 is 0, or $S - X$, whichever is larger.

■ **TABLE 6.5**

CALCULATION OF A EUROPEAN CALL VALUE

S	$e^{-rf(T-t)}$	d_1	$N(d_1)$	$Se^{-rf(T-t)}N(d_1)$
$1.55	0.983471	−0.003368	0.486567	$0.741713

X	$e^{-r(T-t)}$	d_2	$N(d_2)$	$-Xe^{-r(T-t)}N(d_2)$
$1.55	0.99005	−0.12028	0.45213	−$0.693829
			Call	$ 0.0479

DELTA HEDGING

Figure 6.8 plots the values in Table 6.6. This plotting illustrates the relationship that Black and Scholes used to identify their option-pricing formula. As the spot value of the currency increases or decreases, the value of the call increases or decreases by precisely identifiable amounts. The slope of the call value curve in Figure 6.7 identifies the relationship between changes in the value of the call and small changes in the price of S. Figure 6.7 illustrates this relationship for a change in the price of the currency from $1.55 to $1.57. For this $0.02 increase in the price of the currency, the call increases by $0.01, from $0.048 to $0.058. The slope of this sector of the curve of the call values is approximately 0.50. The finance literature refers to this value as *delta*, especially in the context of hedging.

When the value of the currency is $1.56, a portfolio of one unit of currency and a short position of two calls is worth $1.454 ($1.56 − 2($0.053)). If the price of the currency jumps instantaneously to $1.57, the value of the portfolio remains $1.454 ($1.57 − 2($0.058)). Similarly, if the value of the currency falls to $1.55, the portfolio is still worth $1.454 ($1.55 − 2($0.048)). This portfolio is riskless with respect to changes in the value of the currency because the changes in the value of one unit

■ **TABLE 6.6**

CALL VALUES FOR A RANGE OF SPOT CURRENCY PRICES

S	Call	S	Call
$1.50	$0.0276	$1.58	$0.0635
1.51	0.0311	1.59	0.0693
1.52	0.0348	1.60	0.0754
1.53	0.0389	1.61	0.0817
1.54	0.0432	1.62	0.0883
1.55	0.0479	1.63	0.0952
1.56	0.0528	1.64	0.1022
1.57	0.0580	1.65	0.1096

of the currency and two calls are equal in size and opposite in direction. The ratio between the spot currency position and the call currency position is 1:2, or 0.50, or delta. Thus, delta is a risk-eliminating hedge ratio between the underlying asset, the currency, and its call. In this case, 0.5 currency units hedges one call. This means that managers can use options as instruments to hedge currencies just as they use forward and futures contracts. One of the significant differences is that delta changes as S changes, that is, the slope changes along the curve in Figure 6.8. Therefore, managers must adjust their hedge positions as the value of the currency changes to maintain a risk-free position.[8]

TIME TO MATURITY

One other important characteristic of options is the relationship between the value of the option and the time before expiration of the option, holding all other parameters constant. Figure 6.9 plots the values of the call we have been examining as a function of the time before expiration. In this example the value of the currency is $1.56. With 0.6 years to expiration, the call is worth more than $0.065. With only 0.3 years to expiration, the call is worth just slightly more than $0.051. The option loses value as time passes, assuming that none of the other parameters change. This is an important implication for purchasers and sellers of options. As we did with the relationship between the call value and the currency price, we can measure the relationship between the call value and time. In this example, the slope of the curve at time 0.35 is approximately 0.6, and this value measures the rate at which the value of the call is declining as time passes.

FIGURE 6.8

VALUE OF A CALL FOR A RANGE OF CURRENCY PRICES

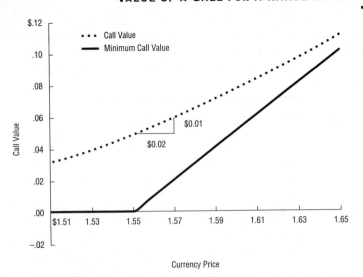

■ FIGURE 6.9

VALUE OF A CALL FOR A RANGE OF TIMES TO MATURITY

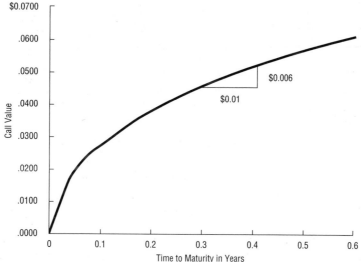

IMPLICATIONS FOR MANAGERS

We have, at various points in this book, made the point that exchange rates vary substantially over time. That variability has been the underlying theme of this chapter. It is the reason that forecasting, hedging with futures and forwards, and option pricing and trading are such important aspects of international finance. At the end of Chapter 5, we made that point with reference to the variability of the German mark from mid-1985 to mid-1986. We saw that this variability caused the cost of aircraft for Lufthansa to vary from DM 1,089 to DM 1,482, depending on how Lufthansa forecast the future value of the U.S. dollar and how the company chose to cope with currency risk. To emphasize that this problem is not limited to a single currency or time period, Figure 6.10 plots the time series of the British pound from January 1976 to December 1993. We have labeled several of the highs and lows during that time period.

From January 1977 to early 1981, the pound appreciated almost 50 percent relative to the dollar. Firms that imported British goods found that their costs increased steadily over this period. Firms that carried British pound accounts payable found that the dollar cost of those payables was higher at the time of payment than expected at the time of purchase. Conversely, U.S. firms selling goods in Britain found that their competitive position steadily improved over this period.

The four years from early 1981 to early 1985 produced a profound reversal of the prior trend. U.S. goods sold in Britain for £1 million in 1981 produced revenues of $2,438,300. The same goods sold for £1 million in 1985 produced revenues of only $1,090,000. Almost any U.S. product that produced a reasonable dollar profit from its sale in Britain in 1981 would still have been profitable in 1985.

   After 1985 there was a substantial appreciation in the value of the pound over the next four years. Since then there have been five periods in which the pound lost or gained approximately 15 percent of its value in relatively short periods of time. Managers must understand the role of forecasting and risk management in response to this volatility.

   Understanding risk management with derivative securities is demanding because few areas of business practice have changed as rapidly as the market for derivative securites and the roles they play in risk management. This chapter has examined that facet of international business in modest technical detail. It would be misleading to suggest that we have presented more than a basic introduction. Each of the three major themes in this chapter, forecasting, hedging with futures and forwards, and options trading, is properly the subject of a complete book, not a part of a chapter. Highly trained and highly compensated individuals build careers specializing in one of these fields. The material covered in this chapter should accomplish two goals. First, it builds a framework of understanding within which international financial managers can ask the correct questions about currency opportunities and risk. Second, it establishes a solid foundation on which the reader can build a more complete understanding of sophisticated currency risk management.

■ **FIGURE 6.10**

**TIME SERIES OF THE BRITISH POUND SPOT PRICES
JANUARY 1976 TO DECEMBER 1994**

QUESTIONS AND EXERCISES

6-1. Your firm has just begun to do business in Japan and you anticipate having a significant level of yen receivables in the future. To manage this risk exposure, you are considering subscribing to a currency forecasting service. The following table reports the forecasts made by each of four services, A, B, C and D, for the last five months. On the basis of this limited data, evaluate the forecasting abilities of the services and their potential value to you. (You interpret the table as follows: On January 15, the forward and spot rates of the yen were $0.008778 and $0.08752, respectively. Firm A forecast that the yen spot rate on February 15 would be $0.009190 yen. The actual spot rate on February 15 was $0.009654.)

			Forecasts by Services			
Time	Forward	Spot	A	B	C	D
January 15	$0.008778	$0.008752	$0.009190	$0.009015	$0.008800	$0.087520
February 15	0.009681	0.009654	0.010137	0.009944	0.009700	0.090000
March 15	0.008941	0.008912	0.009358	0.008645	0.009000	0.092000
April 15	0.009223	0.009191	0.009651	0.009421	0.009300	0.090000
May 15	0.008843	0.008815	0.009256	0.008639	0.009000	0.090000
June 15	—	0.009111	—	—	—	—

6-2. A small firm in New Mexico, HOTCHILI, has discovered a market for chili in Germany. At the middle of each month the firm ships DM 1,000,000 of green and red chili. HOTCHILI has agreed to price its product in marks as a concession to its customer, a German wholesaler. The German wholesaler pays about one month after the chili is shipped. This is a very good business, but HOTCHILI is concerned about the variability of the mark exchange rate. The following table indicates the recent price history of the exchange rate and the corresponding prices for the mark futures contract. HOTCHILI has been recording its sales on the basis of the spot rate at the time of shipping and then adding or subtracting a gain or loss on the exchange rate.

	Futures	Spot
January 15	$0.662	$0.649
February 15	$0.690	$0.672
March 15	$0.719	$0.695
April 15	$0.641	$0.625
May 15	$0.684	$0.665
June 15	$0.620	$0.605
July 15	$0.648	$0.635

Calculate the gain or loss on the exchange rate each month. On average, has HOTCHILI gained or lost?

REFERENCES

Black, Fischer, and Myron Scholes. "The Pricing of Options and Corporate Liabilities." *Journal of Political Economy*, May 1973, pp. 637–659.

Cox, J. C., Stephen A. Ross, and Mark Rubinstein. "Option Pricing: A Simplified Approach." *Journal of Financial Economics*, September 1979, pp. 229–263.

Eaker, Mark R., and Dwight M. Grant. "Cross-Hedging Foreign Currency Risk." *Journal of International Money and Finance*, March 1987, pp. 85–105.

Frenkel, Jacob A. "Flexible Exchange Rates, Prices, and the Role of "News": Lessons from the 1970s." *Journal of Political Economy*, August 1981, pp. 665–705.

Garman, Mark B., and Steven W. Kohlhagen. "Foreign Currency Option Values." *Journal of International Money and Finance*, December 1983, pp. 231–237.

Giddy, Ian H. "Foreign Exchange Options." *The Journal of Futures Markets*, Summer 1983, pp. 143–166.

Goodman, Stephen H. "Foreign Exchange Rate Forecasting Techniques: Implications for Business and Policy." *Journal of Finance*, May 1979, pp. 415–427.

Grabbe, J. Orlin. "the Pricing of Call and Put Options on Foreign Exchange." *Journal of International Money and Finance*, December 1983, pp. 239–253.

Hull, John. *Options, Futures, and Other Derivative Securities*, 2nd ed. Englewood Cliffs, N.J.: Prentice–Hall, 1993.

Kerkvliet, Joe, and Michael H. Moffett. "The Hedging of an Uncertain Future Foreign Currency Cash Flow." *Journal of Financial and Quantitative Analysis*, December 1991, pp. 565–580.

Levi, Maurice. "Spot versus Forward Speculation and Hedging: A Diagrammatic Exposition." *Journal of International Money and Finance*, April 1984, pp. 105–109.

Meese, R. A., and K. Rogoff. "Empirical Exchange Rate Models in the Seventies: Do They Fit Out of Sample!" *Journal of International Economics*, February 1983, pp. 3–24.

Perold, Andre F., and Evan C. Shulman "The Free Lunch in Currency Hedging: Implications for Investment Policy and Performance Standards." *Financial Analysts Journal*, May-June 1988, pp. 45–50.

Recall that:

S = the spot price of the foreign currency.

X = the exercise price of the call.

r = the risk-free domestic rate of interest.

rf = the risk-free foreign rate of interest.

$T-t$ = the amount of time before the expiration of the option.

$d_1 = [\ln(S/X) + (r - rf + \sigma^2/2)(T-t)]/[\sigma(T-t)^{1/2}]$

$d_2 = d_1 - \sigma(T-t)^{1/2}$

σ = the volatility of the option.

$N(x)$ = the area under a normal curve between $-\infty$ and x.

The value of a European put written on a currency is

$$Xe^{-r(T-t)}N(-d_2) - Se^{-rf(T-t)}N(-d_1)$$

and as with the case of a call,

$$d_1 = [\ln(S/X) + (r-rf + \sigma^2/2)(T-t)]/[\sigma(T-t)^{1/2}]$$

$$d_2 = d_1 - \sigma(T-t)^{1/2}$$

Replicating Table 6.5 for the value of the put, we have

Calculation of a European Put Value

S	$e^{-rf(T-t)}$	d_1	$N(-d_1)$	$-Se^{-rf(T-t)}N(-d_1)$
$1.55	0.983471	−0.003368	0.51343	−$0.78267

X	$e^{-r(T-t)}$	d_2	$N(-d_2)$	$Xe^{-r(T-t)}N(-d_2)$
$1.55	0.99005	−0.12028	0.54787	$0.84075
			Put	$0.0581

Area Under the Normal Curve from $-\infty$ to x

x	N(x)	x	N(x)
−3.00	0.00135	−1.50	0.06681
−2.95	0.00159	−1.45	0.07353
−2.90	0.00187	−1.40	0.08076
−2.85	0.00219	−1.35	0.08851
−2.80	0.00256	−1.30	0.09680
−2.75	0.00298	−1.25	0.10565
−2.70	0.00347	−1.20	0.11507
−2.65	0.00402	−1.15	0.12507
−2.60	0.00466	−1.10	0.13567
−2.55	0.00539	−1.05	0.14686
−2.50	0.00621	−1.00	0.15866
−2.45	0.00714	−0.95	0.17106
−2.40	0.00820	−0.90	0.18406
−2.35	0.00939	−0.85	0.19766
−2.30	0.01072	−0.80	0.21186
−2.25	0.01222	−0.75	0.22663
−2.20	0.01390	−0.70	0.24196
−2.15	0.01578	−0.65	0.25785
−2.10	0.01786	−0.60	0.27425
−2.05	0.02018	−0.55	0.29116
−2.00	0.02275	−0.50	0.30854
−1.95	0.02559	−0.45	0.32636
−1.90	0.02872	−0.40	0.34458
−1.85	0.03216	−0.35	0.36317
−1.80	0.03593	−0.30	0.38209
−1.75	0.04006	−0.25	0.40129
−1.70	0.04457	−0.20	0.42074
−1.65	0.04947	−0.15	0.44038
−1.60	0.05480	−0.10	0.46017
−1.55	0.06057	−0.05	0.48006
−1.50	0.06681	0.00	0.50000

$N(-x) = 1.00 - N(x)$

CASE 6.1 ▬▬▬▬▬▬
VIDEO SYSTEMS, INC.

"Kathy, as we become more international in our transactions, we've just got to develop currency forecasts. Without accurate forecasts, I don't see how we can budget and plan for the manufacturing facility in England, make financing decisions, or decide which of our foreign currency receivables and payables to hedge."

"I agree, John, but neither you nor I have currency expertise. I took an international finance class in graduate school, but I don't recall learning much about forecasting. What I do remember is that it's probably not possible to do at all."

Katherine DeFoe, assistant treasurer of Video Systems, Inc., and John Venturya, the company's manager of financial planning, had met on a rainy Monday in early 1990 to review Video System's fiscal year budget. The company manufactured video equipment for commercial studios. Established in 1978 in Portland, Oregon, Video Systems operated plants in Oregon and Cambridge in the United Kingdom.

"There are hundreds of forecasting services," Kathy continued, "from tiny one-person operations to large econometric firms. But I don't have much confidence in them. Billions of dollars worth of foreign exchange are traded every day in New York, London, and Tokyo. If these so-called seers could really predict exchange rates, they wouldn't be selling their forecasts, they would be betting on them! Instead, they prepare some glossy brochures and try to get us to pay for the forecasts. When they happen to be right, they call up and gloat, but when they're wrong, which is most of the time, they won't return phone calls."

"I don't entirely agree with you, Kathy, and we do need to do something. It's frustrating, and I need to prepare budgets for the English plant. I've looked at their plans, but they are in pounds, and I have to convert the operating forecasts to dollars."

"Good luck and I don't envy you."

"Hey, keep the sympathy; I want help."

"John, you know I'd help if I could, but really, all I remember is my professor saying how hard forecasting was. The guy seemed to do a lot of consulting, but I can't figure out what he could tell anyone. And I got a B- in the course."

"Look, Kathy, I've already started on this, so how about looking at what I've done? I've got some interesting results. I'm not so sure this is as difficult as you or your professor think. Let me show you these results.

"I called over to the foreign exchange department of the bank and asked them for some exchange rate data. They gave me spot and forward rates for the British pound for 1975 through 1987 [Exhibit 6.1]. I remembered reading that two ways you might forecast future exchange rates are by using today's spot rate or using the forward rate; so I gave them a try."

"Hold it. I thought you would need to take into account all types of economic variables like interest rates, inflation rates, money supply, and so on. Where did you get that information and how did you use it?"

■ EXHIBIT 6.1

VIDEO SYSTEMS, INC.
■ DATA FOR THE BRITISH POUND, JULY 1975–DECEMBER 1987
(FORWARD RATES ARE FOR THREE-MONTH CONTRACTS)

Date	Forward	Spot	Date	Forward	Spot	Date	Forward	Spot
7507	$2.137	$2.147	7909	$2.192	$2.198	8311	$1.464	$1.465
7508	2.105	2.111	7910	2.077	2.076	8312	1.463	1.451
7509	2.029	2.041	7911	2.192	2.196	8401	1.404	1.404
7510	2.067	2.076	7912	2.202	2.224	8402	1.489	1.489
7511	2.014	2.017	8001	2.257	2.268	8403	1.447	1.443
7512	2.005	2.024	8002	2.255	2.279	8404	1.404	1.397
7601	2.018	2.029	8003	2.162	2.167	8405	1.388	1.385
7602	2.023	2.027	8004	2.255	2.266	8406	1.366	1.353
7603	1.899	1.916	8005	2.343	2.330	8407	1.303	1.306
7604	1.828	1.844	8006	2.323	2.362	8408	1.309	1.311
7605	1.756	1.764	8007	2.304	2.338	8409	1.238	1.248
7606	1.752	1.781	8008	2.401	2.393	8410	1.225	1.217
7607	1.767	1.784	8009	2.373	2.388	8411	1.193	1.199
7608	1.773	1.775	8010	2.423	2.438	8412	1.154	1.157
7609	1.626	1.678	8011	2.360	2.359	8501	1.120	1.128
7610	1.562	1.606	8012	2.419	2.385	8502	1.073	1.090
7611	1.649	1.648	8101	2.366	2.386	8503	1.232	1.243
7612	1.664	1.702	8102	2.200	2.204	8504	1.225	1.244
7701	1.697	1.714	8103	2.248	2.244	8505	1.290	1.273
7702	1.711	1.709	8104	2.149	2.140	8506	1.296	1.295
7703	1.707	1.720	8105	2.078	2.069	8507	1.408	1.429
7704	1.715	1.719	8106	1.945	1.943	8508	1.388	1.400
7705	1.713	1.718	8107	1.845	1.856	8509	1.385	1.401
7706	1.711	1.720	8108	1.840	1.837	8510	1.437	1.443
7707	1.734	1.737	8109	1.809	1.801	8511	1.489	1.483
7708	1.742	1.743	8110	1.878	1.845	8512	1.439	1.445
7709	1.753	1.746	8111	1.959	1.970	8601	1.406	1.412
7710	1.835	1.832	8112	1.859	1.908	8602	1.438	1.469
7711	1.817	1.815	8201	1.879	1.884	8603	1.458	1.485
7712	1.920	1.906	8202	1.816	1.816	8604	1.535	1.545
7801	1.953	1.950	8203	1.792	1.782	8605	1.472	1.482
7802	1.940	1.934	8204	1.825	1.788	8606	1.532	1.530
7803	1.860	1.856	8205	1.781	1.791	8607	1.487	1.490
7804	1.815	1.831	8206	1.746	1.738	8608	1.491	1.478
7805	1.839	1.822	8207	1.741	1.740	8609	1.430	1.450
7806	1.840	1.860	8208	1.722	1.721	8610	1.398	1.400
7807	1.927	1.932	8209	1.698	1.693	8611	1.432	1.436
7808	1.938	1.943	8210	1.677	1.673	8612	1.472	1.475
7809	1.958	1.972	8211	1.632	1.612	8701	1.505	1.530
7810	2.065	2.090	8212	1.630	1.615	8702	1.544	1.544
7811	1.941	1.949	8301	1.518	1.531	8703	1.596	1.605
7812	2.041	2.035	8302	1.561	1.521	8704	1.662	1.665
7901	1.978	1.996	8303	1.483	1.479	8705	1.629	1.626
7902	2.024	2.023	8304	1.562	1.562	8706	1.610	1.610
7903	2.065	2.069	8305	1.602	1.609	8707	1.587	1.593
7904	2.067	2.058	8306	1.528	1.530	8708	1.630	1.626
7905	2.069	2.066	8307	1.515	1.521	8709	1.618	1.630
7906	2.161	2.168	8308	1.497	1.493	8710	1.719	1.713
7907	2.235	2.281	8309	1.495	1.496	8711	1.830	1.831
7908	2.260	2.251	8310	1.493	1.495	8712	1.883	1.871

"I didn't. I used market information. You know, it's like the stock market: all the information is reflected in the existing price or, in this case, the existing exchange rate."

"But, John, you said either the spot or forward rate. Which one is the right one?"

"Well, Kathy, I'm not positive about the theory, but my results indicate that it doesn't seem to make much difference. Both seem to work very well. I decided to look at the relationship between the current spot rate and the spot or forward rate three months earlier. Look at these two scatter plots [Exhibit 6.2]. See, both relationships look linear, so I used the Lotus 1-2-3 regression option to fit lines to the data, and here are the results [Exhibit 6.3]."

"Wow! Look at those R^2's, John. Looks like you've really found something."

"I thought you'd be impressed. As you can see, it looks like either one would do a pretty good job."

"What's this other regression?"

"Well, that's an idea that didn't pan out the way I thought it would, for reasons I still don't understand. I figured that maybe I could get a better model by using the difference between the current spot and forward rates to predict the change in the spot rate between now and three months in the future, but as you can see, the model turned out to be awful."

"Yeah, the R^2 is the pits. Did you try anything else?"

"Well, as a matter of fact, I did. Look at this time series graph of spot rates [Exhibit 6.4]. Since there is clearly a pattern, I tried to fit a simple exponential-smoothing model. Turned out, though, that the best smoothing constant alpha I could come up with was 1, which minimized the MSE at around .01145."

"What's an 'MSE'?"

"It stands for mean squared error, or average squared difference between the model's forecast and the actual spot rate. All I know is that it should be as small as possible, and an alpha of 1 makes it that way."

"So is this model any better than your regression models?"

"I was hoping you could answer that because I'm not sure. I did try one other thing, though, that gave me an even better time series model. Notice on the time series that there seems to be a fairly stable trend over the last two-and-a-half years. I decided to try to fit a double-exponential-smoothing model to just this data, where I allowed for trend as well as level. Doing this, the best model I could come up with had an alpha of .04 and beta of .6, producing an MSE of .00384. As you can see, this is quite a bit better than the previous time series model, but I'm a little concerned that the values of the two smoothing constants are not within the range my graduate school note indicates they should be."

"But still no idea of how to compare it to the regression models?"

"No, so I decided to try one other regression model. If there really is a clear trend over the last two-and-a-half years, why not try a regression model that relates month to month spot rates over that period? So I numbered all the months from June 1985 through December 1987 consecutively—1, 2, 3, etc.—and regressed that against spot price. Unfortunately, the resulting model [Exhibit 6.5] doesn't appear to be as good as my first two, since it has a lower R^2."

VIDEO SYSTEMS, INC.

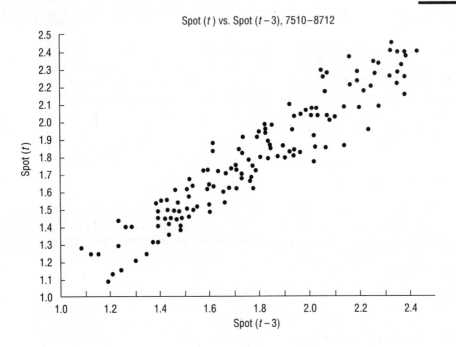

Spot (*t*) vs. Spot (*t* − 3), 7510−8712

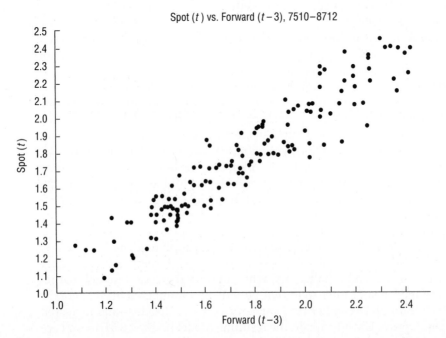

Spot (*t*) vs. Forward (*t* − 3), 7510−8712

■ EXHIBIT 6.3

VIDEO SYSTEMS, INC.
■ **REGRESSIONS ON DATA FROM JULY 1975–DECEMBER 1987**

Model: $spot(t) = a + b \times spot\ (t - 3)$

Regression output

Constant	0.111285
Std err of Y est	0.105617
R^2	0.890953
Number of observations	147
Degrees of freedom	145
X coefficient(s)	0.933397
Std err of coef.	0.027118

Model: $spot(t) = a + b \times forward\ (t - 3)$

Regression output

Constant	0.114011
Std err of Y est	0.107267
R^2	0.887519
Number of observations	147
Degrees of freedom	145
X coefficient(s)	0.934507
Std err of coef.	0.027628

Model: $spot(t) - spot(t - 3) = a + b \times [forward\ (t - 3) - spot\ (t - 3)]$

Regression output

Constant	–0.00735
Std err of Y est	0.107719
R^2	0.001349
Number of observations	147
Degrees of freedom	145
X coefficient(s)	–0.26905
Std err of coef.	0.607781

"John, I'm really confused. Sounds like we should just go back and use one of your first two models, either the previous spot rate or the previous future rate."

"I know, Kathy, but I'm still bothered by the fact that maybe one of these other models is better and we just don't know enough to be able to tell it. I just got the 1988 data on the British pound from the foreign exchange department [Exhibit 6.6]. Maybe we can use these rates to test the different models to see which one is really best."

■ EXHIBIT 6.4

VIDEO SYSTEMS, INC.
■ TIME SERIES OF SPOT RATES OF BRITISH POUND, 7507–8712

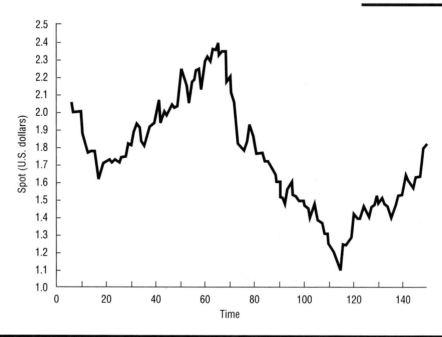

■ EXHIBIT 6.5

VIDEO SYSTEMS, INC.
■ REGRESSION ON DATA FROM 8506–8712

Model: Spot(t) = a + $b*t$

Regression Output	
Constant	–0.06837
Std err of Y est	0.068100
R^2	0.720756
No. of Observations	31
Degrees of Freedom	29
X coefficient(s)	0.011831
Std err of coef.	0.001367

VIDEO SYSTEMS, INC.
■ DATA FOR THE BRITISH POUND, JANUARY 1988–DECEMBER 1988
(FORWARD RATES ARE FOR THREE-MONTH CONTRACTS)

Date	Forward	Spot
8801	$1.761	$1.766
8802	1.772	1.775
8803	1.881	1.888
8804	1.872	1.876
8805	1.836	1.837
8806	1.704	1.712
8807	1.702	1.711
8808	1.682	1.685
8809	1.681	1.691
8810	1.756	1.765
8811	1.848	1.851
8812	1.799	1.809

EXPOSURE MEASUREMENT AND MANAGEMENT

7

CHAPTER

KEY CONCEPTS

THE THREE DEFINITIONS OF EXCHANGE RATE
EXPOSURE: ECONOMIC, TRANSACTION, AND
TRANSLATION

THE THEORETICAL MEASUREMENT OF ECONOMIC
EXPOSURE AND A PRACTICAL APPROACH
TO MEASURE IT

THE RELATIONSHIP BETWEEN EXPOSURE AND
PURCHASING POWER PARITY

THE USE OF ELASTICITIES TO DETERMINE A FIRM'S
ECONOMIC EXPOSURE

A FRAMEWORK FOR CATEGORIZING THE EXPOSURE OF A
BUSINESS BASED ON THE DEPENDENCE OF ITS
REVENUES AND COST STREAMS ON
EXTERNAL MARKETS

THE BASICS OF TRANSLATION OR ACCOUNTING
EXPOSURE

THE CHARACTERISTICS OF AN EXPOSURE MANAGEMENT
SYSTEM

INTRODUCTION

How sensitive is a firm's value to changes in exchange rates? That is the question that exposure measurement attempts to answer. It is an important question for the manager of a firm that engages in international transactions. It has implications for planning financial and nonfinancial strategy, for assessing a firm's riskiness, and for preparing its financial statements. Unfortunately, it is a very hard question to answer. In fact, part of the difficulty is that there are too many answers, and there is little agreement as to which is correct. Part of the disagreement stems from different objectives of exposure measurement and part of it from different assumptions or views about what generates exposure.

In response to the divergent views and uses of exposure measures, firms should develop multiple exposure management systems. Two of the systems should be designed to conform with external objectives: tax compliance and accounting requirements. The third system should fulfill the firm's need to make internal operating and financial decisions. It is important to recognize that the requirements of the external systems make those systems inappropriate for the internal role. The first two are established by authorities and apply to all firms; the third should be customized for the individual firm.

EXPOSURE DEFINED

As we discussed in previous chapters, *foreign exchange exposure* refers to the change in the value of an asset, liability, or portfolio of assets and liabilities caused by a change in exchange rates. The narrowest definitions of exposure measure only the changes in the value of assets or liabilities that are denominated in a foreign currency. For example, a British multinational with a Swedish subsidiary tries to measure its exposure to changes in the pound/krona exchange rate by estimating how the pound value of the assets and liabilities of the subsidiary change as the exchange rate fluctuates. A broader definition of exposure recognizes that exchange rate changes affect not only the foreign currency–denominated assets and liabilities held by a firm or its subsidiaries but also the firm's operations. In the case of the British multinational, its value might be affected by the change in the exchange rate if it imports Swedish materials or competes for sales at home or abroad with Swedish companies. Those changes do not show up immediately as changes on the balance sheet, but they clearly alter the going concern value of the firm.

A mathematical expression for exposure can be derived from the expression for the value of a firm as a discounted stream of future cash flows:

$$V_j = \sum_{t=1}^{n} C_t/(1+r)^t \qquad (7.1)$$

Where V_j is the value of the firm, C_t is the net cash flow at time t and r is the appropriate discount rate. Expression (7.1) can be modified to reflect the fact that the home or domestic currency of the firm might differ from the currency of the various cash flows.

$$V_j = \sum_{i=1}^{m}\sum_{t=1}^{n} C_{it} S_{it}/(1+r)^t \qquad (7.2)$$

V_j is now the home currency value of the firm, C_{it} is the net cash flow denominated in currency i accruing in period t, and S_{it} is the exchange rate at time t expressed in units of currency j, the home currency, per unit of the ith currency.

The expression is less intimidating than it appears. In terms of the preceding example, V_j is the value of the British multinational in terms of its domestic currency, pounds. C_{it} includes its cash flows in all currencies including the Swedish krona, and S_{it}, all the exchange rates that influence the firm's value. The narrow type of exposure described earlier arises from having krona cash flows that are now valued at the new exchange rate. The broader exposure measure includes how all the non-krona cash flows are affected by changes in the krona exchange rate. Exposure for any currency is the partial derivative of V_j with respect to that currency exchange rate with j. In discrete terms, exposure equals $V_{1j} - V_{0j}$ when the only event distinguishing times 1 and 0 is the change in exchange rate.

Although it is conceptually useful to derive a mathematical expression for exposure, it is not very helpful operationally. It is possible in theory to measure the total exposure of the firm to an exchange rate change, but it is not practical to do so. Theoretically, V_j is the market value of a company that is equal to the number of shares outstanding times the share price. The firm's exposure, therefore, can be defined as the way that V_j changes when the exchange rate change occurs. This approach is no different than that used in many of the studies analyzing the behavior of stock prices to new information using regression techniques. The difficulty is that exchange rate changes are likely to explain a very small portion of the variability in stock prices so that statistically little would be learned from regressing changes in the market value of a stock, say IBM, against changes in an exchange rate. So many other factors influence the stock price that the exchange rate effect is swamped.

In practice, the approach taken to estimating exposure is to disaggregate the firm's assets and liabilities and ask what the exposure is on each type. The sum of the individual asset or liability exposures for each currency of relevance to the firm is then considered the firm's exposure in that currency. This approach focuses almost exclusively on balance sheet exposure, which is the narrow interpretation. It, in turn, might be modified to reflect the broader, operational measure. Later in this chapter, we discuss how to accomplish that. At this point, it is necessary first to develop an understanding of what causes a balance sheet exposure.

The key to determining the degree of exposure of an asset or liability is the relationship between price changes measured in the currency of denomination of the asset or liability and the changes in exchange rates. Assets and liabilities are not exposed when the domestic currency price changes are precisely offset by exchange rate changes. They are exposed when the price and exchange rate changes do not offset each other. The examples in Table 7.1 indicate how the price and exchange rate effects interact for a fully exposed asset, accounts receivable, and an unexposed asset, gold.

■ TABLE 7.1

THE EFFECTS OF EXCHANGE RATE CHANGES ON
EXPOSED AND UNEXPOSED ASSETS

Assets	French Francs	Dollars 1FR = $0.125	Dollars 1FR = $0.0625	Dollars 1FR = $0.15
Accounts receivable	10,000,000	$1,250,000	$ 625,000	$1,500,000
Gold (3,125 ounces)	10,000,000	$1,250,000	$1,250,000	$1,250,000
Dollar price of gold (per ounce)		$ 400	$ 400	$ 400
Franc price of gold (per ounce)		3,200	6,400	2,667
Market value of 3,125 ounces in francs		FR 10,000,000	FR 20,000,000	FR 8,333,333

The exposed asset has an initial value of 10,000,000 French francs (FR) equal to $1,250,000 at the prevailing exchange rate of FR1 = $0.125. The unexposed asset, gold, also has a value of FR10,000,000, because there are 3,125 ounces of gold and the price of gold is FR3,200 per ounce. After a depreciation of the franc to $0.0625, the accounts receivable have a dollar value of $625,000. On each franc of value, the asset has lost the full amount of the exchange rate change. It is in that sense that the asset is fully exposed. Changes in exchange rates bring about a 1-for-1 change in the dollar value of the asset. Had the franc appreciated in value to $0.15, the exposed asset's dollar value would have risen to $1,500,000.

The types of assets that are fully exposed include assets whose domestic currency value is fixed for whatever reason. Cash held by a firm or individual is the clearest example, but in addition, most receivables or financial assets are fully exposed. Their domestic currency values do not change as exchange rates change. A firm that owes £100,000 or DM1,000,000 will continue to have that obligation in pounds or marks regardless of the value of the domestic currency. The dollar, yen, and franc values of the obligation change as the exchange rates vary; that is exposure.

Assets or liabilities whose value is not affected by exchange rate changes are not exposed. In the case of gold, we assume that the dollar value of gold does not change when the franc devalues. This is a reasonable assumption for gold and for any product such as oil, wheat, or lumber, that trades in the world market and for which French supply or demand is small. Global markets establish the prices of basic commodities. For example, the price of gold conforms to the law of one price. Gold sells everywhere at the same price regardless of the currency in which it is denominated. If gold is more expensive in Switzerland than in England, arbitrage occurs. Traders buy in the cheaper market and sell in the more expensive market. Consequently, changes in the domestic currency price of gold occur to equalize the value of gold after an exchange rate change. For example, when the franc changes value, the dollar values (or pound values) of these assets do not change. Rather, their domestic (franc) values change. The last row of Table 7.1 reflects that relationship. The change in the domestic value has precisely offset the change in the exchange rate.

As we suggested, gold is an extreme example of an asset that is priced in the world market. Gold is not unique in this respect. Most widely traded raw materials or commodities also hold their values despite changes in exchange rates. The same is true, to a lesser degree, of most real (nonmonetary) assets. That is the case because one of the major factors leading to exchange rate changes is relative inflation, which also affects the domestic currency value of an asset.

Consider the example of a U.S. firm with a British subsidiary. The subsidiary has an inventory consisting of cashmere sweaters that are sold to British retail stores. The value of the inventory is £1,000,000 or $1,500,000 when the exchange rate is $1.50 = £1. Britain experiences an increase from zero inflation to a 1 percent rate of inflation. The U.S. rate of inflation is zero. Purchasing power parity (PPP) holds, and the British pound depreciates by 1 percent relative to the dollar and is worth $1.48515 ($1.50/1.01). It appears that the inventory of sweaters has a lower dollar value than before, but that is not necessarily the case. If the sweaters increase in value in terms of pounds at the overall British inflation rate, they are worth

£1,010,000 after the inflation. At $1.48515 per pound, the sweaters have a dollar value of $1,500,000. There has been no change in the dollar value of the inventory and, hence, no loss incurred due to the depreciation of the pound. The key is that PPP held and the sweaters' prices kept pace with inflation.

What would have happened if the sweaters had not increased in price by as much as the general rate of inflation? If, for example, either competition or price controls restricted the price rise to .8 percent, the dollar value would have fallen. The inventory would be worth £1,008,000, or $1,497,000. The loss due to the depreciation of the pound is $3,000.

Because PPP refers to price changes that are measured by broad indices, it is to be expected that many assets change in price by a different amount. Therefore, most real assets have some degree of exposure.

A FRAMEWORK FOR MEASURING EXPOSURE

We now elaborate on the way to view the exposure of cash flows to exchange rate changes. To do that, we define the value[1] of an asset, liability, or cash flow in the home currency, C^*, as the product of the cash flow in the foreign currency, C, and the exchange rate S.

$$C^* = CS \qquad (7.3)$$

One important influence that can cause changes in the home country value of the cash flow is a change in the inflation rate in the foreign country. A change in the inflation rate may have an effect on the size of C and likely on the price of the foreign currency, S. The sensitivity to changes in inflation of C and S indicates how inflation affects the value of C^*. All of these sensitivities can be measured as elasticities with respect to inflation, that is the percentage changes in C^*, C and S relative to the percentage change in 1 plus the inflation rate. The relationship[2] among the elasticity of the cash flow in the home currency, e_{C^*}, the elasticity of C, e_C, and the elasticity of S, e_S, is

$$e_{C^*} = e_C + e_S \qquad (7.4)$$

The percentage change in domestic value is the sum of the percentage changes in the foreign value and the exchange rate. When C exactly keeps pace with inflation (when C is constant in real terms), e_C equals 1. When cash flows rise less

---

[1] This approach ignores the complication of discounting. When discounting is included, the arithmetic is more complicated, but the basic results are the same.

[2] Let i represent 1 plus the rate of inflation as in the sweater example i changed from 1.00 to (1.01). $C^* = CS$ and C and S both may vary with changes in i. Then

$$\delta C^*/\delta i = S(\delta C/\delta i) + C(\delta S/\delta i)$$

Dividing both sides of this equation by i/CS and remembering that $C^* = CS$ produces

$$(\delta C^*/C^*)/(\delta i/i) = (\delta C/\delta C)/(\delta i/i) + (\delta S/S)/(\delta i/i)$$

$$e_{C^*} = e_C + e_S.$$

quickly than inflation, e_C is less than 1; when they rise more quickly, e_C is greater than 1. When PPP holds, S is constant in real terms and the percentage changes in the exchange rate and the inflation rate are equal, but opposite in sign. In that case, e_S is −1. When the exchange rate declines more quickly than inflation increases, e_S is less than −1; when the exchange rate declines less quickly than the inflation rate, e_S is greater than −1.

When both C and S are constant in real terms, there is no change in C^* because

$$e_{C^*} = e_C + e_S = +1 - 1 + 0 \qquad (7.5)$$

When inflation increases and both C and S fall in real terms, then C^* also declines because e_C is less than 1 and e_S is less than −1. Conversely, when inflation increases and both C and S increase in real terms, then C^* increases because e_C is greater than 1 and e_S is greater than −1. The net effect when one variable rises in real terms and the other falls in real terms depends on the relative strength of the two effects.

Compare this discussion with the results found in the sweater example. When PPP held and the sweaters' price kept pace with inflation, the dollar value did not change. That is the case described in equation (7.5): The percentage change in C^* is zero because the PPP effect ($e_S = −1$) and the sweaters' price keeping pace with inflation ($e_C = 1$) exactly offset each other. This example corresponds to a constant real exchange rate and a constant real cash flow. Changes in the inflation rate have no effect on the value of C^*.

Now, alter the assumption so that the price of the sweaters goes up by 0.8 percent when inflation increases from 0 to 1 percent, but PPP still holds. Then e_S is still −1 while e_C is 0.8 percent, or 0.8. The inability to fully adjust prices in the domestic currency generates exposure.

$$e_{C^*} = e_C + e_S = +0.8 - 1 = -0.2 \qquad (7.6)$$

What exactly does the e_{C^*} of −0.2 mean? It is a measure of potential value changes (in this case, losses associated with an increase in the inflation rate) from inflation-created changes in the foreign cash flow and the exchange rate. The U.S. multinational has a £1,000,000 position that has an exposure of −0.2 or −20 percent. A 1 percent increase in the inflation rate in Britain changes the U.S. dollar cash flow by −0.2 percent. In the sweater example, the value of the cash flow was originally $1,500,000 and −0.2 percent of this is $3,000. This is the change in value calculated above.[3]

Change in Dollar Value = $1,500,000 − [(1.50$/£]/1.01][£1,008,000] = $3,000

Table 7.2 contains the simple balance sheet of a British subsidiary of a U.S. company. It can be used as the basis for an extended example of the application of exposure measurement. The first step is to estimate or derive the elasticities.

---

[3] Remember that $e_{C^*} = (\delta C^*/C^*)/(\delta i/i)$. Therefore, when you multiply e_{C^*} by the percentage change in the inflation rate, the product is the percentage change in C^*. When you multiply the percentage change in C^* by the value of C^*, the product is the dollar change in C^*.

▪ **TABLE 7.2**

BRITISH PRODUCTIONS LTD. JUNE 30, 1994
(MILLIONS)

Assets		Liabilities	
Cash	£ 8	Accounts payable	£16
Accounts receivable	16	Other liabilities	12
Inventories	23		
Total current assets	47	Total current liabilities	28
Net plant and equipment	44	Long-term debt	24
		Net worth	39
Total assets	91	Total liabilities	91

Analysts familiar with the firm, its real assets, and the industry must estimate values for e_C for different types of cash flows, or, as in this example, assets and liabilities. They will be determined by such factors as the degree of competition, the use of long-term fixed price contracts, and government regulation.

The firm in this example has two categories of real assets, inventories and plant and equipment. Assume that the first has an e_C of 0.9 and the second an e_C of 0.8. The value of e_S can be estimated by empirically measuring how well PPP has held in the past and assuming that it will hold to the same degree in the future. In this example, assume that $e_S = -0.75$.

Table 7.3 uses these elasticities to calculate the currency exposure of this firm. It is convenient to define the exposure of each asset or liability as the product of its pound value multiplied by the e_{C*} appropriate for it. This firm's cash and accounts

▪ **TABLE 7.3**

EXPOSURE CALCULATIONS FOR BRITISH PRODUCTIONS LTD.
(MILLIONS)

Assets	Value (C)	e_C	e_S	e_{C*}	$(C)(e_{C*})$
Cash	£ 8	0	−0.75	−0.75	−£ 6
Accounts receivable	16	0	−0.75	−0.75	−12
Inventories	23	0.95	−0.75	0.2	4.6
Net plant and equipment	44	0.85	−0.75	0.1	4.4
Asset exposure	—	—	—	—	−15
Liabilities					
Accounts payable	16	0	−0.75	−0.75	−12
Other liabilities	12	0	−0.75	−0.75	− 9
Long-term debt	24	0	−0.75	−0.75	−18
Liabilities exposure	—	—	—	—	−39
Net exposure	—	—	—	—	−£24

receivable do not keep pace with inflation because they are monetary assets. The firm's inventory and net plant and equipment do tend to keep pace with inflation. Because they are the larger portion of the assets, the total asset exposure is quite small, –£15 million. The negative sign indicates that an increase in the rate of inflation decreases the dollar value of the assets. The current liabilities and long-term debt are monetary liabilities, and their pound values do not change with changes in the inflation rate. Notice that net worth is not treated individually because it is a plug or residual item. The total liabilities exposure is quite large, –£39 million. This means that an increase in the inflation rate decreases the dollar values of the liabilities. Note that this is advantageous for the U.S. parent. Therefore, the net exposure of this subsidiary is found by subtracting the liability exposure from the asset exposure. In this case, it is +£24 million (–£15 + £39) or, at an exchange rate of 1.50$/£, $36 million. If the British inflation rate increases from 0 to 1 percent, the dollar value of this subsidiary increases by $360,000.

This example is simplified because it does not identify the exact timing of the cash flows associated with each asset and liability. If a firm does that, it can express the value of each asset and liability in terms of the discounted values of these cash flows and follow a very similar approach to measuring exposure. This example is also simplified, because it discusses how value changes when exchange rates change but does not consider other factors that may influence values. Again, it is feasible to include other influences in a slightly more complex format. A firm that calculates its exposure accurately is in position to manage its currency exposure better by increasing or decreasing its exposure in response to its currency forecasts and its tolerance for risk.

MEASURING THE EXPOSURE OF A BUSINESS

Implementing the broader interpretation of exposure is more difficult than looking only at assets and liabilities, yet firms should examine the impact of exchange rate fluctuations on the volume of cash flows as well as the value. No formal framework is available for evaluating operational exposure. Rather than arriving at a number that can be used to project losses or gains due to currency fluctuations, most approaches to measuring operational exposure attempt to categorize business activities according to their sensitivity to currency movements. An exposed operation is one whose foreign currency cash flows change dramatically, whereas a nonexposed operation experiences little change.

Flood and Lessard[4] develop a conceptual approach to determine operating exposure. They make the point that because operating exposure measures the impact of exchange fluctuations on future revenues, costs, and profits, it cannot be determined by examining current accounting statements. Assessing operating exposure requires an analysis of the firm's competitive environment. It also reques an analysis of the firm's outputs and inputs and answering two main questions: What is the appropriate currency for pricing? Are the markets local or global?

[4] Eugene Flood, Jr., and Donald R. Lessard, "On the Measurement of Operating Exposure to Exchange Rates: A Conceptual Approach," *Financial Management*, Spring 1986, pp. 25–37.

The currency question basically concerns the relevancy of *the law of one price*. Is the good's price determined in local markets or in the global market? If it is priced locally, local supply and demand factors dominate and deviations from the law of one price might exist. This is true if sales are predominantly local and either tariffs, quotas, or high transaction costs precluded import competition. Household services and labor are examples of locally priced products and inputs.

A global market-priced product or input exists when trade is relatively easy or control of trade difficult. Most basic commodities have global prices. When a good is globally priced, changes in local supply and demand have little impact on price. It is more likely that quantity adjustments lead to increased imports or exports, depending on whether supply or demand factors shift.

To illustrate the range of operating exposures, Flood and Lessard categorize firms into one of four types: exporter, local market, importer, and world market. The taxonomy is based on the sourcing and selling patterns of the firm.

1. Exporter firms source their inputs in local markets and sell their products in competitive world markets.

2. Local market firms source their inputs and sell their products in local markets.

3. Importer firms source their inputs in competitive markets and sell in local markets.

4. World market firms source their inputs and sell their products in competitive world markets.

The impact of an exchange rate fluctuation on the operating margin of the different types of firms can be seen with a simple example based on data given in Table 7.4. The example takes the viewpoint of a U.S. firm with a British subsidiary. The parent's concern is the dollar value generated by operations. Notice that the change in the exchange rate is a 10 percent real appreciation of the pound relative

▪ TABLE 7.4

OPERATING EXPOSURE

Initial price	£100 = $150
Initial cost	£ 80 = $120
Contribution margin	£ 20 = $ 30

There is a 10% real appreciation in the value of the pound.

	Exporter	Local Market	Importer	World Market
New price	$150	$165	$165	$150
New cost	132	132	120	120
New contribution margin	18	33	45	30
Change in contribution margin	–40%	10%	50%	0%

to the dollar. A real exchange rate fluctuation represents a deviation from PPP. When the pound appreciates 10 percent in real terms, it increases from $1.50 to $1.65 without any difference in relative inflation. A currency change consistent with PPP has no impact on relative prices and costs regardless of the type of firm. When a real exchange rate change occurs, the sensitivity of the firm to the change depends on the firm's structure. That is apparent from the bottom half of Table 7.4, which reports the effects on the contribution margins for each of the four types of firms.

The exporter firm has a large decline in its margin; the local market and importer firms experience margin increases. Only the world market firm has no exposure and a constant margin. The lack of exposure for the world market firm comes about because neither its costs nor its revenues are determined in pounds, the currency whose value has changed. Although the firm is located in Britain, it is in effect a dollar-based business, at least in terms of its operations. All the other firm types experience some change in margins because either their prices or costs are determined by pounds.

ACCOUNTING MEASURES OF EXPOSURE

The final approach to measuring exposure is that prescribed by the accounting authorities. The required accounting treatment varies greatly among countries. Differences result from varying objectives of the local accounting rule-making body and different attitudes toward price-level accounting. The latter is important because of the relationship between inflation and exchange rate movements. Those differences highlight the fact that even accounting measures are subjective or arbitrary. No single correct measure exists. Each firm must comply with the accounting rules established by its national policy-making group. Firms should not be misled and believe that the resulting exposure measure is necessarily the measure that management should use to monitor and adjust its position.

Accounting measures of exposure or translation are primarily concerned with the choice of exchange rates for the preparation of consolidated financial statements. Because many companies have operations in several countries (some in more than 100), it is necessary to convert or translate foreign currency values into the currency of the parent company. The basic choice confronting preparers of accounting statements is whether to use the current exchange rate or the historic rate that existed at the time the asset or liability was acquired. If a firm uses the current rate, the position is exposed because changes in the current rate cause changes in the home currency value of the asset or liability. When the historic rate is used, the value is unaffected by exchange rate changes and the asset or liability is not exposed.

The three prevalent methods of translation that differ from one another regarding the categories of assets and liabilities that are translated at current or historic rates are as follows.

1. *Current/noncurrent method* in which assets and liabilities with maturities of one year or less are translated at the current rate and those with longer maturities at an historic rate.

2. *Monetary/nonmonetary method* in which financial assets and liabilities are translated at the current rate and nonfinancial assets and liabilities at an historic rate.

3. *All-current* method in which all positions are translated at the current rate.

We illustrate the differences among the methods with an example. Table 7.5 reproduces the balance sheet of British Productions Ltd. from Table 7.2. In addition, Table 7.5 identifies the accounting exposures under each of the three translation methods and the effects of an appreciation of the pound from $1.50 to $1.55 on the dollar value of the parent's holdings.

■ TABLE 7.5

**IMPACT OF TRANSLATION METHODS ON BRITISH PRODUCTIONS LTD.
(MILLIONS)**

Assets	Beginning Balance Sheets		Exposure Measurements			Adjusted Balance Sheets		
	A	B	C#	D#	E#	C	D	E
Cash	£ 8	$ 12.00	£ 8	£ 8	£ 8	$ 12.40	$ 12.40	$ 12.40
Accounts receivable	15	22.50	15	15	15	23.25	23.25	23.25
Inventory	23	34.50	23		23	35.65	34.50	35.65
Property	44	66.00			44	66.00	66.00	68.20
Total assets	£90	$135.00	46	£ 23	£ 90	$137.30	$136.15	$139.50
Liabilities								
Accounts payable	£16	$ 24.00	£–16	£–16	£–16	24.80	24.80	24.80
Other	11	16.50	–11	–11	–11	17.05	17.05	17.05
Long-term debt	23	34.50		–23	–23	34.50	35.65	35.65
Net worth	40	$ 60.00				60.95	58.65	62.00
Total liabilities	£90	$135.00	£–27	£–50	£–50	$137.30	$136.15	$139.50
Total exposure			£ 19	£–27	£ 40			

A is the beginning pound balance sheet.
B is the beginning dollar balance sheet valued at £1 = $1.50.
C# is the current/noncurrent exposure in pounds.
D# is the monetary/nonmonetary exposure in pounds.
E# is the all-current exposure in pounds.
C is the dollar balance sheet valued using the current/noncurrent translation method after the pound appreciated to £1 = $1.55. There is $0.95 million addition to owners' equity.
D is the dollar balance sheet valued using the monetary/nonmonetary translation method after the pound appreciated to £1 = $1.55. There is a $1.35 million reduction in owners' equity.
E is the dollar balance sheet valued using the all-current translation method after the pound appreciated to £1 = $1.55. There is a $2.00 addition to owners' equity.

The net worth is the residual or balancing account that reflects the effects of translation. Changes in net worth represent accounting gains or losses. It is apparent from Table 7.5 that each of the translation methods results in a different translated balance sheet and a different gain or loss. These range from a loss of $1.35 million to a gain of $2.00 million, demonstrating that the choice of accounting method makes a material impact on the preparation of financial statements.

In the example, the all-current method (E) generates the largest gain because the pound appreciates and this method has the largest positive exposure, £40 million. On each pound, the U.S. parent gains $0.05 for a total reported gain of $2.00 million. The current/noncurrent method (C) has a positive exposure of £19 million. This produces a reported gain in net worth of $0.95 million. The monetary/non-monetary exposure is –£23 million. Because the exposure is negative, the appreciation of the pound leads to a reported loss of $1.35 million: The dollar value of the subsidiary's liabilities increases by more than the increase in the dollar value of the assets.

None of the translation methods produce an accounting exposure equal to the economic exposure illustrated in Table 7.3. Two elements of the measurement process cause the differences. The first is the choice of exposed items. Under the current/noncurrent method, for example, long-term debt is not exposed even though its dollar value clearly changes because it is a financial liability. The second element is the treatment of exposed assets. The accounting treatments assume implicitly that the inflation and exchange rate elasticities, e_C and e_S are 1 and 0, not an intermediate value based on empirical evidence.

The justification for the accounting approach is that it is more objective than others. Price-level accounting, which tries to value all assets at their market value, is considered too subjective by many accounting rule-making bodies, including that of the United States. It is beyond the scope of this text to critique the accounting treatment. It is sufficient to note the differences in the various approaches and emphasize that although management must follow approved accounting methods in the preparation of financial statements, those methods need not be the basis for managerial responses to exposure.

◼ FINANCIAL ACCOUNTING STANDARDS BOARD *STATEMENTS NO. 8 AND NO. 52*

Financial Accounting Standards Board *Statements No. 8* and *No. 52* detail U.S. accounting treatment for translation. Prior to the release of *Statement No. 8* in 1976, U.S. firms had considerable latitude in their choice of translation method. *Statement No. 8* changed that by requiring firms to use the monetary/nonmonetary approach. The only exception was for real assets valued at the lower of cost or market when the market was lower and the assets were translated at the current, rather than the historical, rate.

Statement No. 8 was very controversial. Some financial managers criticized the choice of translation method, and most criticized the requirement that gains and losses be reported quarterly on the income statement. In periods of volatile exchange rates, this requirement forced firms to show gains and losses due to translation, even though the effects had no impact on cash flows. Many corporate officials maintained that this had a material effect on earnings per share and on stock prices. The academic literature on the subject suggested that the markets were able to evaluate the economic impact and that the volatility of reported earnings brought about by implementing *Statement No. 8* had no effect on stock prices.

The Financial Accounting Standards Board responded to the criticism by replacing *Statement No. 8* with *Statement No. 52*. *Statement No. 52* made two significant changes in the treatment of translation. First, it replaced, for most cases, the monetary/nonmonetary method with the all-current method, the exception being for cases in which remeasurement is necessary.

To understand remeasurement, it is necessary to introduce the concept of *functional currency*, which is the primary currency in which the operating entity conducts its transactions. The Financial Accounting Standards Board allows firms to determine the functional currency for their subsidiaries according to guidelines established in *Statement No. 52*. Normally, the functional currency is determined by geography but not always. For instance, if a subsidiary primarily engages in intracompany transactions, the functional currency is the parent's currency.

Remeasurement involves the conversion of the subsidiary's assets and liabilities into the functional currency. Remeasurement is performed according to the monetary/nonmonetary criterion established by *Statement No. 8*. For example, a German subsidiary of a U.S. company might have as its functional currency marks but have pound- and franc-denominated assets and liabilities. Before translating these accounts to dollars, the nonmark accounts are remeasured in marks by the monetary/nonmonetary method. Translation then converts the functional currency balance sheet, marks in this case, to dollars. *Statement No. 52* requires translation by the all-current method.

The second change brought about by *Statement No. 52* allows firms to show translation gains and losses as adjustments to the parent's equity as opposed to reporting them as additions or reductions to earnings. The second change muted the criticism concerning volatility and substantially eliminated the complaints about translation accounting.

EXPOSURE MANAGEMENT SYSTEMS

When a firm has chosen an exposure measurement method, it must establish an exposure management system. The exposure management information system must be designed to fit the requirements and capabilities of the parent and its operating units. Too frequently, information systems produce more data than management can process effectively. Such systems do not enhance decision making. Management must determine how actively it intends to manage or alter its exposure. For example, if management wants to adjust positions frequently to reflect their rapidly changing views of exchange rates, the information system must update exposure estimates frequently.

An exposure management systems should be designed with several key elements in mind:

1. The system should be forward looking. It should anticipate changes in rates, balance sheets, and operations. Historic measures are of limited value because they preclude actions to alter the level of exposure.

2. Frequency of reporting should be determined by the intention of management to manage exposure and the economic environment. The greater the desire to actively manage and the more volatile the environment, the more frequent the reporting.

3. Reporting requirements should reflect the size and the importance of the operating units. Smaller units should report less frequently if reporting is potentially burdensome.

4. Reports should be made to a centralized treasury department that functions as the exposure manager. It is important that exposure management be done with a global perspective.

The exposure measurement system should be integrated into the firm's financial planning system. Financial and operating decisions generate exposure. Measuring and managing exposure independent of other elements of the firm's operations and financial choices is a mistake. We raised the issue of trade-offs earlier with the example of a conflict between operating exposure and financial exposure. The exposure management system must be an integral part of the financial planning system to allow the identification of potential trade-offs or conflicts.

IMPLICATIONS FOR MANAGERS

Translation, the accounting measure of exposure, is well defined by accounting rules in different countries. Managers have no choice but to follow the prescribed translation method in the preparation of financial statements. Therefore, it is tempting to use accounting measures to manage a firm's exposure. That temptation should be avoided.

Accounting measures are relatively arbitrary. They do not reflect the operational or strategic exposure of the firm because the accounting measures fail to reflect economic values. Managers want to understand the economic implications of their decisions. To do that, it is necessary to measure exposure in the context of the firm's operating strategy and its competitive environment.

This chapter has provided two frameworks for measuring economic exposure that are complementary. One gives a classification scheme that indicates whether the exposure is on the cost or revenue side of the income statement. The second uses elasticity to measure the sensitivity of revenue and cost streams to changes in exchange rates. Using the two approaches in combination allows an external analyst or internal manager to identify and measure the impact of exchange rates on the value of a firm.

Within the firm, it is essential to approach the measurement and management of exposure in a systematic fashion. The issue of exposure, however, should be raised before operational decisions are made. Once a plant has been built or a contract signed, it might be too late to effectively manage the exposure related to the decision. Building a facility in Brazil might appear to be the most cost-effective way to produce a good, but it creates a long-term exposure that should be identified before, not after, the plant is constructed.

QUESTIONS AND EXERCISES

7-1. The manager of a large U.S. city arranges for the city to borrow $50 million in marks, for five years at a fixed interest rate of 6 percent per annum, with interest paid annually. The reason for borrowing in marks is that the comparable dollar loan cost is 7.5 percent per annum. The spot rate is $0.55. Six months after taking out the loan, the spot rate increases to $0.62. If the rate remains unchanged for the next five years, what is the effective dollar interest rate on the loan?

7-2. A corporate treasurer is considering raising $35 million from two alternative sources. One is a domestic loan with a fixed interest rate of 10 percent. The other is a Swiss franc loan with a fixed interest rate of 8 percent. The term of both loans is seven years and interest is paid annually.

a. What constant rate of annual appreciation in the Swiss franc makes the dollar cost of the Swiss loan 10 percent?

b. What is the firm's economic exposure if it borrows in Swiss francs?

c. If the treasurer selects the Swiss franc loan and expects the franc to appreciate sufficiently over time to raise the average dollar cost to 10 percent, how might she engage in selective hedging in order to achieve a dollar cost lower than 10 percent?

7-3. Listed below is the balance sheet for a German subsidiary of a U.S. firm and its translation into U.S. dollars at the current price of $0.50 per mark.

GERMAN SUBSIDIARY BALANCE SHEET AND U.S. TRANSLATION (THOUSANDS)

	DM	DM Price = $0.50
Cash	2,000	$ 1,000
Accounts receivable	5,000	2,500
Inventory	20,000	10,000
Fixed assets	50,000	25,000
Total assets	77,000	38,500
Accounts payable	9,000	4,500
Long-term debt	34,000	17,000
Equity	34,000	17,000
Liabilities and equity	77,000	38,500

a. Calculate the U.S. firm's accounting exposure under three alternative translation methods, the current/noncurrent method, the monetary/nonmonetary method, and the all-current method.

b. The U.S. firm anticipates that the mark will appreciate to $0.60. Produce pro forma U.S. dollar translations of the balance sheet at this new price of the mark under each of the three alternative accounting methods.

c. Relate the change in the equity account found in part (b) for each of the three methods to the exposure calculations in part (a).

7-4. As Jack Eaton, treasurer of Auld Products, analyzes the balance sheets of the company's two overseas subsidiaries, he is becoming increasingly aware that Financial Accounting Standards Board *Statement No. 52* affects the accounting exposure of the corporation. His concern is that changes in the value of the two currencies used by the subsidiaries might have a significant impact on Auld's profitability. The subsidiaries are located in Germany and France, and their balance sheets as of May 31 are as follows.

	France	Germany
Cash	1,000	1,250
Accounts receivable	1,150	2,850
Inventory	2,100	1,400
Net plant and equipment	4,240	3,000
Total assets	8,490	8,500
Accounts receivable	3,250	2,800
Taxes payable	600	900
Dividends payable	600	1,500
Equity	4,040	3,300
Total liabilities and equity	8,490	8,500

The numbers used in the balance sheet are in francs for the French subsidiary and marks for the German subsidiary. As of May 31 and at the time the various assets and liabilities were acquired, 1FR = $0.25 and 1DM = $0.50.

The dividend payable by the French firm is denominated in francs and the subsidiary owes the parent FR600. The dividend payable on the books of the German firm is denominated in dollars and owed to the U.S. parent. Each of the subsidiary's functional currency is its own domestic currency.

a. Calculate the parent's translation exposure in francs and marks according to *Statements No. 8* and *No. 52*.

b. An economist tells Eaton that the franc is going to decline to $0.20 and the mark is going to appreciate to $0.60. If this occurs, what will Auld's translation gains or losses be, according to *Statements No. 8* and *No. 52*?

c. How can Eaton reduce his exposure in each case? What are the costs?

7-5. The management of Plantation Products, Ltd., is trying to determine what its balance sheet should look like. Management is most concerned with the operating aspects of the business, but they must respond to the owners, who are putting pressure on them to reduce Plantation's exposure to translation gains and losses. Plantation Products is a joint venture of three companies, each of which comes from a different country and each of which has a different accounting rule for measuring translation exposure. One parent firm uses the all-current method, another the monetary/nonmonetary method, and the third, the current/noncurrent method. Consequently, each parent is inclined to structure the joint venture's balance sheet a little differently than the others, and Plantation's management is stuck in the middle.

Plantation's balance sheet as of December 31, 1994, in local currency, the plantain, is the following:

BALANCE SHEET
DECEMBER 31, 1994
(OOO PLANTAINS)

Cash	1,200
Accounts receivable	1,500
Inventory	2,250
Net plant and equipment	1,350
Total assets	6,300
Short-term liabilities	1,640
Long-term liabilities	2,500
Equity	2,160
Total liabilities and equity	6,300

At current exchange rates, the plantain equals 0.50 of each of the owner's currencies, but there are indications that it is going to be devalued by 20 percent. Assuming that is true, what argument would each of the joint venture partners use to urge management to restructure Plantation's balance sheet and why?

7-6. The chief executive officer of one of the largest U.S. multinational corporations believes that the best way to maximize shareholder value is to maximize earnings per share. The company is based in the United States and has operations in 46 countries and markets products in over one hundred countries. However, the CEO believes that the stock market is interested in dollar earnings and has decided to base the performance evaluation of the various subsidiaries on their contribution to dollar earnings per share. Do you agree with the CEO's policy? Explain your reasoning.

7-7. The following are the balance sheets for Imperial Oil, a Canadian integrated oil company, for 1991 and 1992. Exxon owns 70 percent of Imperial Oil and consolidates that proportion of Imperial Oil's balance sheet with its own. At the end of 1991, the value of the Canadian dollar was $0.8654, and at the end of 1992 it was $0.7865. Imperial Oil earned C$195 million and paid total dividends of C$349 million. Determine the effect of the change in the value of the Canadian dollar on Exxon's shareholders' equity, assuming that all dividends that were paid at year end and that Exxon uses the all-current method of translation.

IMPERIAL OIL BALANCE SHEETS
(THOUSANDS OF CANADIAN DOLLARS)

	Fiscal year ending December 31	
	1991	1992
Assets		
Cash	$ 286,000	$ 265,000
Marketable securities	7,000	757,000
Receivables	1,052,000	1,008,000
Inventories	782,000	608,000
Total current assets	2,127,000	2,638,000
Net property and equipment	10,760,000	9,965,000
Investment in subsidiaries	245,000	216,000
Intangibles	400,000	373,000
Total assets	$13,532,000	$13,192,000

Annual liabilities		
Fiscal year-end	12/31/91	12/31/92
Notes payable	$ 58,000	
Accounts payable	1,471,000	$ 1,316,000
Income taxes	110,000	247,000
Total current liabilities	1,639,000	1,563,000
Deferred charges	1,699,000	1,577,000
Long-term debt	2,356,000	2,243,000
Other long term liabilities	1,048,000	1,173,000
Total liabilities	6,742,000	6,556,000
Common stock net	2,977,000	2,977,000
Retained earnings	3,813,000	3,659,000
Shareholder equity	6,790,000	6,636,000
Total liabilities and net worth	$13,532,000	$13,192,000

REFERENCES

Adler, Michael, and Bernard Dumas. "Exposure to Currency Risk: Definition and Measurement." *Financial Management,* Summer 1984, pp. 41–50.

Aliber, Robert, Z., and Clyde P. Stickney. "Accounting Measures of Foreign Exchange Exposure: The Long and Short of It." *The Accounting Review,* January 1975, pp. 44–57.

Carsberg, Bryan. "FAS #52—Measuring the Performance of Foreign Operations." *Midland Corporate Finance Journal*, Summer 1983, pp. 48–55.

Flood, Eugene, Jr., and Donald R. Lessard. "On the Measurement of Operating Exposure to Exchange Rates: A Conceptual Approach." *Financial Management*, Spring 1986, pp. 25–37.

Garner, C. Kent, and Alan C. Shapiro. "A Practical Method of Assessing Foreign Exchange Risk." *Midland Corporate Finance Journal*, Fall 1984, pp. 6–17.

Hekman, Christine R. "Measuring Foreign Exchange Exposure: A Practical Theory and Its Application." *Financial Analysts Journal*, September/October 1983, pp. 59–65.

Lessard, Donald R., and David Sharp. "Measuring the Performance of Operations Subject to Fluctuating Exchange Rates." *Midland Corporate Finance Journal*, Fall 1984, pp. 18–30.

Shapiro, Alan C., "Defining Exchange Risk." *The Journal of Business*, January 1977, pp. 37–39.

INTRODUCTION

In January, 1990, Mr. Gaston Cevallos, Assistant Treasurer of Dow Europe, the European management unit of Dow Chemical Company, reflected on the effectiveness of modifications made to the company's foreign exchange management systems the previous year. On January 1, 1989, Dow Europe had (a) switched from the United States dollar (USD) to the ECU (European Currency Unit) as a basis for inter-company transactions, (b) changed to the local currency as the "functional currency" when translating foreign subsidiary financial statements to the USD, and (c) implemented a system for projecting the sensitivity of cash-flows to foreign currency movements. The three measures were intended to provide more efficient and representative management of the transaction, translation, and economic exposure faced by Dow.

For Dow, efficient foreign exchange (forex) management was exceedingly important. The company's two primary product areas, chemicals and plastics, were global industries characterized by low margins and dominated by large multinational corporations. Both industries were extremely cyclical, vulnerable to changes in the price of oil and fluctuations in economic growth. The characteristics of the industries placed a premium on efficient financial management of which foreign exchange management was an integral part. Dow had always taken a very aggressive approach to forex management and had developed a wide reputation within the industry as a company unwilling to rest on its laurels.

Responsibility for forex management was held primarily by the treasury department. A number of foreign exchange management systems had been in place at Dow, but the need for adjustments to the systems had become apparent during the 1980's as strong growth in Dow Europe's operations and fluctuations in the USD exposed weaknesses. Further, managers of the treasury department felt that certain exposures to foreign currency movements were not accurately identified and a more integrated approach would directly benefit the company. The question Mr. Cevallos asked himself was whether the changes made were really worthwhile, or had Dow Europe merely substituted one set of problems for another.

I. COMPANY BACKGROUND

THE DOW CHEMICAL COMPANY

The Dow Chemical Company was founded in 1897 by Herbert Dow in Midland, Michigan to produce chlorine extracted from extensive local brine deposits. Following World War II, the company began developing petroleum based chemicals and plastics as the demand for these products increased. By 1989 Dow Chemical had grown to be the sixth largest chemical company in the world with sales of $17,600 million and profits of $2,487 million. (Exhibits 7.1A and 7.1B are summary financial statements of The Dow Chemical Company.) The five largest chemical companies ranked in order by sales in 1989 were BASF (West Germany), Hoechst (West Germany), Bayer (West Germany), Imperial Chemical Industries (United Kingdom) and Du Pont (USA).

The company had undertaken significant diversification efforts in the late 1980's to reduce vulnerability to the cyclical commodity chemicals industry. These efforts included a joint venture with Eli Lilly in agrichemicals, a purchase of 67% of Marion Laboratories, an American pharmaceutical company, and continued investments in specialty chemicals. By the end of the 1980's, Dow management considered its primary diversification plans realized.

Dow Chemical had traditionally focused on the production of bulk chemicals, used largely as raw materials in a wide variety of industrial processes, and industrial plastics for everything from car bumpers to compact disks. These commodity chemicals and plastics businesses typically had a low value-added component as the technology required was readily available and the large number of companies in the industries assured competition. A further complication was that chemicals and plastic plants were extremely expensive to build and, once completed, difficult

■ EXHIBIT 7.1A

DOW EUROPE

■ SELECTED FINANCIAL RESULTS FOR DOW CHEMICAL COMPANY, MIDLAND, MICHIGAN

Income Statement		1989	1988	1987	1986
Net Sales		$17,600	$16,682	$13,377	$11,113
Operating costs and expenses	Cost of sales	10,478	9,806	8,660	7,727
	Insurance and finance company operations, net expense (income)	(59)	(28)	20	(57)
	Research and development expenses	873	772	670	605
	Sales, Marketing and other	2,298	2,083	1,762	2,104
	Total operating costs and expenses	13,590	12,633	11,112	9,774
Operating Income		4,010	4,049	2,265	1,339
Other income (expense)	Equity in earnings of 20%–50% owned companies	138	89	43	(6)
	US interest and other	(271)	(288)	(220)	(127)
	Gains on foreign currency transactions	58	5	39	30
Income before provision for taxes on income and minorities		3,935	3,855	2,127	1,236
Provision for taxes on income		1,436	1,450	882	495
Minority interests' share in income		12	7	5	0
Net income		2,487	2,398	1,240	732
Net income available for common stockholders		$ 2,487	$ 2,398	$ 1,240	$ 732
Earnings per common share		$ 9.20	$ 8.51	$ 4.31	$ 3.82

SOURCE: Annual reports.

■ EXHIBIT 7.1B

DOW EUROPE
■ SELECTED FINANCIAL RESULTS DOW
CHEMICAL COMPANY, MIDLAND, MICHIGAN

Balance Sheet		1989	1988	1987	1986
	Assets				
Current Assets	Cash and cash equivalents	$ 117	$ 225	$ 21	$ 17
	Marketable securities	172	0	397	348
	Accounts and notes receivable	4,219	3,768	3,229	2,381
	Inventories	2,832	2,370	2,105	1,940
	Total current assets	7,340	6,363	5,752	4,686
Investments	Capital stock in accumulated earnings of 20%–50% owned companies	1,111	1,053	1,064	952
	Other investments	1,089	903	684	493
	Noncurrent receivables	487	267	399	378
	Total investments	2,687	2,223	2,147	1,823
Plant properties	Plant properties	17,334	15,360	13,502	12,715
	Less-accumulated depreciation	9,692	8,784	7,951	7,368
	Net plant properties	7,642	6,576	5,551	5,347
Other	Goodwill	3,997	691	485	303
	Deferred charges and other assets	500	386	421	394
	Total	$22,166	$16,239	$14,356	$12,553
	Liabilities and Stockholders' Equity				
Current liabilities	Notes payable	$ 2,206	$ 328	$ 129	$ 221
	Long-term debt due within one year	80	104	50	58
	Accounts payable	2,274	1,873	1,583	1,177
	United States and foreign taxes on income	263	605	511	346
	Accrued and other current liabilities	1,661	1,265	1,182	1,135
	Total current liabilities	6,484	4,175	3,455	2,937
Long-term debt		3,855	3,338	3,779	3,404
Deferred taxes and	Deferred income taxes	642	567	527	441
other liabilities	Other noncurrent obligations	1,119	857	790	563
	Total deferred taxes and other liabilities	1,761	1,424	1,317	1,004
Minority interest in subsidiary companies		595	47	36	30
Stockholders' equity	Common stock	818	545	541	535
	Additional paid-in capital	621	923	817	725
	Misc. equity	761	—	—	—
	Retained earnings	8,999	7,167	5,226	4,436
	Cumulative translation adjustments	205	182	95	37
	Treasury stock, at cost	(1,933)	(1,562)	(910)	(555)
	Net stockholder's equity	8,718	7,255	5,769	5,178
	Total	$22,166	$16,239	$14,356	$12,553

SOURCE: Annual reports.

to convert to a different type of product. The primary feedstock for Dow's product line, as with all chemicals and plastics producers, was naphtha, a petroleum derivative, and natural gas, both of which were widely traded. Dow successfully competed in this environment by concentrating on process technology in order to become the low cost producer in the industry.

The 1980's were a tumultuous period for the large chemical giants. The second oil shock in 1979, and the 1982 recession reduced profits at most of the multinational chemical manufacturers. Straddled with excess capacity and very high raw material costs, there was little any of the companies could do but wait and hope for a recovery. Beginning in 1983 the needed recovery did come and demand gradually absorbed excess capacity in the industry. Continued strong demand, combined with falling prices for raw materials, extended the recovery through the late 1980's giving the industry a prolonged period of record profits.

THE DOW ORGANIZATION

Dow Chemicals had a three dimensional organizational structure which had evolved out of necessity. The three axes to the structure were product line, geographical region, and functional area. Preliminary work had also begun on an additional reporting line focused on certain global industries, such as automobiles, where customers purchased a wide variety of products throughout the world. Although complex, the organization was seen as effective given the nature of the company and the operating environment. The importance of any individual line of authority varied according to the specific conditions. The treasury group, for example, was organized with very strong functional lines although individual treasurers were geographically based. Generally, however, the most cohesive lines of authority were based on geographical regions.

Products were organized into four primary groups: chemicals (31%), plastics (41%), consumer specialties and pharmaceuticals (18%), and hydrocarbons and miscellaneous (10%). (Sales as a percentage of total company sales are indicated in parentheses.) Geographically, the company was sectioned into five areas: US, Canada, Latin America, Pacific and Europe. These five areas were further subdivided into regions. The regional subsidiaries were responsible for operations in either a group of countries or a single country if the internal market was particularly important. In the annual report results were only shown as US, Europe and Rest of World.

DOW AS AN INTERNATIONAL COMPETITOR

It was not until WW II that Dow began operations overseas by building a manufacturing plant in Canada. The company's first sales office outside of North America was established in Europe in the early 1950's. As the European economy regained strength following the end of the war, Dow gradually increased its European presence. However, the company continued to manufacture in the US almost all of the products it sold in Europe well into the 1960's. It was the growing international nature of chemical production as well as company policy to avoid dependency on a single country that pushed Dow to build up overseas operations at an increasing rate after the mid 1960's.

Once committed to establishing production sites overseas, Dow expanded quickly. By the mid 1980's, 75% of European demand for Dow products was supplied by local European production. In 1989, only 5% of Dow's European sales consisted of products manufactured in the US.

Dow's international character was also reflected in the distribution of employees. In 1989, about half of Dow's employees were based outside the US. The same year, Dow also had sales of at least 100 million USD in 16 different countries.

Dow's extensive overseas operations sheltered it from significant losses stemming from economic deterioration in any individual country or region but were of little benefit when recessions spread throughout the world, as was the case in 1981–1982.

DOW EUROPE

Dow Europe managed Dow Chemical Company's operations in Europe, the Middle East and Africa from its offices in Horgen, Switzerland, an idyllic village 15 kilometers south of Zurich. The European management structure was further broken down into 8 regional units: Germany, France, Italy, Iberica, United Kingdom, Benelux, Nordic and MEAF (Middle East, Africa, Eastern Europe, Austria and Switzerland). The Regional management units reported to Dow Europe headquarters. Regional treasurers had direct reporting responsibility both to the general manager of the region and the Treasurer of Dow Europe. Dow Europe's Treasurer reported to both the Treasurer of Dow Chemical in Midland and the President of Dow Europe. Each of the Regionals management units had responsibility for a number of legal entities.

Manufacturing operations were located in each of the regions. The most important production sites were located in Holland, Germany, and Spain. (Dow Holland operated the largest production facility in Dow Europe and the third largest for Dow World-wide). Other regionals had production sites which varied in size although most were relatively small. The MEAF regional, which had the highest sales volume, had virtually no production. The structure was complicated, although not unwieldy, and provided for many situations in which foreign exchange management was necessary.

TREASURY ORGANIZATION

Treasury department operations at Dow reflected the company's philosophy of keeping decision making responsibility centered at the lowest possible level. In Midland, the corporate treasury department focused its operations on long-term finance and global functional responsibilities. The balance of the corporate treasury office's efforts were directed at enhancing the performance of the subsidiaries' treasuries through policy development and leadership.

The Dow Europe treasury office in Horgen, one of the 5 Dow area offices, was responsible for financial planning and strategy for the treasury unit, mergers and acquisitions operations, and funding coordination for the company's European area operations. The Horgen office also developed bank relationships and the necessary financial vehicles to insure that regional units had access to financing. It was at the area level that Dow also centered most of its foreign exchange management. (Exhibit 7.1c is an organizational chart of the treasury department of Dow Europe.)

The regional treasuries were where operational activities including credit, collections, cash management, project financing, and legal entity monitoring took place. (Exhibit 7.1D shows areas of responsibility within Dow Treasury.)

As Dow's international commitments grew from a large exporter of products manufactured in the United States to a multinational corporation with production facilities in 31 countries and sales offices throughout the world, the complexity of international transactions dramatically increased. It was the responsibility of the Treasurer of Dow Europe to insure that foreign exchange management in the area was conducted efficiently and the funding needs of both the subsidiaries and the parent company were met.

■ **EXHIBIT 7.1c**

DOW EUROPE

■ **ORGANIZATIONAL CHART, DOW EUROPE TREASURY DEPARTMENT**

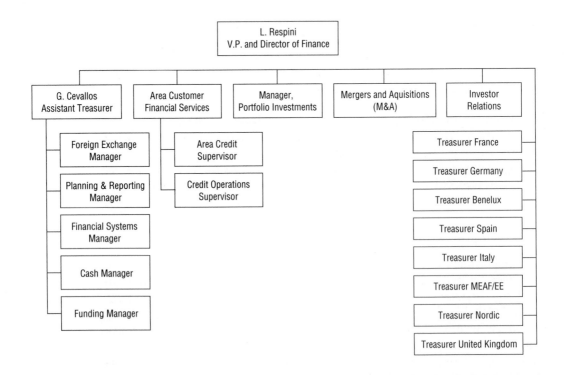

▪ EXHIBIT 7.1D

DOW EUROPE
▪ **DOW TREASURY ORGANIZATION**

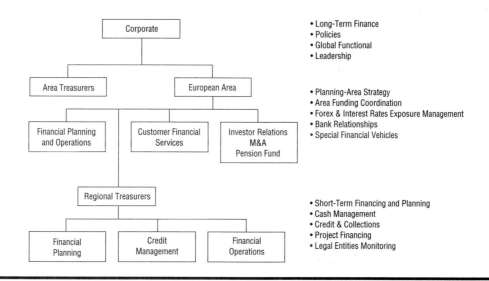

- Long-Term Finance
- Policies
- Global Functional
- Leadership

- Planning-Area Strategy
- Area Funding Coordination
- Forex & Interest Rates Exposure Management
- Bank Relationships
- Special Financial Vehicles

- Short-Term Financing and Planning
- Cash Management
- Credit & Collections
- Project Financing
- Legal Entities Monitoring

II. DOW'S APPROACH TO FOREIGN EXCHANGE EXPOSURE

Three types of foreign exchange exposure are generally defined: transaction, translation and economic. *Translation* exposure occurs when one currency must be converted to another. For example, transaction exposure may occur between the time a foreign currency denominated transaction is initiated and the time payment is received. During the time between a sale is made and the payment received, the relative values of the currencies may change resulting in a change in the value of the transaction. *Translation* exposure occurs when a subsidiary's financial statements, denominated in a currency other than that of the consolidating company's, are restated in the reporting currency of the parent company. *Economic* exposure is the long-range exposure of cash flows to changes in exchange rates.

DOW'S SYSTEM FOR MANAGING TRANSACTION EXPOSURE

In the mid 1960's, when 100% of Dow's European sales were of products produced in the US, the related foreign exchange management issues were limited. Dow would sell, for example, 100 cubic meters of Styrofoam to a French packaging company which would pay for the transaction in FFR (French francs). Dow would then convert the FFR to USD using one of the company's US banks. Dow had foreign exchange transaction exposure between the time the contract was made and the time payment was received, but forward purchases of USD for FFR adequately hedged the exposure. The local Dow sales office had only minimal expenses in FFR and was not overly concerned with the exchange rates; foreign exchange management was Midland's responsibility.

As local operations and production sites proliferated, the currency issues faced by the company became more pronounced. By the mid 1980's local production accounted for 95% of Dow Europe's sales, of which 30% were denominated in currencies other than the currency of the particular subsidiary involved in the transaction. Regardless of where the currencies came from (sales were denominated in 14 different currencies on a regular basis), Dow needed a system for managing the large volume of foreign currencies generated by the company's sales structure.

Dow Chemical had four primary types of sales transactions, three of which generated transaction exposure for the subsidiaries. Differences in the characteristics of each type necessitated special methods of handling the resulting exposure. The types were broken down as follows: (An example of each is provided.)

1. Transactions with local customers in local currencies: a German company purchases Styrofoam from Dow Germany and pays in DM, Dow Germany's operating currency.

2. Transactions between Dow subsidiaries with different operating currencies (Dow referred to this type of transaction as intercompany rather than intracompany): Dow Germany, which used DM as the operating currency, purchases agrichemicals for resale from Dow UK, which used pounds Sterling as the operating currency.

3. Local customers paying with non-local currency: similar to situation (1) except the customer desires to make payments in French francs to reduce its excess balances in that currency. (For competitive reasons Dow's policy was to permit the customer to choose the currency.)

4. Non-local customers paying with non-local currency: customers from other countries occasionally approach Dow units outside their normal country of operations for purchases of specialized products. This was discouraged by Dow but was occasionally necessary.

For Dow subsidiaries, transactions of types 2, 3, and 4 generated transaction exposure between the subsidiary's operating currency and the currency used in the transaction. For intercompany transactions (type 2) Dow Europe had established a clearing system which allowed the company to offset large currency exposures. The intercompany clearing system was not suited to third-party transactions (types 3 and 4) and, for these, an in-house factoring procedure had been devised.

DOW'S INTERNAL FACTORING SYSTEM

When Dow first initiated foreign currency sales, the company established a re-invoicing system to centralize the management of foreign exchange. Under the reinvoicing system adopted by Dow, as with other reinvoicing systems, following a sale, the sales unit sent an invoice to the reinvoicing center. The reinvoicing center then issued a new invoice to the customer and at the same time assumed responsibility for collection of the receivable. The sales unit received payment from the reinvoicing center in its local currency. Complications with postal delays, excessive paper work (reinvoicing required two sets of invoices to be produced) and separation between the customer and particular subsidiary handling the sale, led Dow to abandon the system in the early 1980's.

After the reinvoicing system was abandoned, Dow operated for short while without centralized intercompany transactions. Instead, all sales to third parties were handled by the regions as was any related foreign exchange management. The lack of a centralized foreign exchange system was not entirely out of character with the goals of Dow Europe. It had long been a policy of Dow Europe and Dow Chemical to place responsibility for decision making with managers as far down the corporate hierarchy as feasible.

Centralized forex allowed a number of advantages including funding of receivables and easier collection of cross-border receivables, which eventually enticed Dow managers to develop a new internal factoring system. Under the new system, regions sold their third-party receivables denominated in non-local currencies to Dow Factoring, a wholly owned subsidiary of Dow Europe, incorporated in Switzerland and based in Horgen. The price at which Dow Factoring purchased these receivables was at a discount to the face value. Dow Factoring took over both the responsibility for collection and the resulting foreign exchange exposure.

By 1988 local trade made up the bulk of Dow Europe's USD 6 billion in sales to external customers (as opposed to internal sales). Factored sales constituted a fourth of all sales approximately half of which were denominated in USD. Geographically 45% of factored sales were from the MEAF region, with the balance coming from the rest of Europe.

NETTING Centralizing forex management also permitted extensive netting. Dow Factoring maintained a cash pool which consisted of balances in a number of currencies in which Dow had significant sales. Netting occurred, for example, when FFR, received in a transaction between a customer in France and Dow Germany, was used to pay the factored receivables of Dow France. NGL (Dutch guilders), DM (West German marks), GBP (British pounds), and FFR were the primary currencies Dow paid out because of the extensive operations in those countries. Frequently, to meet the needs of the netting system, Dow had to purchase Belgian francs, Spanish pesetas, and Dutch guilders as these currencies did not generally enter into the system through normal transactions. Most other currencies were in plentiful supply and the excess balances were sold in bulk for USD. Because of the size of these foreign exchange transactions, Dow was able to command meaningful price reductions over that for smaller transactions.

DOW'S CLEARING SYSTEM FOR INTERCOMPANY TRANSACTIONS

The internal factoring system was used only for third-party transactions (types 3 and 4 on page 238). Transactions in Europe between Dow units (type 2) were handled via an intercompany clearing system.

Prior to January 1, 1989 intercompany transactions were invoiced to USD and subsidiaries maintained intercompany receivables and payables on their balances sheet in USD. For convenience, a company-wide exchange rate, or bookrate as it was known at Dow, was established for each currency at the beginning of every month. The bookrate was used for accounting conversions, including intercompany transactions, factoring, translation, etc., throughout the company during the month.

All intercompany transactions were conducted through Dow Europe S.A. Settlement occurred once monthly, at which time cumulative transactions for the month were processed. After establishing the net positions of each subsidiary, positive net intercompany balances were paid to the subsidiaries in a currency of their choice, usually their local operating currency. Correspondingly, negative net positions were the clearing system were usually paid by the subsidiary in its local currency. The exchange rate used to determine payments was set on the morning of the day the clearing was run. Transaction exposure between the time of the sale and the clearing date was easily hedged under the system: the subsidiaries needed only to hedge their USD receivables from one bookrate to the next. The USD was selected for intercompany invoicing because it was the operating currency of Dow Europe and the currency of the parent company, Dow Chemical.

NETTING The netting of debits and credits in individual currencies was the primary benefit of the clearing system and had been the original objective of the system when developed in the 1960's. Netting, for example, occurred when FFR received from one transaction were used to settle FFR obligations arising from other transactions. There were other advantages to the centralized clearing system which overall resulted in reduced costs and better management.

As a result of monthly intercompany transactions, Dow Europe S.A., the entity under which the clearing system was managed, had simultaneous credit and debit positions in various European currencies at the end of the month. Many of these positions were netted against each other. After netting debits and credits where possible, positive net balances in some currencies (almost always Spanish pesetas and Belgian francs) and negative balances in others (frequently USD and Dutch guilders) remained. Dow Europe S.A. set the bookrate on the morning of the last business day of the month and entered the spot market to buy and sell the necessary currencies. All subsidiary balances were settled at the bookrate. Any gains or losses between the time the bookrate was set and the actual trade time, a few hours at most, were incurred by Dow Europe. Because spot market currency transactions were settled in two days, transactions with subsidiaries clearing the accounts were conducted on the second business day of the new month.

In 1988, the clearing system handled USD 6 billion in intercompany transactions, USD 2.5 billion of which was netted.

PROBLEMS WITH THE SYSTEM By the late 1980's, the intercompany clearing system had been operational for many years and senior managers in Midland were generally satisfied with its performance. The only significant problem with the existing system was that receivables and payables associated with the clearing system were denominated in USD on the balance sheets of the subsidiaries. While many of the subsidiaries positions were netted out as the month progressed, some subsidiaries were chronically long or short relative to the USD. Dow Holland, for example, was a major recipient of intercompany transfers and had large USD receivables on the books at any particular time. The value of this balance in NGL terms, Dow Holland's operating currency, was dependent on the value of the USD. Depreciation of the USD to the NGL reduced the value of Dow Holland's USD receivables. These unrealized losses, for Dow Holland and other subsidiaries, were frequently enough to wipe out the subsidiary's accounting income in the local currency for the period.

From the US perspective, however, the USD results after consolidation were generally unaffected. The transaction loss for one subsidiary would usually be offset by an equal gain for another subsidiary which was able to pay its obligation to the clearing center with its more valuable local currency as the USD devalued. Because the transaction losses and gains for individual subsidiaries typically evened out over the month in USD terms, Dow Chemical in Midland was largely unconcerned with the issue: the value of the subsidiary as measured in the local currency was not of great interest to Dow.

The subsidiaries, however, were concerned about the impact of fluctuations in the USD on their net worth. For tax purposes, local funding requests and, in a few isolated cases, profit sharing, Dow subsidiaries were required to produce financial statements denominated in the local currency. The recipients of the subsidiary financial statements who used the profit figures to calculate tax liabilities and credit ratings were understandably distressed to see wide swings in profits.

The magnitude of the problem was dramatic at times. Between November 1979 and January 1984 the USD appreciated against the DM almost 100%. Over the next two years the trend reversed and by August, 1987 the USD had fallen below the November, 1979 rate. The USD relative to other European currencies was equally variable. (Exhibit 7.1E.) The increase in the number of companies using the clearing system from 8 in 1972 to 90 subsidiaries 15 years later (including some non-European companies), increased the pressure on the treasury group to improve the system. The most promising alternative to the USD for an intercompany invoicing currency was the ECU, especially given its relation to the major European currencies. (Exhibit 7.1F.)

THE STUDY At Dow Europe the concept of using the ECU as the base currency for intercompany transactions had developed over an extended period. The treasury department managers had been aware of the ECU and, at least theoretically, the potential benefits which its use would give. Additionally, Dow was able to observe how other companies had adapted to the ECU for various purposes and watch the increasing liquidity of the ECU in international financial markets. The culmination of the concept, however, was dependent on achieving the necessary support within the organization. This support materialized with the appointment in Midland of a new corporate Treasurer, Petro Reinhard, formerly the Treasurer of Dow Europe. Under the new Treasurer, the treasury staff at Horgen was charged with conducting a study analysing the potential savings that would result from using the ECU

■ **EXHIBIT 7.1E**

DOW EUROPE
■ DEUTSCHE MARK PER U.S. DOLLAR (NOVEMBER 17, 1979–
NOVEMBER 17, 1989)

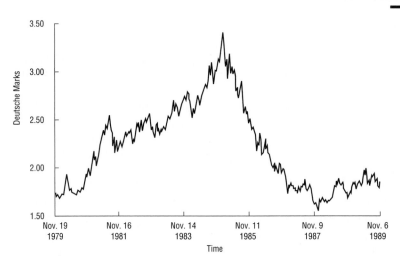

■ **EXHIBIT 7.1F**

DOW EUROPE
■ VALUE OF 1ECU IN TERMS OF US$, DM, AND FF OVER PAST FIVE
YEARS (FROM JUNE 5, 1983 TO JUNE 5, 1988 WEEKLY REBASED)

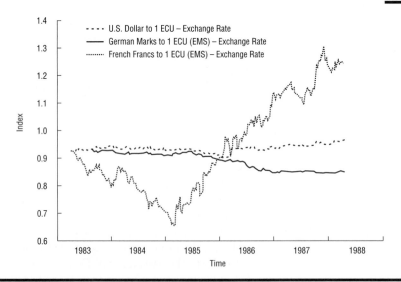

SOURCE: Company document.

as the intercompany invoicing currency and the relations of the subsidiaries that would be most affected by the new system.

As part of the study, simulations of the clearing process with the ECU instead of the USD were conducted using the transactions from the previous year. Results from this trial showed substantially reduced gains and losses from foreign exchange movements. The ECU was clearly able to reduce fluctuations in earnings due to changes in the value of the balance sheets of the subsidiaries.

Responses from the subsidiaries was also highly positive on the proposed modifications. (See letters from Dow UK, Exhibit 7.1G and Dow Nordic, Exhibit 7.1H.) However, some regional treasurers supported the continued use of the USD or a switch to the Deutsche mark as opposed to the ECU. Regardless of the higher

■ EXHIBIT 7.1G

Dow Europe
■ Letter from Dow UK as Part of Study
Regarding Adoption of ECU

Proposal to Use Ecu as Invoicing Currency for Intercompany Trade within Europe

Introduction
We basically see no reason not to shift to the ECU as intercompany currency. Our controllers are fully supportive of the move and assure us that the transition would occur without pain.

It is obvious that on the positive side the ECU/S exchange rate would be less volatile than the $/S exchange rate and in any case since over 80% of our intercompany trade is with ECU countries, the ECU would more closely reflect the underlying reality.

It can, of course, be argued that the choice of intercompany currency does not really matter from an overall company point of view since the gains in one Dow company are mirror-imaged by losses in another Dow company. This is only true from a before tax point of view.

The main advantage of the ECU as intercompany currency would come if hedging had to be done locally, as it would facilitate defending hedging cost allowance in front of local tax authorities.

Local Regulations
There are no permits required or restrictions of any kind in the UK.

Settlement of Invoices
Settlement of invoices can be done in ECU via all the major UK bank: Barclays, Midland, Nat West, Lloyd, Bank of Scotland, etc.

Legal Entity Results
The attached graph shows that the UK line 24 was in 1987 and what it would have been with the ECU as intercompany currency. Since the $ went down in 1987 and the UK is a net intercompany importer, it is obvious that to have the $ as intercompany currency increased local profit. The currency gains being trade related are added to our trading income which is taxed at 35%. So our tax bill increased by 35% of $5.5MM or about $2MM.

Business Considerations
Besides hedging and related tax allowances (which in my view are as much "business" as anything else), we should mention that using the ECU as intercompany currency would facilitate discussions with the Health Authorities regarding the pricing of our pharma business in the UK. It is hard to quantify the impact but it would certainly help.

SOURCE: Dow Europe.

- **EXHIBIT 7.1H**

DOW EUROPE
- **LETTER FROM DOW NORDIC REGARDING**
PROPOSED ADOPTION OF ECU

Re: Interco Inv. Currency
Main Nordic currencies (SEK and FIM) are based on a basket carrying both USD and EEC currencies. Considering Nordic as almost 100% net buyer interco, local currency would be the best from our point.

The other alternatives are more or less volatile, here showing last 12 months changes in regard to SEK.

Ecu	4%	Revalued	Against SEK
DM	6%	Revalued	Against SEK
USD	12%	Devaluation	Against SEK

Our advise therefore:

1. Yes, we favor a change
2. Less currency volatility in exposure, however except USD there might be need of increasing consolidating efforts
3. A. Local currency
   B. ECU
   C. DM
   D. USD

Note: From DCE point ECU is probably preferable B/C net receiver interco would get currency exposure with the local currency approach.

Uncertainties about development of ECU and perhaps Nordic participation within the EMS also favours ECU in the long run.

SOURCE: Dow Europe.

liquidity of the DM, Dow wanted to avoid damaging national sensitivities and chose the ECU. The need for change was clear, and, although the problems with the USD were not shared evenly by all subsidiaries, the advantages of the ECU were overwhelming. Dow began using the ECU for intercompany transactions on January 1, 1989.

THE ECU[1] The ECU was created as part of the European Monetary System (EMS) established on March 13, 1979. The EMS was a system of managing the exchange rates between the currencies of member nations. The EMS was closely tied to the European Economic Community and in essence was the mechanism to help draw the member nations towards eventual monetary union. The concept behind the ECU was as a common measure of value among the member nations. Instead of choosing an existing currency, a basket currency was chosen as it would both limit the fluctuations relative to any currency within the basket and avoid the political

---

[1] The name of the ECU had a double significance as both an acronym for the European currency unit and as the name of a coin used in Europe during the middle ages.

■ TABLE 7.1A

COMPOSITION OF THE ECU BY PERCENTAGE
WEIGHT OF NATIONAL CURRENCY

22.8.86		20.9.89
34.2	30.1	Deutsche marks
19.0	19.0	French francs
12.8	13.0	British pounds (*)
10.8	9.4	Dutch guilders
9.6	10.1	Italian lira
8.8	7.9	Belgian/Lux. francs
2.8	2.4	Danish kroner
1.2	1.1	Irish pounds
0.8	0.8	Greek drachma (*)
—	5.3	Spanish peseta
—	0.8	Portuguese escudo (*)
100%		100% Total

* These countries did not participate in the exchange rate
management system of the EMS.

SOURCE: Euromoney

complications of existing national currencies. The ECU, because of its multiple currency base (all of which, except the British pound, Greek drachma and the Portuguese escudo, were managed relative to each within certain limits under the terms of the EMS), would be more stable than any individual currency, facilitating trade. (The composition of the ECU in 1986 and 1989, before and after the inclusion of the Spanish peseta and the Portuguese escudo, is shown in Table 7.1A.)

Each currency's participation in the ECU was determined by the strength of the country's economy and currency. Following its inception the ECU had grown in stature to the extent that in 1989 it was the fifth most used currency for Eurobonds. The USD was still the most popular followed by the Deutsche mark, British pound and the Japanese yen.

Most of the currencies in which Dow Europe conducted transactions were included in the ECU. The ECU was attractive for Dow's intercompany invoicing for two reasons, 1) the ECU was an average of currencies so that any one currency fluctuated less against the ECU and, 2) as mentioned above, 9 of the 12 currencies in the ECU were managed through the EMS to reduce fluctuations. The change to the ECUwas initially only considered for the European area although some non-European based subsidiaries had shown interest in the system. Dow had to request special permission from certain countries including Spain, Germany and Italy, in order to allow subsidiaries based in those countries to participate in ECU-based clearing. Turkey prohibited companies from using the ECU for any reason and Dow's subsidiaries there continued to invoice in USD for intercompany transactions. Sales handled through the clearing center had to be recorded in the full amount (unnetted) on the companies' books for tax purposes. Even still, local authorities occasionally required more detailed documentation regarding the bookrate used in transactions.

With the switch to the ECU for intercompany invoicing, Dow subsidiaries still had large non-local currency items on their balance sheets. However, because these positions were denominated in ECU, fluctuations in value were anticipated to be minimized relative to the USD. The subsidiaries were still exposed on a transaction between one bookrate and another as before. This exposure was relatively easily covered by hedging, usually with forwards. Dow Europe's diverse currency positions resulting from the clearing operations offered the company opportunities to write forward contracts to subsidiaries to hedge their positions. Although Dow encouraged subsidiaries to hedge their positions only when necessary, treasury managers in Horgen believed that the subsidiaries were almost always hedged.

CHANGE OF THE FUNCTIONAL CURRENCY

At the time Dow began studying the currency used in intercompany invoicing, the treasury department also was aware of a related problem, concerning the use of the USD as the functional currency. Under the rules for translation then in use, fixed assets of foreign subsidiaries were translated to USD using a historical (rather than current) exchange rate.[2]

Translating at historical rates, however, masked any potential changes in the value of the assets resulting from exchange rate changes. In reality, the USD value of foreign fixed assets changed with the exchange rate, but under the rules of FAS no. 8 these changes were not apparent. Furthermore, the FAS no. 8 rules, transaction and translation gains and losses were not separated. The total undifferentiated figure was taken through the income statement mixing the two exposures and making them difficult to manage.

Switching to the local currency as the functional currency under FAS no. 52 had two advantages for Dow: (1) it permitted the use of the current exchange rate rather than historical rates for the translation of fixed assets, and (2) it separated transaction and translation gains and losses when consolidating. With the local as the functional currency transaction gains and losses went to the income statement as before, but translation results bypassed the income statements and went directly to a "special equity" account on the balance sheet.

Using the current rate for translating fixed assets revealed USD 1.6 billion in exposed assets held by foreign subsidiaries. The new rules of FAS no. 52 did not alter Dow's exposure nor affect the local book of the subsidiaries stated in local currencies. The exposure had existed all along; the new system simply made the two exposures explicit and therefore easier to manage.

---

[2] In 1983, US based multinational companies were required to choose a functional currency for translation purposes under the rules of FAS no. 52. Dow chose the US dollar as the functional currency for its foreign subsidiaries. With the dollar as functional currency, the FAS no. 52 translation rules were the same as under FAS no. 8, which required the use of historical rates for translating fixed assets.

MANAGING THE EQUITY EXPOSURE

Dow made a decision to actively manage the USD 1.6 billion in equity exposure. Some of the exposure was neutralized by local borrowing to match assets and liabilities currency by currency at the subsidiary level. The remaining balance sheet exposure was hedged using forward currency contracts and options if management's forecasts indicated forex movements in an adverse direction. The company was aware that balance sheet numbers reflected historical costs and were potentially misleading as a basis for hedging. A Dow executive said, "The exposure is real, so we manage it. We know the numbers are wrong, but we work with what we have, and that's the balance sheet."

DOW'S SYSTEM FOR MANAGING CASH FLOW EXPOSURE

"A lot of people talk about economic exposure to foreign exchange risk," commented Gaston Cevallos. "Academics and others give advice about it. But very few companies actually do anything. We wanted to take the additional setups of (a) measuring economic exposure, and (b) doing something about it."

Dow Europe's system for managing cash flow exposure began with a projection of cash flows each of the eight regions one year ahead (regions are Germany, France, Italy, Iberica, United Kingdom, Benelux, Nordic, and MEAF, the latter comprising Middle East, Africa, Eastern Europe, Austria and Switzerland). These flows were referred to as "projected actual" flows.

In 1987, Dow Europe sold USD 4.3 billion of products. Sales were invoiced in various European currencies, but the currency of the invoice was not necessarily the currency to which the selling price was most sensitive, i.e., the "economic currency." The next step in the process was to determine the economic currency for each product group and each major element of cost.

The analysis was made by taking a representative sample of products from each product group and interviewing the product marketing manager in each case. Questions concerned the general characteristics of the market, who the competitors were, how pricing was determined, and what factors had the largest impact.

Based on these interviews, a rating was given to each product group that signified the extent to which the product price was sensitive to movements in US dollars. A rating of "0" meant that the product was dollar-sensitive and that prices quoted in European currencies likely would adjust immediately upon moves in the USD exchange rate. A rating of "100" meant that the product was European-currency sensitive and that prices quoted in European currencies likely would be completely unaffected by changes in the USD exchange rate. "European currency" in this context meant the currency of the country in which the sale was made.

The product rating in a sense was a measure of Dow's ability to pass on changes in exchange rates to customers. If a product were completely dollar-sensitive (rating of 0), forex changes could be passed on immediately. If insensitive (rating 100), changes could not be passed on.

A similar analysis was done for costs. Each major element of cost was given a rating on the same scale used for revenues.

CASH FLOW ADJUSTMENT The "actual" cash flows projected were then transformed into "economic" cash flows by multiplying them by the ratings described above. This procedure split each cash flow into two components, a dollar component and a non-dollar component.

Revenues and costs were then aggregated to get economic cash flows for Dow Europe overall in terms of dollar and non-dollar exposure. Once economic exposure was calculated for each region, it was then aggregated for Dow Europe.

The results of the calculations showed Dow Europe to be short some currencies and long others. The net position was long European currencies relative to the USD. According to Mr. Cevallos, if the estimated long position was correct and the USD weakened against European currencies by 1 percent, Dow Europe would see its profits increase by 1 percent of the net exposure. The additional profit would show up in improved profit margins, rather than as explicitly identified forex gains.

Once the cash flow exposure was determined, hedging simulations were carried out to determine the results of alternative hedging strategies. Three strategies were tested: (1) use of forward contracts in each European currency; (2) use of forward contracts in a proxy currency, first the ECU and then the Deutsche mark; and (3) using currency options, with the DM as a proxy.

RESULTS

Based on the results of the analysis, Dow Europe management reached two key conclusions: first, Dow Europe had significant cash flow exposure, and second, they were confident enough of the system to use it as the basis for a hedging strategy.

The ECU was chosen as the hedging instrument. According to Cevallos, the results using ECU were "close enough to those achieved using individual currencies." To fully hedge the long position, Dow Europe would sell ECU forward against the dollar for one year in the amount of the position. The policy adopted was to hedge when there was a clear consensus within the treasury unit that the dollar was likely to strengthen. If it was felt that the odds favored a weaker dollar, no hedge was implemented.

This practice reflected in part Dow's confidence in their own ability to forecast the dollar, but also the realities of typical accounting systems. According to Cevallos, "accounting treats forex gains and losses in isolation. To some, a hedge looks like speculation. If we show a loss on forex, we have a difficult time convincing people that it was one side of a hedge, and that the offsetting gain is somewhere in operations. We can't point to the gain. So we want to avoid showing forex losses."

The system was implemented in 1989. According to Luciano Respini, Vice President for Finance and Treasurer of Dow Europe, in early 1989 Dow's board in Midland gave them permission to manage USD 100 million of the total exposure. Based on results in 1989, that authority was increased to USD 250 million in 1990. "If the accountants would let us relate the gains and losses," commented Respini, "the board would let us manage the entire amount. Top management doesn't want to have to explain 'forex loss' to shareholders and financial analysts, even when it was one side of a hedge with a gain on the other side. If it weren't for the accounting treatment, we'd have authority to manage the whole thing."

During 1989, the dollar strengthened against the ECU during the first half, and weakened during the second half, finishing the year at about the same level at which it started. Unhedged, according to Cevallos, Dow would have had a cumulative loss through July, but essentially a wash for the year. On the hedge, there was a gain during the first half, a loss during the second, and a small gain for the year.

III. RESULTS OF THE CHANGES

The use of the ECU for intercompany transactions, the change to the local currency as the functional currency, and the cash flow exposure system generated extensive benefits for Dow. Dow believed its decisions regarding foreign exchange management were more realistic as a result of the increased awareness. Additionally, the changes improved security and reduced costs.

Regarding the system for managing economic exposure, Mr. Cevallos recalled: "Initially there was some skepticism, especially from the manufacturing and commercial people. They thought the system was an excuse to speculate."

He continued, "In our system, the numbers may be wrong, but the direction is right. The program is still very experimental. We are doing something about economic exposure, in a cautious way."

Dow's international scope made transaction, translation and economic exposure an inescapable management problem. The questions Mr. Cevallos faced were whether the new systems were effective in identifying the exposures, and whether the techniques developed to address the situation were sufficient for the purposes of the company.

CASE 7.2 ▬▬▬▬▬
WESTERN MINING*

Western Mining Corporation Holdings is a world-scale mining company as well as one of the larget corporate groups in Australia. It is the largest gold producer in Australia, produces 10 percent of the Western world's nickel, owns 44 percent of Alcoa of Australia (which is 51 percent-owned by the Aluminum Company of America), and has producing interests in oil and gas, copper, uranium, and talc.

Western Mining is exposed to foreign exchange risk by virtue of its (1) borrowings in foreign currencies, (2) income in foreign currency, and (3) competition with producers whose costs are denominated in a foreign currency. The Treasury Department of Western Mining has accordingly made a considerable effort to understand the company's currency exposures, and to develop appropriate policies for managing those exposures. Although we have found it difficult to define and quantify such exposures with much precision, our analysis has led nevertheless to a radical change in our perception of our real, underlying exchange risk. And this change in view has in turn resulted in the adoption of a new currency management policy that represents a significant improvement over our past practice (not to mention the policies of our Australian competitors).

This article discusses how we arrived at these policy changes—a process that may be of interest to other firms attempting to identify and manage their currency risks. Such companies, we think it important to add, are not only those that operate internationally but may also include wholly domestic companies that compete against imports.

SOME HISTORICAL PERSPECTIVE ▬▬▬▬▬▬▬

In the late 1960s, the early 1970s, and again in the early 1980s, Australian mining companies undertook major capital investments in very large-scale minerals projects. In the 60s and 70s, the equity and debt markets in Australia were neither large nor sophisticated enough to provide adequate funding for such projects. As a result, a significant portion of the necessary capital was raised in the developing Euro-dollar market. And even during the "mining boom" of the early 1980s, when Australian capital markets had developed sufficiently to finance a large portion of the investment, Australian mining companies continued, with few exceptions, to fund themselves with borrowings in U.S. dollars.

Most of the commodities to be produced from these new investments were intended for export and were—and continue to be—priced in U.S. dollars in

*I wish to acknowledge the contributions of my colleagues in the Treasury Department—Basil Jenkins, Alan Knights, and Julian Thornton—to the development of understanding of Western Mining's foreign exchange exposure and of strategies to manage it. The assistance provided by Kees Scholtes and his currency advisory team at S.G. Warburg and Company is gratefully acknowledged. I would also like to thank Don Morley, Director of Finance and Administration, for his advice and guidance and for his cooperation in the publication of this article. Finally, I would like to thank Professor Clifford Smith and Charles Smithson for their helpful comments, and, especially, Don Chew, for his support, patience, and perserverance in preparing this article—Peter J. Maloney, Western Mining Corporation. This case is an edited version of an article written by Peter J. Maloney and reprinted with the permission of the *Journal of Applied Corporate Finance.*

international markets.[1] Because most Australian mining companies receive a major revenue stream denominated in U.S. dollars, the conventional wisdom was that the Australian mining industry was exposed to significant, long-term U.S. dollar exchange rate risk. It was widely believed, for example, that if the Australian dollar appreciated sharply against the U.S. dollar, Australian mining firms would suffer a significant dollar revenue (both immediately and over the long term).

Given such an exposure, the conventional wisdom also held that borrowing in U.S. dollars would provide a "natural hedge" against their U.S. dollar revenue stream. In fact, so convinced were Australian mining companies of their exposure to the U.S. dollar that, when forward currency markets began to develop in the mid-1970s, such companies began to supplement the hedge provided by U.S. dollar debt with forward exchange contracts. They entered into arrangements whereby they sold forward their future U.S. dollar revenue stream, often hedging up to 100 percent of forecast revenue with a combination of debt servicing and forward contracts—sometimes for periods out to 10 years, although two to five years was more common.

In the early and mid-1980s, when the Australian dollar declined sharply against the U.S. dollar, the "natural hedge" proved not to be a hedge at all, but rather an uncovered short position in the U.S. dollar. As expected, the decline in the Australian dollar increased the cost of servicing U.S. dollar debt. And, for a number of mining companies having just completed large new projects or expansions, such borrowings comprised the majority of their balance sheet liabilities. Those companies that had also sold forward some or all of their expected U.S. dollar revenue stream also suffered further foreign exchange losses as these contracts matured. On the asset side, however, the positive effect of the stronger U.S. dollar on dollar-denominated revenues was offset by a prolonged slump in mineral commodity prices; and thus the expected increase in revenue did not materialize. Thus, squeezed between flat or even falling revenues and rising funding costs, many mining companies began to declare annual foreign exchange losses due to revaluation of U.S. dollar debt that greatly reduced (and, in some cases, completely wiped out) the profits from operations.

WESTERN MINING POLICY

Although it too experienced some currency losses, Western Mining fared better than many of its competitors because it had relied more on the equity markets to finance its capital expenditures and had not participated in any major new projects

---

[1] The basis of the pricing differed: in some cases the price was publicly quoted on commodity markets changing from day to day; in other cases, such as nickel, the price was predominantly set in U.S. dollars by what was known as a "producer price" mechanism (but is now priced on a public commodity market); in other cases, because of product quality differentials, for example in iron ore and coal, there was no one world market price-contracts and pricing terms were negotiated on an annual basis with consumers, but, invariably, prices in these contracts were set in U.S. dollars. Even when some production was sold in the domestic market, the price was effectively the U.S. dollar price.

in the early 1980s. In 1984, however, the company contemplated investment in a new copper, uranium and gold mine, with expected capital costs of about $750 million. Under arrangements with a joint venture partner, the company planned to finance its share of the mine solely with debt, thereby increasing its total debt by a magnitude of two or three times. When confronted with the need to decide the currency denomination of the debt, the Treasury Department concluded that the "traditional" rationale for borrowing in U.S. dollars was probably no longer valid, and for two reasons:

First, in recent years the depth of the Australian dollar debt market, both in Australia and overseas, had increased to the extent that Western Mining could now conceivably fund all of its debt in Australian dollars. Also the growth of debt markets in other foreign currencies and the explosive growth of capital markets products, such as interest rate and currency swaps, had make it possible for borrowers in foreign currencies, such as U.S. dollars, pounds sterling and Japanese yen, to convert a foreign currency liability into an Australian dollar liability.

Second, there were apparent flaws in the economic arguments used to justify the "natural hedge" approach. We questioned whether mining companies really had an economic exposure to the U.S. dollar. Obviously, once a sale was made, and the amount and timing of U.S. dollar receipts was known (although still subject to credit risk), the firm clearly had a "transactional" exposure; and short-term U.S. dollar debt was an effective hedge against such an exposure. But, for sales one year, two years, or ten years ahead, was there an economic exposure from fluctuations of the U.S. dollar that should be hedged by U.S. dollar debt and forward sales?

We accordingly began to consider whether borrowing in a basket of currencies might not provide a better hedge than U.S. dollar debt against fluctuations in our home revenues. We also considered the alternative of borrowing exclusively in Australian dollars, in part because it would eliminate any exposure of our liabilities to exchange rates. Our reasoning was as follows:

1. The economic price of a given commodity is set by the supply of that commodity as well as the demand for it. Supply is determined by such factors as the discovery of new mineral deposits, and the costs of extracting and treating minerals, both in Australia and in other mineral-producing countries. The cost of extracting minerals and the ability to compete against other producers is determined, to some extent, by exchange rates. For example, a sustained depreciation of the Canadian dollar relative to the Australian dollar would likely improve the competitive position of Canadian producers relative to Australian producers. Demand is determined largely by economic growth in the developed economies and by technological change, which might either increase consumption or result in substitution or reduced requirements. But it, too, can be affected by exchange rate changes in the major consuming countries.

Ultimately, the factors that affect supply and demand for a given commodity determine the price of that commodity, and not the currency in which it happens to be priced. As a result, to the extent Western Mining faces any consistent (and thus hedgeable) foreign currency exposure, that exposure is likely to be a variety of different currencies, the movements of which could affect the company in unpredictable ways.

To illustrate how such thinking might be applied, consider the following simple example. If the U.S. dollar appreciates by 10 percent against all other currencies and the price of nickel immediately goes up by 10 percent, this price increase will have two effects: (1) it will gradually reduce the demand for nickel in countries that pay 10 percent more—that is, all countries other than the U.S.; and (2) unless demand falls off sharply, it will encourage and increase in the supply of nickel. Consequently, the price of nickel would tend to fall back to its equilibrium price before the appreciation of the U.S. dollar. (Economists would likely identify this line of reasoning as a form of the theory known as "purchasing power parity.") In such a case, an Australian producer funding it operations with U.S. dollar debt would experience an only temporary increase in revenues, but a permanent increase in the cost of servicing its U.S. dollar debt and settling its forward exchange contracts.

2. We were also impressed by the argument that the Australian economy was so dependent on commodity exports (agricultural commodities as well as minerals) that a general decline in world commodity prices would be expected to lead to a decline in the Australian dollar; and, conversely, that an increase in commodity prices would most likely lead to a strengthening of the Australian dollar. Although there is some academic work in support of this view,[2] our experience in the early 1980s was perhaps the most compelling argument. During that period, as mentioned, commodity prices and the Australian dollar declined together. For Australian mining companies, this meant that their revenues from overseas commodity sales were shrinking at the same time as the costs of servicing their U.S. debt and settling their forward contracts were sharply increasing.

Given either or both of the above arguments, it seemed clear to us that taking a short position in U.S. dollars, whether by borrowing or selling forwards, would not stabilize—and would in fact likely add to the volatility of—our home country operating profits. And our first response, based on the above reasoning, was to consider whether we may not be better served by borrowing in Australian rather than U.S. dollars. To the extent we accepted the view that the strength of the Australian dollar depends systematically on the general level of commodity prices, borrowing Australian dollars could be expected to reduce the volatility of our home country earnings and cash flows. (And, to show how sharp a reversal this change in thinking represented, we even considered the forward *purchase* of U.S. dollars as a means of offsetting the decline in revenue due to falling commodity prices.)

---

[2] I am not aware of any economic research regarding the relationship between the value of the Australian dollar and commodity prices in general. However, an Australian economist has put forward the proposition that the growth in mineral exports would likely result in, amongst other things, a higher value for the Australian dollar (see R.G. Gregory, "Some Implications of the Growth of the Mineral Sector," *Australian Journal of Agricultural Economics*, August 1976). This proposition was supported in varying degrees by a number of other respected economists (see Richard H. Snape, "The Effects of Mineral Development on the Economy," seminar paper 1977, and Andy Stoeckel, "Some General Equilibrium Effects of Mining Growth on the Economy," *Australian Journal of Agricultural Economics*, April 1979). It is reasonable to assume that an increase in mineral prices would have the same effect as an increase in the volume of mineral exports.

It is important to recognize, however, that the prescription for borrowing in Australian dollars is based largely on the likelihood of a scenario in which the U.S. dollar either appreciates or depreciates against all other currencies (what is referred to as a "unilateral" movement in the U.S. dollar). But how realistic is the expectation that the dollar will move in this fashion? What if we instead considered the possibility of such a "unilateral" shift in the value of the *Australian* dollar? That is, how would our financing policy change if the Australian dollar were expected either to increase or decrease by 10 percent against all other currencies?

Under this scenario (which is undoubtedly as artificial as "unilateral" movements in the U.S. dollar), the home country revenues and the costs of servicing U.S. dollar debt would move together, thus bringing us back to the accepted wisdom that U.S. dollar debt should be used to hedge U.S. dollar revenues. In such a case, however, denominating the debt in *any* currency other than Australian dollars would have provided an equally effective hedge. That is, as long as one clings to the assumption of a unilateral movement in the Australian dollar, then hedging home country revenues with debt denominated in yen or pounds sterling or Swiss francs is equally effective as borrowing in U.S. dollars.

SOME EVIDENCE

These two currency scenarios and their associated policy prescriptions—one based on unilateral movements in the U.S. dollar and the other on unilateral changes in the Australian dollar—are of course polar opposites. And, as extreme positions, they are best thought of as caricatures of a complex economic reality that lies somewhere in between.

In 1984, in an attempt to determine which of these two models offers a better approximation of the real world, Western Mining engaged its U.K.–based merchant bank to carry out some statistical analysis of the relationship between movements in the price of a number of commodities against both the U.S. dollar and an SDR currency basket. More precisely, the bank calculated "correlation coefficients" designed to measure the extent of co-movement between (a) commodity prices expressed in U.S. dollars and the value of the U.S. dollar against the other major currencies (the SDR/U.S. dollar rate and other currency baskets were used) and (b) commodity prices expressed in a basket of currencies and the value of the U.S. dollar.

The reasoning behind this exercise was that a stronger negative or even positive correlation between the U.S. dollar and dollar-priced commodities than that between the dollar and commodity prices based in other currencies would indicate that high U.S. dollar commodity prices were associated with a falling U.S. dollar and vice versa (and thus that U.S. dollar debt does not reduce, but instead accentuates, the volatility of home country earnings). By the same token, a much less negative correlation between the U.S. dollar and commodity prices expressed in a basket of currencies offers a more effective hedge than U.S. dollar debt.

The results of the analysis supported the conclusion that there is a strong inverse relationship between the U.S. dollar and commodity prices. For example, the

■ **TABLE 7.2A**

CORRELATION OF MONTHLY MOVEMENTS IN SDR/U.S. DOLLAR
EXCHANGE RATES AND COMMODITY PRICES

| Commodity | U.S. Dollar | | SDR | | SGW DM Basket | SGW Sfr. Basket |
	through 12/83	through 8/86	through 12/83	through 8/86	through 8/86	through 8/86
Gold (1973-86)	−0.233	−0.065	−0.101	0.117	0.076	0.140
Nickel (1976-86)	−0.398	−0.270	−0.371	0.236	0.129	0.300
Aluminum (1976-86)	−0.447	−0.317	−0.214	0.014	−0.065	0.059
Copper (1976-86)	−0.085	0.463	0.465	0.745	0.700	0.691
Silver (1973-86)	−0.356	−0.282	−0.267	−0.166	−0.196	−0.205

A correlation coefficient with an absolute value greater than or equal to 0.17 indicates a 95 percent probability that a relationship exists between the two variables.

correlation coefficient for nickel was −0.398 (which means, loosely speaking, that a 10% increase in the dollar was associated on average with a 4% decrease in the price of nickel). Unfortunately, however, the results also showed an almost equally strong negative correlation (−0.371) between nickel prices and the SDR. In short, the results appeared to suggest that neither funding in U.S. dollars nor in a basket of currencies provided an effective hedge against U.S. dollar-denominated currency revenues.

In the middle of 1986, we asked our bank to prepare a further study of our currency exposure and to make recommendations as to the appropriate currency management policy. The results of this statistical work (summarized in Tables 7.2A and 7.2B), although clearly confirming the earlier finding that U.S. dollar borrowings would accentuate rather than reduce the volatility of commodity revenues, nevertheless also provided only moderate support for funding in a basket of currencies rather than just U.S. dollars.

■ **TABLE 7.2**B

Commodity	Currency Denomination	Co-efficient of Variation (std. dev./mean)	
		through 12/83	through 8/86
Gold	U.S.	59.6	52.0
(1973-86)	SDR	57.7	50.4
	SGW DM basket	57.5	50.1
	SGW Sfr. basket	57.9	50.7
Nickel	U.S.	18.6	17.4
(1976-86)	SDR	16.6	16.5
	SGW DM basket	16.2	15.9
	SGW Sfr. basket	16.7	17.0
Aluminum	U.S.	30.7	27.3
(1976-86)	SDR	28.5	25.5
	SGW DM basket	28.7	25.4
	SGW Sfr. basket	29.1	26.1
Copper	U.S.	16.2	16.8
(1976-86)	SDR	18.3	22.3
	SGW DM basket	17.2	21.0
	SGW Sfr. basket	17.0	20.5
Silver	U.S.	77.0	71.8
(1973-86)	SDR	71.7	65.4
	SGW DM basket	73.2	67.1
	SGW Sfr. basket	73.1	67.1

PART

INTERNATIONAL INVESTMENT

8

CHAPTER

KEY CONCEPTS

DIRECT FOREIGN INVESTMENT AND ITS STATISTICAL MEASUREMENT ▬

CORPORATE MOTIVES FOR UNDERTAKING DIRECT FOREIGN INVESTMENT ▬

THE ECONOMIC THEORY RELATING TO DIRECT FOREIGN INVESTMENT ▬

THE CHOICE OF LICENSING OR EXPORTING AS AN ALTERNATIVE TO FOREIGN DIRECT INVESTMENT ▬

A CHECKLIST FOR MAKING THE FOREIGN INVESTMENT DECISION ▬

METHODS OF EVALUATING AND MANAGING THE RISKS CONNECTED WITH FOREIGN INVESTMENT ▬

INTRODUCTION

Why do firms establish foreign operations? There is a short, obvious answer: because they believe they are profitable. But behind that intuitive response stands a great deal of uncertainty about the factors that make foreign investment desirable. It is more difficult to manage a firm that operates in many countries than a firm that operates in only one country. The firm must master regulations and tax and employment policies and must become attuned to different cultures and ways of doing business. These differences make it inherently more difficult to manage foreign activity and place the multinational corporation (MNC) at a disadvantage relative to domestic competitors. To make foreign investment profitable, there must be offsetting factors that allow the multinational to compete. The development of the different theories of foreign investment represents attempts to identify those factors.

As will become apparent in the chapter, there is no definitive theory of what motivates foreign investment. The likely explanation is that foreign investment is largely in the domain of the class of firms that economists understand least: oligopolies and firms in monopolistically competitive markets. Economic theory has much to say about how firms behave in perfectly competitive markets or how a monopolist behaves. However, for the spectrum between the two extremes, there is no well-accepted theory. Because it is in that spectrum that we find most MNCs, a single, unifying theory of direct foreign investment has eluded researchers.

Not having a well-accepted theory about foreign investment is not an important problem for managers. They engage in foreign investment because they believe that it is important to their firms. The absence of a unifying theory means that there is no convenient framework for analyzing investment decisions. Understanding the motives for foreign investment requires an understanding of many potential incentives. Managers assessing a foreign investment opportunity need to analyze the whole array of potential benefits and compare them to the risks.

This chapter focuses on the strategic aspects of direct foreign investment. It is a wide-ranging and general discussion. Subsequent chapters will look at the narrower financial aspects of operating in foreign countries.

WHAT IS FOREIGN DIRECT INVESTMENT?

For statistical purposes, foreign direct investment (FDI) is usually considered ownership of 10 to 25 percent of the equity of a firm by a nonresident of the country in which the firm operates. The percentage varies, depending on the government or agency collecting the statistics, but there is general consensus that FDI is ownership with the intent to control. Portfolio investment, in contrast to FDI, is the ownership of foreign securities with neither the ability nor the desire to control the management of the assets that give the securities value. Once the issue focuses on control, the choice of a particular percentage of ownership to distinguish FDI from portfolio investment is relatively arbitrary. The discussion in this chapter is concerned with investment related to control.

Because much of what is written about FDI is in the context of its impact on developing countries and the strains that exist between the host countries and the firms, it is easy to assume that most FDI is made in developing countries. That is decidedly not so. Table 8.1 provides some general evidence about the flow of investment capital from 1981 to 1991. It documents that throughout the period, most FDI has been made in industrialized countries. More detailed statistics would reveal that the increase in investment in developing countries has been concentrated in a few nations. Brazil, Mexico, Hong Kong, Malaysia, the Philippines, and Singapore have been major recipients of FDI.

Investment flows increased dramatically through the 1980s and then declined even faster in 1991. Two factors contributed to this rapid growth. One is the rapid rate of economic growth in the latter half of the 1980s. The other is an increasingly liberal attitude toward investment on the part of host countries.[1] The increase in in-

---

[1] Organization for Economic Co-operation and Development, *OECD Economic Outlook*, December 1991.

■ TABLE 8.1

FOREIGN DIRECT INVESTMENT INWARD FLOWS BY REGION, 1981–1991
(MILLIONS OF U.S. DOLLARS)

Host Region	Average 1981–86	1987	1988	1989	1990	1991
Developed regions	$ 41,797	$109,455	$129,856	$167,504	$171,907	$107,793
Western Europe	17,402	41,482	60,489	88,250	108,822	84,065
North America	21,249	62,418	61,065	70,753	52,158	16,034
Other	3,145	5,555	8,302	8,502	10,927	7,964
Developing regions	13,270	25,303	30,204	28,644	31,345	38,768
Africa	1,709	2,344	2,795	4,814	2,085	2,514
Latin America and the Caribbean	5,759	10,950	11,451	8,326	9,950	15,235
Western Asia	418	255	690	447	494	794
East, south, and southeast Asia	5,230	11,636	15,025	14,774	18,454	19,967
Other	154	119	243	283	363	258
Central and Eastern Europe	18	12	15	11	89	1,793
Total	$110,151	$269,529	$320,135	$392,308	$406,594	$295,185

SOURCE: *World Investment Report*, 1993, United Nations.

vestment activity in Eastern and Central Europe reflects the major structural changes in those economies. As these countries become more market oriented, it is likely that they will attract increasing amounts of FDI. The decline in investment flows in 1991 demonstrates how sensitive the decision to invest is to economic slowdown, which occurred in 1991.

Statistics on FDI are not particularly good. Within the balance of payments statistics are measures for international capital flows. These statistics indicate the amount of new funds that have moved out of or into a country during a year, but those numbers do not adequately quantify the amount or importance of FDI. Firms have been making foreign investments for hundreds of years. As a result, aggregating recent annual flows gives only a partial measure of the stock or total amount of FDI in a nation. In many nations, the bulk of FDI occurred prior to the statistical record keeping. Countries track FDI flows using different definitions. The threshold level of ownership for measuring control that countries use ranges from 10 to 25 percent and countries categorize retained earnings differently. The latter difference is especially important because an increasing percentage of FDI has come in the form of reinvested earnings. Some countries do not treat these as additions to foreign investment and, hence, they understate the amount of FDI.

Another source of understatement is the use of book values to measure investment. When stock figures are compiled, they represent cumulative summations of annual flows. The market value of the original investment is likely much higher. For example, a foreign investor who acquired New York city real estate in the 1970s would now own assets worth much more than their book values as recorded in U.S. foreign direct investment statistics. More generally, most ongoing investments have a market value that exceeds the book value, so the use of book values is a cause of major distortions in FDI analysis.

Another problem with the statistics is that they measure equity holdings, which are a misleading measure of control. By using financial leverage and a holding company form of organization, a foreign entity can multiply its operating control far beyond its equity position. Real estate investments provide a good example.

Assume that a German firm invests £5,000,000 in a wholly owned British subsidiary and that subsidiary borrows £95,000,000 in London to purchase an office building. The value of the property controlled by the German firm is £100,000,000, yet the amount shown as FDI is only £5,000,000.

WHY OPERATE IN FOREIGN COUNTRIES?

For some firms, foreign operations are synonymous with being in business. International airlines, shipping companies, and worldwide hotel chains obviously must have facilities in many countries. The same is true in some sense for banks, insurance companies, and consulting firms that operate globally. In each of those industries, firms can choose to operate only domestically, but there are also market niches that require international operations. The decision to be in the international segment is a decision to be a foreign investor. That differs from the decision facing manufacturers because they can serve foreign markets through exports without the need for foreign investment.

The oldest multinationals went overseas primarily because they were established for that purpose. They operated in extractive resource industries or plantation industries. British companies invested in the United States, Canada, India, and countries in Africa because crops such as tobacco, cocoa, tea, and cotton grew there, not in England. Royal Dutch Petroleum grew and invested overseas to gain access to oil reserves. Similarly, other companies went overseas to find tin, gold, copper, bauxite, diamonds, and a host of other minerals. These early examples of FDI also tended to concentrate in the regional or colonial spheres of influence of the host country. U.S. firms tended to invest most heavily in Latin America. British companies invested in commonwealth nations and Japanese companies in Asia. There are still tendencies for countries to operate in familiar regions, but competition for markets and the demise of the colonial system have led firms to consider broader geographic areas.

The same two factors, an emphasis on markets and the elimination of colonies, as well as the rise of nationalist feelings about natural resources, led to a shift in FDI after World War II. Newly independent countries expropriated or nationalized resource related firms to establish local control over resources and reduce dependence on former imperial powers. Therefore, FDI in the manufacturing and service sectors grew relative to investment in the natural resource sector.

Nationalism played an important part in the shift, but changes in the capital markets facilitated implementation of nationalist policies. The development of the Eurocurrency market and the availability of bank loans to less developed countries allowed those countries to finance development projects and implement nationalistic policies without private foreign equity capital. As a result, many nations restricted FDI. Problems related to debt repayment in the 1980s have generated new more receptive policies toward FDI, but the poor economic environments in many developing countries have discouraged investment. The issues of restrictions and the role of FDI in the development process will be discussed in detail in later sections of this chapter and in Chapter 11. At this time, the main point is that a variety of political and economic factors influence the pattern of FDI.

A firm can follow many alternative paths to become an international company. Figure 8.1 illustrates a representative path. It shows a firm beginning as a purely domestic manufacturer and distributor, beginning to export, and then expanding its sales and support facilities to foreign countries. The final step is to manufacture the product in foreign countries for sales in those markets and possibly in the home market as well.

The initial motivation to export is the opportunity to earn extra profits by exporting relatively small volumes at prices high enough to cover the extra costs of transportation and foreign distribution. When foreign sales are large enough, it is economical to create a foreign sales office. This reduces travel and communication costs and allows for closer contacts with foreign customers. Close customer contact is especially important for products that require service after sale. A network of authorized dealers or repair facilities can address the need. For companies such as IBM, Hewlett Packard, Phillips, and Siemens, which extol their service and technical expertise, there is a perceived need to provide service directly. That means investing in service facilities in foreign countries.

The final step, manufacturing in a foreign country, is a less automatic step. Once foreign markets become an important part of a company's total sales, local manufacturing offers some advantages. It reduces transportation costs, generates goodwill by becoming a local employer, and facilitates modification of products to appeal to regional preferences.

The decision to manufacture in a foreign country, however, can have surprising results. For example, Volkswagen has had mixed experiences. Its operations in Brazil and Mexico have been extremely successful in terms of market share and profitability. The Mexican plant has continued to manufacture the Beetle, which is suitable for the Mexican market and to export it to other developing countries. On the other hand, the Volkswagen decision to manufacture its Golf (Rabbit) model in the United States was not successful. Aside from operating difficulties in its Pennsylvania facility, Volkswagen lost its reputation as a quality manufacturer

■ FIGURE 8.1

A PATH TO FOREIGN INVESTMENT

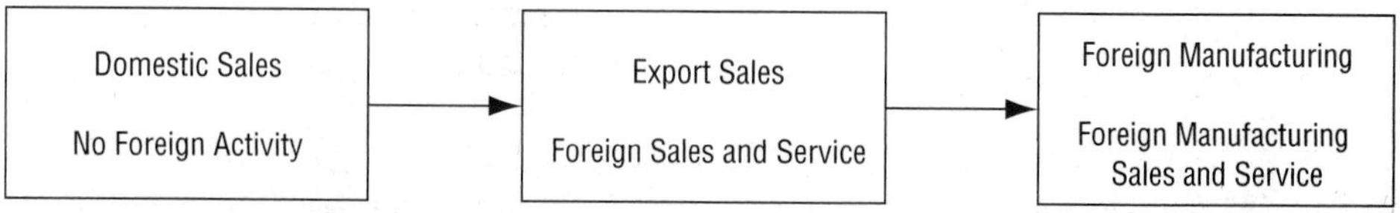

Domestic Sales No Foreign Activity	→	Export Sales Foreign Sales and Service	→	Foreign Manufacturing Foreign Manufacturing Sales and Service

■ FIGURE 8.2

VERNON'S PRODUCT LIFE CYCLE

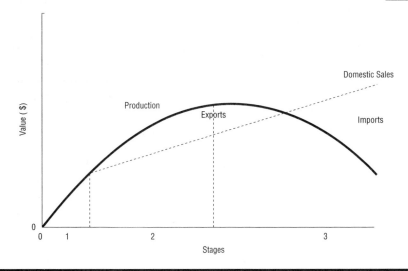

with its U.S.–produced cars. Consumers perceived the U.S.–made cars as inferior to the German–made cars. Volkswagen's sales and profits plummeted.

Ray Vernon has proposed a theory of foreign investment that is consistent with the general scenario described in the text and illustrated in Figure 8.1.[2] His is the *product life cycle theory* of foreign investment that focuses on the stages that individual products go through from initial development to market maturity. Vernon's product life cycle theory is usually represented by a graph such as the one in Figure 8.2.

The initial stage of the cycle involves product innovation and market development. There is a great deal of uncertainty about both the design and manufacturing of the product as well as its reception in the market place. During this stage, innovation and flexibility play important roles. Good communication is necessary within the firm and between the firm and the market to respond to problems of design, performance, or service during the process of bringing the product to market. Because the extent of the market is unknown and there is little immediate competition, the firm emphasizes domestic sales. The initial product stage emphasizes local production and sales. Exports are zero or insignificant. Exports become important in the second stage.

Once manufacturing goes beyond the innovation and introduction stage and there is domestic market acceptance, the firm expands its sales horizons to include foreign markets. Part of the reason is the firm's need to sustain growth as the do-

[2] Raymond Vernon, "International Investment and International Trade in the Product Cycle," *Quarterly Journal of Economics*, February 1967.

mestic market becomes saturated. Because market success attracts competitors, there is additional pressure to seek new markets. Export markets represent an additional opportunity. For many products, it is important to increase production and sales volume to achieve economies. Export sales provide the advantage of larger volume. Early penetration of export markets can also preempt the development of foreign competitors. In this second stage, initial foreign investment occurs in order to provide the sales support needed for exports.

In the third stage, the firm makes larger foreign investment. This stage begins when product standardization allows for dispersed manufacturing, and this may permit the use of lower-cost labor inputs. Manufacturing no longer needs to take place near engineering and product development staffs. The movement of electronic and related consumer products manufacturing from the United States and Japan to South Korea, Malaysia, Singapore, and Taiwan is consistent with this third stage of the product cycle. Some varieties of semiconductors have moved through the product cycle extremely rapidly. In a period of a few years, they have progressed from being produced by the most sophisticated electronics companies in developed countries to widespread manufacturing by relatively small firms using semiskilled labor and borrowed technology.

The original manufacturing locations and processes may become noncompetitive in this third stage. The foreign manufacturing facilities may begin to supply the home market, converting it from an exporter to an importer. The developers of the product still control it, but its manufacture takes place in other countries. In the final stage, when the profit margins have become very slim, the technology-intensive firms might abandon the product entirely. Competition eliminates the return to technology and replaces it with normal economic profits. For the technologically innovative firms, the lower level of profits is not attractive. They want to use their resources and competitive advantages to reap the higher profits consistent with the first two stages.

Not every manufacturing-related foreign investment follows the product life cycle pattern but enough do to make it an important theory. An understanding of the theory provides useful insights for the people responsible for a firm's strategic planning. It indicates when in a product's life the manufacturer should be looking to export, when to shift production, and when to leave the market to others.

The product life cycle theory provides more understanding of investment from industrial to developing countries than it does for investment between industrial countries. Although product standardization and market expansion might make foreign investment more attractive, it is unlikely that U.S. firms will invest in Europe, or European firms in the United States, to benefit from reduced costs. Manufacturing inputs are close enough in costs in the industrialized countries to be offset by the disadvantages of foreign production. Other reasons explain investment flows between industrialized countries.

INVESTING IN INDUSTRIALIZED COUNTRIES

Industrialized countries are less likely to offer the attraction of natural resources or lower labor costs to foreign investors. Moreover, they are more likely to have domestic firms in the same industry. Japanese automobile firms investing in the United States must compete against General Motors, Ford, and Chrysler. IBM must compete against Olivetti in Italy, Nixdorf in Germany, and Hitachi, among others, in Japan. In fact, it is difficult to name an industry in which foreign firms do not find at least one major domestic competitor in the larger industrial countries. So why is there FDI between these countries?

Several studies have examined why non–U.S. firms established operations in the United States. Ajami and Ricks[3] used survey results to rank the motives of firms investing in the United States during the period 1974 to 1978. Table 8.2 lists the 25 most frequently cited motives in order of their importance indicated by the survey response. In addition, the motives have been placed in categories to provide a better overview of the investment decision.

The categories have been selected according to the driving factor behind the particular motive or response. Those motives that relate to sales, growth, or markets are grouped as market driven. Firms are either seeking new markets or responding to competition and trying to protect existing markets. The environmental category includes items that reflect the general political, legal, and economic climate in the United States and the home country. Attitudes toward investment, the level of regulation, and the relative safety of capital are included in the environmental classification. Technology/resource motives include those responses dealing with either inputs such as labor or managerial know-how and the availability of technology. Financial factors include incentives, exchange rate considerations, and the functioning of the capital markets. The final category, risk-related motives, relates to the benefits of diversification in the strategic sense of reducing reliance on limited markets, governments, or suppliers.

Clearly, the most frequently stated motives are market oriented. Following that group are technology/resource and environmental inducements. From the standpoint of a country that wants to increase foreign investment, one implication of the survey results is not good. Hard-to-influence factors such as population size and income levels are the key features that attract FDI. Those features determine the size and quality of the market. Technology and a generally favorable business climate are also important but less so.

FDI has been concentrated among the industrial countries and a few less-developed countries. Those less-developed countries have either been technology- or resource-rich countries or countries with attractive markets such as Mexico, Brazil, and Indonesia. The intense interest that so many firms have shown in China is additional evidence of the importance of markets. Although China is currently a relatively poor country, the prospect of one billion consumers has been enough to offset the frustrating and difficult task of doing business in China. Firms believe that by investing early, they will reap large benefits from being able to sell in the world's most populated shopping center.

More recent FDI in the United States has also been market oriented. All of the major Japanese automobile makers, Toyota, Nissan, Mazda, and Honda, have in-

---

[3] Riad Ajami and David Ricks, *Motives for Non-American Firms investing in the United States* (Columbus: Ohio State University, 1980).

■ **TABLE 8.2**

Rank	Category	Motive	Average Importance
1	A	Extremely large U.S. market	1.84
2	A	General need for growth	2.15
3	A	Search for new markets	2.17
4	B	Attractive political climate	2.41
5	A	Desire to preserve markets that were established by exporting	2.46
6	B	Attractive U.S. attitude toward foreign investment	2.48
7	D	General desire for higher profits	2.81
8	C	Desire to acquire technologies	2.84
9	E	Desire for geographic dispersion as a means to spread risks	3.10
10	C	Desire to compete abroad by employing technological, managerial, or financial advantages	3.25
11	C	U.S. managerial and marketing know-how and innovations	3.33
12	C	Attractive U.S. technology	3.41
13	C	Traditional U.S. receptivity to new products, methods, and ideas	3.48
14	E	Fear of further investments at home because of political unrest	3.53
15	B	Comparatively low U.S. government control over business	3.64
16	E	Direct investments may be the only way to surmount risks	3.78
17	C	Skill and efficiency of U.S. labor force	3.89
18	D	Desire to enjoy local incentives	3.94
19	D	Declining value of the U.S. dollar	4.00
20	D	Attractive U.S. capital markets	4.12
21	C	Attractive U.S. supplies of important natural resources	4.23
22	E	Desire to hold land or other foreign assets as a hedge against domestic inflation or as a store of value	4.30
23	E	Desire to reduce dependence on other firms	4.33
24	A	Need to be closer to customers to provide better service	4.43
25	C	Need to ensure supplies of resources	4.56
	A	Markets	
	B	Environmental	
	C	Technology/Resource	
	D	Financial	
	E	Risk	

vested in plants in the United States. The key reason for this foreign investment appears to be quotas on imported cars and the threat of future restrictions.

ADVANTAGES OF THE MULTINATIONAL CORPORATION

Most FDI is made by firms that operate in industries characterized by imperfect competition. Within those industries, firms prosper by differentiating their service or product or based on proprietary expertise. They often hold patents and copyrights that protect them from competition. These features offset the disadvantages of operating in foreign countries. Industries in which either intangible product or management skills are important or in which barriers to entry are possible are prime candidates for FDI.

One way to differentiate a product is through intensive marketing. Examples of such products marketed internationally by multinational corporations include over-the-counter drugs, household products, premium clothing, and toiletries. Burroughs-Wellcome and Glaxo are large British pharmaceutical firms that operate worldwide. Hoffman-La Roche, a Swiss firm, and Schering-Plough, a U.S. firm, are other multinational pharmaceutical companies. They benefit from patent protection, which allows them to exploit their proprietary knowledge. Coke and Pepsi, Procter & Gamble, Unilever, Richardson Vicks are also companies with long traditions of foreign investment. Their products are generally not very different from the competition, but they are canny, sophisticated marketers who have been able to differentiate their brands in the minds of the public, and that allows them to charge higher prices to offset the added costs of doing business abroad.

Other industries, such as textiles and steel, have not been able to differentiate their products or to develop proprietary knowledge that would create competitive advantages. Firms in these industries do not tend to invest internationally, even though they might be very large companies. For the most part, they deal in standardized products for which price considerations are paramount. The technology they use is widely available and relatively easy to duplicate. As a result, many countries have domestic steel and textile industries that compete in local and export markets on the basis of price. Firms trying to operate in a foreign environment would be unable to overcome the foreign handicap.

Retailing is another industry that has not, to date, seen much FDI, although that is beginning to change. A number of very successful U.S. companies, such as Toys R Us and Wal-Mart, are investing internationally. The major exception has been at the very high-priced specialty stores that sell their own private label merchandise. Even a spectacularly successful company such as the Italian firm, Benetton, which has stores throughout the world, has expanded through franchising, not FDI. The stores are almost all privately owned and stock the Benetton merchandise the owners consider suitable for their location. In retailing, knowledge of the domestic market has outweighed any benefits that might be associated with a well-known store name. That might be the reason that a famous company such as Harrods of London has not tried to open in New York or Toronto.

A Checklist to Follow in Making FDI Decisions

The decision to invest in foreign countries is, more than anything else, a strategic decision. It presents a different and more difficult management challenge than the firm confronts in its domestic market. It is imperative that a firm assess its preparedness and ability to compete internationally. Failure to conduct a thorough analysis of the firm's competitive position, including its marketing capability, its personnel, its technological strengths, and its financial capacity, will jeopardize the venture. The firm's foreign investment strategy must be consistent with its own strengths and weaknesses?

■ TABLE 8.3

INVESTING IN FOREIGN OPERATIONS: A CHECKLIST FOR MAKING THE FDI DECISION

Eliminating

1	Current domestic operational problems preclude diluting management attention.
2	Domestic operation has essentially nontransferable expertise.

Limiting

3	The firm has no unique technology or marketing skills.
4	Domestic technical standards differ significantly from global standards.
5	Most major global markets are dominated by competitors.

Positive

6	The firm has a record of divisional success.
7	A technological comparative advantage exists now or is forthcoming.
8	The firm has a track record of marketing success.
9	The firm has a strong domestic market position.
10	Real global market growth is higher than 5%.
11	There are emerging international markets.
12	Real domestic market growth is higher than 10%.
13	The firm is an accepted domestic market leader.

Compelling

.14	Competitors sourcing abroad and tying up supplies of necessary components threaten the domestic market position.
15	Domestic markets are threatened by competitive expansion.
16	Export markets served by domestic production are threatened by trade barriers.

SOURCE: *Multinational Management*, 1982.

David Ruttenberg[4] has developed a checklist that identifies the major areas a firm should consider when deciding to invest internationally (see Table 8.3). He has also categorized the items on the list according to whether they enhance or diminish the option to go into foreign markets. The four categories are eliminating, limiting, positive, and compelling. A strong negative assessment in an eliminating category item militates against investing. Strong positive evaluations of the compelling category items support investing.

The problem, of course, is that the signals received from the checklist are often contradictory. It is possible, for instance, that a firm facing an aggressive expansion into its domestic market (a compelling circumstance) might also have current domestic operational problems that preclude diluting management attention (an eliminating condition). When the analysis is not clear cut, the firm must weigh carefully the information and examine carefully all of its options to investing internationally, including licensing, or exporting.

---

[4] David Ruttenberg, *Multinational Management*, (Boston, Mass: Little Brown, 1982).

RECOGNIZING THE RISKS OF FOREIGN INVESTMENT

Foreign investment is generally riskier than domestic investment. Most firms believe that capital invested in other countries is subject to greater risks from potential expropriation and capital or exchange rate restrictions. Such restrictions occur most frequently when countries change governments or when economic conditions such as a recession or balance of payments difficulties generate changes in policies. Because the most dramatic and frequent changes of government and policies take place in less developed countries, those countries are perceived as being riskier than countries with mature industrialized economies and having relatively stable political systems. Less developed countries also have the most volatile economies, so economic polices are the most volatile.

It is important, however, to realize that generalizations about government and economic stability mask exceptions. Italy has a mature industrial economy but has had more changes of government since World War II than most Latin American countries. Even with their stable democracies and mature economies, England and France experience dramatic changes in economic policies and in their governments' attitudes toward capital when power shifts between parties. When she was elected Prime Minister, Mrs. Thatcher denationalized or privatized great chunks of the British economy. Her government also deregulated financial institutions and removed foreign exchange restrictions that had been in place for years. Yet a return of the Labor party to power might lead to renationalizations and more stringent regulations. In France, the socialist government surprised most people by reducing the state influence in the French economy. That trend was extended by the conservative policies of Jacques Chirac, who became prime minister in 1986. The point to remember is that change occurs and that firms must monitor the political and economic environment of the countries in which they operate. Part of the added cost and complexity of doing business abroad is the expense of gathering and analyzing information.

EVALUATING AND MANAGING RISK

Identifying, estimating, and adjusting for risk are major aspects of the foreign investment evaluation process. Ignoring risk in making capital budgeting decisions leads to suboptimal allocations of capital, so it is important to consider risk. Managers can reduce risk through the decisions they make in planning and managing an investment. The keys to reducing risk are monitoring information, anticipating policy, and adapting to change.

Monitoring information involves establishing an intelligence network that provides political, social, and economic information pertaining to events in the host country. For large firms with extensive worldwide investment, such as the major petroleum companies, the intelligence-gathering process can be almost entirely in-house. The same is true for multinational banks with extensive branch systems. Area or divisional personnel can be assigned the primary responsibility for collecting information and forwarding it to headquarters for evaluation.

Many large companies now have staff economists and political scientists who assess country risk. Although these staff people are important in the monitoring process, their analysis should be used in conjunction with evaluations of line personnel who are stationed in the country. Relying solely on either staff or line personnel can provide biased analysis. Staff evaluations tend to be more objective, but because they are done at a distance from a country, they often ignore insights that can be gained only by extensive experience living in an area. Line personnel have that experience but are often unwilling to recognize or admit negative aspects about their own nation or the country for which they have managerial responsibility, in part because negative information might adversely affect their own activities. For example, bank calling officers or branch managers are the appropriate line personnel to provide country information, but their personal interest is in expanding loans or the sale of other bank services. This basic conflict often introduces a bias into the information-gathering process.

Small firms do not generally have the resources to develop their own information networks. Instead, they rely on information purchased from firms organized for that purpose. Even if the company's primary information sources are external, it should still establish an internal monitoring system as a secondary source. Area personnel should file informal country evaluations and headquarters staff should visit the country on a regular basis. Their assessments should be matched against those of the external source to check for consistency and accuracy. A firm should not become too dependent on a single source or too complacent to change to another advisory service if its current one is missing many trends or changes.

Managers should evaluate the information to anticipate governmental policy changes and attitudinal changes in the host country. Some changes affect the general operating environment of the firm whereas others have a direct impact on the operating or ownership structure of the firm.

Environmental changes can be both general and specific. Among the former are macroeconomic policies that attempt to stimulate or restrict economic activity. For example, countries with accelerating inflation or difficulty servicing external obligations are likely to pursue restrictive monetary and fiscal policies. The effect of these policies is a reduction of sales in the host country. Other changes related to macroeconomic policy are the imposition of price and wage controls or currency restrictions. If management anticipates the policies, it can take steps to reduce their impact: It might raise prices prior to the imposition of price controls or make foreign currency payments before the local currency becomes inconvertible.

A firm might pursue other longer-term policies to reduce risk. Labor unrest in the form of strikes varies in severity from country to country. Where strikes are frequent, a firm might choose less labor-intensive technology or adopt employment policies that reduce the threat of strikes. For example, a large U.S. electronics firm with major manufacturing facilities in Great Britain has a totally nonunion labor force in that highly unionized country. It has been able to maintain that status by having generous benefits and an open employee-management relationship. These policies entail some added costs but reduce the risk of labor strife. The company has not lost manufacturing time due to strikes and has added flexibility to establishing its seniority and compensation system.

Specific policies that arise from concerns about the economic environment can directly affect a firm's operating structure. Examples include requirements concerning the value of local content in manufacturing, domestic nationals in management positions, pricing to subsidize local consumption, and investment in infrastructure. Likewise, regulations that affect transfer pricing or establish restrictions on licensing arrangements and royalty payments affect a firm's operating structure.

The final type of investment risk involves government interference with the ownership of the investment. Governments can seize the wealth of foreign investors in numerous ways including punitive taxes, required partnership with local firms, nationalization with some compensation and outright expropriation. Regardless of the form it takes, it is unlikely that any involuntary change in ownership structure benefits the original investors. If it did, it would not be involuntary. Often, significant economic or political events precede increased interference or changes in attitudes toward foreign investment. This makes the monitoring information and anticipating policy changes worthwhile: They allow a firm to reduce its exposure while there is still time to maneuver.

Adapting to change is essential. Firms must adjust their polices and practices in response to changes in the legal, political, social, and economic environments. Sometimes those adjustments are undesirable on other grounds but necessary in order to reduce risk related to investing in foreign countries. Entering into a *joint venture* with a foreign partner is an important example.

Joint ventures represent shared ownership and control of operating entities by two or more independent firms or groups of investors. It has been common for less developed countries to require foreign firms to invest through a joint venture with a domestic partner. This requirement arises from a sense of nationalism, a desire that some of the returns on capital investment be retained in the host country, and a desire to have local companies gain experience in partnership with foreign companies. At other times, firms voluntarily seek out joint venture relationships because it is to their advantage to do so. For example, one firm may have capital or an established distribution network and its partner may have special technological skills or a brand name. The joint venture activity in the U.S. automobile market represents one example of matching contributions: American Motors Corporation had a dealer network, and Renault had a car design it wanted to introduce to the United States. In another example, Toyota brought its small car technology to a joint venture with General Motors Corporation, which had a strong market position.

Despite some major exceptions, survey research has indicated that the majority of U.S. firms oppose joint ventures, especially with local partners. The reasons relate to control. The local partner acquires access to technology and pricing information that might make it a formidable competitor at some future date. Differences in objectives might lead to disputes over dividend policies, transfer pricing, financial structure decisions, licensing agreements, and efforts by the foreign partner to rationalize production among its worldwide subsidiaries.

The advantages of joint ventures include access to markets that might otherwise be unavailable and a reduction in the probability of government interference directed toward foreign investors. Having local nationals involved in ownership and management may deflect criticisms aimed at foreign investors.

The choice of a local partner is important. Under the best of circumstances, the local partner brings to the enterprise skills or attributes other than a convenient nationality. If nationality is in fact the only contribution, the foreign investor should try to find a partner that is reliable and in the mainstream of local politics.

Finally, there is a classic method for managing the risk of foreign investment—insurance. A number of developed nations, including the United States, have governmental or quasigovernmental programs for insuring foreign investment against the risk of war, expropriation, or currency inconvertibility. There is also a private insurance market organized through the auspices of Lloyd's of London. In the United States, the Overseas Private Investment Corporation (OPIC) provides insurance for U.S. private investments in less developed countries and project financing. Its fees vary, depending on the type of coverage and, to some extent, on the risk related to the investment. OPIC has been very successful at marketing its programs, and the majority of nonpetroleum investments in less developed countries have some form of OPIC coverage.

The decision to buy OPIC insurance must be made along the lines of risk management decisions in general. Firms need to weigh the costs against expected losses and their willingness and ability to bear those losses. Buying OPIC coverage might create a moral hazard situation for firms. Having protection could lead firms to ignore other risk-reduction policies and contribute to a higher incidence of loss. Ultimately, this results in higher premiums or a decline in insurability. Because settlements under OPIC are usually the result of a long negotiating process, firms should avoid the attitude of "Why worry? We're insured."

Finally, investors should not associate political risk only with investments in less developed countries. Each of the types of risk discussed in this section are or have been present in almost every nation. Certainly, the environmental factors are omnipresent, and attitudes toward foreign investment change over time in developed countries. The investor might have recourse under the law in those nations, but the interference in business operations and the loss of wealth are real possibilities that must be considered in making investments.

IMPLICATIONS FOR MANAGERS

When a firm makes the decision to invest overseas, it needs to have a clear understanding of why it is doing so. Overseas operations are more difficult to manage than domestic ones. Differences in laws, tax policies, languages, culture, and local competition must be overcome in order to be successful. None of that is easy or costless. Managers need to estimate those costs and determine what advantages their firms have to offset them.

In many cases, the answer lies with the competitive advantages of the firm. It might have proprietary technology, protected trademarks, or market power by virtue of the firm's size relative to its competitors. The key task for the manager is to understand what her firm has that will overcome the inherent disadvantages of investing overseas. With that understanding in mind, the firm can determine whether overseas expansion is desirable. The 16-point checklist in this chapter can be utilized to determine if the time is right or if another route to achieving foreign sales should be followed.

QUESTONS AND EXERCISES

8-1. During the 1980s, balance of payments statistics indicated that the United States had become a net debtor internationally. What does that mean and do you think that it accurately reflects the economic position of the United States vis-à-vis the rest of the world?

8-2. Many countries have imposed restrictions of foreign direct investment. Mexico has done it in the petroleum industry, the United States in broadcasting and defense industries, and Brazil in computers and related technology. What are the arguments to support such policies and what are the economic effects?

8-3. Using the checklist in Table 8.3, choose an industry or company that you are familiar with and determine whether foreign investing is desirable. If you cannot think of one, use Disney and its decision to invest in Europe, BMW and its decision to invest in the United States, or McDonald's decision to invest in Russia.

REFERENCES

Ajami, Riad, and David Ricks. *Motives for Non-American Firms investing in the United States.* Columbus: Ohio State University, 1980.

Organization for Economic Co-operation and Development. *OECD Economic Outlook,* December 1991.

Ruttenberg, David. *Multinational Management,* Boston, Mass.: Little Brown, 1982.

Vernon, Raymond. "International Investment and International Trade in the Product Cycle." *Quarterly Journal of Economics,* February 1967.

INTERNATIONAL PAPER:
THE AUSSEDAT-REY ACQUISITION

> If these takeovers continue like this, there will not be a single French company left which is capable of resisting the weight of money from overseas.... These companies can count on me to put in place a system which will prevent the ruin of the French economy [and] prevent its pillage, especially within the Europe of 1993.
>
> President Francois Mitterrand,
> during a nationally televised
> interview, February 12, 1989[1]

Although the international business community anticipated that Mitterrand would respond to the spate of foreign takeovers in France, the timing and pugnacity of his comments were nonetheless unsettling to International Paper's (IP) senior management. IP had one month earlier, on January 17, announced its bid of 675 French francs (FR) per share for Aussedat-Rey (AR), France's second largest paper company, but the transaction remained under French government review. The tone of the president's comments threatened IP's bid by suggesting possible government intervention. Mitterrand possessed the authority to block the purchase on the grounds of national self-interest, and even if the government approved IP's bid, comments in the French press and the delay in government approval indicated that the deal might be in jeopardy. Rumors abounded that a French or European consortium was contemplating a counteroffer for AR. Mitterrand's implicit suggestion of support for a "French Solution" would only encourage other bidders.

Short on cash and in need of substantial capital investments to remain competitive, AR had approached IP in November 1988 with the idea of a strategic partnership. As the world's largest paper company, IP possessed the financial resources to support AR's investment strategy. In return, AR would provide IP with a strong presence in Europe, which was particularly appealing in light of apprehensions that a "Fortress Europe" might arise from the European Community in 1992. Furthermore, IP management saw potential synergies from the acquisition in manufacturing, distribution, and personnel.

IP managers now wondered what actions, other than increasing the price, they could take to promote the success of their bid. If forced to raise the price, to what level could IP go while still providing an adequate return for its shareholders?

THE U.S. PAPER INDUSTRY IN THE 1980S

U.S. paper manufacturers experienced a period of unprecedented change in the 1980s as a wave of consolidation swept the industry. At the beginning of the

---

[1] "Mitterrand Attacks "Predatory Money," *The International Hearld Tribune,* February 12, 1989.

■ EXHIBIT 8.1A

INTERNATIONAL PAPER
■ SELECTED FINANCIAL DATA ON THE TEN LARGEST PAPER COMPANIES
IN THE UNITED STATES FOR FISCAL YEAR 1988
(IN MILLIONS OF U.S. DOLLARS)

	Sales	Net Income	Debt/ Equity	Average Price/ Earnings	Beta
Weyerhaeuser	$10,004*	$565	1.04	9.5	1.25
International Paper	9,533	754	.38	6.7	1.25
Georgia-Pacific	9,509	467	.95	7.0	1.25
James River	5,872	255	.82	9.3	1.25
Champion International	5,129	457	.57	7.2	1.25
Scott Paper	4,726	308	.72	9.3	1.10
Mead Corp.	4,463	240	.59	10.5	1.40
Boise Cascade	4,095	289	.55	7.1	1.25
Stone Container	3,743	325	.72	5.7	1.65
Union Camp	2,661	295	.40	8.1	1.25

*Although Weyerhaeuser eclipsed IP in total revenues, a larger proportion of IP's sales were paper related.

SOURCE: *Value Line*, October 27, 1989.

decade, the 10 largest companies accounted for 53 percent of total U.S. paper production. By the end of 1988, the five largest companies accounted for roughly the
same amount.[2] The large integrated companies listed in Exhibit 8.1A dominated the
commodity markets in newsprint, reprographic (photocopy), and uncoated printing paper. Smaller, usually nonintegrated, specialty companies occupied the low-
volume niche markets in fine writing, fancy coated, and single-use papers.[3]

To a large degree, the trend toward consolidation was symptomatic of the
unique economics of the paper industry. Paper manufacturers, unable to differentiate their commodity grades significantly, pursued competitive advantages
through investments in equipment and processes to increase productivity and
lower costs. Investments in the paper industry, whether for new machines or up-
grades, were made in large amounts and on single projects. Costs for a new mill
ranged from $30 million for a small specialty mill to $1 billion for a large integrated
mill. Such investments were beyond the means of most moderately sized companies, but by combining their operations, paper companies acquired the financial
resources to support the high capital expenditures.

The integrated producers' efforts to diversify their earnings streams also contributed to industry consolidation. Compared with commodity grades of paper,

[2] Unless noted otherwise, information is from International Paper.

[3] Integrated paper companies produced 100 percent of their pulp needs. Many also sold pulp on the
open market to nonintegrated mills.

specialty papers provided relatively high margins and less sensitivity to general economic activity. Because the commodity producers could not readily adapt their large machines to produce specialty grades economically, these companies entered specialty markets through acquisitions.

In addition to increased scale, consolidation led to forward integration in the industry. Through acquisitions, large producers acquired not only additional capacity but also the acquired companies' captive "merchants" (distributors). In many cases, these newly acquired distribution channels provided the integrated producers with access to previously untapped markets. The role of merchants was expected to become increasingly important in the 1990s because of the high growth rates of merchant products such as reprographic and commercial printing papers.

In the United States, demand for printing and writing papers was growing at rates exceeding the rise in real gross national product. This trend resulted largely from office automation and the rise of the service economy. Industry forecasts expected total U.S. consumption (in tons) of printing and writing paper to increase 4 to 5 percent per year between 1986 and 1991, with certain grades showing much greater growth. Business papers (reprographic and writing), for example, were projected to grow at an annual rate of 7 percent over the period.[4] Within this sector, demand for reprographic paper was expected to increase 6 to 8 percent a year through 1991.

Paper prices fluctuated considerably in the short run; during 1988, certain grades of paper experienced price changes exceeding 14 percent.[5] Despite this volatility, industry analysts predicted that average paper prices would deteriorate 1.1 percent per year in the long term because of competitive pressures and falling production costs.

A vast majority of U.S. manufacturers' sales and profits were made domestically. The only appreciable U.S. paper-related exports were pulp, packaging, and wood products. Approximately 12 percent of U.S. purchases of writing and printing paper was imported.[6]

THE EUROPEAN PAPER INDUSTRY[7]

In many respects, the European paper industry was similar to its U.S. counterpart. A number of large producers dominated the commodity markets of the industry, while smaller specialty producers occupied niches. Unlike those in the Unites States, few European companies were fully integrated. In 1988, Europe imported approximately 60 percent of its pulp needs. In order of importance, Europe's major pulp suppliers were Scandinavia, Canada, Brazil, and the United States.

---

[4] James Y. Bryce, "The Paper Revolution: Not Over by a Long Shot," *Office*, April 1988, 68–72.

[5] American Paper Institute, "Annual Statistical Summary, 1988," August 1989, 33.

[6] Ibid, 57–58, 8.

[7] *European* refers to the 12-nation European Economic Community (EEC). Scandinavia is treated as a separate region.

■ **EXHIBIT 8.1B**

INTERNATIONAL PAPER
■ EUROPEAN AND SCANDINAVIAN PAPER COMPANINES IN 1987
(SALES IN MILLION OF U.S. DOLLARS)

Company	Country	Sales	World Rank 1988	World Rank 1987
MoDo	Sweden	$3,188	12	41
Stora	Sweden	2,976	13	12
Svenska Cellulosa	Sweden	2,726	15	20
Jefferson Smurfit	Ireland	2,369	18	18
Feldmuhle	West Germany	2,035	24	21
PWA	West Germany	1,949	26	25
Wiggins Teape	United Kingdom	1,828	28	23
Kymenne	Finland	1,798	30	32
Enzo-Gutzeit	Finland	1,690	31	31
Arjomari-Prioux	France	1,386	39	46

SOURCE: *Pulp and Paper International*, September 1989.

In addition to a lack of integration, the European paper industry differed from the U.S. industry in scale. Eight of the 10 largest paper companies in the world were American. As Exhibit 8.1B shows, the largest European company, Jefferson Smurfit, ranked 18th globally. A greater proportion of European companies were also private or closely held public corporations. In many instances, banks were major shareholders. Also, European manufacturers had traditionally controlled the merchants, a situation that had only recently developed in the United States.

European paper makers were running near or at capacity because of rising consumption. In 1988, European demand (in tons) for paper and paperboard increased 6.9 percent, as opposed to global growth of 3 to 4 percent.[8] In France, demand increased 8.2 percent. Within the French market, consumption of reprographic paper increased 10 percent in 1988.[9] Europe was generally acknowledged to trail the United States in office automation by approximately five years. Consequently, much of the demand growth experienced in the United States during the recent past had not yet occurred in Europe. A corollary to this situation was the disparity in per capita paper consumption among various countries in 1988: France used 140 kilos, while West Germany used 190, the Scandinavian countries used 220, and the United States used 300.[10] In light of the European movement toward office automation and the continent's relatively low per capita consumption,

---

[8] "Costs Are Still Too High," *Logistique Magazine*, April 21, 1989.

[9] Aussedat-Rey annual report, 1988.

[10] "A Solid Timber Sector," *Le Monde*, March 14, 1989.

most forecasts projected that European, and particularly French, growth in the consumption of business papers between 1986 and 1991 would exceed that of the United States.

Although the total European market for paper was only half that of the United States, the continent was very attractive to paper manufacturers. Scandinavian companies were moving aggressively to tighten their strong hold on the commodity markets by acquiring European companies. European producers of specialty papers were also actively seeking takeover or merger candidates. The consolidations were for the same reason as in America—to achieve a mass sufficient to support the large investment necessary to compete in an increasingly global market place. As Bo Wergens, president of the Swedish Association of Pulp and Paper Manufacturers, commented:

> In the future our biggest competitors in Europe will be the Americans. With the profit they are raking in at the moment, thanks to the excellent economic climate of the industry, American paper companies will take over considerable parts of the [European] market bit by bit. The only solution for us is to invest more and more and to buy European companies before they do.[11]

INTERNATIONAL PAPER

With sales of $9.5 billion, IP was the largest paper company in the world (see Exhibit 8.1c for selected financial data). The company operated 28 pulp and paper mills producing 7.7 million tons of paper, or slightly over 13 percent of total U.S. production. IP sold a million tons of pulp on the open market. It also operated 78 packaging plants, 5 envelope companies, and 25 merchants with over 140 distribution centers. With 7 million acres of timberland, the company was the largest private landowner in the United States.

Traditionally, IP had operated in all the major markets of the paper industry. In 1984, however, management altered strategy to target growth markets, reduce costs in commodity businesses, and exploit brand recognition and distribution relationships to expand the value-added market segments. Various businesses were sold (newsprint, oil, and gas), and resources were reallocated to major sectors: Pulp and Paper, Paperboard and Packaging, Distribution, Timber and Wood Products, and Specialty Products.

IP's paper operations were concentrated in various commodity grades of coated and uncoated papers. Coated papers were used for magazines, catalogs, direct-mail advertisements, and newspaper inserts. Uncoated papers were used for writing, photocopying, printing, and converting (forms and envelopes).

In 1986, IP acquired the Hammermill Paper Company for $1.1 billion, which strengthened IP's market position in the fast-growing business papers market.

---

[11] "The Home Stretch for Aussedat-Rey," *Le Journal des Finances*, March 11, 1989.

■ EXHIBIT 8.1c

INTERNATIONAL PAPER
■ BALANCE SHEETS AND INCOME STATEMENTS
AS OF DECEMBER 31, 1988
(IN MILLIONS EXCEPT SHARE DATA)

	1988	1987
Assets		
Current assets		
Cash & investments	$ 122	$ 233
Accts & notes rec.	1,153	998
Inventories	971	852
Other current assets	97	80
Total current assets	$2,343	$2,163
Property, plant, & equipment (net)	$5,456	$5,124
Timberlands	772	780
Investments	88	109
Goodwill	304	170
Deferred charges & other assets	499	363
Total assets	$9,462	$8,710
Liabilities and Shareholders' Equity		
Current liabilities		
Notes payable & current maturities of long-term debt	$ 252	$ 495
Accounts payable	672	542
Accrued payroll	138	149
Accrued income tax	128	58
Other accrued liabilities	372	262
Total current liabilities	$1,562	$1,506
Long-term debt	$1,853	$1,937
Deferred income tax	892	684
Minority int. & other	276	209
Preferred stock	322	322
Common stock ($1 par value; issued 1988, 116.7MM shares; 1987, 116.5MM shares)	117	116
Paid-in capital	1,149	1,128
Retained earnings	3,482	2,933
Treasury stock (1988, 6.0MM shares; 1987, 5.0MM shares)	191	125
Total shareholders' equity	$4,557	$4,052
Total liabilities & shareholders' equity	$9,462	$8,710

continued on next page

Following the Hammermill purchase, IP assumed market leadership in reprographic paper. One of every four sheets of paper used in a copy machine in the United States was estimated to be an IP product.[12]

---

[12] "International Paper: Europe Targeted," *Le Figaro,* April 2, 1989.

	1988	1987	1986
Revenue			
Net sales	$9,533	$7,763	$5,550
Other income (net)	24	58	53
Gain on stock			33
	$9,557	$7,821	$5,586
Costs & expenses			
Cost of goods sold	$6,715	$5,697	$3,991
Depreciation	446	398	326
Distribution expense	383	352	302
Sales, general, and administrative	561	447	355
Taxes	89	79	69
Earnings before interest and taxes	$1,363	$ 848	$ 543
Interest	165	167	89
Earnings before taxes	$1,198	$ 681	$ 454
Income tax expense	444	274	149
Net income	$ 754	$ 407	$ 305
Preferred dividends	21	20	21
Earnings to common	$ 73	$ 407	$ 305
Earnings per share	$ 6.57	$ 3.68	$ 2.89

SOURCE: International Paper Company annual report, 1988.

As part of the Hammermill transaction, IP acquired Carter Rice and Western Paper, two large paper merchants. IP had not previously owned a captive merchant. Despite IP ownership, a majority of the products that Carter Rice and Western Paper sold came from other companies. Only 20 percent of IP's products were to be sold through its captive distributors. IP nevertheless continued to acquire merchants as a means of entering new markets.

In conjunction with IP's move into fine writing papers, management devoted substantial resources to peripheral product lines. At the end of 1988, IP's Specialty Products sector included a manufacturer and marketer of photographic paper, one of the largest processors of paper mill by-products, and a manufacturer of non-woven fabrics. This sector also included Masonite, the world's largest producer of composite wood products for home construction. Exhibit 8.1D contains sector information.

From 1981 to 1989, IP invested more than $6 billion to improve productivity and reduce costs. As a result, per ton production costs of printing, writing, and reprographic papers fell 5 percent from 1982 levels. Per ton pulp costs fell 18 percent over the same period. By 1989, IP was considered to be among the industry's low-cost producers in many product lines. According to management, cost reductions,

■ EXHIBIT 8.1D

INTERNATIONAL PAPER
■ OPERATING RESULTS BY INDUSTRY SECTOR
FOR THE YEARS ENDED DECEMBER 31
(IN MILLIONS)

	1988	1987	1986
Net sales			
Pulp & paper	$3,060	$2,452	$1,905
Packaging	3,267	2,983	2,372
Distribution	1,870	1,521	589
Wood & timber	795	790	617
Specialty prod.	822	310	203
Less: Intersector	281	293	186
Net sales	$9,533	$7,763	$5,500
Operating profit			
Pulp & paper	$ 628	$ 287	$ 248
Packaging	564	432	195
Distribution	36	34	13
Wood & timber	124	139	116
Specialty prod.	110	43	13
Other items*			43
Operating profit	$1,462	$ 935	$ 628
Interest expense (net)	$ 165	$ 167	$ 89
Corporate items (net)	99	87	85
Earnings before taxes	$1,198	$ 681	$ 454

*Includes gain on sale of New York headquarters.

SOURCE: International Paper Company annual report, 1988.

combined with a shift in the product mix to less price-sensitive grades, had reduced the historical volatility of IP's earnings. "Overall, we have become more stable...," commented Chief Executive Officer John Georges. "It is part of our strategy of internal investments and part of our strategy of acquisitions."[13] While a vast majority of IP's earnings remained in cyclical businesses, management believed the changes would enable the company to meet the stated goal of an average 15 percent return on equity (ROE) through a business cycle.

Notwithstanding its name, IP's revenue stream had little geographical diversity: no more than 10 percent of sales were made overseas (primarily pulp and packaging). Consequently, IP's performance was extremely sensitive to growth rates in the U.S. economy.

AUSSEDAT-REY

With 20 percent of the French market, AR was the second largest paper company in its home country and the twelfth largest paper company in Europe. The com-

[13] "No Lumbering Giant: IP Races to New Peaks in Earnings," *Barrons*, January 2, 1989, 25–26.

pany operated eight mills, producing 180,000 tons of pulp and 500,000 tons of paper a year. Through its subsidiaries, it also had interests in building products and in paper-products distribution. Members of the founding family controlled 20 percent of the company's stock.

AR's paper operations, which accounted for 68 percent of total company sales, were concentrated in three market sectors: specialty papers, publishing and advertising papers, and reprographic paper. The latter accounted for the largest proportion of AR's paper sales.

Specialty papers included high-end, colored, and coated reprographic paper for laser printers as well as heavy weighted papers for security printing and optical character reading. AR's publishing and advertising products included coated papers for magazines, labels, and impactless printers. Reprographic papers were essentially commodity grades for photocopy machines. AR, with a 10 percent market share, was the leading producer of reprographic paper in Europe.

AR also operated the second largest paper merchant in France, with a market share of approximately 20 percent. This business accounted for 31 percent of total sales. Approximately 16 percent of AR's paper products were sold to its captive merchant.

AR exported 35 percent of its paper production, with 90 percent of all exports going to European countries. AR's policy was to expand its presence in each strategic country or region worldwide, with the goal of increasing foreign sales to 53 percent of total revenue by 1989.[14]

Polyrey, a wholly owned subsidiary of AR, was the leading French producer of high-quality decorative panels for household and office use and accounted for 12 percent of company sales. Some 40 percent of the division's products were sold overseas, and Polyrey controlled 5 percent of the European market for decorative panels.

Despite restructuring in 1986 to reduce costs and increase output, AR's results fell below management's target of a 5 percent return on sales. (See Exhibit 8.1E for selected financial data and stock price information.) The cause was primarily that AR was a net buyer of pulp; it purchased approximately 50 percent of its fiber needs on the open market. Between 1987 and 1988, pulp prices in France increased 19 percent. AR's 1988 annual report stated that the company's deteriorating margins during the period reflected its inability to pass these costs on to customers.

Ironically, AR's Saillat mill in Limosine, France, had ready access to one of the largest stands of mature timber in Europe, but the company was unable to use this low-cost resource fully because of the mill's limited pulp capacity. (Saillat was the company's primary reprographic paper mill.) Pulp produced from these forests would cost an estimated 25 percent less than pulp imported from Scandinavia.[15]

AR planned to invest a total of FR2.2 billion over three years at Saillat, but even though AR's performance in 1987 bolstered its financial condition, the company's resources remained insufficient to fund such an expansion program. Management thus began to pursue interested investors in spring 1988.

---

[14] "Aussedat-Rey: The Local Politicians Face to Face with Development," *Sud Quest,* January 7, 1989.

[15] "Paper Manufacturers Are Betting on Increase," *Le Monde,* April 28, 1989.

■ **EXHIBIT 8.1E**

	1988	1987
Assets		
Current assets		
Cash & investments	FF 112	FF 71
Receivables	1,366	1,219
Inventories	699	605
Other current assets	196	180
Total current assets	FF 2,373	FF 2,075
Property, plant, & equipment (net)	1,015	841
Investments	150	94
Other assets	95	94
Total assets	FF 3,633	FF 3,104
Liabilities & Shareholders' Equity		
Current liabilities		
Accounts payable	FF 1,238	FF 1,097
Notes payable	151	96
Current maturities	104	49
Deferred income taxes	67	44
Total current liabilities	FF 1,560	FF 1,286
Long-term debt	1,230	1,163
Other liabilities	43	39
Total liabilities	FF 2,833	FF 2,488
Minority interest	57	73
Share capital	160	138
Paid-in capital	287	218
Revaluation surplus	9	11
Retained earnings	287	176
Total shareholders' equity	FF 743	FF 543
Total liabilities & shareholders' equity	FF 3,633	FF 3,104
Net sales	FF 4,851	FF 4,485
Other income	26	19
Total revenue	4,877	4,504
Purchase costs of sales	2,826	2,543
Payroll	904	894
Finance costs (net)	127	132
Other Operating costs (net)	859	798
Income before taxes	161	137
Tax expense (benefit)	38	(4)
Net income	FF 123	FF 141
Minority interests	1	10
Net income per common share	FF 43.1	FF 48.4
Average number of shares	2,847,000	2,703,000

continued on next page

■ EXHIBIT 8.1E

(CONTINUED)

Stock Price and Volume Averages
(prices in French francs)

Period	Average Price	Percentage Change	Number of Shares Traded	Percentage of Common Stock Traded
Nov. 1987	330	—	377,089	13.7%
Dec. 1987	323	−2.1%	397,259	14.4
Jan. 1988	290	−10.2	246,385	8.3
Feb. 1988	365	25.9	672,193	22.7
Mar. 1988	390	6.8	360,131	12.2
Apr. 1988	482	23.6	533,149	18.0
May 1988	515	6.8	342,745	11.6
June 1988	526	2.1	315,156	10.6
July 1988	514	−2.3	284,955	9.6
Aug. 1988	514	0.0	190,264	6.4
Sep. 1988	511	−0.6	172,789	5.8
Oct. 1988	572	11.9	1,312,952	44.3
Nov. 1988	556	−2.8	114,719	3.9

Trading suspended January 12, 1989, at FR612 per share

Note: The percentage of common stock traded was calculated on the basis of 2,757,000 shares for 1987 and 2,962,807 shares for 1988. At the time of IP's valuation, 3,213,000 shares, on a fully diluted basis, were outstanding.

SOURCES: Aussedat-Rey annual report 1988; and for stock price and volume averages, Lazard Freres.

THE AUSSEDAT-REY TRANSACTION

IP began looking toward the growth market of Europe in the mid-1980s. Initially, it focused on purchasing a merchant to distribute specialty grades such as heavy-weight, colored, and opaque papers. IP recognized that European merchants held much greater influence in the markets than their American counterparts, but forward integration also limited acquisition candidates. Independent merchants with sizable market shares were rare. Therefore, IP turned to the European producers. In April 1988, AR approached IP with the proposition to form a joint venture.

In return for an investment of FR1.2 billion to install a new paper machine at the Saillat mill, AR offered IP a number of alternative arrangements, including a stake in one of its subsidiaries or a minority interest in AR itself. IP management rejected this bid for two reasons. First, IP's engineers did not see the immediate need for upgraded paper capacity. Instead, they recommended management first invest in upgraded pulp and power capacity to make Saillat the low-cost European producer of reprographic paper. Second, and more important, IP's policy was not to take minority interests. It preferred to apply its expertise through direct management.

In late November, AR's investment banker, Goldman Sachs, informed IP that AR had considered its position and would be receptive to a tender offer for the whole company. Jacques Calloud, AR's chairman and a member of the founding family, placed four conditions on any deal: (1) AR must remain an independent subsidiary and be the core of IP's European operations, (2) existing management must be retained, (3) IP must commit to AR's expansion plans at the Saillat mill, and (4) a mutually agreeable price must be reached.

Total ownership appealed to IP. Aside from the tissue operations of Scott and James River, no American company had a significant presence in Europe, but purchasing AR would provide IP with a major foothold on the continent. AR possessed a strategically positioned merchant chain and a diversified product line of specialty and commodity papers. AR's dominant European position in the reprographic market was particularly appealing given IP's similar position in the United States.

Complementary product lines also existed between Polyrey and Masonite. In addition, as a net buyer of pulp, AR would allow IP to integrate almost one-third of its market pulp sales, thus reducing IP's exposure to commodity price fluctuations. Certain grades of IP paper could also be distributed through AR's captive merchants.

A French presence was especially attractive because of France's relatively cheap labor and abundance of inexpensive timber. France, in addition to being a large market in its own right, also bordered on the principal growth markets of the future—Spain and Italy. Recent acquisitions had significantly reduced the number of independent French paper manufacturers, which prompted IP to view AR as its last chance to acquire a French company of appreciable size.

IP management commented on the potential synergies in the transaction:

> After the takeover of Aussedat-Rey, the two companies will combine their marketing and production capacities in order to increase their profitability and to reinforce their share in respective markets, as much in France as in Europe. In this respect we will follow the policy already adopted by Aussedat-Rey under the management of the present team.[16]

Estimates of tonnage growth rates, price trends, and synergies that would result from acquiring AR are included in the pro forma financial statements of Exhibit 8.1F. The exhibit also includes exchange rate information.

Both IP and AR managers wished to transform the company into a major European paper producer. Accordingly, IP agreed to Calloud's condition that existing management be retained. IP agreed only to operate AR as *one* of its major European units, however, not the core of its operations on the continent.

To keep AR competitive, IP agreed to a major investment in the Saillat facility. Given its engineers' recommendations, IP committed to invest up to FR2 billion to increase pulp capacity and to rebuild and expand the existing paper machines.[17] Subsequent investments for incremental paper-making capacity would depend on

---

[16] "Aussedat-Rey: The Takeover Is a Roaring Success," *T.P.G.*, March 23, 1989.

[17] These investments are not reflected in the Exhibit 8.1F pro formas.

■ EXHIBIT 8.1F

INTERNATIONAL PAPER
■ AUSSEDAT-REY PROJECTED CASH FLOWS
(IN MILLIONS OF FRENCH FRANCS)

	Sales	Earnings before Interest and Taxes	Depreciation	Taxes	Capital Expenditure	Increase in Working Capital
1988	4,806	325	126	46	275	71
1989	5,154	438	156	100	260	100
1990	5,339	470	160	113	250	53
1991	5,606	505	200	177	307	66
1992	5,886	565	220	198	322	70
1993	6,180	612	240	214	339	73
1994	6,489	681	255	238	355	77
1995	6,814	729	270	255	373	81
1996	7,154	823	285	288	392	85
1997	7,512	886	300	310	411	89

Exchange Rate Information (trades of $1MM or more)

FF to $

Dec. 30, 1988	6.0590
30-day forward	6.0552
90-day forward	6.0470
180-day forward	6.0365

Notes: (1) Revenues reflect volume increases and long-term price trends. An effective tax rate of 35 percent
was assumed beginning in 1991. All numbers compiled as of November 1988.
(2) All numbers are disguised.
SOURCE: *The Wall Street Journal*, December 31, 1988.

future market conditions. AR's board emphasized the importance of these investments in its announcement of the agreement (January 17, 1989):

The new partnership will allow Aussedat-Rey to develop its position as a major
European producer of reprographic paper and reinforce its strong standing in the production and distribution of printing and writing papers and decorative panels, thereby
responding to the consolidation and considerable investments that characterize the
paper industry today.

While IP could pinpoint numerous benefits of the acquisition, many uncertainties complicated a valuation of AR. Certain positive factors, such as IP's financial wherewithal and marketing capabilities, were difficult to quantify and thus not
necessarily reflected in the numbers. On the other hand, recent mergers in Europe
and Scandinavia had formed formidable competition. Europe was also an unfa-
miliar market. IP management wondered how much weight should be put on the
projections.

■ EXHIBIT 8.1G

INTERNATIONAL PAPER
■ VALUATION OF AUSSEDAT-REY ASSETS AS OF NOVEMBER 1988
(FRENCH FRANCS IN MILLIONS)

Facility	Yaakko Poyry Valuation	AR Ownership	Asset Value Not Including Working Capital
Saillat	FF 1,080	100%	FF 1,080
Lancey	642	85	546
Maresquel	558	60	345
Anould	264	100	264
Cran	156	60	94
Robertson	138	60	83
Pont De Claix	150	100	150
Distribution	385*	100	385
Polyrey	FF 865*	100%	865
Grand Total			FF 3,812

*Casewriter's estimates.

Notes: (1) Valuations based on replacement costs minus depreciation.
(2) AR commissioned Yaakko Poyry to perform the valuation and made the report available to IP.

Uncomfortable with a bid based solely on a discounted cash flow analysis, IP also took into account a valuation of AR's assets by Yaakko Poyry, an independent Finnish appraiser (see Exhibit 8.1G). With this additional information, and knowledge of the other recent acquisitions outlined in Exhibit 8.1H, IP arrived at a value for AR and, in early January, submitted a bid of FR675 per share. AR management accepted, and an agreement of intent was signed in mid-January 1989.

If successful, IP planned to finance the purchase with French franc borrowings at an estimated rate of 9.4 percent. The company anticipated entering into a swap agreement that would mitigate its foreign exchange risk. IP's all-in rate in French francs, including the cost of the swap, was estimated to be 9.65 percent, which was comparable to rates on IP's dollar-denominated debt in the United States. The three-month Treasury bill and U.S. long bond were yielding 8.48 percent and 9.08 percent, respectively. IP assumed that AR's earnings would be reinvested in France rather than be repatriated.

MITTERRAND'S RESPONSE AND COUNTERBIDS

Mitterrand's highly political comments (general elections were scheduled for March) were not directed at IP's bid in particular but addressed the perception among certain groups in France of a growing foreign hegemony over French industry. At the end of 1987, foreigners controlled almost 11 percent of all French

■ EXHIBIT 8.1H

INTERNATIONAL PAPER
■ SELECTED FINANCIAL INFORMATION ON RECENT ACQUISITIONS OF
PAPER COMPANIES IN FRANCE AND THE UNITED STATES
(IN MILLIONS)

Target/Buyer	Acquisition Price	Acquisition P/E	Acquisition Price/ Book Value	Acquisition Price/ Sales
France				
Guerimand-Voiron/ Arjomari-Prioux (6/88)	FF 1,050	15.1X	2.6X	1.1X
Arjomari-Prioux (35%)/ Saint-Louis (6/88)	1,750	14.1	3.2X	0.7
Corbehem (50%)/ Feldmuhle (4/88)	575	10.0	N.Av.	0.5
Peaudouce/ Moynlick (1/88)	1,960	18.0	N.Av.	0.7
Kaysersberg (50%)/ James River (10/87)	FF 1,500	22.6X	N.Av.	0.7X
United States				
Fort Howard Corp./ Morgan Stanley (1/88)	$3,580	22.5X	2.7X	2.0X
Acco World Corp./ Amer. Brands (6/87)	611	25.9	5.9	2.5
Owens Illinois/ KKR (12/86)	3,678	20.4	2.2	1.0
Ampad/ Merell Corp. (11/86)	119	23.4	2.0	0.9
C.Z. Distrib./ Mead Corp. 9/68	250	N.M.	2.8	0.3
Hammermill Paper/ Int'l Paper (8/86)	$1,130	24.8X	2.0X	0.6X

SOURCE: Laz'Freres.

industrial firms, whereas 15 years previously, they controlled only 6.7 percent. These figures neglected French investment overseas, however. By the government's own account, in 1987 and 1988, French overseas investments were twice the amount foreigners invested in France during those years.[18] In the United States alone, French companies had recently acquired or bid for Triangle Industries (American Can) and Honeywell. Nevertheless, as France's second largest paper company, AR's future would be of interest to the government.

---

[18] "France Attracts Foreign Investment," *Les Echos,* March 22, 1989.

The French Treasury had two months to rule on an acquisition involving a non-EEC company. Prior to the president's comments, IP had not received any negative indications from the Treasury, and no alternative bidders had surfaced, despite rumors to the contrary. The French press speculated that either Modo or Kymenne, the largest Scandinavian manufacturers of reprographic paper, would offer a European solution in an attempt to protect their markets.[19] Any chance of a French solution had been ruled out after AR failed to find a French investor in spring 1988.[20] Therefore, the emergence of Arjomari-Prioux (Arjomari), France's largest paper company, as a likely suitor two weeks after Mitterrand's comments was unexpected.

Lacking sufficient funds to mount a takeover on its own, Arjomari formed a partnership with its 34 percent stockholder, the Saint-Louis Group. Together, they proposed a "100 percent French" alternative of FR675 per share, or approximately FR2.2 billion, for all the AR shares outstanding. They also pledged to invest a total of FR2 billion in the AR mill system. Barnard Duman, director of the Saint-Louis Group, explained Arjomari's position:

> To put together an Arjomari-Aussedat unit is an unparalleled chance to create a French paper group of European size. The unit would record sales of FR13 billion and have a cash flow of 1 billion FR. It would help redress the [trade] balance of the French paper industry, at present with a deficit of FF4.6 billion.[21]

In defending Arjomari's previous apathy toward AR, Duman stated:

> In March of 1988, Aussedat-Rey was not interested in selling but only in increasing capital by FF2 billion by means of the inclusion of a new investor. To have a minority holding in Aussedat-Rey did not interest us. The agreement made between Aussedat-Rey and International Paper was a surprise to us.[22]

While the Arjomari bid seemed to be legitimate, it was contingent on the government rejecting IP's bid. The French press immediately dubbed the Arjomari proposal the "Seduction Plan."[23] Duman commented:

> There must be a problem [with the IP bid]; otherwise the government would have given the go-ahead signal.... [I] would like to help the French government in the wake of such a delicate decision ...[and] the solution would be positive for the shareholders.[24]

The possibility of a French Solution put increased pressure on the government to block IP's bid. As one paper-sector analyst suggested, "This is the last opportunity for France to pull together a major French paper maker. It's a test case for Mitterrand's government."[25]

---

[19] "The Price of the Takeover of Aussedat-Rey," *Liberation,* January 18, 1989.

[20] AR had offered the joint venture proposal to various European and Scandinavian firms but found no interest.

[21] "Saint-Louis Insists on the Association of Aussedat-Rey with Arjomari," *La Tribune De L'Expansion,* February 28, 1989.

[22] "Arjomari's French Solution for Aussedat-Rey," *Agence Economique et Financiere,* February 28, 1989.

[23] "Aussedat-Rey: French Green Light for International Paper Probable," *Les Echos,* March 1, 1989.

[24] "Arjomari Ready to Invest FF2.4 Billion in Aussedat-Rey," *Les Echos,* February 28, 1989.

[25] "International Paper Bid a Test for Mitterrand," *Reuter,* February 14, 1989.

Arjomari's proposition was anything but subtle; it provided nationalists within Mitterrand's cabinet a way to push their agenda. IP management concluded that, if it did not respond, the government was likely to block its bid. IP's options were numerous.

First, IP could mobilize various French and U.S. resources to step up its own political pressure on the French government. As a former chairman of the European Pulp and Paper Association, Calloud was influential in the industry and had contacts within the government. His repudiation of the Arjomari initiative and the friendly nature of IP's deal guaranteed his ongoing support. Lazard Freres, IP's investment banker, was also well connected politically and could exert leverage on the Treasury. From the U.S. side, the U.S. embassy and the special trade representative could be enlisted to push IP's position. Historically, U.S. firms had received a cool welcome in France, while French companies had expanded freely within the United States—a discrepancy of which the U.S. government was aware. If Mitterrand rejected IP's bid, U.S. officials might suggest the possibility of reciprocation by the Securities and Exchange Commission on French acquisitions pending in the United States.

IP's second option was to raise its bid prior to the Treasury's decision. Such a move might make it more difficult for the government to reject the bid, but any increase in price would have to be justified economically as well as strategically. Throughout the process, however, IP had made no indication that it was willing to increase its offer. Throwing additional money at the deal might also smack of President Mitterrand's characterization of foreign takeovers as "roving, predatory money" and "gangsterism of the strongest."[26] Furthermore, an increased bid might not guarantee that Arjomari would withdraw its offer. Many French paper-sector analysts thought a takeover battle was possible; commented one, "Arjomari is going to get all the big French groups with any interest in paper involved."[27] The combined financial resources of the Saint-Louis Group, Arjomari, and others could make AR very expensive.[28]

Recent indications from the French treasury were that IP's bid would most likely be approved, although the outcome was still far from certain. IP executives were thus considering the following questions: If IP were to raise its bid, what should it offer? How much should IP be willing to pay for AR in a bidding war? IP's answers had to take into account not only the hard numbers but such intangibles as strategic position, the possibility of future acquisitions and/or expansion, and the synergies these might create. More important, IP's decisions had to reflect its stated goal of a 15 percent ROE. As CEO Georges commented in late 1988, "I want to make the company more profitable, to create greater inherent value. I guess I am a builder, not a financial engineer."[29]

[26] "Mitterrand Attacks 'Predatory Money,'" *The International Herald Tribune*, February 12, 1989.

[27] "International Paper Bid a Test for Mitterrand."

[28] Although a consortium had not been formed, the Swedish firm, MoDo, had declared its willingness to "go with" Arjomari.

[29] "No Lumbering Giant."

CASE 8.2

FIRST WACHOVIA CORPORATION

Wayne Williams, a vice president at First Wachovia Corporation, was part of the company's First Wachovia Corporate Services subsidiary, which managed the loan portfolio of less developed countries (LDCs) for both Wachovia and its recent merger partner, First Atlanta Corporation. As shown in the financial information in Exhibits 8.2A and 8.2B, First Wachovia was an $18.7 billion financial institution headquartered in both Winston-Salem, North Carolina, and Atlanta, Georgia. The holding company was formed in December 1985, following the merger of The Wachovia Corporation and First Atlanta.

Williams' particular concern in October 1987 was the international portfolio's Mexican exposure. First Wachovia held more than $200 million in LDC debt in mid-1987, about one-half of which was in Mexican public sector instruments. Although the bank had established loss reserves that more than matched the potential LDC exposure, Williams' goal was to recoup as much of the face value of the debt as possible. In his review of alternatives, Williams had run across a prospectus for the IDI Fund, a limited partnership formed to convert sovereign debt to equity in the Mexican private sector. He needed to determine the feasibility and desirability of participating in the IDI Fund.

LATIN AMERICAN MARKET

The Latin American debt situation had its roots in the flawed lending theory of the 1970s: governments could not go broke. Ever since Mexico had first suspended debt service in 1982, government officials and financial institutions had searched for innovative ways to relieve countries of debt service burdens. The U.S. government supported the restructuring of Latin American debt service schedules. U.S. Treasury Secretary James Baker pushed Latin American governments to formulate growth-oriented strategies emphasizing privatization of state-owned enterprises, direct foreign investment opportunities, and a general loosening of government's grasp on the private sector. He also strongly encouraged commercial banks to resume lending to countries that showed a willingness to redirect their economies. Banks with the largest LDC exposures were willing to work with the foreign governments to keep the lapsed sovereign debt current on their books (Exhibit 8.2c).

In 1982, a secondary market developed for restructured LDC sovereign debt. The market allowed holders of this debt to buy, sell, and trade restructured instruments at amounts less than the face value of the original notes. Discounts in the secondary market ranged from as high as 92 percent for Bolivia to 40 percent for Mexico, as shown in Exhibit 8.2D. Institutions trading in the market preferred to swap sovereign debt rather than sell it outright for a number of reasons. Many had not built sufficient reserves to absorb the losses realized when debt was taken off the books at less than face value. There had been a concern that officials would

This case was written by Laura M. Connelly, MBA 1988, under the supervision of Mark R. Eaker, professor of Business Administration. Copyright © 1988 by the University of Virginia Darden School Foundation, Charlottesville, Va. All rights reserved. Rev. 5/88.

FIRST WACHOVIA CORPORATION
■ BALANCE SHEET
(MILLIONS OF DOLLARS)

	December 31	
	1986	1985
Assets		
Cash and due from banks	$ 2,100.6	$ 1,914.2
Investment securities	4,288.8	4,214.3
Loans and leases	11,747.1	10,702.0
Less allowance for loan losses	163.8	144.5
Net loans and leases	$11,583.3	$10,557.5
Net property and equipment	$ 277.6	$ 253.8
Other assets	439.2	766.7
Total assets	$18,689.6	$17,706.5
Liabilities		
Deposits in domestic offices	$13,185.7	$11,805.3
Deposits in foreign offices	594.9	869.7
Total deposits	$13,780.6	$12,674.9
Federal funds under repo agreements	$ 2,605.4	$ 2,736.9
Borrowed funds: Short-term	492.7	299.5
Long-term	286.8	295.5
Other liabilities	346.6	666.0
Total liabilities	$17,512.1	$16,672.8
Shareholders' Equity		
Common stock, par value $5 a share	$ 268.4	$ 266.7
Capital surplus	119.1	114.1
Retained earnings	789.9	652.9
Total shareholders' equity	$ 1,177.4	$ 1,033.7
Total liabilities and shareholders' equity	$18,689.6	$17,706.5

require an LDC debt holder to write down all of its LDC exposure to realizable market value if a portion was sold outright. The swapping allowed banks to restructure their portfolios without exposing their entire position to a write-off. Bank regulators had indicated that write-offs would not be required.

Debt swaps in the secondary market took a number of forms. Debt-for-debt swaps were completed with either a trade of sovereign debt or a conversion of restructured debt into another instrument, such as a bond, which was exempt from further restructuring. So long as the market value of the swapped debt was equal, no loss was recorded.

The debt/equity swap was an offshoot of the debt-for-debt swap. Chile instituted the first program in 1985, and since then Mexico, Costa Rica, Ecuador, Brazil, Argentina, and the Philippines had followed suit. *Institutional Investor* estimated

FIRST WACHOVIA CORPORATION
■ CONSOLIDATED INCOME STATEMENT
(MILLIONS OF DOLLARS)

	December 31	
	1986	1985
Interest Income		
Loans	$1,117.4	$1,124.8
Other	317.9	362.3
Total interest income	$1,435.3	$1,487.0
Interest Expense		
Interest on deposits	$ 626.1	$ 692.2
Short-term borrowed funds	177.8	198.4
Long-term borrowed funds	26.4	27.9
Total interest expense	$ 830.3	$ 918.5
Net interest income	605.0	568.5
Provision for loan losses	95.4	80.7
Net interest income after provision	$ 509.6	$ 487.8
Other Income		
Other operating revenue	$ 282.7	$ 255.1
Gain on sale of subsidiary	8.9	17.0
Investment securities gains (losses)	12.3	11.3
Total other income	$ 303.8	$ 283.4
Other Expense		
Staff	$ 309.0	$ 285.5
Other	278.1	251.8
Total other expense	$ 587.1	$ 537.3
Income before income taxes	226.3	233.9
Applicable income taxes	32.6	46.2
Net Income	$ 193.8	$ 187.7

that these programs alone would have completed a total of $6 billion in debt/equity conversions by the end of 1987.[1] Because of this success, 15 more countries were investigating ways to institute similar programs by 1988.

In a typical debt/equity conversion program, public sector debt that had been part of a restructuring was eligible to be swapped. A multinational corporation purchased LDC debt in the secondary market at appropriate market discounts on face value. The debt was changed into local currency in cash or negotiable securities at a conversion discount charged by the host government. Each government

---

[1] A Guide to Debt-Equity Converstions," a special sponsored section, *Institutional Investor*, Shearson Lehman Bros., September 1987, 2.

■ EXHIBIT 8.2C

FIRST WACHOVIA CORPORATION
■ LARGEST DOMESTIC LATIN AMERICAN DEBT HOLDERS,
AS OF JUNE 1, 1987

Bank	Exposure* (in billions)	Percentage of Holding Company's Capital
Citicorp	$10.4	149%
Bank of America	7.5	186
Manufacturers Hanover	7.5	199
Chase	7.0	143
JP Morgan	4.6	89

*Includes debt exposure from Mexico, Brazil, Argentina, Peru, and Venezuela.

SOURCE: *A Stunner from The Citi," *Business Week,* June 1, 1987, 43; data from IBCA, Inc.

■ EXHIBIT 8.2D

FIRST WACHOVIA CORPORATION
■ SECONDARY MARKET LDC SOVEREIGN DEBT PRICES
(MAY 1987)

Country	Cents for Each Dollar of Debt
Romania	86–89
Colombia	86–88
Ivory Coast	76–78
Yugoslavia	74–77
Venezuela	72–74
Philippines	70–71
Chile	67–69
Morocco	66–68
Panama	66–68
Brazil	64–65
South Africa	60–65
Argentina	59–60
Mexico	58–59
Ecuador	53–56
Egypt	49–51
Poland	43–45
Nigeria	37–39
Zaire	24–26
Peru	13–15

SOURCE: "Swapping Debt—Just Hot Air?"
Euromoney (London), May 1987, 118.

established conversion discount schedules that were favorable for projects that fueled exports and created jobs and unfavorable for projects that did not fund economically important areas. The conversion fee ranged from 25 percent of the face value of the debt for projects in low-priority industries to a zero discount for certain export-generating projects. After funds were converted to local currency, they were invested in approved local projects as equity. Rules varied about repatriation of funds, but most programs did not allow capital repayment before the scheduled amortization of principal on the restructured debt.

Swaps offered advantages to both LDCs and debt holders. LDC governments were relieved of a portion of their debt-payment burdens and at the same time were able to attract investment to boost exports and create jobs. The conversion of debt through LDC financial networks also promoted the development of local capital markets. For banks, the debt/equity swap offered a tool to cut LDC debt exposure and, in the best case, would result in viable long-term investments at bargain prices for the purchaser.

Financial institutions were active in the swap market as intermediaries in swap transactions. Institutions with Latin American divisions were positioning themselves to be both brokers of LDC debt and managers of equity funds. Specific country knowledge was important because the mechanics of the swap process involved complex regulatory systems in each country. Intermediaries needed experience with documentation and trading skills as well as large networks of local government and business contacts to create viable equity deals. Financial institutions expected eventually to underwrite, resell, and syndicate LDC exposure for debt holders who did not have the capacity or inclination to originate opportunities themselves in foreign countries.

In 1986, secondary market trading in Latin American and other country debt totaled nearly $5 billion, up $3 billion from 1985. *The Banker* estimated that the total debt swapped in 1987 would approach $7 billion.[2] Although growing, this market represented only a fraction of the total Latin American debt exposure of approximately $380 billion. Through early 1987, financial institutions with large Latin American exposure avoided swapping their own loans in the debt/equity program. They were reluctant to report losses from the government conversion fees related to the swapped portfolios. Also, they feared being required to apply the discounts of the swap transactions to the LDC debt that remained on their books.

Recently, however, there had been signs that the participation of the large debt holders in the swap market would increase. In May 1987, Citicorp announced that it was setting up a $3 billion reserve against its Latin American exposure. Chairman John Reed stated that he hoped to get rid of $5 billion in LDC debt over the next three years through the secondary market. The financial community expected that a large part of the amount would be converted through debt/equity swaps. American Express and Bankers Trust tested the accounting treatment of LDC debt left on their books after a swap transaction. Their auditor, Arthur Young, stated that no losses would be realized when the swaps were made, if it were possible to es-

---

[2] "Trading Debt for Equity," *The Banker*, February 1987.

tablish the fair value of the investment. And the remaining debt portfolio would stay on the books at full value. Finally, in August, the Federal Reserve Board ruled that banks could own up to 100 percent of the equity of companies being denationalized in LDCs, a significant boost from the previous rule of 20 percent.

MEXICO

Facing a slowdown in economic activity in the mid-1970s, Mexico turned to public sector spending to stimulate local demand. The government depended on foreign lenders and debt to fund a substantial part of this spending. When oil prices shot up in the late 1970s, the government's spending programs grew unchecked, and foreign investors flocked to support the oil-rich country. By 1982 public sector spending was at an all-time high, and inflation was growing at an alarming rate. Foreign and local investors lost confidence in the government's ability to cut spending, and the country experienced massive capital outflows. These factors set the stage for the foreign debt crisis of 1982.

The Mexican government enacted a well-planned but ineffective stabilization program over the next three years. Heavy public sector borrowing crowded private companies out of the local debt markets. Continued growth of government deficits left no room for private investors to stimulate economic resurgence. Under the theory that present hardships would lead to a higher standard of living in the future, President Miguel de la Madrid responded to the debt crisis with a harsh austerity program. De la Madrid's basic policy was to hold down wages while severely devaluing the peso to stimulate exports and meet payments on the country's $100 billion in foreign debt. One result was the depreciation in the free-market peso exchange rate shown in Exhibit 8.2E.

■ EXHIBIT 8.2E

FIRST WACHOVIA CORPORATION
■ MEXICAN PESO/DOLLAR EXCHANGE RATE

Year	Quarter	Peso/Dollar
1985	1	226.31
	2	239.12
	3	370.50
	4	447.50
1986	1	486.50
	2	644.50
	3	770.50
	4	922.00

SOURCE: U.S. Department of Commerce, *Foreign Economic Trends*, May 1987.

MEXICAN SWAP PROGRAM

De la Madrid was faced with finding a way to gain some liquidity in the Mexican capital markets at a time when the local prime lending rate was over 90 percent. In 1986, the government turned to the debt/equity swap market to attract foreign investment and to reduce the foreign debt load. Section 5:11 of the New Restructure Agreement dated August 29, 1985, declared all public sector debt eligible for swapping. Qualified stocks had the following restrictions:

1. They could be issued only to offshore entities and could not be transferred to a Mexican entity before January 1, 1998.

2. No conversion was allowed into other types of securities.

3. No redemption could be made on a basis more favorable than the repayment schedule of the underlying debt.

Dividends could not be guaranteed but were unrestricted. Swaps had to be approved by the Ministry of Finance and Public Credit and the National Commission on Foreign Relations, and, in some circumstances, the Ministry of Foreign Relations. Following approval, the Mexican government would convert debt at the free-market exchange rate. Discounts were applied to the swapped debt, and funds were directed to private investment projects. The conversion discounts shown in Exhibit 8.2F were based on the government's view of the priority of the project to be funded. The Mexican authorities monitored the program closely, and in early 1987 began to impose a .25 percent application fee to ensure sincerity on the part of foreign investors.

▪ EXHIBIT 8.2F

FIRST WACHOVIA CORPORATION
▪ MEXICAN GOVERNMENT DISCOUNT SCHEDULE
FOR DEBT/EQUITY SWAPS

Percentage Discount*	Qualifying Projects
0	Acquisition of state-owned firms
5	Investment in firm that exports 80% of production
	New investment in firm that creates jobs and brings in high technology
14	Investment that reduces debt to local banks
15	Investment geared toward partial FICORCA prepayment[†]
16	Investment for total prepayment for FICORCA[†]
25	All other approved investments

*The Mexican government would convert the sovereign debt into pesos at the free-market exchange rate prevailing on the closing date after taking the listed discount.

[†]See Exhibit 8.2G.

Because of the potentially inflationary effects of pumping more pesos into the economy, the annual size of the debt/equity program was limited to 7 percent of the budget deficit.[3] In addition, directing pesos toward investments that generated new production lessened the potential inflationary impact. *Euromoney* estimated that $685 million of debt-swap transactions had been completed and $375 million in additional projects were nearing conversion.[4] The average discount rate on the 250 projects approved was 12 percent.

Although the government was applauded for its success in attracting new investment, the swap program was not without its critics. Some large bank debt holders hesitated to enter the Mexican program. Twice after its inception, the program shut down because of political and economic concerns as well as disputes within the government.

Major participants in the program were multinational corporations that bought Mexican sovereign debt in the secondary market. These companies capitalized new entities and existing subsidiaries by buying debt from banks at the free-market discount of 40 percent and then converting into pesos at the government discount rate of 5 to 25 percent. *Institutional Investor* projected that the automobile sector absorbed nearly $500 million and tourism over $300 million of the new investment.[5] The largest conversion projects were Chrysler de Mexico, S.A., $100 million; Nissan Mexicana, $54.4 million; Ford Motor, $21.8 million; Renault Ind. Mex., $14.1 million; GEM, S.A., $9.1 million; and Tramsider, $5.0 million.

Because large bank-led swap funds had not been strong participants in the Mexican swap program, groups of private individuals established smaller investment portfolios. Their mutual funds were made up of the sovereign debt pledged by institutions that were reluctant to manage their own Mexican equity portfolios. The groups had contacts with Mexican entrepreneurs, who supplied management expertise and crucial government connections. The major challenge faced by these private groups was gaining credibility with investors, who had to commit to equity projects that would not unwind for 10 years or longer.

IDI ASSOCIATES

IDI Associates (the Fund) was a limited partnership formed in March 1987 to organize, sponsor, and manage one or more debt/equity swap funds. IDI solicited regional banks willing to pledge their Mexican public sector debt to be swapped for equity in investments deemed appropriate by the Fund. IDI set a minimum Fund size at $50 million and maximum at $75 million. Minimum participation in the Fund was $5 million, and no one bank could contribute more than 24.9 percent of the total Fund. An organization fee equaling 3 percent of the pledged debt was due up front in cash, and management fees of 1.5 percent annually would be deducted from the cash flow paid to the subscribing banks. IDI was also to receive a

---

[3] The 1986 deficit allowed $1.5 billion in swaps.

[4] "Swapping Debt—Just Hot Air?" *Euromoney*, May 1987, p. 117.

[5] "A Guide to Debt-Equity Conversions," p. 10.

FIRST WACHOVIA CORPORATION
■ SAMPLE INVESTMENTS OF IDI FUND

Government-company buyout: A major group in Mexico was preparing to bid for a government-owned producer of proprietary drugs. The government planned to sell the assets at their book value, using the proceeds to retire outstanding liabilities. The total cash price would be $60 million.

FICORCA prepayment: The FICORCA program involved a series of dollar-denominated debt restructurings at favorable interest and exchange rates that were arranged in the early 1980s. An established soft drink bottler wanted to lock in an advantage resulting from FICORCA borrowing. The company carried loans from foreign banks of $12 million, which were restructured in 1983 under the FICORCA program. Because the peso devaluation rate had exceeded the interest rate charged by FICORCA, peso debt carried on the books of the company was priced at a 30 percent discount below the value had the obligation remained dollar denominated. The company had an opportunity to purchase a smaller bottler but did not want to eliminate any portion of the sinking fund designed to meet upcoming FICORCA repayment requirements. The company was therefore requesting an equity investment of up to $5 million to prepay FICORCA.

Mining project: A mining company operated by one of the most reputable groups in Mexico needed funds to expand one of its principal mines. Total cost of the expansion program was estimated to be $20 million.

SOURCE: IDI Information Memorandum.

fee of 1 percent of the amount of any equity investments it sold after conversion, as well as incentive payments when the return on investment exceeded predetermined levels.

IDI's portfolio strategy was based on its belief that the best investment prospects were established Mexican companies. IDI would concentrate on companies in the top 100 of the Mexican economy with revenues from $25 million to $200 million and equity from $15 million to $100 million. The Fund targeted companies that used domestic raw materials and planned to increase export business. Likely investment industries included electronics, machinery, auto parts, chemicals, plastics, and cement. Descriptions of opportunities are presented in Exhibit 8.2G.

IDI wished to round out the Fund portfolio with up to 15 percent debt-for-debt swaps and planned to target potential foreign investors in Mexico willing to swap dollar-denominated debt for Mexican sovereign debt. Management would also consider swapping a portion of its sovereign debt for the dollar-denominated debt of one of its equity investment companies if the company demonstrated the ability to generate cash flow to cover debt service. Exhibit 8.2H shows the structure of the Fund based on a total subscription of $50 million.

After identifying investment opportunities, IDI would direct swap transactions through the government system and monitor the resulting portfolio. Although a passive investor, IDI wanted to be actively involved through attending periodic management meetings and conducting continuous financial analyses of all the Fund's investments. IDI's goal was to be fully invested within two years of

FIRST WACHOVIA CORPORATION
■ IDI FUND ALLOCATION OF PLEDGED DEBT
(THOUSANDS OF DOLLARS)

Assuming a $50 million Fund

Total subscription amount	$50,000
Organization fee	1,500
Available for investment	$48,500
Swapped for debt (15%)	7,270
Available for equity investment	$41,230
Conversion discount (8%)	3,300
Invested in equities	$37,930

SOURCE: IDI Mexico Fund I Information Memorandum.

the Fund's closing. When this was achieved, IDI would begin the search for innovative ways to recoup dollar investments by structuring equity sales to other offshore entities. Exhibit 8.2I shows projected rates of return in optimistic, pessimistic,
and base case scenarios.

J. Hallam Dawson and Amsterdam Pacific Corporation were general managers of the Fund. Dawson, chairman of IDI, was managing director of Dawson
and Company, a West Coast venture capital firm. Amsterdam Pacific was a
California-based investment bank. An advisory board would be formed to counsel
the general managers on initial investments and ongoing portfolio analyses, and
one or more of the three to five people on the board would be from banks pledging
LDC debt.

IDI maintained offices in San Francisco and Mexico. Luis M. de la Fuente, executive vice president of IDI, directed foreign operations. De la Fuente had joined
IDI in February 1987 from Salinas y Rocha, the largest department and furniture
store chain in Mexico and one of the country's 20 largest companies. He was known
as a creative financial manager with extensive experience in operating finances. IDI
was counting on his business, political, and financial connections to be instrumen-
tal in the success of the Fund. Exhibit 8.2J offers further background on the Fund's
management.

RISKS OF DEBT/EQUITY SWAP MARKET

Although the IDI Fund was attractive to First Wachovia, Williams did not want to
lose sight of the risks involved. There were questions about the viability of the
swap market. As larger banks rushed into the LDC debt management business,

■ EXHIBIT 8.21

Line	Item (thousands of dollars)	Year 1	Year 2	Year 3	Year 4	Year 5	Year 6	Year 7	Year 8	Year 9	Year 10
Base Case											
1	Equity investments	37.93	40.85	43.99	47.38	51.03	54.96	47.35	38.25	27.44	14.79
2	Earnings from equity	4.17	4.49	4.84	5.21	5.61	6.05	5.21	4.21	3.02	1.63
3	Dividends	1.25	1.35	1.45	1.56	1.68	1.81	1.56	1.26	0.91	0.49
4	Withholdings on dividends	0.69	0.74	0.80	0.86	0.93	1.00	0.86	0.69	0.50	0.27
5	Net dividends	0.56	0.61	0.65	0.70	0.76	0.82	0.70	0.57	0.41	0.22
6	Loans	7.28	7.28	7.28	7.28	7.28	7.28	5.82	4.36	2.91	1.46
7	Interest	0.65	0.65	0.65	0.65	0.65	0.65	0.52	0.39	0.26	0.13
8	Withholding on interest	0.10	0.10	0.10	0.10	0.10	0.10	0.06	0.06	0.04	0.02
9	Net interest	0.56	0.56	0.56	0.56	0.56	0.56	0.45	0.33	0.22	0.11
10	Tax credits	0.39	0.42	0.45	0.48	0.51	0.55	0.47	0.38	0.27	0.14
11	Management and other fees	0.70	0.75	0.79	0.84	0.90	0.96	0.82	0.66	0.48	0.27
12	Current income	0.81	0.84	0.86	0.89	0.93	0.96	0.79	0.61	0.42	0.21
13	Loan repayments	—	—	—	—	—	1.46	1.46	1.46	1.46	1.46
14	Divestitures	—	—	—	—	—	11.84	12.75	13.73	14.79	15.93
15	Divestiture fee	—	—	—	—	—	0.24	0.25	0.27	0.30	0.32
16	Net cash flows	0.81	0.84	0.86	0.89	0.93	14.02	14.74	15.53	16.37	17.27
17	Internal rate of return 100% = 6.7%										
18	60% = 14.2%										

continued on next page

SOURCE: IDI Mexico Fund I Information Memorandum.

Line	Item (thousands of dollars)	Year 1	Year 2	Year 3	Year 4	Year 5	Year 6	Year 7	Year 8	Year 9	Year 10
	Optimistic Case										
1	Equity investments	37.93	42.21	46.97	52.27	58.16	64.73	57.62	48.09	35.68	19.85
2	Earnings from equity	4.93	5.49	6.11	6.79	7.56	8.41	7.49	6.25	4.64	2.58
3	Dividends	1.48	1.65	1.83	2.04	2.27	2.52	2.25	1.88	1.39	0.77
4	Withholdings on dividends	0.81	0.91	1.01	1.12	1.25	1.39	1.24	1.03	0.77	0.43
5	Net dividends	0.67	0.74	0.82	0.92	1.02	1.14	1.01	0.84	0.63	0.35
6	Loans	8.37	8.37	8.37	8.37	8.37	8.37	6.69	5.02	3.35	1.67
7	Interest	0.75	0.75	0.75	0.75	0.75	0.75	0.60	0.45	0.30	0.15
8	Withholding on interest	0.11	0.11	0.11	0.11	0.11	0.11	0.09	0.07	0.05	0.02
9	Net interest	0.64	0.64	0.64	0.64	0.64	0.64	0.51	0.38	0.26	0.13
10	Tax credits	0.93	1.02	1.12	1.23	1.36	1.50	1.33	1.10	0.81	0.45
11	Management and other fees	0.72	0.78	0.86	0.93	1.02	1.12	0.99	0.82	0.61	0.35
12	Current income	1.51	1.62	1.73	1.86	2.00	2.16	1.86	1.51	1.08	0.58
13	Loan repayments	—	—	—	—	—	1.67	1.67	1.67	1.67	1.67
14	Divestitures	—	—	—	—	—	14.41	16.03	17.84	19.85	22.09
15	Divestiture fee	—	—	—	—	—	0.43	0.48	0.54	0.60	0.66
16	Net cash flows	1.51	1.62	1.73	1.86	2.00	17.80	19.08	20.48	22.01	23.68
17	Internal rate of return 100% = 11.3%										
18	60% = 9.5%										

continued on next page

■ E X H I B I T 8 . 2 1

(CONTINUED)

Line	Item (thousands of dollars)	Year 1	Year 2	Year 3	Year 4	Year 5	Year 6	Year 7	Year 8	Year 9	Year 10
Pessimistic Case											
1	Equity investments	37.93	39.25	40.62	42.04	43.50	45.02	37.27	28.93	19.96	10.33
2	Earnings from equity	3.03	3.14	3.25	3.36	3.48	3.60	2.98	2.31	1.60	0.83
3	Dividends	0.91	0.94	0.97	1.01	1.04	1.08	0.89	0.69	0.48	0.25
4	Withholdings on dividends	0.50	0.52	0.54	0.55	0.57	0.59	0.49	0.38	0.26	0.14
5	Net dividends	0.41	0.42	0.44	0.45	0.47	0.49	0.40	0.31	0.22	0.11
6	Loans	7.28	7.28	7.28	7.28	7.28	7.28	5.82	4.36	2.91	1.46
7	Interest	0.58	0.58	0.58	0.58	0.58	0.58	0.47	0.35	0.23	0.12
8	Withholding on interest	0.09	0.09	0.09	0.09	0.09	0.09	0.07	0.05	0.03	0.02
9	Net interest	0.49	0.49	0.49	0.49	0.49	0.49	0.40	0.30	0.20	0.10
10	Tax credits	0.00	0.00	0.00	0.00	0.00	0.00	0.00	0.00	0.00	0.00
11	Management and other fees	0.70	0.72	0.74	0.76	0.79	0.81	0.67	0.52	0.37	0.20
12	Current income	0.20	0.20	0.19	0.18	0.18	0.17	0.13	0.08	0.05	0.01
13	Loan repayments	—	—	—	—	—	1.46	1.46	1.46	1.46	1.46
14	Divestitures	—	—	—	—	—	9.32	9.64	9.98	10.33	10.69
15	Divestiture fee	—	—	—	—	—	0.09	0.10	0.10	0.10	0.11
16	Net cash flows	0.20	0.20	0.19	0.18	0.18	10.85	11.13	11.42	11.72	12.04
17	Internal rate of return	100% = 1.9%									
18		60% = 8.8%									

continued on next page

Notes to Internal Rate of Return Cases[1]

Line	Item	Note
1	Equity investments	Equals the face value of the debt swapped less an average discount of 8%, plus retained earnings, and adjusted by changes in the real peso/dollar exchange rate of B = 0% per annum, P = −2%, O = +2%.
2	Earnings from equity	Assumes earnings on equity investments in real peso terms (net of Mexican inflation) of B = 11%, P = 8%, O = 13%.
3	Dividends	A 30% payout ratio is assumed.
4	Withholdings on dividends	Currently, the Mexican withholding on dividends paid abroad is 55%.
5	Net dividends	Dividends less the withholding on those dividends.
6	Loans	Debt is swapped for these loans on the following terms: B & P at face value, O at a 15% premium.
7	Interest	B and O = 9%, P = 8%.
8	Withholding on interest	Currently 15% for registered lenders.
9	Net interest	Interest less the withholding.
10	Tax credits	Assumes current, carried back, or discounted carried forward benefit of the amounts withheld of B = 50%, P = 0%, O = 100%.
11	Management and other fees	The management fee is 1.5% of the equity investments plus the loans at the beginning of the year, and other fees are $25,000 per annum.
12	Current income	Net dividends plus net interest plus tax credits less management and other fees.
13	Loan repayments	The principal portion of the loans is assumed to be repaid in equal annual installments at the end of years 6–10.
14	Divestitures	Equity investments are assumed to be sold at their carrying values as defined in Line 1 as follows: 1/5 at the end of year 6, 1/4 at year 7, 1/3 at year 8, 1/2 at year 9, and the balance at year 10.
15	Divestiture fees	1% at the sales price plus an incentive fee of B = 1%, P = 0%, O = 2%.
16	Net cash flows	Current income plus loan repayments plus divestitures less divestiture fees.
17	Internal rate of return	100% The internal rate of return on the full face value of the UMS debt and cash contributed to the fund.
18		60% The internal rate of return on the approximate secondary market value of the contributed debt.

[1] B = Base case, P = Pessimistic case, O = Optimistic case

■ EXHIBIT 8.2J

FIRST WACHOVIA CORPORATION
■ IDI MANAGEMENT DESCRIPTION

J. Hallam Dawson, chairman of IDI

1985–present	Managing director of Dawson and Company, San Francisco, a venture capital firm
1975–1984	Initially ran International Division at Crocker National and then served as its president for three years
1960–1974	In a variety of positions at The First National Bank of Chicago, including head of Latin American lending

Amsterdam Pacific Corporation, general partner

A San Francisco-based investment banking firm affiliated with EBC AMRO Bank Ltd., London, the wholly owned international investment banking subsidiary of the Amsterdam Rotterdam Bank NV. The three managing directors had extensive experience in Mexico.

Luis M. de la Fuente, executive vice president of IDI

1975–1987	Director of finance of Salinas y Rocha
1970–1975	Held a variety of positions at The First National Bank of Chicago in Chicago, Mexico City, and Costa Rica

SOURCE: IDI Mexico Fund I Information Memorandum.

sound equity investments might become difficult to find. Even if attractive investments were found, investors in this mutual fund would still be carrying assets in currencies other than those the banks were using as fund sources. Moreover, further devaluations could be harmful to returns if the appreciation in the portfolio did not keep pace. Williams wondered what precedents would be established for the write-down of swapped debt. IDI accountants stated that, in their opinion, no write-down should be required on the pledge of sovereign debt to the Fund. Required write-downs on conversion of debt to equity would equal the government-mandated discount rate.

In addition to the business concerns, risks were associated with the political system in Mexico. Upcoming elections brought the chance of renewed social unrest, which had accompanied de la Madrid's election in 1982. The mechanics of the political system ensured that de la Madrid's candidate would win the July 1988 election, but a smooth transition was important. Political pressure during the transition period could force de la Madrid to relax the country's austerity program and give in to other demands, such as letting wages outpace inflation. Williams discovered that the effect of political changes had already been felt: Carlos Salinas Gotari, minister of finance, budgets and planning and De la Madrid's chosen candidate, closed down the swap market at the beginning of October 1987 to review its impact on the Mexican economy. A determination that the swap program was fueling inflation could cause a breakdown of the entire system.

Williams weighed these issues against the possible results of pursuing other alternatives. Doing nothing would allow time for Mexico's political situation to become more stable, but with Treasury Secretary Baker advocating further renegotiation, First Wachovia would probably be pressured to step up its participation. On the other hand, selling the Mexican exposure in the secondary market would bring immediate cash flow that could be reloaned to more stable ventures. A final option would be swapping Mexican debt for the debt of another, less risky LDC. Williams wondered, however, if making a bet on the viability of one country would be more efficient than spreading the risk over the entire LDC arena. He now had to set about the task of evaluating which method would be right for First Wachovia.

9

CHAPTER

KEY CONCEPTS

INTRODUCTION

Investment selection is a fundamental business activity. The purpose of this chapter is to illustrate how international and domestic investment selection differ. A firm can invest in an essentially unlimited set of assets. For practical purposes, a firm has a relatively limited amount of capital available for investment. Therefore a firm's managers must budget its capital among the most promising investments. The managers' goal is to select the assets that add the largest value to the firm and thus maximize the shareholders' wealth. We refer to the process of selecting the best investment alternatives as capital budgeting.

The net present value *(NPV) approach to capital budgeting requires managers to compare the cost of an investment to the benefits it produces. We define the cost in terms of after-tax cash outflows that typically occur at the beginning of the investment. The benefits of the investment typically occur over time, and we define the benefits in terms of the after-tax cash inflows over time. Because investment capital has opportunity costs and because people are averse to risk, a dollar of cost today is not equivalent to a dollar of risky benefit in the future. Therefore, we typically* discount *the cash-flow benefits in the future by a* cost of capital *or* required rate of return *that reflects both the timing of the cash flows and their risk. For example, if an investment is expected to cost* C_0 (C_0 *is negative) today and to produce expected cash flows after one and two years of* C_1 *and* C_2 *and the cost of capital is* r *percent per year, the net present value of the investment is*

$$NPV = C_0 + C_1/(1 + r)^1 + C_2/(1 + r)^2 \qquad (9.1)$$

The NPV is a measure of the extent to which an investment increases the wealth of the firm's shareholders. Implementing this capital budgeting approach to investment selection, domestically or internationally, requires two types of estimates, expected cash outflows and inflows and the cost of capital.

There are many complexities that require careful consideration, whether analyzing a domestic or international investment opportunity. For example, how do you compare mutually exclusive investment alternatives and should the discount rate reflect the investment's total risk or only its systematic risk? Corporate finance textbooks address these issues. In this chapter, we address only specifically international complexities of capital budgeting, such as how special tax and financing arrangements enter into the capital budgeting calculations, the way inflation and exchange rate fluctuations should be considered, and the best way to reflect the added risk of international investment. In this chapter, we address these questions by analyzing how international cash flows differ from domestic cash flows and how the international cost of capital differs from the domestic cost of capital.

MEASURING CASH FLOWS TO THE PARENT COMPANY

A major difficulty faced by analysts in evaluating foreign investment cash flows is the divergence between the cash flows generated by the investment project as a free-standing local project and the cash flows accruing to the parent. Several factors contribute to the differences: some are controlled by the investor and others are determined by the firm's operating environment. Regardless of the source of the discrepancy, it is important to recognize that the relevant cash flows are those that accrue to the firm's shareholders. Estimation of those cash flows involves a three-stage process that begins with a forecast of the total or free-standing project flows and ends with the shareholders' cash flows. That process requires identifying the factors that cause the two cash flows to diverge and converting estimated foreign currency flows into the home currency of the shareholders. We discuss four influences that cause the cash flows to diverge, interdependencies between the parent firm and the foreign subsidiary, remittance restrictions, taxation and subsidies.

INTERDEPENDENCIES

International investment is often prompted by defensive motives, for example, import tariffs and quotas, or competitive pressure. For example, when the U.S. government induced Japanese car manufacturers to limit their export of automobiles to the United States, the Japanese increased their investment in U.S. manufacturing facilities. In those cases, some of the sales generated by the project are cannibalized from export sales formerly made by existing divisions of the firm. Sales lost to the foreign investment, that would have been maintained without it, should not be included among the foreign investment's revenues. Alternatively, sales that would have been lost due to trade restrictions or competition, should be attributed to the foreign investment project. An example can help clarify this point. A firm is contemplating a foreign investment that will have sales of 7,000 units per month at a price of $50 per unit. The firm currently services that market with export sales of 5,000 units at a price of $60 per unit. A major competitor is establishing a facility in the same region to avoid import quotas that will take effect in the next year. If the firm does not follow suit and make the investment, its estimated export sales will be 2,000 units at $50 per unit. If it does make the investment, export sales will fall to 1,500 units. What sales revenue should be credited to the foreign investment?

The correct answer is the amount that is incremental to the project compared to what would be generated if the project were not undertaken. That amount is $325,000 per month, the difference between the $425,000 total sales with the expansion and the $100,000 that would be realized without it. The $325,000 represents the $350,000 in sales that the investment generates, less the $25,000 that is cannibalized from existing sales. The remaining decline in export sales ($200,000) is not deducted from the project because those sales would be lost even if the investment were not made. Table 9.1 summarizes this example.

Changes in sales revenues are utilized in Table 9.1 to illustrate interdependencies, but they are only one side of the cash-flow equation. In a more complete analysis, costs must also be considered. If costs are higher at the foreign operation, then the increase reduces the cash flows to the parent. The net impact of the foreign investment on total cash flows is relevant.

Interdependencies of cash flows between the parent company and a foreign subsidiary also show up through *transfer pricing*. Transfer prices are the internally

■ TABLE 9.1

INCREMENTAL CASH-FLOW ANALYSIS

	Current Sales	No Investment Sales	With Investment Sales	With Investment Exports
Units	5000	2000	7000	1500
Price	$ 60	$ 50	$ 50	$ 50
Revenue	$300,000	$100,000	$350,000	$75,000

established prices at which different units of a single enterprise buy goods and services from each other. Foreign investment invariably involves international intracompany transactions. Because of tax effects and currency restrictions, international transfer prices are not always set at market levels. For example, the transfer price for a good sold to a foreign subsidiary might be set at an arbitrarily high level, if the foreign subsidiary is in a high tax jurisdiction. This choice has the effect of shifting earnings from a high tax jurisdiction to a low tax jurisdiction. From a corporate viewpoint, the tax reduction increases total cash flows, but without careful analysis, the source of the cash flows might be identified incorrectly because the effect of that transfer pricing policy is to reduce stated cash flows in the high tax country and raise them in the low tax country. Again, an example is helpful.

A firm is considering investing in a foreign assembly plant that buys components from the parent. The market price of the component is $30. At that price, the contribution margin for the parent is $8. After assembly, which adds $10 to the subsidiary's cost, the subsidiary sells the finished product for $50. The effective tax rates in the parent's and subsidiary's countries are 30 percent and 40 percent, respectively.

If the parent uses the market price of the component as the transfer price to the subsidiary, the after-tax cash flows for the corporation are $11.60: $5.60 at the parent level and $6.00 at the subsidiary level. See Table 9.2 for the calculations. Because of the differences in tax rates, a higher transfer price leads to higher after-tax cash flows for the corporation as a whole. At a transfer price of $40, the subsidiary's profits are eliminated entirely, whereas the parent's after-tax cash flows rise to $12.60. If the $40 transfer price is used in evaluating the foreign investment project and the subsidiary is not credited with its share of the final cash flows, the investment appears unprofitable. As an extreme case, suppose that all of the sales depend on building the assembly plant (because of trade restrictions). The correct cash flows to the project then are the full $12.60, even though none of these show up on the subsidiary's books. Because of the presence of interdependencies, it is important to identify accurately the amount and source of all relevant cash flows.

Note in the example that changing the transfer price alters not only the total tax payment but also the allocation of the tax payments between the foreign and home countries. The host country would be very unhappy with the transfer price in the second case because it would eliminate its tax revenues entirely. Determining the fair transfer price is often difficult and has led to disagreements between firms and governments and to the imposition of policies that in the long run are often counterproductive for all concerned. The restrictions discussed in the next section include rules related to transfer pricing as well as other cross-border funds flows.

REMITTANCE RESTRICTIONS

Countries frequently impose limits on the amount of funds that subsidiaries can pay to their foreign parent in the form of dividends. These policies are generally part of a more comprehensive program to reduce a balance of payments deficit. Descriptions of restrictions in force and changes in policies can be found in *Exchange Arrangements and Exchange Restrictions*, published annually by the

■ TABLE 9.2

IMPACT OF TRANSFER PRICES

Case I

Assumptions

Parent's tax rate	30%		
Subsidiary's tax rate	40%		
Transfer price	$30		

Parent's cash flow per unit		Subsidiary's cash flow per unit	
Sale to subsidiary	$30.00	Sale to public	$50.00
Direct costs	22.00	Purchase price	30.00
Contribution margin	$ 8.00	Assembly cost	10.00
Taxes	2.40	Contribution margin	$10.00
		Taxes	4.00
Net margin after tax	$ 5.60	Net margin after tax	$ 6.00

Case II

New assumption

Transfer price	$40		

Parent's cash flow per unit		Subsidiary's cash flow per unit	
Sale to subsidiary	$40.00	Sale to public	$50.00
Direct costs	22.00	Purchase price	40.00
Contribution margin	$18.00	Assembly cost	10.00
Taxes	5.40	Contribution margin	0.00
		Taxes	0.00
Net margin after tax	$12.60	Net margin after tax	$ 0.00

International Monetary Fund. When making a foreign investment decision, it is important that management understand current policies and make some estimate of restrictions in the future. The latter necessarily involves an evaluation of the host country's balance of payments position.

Restrictions on subsidiaries' dividend payments to their parent companies take a variety of forms, usually allowing payment of only a maximum percentage of annual earnings, retained earnings, or sales. Whatever the form, they defer the receipt of cash flows and thereby reduce the value of those flows. The amount of the loss is determined by the amount of cash flows delayed, the length of the delay, and the opportunities to invest the blocked funds in the foreign country. For example, assume that an investment with a 10-year life generates annual net cash flows of $1 million. Restrictions on dividends limit payments to $400,000 each year for the first 9 years, but allow payment equal to accumulated retained earnings at the end of the 10th year. The appropriate cash flows to consider in this case are the $400,000 per year for the first 9 years and $6,400,000 in the last year. If the funds can be reinvested during the interim, the additional interest income should be included as part of the dividend. If the delayed $600,000 can be invested at 5 percent and those earnings are also available for dividends at the end of the 10th year, the final cash flow will be a $400,000 regular dividend, plus a $6,000,000 deferred dividend plus

$1,547,000 in interest on the deferred dividend. The loss due to deferral is obvious when we introduce a required rate of return on this investment. Assume that value is 15 percent per year. The present value of $1,000,000 per year for 10 years is $5,019,000 if discounted at 15 percent. The present value of $400,000 per year for 10 years, plus $6,547,000 at the end of year 10, is $3,873,000. The difference between $3,873,000 and $5,019,000, $1,146,000 is the present value lost because of the deferral. It occurs because the deferred cash flows earn 5 percent, which is less than the required rate of return of 15 percent.

In the example, cash flows and earnings are considered to be the same. That is usually not the case because of the presence of noncash expenses such as depreciation. The disparity between earnings and cash flows creates some ambiguity about which cash flows are available for repatriation. If the dividend restriction establishes a limit on payments based on earnings, the positive cash flow related to depreciation is not available to the firm for repatriation. Unless these funds can be used beneficially elsewhere in the country, it is usually in the parent corporation's interest to keep depreciation expenses low in order to maximize after-tax income available for foreign dividends. No general rule fits all cases, but it is necessary for managers to understand fully whatever restrictions exist and their implications.

TAXATION

Differences in tax rates have already been shown to enter the cash-flow calculations. Effective tax rates in different countries vary a great deal. From the standpoint of a U.S. investor, the tax rate that applies is usually the higher of the two effective rates. The United States gives credit for foreign taxes but only up to the maximum U.S. rate. Therefore, any taxes beyond that rate reduce the return to the investor. Taxes are such an important element that we discuss them in detail in Chapter 10.

SUBSIDIES

Host countries often offer *subsidies* to firms to encourage them to invest. The host country may target the subsidies to attract specific types of investment, such as high technology investments, or to attract investment to specific regions of the country, such as a region with high unemployment. These inducements can take several forms, including tax relief, preferential financing, exemptions from some regulations, and cash payments. The subsidies increase the net present value of a project. In some cases, the subsidies are large enough to change foreign investments' net present values from negative to positive. In those cases, firms make foreign investments that they would not make without the subsidy. When that occurs, the host country has achieved its objective.

Potential investors need to evaluate the subsidy and consider that governments can also eliminate subsidies. A very conservative approach is to accept only those projects that add to the firm's value without the subsidy. A more reasonable method is to include the value of the subsidy as a separate calculation in the evaluation of the investment. This makes clearer the extent to which the investment's value depends on a government subsidy.

EXCHANGE RATES, CASH FLOWS, AND THE DISCOUNT RATE

VALUATION ALTERNATIVES

In the various examples presented in this chapter, the cash flows are given in dollars even though it is clear that they are generated in some other currency. Conversion from local currency into dollars is consistent with the view that parent or investor cash flows are the relevant flows to analyze. A U.S. firm investing in a foreign country is doing so to earn dollars that it can distribute to its shareholders. That much is straightforward. What is not so simple is the process by which estimated foreign currency cash flows are converted to dollars. That process requires forecasts of inflation, exchange rates, and their impacts on the operating cash flows. In addition, the appropriate choice of currency for cash-flow measurement is related to the choice of a discount rate for cash-flow valuation. Therefore, the analysis that follows discusses both the numerator—the forecast cash flows—and the denominator—the discount rate—of the capital budgeting formula. Because the task is formidable, it is important to start with a structured approach. Once we establish the framework, it is possible to build more complicated relationships into the analysis.

To evaluate the investment using the net present value (NPV) criterion, an analyst has at least four alternatives:

1. Use real foreign currency cash flows and a real foreign currency discount rate.

2. Use nominal foreign currency cash flows and a nominal foreign currency discount rate.

3. Use real dollar cash flows and a real dollar discount rate.

4. Use nominal dollar cash flows and a nominal dollar discount rate.

Real cash flows are nominal cash flows adjusted for inflation using the inflation rate expected or recently experienced in that country. The four alternatives are not as different as they might at first appear. We saw in Chapter 4 that economic theory explicitly links inflation rates, exchange rates, and interest rates. If those theoretical relationships are valid empirically, then the choice among the four alternatives is immaterial: Each leads to the same outcome. Because the empirical evidence supports the theory, in broad terms, some authors have suggested using alternative 1 because it requires the least information. That alternative does not require either inflation or exchange rate forecasts. Unfortunately, the use of real foreign cash flows can obscure some important and relevant factors that might influence the desirability of a particular project. As a result, the approach suggested here is alternative 4, the choice that is most difficult because it requires explicit forecasts of both inflation rates and exchange rates. Making these forecasts enhances the likely accuracy of the investment evaluation, because it requires explicit forecasts, rather than relying on implicit assumptions. In the next section, we present the implicit theoretical assumptions that the other alternatives rely on and demonstrate when the four alternatives are equivalent.

THE FISHER EFFECT

The *Fisher effect* relates interest rates to inflation expectations. Specifically, it hypothesizes that the nominal rate of interest consists of a real or noninflation component and an inflation component. An algebraic presentation and numerical example of the Fisher effect follow:

$$(1 + r) = (1 + r^*)(1 + i) = (1.03)(1.20) = 1.236 \qquad (9.2)$$

where

r = the nominal rate of interest, 23.6 percent in this example

r^* = the real rate of interest, 3 percent in this example

i = the expected rate of inflation, 20 percent in this example

The Fisher effect, as defined in equation (9.2) applies to all countries. When we use foreign country variables, we distinguish them with the subscript f. The academic literature usually assumes that r^* and r^*_f, the real rates of return, are equal. If we assume that the expected rate of inflation in a foreign country is 8 percent, the expression for the Fisher effect for that foreign country is

$$(1 + r_f) = (1 + r^*)(1 + i^*_f) = (1.03)(1.08) = (1.1124) \qquad (9.3)$$

PURCHASING POWER PARITY

Relative purchasing power parity (PPP) relates changes in the exchange rate between two countries to their inflation rates: A change in the exchange rate between two time periods is determined by the relative inflation rates in the two countries. The nation experiencing the higher rate of inflation has a depreciating currency. The nation with the lower inflation rate has an appreciating currency. PPP can be expressed as

$$X_0(1 + i)^t/(1 + i^*_f)^t = X_t \qquad (9.4)$$

where

X_0 = exchange rate expressed in home currency (dollars) per foreign currency unit at time 0; in this case we assume it is $1.80

X_t = exchange rate at time t years from 0

In terms of our earlier one-period example,

$$\$1.80(1.20)/(1.08) = \$2.00$$

EQUIVALENCE OF THE FOUR ALTERNATIVES

If the Fisher effect and purchasing power parity are valid, the four alternatives for calculating the present value of foreign cash flows are equivalent. We first demonstrate this analytically and then illustrate it with an extended example.

Beginning with alternative 1, the present value in the home currency, PV, in the base year, 0, of a real foreign currency cash flow in year t, C_t^*, is

$$PV = (X_0)(C_t^*)/(1 + r^*)^t \qquad (9.5)$$

Alternative 2 calls for discounting a nominal foreign cash flow by a nominal foreign discount rate. Therefore, the nominal flow is $C_t^*(1 + i_f)^t$. The present value of this cash flow, adjusted by the nominal discount rate, is

$$PV = (X_0)(C_t^*)(1 + i_f)^t/(1 + r^*)^t(1 + i_f)^t \qquad (9.6)$$

Because the numerator and denominator both have been multiplied by the same value, $(1 + i_f)^t$, equations (9.5) and (9.6) are identical. But the denominator of equation (9.6) is the right-hand side of the Fisher equation (9.3), so equation (9.6) is equal to

$$PV = (X_0)(C_t^*)(1 + i_f)^t/(1 + r_f)^t \qquad (9.7)$$

which is the mathematical representation of alternative 2. Therefore, alternatives 1 and 2 are equivalent.

To show that alternatives 3 and 4 are equivalent, substitute the PPP expression for X_0 from equation (9.4) into equation (9.6).

$$PV = [(X_t)(1 + i_f)^t/(1 + i)^t][(C_t^*)(1 + i_f)^t]/(1 + r^*)^t(1 + i_f)^t \qquad (9.8)$$

This is equal to

$$PV = (X_t)(C_t^*)(1 + i_f)^t]/(1 + r^*)^t(1 + i_f)^t \qquad (9.9)$$

and

$$PV = C_t/(1 + r^*)^t \qquad (9.10)$$

These are the expressions for alternatives 4 and 3, respectively.

To arrive at PV using alternative 4, equation (9.9), it is necessary to forecast the base year cash flows, C_t, inflation in the foreign country, i_f, and future exchange rates, X_t. Forecasting X_t requires some measure of i to compare with i_f, so a home inflation forecast is also necessary. The denominator in equation (9.9) is equal to $1 + r$, and r, the home nominal rate, is a market determined value.

These relationships and the advantages of using nominal dollar flows can be clarified with an example. Assume that an investment in a French project requires a cash outlay of $1 million or FR5 million at the current spot rate. Sales revenues from the project, which has a five-year life, are estimated to be FR3 million per year at today's prices; costs are FR1.2 million. Both revenues and costs are expected to change by 12 percent per year in line with French inflation. Inflation in the United States is 5 percent per year. For a project of this type, the required real rate of return is 3 percent per year.

With the preceding information, it is possible to evaluate the project according to each alternative. The only additional values necessary to do the various calculations can be determined by assuming that the Fisher effect and PPP hold. Table 9.3 summarizes the cash flows, discount rates, and $NPVs$ of the project for each of the four alternatives for valuing investments.

■ **TABLE 9.3**

ALTERNATIVE CASH-FLOW ESTIMATES WHEN
PURCHASING POWER PARITY HOLDS

Year	Option 1 Real Franc	Option 2 Nominal Franc	Option 3 Real Dollar	Option 4 Nominal Dollar
0	−5,000,000	−5,000,000	($1,000,000)	($1,000,000)
1	1,800,000	2,016,000	360,000	378,000
2	1,800,000	2,257,920	360,000	396,900
3	1,800,000	2,528,870	360,000	416,745
4	1,800,000	2,832,335	360,000	437,582
5	1,800,000	3,172,215	360,000	459,461
Discount rate	3.00%	15.36%	3.00%	8.15%
Net present value	3,243,473	3,243,473	$ 648,695	$ 648,695

Examination of the numbers reveals that the four alternatives give the same result. That being the case, it is easy to understand why some people advocate using real cash flows and real returns. That method requires the least amount of information and the least amount of forecasting. It is important to understand, however, that the equivalent results were derived because the economic relationships, PPP and the Fisher effect, were assumed to hold perfectly and because the cash flows were of a simple form. In the next section, we explain why we prefer a method that does not rely on these assumptions.

DO THE FISHER EFFECT AND PPP APPLY?

WHEN THEY APPLY

A vast body of evidence is available concerning the validity of the Fisher effect and PPP. Although much of the evidence is contradictory and subject to varied interpretations, the general view is that over the long run, the relationships are valid. This means, for example, that PPP does not hold month to month or even year to year but that over a 10- or 20-year period, exchange rates do reflect inflation differentials. In addition, there is evidence that the deviations from PPP are not systematic but random. This implies that it is difficult, if not impossible, to accurately forecast the deviations, making the effort not worthwhile. Thus, analysts use PPP as a working assumption about future rates. Because that is the case, why do we not recommend using alternative 1 instead of alternative 4?

The most important reason we do not recommend alternative 1 is that PPP is a macroeconomic relationship: For an economy as a whole, it tends to be valid. At the microeconomic level, PPP is more problematic. It is based on some aggregate price performance measure such as the consumer price index, wholesale price index, or GNP deflator. Within that aggregate is a great deal of variation. As a result, even if PPP holds for the economy as a whole, it is not valid for every individual product or industry line. Moreover, it is unlikely that both revenues and costs will follow the same trend. If that is not the case, differences will arise between the value generated by each of the alternatives.

A variety of factors can generate deviations in the growth paths of revenues and costs. The most common reason is that wages, which are a major component of costs, and prices are not perfectly correlated. More specifically, firms often contract long term for sales or labor. Those contracts generally are written in nominal terms with an expected inflation component built in. Deviations from the inflation expectations lead to windfall profits or losses, depending on the direction of the forecast error. Along the same lines, other costs are generally not indexed for inflation. The most important of these is depreciation, which in most countries is based on historical costs. Inflation therefore dilutes the value of the tax shield that depreciation generates for the firm.

THE IMPACT OF DEVIATIONS FROM PPP

To demonstrate the impact of these factors, we introduce them into the example in Table 9.3. Assume that the costs of FR1.2 million consist of FR900,000 for labor and FR300,000 fixed value payments. PPP and the Fisher effect hold, so the exchange rates each period will be the same as those implicit in Table 9.3. Table 9.4 provides the NPV for each of the alternatives.

In Table 9.3, the four alternatives give identical results. The choice of nominal or real variables, and the choice of francs or dollars introduces no difference. The dollar values are exactly the franc values converted at the current spot rate of exchange. In Table 9.4, the nominal and real calculations differ. Different inflation

■ TABLE 9.4

ALTERNATIVE CASH-FLOW ESTIMATES WHEN
SOME CASH FLOWS ARE FIXED VALUES

Year	Option 1 Real Franc	Option 2 Nominal Franc	Option 3 Real Dollar	Option 4 Nominal Dollar
0	−5,000,000	−5,000,000	($1,000,000)	($1,000,000)
1	1,800,000	2,052,000	360,000	384,750
2	1,800,000	2,334,240	360,000	410,316
3	1,800,000	2,650,349	360,000	436,764
4	1,800,000	3,004,391	360,000	464,164
5	1,800,000	3,400,918	360,000	492,586
Discount rate	3.00%	15.36%	3.00%	8.15%
Net present value	3,243,473	3,620,251	$ 648,695	$ 724,050

rates for revenues and costs and the deviation of those rates from the expected rates implicit in the nominal discount rate generate the differences. Across currencies, the two nominal *NPV*s and the two real *NPV*s are still equivalent. The first pair are equal because PPP was assumed to be valid, and the second set are equal because the required real return in each currency is the same.

Why then is alternative 4 the best choice? It does not rely on the empirical validity of the PPP and the Fisher effect propositions. If they hold, then the results provided by alternative 4 are still accurate, although more tedious to derive; if they do not hold, then alternative 4 incorporates the deviations. Deviations at the macroeconomic level might be hard to predict, but at the firm level, many deviations are predictable. In the example, depreciation expense is known to have a zero inflation rate. Moreover, financial analysts within the firm have access to information that others do not have. They are more informed about the firm's intentions, costs structures, and sales patterns than anyone else. By using nominal rates, they use that information. Moreover, the detailed development of pro forma financial statements forces the analyst to consider possible problem areas and to be aware of their potential impact on the profitability of a project.

The following example demonstrates the point. For a particular project, labor costs represent 60 percent of variable costs at current prices. During the last decade wages have not kept up with the general rate of inflation, so current real wages represent only 70 percent of the real wage rate of 10 years ago. This has been caused in part by wage controls deliberately set by the government to lag price increases. One result has been increased investment in labor-intensive firms, but another has been labor unrest and union agitation. Consequently, the analyst believes that future wages will rise at a faster rate than prices, thus squeezing the profitability of the project. If the analyst relies on current real costs or past wage patterns, the problem of rapidly rising future costs escapes notice.

Finally, the use of real cash flows assumes that there are no changes in competitive position related to exchange rate changes. The traditional view is that a depreciation of a country's currency makes the country's goods more desirable because they are cheaper and that an appreciation makes those goods more expensive and less desirable. According to this view, when a nation's currency devalues, its exports become cheaper and its imports more expensive. Consequently, foreigners buy more of the nation's goods as do locals who reduce their volume of imports. A similar story with opposite results applies to the case of an appreciation.

The problem with the traditional view is that it ignores PPP and the individual firms' competitive positions, both of which have an impact on whether or not revenues change when exchange rates change. Recall that if PPP holds perfectly, exchange rate changes are determined by and exactly reflect inflation differentials in the two countries. Because the relative cross-border price of a good is determined by the local currency price and the exchange rate, there is no change in the relative price if PPP holds. Any depreciation that lowers the value of the currency is precisely offset by the inflation effect that raises its local currency price. Therefore, currency fluctuations are neutral with respect to sales volumes and base currency revenues. This naive view is inconsistent with observations of the effects that changes in exchange rates have on the competitive positions of firms.

OTHER RELEVANT FACTORS

Once the PPP assumption is relaxed, there is room for relative price changes and competitive adjustments. The net impact depends on the elasticities of supply and demand. They are affected in turn by a variety of factors that should be considered when cash flows are estimated, even if the analyst cannot measure them exactly. Among the more important considerations are these:

1. The absolute and relative sizes of the domestic and export business of the firm.
2. The extent of competition in domestic and foreign markets.
3. Available capacity for expanding sales.
4. The relative importance of local versus foreign content in manufacturing costs.
5. Price restrictions and tariffs.
6. Whether the product is priced for export in local currency or a single major currency.

As indicated previously, each of the factors influences the elasticity of supply or demand either directly or indirectly. For example, if a firm competes solely in a domestic market against other local firms, a devaluation has little impact on sales. It likely reduces demand somewhat because consumers have lower purchasing power due to the devaluation, but the firm does not gain any price advantage from the change in exchange rates. If the firm depends on foreign sources of new materials or components, the devaluation increases its costs. Those increases might not be allowed to be passed on to consumers if local price controls are in effect, a fairly common situation in devaluing countries. The scenario described here applies to many nations that are trying to encourage local manufacturing with protection from exports provided by prohibitive tariffs.

Clearly, evaluating foreign investments involves many factors and many sources of uncertainty. That makes the whole process more difficult but also highlights the importance of including specifically in the analysis nominal foreign currency cash flows and the impact of deviations from parity relationships. It also suggests that *sensitivity analysis* should play an important role in the evaluation process. Analysts must examine how sensitive an investment's cash flows are to various changes that might occur. Sensitivity analysis not only reveals interaction effects that might otherwise go unnoticed but also provides insights into the risk of the investment. More will be said about risk in the next section.

We can summarize our recommendations for valuing foreign investment to this point as a three-step process.

1. Consider the project cash flows as an independent free-standing foreign investment. Estimate cash flows in nominal foreign currency values.
2. Isolate the cash flows that actually accrue to the investor. This step involves looking closely at dividend remittances, transfer payments, and interdependencies between the new foreign investment and existing investments.

3. Convert the investor's foreign currency flows to home currency values in order to produce a set of nominal dollar cash flows to be discounted with a nominal dollar rate of interest.

ADJUSTING FOR RISK

THE NET PRESENT VALUE METHOD

We began this section by describing the net present value of an investment over a two-period time horizon as

$$NPV = C_0 + C_1/(1 + r)^1 + C_2/(1 + r)^2 \qquad (9.1)$$

To this point, we have discussed the estimation of the cash flows, the C's, and we have treated the required rate of return, r, as a real risk-free rate of interest adjusted for inflation. This approach omits one important consideration, risk. Shareholders are averse to risk. If the expected values of two cash flows and their timing are identical, the one with the smaller risk has a larger present value. There are two ways to adjust for risk. Lowering the expected value of the cash flow to the value that would be equivalent, if it were riskless, is one way. This value, known as the *certainty equivalent* of the risky cash flow, is discounted at the risk-free rate of return to produce the present value of the risky cash flow. The certainty equivalent approach has considerable theoretical appeal, but it is not popular because there is no well-established way to calculate certainty equivalents. An alternative approach is to adjust the discount rate to a value higher than the inflation-adjusted risk-free rate of return. This value is called the risk-adjusted discount rate. Used to calculate present values of risky cash flows, the risk-adjusted interest rate lowers the present values relative to those produced using the risk-free rate of return. This approach has the disadvantage of increasing the adjustment for risk as the time horizon increases. We say disadvantage, because the risk may not increase with time.

Table 9.5 illustrates this problem. The risk-free rate of return is 10 percent and the risk-adjusted rate of return is 15 percent. The discount factors are the values $1/(1 + \text{Interest Rate})^t$. The ratios are the values $(1.15)^t/(1.10)^t$. They measure the extent to which the present value is reduced to reflect risk. For the cash flow at

▪ TABLE 9.5

COMPARISON OF DISCOUNT FACTORS

	Time		
Discount Rates	1	2	3
15%	0.870	0.756	0.658
10%	0.909	0.826	0.751
Ratios	0.957	0.915	0.875

time 1, the risk adjustment is 4.3 percent; at time 2, it is 8.5 percent; and at time 3, it is 14.9 percent.

Despite this problem, the risk-adjusted rate of return method is quite popular. One reason is that it is possible to relate the risk-adjusted rate of return to the cost of raising funds for the firm to invest. This cost of capital for the firm is easy to approximate, relative to the other alternative adjustment methods. Using the cost of capital as the risk-adjusted discount rate is often not appropriate. The discount rate should reflect the systematic risk of the investment being valued and the cost of capital reflects the risk of the whole firm. This is an especially important issue with respect to foreign investment, where the project risk is likely quite different from the risk of the firm as a whole. There are two possible responses to this objection. One response is to estimate the cost of capital for firms that resemble the investment project being valued. This is easier to describe than to implement because it is difficult to identify comparable firms. The other response is to suggest using the firm's cost of capital as a point of departure and adjusting it arbitrarily to reflect the estimated relationship between the riskiness of the project and the firm as a whole. Firms that have adopted this approach have, in some cases, added a separate adjustment to the discount rate for foreign investments.

ADJUSTED PRESENT VALUE METHOD

The *adjusted present value* (APV) method offers a slightly different approach to risk adjustment. It is based on adjusting the discount rate, but it customizes the adjustment to match the different risk characteristics of the individual components of the cash flows. This approach has been applied to both domestic and international project evaluation.

The APV method begins with the premise that the project's cash flows can be decomposed into their constituent parts. Each is discounted at a different rate, reflecting the risk associated with it. With regard to an international project, the cash-flow streams might consist of dividend remittances from operating income, royalties or other transfer payments, depreciation-related tax savings, and the benefits from a subsidized loan. An argument can be made that these cash flows, beginning with operating income, are subject to decreasing risk or uncertainty. Therefore, progressively lower discount rates are appropriate for each set.

It has been suggested that the operating flows be discounted using an all-equity rate that reflects the risk of a similar project if it were funded without financial leverage. The subsidy benefits should be discounted at the risk-free rate because they are not subject to operating uncertainty. The remaining flows would be discounted at rates somewhere between the two, reflecting their relative risk. Although the APV has considerable theoretical and intuitive appeal, it is much easier to describe than to implement. Choosing the various discount rates is not easy.

IMPLICATIONS FOR MANAGERS

Foreign exchange uncertainty complicates the capital budgeting process when cross-border cash flows are involved. The impact is on both the estimate of cash flows and the choice of the appropriate discount rate. The financial manager of a multinational corporation must determine how to adjust the cash flows and discount rate to reflect the added dimension that currency brings to the capital budgeting process.

From a purely theoretical perspective, if the parity relationships hold perfectly, then there are four alternatives that work equally well, as indicated in the chapter. However, in practice, it is clear that there are deviations from theory and, as a result, the four alternatives provide different conclusions. We have suggested that the most demanding of the four approaches, nominal dollar cash flows and a nominal discount rate, be used. It forces the financial managers to explicitly forecast inflation rates and exchange rates as well as to identify those cash flows that might be affected by subsidies, transfer prices, and other variables.

One reason for the extra effort is that the approach will lead to better, more accurate estimates when the parity conditions do not hold. Another, and perhaps more important, reason is that by explicitly modeling the various cash flows, the manager becomes more aware of the impact of changes in the estimates. This makes sensitivity analysis of the cash flows possible and it is a powerful tool for understanding the riskiness of the investment.

The approach favored in this chapter balances the theory with the practical realities. We focus attention on the central importance of currency valuation and its relationship to prices and interest rates. The various parity relationships are not just invoked automatically or seen as analytical shortcuts. Instead, they are viewed as a framework for understanding how economic and business considerations might change the cash flows and their values. it is difficult, perhaps impossible, to forecast prices and exchange rates over the life of a project. That difficulty is recognized fully, but the requirement of making explicit and reasonable assumptions will help the manager understand fully what the success or failure of the project depends upon.

QUESTIONS AND EXERCISES

9-1. A consumer goods manufacturer is currently selling 250,000 gross of its product to Mexican wholesalers. If the firm builds a factory in Mexico, it will be able to sell 400,000 gross in Mexico and to increase its exports to other Latin American countries by 50,000 gross. If it does not build a plant in Mexico, it will lose significant market share and its sales will fall to 150,000. In that case, it will divert exports to other Latin American countries and increase sales there by 30,000 gross. What is the sales increase attributable to building the plant in Mexico?

9-2. A firm operating in a foreign country often sends its executives there to act as consultants. When it does so, it bills the subsidiary for their time at the rate of $2,000 per day. The actual cost of the executives' time averages $800 per day. The firm bills its foreign subsidiary for an average of 500 days per year of executive time. The corporate tax rate in the foreign country is 50 percent, and the tax rate in the United States is 40 percent.

   a. What is the size of the understatement in the foreign subsidiary's income before tax and the overstatement in the parent's income before tax that this practice creates?

b. What is the size of the underpayment in foreign taxes and overpayment in domestic taxes?

c. How much does the firm gain from this practice?

d. How might the foreign country control this practice?

9-3. Two students studied Table 9.3 in the chapter and decided that there was a fifth method of calculating the *NPV* of a foreign investment. This fifth method involved using nominal French franc cash flows in each year. The students converted these to dollar cash flows by forecasting the value of the FR in each year. They discounted the dollar cash flows by the real U.S. interest rate. To make their method equivalent to those in Table 9.3, they made their forecasts of the FR, assuming that PPP held. The problem with this effort is that they calculated a different *NPV* for the investment. Listed below is their addition to Table 9.3. How did they calculate their forecasts for the values of the FR and their dollar cash flows? What do the students need to do to correct their method?

	Option 2		Option 5
Year	Nominal French Franc	French Franc Forecast	Real Dollar
0	–5,000,000	$0.2000	($1,000,000)
1	2,016,000	0.1875	378,000
2	2,257,920	0.1758	396,900
3	2,528,870	0.1648	416,745
4	2,832,335	0.1545	437,582
5	3,172,215	0.1448	459,461
	15.36%		3%
	3243473	NPV FR	
	$ 648,695	NPV $	$ 907,609

9-4. A U.S. manufacturer is planning to open a factory in Mexico to supply the local market. The factory costs $1,000,000 and has a useful life of seven years. The manufacturer has developed the following real dollar pro forma cash-flow statement for the plant, which it expects to apply in each of the seven years. The required rate of return on the plant is 12 percent in real terms, and the tax rate in both countries is 40 percent. The manufacturer is concerned with the possibility that inflation in Mexico and the changing value of the peso may affect the feasibility of making this investment in Mexico.

Sales	$2,000,000
Cost of sales	–1,600,000)
Selling costs	(110,000)
Depreciation	(142,857)
Net income before tax	147,143
Taxes	(58,857)
Net income after tax	88,286
Cash flow after tax	231,143
NPV	

a. What is the real dollar NPV of this plant?

b. Assume that U.S. inflation is 0 percent per year and inflation in Mexico is 10 percent per year. What is the NPV of the investment in Mexico if the real value of the peso is unchanged over the period?

c. Repeat part (b), assuming that the real value of the peso appreciates 2 percent per year.

d. Why might the real value of the peso appreciate over time?

9-5. A U.S. firm planning an investment in Argentina has been offered a choice of two tax incentives. The firm can either pay two-thirds of its tax liability each year, or it can pay 100 percent of its taxes but defer payment for 10 years.

a. Assuming that the firm's income and income taxes will be approximately equal each year for the 10-year period, which is the better alternative if the appropriate discount rate for this type of incentive is 6 percent per year?

b. Which is the better alternative if the appropriate discount rate is 10 percent per year?

9-6. In an effort to attract foreign investment, the state of Tennessee has offered a foreign manufacturer a $50 million loan with an annual interest rate of 3 percent. Interest is payable annually, and the term of the loan is 15 years. The firm pays a tax rate of 40 percent on income, and its normal after tax cost of debt is 6 percent. How much is this financial subsidy worth?

REFERENCES

Kim, S. H., and T. Crick. "Foreign Capital Budgeting Practices Used by U.S. and Non-U.S. Multinational Companies." *Engineering Economist,* Spring 1984, 207–215.

Lessard, D. R. "Evaluating Foreign Projects: An Adjusted Present Value Approach." In International Financial Management, 2nd ed. Ed. D. R. Lessard. New York: John Wiley, 1985.

Shapiro, A. C. "Capital Budgeting for the Multinational Corporation." *Financial Management,* Spring 1978, 7–16.

———. "International Capital Budgeting." *Midland Journal of Corporate Finance,* Spring 1983, 26–45.

Stonehill, A. I., and L. Nathanson. "Capital Budgeting and the Multinational Corporation." *California Management Review,* Summer 1968, 39–54.

GRAND METROPOLITAN PLC

Grand Metropolitan PLC is the world's largest wine and spirits seller, and the only one analysts expect will show volume gains this year. Its Burger King hamburger chain, the world's second biggest, has just completed a turnaround. So why is the price of GrandMet shares in New York, compared with its earnings, 10 percent below the average price/earnings ratio of the companies in the Standard & Poor's 500 index? And more important, why have rumors surfaced that GrandMet, valued at more than $14 billion in the stock market, may be a takeover target?[1]

It is our goal to build on GrandMet's strengths and continue to create sustainable competitive advantage in our businesses, which is the bedrock of shareholder value and wealth.[2]

By April 1992, senior managers of Grand Metropolitan PLC could look back on a flurry of financial activity. GrandMet had just acquired Cinzano, the Italian vermouth and wines company, for £100 million. In the United States, GrandMet was negotiating a joint venture in which it would receive £39.5 million in exchange for the U.S. flour-milling business it had acquired when it bought Pillsbury in 1989. In 1991, the group sold off about £800 million in businesses in its effort to focus on core activities: food, drink, retailing.

In spite of the world recession, Grand Metropolitan beat market forecasts in 1991 with a 4.8 percent increase in pretax profits, which brought the group to a record £963 million. This success was accomplished in what Chairman Sir Allen Sheppard believed was "one of the toughest years in Grand Metropolitan's history." Sheppard emphasized that the positive results demonstrated the validity of GrandMet's strategic intent to focus on its core businesses. While conceding that "1992 will be another tough year," he reiterated the company's goal "to constantly improve on rather than match previous achievements." The 1991 annual report carried the slogan "adding value" imprinted under the company name. Achieving the goal, however, might mean selling off some of the group's poorly performing businesses, such as Pearle Vision. Furthermore, in the previous year, rumors had circulated that GrandMet might be a takeover target.

THE COMPANY ▬▬▬▬▬▬

With a total 1991 turnover (sales) of £8.75 billion, Grand Metropolitan ranked among Britain's 10 largest companies. It acted as a pure holding company for a group of business units that were widely diversified both geographically and in terms of products. Exhibit 9.1A presents a summary and description of GrandMet's three major operating sectors: foods (30 percent of 1991 trading profit), drinks

---

[1] Peter Waldman, "Sir Allen Cools the Pace at Grand Met," *European Wall Street Journal*, October 8, 1991.

[2] 1990 Annual Report to Shareholders, Grand Metropolitan PLC.

This case was prepared by Philippe Demigne, Jean-Christophe Donck, Bertrand George, and Michael Levy with Professor Robert F. Bruner. The financial support of the Citicorp Global Scholars Program is gratefully acknowledged. Copyright © 1992 by the Darden Graduate Business School Foundation, Charlottesville, Va., and INSEAD, Fontainbleau, France. Rev. 7/93.

GRAND METROPOLITAN PLC

FOOD Trading Profit £300 m (30%)	DRINKS Trading Profit £454 m (46%)	RETAILING Trading Profit £236 m (24%)
Pillsbury Brands (US) Baked goods (biscuits, sweet foods, pizzas); fresh, frozen, and canned vegetables; milled flour and processed food. Brands included Pillsbury, Janos, Green Giant, Totino's.	**International Distillers and Vintners (worldwide)** Production and distribution of wines and spirits.	**Grand Metropolitan Retailing (UK)** Management and operation of one small restaurant chain, Old Orleans, and around 1,540 managed pubs, both unbranded and under the Chef & Brewer, Clifton Inns, and Country Carvery brand names.
Pillsbury Food Group (Europe) Prepared meals; baked goods (cookies, cakes, gateaux, pies, savoury pastries); savoury products (meat pies, sausages, burgers & buns). Brands included Erasco, Jokish, Peter's, Hofmann Menu, Fleur de Lys, Memory Lane, Kaysens, Brossard, Goldstein, Jus-rol, Bélin Surgelés, Vinchon Jeanette.	Owned brands included Smirnoff vodka, J&B rare Scotch whisky, Bailey's Irish Cream liqueur, Malibu liqueur, Croft Original sherry, La Plat d'Or wines, Metaxa Greek brandy, Popov vodka, Gilbey's gin, Bombay dry gin, Cinzano vermouth, Ouzo 12, Inglenook, Almaden, and Beaulieu California wines.	**Pearle Inc. (US, Europe, Far East)** Retailing of eye-care products/ services with over 1,100 stores. Brands included Pearle Vision.
Häagen-Dazs (US, Europe, Far East) Premium ice cream.	Agency brands included Grand Marnier liqueur, Cointreau, Jose Cuervo Tequila, Absolut vodka, Jack Daniels bourbon.	**Burger King (worldwide)** Chain of 6,400 franchised hamburger restaurants in 41 countries.
Alpo Pet Food (US) Cat and dog food. Brands included Alpo, Jim Dandy, Blue Mountain.	Note: This division also previously included Grand Metropolitan Brewing, with owned and licensed beer brands including Webster's, Watney, Foster's, Carlsberg, Budweiser, Holsten. This segment was sold to Courage in February 1991 as part of a pubs-for-breweries swap transaction (Inntrepreneur Estates).	
GrandMet Foodservice (US) Food goods for bakery and catering sectors.		

Property Interests

Grand Metropolitan Estates (UK)
Property management and development.

Inntrepreneur Estates (UK)
50% joint venture with Courage responsible for licensed estate of 7,350 tenanted pubs.

SOURCE: Annual reports of Grand Metropolitan PLC.

(46 percent), and retailing (24 percent). The brands it owned and managed ranked among the best known worldwide: Green Giant, Häagen-Dazs, Alpo, and Pillsbury in foods; Smirnoff, Bailey's, J&B, and Cinzano in drinks; Burger King and Pearle

Vision in retailing. Geographically, 51% of GrandMet's 1991 turnover was generated in the United States, 34 percent came from the United Kingdom, and 10 percent from Continental Europe.

Exhibit 9.1B gives GrandMet's historical financial performance broken down by operating sector and by geographical region. Exhibit 9.1c summarizes the group's consolidated balance sheets and income statements for the past five years.

GrandMet was founded in the late 1940s as the Washington Group, a chain of hotels established by Sir Maxwell Joseph. With the acquisition of the Mount Royal Hotel in 1957, the company changed its name to Mount Royal Ltd. to reflect the fact that, with 712 rooms, this new acquisition was much larger than the group's existing hotels. In 1961, the company was listed on the London stock exchange, and in 1962, the group changed its name to Grand Metropolitan Hotels.

The 1960s saw the first in a series of acquisitions that would move GrandMet into nonhotel businesses. In 1966, the group bought Levy & Franks, owners of the Chef and Brewer pub and restaurant chain. By 1969, GrandMet had expanded into dairy products with the acquisition of Express Dairy (£32 million). During the 1970s, its most important purchases included the Mecca gaming establishments (bought for £33 million, sold in 1985 for £95 million) and Watney (£435 million), the owner of International Distillers and Vintners, which would form the core of GrandMet's drinks division.

GrandMet's pace of acquisition and divestiture accelerated during the 1980s. Its major acquisitions during this decade included the Liggett Group (owner of Alpo pet food, bought for $450 million), Intercontinental Hotels (bought for $500 million, sold in 1988 for $2 billion), Pearle Optical ($385 million), Heublein (U.S. wines and spirits company and owner of Smirnoff vodka, bought for $1.2 billion), and finally, Pillsbury (owner of Burger King and Häagen-Dazs, bought for £3.3 billion).

The 1990s started with a flurry of divestitures, as nearly £800 million in businesses were sold off. By 1992, GrandMet had divested all of its hotels, breweries, gaming establishments, soft-drink bottling plants, fitness products, and all food brands that were judged not to have international branding potential. The result was a group focused on a "core competence": the management of international brands in food, drinks, and retailing. Exhibit 9.1D summarizes the transactions that GrandMet undertook from 1960 through 1992.

FINANCIAL STRATEGY

In an analysts' briefing given by GrandMet in December 1991, Ian Martin, group managing director and chief operating officer, stated that the group's positive financial results "demonstrate the effectiveness of our operational principles, which can be simplified down to just seven words: build brands, cut costs, develop products, all within the framework of total quality."[3] At this same briefing, David Nash, financial director, outlined the financial strategy that supported these operational principles: capitalize brand value, increase interest coverage, and dispose of products that do not provide an adequate return.

---

[3] GrandMet preliminary results briefing, December 5, 1991.

■ **EXHIBIT 9.1B**

GRAND METROPOLITAN PLC
■ DISTRIBUTION OF TURNOVER, PROFITS, AND ASSETS
BY SEGMENT AND REGION

	Absolute Performance					As a Percentage of Totals				
	1991	1990	1989	1988	1987	1991	1990	1989	1988	1987
Drinks										
Turnover	2,425	3,000	2,784	2,581	2,178	32	33	36	47	46
Operating profit	454	473	389	316	257	46	45	45	55	53
Net assets	1,536	1,623	1,626	1,479	1,504	26	26	26	40	49
Operating margin	18.7%	15.8%	14.0%	12.2%	11.8%					
RONA*	**19.2%**	**18.9%**	**15.6%**	**13.9%**	**11.1%**					
Food										
Turnover	3,026	3,506	2,872	1,253	1,047	40	39	37	23	22
Operating profit	300	309	245	84	69	30	29	28	15	14
Net assets	1,997	1,763	2,468	310	260	34	29	39	8	9
Operating margin	9.9%	8.8%	8.5%	6.7%	6.6%					
RONA	**9.8%**	**11.4%**	**6.5%**	**17.6%**	**17.3%**					
Retailing										
Turnover	2,051	2,531	2,040	1,671	1,467	27	28	27	30	31
Operating profit	236	278	230	179	160	24	26	27	31	33
Net assets	2,332	2,785	2,266	1,898	1,290	40	45	36	51	42
Operating margin	11.5%	11.0%	11.3%	10.7%	10.9%					
RONA	**6.6%**	**6.5%**	**6.6%**	**6.1%**	**8.1%**					
United Kingdom and Ireland										
Turnover	2,940	3,685	4,688	3,836	3,559	34	39	50	64	62
Operating profit	385	451	424	364	331	36	42	44	56	58
Net assets	1,816	2,500	2,626	2,700	1,945	30	40	41	64	62
Continental Europe										
Turnover	862	661	471	221	214	10	7	5	4	4
Operating profit	104	81	66	46	36	10	7	7	7	6
Net assets	557	427	330	384	335	9	7	5	9	11
United States										
Turnover	4,433	4,537	3,720	1,758	1,720	51	48	40	29	30
Operating profit	517	475	395	218	185	48	44	41	33	32
Net assets	3,466	3,149	3,314	1,034	759	57	50	51	25	24
Rest of America										
Turnover	216	216	174	54	58	2	2	2	1	1
Operating profit	20	21	20	14	13	2	2	2	2	2
Net assets	128	148	145	50	61	2	2	2	1	2
Rest of World										
Turnover	297	295	265	160	155	3	3	3	3	3
Operating profit	45	54	62	12	6	4	5	6	2	1
Net assets	86	91	68	22	24	1	1	1	1	1

*Return on net assets is computed as EBIAT (earnings before interest and after taxes) divided by net assets (total assets less current liabilities). A benchmark against which to compare RONA is the weighted average cost of capital.

SOURCE: Annual reports of Grand Metropolitan PLC.

■ **EXHIBIT 9.1c**

GRAND METROPOLITAN PLC
■ HISTORICAL FINANCIAL STATEMENTS
(IN £ MILLIONS)

	1991	1990	1989	1988	1987
Balance Sheet					
Total assets	9,187	9,420	9,570	5,846	4,577
Fixed assets					
Intangible assets	2,464	2,317	2,652	588	0
Tangible assets	2,764	3,756	3,839	3,279	2,725
Investments	851	214	144	206	177
Total fixed assets	6,079	6,287	6,635	4,074	2,902
Current assets					
Stocks	1,286	1,349	1,269	761	734
Debtors	1,561	1,541	1,451	874	828
Cash at bank and in hand	261	243	215	138	113
Total current assets	3,108	3,133	2,935	1,772	1,675
Creditors (less than one year)					
Borrowings	(157)	(206)	(362)	(187)	(330)
Other creditors	(2,135)	(2,343)	(2,316)	(1,301)	(1,166)
Total current liabilities	(2,292)	(2,549)	(2,678)	(1,488)	(1,496)
Current assets – Current liabilities	816	584	257	284	179
Total assets – Current liabilities	6,895	6,871	6,892	4,358	3,081
Creditors (greater than one year)					
Borrowings	(2,703)	(2,925)	(3,494)	(702)	(1,142)
Other creditors	(169)	(191)	(231)	(163)	(103)
Total noncurrent liabilities	(2,872)	(3,116)	(3,725)	(865)	(1,245)
Provisions	(569)	(328)	(325)	(55)	(70)
Total assets – Total liabilities	3,454	3,427	2,842	3,438	1,765
Capital and reserves					
Capital	515	508	506	443	441
Reserves	2,907	2,893	2,304	2,964	1,296
Minority interests	32	26	32	31	28
Total equity	3,454	3,427	2,842	3,438	1,765
Profit-and-Loss Account					
Turnover	8,748	9,394	9,298	6,029	5,706
Cost of sales	(7,473)	(8,119)	(8,159)	(5,262)	(5,016)
Depreciation	(204)	(216)	(190)	(125)	(126)
Trading profit	1,071	1,059	949	642	564
Income of related companies	10	23	18	12	8
Other income	18	79	80	39	14
Net interest	(171)	(239)	(280)	(93)	(120)
Exceptional items	35	(3)	(35)	(25)	(9)
Pretax profit	963	919	732	576	456
Taxation	(298)	(279)	(216)	(155)	(120)
Net income	665	640	516	421	336
Minority interests	(7)	(6)	(8)	(8)	(2)
Extraordinary items	(226)	435	560	290	128
Dividends payable	(218)	(198)	(167)	(129)	(104)
Retained earnings	214	871	901	574	358

SOURCE: Annual reports of Grand Metropolitan PLC.

■ **EXHIBIT 9.1D**

Acquisitions	**Divestitures**

1960s and 1970s

1966 Levy & Franks: pub and restaurant chain
1967 Bateman & Midland Catering: contract catering
1969 Express Dairy: distribution of milk products
1970 Berni Inns: hotels in UK; Mecca: gaming, betting, and amusement centers
1971 Truman Hanbury Buxton: brewing, pubs, and hotels
1972 Watney (incl. IDV): brewing, distribution of wines and spirits

1980s

Acquisitions	Divestitures
1980 Liggett Group (US): cigarettes, wines and spirits, soft-drink bottling, fitness products, pet food (Alpo)	**1984** CC Soft Drinks: soft-drink manufacturer
1981 Intercontinental Hotels: worldwide luxury hotel chain	**1985** Express Dairy (northern area): milk/dairy products; Pinkerton Tobacco (US): chewing tobacco (Liggett); L&M do Brasil: tobacco leaf (Liggett); Mecca Leisure: bingo halls/amusement centers
1983 Childrens' World (US): early education services	
1985 Cinzano (25%): drinks; Quality Care (US): home health-care; Pearle Optical (US): world's largest eye-care products retailing	**1986** Dryborough & Co. (UK), Stern Brauerei (D), Brouwerij Maes (B): brewing; Liggett Group (US): cigarettes
1986 G. Ruddle & Co.: brewer	**1987** Compass Group: contract and other services; Childrens' World (US): child care products; Quality Care (US): home health-care products; Diversified Products (US): fitness products (Liggett); McGuinness Distillers: Canadian spirits
1987 Heublein (US): wines and spirits; Almaden Vineyards (US): wines; Saccone & Speed and Roberts & Cooper: wines and spirits; Dairy Produce Packers: dairy products; Martell (10%): cognac; two pet-food manufacturers (US)	
1988 Vision Express and Eye & Tech (US): optical superstores; Kaysens: frozen desserts; Peter's Savoury Products: meat and pastry products; William Hill Org.: retail betting; Wienerwald/Spaghetti Factory: German and Swiss restaurants	**1988** Hotel Meurice (F); Atlantic Soft Drink Co./Pepsi-Cola San Joaquin Bottling Co. (US); Intercontinental Hotels
1989 The Pillsbury Company (US): international food group: Burger King, Green Giant, Häagen-Dazs; Metaxa: Greek brandy; Ouzo-Kaloyannis (30%): Greek spirits; Brent Walker: pubs; UB Restaurants: Wimpy, Pizzaland, and Pizza Perfect fast-food chains	**1989** Steak & Ale/Bennigans (US): restaurant chain; London Clubs: London casino business; Van De Kamp's: branded frozen foods; Bumble Bee: branded seafood; William Hill: retail betting

continued on next page

■ EXHIBIT 9.1D

Acquisitions	Divestitures
1990s	

Acquisitions	Divestitures
1990 Remy Martin-Cointreau (20%): joint-venture spirits/liqueurs; Anglo Espanola de Distribucion: Spanish wines and spirits distributor; Jus-rol: food manufacturer **1991** Belin Surgelés (France): frozen cakes and pastries; Inntrepreneur Estates (50%) joint venture with Courage: management company for all Courage and 3,570 GrandMet pubs under pubs-for-breweries swap **1992** Cinzano: remaining 75%	**1990** Berni Inns: family restaurant chain **1991** Pizzaland/Pastificio: pizza/pasta restaurant chains; Perfect Pizza: take-away/delivery pizza chain; Watney Truman, Ruddles Brewery, Samuel Webster and Wilsons: breweries; 4 Pillsbury flour mills (US); 3,570 managed and tenanted pubs to Inntrepreneur Estates; The Dominic Group: off-license chain; Express Dairy: liquid milk products; Eden Vale: chilled products

SOURCE: Annual reports of Grand Metropolitan PLC and IBCA report, "Grand Metropolitan" (October 1991).

BRAND VALUATION: In 1988, GrandMet was the first U.K. company to begin the practice of assessing the value of recently acquired brands and then capitalizing that value on the balance sheet. As shown in Exhibit 9.1c, the value of the brands (principally, Smirnoff, Pillsbury, Green Giant, and Burger King), consolidated under the label "Intangible assets," constituted 40 percent of 1991 fixed assets and 27 percent of the company's 1991 total assets.

INTEREST COVERAGE AND DEBT POLICY: Senior management was committed to reducing GrandMet's financial gearing (leverage) and noted in announcing the results for 1991 that the ratio of debt/capital had fallen by 9 percentage points in the last year and that the firm's interest coverage ratio had risen from 4.8 times to 6.6. Exhibit 9.1E shows the historical evolution of GrandMet's debt structure in terms of its maturity profile and currency profile.

INVEST IN PROJECTS MEETING GROWTH CRITERIA: At the December 1991 analysts' briefing, CEO Sheppard outlined GrandMet's investment policy as follows: "In addition to Brewing, we have continued to exit those businesses whose future potential earnings do not meet our growth criteria. All these decisions were driven by a thorough analysis of income growth prospects."[4] As Exhibits 9.1B and 9.1c indicate, during the 1987–1991 fiscal years, GrandMet had generated a compound growth rate in pretax profits of 20.5 percent per year. Implicit in Sheppard's statement was the assumption that only those investments that would not jeopardize this growth trend would be undertaken.

---

[4] Ibid.

GRAND METROPOLITAN PLC
■ DEBT PROFILE

	1991	1990	1989	1988	1987
Debt Maturity					
Current	5%	7%	9%	21%	22%
1 to 2 years	2	58	11	19	25
2 to 5 years	77	30	69	14	28
Over 5 years	16	5	11	46	25%
Debt Currency					
U.S. dollar	77%	79%	11%	8%	11%
Pound sterling	18	15	9	47	33
Deutsche mark (DM)	2	1	1	0	0
Multicurrency	0	0	77	34	47
Various	3	5	3	10	8

Market Value of Equity (as of April 15, 1992)

Common shares prices	£9.48 per share
Shares outstanding	1,005,896,041
Market value of equity	£9,535,894,468

SOURCES: Annual reports of Grand Metropolitan PLC; *The Wall Street Journal.*

GROUP COST OF CAPITAL

Were GrandMet's financial objectives consistent with the creation of value? To approach this question, analysts often used the discounted cash flows of any project as a measure of value creation. This method required knowledge of the opportunity cost of capital for investments of similar risk. One commonly used discount rate was the weighted average cost of capital (WACC), defined as

$$\text{WACC} = (1 - T)\, i \left(\frac{D}{V} \right) + K_e \left(\frac{E}{V} \right)$$

where T is the corporate tax rate, i is the pretax cost of debt, D is the market value of debt, E is the market value of equity, K_e is the cost of equity, and V is the market value of the firm's assets ($V = D + E$).

In basic terms, the WACC blends the requirements of the different providers of capital—bondholders and shareholders. A separate WACC could be calculated for each of the three operating sectors as well as for the entire company.

CAPITAL STRUCTURE WEIGHTS: Exhibit 9.1F gives the book value and market value weightings for the company's capital structure.

COST OF DEBT AND PREFERRED STOCK: Exhibit 9.1G estimates the weighted average pretax cost of debt for GrandMet in both pounds sterling and U.S. dollars. The 1990 annual report stated:

The group interest expense is arranged centrally and is not attributable to individual activities or geographical areas.... The group has arranged interest rate swaps which have the effect of fixing the rate of interest at an average of 8.6 percent on US dollar and Deutschemark borrowings totalling £616 million.... In addition, the interest rate on borrowings of £1,070 million has been capped for 1 year by the purchase of interest rate caps at a rate of 9 percent. The interest rates shown ... are those contracted on the underlying borrowings before taking into account any interest rate protection.

The firm noted that most of the commercial paper borrowings were classified as "mid-term" (i.e., longer in maturity than one year but shorter than long term), because the firm intended to roll over the maturing commercial paper indefinitely.

The statutory maximum corporate income tax rate prevailing in the United Kingdom in 1992 was 35 percent. In the United States, it was 34 percent.

Exhibit 9.1G also presents the cost of preferred stock (calculated as the annual dividend divided by the market value of the stock) and the cost of convertible debt. Convertible debt was recognized to be a hybrid, a mixture of "straight" debt and equity. Therefore, the cost of the convertible debt, 9.75 percent, was estimated[5] as an average of the cost of equity and cost of debt, weighted by proportions implicit in the convertible; that is, 9.75 percent was not simply the yield on the bond portion of the convertible.

■ **EXHIBIT 9.1F**

GRAND METROPOLITAN
■ **SUMMARY OF PERCENTAGE WEIGHTS OF**
THE VARIOUS CLASSES OF CAPITAL

	Pound Outstandings		Pound Weights*		U.S. Dollar Outstandings		U.S. Dollar Weights	
	Book (1)	Market (2)	Book (3)	Market (4)	Book (5)	Market (6)	Book (7)	Market (8)
Specified debts†	1,777.4	1,794.8	33.0%	15.6%	3,107	3,137	33.0%	15.6%
Unspecified debts‡	87.0	87.0	1.6	0.8	152	152	1.6	0.8
Convertible debt	52.0	63.0	1.0	0.5	91	110	1.0	0.5
Preferred stock	12.2	6.3	0.2	0.1	21	11	0.2	0.1
Common stock	3,454.0	9,535.9	64.2	83.0	6,038	16,669	64.2	83.0
Total capital	5,382.6	11,487.1	100.0%	100.0%	9,409	20,079	100.0%	100.0%

* The pound weights are calculated by dividing the pound outstanding in each class of capital by the total amount of £ capital. The U.S. dollars weights are estimated the same way.

† The balance sheet listed eight separate classes of debt capital to which costs could be attributed: bank loans, commercial paper, guaranteed notes, guaranteed debentures, debenture stock, and bonds.

‡ The balance sheet listed £87 million of debt outstanding without citing a specific cost. Presumably, this debt consisted of a number of small issues. One way to treat those issues in cost-of-capital estimation is to assume that their average cost is equal to a weighted average cost of all the other specified debt securities.

[5] By the casewriters.

GRAND METROPOLITAN PLC
■ ESTIMATION OF AVERAGE OF DEBT AND PREFERRED STOCK

	Currency	Yield on Book Value	Yield on Market Value	Pound Yields — Book Value	Pound Yields — Market Value	U.S. Dollar Yields — Book Value	U.S. Dollar Yields — Market Value
Bank loans and overdrafts	£	9.54%	9.54%	9.54%	9.54%	7.86%	7.86%
Commercial paper	US$	5.93	5.93	7.58	7.58	5.93	5.93
Guaranteed notes 1996	US$	8.13	7.97	9.81	9.65	8.13	7.97
Guaranteed notes 2001	US$	8.63	7.87	10.32	9.55	8.63	7.87
Guaranteed debentures 2011	US$	9.00	8.02	10.70	9.70	9.00	8.02
Commercial paper	£	10.80	10.80	10.80	0.80	9.10	9.10
Debenture stock 2008	£	12.13	11.15	12.13	11.15	10.40	9.44
Bonds 1992	DM	6.63	8.57	6.93	8.88	5.29	7.21
Weighted average cost of debt		**7.15**	**7.13**	**8.69**	**8.63**	**7.03**	**6.96**
Subord. convert. bonds 2002	**£**	**6.25**	**9.75**	**6.25**	**9.75**	**4.62**	**8.07**
Preferred stock issues							
4.75%	£	4.75	10.05	4.75	10.05	3.14	8.36
6.25%	£	6.25	10.15	6.25	10.15	4.62	8.46
5.00%	£	5.00	10.35	5.00	10.35	3.39	8.66
Weighted average cost of pfd.		**5.31%**	**10.27%**	**5.31%**	**10.27%**	**3.76%**	**8.57%**

Note: The weighted average costs are based on the following estimated weightings:

	Securities Outstanding*	Book Value — Pound	Book Value — U.S. Dollar	Book Percentage Weights — Pound	Book Percentage Weights — U.S. Dollar	Market Outstdg.	Market Value — Pound	Market Value — U.S. Dollar	Percentage Weights — Pound	Percentage Weights — U.S. Dollar
Bank loans and overdrafts	£ 280	280	489	15.8	15.8	£ 280	280	489	15.6	15.6
Commercial paper	$1,696	970	1,696	54.6	54.6	$1696	970	1,696	54.1	54.1
Guaranteed notes 1996	$ 170	97	170	5.5	5.5	$ 171	98	171	5.5	5.5
Guaranteed notes 2001	$ 170	97	170	5.5	5.5	$ 178	102	178	5.7	5.7
Guaranteed debentures 2011	$ 169	97	169	5.4	5.4	$ 185	106	185	5.9	5.9
Commercial paper	£ 139	139	243	7.8	7.8	£ 139	139	243	7.7	7.7
Debenture stock 2008	£ 50	50	87	2.8	2.8	£ 54	54	94	3.0	3.0
Bonds 1992	DM137	47	82	2.6	2.6	DM136	46	80	2.6	2.6
Total specified debts		1,777	3,107	100.0	100.0		1,795	$3,137	100.0	100.0
Various unspecified debts	£ 87	87	152							
Subord. convert. bonds 2002	£ 52	52	91			£ 63	63	110		
Preferred stock issues										
4.75%	£ 1.2	1.2	2.1	9.8	9.8	£ 0.56	0.56	1.0	9.0	9.0
6.25%	£ 3.3	3.3	5.8	27.0	27.0	2.03	2.03	3.5	32.1	32.1
5.00%	£ 7.7	7.7	13.5	63.1	63.1	3.72	3.72	6.5	58.9	58.9
Total preferred stock	£ 12.2	12.2	21.3	100.0	100.0	£ 6.31	6.31	11.0	100.0	100.0

*Currencies were translated to U.S. dollars or pounds sterling at the following rates of exchange prevailing in mid-April 1992: dollar/pound = 1.748; DM/pound = 2.917; DM/dollar = 1.669.

COST OF EQUITY: Several methods could be used for estimating the cost of equity. One approach was based on the theory that the current stock price was simply the discounted flow of future dividends. In this model, the after-tax cost of equity (K_e) could be approximated by

$$K_e = \left(\frac{DIV}{P}\right) + g$$

where DIV is the current dividend per share, P is the current share price, and g is the expected growth rate of dividends to infinity.

Another approach was based on the capital asset pricing model. This model explicitly sets required returns by considering the risk of the investment, where risk is defined with respect to a fully diversified portfolio. This model leads to the following expression for the expected after-tax cost of equity:

$$K_e = R_f + \beta \, (R_m - R_f)$$

where R_f is the risk-free rate (typically a government bond rate), β is beta,[6] and $R_m - R_f$ is the stock market risk premium.

Exhibit 9.1H gives information for GrandMet relevant to measuring cost of equity, and Exhibit 9.1I presents the financial market conditions in the United States and United Kingdom in April 1992. Which risk-free rate should one use—the U.S. rate (because half the company's revenues were dollar denominated) or the U.K. rate? How should the decision maker decide on which maturity to use (2 years, 10 years)? What did *risk free* really mean? The same questions arose in the case of the market risk premiums. Should the decision maker use the historical long-term geometric averages or short-term ones? With which market(s) should the decision maker be concerned?

The most recent Risk Measurement Service report from the London Business School reported that GrandMet had a beta of 1.14 with respect to the London stock market.[7] *Value Line,* the U.S. investment information service, however, had estimated GrandMet's beta at 0.8 with respect to the New York stock exchange.[8] What might account for the difference between these two numbers?

---

[6] In technical terms, beta is the normalized covariance of the asset's return with respect to the market return—basically, a measure of how the company's returns vary with respect to overall market fluctuations. A company with a beta of 1.0 experiences as much volatility as a broad portfolio of stocks, and it varies synchronously with the market. A company with a beta of less than 1.0 is less risky than the market portfolio. A beta greater than 1.0 indicates greater risk than the market portfolio.

[7] Risk Measurement Services (RMS) estimated betas using five years of *monthly* returns. The returns included dividends and capital gains or losses. RMS noted, "Betas may change because the company changes. For example, if a company becomes more highly geared, the beta of its shares will increase. Similarly, if it acquires a less risky firm, the beta of the shares after the merger will be lower than before. You may find it helpful to bear this in mind when interpreting the estimates...," (London Business School, "Your Questions Answered," *Risk Measurement Services,* October 1991, 63–65.)

[8] *Value Line* estimated its betas by regressing *weekly* percentage changes in the price of a stock against the weekly percentage changes in the New York Stock Exchange Composite Index over a period of five years. *Value Line* noted, "There has been a tendency over the years for high Beta stocks to become lower and for low Beta stocks to become higher. This tendency can be measured by studying the Betas of stocks in consecutive five-year intervals. The Betas published in the *Value Line Investment Survey* are adjusted for this tendency and hence are likely to be a better predictor of future Betas than those based exclusively on the experience of the past five years." ("How to Use the Value Line Investment Survey: A Subscriber's Guide," *Value Line Investment Survey,* 1985, 57.)

EXHIBIT 9.1H

GRAND METROPOLITAN PLC

■ INFORMATION ON COMPARABLE COMPANIES

	Sales (in US$ m)	Dividend Yield	Price/Earnings Ratio	Interest Coverage	Debt to Capital		Debt to Equity			Tax Rate	Beta	Expected Growth — Rate in:	
					Book Value	Market Value	Book Value	Avg. Market Value				Sales	Dividends
Grand Metropolitan	**15,222**	**3.4%**	**13.3**	**6.6**	**35%**	**17%**	**55%**	**21%**		**31%**	**1.14UK .80US**	**6.5%**	**12.0%**
Restaurant/Retailing													
Forte (U.K.)	4,600	5.7	14.1	2.4	27%	30%	36%	42%		16%	1.18	12.3	10.6
McDonald's	6,695	0.8	17.3	4.0	42	2	72	2		34	0.95	12.0	13.5
Luby's	328	3.5	14.2	nil	1	0	1	0		34	0.90	10.0	9.0
National Pizza	305	0.0	16.9	3.3	49	37	96	58		36	1.00	15.5	0.0
TCBY Enterprises	129	3.9	26.8	7.8	14	3	16	3		35	1.25	9.0	23.0
Wendy's Int'l	1,060	2.0	20.7	5.9	33	23	49	30		34	1.15	6.0	0.0
Average	**2,186**	**2.7**	**18.3**	**3.9**	**28%**	**16%**	**45%**	**23%**		**31%**	**1.07**	**10.8%**	**9.4%**
Food Processing													
Argyll Group (UK)	7,830	4.3	13.5	12.9	32	14	47	16		28	0.72	19.8	18.3
Assoc. Brit. Foods (UK)	6,110	3.2	9.6	8.3	19	19	23	23		32	0.47	2.3	14.9
Borden	7,235	3.6	14.1	3.9	43	20	75	25		36	1.15	5.5	9.5
Cadbury-Schweppes (UK)	5,475	3.6	17.4	3.8	38	17	62	21		28	0.83	10.9	14.3
Campbell Soup	6,204	1.8	21.1	5.9	30	8	43	9		40	1.00	7.5	15.5
CPC International	6,189	2.7	15.3	6.5	38	12	61	14		40	1.10	8.5	12.5
Dean Foods	2,158	1.9	16.1	9.5	26	10	35	12		42	0.90	8.0	7.0
Dreyer's Grand Ice Cream	355	0.7	31.6	4.2	31	22	45	28		40	1.05	16.5	0.0
Flowers Industries	825	4.1	20.0	5.2	35	14	54	16		40	0.85	5.5	6.5
General Mills	7,153	2.3	23.3	8.6	39	6	64	6		39	1.00	11.0	15.0
Heinz	6,800	2.8	19.4	7.6	10	2	11	2		38	1.00	8.5	11.0
Michael Foods	455	1.3	14.7	4.1	35	26	54	36		36	1.15	9.5	19.0
Quaker Oats	5,491	2.8	17.8	5.6	40	13	67	15		43	0.90	9.0	11.5
Ralston Purina	7,375	2.2	15.8	4.1	70	18	233	23		40	0.90	9.5	11.0
Sara Lee	12,831	1.9	22.0	6.6	29	6	41	7		36	1.00	7.0	13.5
Tate & Lyle (UK)	5,680	3.7	10.1	3.1	52	32	110	47		29	1.10	14.7	14.3
Tesco (UK)	11,050	3.3	13.2	4.0	19	10	23	11		32	0.73	13.6	22.8
Unilever (NL and UK)	42,250	3.2	15.1	4.6	22	31	28	44		35	0.86	8.5	9.5
United Biscuits (UK)	4,225	5.0	13.7	8.5	32	14	48	16		33	0.88	6.1	12.2
Universal Foods	834	2.6	14.7	7.2	34	13	52	15		37	0.90	9.0	12.5
Average	**$7,326**	**2.9%**	**16.9**	**6.2**	**34%**	**15%**	**59%**	**19%**		**36%**	**0.92**	**9.5%**	**12.5%**

continued on next page

EXHIBIT 9.1H

CONTINUED

	Sales (in US$ m)	Dividend Yield	Price/ Earnings Ratio	Interest Coverage	Debt to Capital		Debt to Equity		Avg. Tax Rate	Beta	Expected Growth Rate in:	
					Book Value	Market Value	Book Value	Market Value			Sales	Dividends
Drinks												
Allied Lyons (UK)	8,940	4.1%	23.4	2.3	43%	30%	75%	44%	29%	0.97	9.2%	14.6%
Anheuser-Busch	10,996	2.0	15.7	8.2	38	15	61	18	38	1.00	7.0	12.0
Bass (UK)	7,630	4.8	10.6	4.3	29	38	40	62	26	0.77	10.1	16.5
Brown-Forman	1,250	2.8	14.7	23.5	14	4	16	4	35	1.20	9.5	11.5
Coors	1,917	2.3	15.2	10.3	13	10	15	11	39	0.85	5.0	0.0
Guinness (UK)	6,110	2.5	15.9	4.7	31	18	44	22	28	1.01	24.2	21.1
Labatt (Canada)	4,400	3.0	14.3	2.9	33	28	49	38	34	0.75	2.0	6.5
Molson (Canada)	2,500	2.1	13.9	3.3	45	37	82	59	34	0.75	5.0	13.0
Scottish & Newcastle (UK)	2,398	5.0	13.5	5.8	23	20	31	25	33	0.59	19.3	16.5
Seagram (Canada)	5,000	1.7	17.2	3.1	29	26	41	35	22	1.10	5.0	12.0
Whitbread (UK)	3,585	5.2	10.7	5.6	15	15	17	17	24	0.70	6.1	15.9
Average	**4,975**	**3.2%**	**15.0**	**6.7**	**28%**	**22%**	**43%**	**30%**	**31%**	**0.88**	**9.3%**	**12.7%**

Notes:
U.S. and Canadian companies: 1991 and expected annual growth rates until 1997.
U.K. companies: 1990 and average annual growth rates of the last five years.

■ EXHIBIT 9.1H

(CONTINUED)

Restaurant

Forte (UK)	Active in contract catering and hotel- and motel-chain management.
Luby's Cafeteria (US)	Operates a chain of cafeterias.
McDonald's (US)	Licenses and operates a fast-food hamburger chain.
National Pizza (US)	Largest franchisee of PepsiCo's Pizza Hut chain.
TCBY Enterprises (US)	Largest franchisor of soft-frozen yogurt stores.
Wendy's Int'l (US)	Licenses and operates a chain of quick-service hamburger restaurants.

Food Processing

Argyll Group (UK)	One of the leading food retailers in the United Kingdom.
Assoc. British Foods (UK)	Operator of grocery stores, retail bakeries, beauty shops.
Borden (US)	Diversified producer of packaged food (dairy, snacks, pasta, popcorn, jams, potato chips) and adhesives (Elmer's Cement, Crazy Glue).
Cadbury-Schweppes (UK)	Manufacturer of bottled and canned soft drinks, candy and other confectionary products, food preparations.
Campbell Soup (US)	A leading manufacturer of canned soups, spaghetti, fruit and vegetable juices, frozen foods, salads, bakery products, olives, pickles.
CPC International (US)	A leading producer of grocery products (soups, mayonnaise, peanut butter, pasta, baked goods) and a large corn refiner (corn syrups, dextrose, starches).
Dean Foods (US)	Manufactures, distributes dairy products (fluid milk, ice cream, cheeses) and processes canned and frozen vegetables, sauces, powdered drinks, and creamers.
Dreyer's Grand (US)	Manufacturer and distributor of premium ice cream products.
Flowers Ind. (US)	Producer of bakery and snack-food goods.
General Mills (US)	Processes and markets consumer foods (cereals, flour, seafood, yogurt) and operates restaurants.
Heinz (US)	Manufactures soups, ketchup, baby foods, cat food, frozen potatoes.
Michael Foods (US)	Producer and distributor of egg and egg products, frozen potato products, ice cream products, refrigerator-case products.
Quaker Oats (US)	Produces foods (cereals, breakfast products, beverages) and pet foods, owns Fisher-Price toys.
Ralston Purina (US)	World's largest producer of dry dog and cat foods and dry-cell batteries.
Sara Lee (US)	Diversified, international, packaged consumer goods (Hanes, Dim), with operations in coffee, specialty meats, frozen baked goods, and food-services distribution.
Tate & Lyle (UK)	Producer and distributor of sugar products, beverages, food products.
Tesco (UK)	One of the leading food retailers in the United Kingdom.
Unilever (NL and UK)	One of the world's largest producers and marketers of branded and packaged consumer goods.
United Biscuits (UK)	Maker of biscuits, cookies and crackers, snack foods, frozen foods and owner/operator of fast-food restaurant chain.
Universal Foods (US)	International manufacturer and marketer of value-added food products and ingredients for food processing, baking, food-service and retail markets.

Drinks

Allied Lyons (UK)	Active in beer and retailing, wines, spirits, eating and drinking places.
Anheuser-Busch (US)	Largest U.S. brewer, also active in baked and snack goods, frozen foods, theme parks.
Bass (UK)	Active in malt beverages, amusement and recreation, hotels and motels, soft drinks.
Brown-Forman (US)	A leading wine and spirits producer and importer, producer of fine china, crystal, and luggage.
Coors (US)	U.S. brewer.
Guinness (UK)	Active in malt beverages, wines, brandy spirits, liquors.
Labatt (CN)	One of Canada's leading brewers, also active in foods, dairy products, fruit juices.
Molson (CN)	Engaged in brewing, cleaning and sanitizing, and retail merchandising.
Scottish & Newcastle (UK)	Active in malt beverages, wine and liquor stores, hotels and motels, soft drinks.
Seagram (CN)	One of the world's largest wine and spirits distillers/producers.
Whitbread (UK)	Maker of malt beverages, operator of hotels and motels, bottler of soft drinks, active in recreation.

SOURCES: *Value Line; Risk Measurement Services,* January–March 1992 (London Business School); Compact Disclosure (Digital Library System, Inc.); casewriters' estimates.

■ **EXHIBIT 9.1I**

GRAND METROPOLITAN PLC
■ CAPITAL MARKET CONDITIONS, APRIL 1992

U.K. Gilt and U.S. Treasury Bond Yields (April 8, 1992)

Term	U.K. Gilts, Yield to Maturity	U.S. Treasuries, Yield to Maturity
1	10.50%	4.45%
2	20.40	5.29
3	10.30	5.95
5	10.00	6.82
10	9.80	7.45
15	9.60	7.59
20	9.60	7.83

Foreign Exchange Rates
$/£ = 1.748
DM/£ = 2.917
DM/$ = 1.669

Long-Term Expected Rates of Inflation
United Kingdom   4.3% annually
United States   2.7% annually
Germany   4.0% annually

Equity Market Risk Premium

Market	Geometric Estimated Current Premium	Arithmetic Mean Historical Premium	Mean Historical Premium
London	3.9%	4.1%	6.9%
New York	2.7	5.6	8.4

SOURCES: *Financial Times; The Wall Street Journal*, OECD, *Economic Outlook*, June 1992 Banque Degroof, Belgium.

BUSINESS SEGMENT CAPITAL COST ESTIMATION

How should one estimate the cost of equity for each of GrandMet's individual sectors? Should each segment have a different risk-free rate based on different project lifetimes? How should one determine the beta for each sector? Finally, how should one determine the weights necessary to combine the business segments into an overall WACC for GrandMet? Should one base the weighting factor on revenues, profits, or some other measure?

The decision maker knew that he could examine the capital structures of comparable companies to facilitate the evaluation GrandMet's gearing in each of its segments. Therefore, he collected the information in Exhibit 9.1H on various companies that competed with GrandMet in each of its operating sectors. Would the fact that this information reflected only book values dramatically affect the estimation of overall cost of capital? Which tax rate should he use, the U.S. marginal rate, the U.K. marginal rate, or some effective rate?

In evaluating GrandMet's performance, analysts wondered whether the cost of capital should be the same in London as in New York. If differences among local capital markets (such as those induced by country risk) existed, one might be able to diversify the differences away by holding a portfolio of international investments. Using this kind of assumption could free an analyst to work with local costs of capital.

The assumption of purchasing power parity implied the following relationship between home and foreign local costs of capital:

$$\text{Local } K = (1 + \text{Home } K)\left\{\frac{1 + \text{Local inflation rate}}{1 + \text{Home inflation rate}}\right\} - 1$$

This equation implies that real risk-free rates, equity risk premia, and betas are constant across countries. Little evidence either to prove or refute such an assertion existed, although in competitive world capital markets, arbitrage activity would tend to drive the three elements into equilibrium. Using home capital costs to discount cash flows translated into home currencies would be a conservative response to these uncertainties.

CONCLUSION

Analysts noted with interest the circulation of rumors that the company might be the target of a takeover attempt. Had the company performed that badly? Were all segments of the group's business portfolio performing equally well? Might one or two of them be targeted for aggressive restructuring? The decision maker decided to compare the returns on net assets in Exhibit 9.1B against the segment WACCs.

CASE 9.2

OLIN CORPORATION

Bill Schmitt, vice president for International Operations for Olin Corporation, was preparing a presentation concerning a project that would expand Olin's involvement in Brazil. Schmitt and his team were proposing to establish a joint venture that would be 50 percent owned by Olin's Brazilian subsidiary and 50 percent owned by a subsidiary of a leading private Brazilian company, Votorantim. The joint venture, to be called Nordesclor, would construct a calcium hypochlorite plant to produce HTH, Olin's registered brand name for its swimming pool chemical treatment product. At this time, there was no HTH manufacturing facility in Brazil. Olin Brasil currently imported HTH from an Olin plant in Tennessee, had it repackaged, and sold it directly through local pool shops. Olin had begun discussions with Votorantim five years earlier, in 1983, but had decided to find out more about the Brazilian market for HTH before investing in a local production arrangement. A market research survey and subsequent new marketing program had dramatically increased HTH's market share, and Schmitt believed many benefits could be gained by moving to local production. Because this would be the first time Olin Chemicals had made a major investment in Brazil, Schmitt wanted to prepare a presentation highlighting all the advantages of this international investment and addressing any concerns the board of directors might put forth.

OLIN CORPORATION

Olin Corporation was a diversified company whose business was concentrated in chemicals, metals, and applied physics, with special emphasis on electronic materials and services, aerospace/defense, and water quality management. Olin's international operations contributed approximately 20 percent of the company's total sales. (See Exhibit 9.2A for financial data for 1986 and 1987.) One of Olin's goals was to double the sales and profit contributed by its international businesses by 1991. Because little growth was projected for exports, the company estimated that overseas operations and joint ventures had to grow at a 20 percent compound annual rate to meet this objective. In early 1988, International Pool Chemicals appeared to be especially promising to Olin as a growth area.

Olin had been producing swimming pool chemicals for over 30 years and had always prided itself on consistently providing the highest quality products in the market. Plants in Charleston, Tennessee, and in South Africa produced its total supply of HTH. Olin had begun exporting HTH to various Latin American markets, including Brazil, in the 1960s, and the Latin American region had become one of Olin's most successful in terms of profitability and market share. Olin's Brazilian segment was actually more profitable than its domestic calcium hypochlorite business on a per pound basis.

Olin had found, however, that it was becoming increasingly difficult to obtain import permits from the Brazilian government in sufficient quantity to support

This case was written by Mark R. Eaker, professor of Business Administration. Copyright © 1989 by the University of Virginia Darden School Foundation, Charlottesville, Va. All rights reserved.

OLIN CORPORATION
■ FINANCIAL HIGHLIGHTS
(IN MILLIONS, EXCEPT PER SHARE AMOUNTS)

	Years Ended December 31	
	1987	**1986**
Net sales and operating revenues	$1,930	$1,732
Operating income (loss)	149	106
Net income (loss)		
Continuing operations	78	75
Discontinued operations	—	—
Net income (loss)	$ 78	$ 75
Per share (assuming full dilution)		
Continuing operations	$ 3.32	$ 3.13
Discontinued operations	—	—
Net income (loss)	$ 3.32	$ 3.13
Net cash flows from operating activities	$ 206	$ 173
Net cash used by investing activities	157	135
Research and development expenditures	62	56
Depreciation	114	111
Cash dividends		
Total	37	34
Per share	1.60	1.525
Average shares outstanding		
(assuming full dilution as of December 31)	23.6	25.4
Total assets	$1,685	$1,545
Property, plant, & equipment, net	727	720
Working capital, net	276	210
Long-term debt	392	375
Shareholders' equity		
Total	700	654
Per share	31.81	30.56

Olin's marketing program in that country. Although there was no domestic producer of calcium hypochlorite in Brazil, there were several producers of liquid bleach, the main competitive product. Fortunately for Olin, Brazil was experiencing a shortage of liquid bleach, and the pool sanitizer market was not deemed important to the liquid bleach producers. Once the shortage eased, however, or a domestic company chose to produce calcium hypochlorite, Olin company officials were concerned that Brazil might block the importation of HTH completely. Mexico had taken such actions several years ago, whereupon Olin had lost 1,500 tons of annual sales.

BRAZIL

Rich natural resources helped make Brazil a growing economic power and one of the world's leading Third World industrial nations. Brazil was a leading global producer of many agricultural goods, including orange juice, cacao beans, cattle, corn, soybeans, and sugar cane. Brazil also produced 30 percent of the world coffee crop and grew more bananas than any other nation. Huge supplies of nuts, timber, and other products came from its forests, and mining operations produced large quantities of iron ore and manganese for export as well as for domestic use. Brazil also produced a large range of finished goods for the global market. The manufacture of metal products was the nation's chief industrial activity. In addition, Brazil ranked among the world leaders in automobile and truck manufacturing. Among its population of 141 million, Brazil had a complex and well-developed domestic consumer market, the strongest in Latin America.

RECENT ECONOMIC AND POLITICAL DEVELOPMENTS IN BRAZIL. In 1985 Brazil returned to a democratic government following 20 years of military rule. After four years of deep recession, the economy started growing again in 1984 and picked up significantly in the following year. (See Exhibit 9.2B for a summary of economic statistics on Brazil.) The economic upturn looked to be short lived, however, as hyperinflation threatened to wipe out the gains of the 1985 impressive 8.0 percent growth in gross domestic product (GDP). Inflation was projected to reach levels of 460 to 500 percent in 1986, higher than at any time in Brazilian history. Facing declining political support, the fledgling civilian government of President Jose Sarney responded on February 26, 1986, by announcing a sweeping anti-inflation program known as the *Cruzado Plan*. Among the plan's three major provisions were a freeze on prices; a phased end to indexing of wages, rents, and interest rates; and the creation of a new currency, the cruzado (Cr), worth 1,000 of the old cruzeiro. Just before the new policies were announced, the cruzeiro was trading for Cr13,700 per U.S. dollar at the official rate and Cr23,000 on the black market.

The plan essentially boosted wages while holding prices constant, and following its implementation, the economy experienced an unparalleled spending spree. Emphasis shifted from exports to internal consumption and imports poured in. The program had overwhelming political support; the government won a landslide victory in the November 1986 elections.

The plan was ill conceived, however, or at the least poorly executed. Although inflation did halt temporarily, the plan failed to freeze either wages or government spending. In early 1987, the plan disintegrated, and inflation took off. Through price controls, the government had merely addressed the symptoms of inflation, not the cause. The high consumption levels of 1986 had also sharply reduced the balance of trade surplus and, to protect foreign exchange reserves, the government suspended interest payments on the $67 billion of its debt that was owed to foreign banks.

LONG-TERM OUTLOOK. To assist it in evaluating the business climate in Brazil, Olin had commissioned a study by a well-known analyst. Its overview stated:

OLLIN CORPORATION

■ BRAZIL—SUMMARY ECONOMIC STATISTICS

	1976	1977	1978	1979	1980	1981	1982	1983	1984	1985	1986	1987
GDP (1980 prices; millions of cruzados)	10,305	10,992	11,542	12,279	12,639	12,216	12,328	12,157	12,696	13,750	14,876	N/A
CPI	18	26	36	55	100*	206	407	984	2,924	9,556	23,436	77,258
Bank discount rate	28%	30%	33%	35%	38%	49%	49%	156%	215%	219%	50%	392%
Trade balance (millions of $)	(2,386)	(100)	(1,158)	(2,717)	(2,823)	1,185	778	6,469	13,086	12,466	8,348	N/A
Current account balance (millions of $)	(6,562)	(5,112)	(7,036)	(10,478)	(12,806)	(11,751)	(16,312)	(6,837)	42	(273)	(4,477)	N/A
Cruzados/$	.012	.016	.021	.043	.066	.128	.253	.984	3.184	10.490	14.895	72.251

*Data that follow are not comparable to data earlier in series.

SOURCE: International Monetary Fund, *International Financial Statistics* (Washington, D.C., various issues).

Brazilian managers will face the reality of an improved business environment with higher profits earned on an annual average than heretofore. The image will be different. In the transition to democracy, government management of the economy and of business has become more temperamental. While economic growth and profits will remain relatively high, there will be more stop/go of the economy and a more erratic government regulatory environment. Corporate managers will have to spend more time in Brasilia, lobbying for their industry, and more time at corporate headquarters, explaining why the bad news reported in the media is not so bad. The key to understanding the emerging Brazilian environment and the benefits to be gained from it is to understand its complexities.[1]

The study included nine specific forecasts of changes that would occur in Brazil. Excerpts from the study on each forecast follow:

1. Economic decisions will be subject to political decisions unlike any time since 1964. Economic crises caused by poor policy choices will be more frequent in the near term and diminish in the out years.

2. Poor economic and regulatory news in 1987 will obscure the strengths of the economic system for the short term. These 1987 problems are the product of domestic political maneuvering, the aftereffects of the Plan Cruzado, and the debt crisis.

3. After a poor 1987, the Brazilian economy will perform well and expand over the next four years. Between 1988 and 1991

   • Real growth will run between 3 and 5 percent every year.

   • Annual inflation will run between 80 and 120 percent, declining in the out years.

   • The cruzado will be maintained at a slightly undervalued level.

   • Brazil will continue to run a balance of trade surplus, but the ongoing debt crisis will not be resolved.

4. The fundamental strengths of the Brazilian economy remain. These include a sophisticated industrial structure, diverse markets, the nation's size and untapped resources, and a sophisticated elite.

5. Brazil will not "take off" into the developed world this century. Among the factors limiting growth are the ongoing debt crisis, a dearth of capital, a highly inflationary environment, and weak industrial and social infrastructure.

6. While populist sentiment will become more prevalent than heretofore in Brazilian political life, Brazil is not risking a return to economic nationalism. The position of foreign investment is likely to strengthen over the next five years as Brazil seeks new sources of capital and technology.

7. Brazilian trade policy will be buffeted by domestic and international forces. Most of the economy today depends on public policy that promotes

---

[1] The quoted material comes from the consulting report prepared for Olin.

exports. This reality will compel Brazil's leaders to continue to favor traders.

8. While the political system will face a series of tests and crises over the next five years, the outlook for stability is good.

9. Regionalism continues to be an extremely powerful political force, exercising a conservative influence on the nation.

THE BRAZILIAN MARKET FOR HTH

SWIMMING POOL SANITIZER MARKET. Currently, Olin's HTH brand has 35 percent of the pool sanitizer chemical market in Brazil, based entirely on imports. This market share was up from 19 percent in 1984 when Olin Brasil was selling approximately 400 tons of HTH in the pool market. At that time, because of the high import duties in Brazil, Olin's HTH was 10 times as expensive (on an equivalent chlorine basis) as liquid bleach, its main competition. Additionally, Olin was spending only a nominal amount on advertising and promotion. In 1984 a marketing study was conducted to gain a better understanding of the residential pool market and the competing products used to sanitize these pools. Olin subsequently developed a new marketing program, aimed at furthering the penetration of HTH and increasing the consumption dosage per pool. One of the key elements of this plan was to reduce the transfer price from Olin U.S. to Olin Brasil so that the ratio of retail sales prices between HTH and competing products went from 10:1 to 4:1. Advertising and promotion were increased five times, and various sales incentive promotions and education seminars were implemented. The program was a tremendous success; sales of HTH went from 360 tons per year in 1984 to 1,500 tons per year in 1987, an increase of 61 percent compounded annually. Were it not for difficulties in obtaining import permits, Olin believed it could have sold up to 2,000 tons in 1987. The HTH brand name had achieved the strongest consumer franchise in the pool market, despite the fact that HTH® was still significantly more expensive than liquid bleach. The main attraction of liquid bleach was its price, but recent chlorine shortages had benefited HTH. No capacity increases for bleach had been announced, and Olin expected the shortage to persist for the next two to three years.

INDUSTRIAL AND POTABLE WATER MARKETS. The joint venture would also allow Olin to serve the industrial and potable water markets in remote areas of Brazil. Import quota restrictions had not permitted Olin to develop these markets, which were presently being served by liquid bleach and chlorite of lime. Olin believed that HTH could be very competitive in both markets as a superior treatment agent, because both bleach and chlorite of lime lost significant strength during long-distance transportation in the tropical climate. The total market for industrial and potable water was estimated to be equivalent to 6,000 tons per year of HTH.

EXPORT MARKETS. Exports to neighboring Latin American countries represented a potential third market for HTH. Presently, Olin sold little HTH to these markets; thus, any volume would be totally incremental. Nordesclor would have significant advantages from regional bilateral trading agreements, the benefits of which accrued only to local producers. Olin expected exports to neighboring Latin American countries to peak at 750 tons per year, although the market potential could be significantly higher.

VOTORANTIM. The proposed joint venture partner was one of Brazil's strongest companies, ranking second to Volkswagen among all Brazilian manufacturing firms in terms of net worth. It was privately owned and managed by three brothers and a brother-in-law. It had 1986 sales of approximately $2 billion. Votorantim had an excellent reputation as an ethical firm committed to expanding employment through reinvestment of profits. In 1987 it had over 54,000 employees.

Votorantim was highly vertically integrated and diversified. It was the largest Brazilian producer of cement, aluminum, zinc, and lime. Votorantim also was a significant producer of steel, cellophane and paper, sugar, and heavy equipment. The company owned 17 hydroelectric plants that provided power to its own plants as well as surrounding municipalities. Investments in the chemical industry were currently a modest part of Votorantim's portfolio that the owners were interested in expanding.

THE PROPOSED PROJECT

The proposed Nordesclor joint venture[2] would construct and operate a 3,100 metric ton per year hypochlorite plant. The plant could be easily expanded to double its initial capacity. The joint venture would be half owned by Olin Brasil and half by Cia. Agro Industrial Igarassu, a subsidiary of Industrial Votorantim. Because of requirements that the venture be Brazilian, Olin would have 40 percent of the voting stock and 60 percent of the nonvoting preferred stock. Profits would be split equally. Olin was confident that it had sufficient control to ensure that the production and marketing standards would be the same as Olin achieved elsewhere in the world.

The plant would be located at Igarassu, Pernambuco, in the northeastern part of Brazil. The region was a development target of the central government, so the project would enjoy a 10-year tax holiday. In addition, the plant would be next door to a chlor-alkali facility owned by Votorantim that would provide the chlorine and caustic soda required by Nordesclor under a long-term preferential supply contract. Lime was to be supplied under a similar arrangement by another Votorantim affiliate, Cal e Tintas.

Proven Olin technology would be used in the manufacturing process, and Olin had complete control over the project execution, plant start-up, and operation of the plant. The front-end engineering would be done by Olin, and an experienced Brazilian engineering firm had been identified to engineer the facility. Exhibits 9.2c and 9.2d set forth the projected timetable for the project and the prospective organization chart for the plant, respectively.

---

[2] The numbers related to the project have been disguised to protect proprietary information.

■ EXHIBIT 9.2c

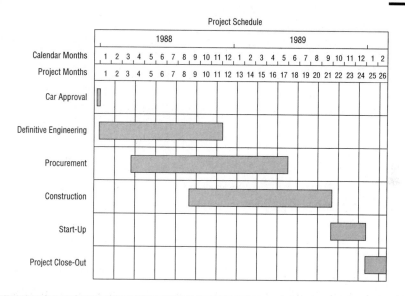

■ EXHIBIT 9.2D

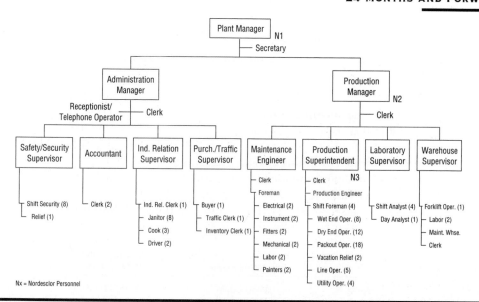

■ EXHIBIT 9.2E

OLIN CORPORATION
■ BRAZILIAN SWIMMING POOL MARKET

	Calcium Hypochlorite	Liquid Bleach	All Other	Total Volume
1983 share %	20	52	28	
Volume (metric tons)	636	1,652	890	3,178
1984 share %	17	57	26	
Volume	635	2,130	971	3,736
1985 share %	24	55	21	
Volume	1,002	2,296	877	4,175
1986 share %	30	53	17	
Volume	1,622	2,865	918	5,405
1987 share %	33	51	16	
Volume	1,896	2,931	920	5,747
1988 share %*	35	49	16	
Volume	2,346	3,285	1,073	6,704
1989 share %*	37	49	14	
Volume	2,603	3,447	985	7,035
1990 share %*	40	48	12	
Volume	3,131	3,757	939	7,827
1991 share %*	41	48	11	
Volume	3,560	4,167	955	8,682
1992 share %*	42	48	10	
Volume	4,007	4,579	954	9,540
1993 share %*	42	48	10	
Volume	4,344	4,966	1,035	10,345
1994 share %*	42	48	10	
Volume	4,344	4,966	1,035	10,345

*Projected.

PROJECT ECONOMICS. Olin's market projections for HTH are given in Exhibits 9.2E and 9.2F. Sales for 1988 and 1989 would continue on an imported basis, with the plant scheduled to come on line in 1990. The current market price of HTH® to dealers in the swimming pool market was $3.30/kg (kilogram). The prices for the nonpool and export markets were currently $1.30/kg and $1.63/kg, respectively.

Direct variable costs were expected to run $267.86/MT (metric ton) for raw materials and $157.59/MT for utilities and power. Additionally, each market had its own packaging and freight costs as listed below:

	Swimming Pools	Industrial and Potable Uses	Export
Packaging	$250.00/MT	$100.00/MT	$25.00/MT
Freight	80.00/MT	80.00/MT	80.00/MT

OLIN CORPORATION

■ MARKET PROJECTION FOR HTH

	Number of Pools (M)	Growth (%)	HTH Share %	HTH Pools (M)	Consumption Kg/Pool/Yr	Pool (MTY)	Pool (MTY)	Non-export (MTY)	Total (MTY)
1983	150		18	27.0	13.0	351	—	—	351
1984	173	15	13	22.5	13.7	308	—	—	308
1985	198	15	23	45.5	14.0	638	—	—	638
1986	250	25	25	62.5	18.0	1,125	—	—	1,125
1987	268	7	31	83.1	16.4	1,363	—	—	1,363
1988*	295	10	35	103.3	18.0	1,856	—	—	1,856
1989*	333	13	37	123.2	18.0	2,218	—	—	2,218
1990*	373	12	40	149.2	18.0	2,686	275	200	3,161
1991*	414	11	41	169.7	18.0	3,055	550	350	3,955
1992*	455	10	42	191.1	18.0	3,440	825	500	4,765
1993*	498	9.5	42	209.2	18.0	3,765	1,100	750	5,615
1994*	543	9.0	42	228.1	18.0	4,105	1,093	750	5,948
							$3.30/kg	$1.30/kg	$1.63/kg

*Projection.

An additional incremental variable cost of $353,000 was budgeted beginning in 1995.

Selling and administrative expenses were projected at 7 percent of net sales, advertising and promotion was expected to run 2 percent of the net pool sales, and provision for bad debts was allowed at 1 percent of net sales. Fixed utilities were $31,000 per year. Operating and supervisory labor was budgeted at $1,906,000 for the first year of operation, declining to $1,176,000 in year 2 and leveling off at $978,000 for the remaining periods. Miscellaneous expenses were expected to be $1,042,000 per year. A 10-year depreciation schedule for the plant is given in Exhibit 9.2G, and Exhibit 9.2H lays out the expected working-capital increases.

FINANCING ALTERNATIVES. The capital required to finance the joint venture was expected to total $25 million, which was to be provided equally by Olin and Votorantim. Olin's contribution would include $2.5 million of engineering and training expenses, which would be incurred in the United States. These funds could be classified as either debt or equity.

There were several alternatives available to Olin to arrange the remainder of the financing. One of those would be for Olin to invest additional new funds into its subsidiary, which would in turn put the funds into Nordesclor. Another option, which would be used in conjunction with other funding, was made possible by the location of the proposed project. Because the project was to be located in the economically depressed Northeast, special government investment funds were available and could provide up to $5 million of medium-term (six-year) funds to the joint venture at an interest rate of 8 percent plus a factor reflecting annual inflation.

Olin was also considering a debt/equity swap. The advantage of a swap was that it offered the opportunity to acquire the necessary cruzados at a below-market exchange rate. There appeared to be two different ways in which a swap could be effected: one was through a formal government-sponsored program and the other involved a direct equity participation of a major bank.

■ **EXHIBIT 9.2G**

OLIN CORPORATION

■ **TEN-YEAR DEPRECIATION SCHEDULE FOR NORDESCLOR PLANT**

Year	Thousands of Dollars
1	2,054
2	2,116
3	2,177
4	2,239
5	2,301
6	2,362
7	2,424
8	2,485
9	2,547
10	2,547

OLIN CORPORATION
▪ WORKING CAPITAL PROJECTIONS

Year	Thousands of Dollars
1	2,072
2	860
3	889
4	890
5	772
6	633
7	619
8	621
9	619
10	619

The Brazilian government adopted measures on November 18, 1987, to reintroduce a debt/equity conversion program, subject to satisfactory completion of its current debt renegotiations. The details of the program were still not final, but Schmitt believed that Olin would be able to obtain the required funding for the Nordesclor project at approximately 60 percent of face value.

As currently understood, the program would provide for $1.5 billion in debt conversions. Preference would be given to projects in the Northeast. The basis for dividend repatriation, registered capital, would be the face amount of the debt acquired for conversion.

The actual savings would depend on two factors, the amount paid for the debt on the secondary market and the conversion discount applied by the Brazilian central bank. Olin would arrange with one of its commercial bankers to acquire debt eligible for conversion. The price would be established in a secondary market and would reflect supply and demand for such paper. Olin would then have to participate in an auction process for the right to convert the debt to cruzados that could be used to fund the Nordesclor project.

The debt/equity swap program offered obvious advantages, but Olin was concerned about its viability. Brazil had had a program in place before but had suspended it in 1984.

The second debt/equity swap involved an ad hoc swap with a participating financial institution. The bank would act as an intermediary and make an investment in the Brazilian subsidiary on behalf of Olin. During the term of the investment, the bank would receive guaranteed annual U.S. dollar dividends. At the end of the required term, 12 years in this case, the bank would be repaid 100 percent of its investment.

As the bank had outlined the transaction to Olin, it would invest $7,731,000 worth of cruzados in the preferred shares of an Olin Brazilian subsidiary. At the end of the 12-year period, the bank would put the shares to Olin Corporation for the full amount of its investment. The shares would carry a 4 percent annual dividend based on the dollar value of the investment.

The bank assured Olin that it had completed similar transactions in the past, although Central Bank approval would be necessary.

GETTING THE MONEY OUT

Under any financing arrangement, cash remittances to the United States would be limited to Olin Brasil's share of net income. In addition, a withholding tax was applied based on the ratio of the remittance to registered capital. The following schedule applied:

Percentage of Registered Capital	Withholding Tax
16	25
16–25	40
25–50	50
Over 50	60

Olin planned to hold the tax rate at the 25 percent level.

Registered capital consisted of new funds invested in Brazil and additions to retained earnings. Under the ad hoc swap, the bank's investment would be considered registered capital. In addition, Olin was confident that any unremitted cash could be invested at an annual rate of 15 percent. Those earnings would also be remittable subject to the 25 percent withholding.

Finally, the tax rate in Brazil was 45 percent. Because of the location of the project in a region designated as a development target of the central government, the project would benefit from a 10-year tax deferral. The deferral meant that taxes would be used in determining net income but that no cash payments would be made during the first 10 years. There would be no additional tax obligation in the United States.

THE DECISION

As he began to determine what points to emphasize in his presentation, Schmitt worked on "selling" the project. The inside directors were committed to international expansion, but several outside directors were sure to raise the issue of additional risk. Two of them worked for firms that had had bad experiences in Brazil. Their industries, pharmaceuticals and computers, were subject to extensive regulations favoring domestic Brazilian companies, which had cost the U.S. firms a great deal of money. Schmitt was certain that those experiences would be recounted for the whole board to hear, yet he needed the board's approval to go ahead. And Schmitt needed to determine the best way to finance the project.

OVERVIEW OF CORPORATE TAX CONSIDERATIONS

10

CHAPTER

KEY CONCEPTS

■ THE DIFFERENT TAXABLE ENTITIES THROUGHOUT THE WORLD AND THE FACTORS THAT AFFECT A FIRM'S ELECTION OF A TAXABLE ENTITY

■ THE BASIC CORPORATE INCOME TAX IMPOSED BY CENTRAL GOVERNMENTS AND SPECIAL PROVISIONS THAT MAY ALTER THE BASIC CORPORATE TAX RATE

■ THE WITHHOLDING TAXES THAT TAX AUTHORITIES MIGHT IMPOSE ON INCOME DERIVED IN THEIR COUNTRY BY NONRESIDENT CORPORATIONS

■ THE VARIATION IN THE DETERMINATION OF CORPORATE PROFITS FROM COUNTRY TO COUNTRY AS A RESULT OF THE DIFFERENCES IN TAXABLE REVENUES AND DEDUCTIBLE EXPENSES

■ THE MEANING OF *THIN CAPITALIZATION RULES*

■ THE EFFECT OF ESTABLISHED TRANSFER PRICES ON TAXABLE INCOME

■ THE DIFFERENCE BETWEEN THE CLASSICAL SYSTEM AND THE IMPUTATION SYSTEM FOR TAXING CORPORATE EARNINGS DISTRIBUTED TO SHAREHOLDERS

■ THE DIFFERENT TYPES OF GOVERNMENT TAX INCENTIVES THAT MAY BE OFFERED BY A COUNTRY

INTRODUCTION

Tax considerations influence investing and financing decisions in the home country. Because tax regulations are often complex, the corporate treasurer usually relies on a cadre of tax experts for input in decision making. Making decisions in foreign countries, however, requires an understanding of domestic tax regulations as well as foreign tax regulations. For foreign tax regulations, corporate treasurers rely on tax experts who are acquainted with such regulations.

Taxes paid by corporate enterprises can be classified into two types: income taxes and indirect

taxes. The former includes taxes paid to the central government based on corporate income and possibly any local income taxes. Indirect taxes include real estate value-added and sales taxes, as well as miscellaneous taxes on business transactions. Our purpose in this chapter is to provide an overview of the key corporate income tax issues that affect investing decisions (covered in Part III of this book) and financing decisions (covered in Part IV of this book) in foreign countries.[1]

ESTABLISHING A BUSINESS ENTITY

The United States has several forms of taxable entities: individuals, partnerships, and corporations. The choice of the structure is determined by a myriad of factors, including the minimization of taxes (income taxes and other business taxes), the desire for limited liability, and the ease with which ownership can be transferred. The same factors also influence the structure a firm elects when establishing a subsidiary in a foreign country. The form of business entity chosen by major commercial entities in the United States is the corporation.

As examples of the business entities that are available outside the United States, let's look at Germany and France. Germany has six forms of commercial enterprises: (1) the corporation (Aktiengesellschaft—abbreviated AG), (2) limited liability company (Gesellschaft mit beschrankter Haftung—GmbH), (3) general commercial partnership (offene Handelsgesellschaft—oHG), (4) limited partnership (Kommanditgesellschaft—KG), (5) limited partnership with share capital (Kommanditgesellschaft auf Aktien— KGaA), and (6) branch of a domestic or foreign company (Zweigniederlassung). Corporate income taxes are assessed on AGs, GmbHs, and nonresident companies that establish German branches. The other forms are not taxed at the entity level but at the individual level; that is, the income is allocated to the individual partners who are then taxed at their appropriate tax rate. The preferred form used by foreigners is either the GmbH or a branch.

The principal forms of French commercial enterprises are (1) the corporation (société anonyme—abbreviated SA), (2) limited liability company (société à responsabilité limitée—SARL), (3) general partnership (société en nom collectif—SCS), (4) partnership limited by shares (société en commandite par actions— SCPA), (5) joint ventures, and (6) branch (succursale). The commercial entities liable for corporate income taxes are SAs, SARLs, SCPAs, and nonresident companies with branches. The other entities may elect to be taxed as corporate entities or as individuals. Foreign entities predominately use SAs and SARLs.

CORPORATE INCOME TAX RATES

The basic corporate income tax imposed by central governments is a fixed percentage or an increasing percentage of the statutorily determined corporate in-

---

[1] We use as examples in this chapter the corporate tax rates and tax accounting treatments outside the United States that prevailed in mid-1993. They are used here simply to show the diversity of tax laws.

come. The rate varies significantly from country to country. Countries typically tax resident corporations on worldwide income regardless of whether the income is repatriated. Nonresident corporations, that is, corporations whose corporate seat and place of management are outside the country, are typically subject only to corporate taxes derived from within the country.

To list the basic tax rates would be misleading for several reasons. First, the calculation of corporate income varies based on the types of revenues that may or may not be included as taxable and permissible deductions. Second, there may be a refund for corporate income distributed to shareholders that lowers the effective tax rate or an additional corporate tax paid on distributed income that raises the effective tax rate. Third, there may be a different tax rate based on the characteristics of the commercial entity, such as its size. Fourth, the effective tax rate may be different for undistributed income and income distributed to shareholders. Finally, the tax rate can vary for resident and nonresident business entities. We'll see examples as we proceed.

In the United States, the basic corporate income tax rate is 35 percent. The basic corporate tax rates in Spain, Portugal, and Austria are a flat 35 percent, 36 percent, and 30 percent, respectively. In Taiwan (Republic of China), both domestic and foreign companies are taxed on a progressive basis as follows: 0 percent on taxable income less than Taiwan dollars (NT) 50,000, 15 percent up to NT 100,000, and 25 percent in excess of NT 100,000. Several countries impose no tax or minimal tax rates. These countries are referred to as *tax havens*.[2] Switzerland and Hong Kong are examples.

The tax rate can vary not only by the amount of taxable income but also by other factors as indicated in the following two examples. In Japan, the corporate tax rate differs for corporations whose issued capital is more than ¥100 million and for those for which it is less than ¥100 million. It is 37.5 percent for the former and 28 percent for the latter. In Korea, the basic corporate tax rate is 20 percent for income up to 80 million won and 30 percent above that amount. However, the latter rate is 33 percent for certain closed corporations that are not listed on the Korean Stock Exchange and have a certain amount of paid-in capital or net equity. Thailand is another country with a differential tax rate for listed and unlisted corporations. The corporate tax rate is a flat 30 percent for corporations whose stock is listed on the Securities Exchange of Thailand; for corporations not listed, the corporate tax rate is 35 percent.

Special provisions may alter the basic corporate tax rate. The most common type is the favorable tax treatment granted to the tax entity if an asset sold produces a capital gain. In the United States, the capital gains tax rate is less than the tax rate on ordinary income. Hong Kong has no tax on capital gains. In Nigeria, the capital gains tax rate is 20 percent, one-half the rate on ordinary business income. The capital gains tax rate can depend on the length of time the asset was held. For

---

[2] Some entities use tax havens to avoid or reduce taxes. The use of tax havens by U.S. entities was significantly reduced by the Tax Reform Act of 1986. Banks establish subsidiaries in tax havens to take advantage of lower reserve requirements than in the parent bank's country of residence.

example, in Ireland, where the basic corporate tax rate is 40 percent, the tax on capital gains is higher than on ordinary business income (50 percent) if the asset is held for no more than three years; however, it is 35 percent if the asset is held between three years but not more than six years and 30 percent if held more than six years.

The amount of income distributed to shareholders can affect the effective tax rate. In Germany, the basic corporate income tax rate is 50 percent of undistributed profits for resident corporations and 46 percent for nonresident corporations. For resident corporations there is a refund of 14/50 of the tax paid for income distributed to shareholders, thereby reducing the effective tax rate to 36 percent. Distributions made by nonresident corporations to the foreign head office are not entitled to a tax refund. In contrast, under Italian tax law, the basic corporate income tax rate is 36 percent; however, if the dividend exceeds 46 percent of taxable income, an additional tax of 56.25 percent of the excess is imposed.

Municipal or local corporate income taxes may be imposed on commercial enterprises. They may be based on corporate income or on the corporate income tax liability due to the central government. Taxes paid to a municipal or local government may or may not be deductible for purposes of calculating corporate income reported to the central government. Many states and major cities in the United States impose a corporate income tax. In Japan, prefectural and municipal governments impose an "inhabitants" tax. The rate is based on both the corporate income tax paid to the Japanese government and the number of employees. In Portugal, most municipalities impose a tax of 10 percent of the federal taxes paid. Because the Portuguese basic corporate tax rate is 36 percent, the imposition of a municipal tax increases the effective combined tax rate to 39.6 percent.

A country's tax authorities withhold taxes on income derived in their country by nonresident corporations. The withholding tax rate may vary, depending on the type of income: dividends, interest, or royalties. Major trading countries often negotiate tax treaties to reduce the double taxation of corporate income. Table 10.1 shows the treaty withholding tax rates between the United States and foreign countries. Notice that the tax rate for all three types of income within each country is less than the basic United States corporate tax rate of 34 percent at the time the table was constructed.

A corporation's effective tax rate on its worldwide income therefore depends on tax treaties between its home country and all the foreign countries where it has established a nonresident corporation. Moreover, the rate also depends on whether a corporation is permitted a credit by the tax authorities in its home country against taxes paid in foreign countries. Many countries permit this credit, called a *foreign tax credit*. The limitation is usually that the tax credit paid to a foreign country may not exceed the amount that would have been paid in the home country.

DETERMINING TAXABLE INCOME

Varying definitions of taxable revenue and deductible expenses cause the determination of corporate profits to vary from country to country. By far, the largest variance can be attributed to the differences in the treatment of items that are deductible for tax purposes. Different methods of treating noncash expenses such as

■ TABLE 10.1

U.S. TREATY WITHHOLDING TAX RATES

	Dividends %	Interest %	Patent and Know-How Royalties %
Australia	15	10	10
Austria	15/5[a]	0	0
Barbados	15/5[a]	12.5	12.5
Belgium	15/5[a]	15	0
Canada	15/10[a]	15	10
China	10	10	10
Cyprus	15/5[a]	10	0
Denmark	15/5[a]	0	0
Egypt	15/5[a]	15	15
Finland	15/5[a]	0	0
France	15/5[a]	0	5
Germany	15[c]	0	0
Greece	30	0/30[b]	0
Hungary	15/5[a]	0	0
Iceland	15/5[a]	0	0
India[d]	25/10[a]	15	15
Indonesia[d]	15	15	15
Ireland	15/5[a]	0/30[b]	0
Italy	15/5[a]	15	10
Jamaica	15/10[a]	12.5	10
Japan	15/10[a]	10	10
Korea	15/10[a]	12	15
Luxembourg	15/5[a]	0	0
Malta	15/5[a]	12.5	12.5
Morocco	15/10[a]	15	10
Netherlands	15/5[a]	0	0
New Zealand	15	10	10
Norway	15	0	0
Pakistan	30/15[a]	30	0
Phillippines	25/20[a]	15	15
Poland	15/5[a]	0	10
Romania	10	10	15
Spain[d]	15/10[a]	10	10
Sweden	15/5[a]	0	0
Switzerland	15/5[a]	5	0
Trinidad and Tobago	30	30	15
United Kingdom	15/5[a]	0	0
USSR	30	0	0

Various exceptions or conditions may apply, depending upon the terms of the particular treaty. Treaties with several other countries have been signed but are not yet in force.

a. The withholding rate is reduced to 5% (10% in the case of Canada, India, Jamaica, Japan, Korea (South), Morocco, and Spain; 15% in the case of Pakistan; and 20% in the case of the Phillippines) if, among other conditions, the receipt is a corporation owning a specified percentage of the voting power of the distributing corporation.

b. The exemption does not apply if the receipient controls directly or indirectly more than 50% of the voting power in the paying corporation.

c. A new treaty with Germany has been signed and is expected to enter into force in 1991. Among other changes, the new treaty would reduce the dividend withholding rate to 5 percent if certain conditions are met.

d. The treaty has various effective dates for different taxes, but none earlier than January 1, 1991.

SOURCE: *Worldwide Corporate Tax Guide and Directory,* Ernst & Young International Business Series, 1991 ed. (New York: Ernst & Young, January 1991), 370.

depreciation and inventory valuation can affect the calculation of taxable income. Two other considerations affect the determination of taxable income. Both of these matters relate to the deductibility of items that foreign tax authorities view as legitimate expenses but are incurred to minimize taxes in the foreign country. The first is the deductibility of interest expense when that expense may be viewed as excessive. The second is the inflation of expenses associated with the sale or purchase of goods and services by a nonresident company with an associated company (that is, a parent company or another subsidiary of the parent) outside the foreign country. We next discuss each of these factors.

DEPRECIATION

In the case of depreciation, the key factors in determining the permissible allowance are (1) the amount that may be depreciated each year, (2) the period over which the asset may be depreciated, and (3) the total amount that may be depreciated. The amount that may be depreciated each year may be set by legislation or may be calculated from a statutorily acceptable depreciation method (e.g., straight line or accelerated). The statutorily prescribed period over which the asset may be depreciated can be set forth by legislation or can be based on the economic life of the asset. Finally, the total amount that the tax laws permit an entity to depreciate an asset may be its cost or the cost reduced by some prescribed amount (the most common being the estimated residual value).

For example, the U.S. tax code groups assets into six classes of personal property (such as machinery and equipment) and into two classes of real property (such as plants and buildings). For each class, a recovery period and depreciation rate for each year of the recovery period are statutorily prescribed. In Japan, depreciation is determined using either straight-line or declining balance methods. The life of an asset is its estimated useful life. Statutory lives are 45 to 65 years for office buildings, 22 to 45 years for warehouses, 3 to 15 years for furniture and fixtures, and 3 to 5 years for automobiles and trucks. The asset may be depreciated down to 5 percent of its residual value.

In Spain, the depreciation allowance taken for tax purposes is generally the same as that for financial reporting purposes as long as the amount deducted does not exceed the tax law maximum. In Singapore, depreciation reported in the financial statement is not allowed for tax reporting. For new industrial buildings, an initial allowance of 25 percent of the construction cost is permitted with the balance typically deductible on a straight-line basis at 3 percent per annum. The rate applied to most plants and machinery is 33 percent, and a straight-line method is used. Capital expenditures for the installation of computers, prescribed automation equipment, and robots is 100 percent deductible in the year of acquisition.

INVENTORY VALUATION

The method of valuation of inventory affects taxable income through its effect on the cost of goods sold. The relationship is as follows:

Beginning inventory
+ Purchases
_____
Goods available for sale
− Ending inventory
_____
Cost of goods sold

The lower the calculated ending inventory, the higher the cost of goods sold and the lower the taxable corporate income.

The acceptable methods for valuing inventory vary from country to country. For example, in Australia, end-of-year inventory may be valued using one of the following methods: cost, market selling price, or replacement value. In France, the lower amount of either cost or year-end market value is used to value inventories. An averaging method or the first-in, first-out method is used to determine which is lower, the cost or market value; the last-in, first-out method may not be employed.

The tax code specifies the types of costs that may be included when determining the cost of inventory. For example, in many countries, the cost of manufactured goods must include direct labor and material costs, as well as manufacturing overhead; selling costs may not be included. In Finland, inventory is valued at the lowest of direct acquisition cost on a first-in, first-out basis; replacement cost, market value, and direct acquisition costs exclude manufacturing overhead. In Sweden, direct costs plus a reasonable proportion of indirect costs may be included in determining the cost of inventory manufactured for tax purposes; interest cost may not be included. In Italy, the cost of production and associated direct overhead expenses are included in cost, but the latter excludes interest and general overhead expenses. In Spain, appropriate overhead may be included in costs.

Obviously, what is defined as overhead cost may vary from country to country.

INTEREST EXPENSE

In most countries, the interest expense associated with borrowed funds is tax deductible. Dividends, in contrast, are treated as distributed profits and are not tax deductible. (However, as explained later, some countries allow the dividend-paying company to receive a tax credit for distributed profits.) This difference is particularly important when a parent company provides financing to a foreign subsidiary. Interest paid by a subsidiary to its parent is deductible for the subsidiary but taxable for the parent. Dividends, in contrast, are taxable for both the subsidiary and the parent.

An increasing number of firms have employed financing arrangements to take advantage of the tax advantage associated with debt. It can be done in two ways. First, a financing agreement can be called "debt" even though it is effectively a form of equity. For example, an instrument may be called a debt obligation but, unlike legitimate debt, it allows the "borrower" to miss periodic payments if sufficient cash flow is unavailable. Or the priority of the "creditors" can be subordinated to all other creditors and to preferred stockholders. Both of these provisions indicate that the instrument may be more appropriately classified as a form of equity rather than debt. Second, several companies have employed capital structures that predominately consist of debt. Such companies are commonly referred to as *thin capitalization companies.*

In some countries, tax authorities have challenged whether, in fact, some of the debt should be appropriately recharacterized as equity for tax purposes, thereby eliminating the deductibility of interest for the reclassified portion. For example, in the United States, a section of the tax code enacted in 1969 gives the Internal Revenue Service the right to define what are debt and equity for income tax purposes. The IRS employs some general guidelines in making its determination. Basically, it is looking for characteristics of the debt instrument suggesting that it is a disguised form of equity. Ireland has provisions in its tax code for recharacterizing instruments as equity. The United Kingdom has specific provisions that address the recharacterization of a security from debt to equity. Greece has some general provisions that permit the tax authorities to challenge a specific agreement; however, the burden of proof is on the tax authorities.

The recharacterization of debt to equity may be due to the terms of the individual agreement or security regardless of the ratio of debt to equity. When a company's debt-to-equity ratio is high, tax authorities may seek to recharacterize a portion of the debt to equity for tax purposes. The Committee on Fiscal Affairs of the Organization on Economic Cooperation and Development (OECD) addressed the issue of thin capitalization in a 1987 publication, *The OECD Report on Thin Capitalization.* The report identifies the general issues but does not provide any guideline as to what is an excessive debt-to-equity ratio.

The United States has no specific formulas for determining whether there is excess leverage. However, it does have provisions that recharacterize certain types of low quality–rated debt (i.e., junk bond or high yield debt) as equity.

The following are some examples of countries that have thin capitalization provisions. The Canadian Income Tax Act includes specific provisions for thin capitalization when interest is paid to nonresidents. More specifically, interest deductibility is denied on that portion of debt that exceeds three times the interest-paying company's equity. In 1987, the tax laws of Australia were amended to deny interest deductibility to resident companies controlled by foreign entities when the debt of the resident company exceeds a statutorily specified multiple of the foreign controller's equity in that company.

In 1989 two cases in Norway, one involving British Petroleum and the other involving Amoco (a U.S. company that established an operating subsidiary in Norway), rendered a decision that certain provisions in the Norwegian tax law could be used to impose thin capitalization restrictions. For example, in the Amoco case, the operating subsidiary's debt to debt-plus-equity ratio was 1.7 percent. The tax authorities argued that for tax purposes, 20 percent of the debt plus equity should be treated as debt. The court ruled that 10 percent was to be recharacterized.

Tax authorities or finance ministries use other methods to attempt to curtail what they perceive to be an abuse of borrowing to benefit from interest deductibility. One way is to place an explicit restriction on the amount of interest that may be deductible. A second way, which Germany and Italy use, is for tax authorities to enact commercial or civil laws restricting the amount of debt. German company law specifies a fixed minimum amount of equity for companies engaged in different business activities. The Italian Civil Code, with some exceptions, permits a company to issue bonds only up to a certain amount of equity.

To restrict resident companies controlled by foreign entities from being thinly capitalized, some countries, requiring approval of the investments by foreign entities, do not grant that approval unless they deem the capitalization adequate. In New Zealand, when a foreign entity owns 25 percent or more of a company, it may have to obtain permission from the New Zealand Overseas Investment Commission to establish a nonresident subsidiary. When approval is necessary, minimum equity or maximum debt levels may be imposed. In Cyprus, regulation of foreign investments grants the Central Bank the right to deny approval if equity is not viewed as adequate. Or countries can use restrictions on the transfer of funds abroad to mitigate the problem of thin capitalization. The Bank of Japan, for example, has the right to question what it deems to be excessive interest payments of a Japanese company to its foreign entity if the amount transferred is ¥30 million or more.

INTERCOMPANY TRANSACTIONS AND TRANSFER PRICES

As just explained, to minimize taxes in foreign countries with high tax rates, a firm may use excessive debt in controlled entities. To further reduce taxes, the interest rate on the "loan" may be above market rates. An excessive interest rate charged to subsidiaries in high tax countries is but one expense that a company with foreign operations can consider to reduce worldwide taxes.

It is common for a company's subsidiaries in different countries to buy and sell goods from each other. The price for the goods in such intercompany transactions is called a *transfer price*. Establishing transfer prices to promote goal congruence within a multinational company is a complicated topic. In practice, goal congruence seems to be of secondary importance to the minimization of worldwide taxes—income taxes and import duty taxes—in the establishment of transfer prices.[3]

The following illustration demonstrates how the establishment of a transfer price affects income taxes. Suppose that a parent company resides in the United States where it faces a marginal tax rate of 35 percent and has only one subsidiary located in a foreign country where the marginal tax rate is 42 percent. The parent company manufactures a product for U.S.$20 a unit and sells 100,000 units to the subsidiary each year. The subsidiary, in turn, further processes each unit at a cost of $10 per unit and sells the finished product for $80 per unit. The parent company's sale represents its revenue, and the subsidiary's purchase represents part of its production cost. It is assumed that fixed costs for the parent and the subsidiary are $1,000,000 and $500,000, respectively.

The top panel of Table 10.2 shows the taxes and the net income of the parent, the subsidiary, and the company as a whole if the transfer price is set at $40 per unit. The bottom panel of the table shows the same analysis if the parent company sets

---

[3] R.L. Benke, Jr. and J.D. Edwards, *Transfer Pricing: Techniques and Uses* (New York: National Association of Accountants, 1980).

a transfer price of $60 per unit. Notice that by increasing the transfer price from $40 to $60, worldwide income increases by $140,000, the same amount by which worldwide taxes decline.

■ **TABLE 10.2**

ILLUSTRATION OF EFFECT OF TRANSFER PRICE ON
WORLDWIDE NET INCOME

Assumptions: Units sold by parent = 100,000
U.S. parent tax rate = 35%
Subsidiary tax rate = 42%

	Price and Costs in U.S. dollars	
	Parent	**Subsidiary**
Selling price	Transfer price	$ 80
Unit variable manufacturing cost	$ 20	Transfer price + $10
Fixed manufacturing costs	$1,000,000	$500,000

	Transfer price = $40	
	U.S. Parent Company Alone	**Subsidiary**
Revenue	$4,000,000	$8,000,000
Variable manufacturing costs	2,000,000	5,000,000
Fixed manufacturing costs	1,000,000	500,000
Taxable income	$1,000,000	$2,500,000
Income taxes	350,000	1,050,000
Net income after taxes	$ 650,000	$1,450,000
Worldwide income taxes = $1,400,000		
Worldwide net income after taxes = $2,100,000		

	Transfer price = $60	
	U.S. Parent Company Alone	**Subsidiary**
Revenue	$6,000,000	$8,000,000
Variable manufacturing costs	2,000,000	7,000,000
Fixed manufacturing costs	1,000,000	500,000
Taxable income	$3,000,000	$ 500,000
Income taxes	1,050,000	210,000
Net income after taxes	$1,950,000	$ 290,000
Worldwide income taxes = $1,260,000		
Worldwide net income after taxes = $2,240,000		

TAXATION OF DISTRIBUTED EARNINGS

In the United States, corporate earnings distributed to shareholders are taxed twice: at the corporate level and when distributed to shareholders. No tax relief is given to either the distributing corporation or shareholder.[4] Under this system of taxing distributed earnings, referred to as the *classical system*,[5] the corporation and the shareholders are treated as distinct taxable entities.

Although the classical system for taxing distributed earnings is found in other countries, some countries give shareholders credit for the taxes that the corporation paid on the distributed earnings. Shareholders then gross up dividends received by the amount of the tax paid by the corporation and correspondingly receive a tax credit for the same amount. For example, suppose a corporation realizes pretax income of $10 per share and pays a 40 percent tax, or $4 per share. The earnings per share after taxes is then $6. Suppose the entire $6 per share is distributed to shareholders. Then a shareholder receiving $6 reports taxable income of $10 (the pretax income per share) but receives a tax credit of $4 (the tax paid by the corporation). As a result, the pretax income of $10 is taxed only once. This system for taxing distributed earnings is referred to as the *imputation system*. Countries that have adopted it usually do not allow nonresident corporations that receive dividends from resident corporations to claim the credit except when a double tax treaty specifically provides for it.[6]

TAX INCENTIVES

Government incentives to induce commerce and/or foster the development of designated economic sectors or geographical regions can be in the form of either below-market interest rates on loans or tax incentives.

Tax incentives granted by a country can be one or more of the following: (1) a tax credit, (2) a reduced tax rate, (3) a special tax deduction, and (4) a tax holiday. The following are examples of each type of tax incentive.

A *tax credit* is a reduction of taxes by an amount equal to the tax credit.[7] For example, if a corporation in the United States has a tax liability prior to any tax credit of $10 million and a tax credit of $2 million, its tax liability is reduced to $8 million. In the United States, at one time the major tax credit was the investment tax credit, which has been repealed. There are still other types of tax credits granted under the tax code of the United States.

---

[4] The exception is when the shareholder is another corporation. There is an intercorporate dividend tax exclusion in such instances. More specifically, under the current tax law, only 30 percent of the dividends distributed is taxable to the corporation receiving the dividends.

[5] *Taxation in Europe: 1991 Edition*, International Tax and Business Guide (New York: DRT International, 1991), 1.

[6] Ibid., 1.

[7] It is important to understand the difference between a tax credit and a tax deduction. A *tax deduction* is a reduction of taxable income by the amount of the deduction. The *reduction in taxes* equals the product of the marginal tax rate and the amount of the deduction.

Spain and Japan are examples of countries with tax credits on investments. In Spain, where the tax code permits a credit of 5 percent of the amount invested in fixed assets, a 5 percent tax credit is allowed for certain types of investments made outside the country to stimulate overseas commerce. In Japan, federal tax law provides a tax credit for incremental research and development expenditures.

Examples of countries with tax incentives in the form of reduced tax rates are Greece and Nigeria. In Greece, on certain large projects, the tax rate generated from the project may be reduced by five percentage points. In Nigeria, where the normal corporate tax rate is 40 percent, a corporation with gross sales of less than Naira 500,000 is assessed a tax rate of only 20 percent for the first three years if it is engaged in manufacturing or agricultural production or mining solid materials.

The following countries offer special deductions. In Greece, normal depreciation is based on the straight-line method. Certain investments, however, may be depreciated on an accelerated basis. In Belgium, depreciation at twice the normal straight-line rate is allowed for investments made by small and medium-sized companies as well as for investments made in designated development areas. Australian tax law permits special deductions to be made for expenditures on research and development. Malaysia allows a double deduction for research and development expenses to encourage investment in those areas.

In an attempt to stimulate economic investment in designated regions of their countries, some central governments grant *tax holidays,* which allow either a total or partial exemption from taxes for a specified period of time. For example, the Italian government offers a 10-year tax holiday for investments in designated areas such as southern Italy, Sardinia, and Sicily, to stimulate economic development. The French government grants tax holidays for business entities established in designated enterprise zones; businesses may be exempt from corporate income taxes for the first 10 years.

Tax holidays are also granted for other types of investments. Sri Lanka grants tax holidays for export-oriented industries and designated agricultural activities. The French tax law allows tax holidays for certain new business activities; the commercial entity may be exempt from taxes for the first two years and partially exempt for the next three years.

In Thailand, the Board of Investment has myriad tax incentives on qualified investments and for investments in areas designated as investment zones. Incentives include reduced business taxes, additional depreciation allowance, double deductions for certain expenditures, and tax holidays.

The People's Republic of China grants refunds to joint ventures that reinvest their earnings in China. Forty percent of the tax paid is refunded if the investment lasts for at least five years. The tax paid is fully refundable if the investment is in technologically advanced or export-oriented enterprises.

IMPLICATIONS FOR MANAGERS

Corporate taxes in a foreign country have managerial implications for investing and financing decisions. Investing or capital budgeting analysis requires an estimation of the cash flow from a contemplated project. Proper cash-flow analysis should consider taxes not as reported in a corporation's financial statement but those projected for tax-reporting purposes. Permissible depreciation methods and inventory valuation methods affect the projected cash flow. Moreover, when properly incorporated into a cash-flow analysis, tax incentives available may influence the country, geographical location within the country, and type of business activities that offer the greatest investment opportunities.

The tax law influences the financing decision—the capital structure and the dividend policy. The existence of thin capitalization rules in a country may affect a foreign subsidiary's capital structure. Debt arrangements between a parent company and its foreign subsidiary must be structured to minimize the risk that the agreement will be recharacterized as equity. Even the decision to list a corporation's stock on an exchange is prejudiced by the tax code in countries where the tax rate is higher for unlisted stocks relative to listed stocks.

Finally, ordinary business activities between a parent and foreign corporation are structured to minimize worldwide taxes. In particular, intercorporate transfer prices are influenced more by the desire to minimize taxes than to achieve goal congruence.

QUESTIONS AND EXERCISES

10-1. Why would a simple listing of the basic tax rates by country be misleading?

10-2. How do the different methods for the treatment of noncash expenses by countries affect the determination of corporate profits?

10-3. What is the controversy regarding the classification of corporate funds as debt or equity?

10-4. What is meant by a *thin capitalization company?*

10-5. What might the tax authorities of a country do if a corporation is viewed as a thin capitalization company?

10-6. The Rotundo Corporation is a U.S. corporation with subsidiaries in several countries. Suppose that the U.S. corporate marginal tax rate is 35 percent and that one of its subsidiaries is operating in a foreign country where the marginal tax rate is 47 percent. Rotundo Corporation manufactures a product for U.S.$60 a unit and sells 50,000 units to the subsidiary each year. The subsidiary, in turn, further processes each unit at a cost of $40 per unit and sells the finished product for $240 per unit. The fixed costs for Rotundo Corporation and the subsidiary are $2,000,000 and $1,000,000, respectively.

a. What are the taxes and the net income of the parent, the subsidiary, and the company as a whole if the transfer price is set at $90 per unit?

b. What are the taxes and the net income of the parent, the subsidiary, and the company as a whole if the transfer price is set at $120 per unit?

c. Given your answers to parts (a) and (b), how does the choice of a transfer price affect the company as a whole?

10-7. What is meant by the *classical system* of taxing distributed earnings?

10-8. What is meant by the *imputation system* of taxing distributed earnings?

10-9. Is the classical system or imputation system followed in the United States?

10-10. Is the classical system or imputation system followed outside the United States?

10-11. What is a *tax credit?*

10-12. What is a *tax holiday?*

REFERENCES

Benke, R. L., Jr., and J. D. Edwards. *Transfer Pricing: Techniques and Uses.* New York: National Association of Accountants, 1980.

Taxation in Europe: 1991 Edition, International Tax and Business Guide. New York: DRT International, 1991, p. 1.

Gaspar de Guzman, controller for Castile Foods Company's agricultural products processing operations in Spain, felt a deep personal responsibility for the financial performance of the companies under his supervision. He was distressed by the situation of El Almirantazgo de los Paises Septentrianales (A.P.S.), S.A. in particular, for the company's recent operating losses and restructuring costs were accentuated by interest expense and by A.P.S.'s nontax-paying position. Sr. de Guzman felt that a recapitalization of the company would have benefits for Castile, but he knew that he had to present his argument in a fashion that would earn the support of the corporate vice president of finance, Phyllis Forth. He also knew it would be necessary for him to understand the risks and benefits of his proposal for the parent company, Castile Foods Company, as well as for A.P.S. Finally, he did not believe that he had very much time to develop his recommendation, because the corporate budget for fiscal year 1993, which began in August 1992, had to be completed in a few weeks.

De Guzman wanted to propose a restructuring of A.P.S.'s financing to reduce the overall after-tax cost of financing for Castile Foods. Any recommendation he made would have to accommodate the tax treatments of interest, dividends, and earnings in the United States as well as Spain. In addition, however, he believed that interest rate differentials, exchange rate fluctuations, and A.P.S.'s future profitability would necessarily be addressed in any recommendation.

BUSINESS BACKGROUND

Castile Foods is a national U.S. manufacturer and distributor of brand named commodity food products. A.P.S. is a wholly owned subsidiary of Castile Foods and has two sites in Spain that process and pack Spanish agricultural products for the international and Spanish markets. Historically, over 80 percent of sales has gone to Castile Foods subsidiaries in the United States, and most of these imports are sold under locally known brand names to the grocery trade and food service companies. Retail competition is mostly based on price, with a large "private label" segment in food stores. Food service competition depends on regularity and flexibility of supply and on parent company support at the food service operator level in providing product use ideas.

Although marginally profitable at the operating level in prior years, A.P.S. was projecting an operating loss of 573 million pesetas (PTA) ($5.6 million at the February 1992 exchange rate of PTA 103/$) in FY1992. These losses arose from the costs of consolidating manufacturing operations in Spain and from an inability to increase factory prices in the face of a strengthening of the value of the peseta against other currencies in comparison to historic levels. By the end of FY1992, A.P.S. was projecting PTA 887 million of accumulated operating losses on a local

---

This case was prepared by Mark R. Eaker, professor of Business Administration. Copyright © 1992 by the University of Virginia Darden School Foundation, Charlottesville, Va. Historical data are from public sources in Spain; names have been changed at the request of the parent company. All rights reserved.

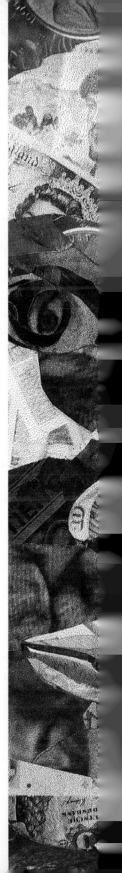

A.P.S., S.A.

■ **A.P.S. INCOME HISTORY AND FY1992 PROJECTION**
(PTA MILLIONS)

	FY1989	FY1990	FY1991	FY1992 Projection
Sales	4,724	6,062	4,199	3,232
Operating Expenses	4,526	5,985	3,912	3,613
Other expense	53	(191)	231	192
Net income on local basis*	145	268	56	(573)
Year-end tax loss carry forwards†	—	323	314	887

*Income in FY1989 through FY1992 does not reflect the results of a substantial investment in processing equipment in FY1992, which was expected to lower costs in future years. Results include the effect of a sale of assets in FY1990 and of restructuring costs, primarily severance, in FY1992.

†Tax losses include additional losses in FY1991 because of the local basis recognition of transactions in FY1990.

SOURCE: Registro Mercantil—Deposito de Cuentas. Because net income numbers include the effects of transactions that would be excluded under U.S. accounting rules, it is difficult to develop meaningful inferences in U.S. accounting terms about A.P.S.'s operating performance from this exhibit. Nonetheless, these published results are directionally and proportionally correct.

tax basis. Of these losses, PTA 314 million would expire in July 1994 and the balance in July 1997. Based on its historical performance, A.P.S. could expect annual earnings before interest and taxes (EBIT) in the range of PTA 200 million to PTA 400 million commencing in FY1993. Recent financial results as published in the regional Spanish Registro Mercantil (Business Registry) and projections for 1992 are shown in Exhibit 10.1A. A.P.S.'s range of earnings possibilities and their effects on A.P.S.'s interest expense and accumulated tax losses are presented in Exhibit 10.1B.

A.P.S.'S FINANCING

A.P.S. was financed by equity, by intercompany loans provided by Castile Foods from the United States, and by peseta debt provided by local banks. These amounts were roughly equity of PTA 1,440 million, intercompany dollar loans of $11 million, and local bank debt of PTA 250 million in March of FY1992. Because local debt was more costly than U.S.–sourced funds regardless of the currency chosen, intercompany loans were generally advantageous for other than short-term requirements. The point that concerned Sr. de Guzman was that A.P.S., with an operating loss in FY1991 and another projected for FY1992, would be unable to take immediate advantage of the tax deductibility of interest expenses in Spain. At the same time,

■ EXHIBIT 10.1B

A.P.S., S.A.
■ POSSIBLE A.P.S. EARNINGS AND TAX LOSS USE
(IN PTA MILLIONS)

	FY1993	FY1994	FY1995	FY1996	FY1997
First Scenario					
No equity contribution					
EBIT forecast	176	204	234	280	330
Interest (expense)	(133)	(125)	(108)	(89)	(58)
Tax at 35%	0	0	0	0	(16)
Net income	43	79	126	191	256
Local adjustment	10	10	10	10	10
Taxable income	53	89	136	201	266
Balance of tax losses					
Expiring 1994	(261)	(172)	0	0	0
Expiring 1997	(573)	(573)	(437)	(236)	0
Equity contribution					
EBIT forecast	176	204	234	280	330
Interest (expense)	(28)	(7)	20	52	77
Tax at 35%	0	0	0	(47)	(146)
Net income	148	197	254	285	261
Local adjustment	10	10	10	10	10
Taxable income	158	207	264	295	271
Balance of tax losses					
Expiring 1994	(156)	0	0	0	0
Expiring 1997	(573)	(522)	(258)	0	0
Memo					
Interest rate					
Assumption	12.3%	12.3%	11.8%	11.8%	10.8%
Second Scenario					
No equity contribution					
EBIT forecast	198	230	263	315	372
Interest (expense)	(131)	(120)	(99)	(76)	(42)
Tax at 35%	0	0	0	0	(67)
Net income	67	110	164	239	264
Local adjustment	10	10	10	10	10
Taxable income	77	120	174	249	274
Balance of tax losses					
Expiring 1994	(237)	(117)	0	0	0
Expiring 1997	(573)	(573)	(399)	(150)	0
Equity contribution					
EBIT forecast	198	230	263	315	372
Interest (expense)	(26)	(2)	29	63	89
Tax at 35%	0	0	0	(96)	(165)
Net income	172	228	292	282	296
Local adjustment	10	10	10	10	10
Taxable income	182	238	302	292	306
Balance of tax losses					
Expiring 1994	(132)	0	0	0	0
Expiring 1997	(573)	(467)	(165)	0	0

continued on next page

■ EXHIBIT 10.1B

(CONTINUED)

	FY1993	FY1994	FY1995	FY1996	FY1997
Third Scenario					
No equity contribution					
EBIT forecast	220	255	293	350	413
Interest (expense)	(130)	(116)	(91)	(62)	(26)
Tax at 35%	0	0	0	0	(117)
Net income	90	139	202	288	270
Local adjustment	10	10	10	10	10
Taxable income	100	149	212	298	280
Balance of tax losses					
Expiring 1994	(214)	(65)	0	0	0
Expiring 1997	(573)	(573)	(361)	(63)	0
Equity contribution					
EBIT forecast	220	255	293	350	413
Interest (expense)	(25)	3	38	74	100
Tax at 35%	0	0	0	(144)	(183)
Net income	195	258	331	280	330
Local adjustment	10	10	10	10	10
Taxable income	205	268	341	290	340
Balance of tax losses					
Expiring 1994	(109)	0	0	0	0
Expiring 1997	(573)	(414)	(73)	0	0
Fourth Scenario					
No equity contribution					
EBIT forecast	160	179	200	224	251
Interest (expense)	(134)	(129)	(116)	(104)	(79)
Tax at 35%	0	0	0	0	0
Net income	26	50	84	120	172
Local adjustment	10	10	10	10	10
Taxable income	36	60	94	130	182
Balance of tax losses					
Expiring 1994	(278)	(218)	0	0	0
Expiring 1997	(573)	(573)	(479)	(349)	(167)
Equity contribution					
EBIT forecast	160	179	200	224	251
Interest (expense)	(29)	(10)	13	41	63
Tax at 35%	0	0	0	0	(106)
Net income	131	169	213	265	208
Local adjustment	10	10	10	10	10
Taxable income	141	179	223	275	218
Balance of tax losses					
Expiring 1994	(173)	0	0	0	0
Expiring 1997	(573)	(573)	(350)	(75)	0

Castile Foods was very profitable and, therefore, in a position to benefit from a tax deduction for interest expense in the United States.

It was evident to Sr. de Guzman that if A.P.S.'s future earnings were PTA 220 million in FY1993 with solid growth in later years (third scenario, Exhibit 10.1B), A.P.S. would have tax losses of $220,874 expiring in 1994 (PTA 65 million × 35% tax rate/PTA 103/$) and would not become tax paying until 1996. On the other hand, if A.P.S.'s future earnings were as shown in the fourth scenario in Exhibit 10.1B, A.P.S. would have tax losses of $1,308,252 (PTA 385 million × 35% tax rate/PTA 103/$) expiring in 1994 and 1997 and would not become tax paying until 1998. In all scenarios, A.P.S. was faced with the prospect of interest expense without the benefit of a contemporaneous tax deduction.

The solution that was intuitively attractive to Sr. de Guzman was a direct equity contribution from Castile Foods to A.P.S. The equity contribution would replace the existing intercompany loan from Castile or local bank debt. The economics of an equity contribution would be determined by two components: (1) the cost of transferring capital in and out of Spain and (2) the benefits of moving debt from A.P.S., which was not tax paying, to Castile Foods, which was.

The cost of transferring equity in and out of Spain encompassed a 1 percent noncreditable, incremental, and unavoidable capital tax on equity contributions and a 10 percent withholding tax on dividends. The necessity of paying the 10 percent withholding tax depended on whether the Spanish tax authority classified any eventual return of equity as a capital or a dividend transaction. Also of consequence would be the U.S. tax authority's classification of the repatriation of funds: if a dividend, the amount would be taxed as foreign-source income in the United States, while any withholding tax paid in Spain as well as any income tax paid in Spain on the earnings that provided the dividend would be creditable against U.S. taxes. Unfortunately, the efficiency of such credits was limited by the U.S. authority's position that credits could not be applied at a rate exceeding the U.S. tax rate. Generally, it could be assumed that foreign taxes exceeding the U.S. tax rate of 34 percent could be credited against U.S. income but only in future years. The various possible treatments of return of equity are laid out in Exhibit 10.1C. Alternatively, it was reasonable to assume that Castile would incur comparable financial costs by leaving cash in Spain if A.P.S. became profitable and tax paying in the future.

The benefits of moving debt from A.P.S. to the United States arose from the availability of a tax deduction for interest expense in the United States as opposed to a lost or deferred tax deduction in Spain. Specifically, when Castile is tax paying in the United States, a condition that was reasonable to expect based on Castile's consistent profitability, interest expense in the United States was deductible against pretax profits as it was incurred. A.P.S., in contrast, had accumulated operating losses for tax purposes against which future income could be offset, so interest expense was deductible in Spain only when and if the company became tax paying.

Several questions needed to be answered before an accurate assessment of the costs and benefits of an equity contribution could be gained. First, the annual cash effect of an equity contribution to A.P.S. needed to be quantified. After assuming, for the sake of analysis, the same cost of debt in both Spain and the United States, Sr. de Guzman determined that an equity contribution that prevented a Spanish

A.P.S., S.A.

■ POSSIBLE TAX TREATMENT OF RETURN OF EQUITY CONTRIBUTION

Tax Treatment in

United States	Spain	Tax Consequence	Assessment
Not E&P*	Capital	No tax	Very favorable but very unlikely
Not E&P	Dividend	10% Spanish withholding tax	Very unfavorable but very unlikely
E&P	Capital	Foreign source income in the United States with low effective tax rate and no withholding tax in Spain	Very favorable and possible for some portion of equity contribution
E&P	Dividend	10% withholding tax in Spain and foreign source income in the United States with low effective tax rate	Slightly favorable and likely for some portion of equity contribution
E&P	Dividend	10% withholding tax in Spain and foreign source income in the United States with high (35%) effective tax rate	Unfavorable but unlikely

*E&P = Earnings and profits.

tax loss from expiring would create annual savings after tax of 2.57 percent of the principal amount of the contribution; similarly, an equity contribution that had the effect of accelerating the use of tax losses that would not otherwise expire would create a savings for Castile's of 2.57 percent initially, followed by a reversal of 2.36 percent in a future year. The basis of this calculation is shown in detail in Exhibit 10.1D.

Sr. de Guzman realized that the net present value (NPV) of these cash savings would depend on the efficiency with which the tax losses in Spain were used. He believed that there were four possible earnings patterns: a low range with average EBIT of PTAs 245 million, a medium range with 276 million, a high range of 306 million, and a historic range, which at 203 million was the lowest. Using these forecasts Sr. de Guzman analyzed how the tax losses would be utilized with either an equity contribution or continued borrowing (Exhibit 10.1B).

The next step in determining the gains to be realized from an equity contribution was to calculate the NPV of the cash savings using Castile's cost of capital of 11.5 percent, if appropriate, under these various cases and earnings scenarios.

Of course, any gains would likely be offset by the negative effect of the imposition of the 10 percent withholding tax when the capital and earnings in Spain were repatriated to the United States. Depending on timing, the present value of the withholding tax might have a significant effect on the net benefit of the equity contribution. Sr. de Guzman wondered under what circumstances the withholding tax would cause the net benefit to be positive or negative.

The practical matter was the amount of equity to be contributed. The most desirable approach would be to contribute equity such that the last dollar of equity invested would have a positive expected present value. Sr. de Guzman would have to review the various combinations of earnings scenarios and cases to determine

■ EXHIBIT 10.1D

A.P.S., S.A.
■ ANNUAL CASH EFFECT OF FINANCING
(% OF PRINCIPAL AMOUNT)

	A.P.S. Nontaxpaying	A.P.S. Taxpaying
Cash Cost of Intercompany Loan		
Spain		
Interest expense*	(6.75)	(6.75)
Tax deduction at 35%	—	2.36
	(6.75)	(4.39)
United States		
Interest income	6.75	6.75
Tax at 34%	(2.30)	(2.30)
Interest expense	(6.75)	(6.75)
Tax deduction at 28%[†]	1.89	1.89
Withholding tax in Spain[‡]	(0.68)	(0.68)
Total cost of financing	(7.84)	(5.48)
Cash Cost of Equity		
United States		
Interest expense*	(6.75)	(6.75)
Tax deduction at 28%	1.89	1.89
Total cost of financing	(4.86)	(4.86)
Cash advantage of equity[§]	2.98	0.62

* Assumes five-year dollar costs of funds to equalize interest rate differentials over planning horizons; alternative rates can be achieved by swaps.

[†] Assumes a negative effect arising from the IRS Sec. 861 interest allocation rule, which effectively reduces U.S. tax deduction on domestic interest expense.

[‡] Shows cash effect of 10 percent withholding tax deducted from interest remitted from Spain to the United States; assumes that tax is incremental expense.

[§] Excludes cash cost of 10 percent withholding tax on dividends repatriated from Spain.

the range of possible outcomes. He had to recommend to Ms. Forth some amount that secured a reasonable chance of benefits without taking too much risk of losing money, and he had to put his recommendation forward on an understandable basis so as to address Ms. Forth's characteristic disinclination to put equity overseas.

Assuming that an equity contribution made sense from an economic stand-point, what would be the financial reporting implications of such a transaction? What effect would a capital contribution have on Castile's consolidated balance sheet? How would the possible economic benefits of this transaction affect Castile's and A.P.S.'s income statements? A.P.S. reported its financial results in pesetas but Castile reported in dollars. The issue here, of course, involved the translation of principal amounts of debt and equity as well as interest and, as Sr. de Guzman knew, would be different for A.P.S. and Castile, depending on the currency involved.

RISKS OF AN EQUITY CONTRIBUTION

As with any cross-border equity contribution, Sr. de Guzman knew risks could arise, particularly with respect to tax regulations and foreign exchange. Tax rules could change to have a negative effect on the economics of an equity contribution. Sr. de Guzman wondered, for instance, what effect EC 1992, with its lessening of restrictions on capital transfers, might have on Spain's tax policies. Exhibit 10.1E lists the tax rates applicable to capital transactions in several European countries as of March 1992.

Foreign exchange movements could affect the economic results of the transaction to the extent that the dollar rate of appreciation against the peseta did or did not exceed Spanish/U.S. interest rate differentials. For example, if the dollar were to strengthen sharply in the near term, the economic and accounting benefits of an equity contribution over peseta debt (but not dollar debt) would diminish. Sr.

▪ EXHIBIT 10.1E

A.P.S., S.A.

▪ EUROPEAN TAX RATES 1992

(PERCENTAGE)

	Income	Interest	Dividends
Ireland	10	30	0
Spain	35	10	10
United Kingdom	35	0	5
France	34	0	5
Belgium	39	10	5
Netherlands	40	0	5
Italy	48	15	5
Germany	56	0	5

de Guzman reviewed the interest rate and exchange rate data shown in Exhibits 10.1F and 10.1G: Did the large interest rate differential between Spain and the United States make dollar debt desirable and should Castile enter into a net asset currency hedge by selling pesetas forward against the dollar?

■ EXHIBIT 10.1F

A.P.S., S.A.

■ SPANISH AND U.S. INTEREST RATES (PERCENTAGE)

	Bank of Spain Rate	Kingdom of Spain Bond Yield	U.S. Discount Rate	U.S. Long-Term Bonds
February 1992	12.65	11.32	3.50	7.34
January 1992	12.65	11.55	3.50	7.03
December 1991	12.50	11.87	3.50	7.09
November 1991	12.50	11.79	4.50	7.42
October 1991	12.60	11.62	5.00	7.53
September 1991	12.60	11.58	5.00	7.65
August 1991	12.70	12.09	5.50	7.90
July 1991	12.75	12.15	5.50	8.27
June 1991	12.75	11.92	5.50	8.28
May 1991	12.75	11.86	5.50	8.07
April 1991	13.50	12.53	5.50	8.04
March 1991	13.50	13.15	6.00	8.11
February 1991	14.50	14.13	6.00	7.85
January 1991	14.71	14.52	6.50	8.09
December 1990	14.71	14.54	6.50	8.08
November 1990	14.65	14.59	7.00	8.39
October 1990	14.65	14.86	7.00	8.72
September 1990	14.65	15.14	7.00	8.89
August 1990	14.65	14.67	7.00	8.75
July 1990	14.66	14.45	7.00	8.47
June 1990	14.65	14.49	7.00	8.48
May 1990	14.56	14.63	7.00	8.76
April 1990	14.53	14.79	7.00	8.79
March 1990	14.50	14.86	7.00	8.59
February 1990	14.55	14.62	7.00	8.47
January 1990	14.55	14.49	7.00	8.21
December 1989	14.52	14.49	7.00	7.84
November 1989	14.54	14.00	7.00	7.87
October 1989	14.51	13.81	7.00	8.01
September 1989	14.50	16.24	7.00	8.19
August 1989	14.50	16.47	7.00	8.11
July 1989	14.50	16.64	7.00	8.02
June 1989	13.84	15.86	7.00	8.28
May 1989	13.75	15.39	7.00	8.86
April 1989	13.75	15.33	7.00	9.18
March 1989	13.75	15.50	7.00	9.36
February 1989	13.40	14.89	7.00	9.17
January 1989	12.40	14.17	6.50	9.09

SOURCE: IMF, International Financial Statistics.

■ EXHIBIT 10.1G

SPANISH AND U.S. EXCHANGE RATES

End of Period	Pesetas/U.S. $
February 1992	102.91
January 1992	101.53
December 1991	96.69
November 1991	103.73
October 1991	105.51
September 1991	105.30
August 1991	108.47
July 1991	109.40
June 1991	113.51
May 1991	106.80
April 1991	106.91
March 1991	105.99
February 1991	94.71
January 1991	93.11
December 1990	96.91
November 1990	95.29
October 1990	95.29
September 1990	97.97
August 1990	97.35
July 1990	98.37
June 1990	102.56
May 1990	105.11
April 1990	106.12
March 1990	108.55
February 1990	108.77
January 1990	108.73
December 1989	109.72
November 1989	115.03
October 1989	116.78
September 1989	118.93
August 1989	122.61
July 1989	117.19
June 1989	124.33
May 1989	127.05
April 1989	116.50
March 1989	117.84
February 1989	114.58
January 1989	115.39

SOURCE: IMF, International Financial Statistics.

CASE 10.2

THE PROCTER & GAMBLE COMPANY: MEXICO 1991

Dick Druffel, associate director of Procter & Gamble's International Treasury Division, looked over the proposal from Procter & Gamble (P&G)(Mexico) to borrow an average of $55 million over the next three years. The funds would be used to expand and modernize P&G (Mexico)'s manufacturing capacity and to make strategic prepayments of advertising expenses. As part of P&G's globalization strategy, the finance needs of all P&G subsidiaries were coordinated through the head office in Cincinnati, Ohio, in order to "finance the Company's global business at the lowest cost of capital consistent with taking acceptable risk."[1]

    The proposal had been presented as a "talk piece" to senior financial management two weeks earlier, on October 6, 1991, and had received preliminary approval. Erik Nelson, vice president–Financial Operations, had asked for a complete written analysis of the proposal for the board's consideration in November. Despite the soundness of the plan, Druffel knew that convincing the board to agree to the financing package would be an uphill battle, depending as it did on the stability of the Mexican economy for at least the next five years.

PROCTER & GAMBLE

In October 1837, James Gamble and William Procter each contributed $3,596 to start The Procter & Gamble Company as a soap and candle manufacturer in Cincinnati, Ohio. The two partners had an eye on the future and, before their partnership was signed, bought land near the Miami-Erie Canal, close to the Cincinnati city limits, as a possible site for a soap and candle factory. Cincinnati's location—linked by rail with Cleveland, Ohio, and the major East Coast cities and by river to the Mississippi and thus the port of New Orleans, Louisiana—contributed to its rapid growth as a manufacturing and distribution center. P&G grew with the city and, by 1848, the company was showing an annual profit of $26,000.

    Through careful stockpiling of raw materials and continual experimentation to improve its products, P&G prospered during the Civil War. In 1878, it introduced Ivory soap, which proved an immediate success and catapulted P&G from 40 years of trading in candles, soaps, lard oils, and glycerin into the development of brands that were recognized and requested by consumers. In 1913, P&G started selling directly to retailers in the New York area and, following World War I, expanded its direct selling to retailers nationally. P&G's ability to offer consistent deliveries to retailers paid off in increased profits and a steady flow of business.

---

[1] E.G. Nelson, vice president–Finance Operations, to E.L. Artzt, chairman and chief executive officer, memorandum of October 14, 1991.

Procter & Gamble celebrated its centennial in 1937 with sales of $230 million, 11 manufacturing plants in the United States, five in foreign countries (Canada, England, Cuba, and the Philippines), 12 cottonseed mills, and a cellulose-processing plant in Memphis, Tennessee, that was described as "the largest in the world."[2] At the same time, P&G was developing the brand management system that was to become a fundamental part of its operations. The company continued to broaden its product range, and by 1955, with sales of $966 million and net earnings of $57 million, P&G was reorganized into three separate operating divisions representing the main areas of operations—foods, drugs, and soaps. By the late 1970s, the company had 10 operating divisions worldwide for consumer products and five for industrial products. P&G consistently chose products that moved through grocery stores and drugstores, primarily for use in the home. Its products were typically small-unit, low-priced, packaged goods that were purchased frequently.

As the company's product markets matured in the United States, P&G's strategy of expansion through broadening product ranges gave way to a strategy of aggressive geographical expansion in the 1980s. The company was competing in 26 product categories by 1981, 41 by 1990. By 1970, P&G had operations in 20 countries, by 1980, 22 countries, and by 1990, 46 countries. Net sales and earnings grew accordingly, as Exhibit 10.2A shows, driven by the growth in unit sales. By 1990, P&G's total sales had grown to $24.1 billion, with international sales exceeding $9.6 billion. Net earnings were $1,602 million, up 33 percent from 1989. The company's return on shareholders' equity exceeded 20 percent for the first time since 1950. Exhibit 10.2B shows net sales, net earnings, and asset distribution by geographical areas of operation for 1979 to 1990.

P&G's chairman of the board and chief executive officer, Edwin Artzt, stated: "Virtually every business in the U.S. today is touched in some way by global competition. P&G is very well positioned to pursue a strategy of globalization. If we do it right, it will be our principal engine of growth."[3] In his report to the shareholders for the 1990 fiscal year, Artzt further expanded on P&G's global strategies:

> In the 1990s our major focus will be on global planning. We will plan the growth of our investments on a worldwide basis to achieve maximum competitive advantage. We will take advantage of our strongest technologies and ideas by reapplying and tailoring them to meet consumer needs everywhere. We will market world brands that share global technology and common positioning, but with appropriate regional testing of product aesthetics and form, packaging materials, and market execution to best satisfy local customer demands for quality and value. Product innovation will flow not only from U.S. research facilities, but increasingly from our major technical centers around the world.

---

[2] Oscar Schisgall, "Eyes on Tomorrow," *Advertising Age*, August 20, 1987.

[3] The Procter & Gamble Company, 1990 Annual Report.

THE PROCTER & GAMBLE COMPANY: MEXICO 1991
■ FINANCIAL REVIEW, 1981–1990

(YEARS ENDED JUNE 30; DOLLARS IN MILLIONS EXCEPT PER SHARE AMOUNTS)

	1981*	1982	1983†	1984	1985	1986	1987†	1988	1989†	1990
Net sales	$11,416	$11,994	$12,452	$12,946	$13,552	$15,439	$17,000	$19,336	$21,398	$24,081
Net earnings	$ 668	$ 777	$ 866	$ 890	$ 635	$ 709	$ 327	$ 1,020	$ 1,206	$ 1,602
Net earnings per common share	$ 2.02	$ 2.35	$ 2.61	$ 2.67	$ 1.90	$ 2.10	$ 0.94	$ 2.98	$ 3.56	$ 4.49
Net earnings as percentage of net sales	5.85%	6.48%	6.95%	6.87%	4.69%	4.59%	1.92%	5.28%	5.64%	6.65%
Dividends per common share	$ 0.95	$ 1.03	$ 1.13	$ 1.20	$ 1.30	$ 1.31	$ 1.35	$ 1.38	$ 1.50	$ 1.75

*Excludes in 1981 an extraordinary charge of $75 million ($.23 per common share) associated with the suspension of sale of Rely tampons.

†Net earnings and dividends per common share have been adjusted for the stock splits in 1983 and 1989.

‡Includes in June 1987 a charge of $459 million ($1.36 per common share) associated with a provision for restructuring.

SOURCE: The Procter & Gamble Company, 1990 Annual Report.

■ EXHIBIT 10.2B

THE PROCTER & GAMBLE COMPANY: MEXICO 1991
■ NET SALES, NET EARNINGS, AND ASSET DISTRIBUTION
BY GEOGRAPHICAL AREA, 1979–1990
(DOLLARS IN MILLIONS)

		United States	International	Corporate	Total
Net Sales	1979	$ 6,722	$2,871	$(264)	$ 9,329
	1980	7,637	3,493	(358)	10,772
	1981	8,044	3,750	(378)	11,416
	1982	8,610	3,737	(353)	11,994
	1983	9,074	3,685	(307)	12,452
	1984	9,554	3,737	(345)	12,946
	1985	10,243	3,625	(310)	13,552
	1986	11,210	4,490	(261)	15,439
	1987	11,805	5,524	(329)	17,000
	1988	12,423	7,294	(381)	19,336
	1989	13,312	8,529	(443)	21,398
	1990	**$14,962**	**$9,618**	**$(499)**	**$24,081**
Net Earnings	1979	$ 467	$115	$ (7)	$ 575
	1980	519	148	(27)	640
	1981	556	130	(18)	668
	1982	685	88	4	777
	1983	758	105	3	866
	1984	707	125	58	890
	1985	521	96	18	635
	1986	612	165	(68)	709
	1987	329	120	(122)	327
	1988	864	305	(149)	1,020
	1989	927	417	(138)	1,206
	1990	**$1,304**	**$467**	**$(169)**	**$1,602**
Assets	1979	$3,575	$1,360	$ 745	$ 5,680
	1980	4,219	1,750	603	6,572
	1981	4,397	1,769	795	6,961
	1982	5,054	1,700	756	7,510
	1983	5,344	1,614	1,177	8,135
	1984	6,072	1,740	1,086	8,898
	1985	6,829	1,946	908	9,683
	1986	8,394	3,461	1,200	13,055
	1987	8,483	3,849	1,383	13,715
	1988	8,346	4,751	1,723	14,820
	1989	8,669	5,260	2,422	16,351
	1990	**$9,742**	**$6,516**	**$2,229**	**$18,487**

SOURCE: The Procter & Gamble Company, annual reports.

In response to the global thrust of P&G's operations, global financing strategies were needed to minimize overall costs of financing and to maximize overall returns from investments. In considering the financing requirements of its international operations, P&G broadly examined the costs, and risks, of sourcing funds by

- Having a subsidiary independently borrow the necessary capital in its country of operation and in local currency.

- Having a subsidiary independently borrow in the United States, in U.S. dollars.

- Having the parent company guarantee the borrowings of the subsidiary in the United States.

- Directly investing equity from the parent company into the subsidiary.

Each of the four approaches involved a different combination of interest rate, currency, and sovereign risk. By comparing the anticipated net cost, P&G was able to estimate the reward related to those basic options. With funds sourced in local currency, the most significant risk was typically that of fluctuating interest rates. In cases where funds were sourced from the United States, the risk of devaluation of the local currency and sovereign risk were greater. Sovereign risk represented the possibility that restrictions could be placed on the operations of foreign-owned enterprises by the government of the country of operation; such restrictions could range from capital investment requirements to complete nationalization.

The broad outlines of P&G's global financing strategy were expressed by Erik Nelson:

> When you look at the regions in which we are now operating around the world, they fall into three broad categories. First, there are the developed, "low risk" regions which primarily include North America, Western Europe and Japan. In these areas, our policy is to borrow in local currency without a parent company guarantee.... We might also guarantee debt in situations where doing so would provide an attractive interest rate discount versus non-guaranteed borrowing. We wouldn't expect to see this very often, since real interest rates (nominal rates less inflation) tend to be very comparable to the U.S. over time.
>
> Second, there are a number of countries which we classify as "medium risk." Mexico is one such country. They are characterized by high local currency interest rates (because the governments are trying to keep inflation in check) but significantly lower rates of inflation and devaluation.
>
> Often, the devaluation risk is low enough that the interest rate savings far outweigh the potential devaluation loss. In such cases ... guaranteeing a dollar loan can often produce substantial savings to the Company....
>
> Another option for financing in medium risk countries, would be a capital infusion, with dollars borrowed from the parent company. This is little different from a loan guarantee for borrowing by a subsidiary. The negative to an infusion is that the capital may be blocked by local regulations or involve a substantial dividend withholding tax. This is usually not the case when repaying borrowed money since the withholding tax usually applies to interest but not principal.

Finally, there are the "high risk" countries, with Brazil being the classic example. Here we typically have no choice but to infuse capital. Local interest rates are exorbitant. The devaluation risk and market volatility are so great that guaranteed dollar borrowing is imprudent."[4]

MEXICO

Mexico was a tightly controlled colony of Spain for over 300 years. Independence in 1821 was followed by decades of political struggle, and economic development was slow until the 30 years of internal peace achieved at the end of the 19th century. This period was disrupted by the Mexican Revolution of 1910, which almost completely destroyed the country's economy. Accordingly, although Mexican culture, society, and politics reflected the cumulative development of over 450 years since the Spanish conquest and of the earlier civilizations, the economy of modern Mexico dated from only the 1920s.

Since the 1920s, the Partido Revolucionario Institucional (PRI) dominated Mexico's politics. The PRI presided over 40 years of strong economic growth with accompanying peace and stability, during which "it became widely accepted that political office allowed exploitation of opportunities of personal enrichment while in office."[5] Real economic growth between 1958 and 1970 averaged 6.8 percent per year, which, with population growth averaging 3.5 percent per year, meant about 3.2 percent real economic growth per capita. Inflation was only 2.9 percent per year, and real interest rates were positive and stable.

The discovery of the massive Chiapas oil field in the late 1970s rapidly increased Mexico's economic growth and prosperity, financed by the massive influx of foreign loans during the presidency of Jose Lopez Portillo (1976–1982). An unhealthy side effect of growth during this period was the rapid increase in inflation. With oil priced at the time at $32 per barrel and predicted to rise, to lose by investing in Mexico seemed impossible, but in 1982 the oil price bubble burst and the economy collapsed. Mexico's external debt was driven to unmanageable levels, resulting in the debt crisis of 1982. To restrain capital flight, the government froze all hard currency payments. All debts owed to foreign creditors—such as that owed by P&G (Mexico) to U.S. banks—were taken over by the government and converted to pesos. The government deferred all principal repayment on these debts for five years, and when it became apparent that this period would be extended, many foreign loans were discounted by creditors in return for early repayment. President Portillo's successor, Miguel de la Madrid, embarked on an austerity program of fiscal restraint and structural economic reform that caused high levels of political unrest and internal friction.

Since 1987, Mexican economic policy has featured a series of government/labor/private sector economic pacts that combined traditional austerity measures

---

[4] Nelson to Artzt, memorandum.

[5] *Economics Intelligence Unit Country Profile 1993–1993: Mexico*, 1994, p. 4.

(tight fiscal and monetary policies) with wage, price, and exchange rate controls. The policies had been successful in restoring economic confidence and reducing inflation while avoiding a sharp recession. External debt as a ratio of gross domestic product (GDP) fell from 47 percent in 1989 to 36 percent in 1991 and was expected to decrease further in 1992. The government maintained tight fiscal control and the public sector deficit had fallen accordingly from 4.0 percent of GDP in 1990 to 1.5 percent of GDP in 1991. A federal budget surplus of 0.8 percent of GDP was predicted for 1992, excluding revenue from sales of state-owned enterprises, many of which were privatized, with a reduction from 1,155 directly owned by the government in 1982, to 280 by 1990. Of these, nearly 150 were expected to be sold by the end of 1992. The changes in Mexican economic policy are reflected in the exchange and interest rate data for Mexico for the period 1970–1989 shown in Exhibit 10.2c. Overall economic data for Mexico for 1987–1993 are shown in Exhibit 10.2d.

In 1991, Mexico had a mixed economy, with the government dominant in the areas of public utilities, petroleum, banking, and some manufacturing industries. The economy was becoming broad based, and dependence on petroleum exports

▪ EXHIBIT 10.2c

THE PROCTER & GAMBLE COMPANY: MEXICO 1991
▪ MEXICAN EXCHANGE RATES, INTEREST RATES,
AND INFLATION, 1970–1989

Year	Exchange Rate (pesos per U.S. $)	Treasury Bill Rate	Time Deposit Rate	Commercial Bank Lending Rate	Consumer Price Index*
1970	12.50				21.68%
1971	12.50				22.82
1972	12.50				23.96
1973	12.50				26.62
1974	12.50				33.09
1975	12.50				38.03
1976	20.00				44.11
1977	22.70		11.00%		57.04
1978	22.70	12.75%	12.00	18.20%	66.93
1979	22.80	17.89	16.75	19.90	79.10
1980	23.30	27.73	26.15	28.10	100.00
1981	26.20	33.23	31.82	36.60	127.90
1982	96.50	57.44	52.54	46.02	203.30
1983	143.90	53.78	54.70	63.03	410.20
1984	192.60	49.18	47.78	54.73%	679.00
1985	371.70	63.20	59.48		1,070.98
1986	923.50	88.57	84.68		1,994.16
1987	2,209.70	103.07	97.24		4,623.41
1988	2,281.00	69.15	63.65		9,902.26
1989	2,641.00	45.01%	36.25%		11,883.57%

*Base year for inflation: 1980 = 100%.
SOURCE: *International Financial Statistics Yearbooks 1980, 1985, 1990, 1992*, The International Monetary Fund.

■ EXHIBIT 10.2D

THE PROCTER & GAMBLE COMPANY: MEXICO 1991
■ MEXICAN ECONOMIC DATA, 1987–1993

	1987	1988	1989	1990	1991*	1992*	1993*
Real GDP percentage change	1.70	1.40	3.10	3.90	3.80	4.60	5.30
CPI percentage change	132.00	114.00	20.00	27.00	16.00	12.00	10.00
Devaluation percentage	125.00	65.00	8.30	14.20	5.00	4.80	4.50
Central bank reserves ($bn)	13.70	6.60	6.90	10.00	16.90	15.30	15.00
Govt. exp. as percentage of GDP	15.40	10.80	6.80	4.20	1.60	2.10	3.80
Oil as percentage of total exports	41.80	32.60	34.60	33.30	29.00	25.00	22.00

*Forecast.
SOURCE: The Procter & Gamble Company, Treasury Division.

was reduced: petroleum accounted for only 29 percent of exports in 1991, down from 77 percent in 1982. Agriculture was dominated by the government's support through crop purchases and financing of cooperatives. Private enterprise dominated in manufacturing, mining, commerce, entertainment, and service industries. Key economic indicators for 1990–1991 are shown in Exhibit 10.2E.

The major economic goals of the government of Mexico in 1991 were to lower inflation, modernize the economy, and improve living standards for the poorest segments of society. The policies adopted by the government to control inflation included (1) reducing the fiscal deficit and the public sector internal debt, (2) controlling aggregate demand, (3) trying to temper real wage increases, (4) limiting price increases through rapid growth in imports that forced price competition and through restraints on price increases, and (5) sterilizing a large proportion of capital inflows.

These policies were combined with measures designed to encourage foreign direct investment in Mexico: (1) control of the rate of devaluation of the peso to achieve a target of 5.5 percent devaluation per year; (2) lowered tax rates, with the maximum corporate tax rate declining from 39.2 percent in 1988 to 35 percent in 1991; and (3) relaxed restrictions on the movement of foreign capital. (Exhibit 10.2F shows money and credit data for Mexico for 1986–1991. Comparisons of income tax rates in the United States, Canada, and Mexico are shown in Exhibit 10.2G.) The government planned to continue the current economic policies and hoped to see increased investment and economic growth from the North American Free Trade Agreement.

Mexico's political reform lagged behind its economic reform. The *Economist* reported:

President Salinas, who took office on December 1, 1988, promised a new era of pluralism and consultation as well as more transparency in political life. And, indeed, when the PRI conceded that gubernatorial elections held in Baja California Norte in July 1989 had been won by the PAN [an opposition party] candidate, he seemed to be sticking to his promises. Never before had the PRI lost a state governorship. However, since then,

■ EXHIBIT 10.2E

THE PROCTER & GAMBLE COMPANY: MEXICO 1991
■ KEY MEXICAN ECONOMIC INDICATORS, 1990–1991

	1990	1991
Domestic Economy		
Population (year-end, in millions)	82.40	$ 84.00
Population growth (% change, p.a.)	2.00%	2.00%
GDP, current U.S.$ (billion)	$ 241.90	$ 283.60
GDP per capita, current U.S.$	$2,935.70	$3,376.20
Real GDP growth (% change, p.a.)	4.40%	3.60%
Real GDP per capita growth (% change, p.a.)	2.40%	1.60%
Consumer price index (% change, p.a.)	29.90%	18.80%
Money supply (M1) (% change, p.a.)	62.60%	122.20%
Production and Employment		
Labor force (year-end, in millions)	26.20	26.80
Open unemployment (% of workforce)	4.00%	3.20%
Real industrial production (% change, p.a.)	5.50%	3.10%
Gross fixed investment (% GDP)	18.80%	19.70%
Govt. financial deficit (% GDP)	4.00%	1.50%
Balance of Payments (US$bn)		
Exports (F.O.B.)	$26.80	$ 27.10
Imports (F.O.B.)	$31.20	$ 38.20
Trade balance	$(4.40)	$ (11.10)
Current account balance	$(7.10)	$ (13.30)
Foreign direct investment	$ 2.60	$ 4.80
Foreign portfolio investment	$ 2.00	$ 7.50
Capital account	$ 8.20	$ 20.20
E & OE	$ 2.20	$ 1.20
Foreign-exchange reserves (year-end)	$10.20	$ 17.50
Foreign debt (year-end)	$40.60	$ 35.60
Foreign debt/GDP (%)	40.60%	35.60%
Average exchange rate (pesos per dollar)	2,807.30	3,006.80
Foreign Direct Investment (US$bn)		
Total (cumulative)	$30.30	$33.90
U.S. (cumulative)	$19.10	$21.50
U.S. share (%)	63.00%	63.40%
U.S.–Mexico Trade (US$bn)		
U.S. exports to Mexico (FAS)	$28.40	$33.30
U.S. imports from Mexico (CUS)	$30.20	$31.20
Trade balance	$(1.80)	$ 2.10
U.S. share of Mexican exports (%)	69.80%	70.00%
U.S. share of Mexican imports (%)	64.60%	67.00%

SOURCE: Market reports, 1992 National Trade Data Bank.

■ EXHIBIT 10.2F

THE PROCTER & GAMBLE COMPANY: MEXICO 1991
■ MONEY AND CREDIT DATA FOR MEXICO, 1986–1991
(IN BILLIONS OF PESOS UNLESS OTHERWISE INDICATED; YEAR-END)

	1986	1987	1988	1989	1990	1991
Currency in circulation	3,067	7,339	13,201	18,030	24,689	32,513
Demand deposits	2,468	4,928	7,130	10,279	21,847	72,772
Money (M1), incl. others	**5,790**	**12,627**	**21,191**	**29,087**	**47,439**	**106,227**
M1 growth (%)	67.2	118.0	67.8	37.3	63.1	123.9
Quasimoney	15.500	40,029	22,257	64,731	117,513	140,108
Money (M2)*	**21,290**	**52,656**	**43,448**	**93,818**	**164,952**	**246,335**
M2 growth (%)*	78.4	147.3	(19.0)	115.7	75.8	49.3
Domestic credit	**33,815**	**69,118**	**115,328**	**167,930**	**237,896**	**322,575**
Claims on central government	21,060	37,585	63,915	72,515	85,372	83,276
Claims on local government	92	251	322	1,506	2,695	3,902
Claims on public sector	2,838	5,789	6,737	9,484	6,835	3,321
Claims on private sector	8,758	22,608	41,346	81,693	141,733	228,924
Claims on other financial institutions	1,067	2,885	3,008	2,732	1,261	3,152
Net foreign assets	3,854	23,388	6,493	7,388	9,868	23,958
Memorandum item						
Average cost of funds (CPP, % annual rate)	80.9	94.6	67.6	44.6	37.1	22.6

*M2 does not include money market instruments, an important component of bank funding in 1988–1989. The figures for M2 growth in those years are thus somewhat misleading.

SOURCE: IMF, *International Financial Statistics,* (various issues) as reported in *Economics Intelligence Unit Country Profile 1992–1993: Mexico,* 1994.

■ EXHIBIT 10.2G

THE PROCTER & GAMBLE COMPANY: MEXICO 1991
■ COMPARATIVE TAX RATES: MEXICO, UNITED STATES, CANADA

	Combined Corporate Income Tax			
	Minimum	Intermediate	Maximum	Average
Mexico	—	—	—	35.00%*
United States	34.00%	38.60%	43.10%	38.30
Canada	38.80	43.80	45.80	43.30

*Excludes social contribution taxes of 10 percent.

SOURCE: American Chamber of Commerce of Mexico, *Business Mexico,* 1992.

progress towards political modernization has been erratic.... The numerous elections held since President Salinas came to office have demonstrated that a part of the ruling PRI is strongly opposed to relinquishing power and hence the practice of electoral alchemy has continued.[6]

The PRI won the July 1988 elections by its narrowest margin ever, with presidential candidate Carlos Salinas de Gortari receiving 50.4 percent of the official votes. In prior elections, the PRI had normally captured more than 90 percent of the official votes. The next elections were scheduled for December 1994.

PROCTER & GAMBLE (MEXICO)

Organized in 1948 under the laws of the United Mexican States as a limited liability company *(sociedad anonima de capital variable)*, Procter & Gamble (Mexico) was a wholly owned subsidiary of Procter & Gamble. P&G (Mexico) competed in 18 product categories within Mexico, whose aggregate market size was approximately $2.5 billion. As P&G's largest operating subsidiary in Latin America, P&G (Mexico) was ranked first in 1991 in unit shipments and seventh in revenues among P&G's international subsidiaries. Headquartered in Mexico City, P&G (Mexico) owned two manufacturing facilities and operated another three, including the largest synthetic detergent plant in the world. P&G (Mexico) had 18 product categories, compared with 41 in the United States, and manufactured in Mexico all the established brands that were sold there.

During the 1980s, P&G (Mexico), like most international companies, suffered from the severely restrictive legislative environment in Mexico. Foreign corporations were allowed to expand in Mexico only with proportionately increasing Mexican partnerships. In addition, the debt crisis of 1982 and subsequent freezing of foreign-debt repayments locked P&G into repaying dollar loans with rapidly devaluing local peso income. P&G had been negatively affected by the rule changes that occurred during the period.

In 1990, as Dick Druffel later reported, "We sensed a change in the investment climate in Mexico and regained confidence in our opportunities. We began to lay plans to develop our business in Mexico in line with the dramatically improved business environment."[7] In an August 1991 report on Mexico (Exhibit 10.2H), Treasury Analyst E. Romero predicted a much-improved outlook for business and prepared a proposal for financing capital investment by P&G (Mexico).

Druffel reported that the proposal was

> to grow the business we needed to increase and modernize our manufacturing capacity and [we] were looking to make capital investments of at least $150 million over the three-year period. On top of that, we would need to finance a significant increase in working capital and start-up costs from new-product introductions. At this point, our business plans were far from firm, but were well enough defined that we could begin planning on how to finance them.[8]

---

[6] Ibid.

[7] Dick Druffel, speech at Financial Executive Institute, Mexican conference.

[8] Ibid.

Approximately 20 percent of the capital needs would be in dollars, with the remaining 80 percent in pesos.

The investment program would be financed by cash surpluses generated by P&G (Mexico) and by borrowing. The average indebtedness over the three years

■ EXHIBIT 10.2H

THE PROCTER & GAMBLE COMPANY: MEXICO 1991

FILE MEMORANDUM

August 22, 1991
R.L.: 9/92

Mexico Outlook

The ruling government has been able to achieve economic/political stability in a relatively short period of time by making fundamental changes to economic and fiscal policy. Included among these changes have been a lowering of tax rates, removing restrictions on foreign capital, and tight monetary control. As a result, Mexico is in the fourth year of economic growth, social spending is up, and inflation has dropped to mid-teens. The current government is in control and has strong support as evidenced by its 60% approval rating.

Satisfactory progress has been made on inflation. In May the CPI rose 1%, bringing accumulated inflation YTD to 8%. With no official price increases scheduled for the year, the government objective of 15% for 1991 appears feasible. More skeptical sources are forecasting a 21% inflation rate, which is still well below recent levels.

It is widely assumed that the managed devaluation of .04 pesos per day will continue until year-end, leading to a 5.5% annual devaluation. To date, Mexico has been able to devalue the peso at rates lower than inflation primarily because the demand for dollars has been easily satisfied by significant dollar inflows to capitalize on purposely high peso interest rates. Further, the current predictable daily devaluation policy has made the market comfortable that the peso is under control.

	1988	1989	1990	1991(e)
Inflation	52.0%	20.0%	30.0%	15.0%
Devaluation	40.0	9.5	11.5	5.5

Approval of the Free Trade Agreement is considered to be beneficial for Mexico's exports and growth prospects over the long term. Further, it is felt this will provide additional momentum to keep the free market/economic rationalization programs moving ahead.

On the external side, the improvement on the trade and current accounts last year was almost entirely due to the windfall of temporarily higher oil prices. Recently, there is evidence of deterioration. Some factors contributing to an increasing deficit are: rising imports, fall in oil prices, modest growth in non-oil exports. For perspective the value of exports was 16% higher in the first five months of 1991 compared to a year ago, but imports were 42% higher.

The erosion of the current account will be more than offset by strong private capital inflows (repatriation of capital). In the year to May, approved foreign investment was estimated at US$3.6 bn. Official reserves at the end of March were estimated at US$13 bn, a US$2 bn increase from year-end 1990.

Overall, Mexico currently has the strongest growth in North and Central America. It is estimated that GDP will expand by 4%–5% in 1991 and this despite the U.S. recession. Further, the government continues to maintain an attractive investment environment. Moreover, the current administration will be in office through 1994, making a negative policy shift unlikely.

E. Romero

Distribution: C. P. Slater, R. C. Stewart, R. T. Druffel, J. Martinez

was expected to be $55 million but could vary by as much as 20 percent more or less, depending on the needs of the capital investment program as well as the cash surpluses generated by P&G (Mexico). In August 1991, Romero had prepared comparisons of financing costs based on borrowing in Mexico and in the United States. Equity investment was ruled out because of the relatively short time frame of the financing needed. Two basic options were considered:

- *Borrowing in Mexico, in pesos.* P&G (Mexico) could borrow directly from banks in Mexico on an "as-needed" basis. The P&G parent company would approve the borrowings but would play no active part in securing the loans. Only variable interest loans for short- and medium-term financing were obtainable. Interest rates to P&G (Mexico) would start at about 29 percent but were expected to come down over the three years so that the average interest rate paid would be 22 percent per year. The dollar financing needed would be purchased when needed by P&G (Mexico), using pesos. The main risk in borrowing in pesos was that interest rates might remain high, or even increase. There would, however, be no devaluation risk and no increase in sovereign risk. Another advantage of borrowing in pesos was the closeness of contact and communication between P&G (Mexico) and the issuing banks in Mexico, which would result in greater flexibility in matching drawdowns of funds with investment needs.

- *Borrowing in the United States, in dollars.* There were two ways that P&G could effect borrowing in the United States to provide the financing needed by P&G (Mexico). First, P&G (Mexico) could borrow directly from U.S. banks, with the approval, but not active participation, of P&G. Indications were that the interest rate for such a loan would average 12 percent per year over the next three years. Second, P&G (Mexico) could borrow directly from U.S. banks, with the loans guaranteed by P&G. Citibank had quoted an average interest rate of 7 percent per year for the guaranteed loan. If the loan were not guaranteed by P&G, the risks would be borne largely by the lender, whereas the guarantee would bind P&G to repaying the funds should P&G (Mexico) default. Whether guaranteed or not, the funds would be drawn down by P&G (Mexico) as needed every quarter from the banks in the United States and converted to pesos or used as dollars, depending on investment needs. Both the guaranteed and unguaranteed loans would carry fixed interest rates, removing the risk of floating interest rates. However, sovereign risk and the risk of devaluation of the peso remained.

In preparing the financing cost comparisons (Exhibit 10.2i), Romero projected inflation in Mexico of 14 percent for 1991–1992, declining to 9.3 percent by 1993–1994. The expected devaluations of the peso against the dollar were projected to be 4.7 percent in 1991–1992, declining to 4.3 percent by 1993–1994. Income tax was expected to remain at 35 percent, with the Social Contribution Tax of 10 percent of income bringing the overall tax rate payable by P&G (Mexico) on income to 45 percent per year.

In addition, the effect of the Inflationary Component Tax had to be considered. The Inflationary Component Tax provided monthly tax benefits to corporations

THE PROCTER & GAMBLE COMPANY: MEXICO 1991
■ FINANCING OPTIONS: 3-YEAR SUMMARY

	1991–1992	1992–1993	1993–1994
Assumptions			
Debt at start of year ($mn)	0.00	$40.00	$70.00
Borrowings for cash needs ($mn)	$40.00	$30.00	$40.00
Inflation	14.00%	11.00%	9.30%
Devaluation (40 centavo/day by gov't flat)	4.70%	4.50%	4.30%
Interest rates			
MTN	6.00	6.00	6.00
U.S.$–guaranteed	7.00	7.00	7.00
U.S.$–unguaranteed	12.00	12.00	12.00
Peso	22.00	22.00	22.00
MTN structuring fee ($mn)	$ 0.44	0.00	0.00
Tax			
Income tax	35.00	35.00	35.00
Social contr. tax	10.00	10.00	10.00
Inflationary component tax			
Penalty on liabilities	45.00	45.00	45.00
Benefit on monetary assets	45.00	45.00	45.00
Average investment return			
Peso	18.50	14.40	12.80
Dollar	9.70	8.70	8.00

Cost Comparisons	Financing Method		
	Guar. $	Unguar. $	Peso
3-year average debt ($mn)	$ 55.0	$ 55.0	$ 55.0
Interest rate	7.0%	12.0%	22.0%
Interest expense ($mn)	$(11.6)	$(19.8)	$(36.3)
Structuring fee	0.0	0.0	0.0
Devaluation effect	$ (7.4)	$ (7.4)	0.0
Total pretax cost	$(19.0)	$(27.2)	$(36.3)
Tax relief on debt	$ 8.55	$ 12.2	$ 16.3
Inflationary Component Tax	$ (8.5)	$ (8.5)	$ (8.5)
Total after-tax cost	$(18.95)	(23.5)	$(28.5)
Difference vs. minimum cost	0.0	$ (4.55)	$ (9.55)

equivalent to the book value of monetary assets at month-end, multiplied by the government's official estimate of inflation during the month, multiplied by 45 percent. Similarly, liabilities were penalized by the government by a tax equivalent to the book value of liabilities at month-end, multiplied by the government's official estimate of inflation during the month, multiplied by 45 percent.

As an example, a loan taken out in Mexico for $100,000 for a year in which the official estimate of inflation was 14 percent would result in a tax expense of 14% × $100,000 × 45% = $6,300. The $100,000 invested in the same year would result in a tax credit of the same amount. Thus, the effect of the Inflationary Component Tax was to reward equity investments and discourage speculative investments in assets that would not be shown on a balance sheet in Mexico (such as foreign currency) using borrowed funds.

As an additional financing option, Citibank suggested that if P&G (Mexico) were to increase its borrowings, they would be able to issue medium-term maturity debt notes (MTN), guaranteed by P&G, directly to the U.S. financial markets. The MTN would carry fixed interest rates and terms. Citibank estimated that the interest rate payable could then be reduced to an average of 6 percent per year. If the average borrowings over three years were increased to $80 million, the issue would be large enough to warrant a public placement. Citibank's fees for structuring such an issue would amount to $440,000.

Dick Druffel knew that the estimates of P&G (Mexico)'s borrowing needs could easily be understated. By issuing the MTN, however, P&G would obtain the full amount of borrowing up front, resulting in cash surpluses initially and, possibly, for all three years. The placement of those surpluses could partially offset the costs of borrowing, depending on what returns could be obtained and at what risk levels. Investment returns in Mexico looked attractive, and establishing an investment portfolio would create an asset that would earn Inflationary Component Tax benefits. The question was whether the high yields on investment were an expression by the market of the risks of investment or were being maintained artificially high by the government's economic policies. In either case, borrowing in the United States was exposing P&G to devaluation and sovereign risk. Increasing the borrowing and investing the cash surpluses in Mexico seemed to be doubling that exposure.

There was no doubt in Druffel's mind that conditions in Mexico had changed for the better, but by how much and for how long?

INTRODUCTION

Chapter 8 introduced the concept of foreign direct investment *(FDI), describing the reasons that corporations establish overseas operations and alluding to the variety of risks involved in such activities. This chapter explores in more detail the concept of* political risk, *an important variable in the success or failure of an overseas investment. The importance of political risk analysis has increased dramatically over the past 20 years, an era marked by the rise of the* multinational corporation *(MNC) as well as increasing international turmoil and volatility. The identification, measurement, and management of political risk, whether for the purposes of lending or establishing international operations, requires rigorous analysis and thoughtful strategic planning. We discuss a variety of techniques in this chapter.*

WHAT IS POLITICAL RISK?

For the purposes of this discussion, *political risk* is the exposure to a change in the value of an investment or cash position because of government actions or other nonmarket events that are political in nature. Political risk arises from a country's political environment. The following examples of changes that affect the economic value of FDI are examples of political risk.

- Revisions in tax regulations and exchange controls, especially those that are discriminatory or arbitrary.
- New host country stipulations about local production, sourcing, or hiring practices.
- Introduction of commercial discrimination against foreign-owned businesses.
- New restrictions on access to local borrowing.
- Biased government interference with privately negotiated contracts.
- Expropriation without adequate compensation.
- Damage or destruction of facilities or harm to personnel resulting from political riots or civil war or revolution.

Events creating political risk cover a wide range of possibilities and circumstances, and their effects also vary. A manager should be aware of the full range or types of political risk events that may affect the host country as well as her particular industry, company, or project.

Examples of losses stemming from political risk events abound. Among the most dramatic are those resulting from the obvious trauma of revolutionary upheaval. For example, in December 1977, GTE signed a telecommunications contract worth more than $500 million with the Iranian government. In accordance with the contract, GTE advanced Iran $95 million in open letters of credit, commonly used in the Middle East in lieu of performance bonds. Given its long-time experience and confidence in Iran, GTE did virtually nothing to protect itself from possible political risks and, therefore, the contract did not specify the grounds on which Iran could call the letters of credit. GTE also did not insure any of its risks. After the revolution in Iran, work on the project proved impossible, and the company stood to lose more than $50 million, not including the letters of credit. If those are included, GTE's potential after-tax losses exceed $60 million, making the firm the biggest potential loser in Iran.

The Iranian revolution is not an isolated example. For example, after the Bolshevik revolution of 1917 in Russia, investors found that the new government would not pay interest or principal on bonds issued by the Czars. In 1959, the Cuban revolution led to the expropriation of many U.S.–owned investments.

Many types of political risk exist in addition to those caused by revolutions or coups. Some companies, for example, were victims of political risk in Iran before the revolution. Acts of terrorism while the Shah was still in power were one such source of risk, with the murder of Rockwell International employees being the most dramatic example. Besides acts of violence, political risk can also take the form of legislative or regulatory changes. In Iran, B.F. Goodrich had built the largest tire plant between Europe and the Far East, with assurances of trade and investment protection from the government. The same government that made the guarantees lifted the protection prematurely to accommodate two competitors. This change forced Goodrich from a 24-hour-a-day production schedule to an 8-hour-per-day schedule. Changes in the law or in regulations can also be directed at all or most companies collectively, as when the Shah of Iran, in the 1970s, decided to mandate public stock offerings on the part of Iranian-based corporations to increase worker ownership and participation. The action was expensive and very disruptive to foreign businesses.[1]

Peaceful elections, such as that of Salvador Allende in Chile in 1971, can likewise lead to dramatic changes in the value of FDI, including its complete loss through expropriation. Less dramatic, but nevertheless important, changes occur in countries such as Canada, when more nationalistic parties win elections and change the rules governing FDI. Government interventions in the marketplace, such as price and currency controls, can result from the regular functioning of the electoral process through gains or losses in a political party's power.[2] The privatization program in the United Kingdom under Prime Minister Thatcher in the 1980s and, in contrast, the nationalization policy pursued by President Mitterand in France during the same years are examples of different manifestations of political philosophies in economic terms—with important financial consequences for managers and investors.

For another example of a normally functioning political process affecting international investment, one may look to the EC 1992 single market movement. This change involved enormous political risks and opportunities for global companies. As Europe proceeds with its economic and political unification, companies may be excluded from certain markets because of regulatory changes. For example, countries such as Spain and Portugal are currently enjoying a great deal of foreign investment because of their cheap labor relative to the rest of Europe. These countries may not be so attractive in the future because they must increase wages to comply with the EC 1992 single market program. Companies that made significant investments in Western Europe based on pre-1992 economics may find their investments worth less in the post-1992 world. The importance of keeping up to date with political and regulatory changes can hardly be overstated.

Turning to Eastern Europe, the relative economic and political stability that accompanied the Cold War has become turbulent and unsettled as the former Communist countries attempt the transitions to market economies. A glance at the former Eastern bloc reveals the full panoply of political risk: In Yugoslavia, once prosperous towns and productive factories have been devastated by ethnic fighting and civil war. In Czechoslovakia, the split between the Czechs and Slovaks over the pace of economic reform has led to the breakup of the country, with possible

---

[1] This discussion of Iran is taken from Charles R. Kennedy, Jr., *Political Risk Management: International Lending and Investing under Environmental Uncertainty* (New York: Quorum Books, 1987), pp. 6–7.

[2] This discussion is gleaned from Stephen J. Kobrin, *Managing Political Risk Assessment: Strategic Response to Environmental Change* (Berkeley: University of California Press, 1982), pp. 30–39.

adverse effects for the foreign companies, especially those that invested in the less prosperous Slovak republic. General Electric's much vaunted $150 million investment in the Tungsram lighting plant in Hungary has lost money because the government has not devalued the forint in line with Hungary's soaring inflation. Chevron, which entered into a joint venture agreement with the former Soviet government, now finds itself in the position of having to negotiate with several independent republics. Moreover, Russia is chronically short of hard currency, and its vacillating monetary policy and price reforms cast a long shadow of uncertainty over any prospective investments. Finally, the ethnic diversity in Russia has already generated devastating military conflicts and may produce many more in the future.

As these examples indicate, the global marketplace is uncertain and turbulent. Whether or not particular aspects of this turbulence and uncertainty constitute a risk to business depends on industry, firm, or project characteristics and managerial actions. Thus, the elements of political risk vary widely among different countries and different companies. Even within a country, political risk is usually industry specific and in many cases project specific as well. Rural insurgency, for example, may pose serious problems to a commercial farming operation, but its impact on a company specializing in financial services or insurance might be minimal. Assessing the political risks of foreign direct investment, therefore, involves the analysis both of those elements of aggregate or *country risk* and of those elements of political risk specific to the company or to its project.

Closely related to political risk are country and economic risks; political risk is a subset of country risk. *Country risk* refers to elements of risk inherent in doing business in the economic, social, and political environment of another country. In international lending decisions, for example, bankers typically examine the economic conditions of the country in question, the balance of payments and its management, the effectiveness of the central bank and its policies, principal economic sectors (imports and exports, trends and prospects, flow of funds, and financial intermediation), social conditions, international relations, and the impact of world events on the domestic economy.

Economic risks, such as those resulting from technological changes, the actions of competitors, or shifts in consumer preferences, are not usually politically generated. In many cases, however, there is a close link between political events in a country and its economic risk. For example, the disintegration of the market structure in Lebanon during its civil war, the banning of certain Western products by the Khomeini regime after the success of the Iranian Revolution in 1979, and the uncertainties posed by the breakup of the Soviet Union are clear instances of political events exacerbating economic risks.

Similarly, although most labor strikes are limited in scope and economic in origin (e.g., disputes over wages, benefits, or other work-related issues), many general strikes, such as those in Nicaragua in 1978 and Poland in 1980, are clearly political in nature and have wide-ranging economic repercussions. Even events with clear economic purposes, such as price controls designed to control inflation, often have political overtones. Thus, it should be clear that it is sometimes very difficult to distinguish between economic risk and political risk, and there are few events that are purely one or the other.

Dramatic events such as revolutions or expropriations attract a great deal of attention and might cause a company to shy away from more turbulent parts of the world. Managers should understand that a political event in itself does not necessarily imply an adverse change. In fact, political instability can present opportunities as well as risks to business. For example, Gulf Oil Corporation in 1975 was able to negotiate a very favorable relationship with the Marxist MPLA during the Angolan civil war, and Dow Chemical was able to reenter Chile after the overthrow of Salvador Allende in 1973.

IDENTIFYING AND MEASURING POLITICAL RISK

Prior to the 1973 oil shock, when the oil-producing countries of the Middle East cut oil supply for political/economic reasons, U.S. banks and MNCs enjoyed a fairly stable and predictable international investment climate. After the economically destabilizing events of 1973–1974, that changed and international investors quickly recognized the need to develop formal risk management systems. The Iranian revolution in 1978–1979 further emphasized the need for astute political risk analysis because foreign companies experienced losses there exceeding $1 billion. This forced MNCs to search for more systematic means to assess and manage the political risks of foreign investment. Following the Iranian Revolution, political risk analysts, who had previously focused primarily on macroeconomic factors, upgraded the importance of sociopolitical considerations in their analyses and models.

The two basic types of political risk are those specific to a country, *macro risks*, and those specific to a particular company or project, *micro risks*. Macro and micro risks may be further subdivided into those resulting from legal or governmental action and those resulting from extra legal action. These classifications yield a matrix of possible political risk events, as shown in Table 11.1.

When assessing risk, analysts should first examine macro issues and work down to micro issues that directly affect a given venture. Using that method, an analyst first determines how the nation's politics will develop and then how economic circumstances will affect the political situation. Next, the analyst explores the coun-

■ **TABLE 11.1**

TYPES OF POLITICAL RISKS

	Legal/Government Risk	Extralegal Risk
Macro risks	Investment laws	Revolution
Micro risks	Trade regulations	Terrorism

SOURCE: Charles R. Kennedy, Jr., *Political Risk Management: International Lending and Investing under Environmental Uncertainty* (New York: Quorum Books, 1987), p. 7.

try's policies toward foreign investment, in general, and then in relation to the company's particular business and specific project. Finally, he or she should consider local issues and how they could affect the company and its project.[3]

Given the complexity and variety of sources of political risk, a thorough analysis cannot simply concentrate on purely political factors and events but must systematically include sociocultural, political, economic phenomena, and their interactions on both the macro and micro levels. Factors causing internal political stress include the following:

- Fractionalisation of the political spectrum and the power of resulting factions.
- Fractionalisation by language, ethnic, or religious groups and the power of resulting factions.
- Restrictive measures required to retain power.
- Xenophobia, nationalism, and an aversion to compromise.
- Social conditions, including extremes in population density and the distribution of wealth.
- Organization and strength of a radical left government.
- Dependence on or importance to a hostile major power.
- Negative influence of regional political forces and possibilities of border wars and disruptions arising from such sources of conflict.
- Societal conflict.
- Political instability.

Many political risk analysts also consider macroeconomic factors such as inflation rates, balance of payment deficits, and surpluses. Regardless of the factors incorporated or the styles of analysis, the objective of political risk analysis is always to assess the likelihood of adverse changes resulting from government intervention in the political environment. Again, political instability does not necessarily correlate with political risk: For a manager or investor, the important question remains the impact of political events on a particular company or project.

POLITICAL RISK MODELS

The development of political risk models has become more sophisticated over the past two decades. These models produce measures of political risk that allow managers to determine both the relative and absolute risk of investing in a country. They also provide quantitative measures of the change in risk of countries over time. Most rely on a combination of objective data and subjective estimates. Various forecasting services attempt to quantify the level of political risk for each nation analyzed. They create indices that measure factors such as the stability of

---

[3] This discussion borrows from Kate Bertrand, "Politics Pushes Marketing Foreground," *Business Marketing,* March 1990, p. 54.

■ TABLE 11.2

BUSINESS ENVIRONMENTAL RISK INDEX: VARIABLES AND WEIGHTS

Variables	Weights
Political stability	3.0
Foreign investment attitude	1.5
Nationalization	1.5
Monetary inflation	1.5
Balance of payments	1.5
Bureaucratic delays	1.0
Economic growth	2.5
Currency convertibility	2.5
Contract enforceability	1.5
Labor cost/productivity	2.0
Professional support	0.5
Communications/transportation	1.0
Local management	1.0
Short-term credit	2.0
Long-term capital	2.0

SOURCE: F. T. Haner, "Business Environmental Risk Index, Appendix B," *BERI Ltd. System for Selected Countries*, August 1981, p. 9.

the local political environment, levels of violence, and internal and external conflict.

One example of an expert-generated approach to political risk is the Business Environmental Risk Index (BERI) developed by F.T. Haner.[4] This system uses 15 variables related to political risk. We list the variables and their respective weights in Table 11.2. Another set of measures is the Political System Stability Index (PSSI), which was developed by Dan Haendel.[5] This method generates three equally weighted indices, each determined by ratings to numerous variables. Haendel uses these indices to generate an overall score. The more negative the number, the greater the political risk. We list the PSSI indices in Table 11.3.

IBC developed a third approach, the International Country Risk Guide, that includes elements of both Haner and Haedel's methods. Table 11.4 identifies the 13 risk indicators used by IBC, the points assigned to each indicator, and the ratings for a set of countries as of June 1993 and June 1994. In the IBC framework, a higher number of points implies lower risk. The higher-rated countries tend to be the Western democracies or small, economically advanced Asian countries. Not sur-

---

[4] F. T. Haner, "Business Environmental Risk Index, Appendix B," *BERI Ltd. System for Selected Countries* (August 1981).

[5] Dan Haendel, *Foreign Investments and the Management of Political Risk* (Boulder: Westview Press, 1979).

■ **TABLE 11.3**

POLITICAL SYSTEM STABILITY INDEX AND OPERATIONAL VARIABLES

Socioeconomic Index
  Ethnolinguistic fractionalism
  GNP growth per capita
  Energy consumption per capita

Societal Conflict Index
  Public unrest index
  Riots
  Demonstrations
  Government crises

Internal Violence Subindex
  Armed attacks
  Assassinations
  Coups d'etat
  Guerilla warfare

Coercion Potential Subindex
  Internal security forces per 1,000 population

Governmental Processes Index
  Political competition index
  Legislative effectiveness
  Constitutional changes per year
  Irregular chief executive changes

SOURCE: Dan Haendel, *Foreign Investments and the Management of Political Risk* (Boulder: Westview Press, 1979), p. 108.

prisingly, the higher-rated countries also have the more stable ratings between 1993 and 1994. That stability is an important component of the lower risk profile. The riskier countries are those with more volatile political, economic, and social environments. Liberia and Somalia illustrate this point. In addition to having high-risk profiles (low scores), their risk ratings changed quite dramatically from 1993 to 1994. Liberia's index increased from 7 to 21 and Somalia's increased from 12 to 21. In contrast, Canada's index changed from 79 to 80 and Singapore's index changed from 80 to 77.

Because political risk has a different impact on different companies, generalized political risk indices, such as the ones described above, must be used cautiously and subjected to careful analysis to assess the full impact on a particular company. Note, for example, that governments rarely expropriate foreign investments indiscriminately. Generally, the greater the benefits of a foreign operation to the host country and the more expensive the replacement of such facilities by a purely local operation, the lower the degree of political risk to the company.

■ **TABLE 11.4**

IBC INTERNATIONAL COUNTRY RISK GUIDE

A.	Economic expectations vs. realities	
B.	Economic planning failures	
C.	Political leadership	
D.	External conflict risk	
E.	Corruption in government	
F.	Military in politics	
G.	Organized religion in politics	

H.	Law and order tradition	
I.	Racial and nationality tensions	
J.	Political terrorism	
K.	Civil war risks	
L.	Political party development	
M.	Quality of bureaucracy	

	A	B	C	D	E	F	G	H	I	J	K	L	M	Total June 1994	June 1993
Maximum points	12	12	12	10	6	6	6	6	6	6	6	6	6	100	—
Canada	6	6	6	10	6	6	6	6	4	6	6	6	6	80	79
France	6	5	6	10	6	6	6	6	5	5	6	6	6	79	80
Liberia	1	1	3	5	1	1	3	1	2	3	2	2	1	26	7
Mexico	8	7	6	10	3	6	6	3	5	5	6	4	3	72	69
Singapore	7	7	8	10	4	6	6	6	6	6	6	3	5	80	77
Somalia	1	1	2	8	1	1	2	1	1	1	1	0	1	21	12
United States	7	6	7	10	5	6	6	6	6	6	6	6	6	83	78

MANAGING POLITICAL RISK

The linkage between political events and risks is often rooted in managerial decisions or their absence. Managers can create opportunities during periods of turbulence, but doing so requires good anticipation and advanced planning. To achieve a desired outcome, the firm must understand the multidimensional and complex nature of political risk.

An effective political risk strategy should consist of three interrelated parts. The first task is to identify the elements of political risk that affect foreign direct investment and to develop an intelligence system to monitor and evaluate changing political conditions in the host country. The second task is to allow a company to deal with changing conditions of political risk by integrating the political risk assessment with its strategic planning. The third task is to devise strategies to protect the company from political risk, especially the risk of expropriation.[6] We discuss these tasks in more detail by considering how an MNC can manage its political risk by developing appropriate preinvestment strategies, operating policies, and, in the worst case scenario, postexpropriation strategies.

---

[6] This discussion borrows from Joseph V. Micallef, "Assessing Political Risk," *The McKinsey Quarterly,* Winter 1982, p. 69.

PREINVESTMENT STRATEGIES

An MNC should take steps to control its exposure to political risk. After analyzing the political environment of a country and assessing its implications, an MNC must decide whether to invest there. Having made the decision to invest in a country, an MNC can minimize its political risk exposure by structuring its operating and financial strategy appropriately.

A company can protect its investment in a foreign country by keeping the foreign investment dependent on the parent company. For example, an investment in a foreign country might depend on the parent company to provide essential supplies or access to export markets. Similarly, when the foreign investment depends on research and technology and proprietary technology, concentrating these facilities in the home country reduces the probability of expropriation.

Encouraging investment by citizens of the foreign country is another risk-reducing policy. In addition, the parent might raise capital from the host government rather than employing funds supplied or guaranteed by the parent company. Involving these other parties may help spread financial risk, but it might not provide the cheapest capital. A manager must weigh carefully the costs and benefits of pursuing such a risk-spreading strategy.

Obtaining unconditional host government guarantees concerning the treatment an investment receives is another way to minimize the financial aspects of political risk. Such guarantees enable creditors to initiate legal action in foreign courts against any commercial transactions between the host country and third parties should a subsequent government repudiate the original obligations. Moreover, such guarantees provide an MNC with sanctions against a foreign nation that do not rely on the support of its home government.

OPERATING POLICIES

MNCs can manage political risk by using operating policies to change the division of benefits with the host country. The more beneficial the existing investment is to the host country, the less likely the host government is to covet its ownership. MNCs can increase the benefits by training local workers and managers, developing export markets for the host nation, and manufacturing a wide range of products locally as substitutes for imports. In addition, the MNC can increase its value to the local economy by developing and supporting local suppliers, banks, and other enterprises.

POSTEXPROPRIATION STRATEGIES

The first objective of an MNC that experiences an expropriation should be to reverse it. An MNC can offer a variety of incentives to encourage this action.

- Hiring national mangers.
- Raising transfer prices charged from the locally based firm to other parts of the group.

- Accepting local partners.

- Changing expatriate management.

- Investing more capital.

- Contributing to political campaigns.

- Releasing the host government from concessionary agreements.

- Supporting government programs.

- Suspending dividend payments.

- Surrendering majority control.

- Removing all home country personnel.

- Reorganizing to give greater benefit to the local partners.

If the concessions do not work, the company might begin to apply sanctions. These can take the form of supporting an opposition political party or invoking home government support for the company's position. Political tactics rarely work, however. Alternatively, an MNC can try to make the best of a bad situation by negotiating the most generous possible compensation for the expropriated assets.

An MNC may be able to seek legal redress. The law requires that legal remedy first be sought in the courts of the host country. After exhausting this course of action, an MNC can plead its case in its home country and in international courts. Where host courts are impartial, seeking local redress is likely to be moderately effective. Where the judiciary is subservient to the government, an MNC can expect little success.

Efforts to sue national governments are frustrated by the doctrine of sovereign immunity and the act of state doctrine. The former says that unless a sovereign state consents, it may not be tried in the courts of another state. The latter doctrine implies that a nation is sovereign within its own borders and its domestic actions may not be questioned in the courts of another nation, even if those actions violate international law.

Arbitration of investment disputes is another alternative. In 1966, the World Bank established the International Centre for Settlement of Investment Disputes. Created to encourage foreign direct investment by providing a forum for international investment disputes, the center provides binding arbitration. In practice, its influence is small.

Finally, an MNC can adapt to expropriation and formulate policies to earn profits following it. Many oil companies whose properties have been nationalized or expropriated receive management contracts to continue exploration, refining, and marketing. They recognize that they do not have to own or control an asset to earn profits and create cash flows from it.[7]

---

[7] The discussion on managing political risk is based on Adrian Buckly, "Taking Account of Political Risk," *Accountancy*, July 1987, pp. 80–81.

INSURING AGAINST POLITICAL RISK

Specific government departments of most developed countries sell political risk insurance to cover the foreign assets of domestic companies. For example, the Overseas Private Investment Corporation (OPIC), an agency of the U.S. government whose mission is to promote U.S. FDI in developing countries, underwrites political risk insurance for events such as expropriation, currency inconvertibility, and losses due to civil strife. The World Bank's Multilateral Investment Guarantee Agency provides similar coverage from international investors. Based in London, the U.K.'s Export Credit Guarantee Department offers a confiscation cover scheme for new overseas investments only.

Some private insurers also underwrite political risk coverage. AIG, Inc., of New York has policies that offer coverage for confiscation, expropriation, or nationalization. Lloyd's of London also offers insurance against political risk. Its coverage applies for new and existing investments on a comprehensive, nonselective policy. Fees vary according to country and the type of risk insured, with coverage usually limited to 90 percent of equity participation.

IMPLICATIONS FOR MANAGERS

Managers deal with uncertainty in all areas of their businesses. Changing market conditions, volatile exchange rates, and unexpected competition all affect the outcome of managerial decisions. Political risk tends to be more abrupt and have more drastic effects than other sources of risk. This makes planning for and responding to political risk qualitatively different than planning for and responding to other sources of risk. In this chapter we have developed a framework for dealing with political risk and identified some of the tools available.

It is important to keep in mind that political change is not a problem only in less developed countries. New tax rules, a change in exchange rate or trade regimes, or a policy concerning new health-care requirements for workers are all instances of changes included in political risk. The British government decision to remove the pound from the exchange rate mechanism is one dramatic example of a political risk encountered in a developed country. Understanding such changes is crucial no matter where an MNC conducts business. MNCs require procedures to manage political risks, just as it requires procedures to manage all other significant sources of risk.

Managers dislike uncertainty. They particularly dislike it when it has an impact on long-term investment and strategic decisions. A German automobile company invests in a Brazilian assembly plant because the German company wants to take advantage of lower wages and fewer trade restrictions in Brazil. Its investment is based on an assessment of future Brazilian policies over the 20- or 30-year life of the project. Changes in Brazil's political, social, and economic policies will have profound effects on the success of the German investment.

The German managers must make an effort to judge the degree of uncertainty and its impact on the project. Part of the task is to determine whether the uncertainty is too great to proceed or if whether the structure of the investment should be altered to mitigate the risk. Using political risk models can help identify particular factors that add to the uncertainty of investing in a country as well as to assist a manager in assessing the overall risk climate in a country.

Once an investment is made, the manager must continue to monitor events to anticipate changes in conditions that might diminish the on-going success of the project. Managers that anticipate new threats to their enterprises can react in advance and reduce the costs those threats might entail if they become realities.

QUESTIONS AND EXERCISES

11-1. How do political, country, and economic risks differ from each other? Give a specific example of each type of risk.

11-2. The chapter mentions the end of the Cold War as an example of an event that has altered the political risks in a region. List several ways in which the risk of doing business in the former Czechoslovakia have increased.

11-3. What are the distinctions between macro and micro risks? Give examples of each type.

11-4. What are the key assumptions underlying political risk models? How well do you think the models are at predicting dramatic changes in a country?

11-5. Examine Table 11.4 and indicate why the countries with the highest risk are judged to be risky.

11-6. One way to manage political risk is to form a joint venture with a local firm or investor. How does that reduce risk? How might it increase the riskiness of the investment?

11-7. Look at a recent issue of the *Wall Street Journal*, *Financial Times*, or *New York Times*. Scan the section on world news and for each article that deals with events in a country, indicate how those events affect the business environment in that country.

11-8. The table below provides the country risk measures for Argentina, Brazil, Chile, and Mexico for June 1993 and June 1994. Compare and contrast the measures.

IBC INTERNATIONAL COUNTRY RISK GUIDE

A. Economic expectations vs. realities	H. Law and order tradition
B. Economic planning failures	I. Racial and nationality tensions
C. Political leadership	J. Political terrorism
D. External conflict risk	K. Civil war risks
E. Corruption in government	L. Political party development
F. Military in politics	M. Quality of bureaucracy
G. Organized religion in politics	

	A	B	C	D	E	F	G	H	I	J	K	L	M	Total
Maximum Points	12	12	12	10	6	6	6	6	6	6	6	6	6	
June 1993														
Argentina	7	6	6	10	3	4	6	4	6	6	6	4	3	71
Brazil	6	5	5	10	4	5	6	4	5	5	5	4	3	67
Chile	7	8	8	10	3	4	4	4	5	4	5	4	3	69
Mexico	8	7	7	10	3	6	6	3	5	3	5	3	3	69
June 1994														
Argentina	6	7	8	10	3	5	6	5	6	6	6	5	3	76
Brazil	6	5	4	10	3	4	6	3	5	4	5	3	4	62
Chile	6	7	8	10	3	3	6	5	6	5	6	5	3	73
Mexico	8	7	6	10	3	6	6	3	5	5	6	4	3	72

REFERENCES

Bertrand, Kate. "Politics Pushes Marketing Foreground." *Business Marketing*, March 1990.

Buckly, Adrian. "Taking Account of Political Risk," *Accountancy*, July 1987.

Haendel, Dan. *Foreign Investments and the Management of Political Risk*, Boulder: Westview Press, 1979.

Haner, F. T. "Business Environmental Risk Index, Appendix B." *BERI Ltd. System for Selected Countries*, August 1981.

Kennedy, Charles R., Jr. *Political Risk Management: International Lending and Investing under Environmental Uncertainty*, New York: Quorum Books, 1987.

Kobrin, S.J. *Managing Political Risk Assessment: Strategic Response to Environmental Change.* Berkeley: University of California Press, 1982.

Kobrin, S.J. "Political Risk: A Review and Reconsideration." *Journal of International Business Studies*, Spring-Summer 1979, pp. 67–80.

Micallef, Joseph V. "Assessing Political Risk," *The McKinsey Quarterly*, Winter 1982.

RODALE PRESS IN THE COMMONWEALTH OF INDEPENDENT STATES

Paul Wessel, chief financial officer of Rodale Press, and Chuck McCullagh, Rodale vice president and publisher of its *Bicycling* magazine, were leaving Pennsylvania for a November 1991 visit to the company's joint venture operation in Moscow, which published a Russian-language farming magazine, *Novii Fermer (New Farmer)*. Wessel, his hands behind his head and leaning back in his chair, was ruminating on the history of Rodale Press's business in Russia.

In the two-plus years since Rodale began investigating the joint venture, unforeseen problems had arisen. Five issues of the bimonthly magazine had been published, but the sixth issue had been put on indefinite hold when Wessel and McCullagh learned that their Russian distributor was buying the magazines but not distributing them! Most of the magazines sat in a warehouse outside Moscow. The Russian editor of the magazine was also selecting articles for publication that were utterly beyond the scope of the magazine, and he seemed oblivious to Rodale's advice. As the political situation in Russia became increasingly unstable, moreover, support for the magazine among potential advertisers evaporated. Wessel wondered if the company would ever achieve its goals in Russia.

RODALE PRESS

Rodale Press, with assets of $300 million, is a family-owned publisher of books, magazines, and newsletters, published 50 books a year on health, fitness, homes, and gardens. It also operated four book clubs. The company's magazine titles included *Prevention*, the nation's most widely read health magazine, which offered systemic ways to prevent illness and disease; *Organic Gardening*, a practical guide to organic food growth and preparation methods; *Bicycling*, the world's largest-circulation English-language cycling publication; *Runner's World*, America's leading running magazine; *Men's Health*; *Backpacker*; and *American Woodworker*.

Funded in part by Rodale Press, the Rodale Institute, a nonprofit organization, conducted research and development in the areas addressed by Rodale's publishing businesses. The Rodale Institute developed methods of sustainable agriculture that were more productive, more profitable, and more protective of the land than currently used methods. At the Rodale Research Center, a 305-acre farm in Maxatawny, Pennsylvania, farmers, experts from major universities, the U.S. Department of Agriculture, and the U.S. Agency for International Development worked together on these techniques. The Rodale Institute also worked with governments, nonprofit agencies, and international organizations in developing countries to help them build self-reliance and economic independence through regenerative agriculture and improved use of resources. The findings of these collaborative efforts were disseminated to farmers everywhere through the Rodale

This case was prepared by Virginia M. Syer, MBA 1992, and Bonnie K. Matosich, MBA 1992, under the supervision of Mark Eaker, professor of Business Administration. Copyright © 1992 by the University of Virginia Darden School Foundation, Charlottesville, Va. All rights reserved. Rev. 4/93.

Institute's *New Farm* magazine, books, workshops, and farmer field days. The Rodale Institute was one manifestation of a companywide mission that resonated throughout the Rodale Press. The company's brochure opened with this statement of the mission: " At Rodale Press, we have a vision of the world as it could be. A world where health is recognized as more than simply freedom from disease. Where individuals take control over their lives. Where people protect and enhance the environment. Where neighbors and nations are guided by the spirit of cooperation." The company offered self-improvement classes for its employees, applied a no-smoking policy to all buildings, and encouraged employees to use the Energy Center, a fitness facility that offered exercise classes and team sports. Rodale Press occupied 13 new and renovated buildings sprinkled in and around the rustic town of Emmaus in the hills of eastern Pennsylvania. Fitness House, the company's "cafeteria," was a renovated home decorated with beautiful artifacts selected by Ardie Rodale, the wife of the recently deceased chairman, Bob Rodale. There employees could select healthy, flavorful meals, many of them vegetarian, served family style.

The company was founded in 1930 by J.I. Rodale, a forward-thinking man who saw the need for natural farming techniques to enable Americans to eat better than they were. In 1942 he launched *Organic Gardening,* followed by *Prevention* in 1950. Many recognized Rodale's founder as the father of the modern natural food and natural living movements in America. Bob Rodale, J.I.'s son, led the company from the time of his father's death in 1971 until his own death in 1990. Bob Rodale's personal contacts and interest in the former Soviet Union led to the launch of *Novii Fermer.*

The company's revered chairman had died in a car accident en route to the Moscow airport while actually working on this deal. His passing strengthened the company's resolve to publish the first issue of *Novii Fermer.* At the moment, however, Wessel was questioning whether a commitment to pursue Bob's dream, however strongly felt, would be enough to overcome all the difficulties that the project faced. Rodale's investment to date in the Russian deal, including legal fees and the purchase of some equipment for the venture, was about $1.5 million.

GENESIS OF THE DEAL

With the 1985 ascension of Mikhail Gorbachev to the presidency of the Soviet Union and his policies of *glasnost* (openness) and *perestroyka* (restructuring), U.S. consumer businesses began to eye the Soviet market's 287 million people. In January 1987, the Presidium of the Supreme Soviet of the USSR authorized the establishment of joint ventures, such as factories and government organizations, between foreign companies and Soviet entities. Gorbachev envisioned that this joint cooperation would satisfy Soviet requirements for scarce industrial products, raw materials, and foodstuffs; attract foreign technology, management experience, and material and financial resources; and develop the export base of the country. When the law was first introduced, a foreign partner was entitled to a maximum of 49 percent ownership in a venture. Foreign companies, however, were not allowed to repatriate their profits; that is, they could not convert ruble profits into hard currency. Therefore, Western partner companies had to be willing to invest for what was, by U.S. standards, the incredibly long term or else establish some sort of barter arrangement to bring home profits in the form of salable goods.

The relationships leading to the Rodale joint venture started in August 1989. Yevgenii Gringaut, a Russian working at Vneshtorgizdat, the publishing house of the Soviet Foreign Trade Ministry, had an idea for not merely a magazine but for a whole package of primarily publishing businesses. Many Russians were predicting an explosion of privatized, independent, owner-operated farms, and Gringaut wanted to ride this wave of interest in farming by teaching individual Russian farmers the U.S. approach to agriculture. Because at the time the only way Russians could deal outside the official government ministries was in a joint venture and because Gringaut wanted to focus on U.S. farming, he needed a U.S. farm-oriented publisher as a partner. Gringaut was attracted to Rodale's organic, regenerative approach to agriculture because he himself was a weekend gardener, a breeder of gladiolus. Coincidentally, his top ministry assistant, Vasilii Senatorov, had met Bob Rodale, an ardent cycling enthusiast, while covering international bicycling events. He moved quickly to establish contact. Senatorov subsequently became general director of the the joint venture.

Gringaut wanted the magazine to be an U.S.–style magazine with U.S. editorial content and a U.S. look and quality. A Russian-printed magazine would face considerable quality problems. Russian printers could not print in four colors, obtain high-quality paper, or adhere to deadlines. As a result, Gringaut had no choice but to propose that the venture print the magazine outside Russia. The venture considered a printer in Yugoslavia, but PTS eventually settled on printing the magazine in Helsinki, Finland, since the Finns had long-time commercial ties to Russia. PTS also chose the Finnish printer because the employees spoke English, used the Western banking network, and were "more businesslike" than the Yugoslavs.

The magazine would generate ruble revenues. Operating expenses for the magazine, except for the printing, would be paid in rubles, but operating expenses were projected to be relatively small. Thus, the magazine would have a big ruble profit and a big hard currency deficit.

A farming magazine (see Exhibit 11.1A) was to be the centerpiece of the deal, but it was not the whole deal. In Russia, any profitable deal required connections with hard currency or with tangible goods with which to barter for hard currency. Gringaut had a dacha in a village that adjoined the 50th Anniversary of the October Revolution State Farm in Kudinova, Noginsk, 40 miles east of Moscow. He and the farm director, Nikolai Geleti, had become friends. The state farm had political connections and could provide goods for bartering or paying employees of the joint venture. Moreover, the farm director, also stirred by the promise of capitalism, wanted to construct a sausage factory in which to process the farm's 60,000 pigs. Quality equipment for such a factory, however, would require hard currency amounting to several hundred thousand dollars. Gringaut decided to offer the farm director equipment for the sausage factory in exchange for the farm's participation in the joint venture. Employees of the joint venture would receive high-quality sausage from the factories and their operation and, perhaps at some point down the line, rights to some of the farm's land.

- EXHIBIT 11.1A

RODALE PRESS IN THE COMMONWEALTH
OF INDEPENDENT STATES
- AGRICULTURAL STATISTICS FOR FORMER SOVIET REPUBLICS, 1991

Analysis of Agriculture in Soviet Republic

	Byelorussia	Ukraine	Russia	Lithuania	Latvia	Estonia
Total population (millions)	10.2	51.7	147.4	3.7	2.7	1.6
Total area (mm hectares*)	20.7	60.4	1,707.5	6.5	6.5	4.5
Cultivated	9.5	41.8	217.5	3.6	2.5	1.4
Arable	6.1 (64.9%)	34.1 (83.7%)	133.5 (61/8%)	2.3 (67.7%)	1.7 (68.0%)	1.0 (71.4%)
Hay/Mowing	1.4 (14.9%)	2.0 (5.0%)	22.8 (10.6%)	.3 (8.8%)	.3 (12.0%)	.2 (14.3%)
Pasture	1.9 (20.2%)	4.6 (11.3%)	59.6 (27.6%)	.8 (23.5%)	.5 (20.0%)	.2 (14.3%)
Total Farms	2,733	10,609	26,305	2,222	4,509	1,167
Collective	1,614	7,885	12,200	749	327	173
State	893	2,557	12,832	311	251	136
Peasant	226	167	1,273	1,162	3,931	858
Livestock (millions)	60.5	392.6	N/A	22.5	15.5	8.9
Cattle	7.3 (12.1%)	25.6 (6.5%)	N/A	2.4 (10.7%)	1.5 (9.7%)	.8 (9.0%)
Pigs	5.1 (8.4%)	19.5 (5.0%)	N/A	2.7 (12.0%)	1.6 (10.3%)	1.1 (12.4%)
Sheep/Goats	.6 (1.0%)	93.0 (23.7%)	N/A	.2 (.9%)	.2 (1.3%)	.1 (1.1%)
Poultry	47.5 (78.5%)	254.5 (64.8%)	N/A	17.2 (76.4%)	12.2 (78.7%)	6.9 (77.5%)
Crops	Grain	Grain	Grain	Flax	Grain	Grain
	Potatoes	Potatoes	Sugar beets	Sugar beets	Forage	Forage
	Vegetables	Beans	Sunflowers	Potatoes	Potatoes	Potatoes
	Fruit	Sugar beets	Potatoes	Vegetables	Vegetables	Vegetables
	Flax	Sunflowers	Flax			
		Vegetables				

*1 hectare = 2.47 acres.
N/A = Not Available.

With U.S. equipment and technology, the farm could produce quality sausage and salami. Half of the sausage production would be sold to the Soviet public for rubles. The remaining sausage would generate hard currency when sold in *berioskas* (hard currency stores) and to embassies and hotels catering to foreigners. For the first year of operation, the sausage plant was projected to make profit of $1 million. The operating expenses of the sausage plant, including construction expenses, feed for the pigs, salaries, and utilities, would be denominated in rubles.

Thus, the sausage plant would lose money in rubles but generate a profit in dollars, whereas the publishing operation would make money in rubles and lose money in dollars. The idea was that the two operations would subsidize each other. Whatever fell between the cracks would be profit.

Gringaut also envisioned that the ruble profits would fund a tourism venture and that the venture's publishing services would be sold to other people. Gringaut would hang dozens of different businesses on the initial joint venture.

Gringaut had explained it to Wessel as follows: "Russian law is quite different from U.S. law. In U.S. law, there is a presumption that you can do anything except what the law prohibits. In Russian law, you can do only what the law specifically sanctions; that is, you cannot make a move until the law says you can. So if you want to do anything, no matter how elementary, it has to be written into your charter."

THE DEAL TAKES SHAPE

In August 1989, Gringaut persuaded Bob Rodale to become involved. Wessel and McCullagh were brought in shortly thereafter. The two senior managers had the most international experience in the company. Moreover, as chief financial officer, Wessel negotiated the financial and legal sides of all Rodale deals. The idea was for Wessel to negotiate the deal and leave the day-to-day running of the magazine to its operating staff, U.S. Editor George DeVault, Advertising Manager Tanya Tishin, and the Russians. McCullagh would assume the title of publisher. British by birth and well traveled, McCullagh was also known as Rodale's corporate trouble-shooter. He was already in Europe during Wessel's first visit to Moscow in November 1989, and he met Wessel there. Neither man spoke any Russian.

Rodale had no delusions about generating hard currency returns any time soon. When Wessel was first evaluating the deal, he proposed to Bob Rodale three possible rationales for getting involved: (1) Rodale Press could make some money, (2) Rodale could help the Russian people improve their lives, and (3) the people at Rodale could have some fun. Bob Rodale responded that Wessel had stated the right reasons but in the reverse order.

Wessel met with Gringaut three times in November 1989 to negotiate details. Then he and McCullagh spent a week in Moscow in December 1989 finishing the agreement. The partners signed the agreement in late February 1990. Under normal circumstances, a joint venture agreement required six months for authorization by the Russian government. Gringaut, however, had a contact within the Finance Ministry, a case officer who reviewed joint venture agreements such as this one. During a chance meeting with Gringaut, this contact told him that PTS needed to make some minor changes in the documents. Wessel recalled looking at the list of required changes and thinking that they did not limit the scope of PTS's businesses at all. The authorities were apparently concerned more with the formalities of the documents than with how the documents would empower the joint venture. In May the partners received one of the fastest government approvals in the history of joint ventures, thanks to Gringaut's chance meeting. After registering in May 1990, the joint venture started hiring employees.

The charter specified a timetable of major activities. The pilot issue of *Novii Fermer* was to be published May 15, 1990. At that time, the joint venture would not exist, so Rodale would have to publish the inaugural issue. Gringaut and Rodale had very different ideas about the purpose of this first issue. Gringaut wanted to get a sense of the magazine's reception among Russian farmers; he thus wanted a pilot that represented the content, quality, and focus of the actual magazine. Rodale wanted to use the pilot as a tool to generate interest among U.S. advertisers.

Several staff people in Emmaus handled the project, and they created a pilot that was unrepresentative of the *Novii Fermer* that was to be. Printed in the United States, the pilot issue was of higher production quality than later issues. It was almost entirely in English and featured articles technically beyond Russian farmers' comprehension. Gringaut and the other Russian managers at PTS did not even want copies of the pilot. Advertisers, on the other hand, were excited about the pilot issue, but they had inflated expectations of the permanent magazine. (See Exhibits 11.1b and 11.1c for a copy of the letter Tishin sent to prospective advertisers and for the advertising rates.)

THE START-UP OF OPERATIONS

Organizing the venture's operations and hiring staff took much longer than Rodale had anticipated. Office space in Moscow was in critically short supply. PTS did obtain office space, but, because of a shortage of construction materials, it took seven months to repair the offices. The Russian partners spent four months looking for the secondhand furniture for the offices, which were located in a converted apartment building. Office necessities included a refrigerator so that employees of PTS could purchase food in the morning on their way to work while it was still available in the stores.

Hiring and retaining employees were difficult. Most of those hired had worked for governmental agencies such as the State Press and Publishing Committee or the news agency TASS. They were excited about participating in this operation. The head of the editorial office explained, "In a government organization, yes, you are supplied with paper. You feel stable, but the salary is low, and there is no room for creative efforts. Here I have a lot of freedom to show my creativity." The opportunity to participate in a creative venture, to travel abroad, perhaps even to receive some hard currency compensation did not, for some, outweigh the difficulties of working in the PTS environment. Two of the joint venture's employees resigned because they preferred jobs with more structure and less ambiguity. "They preferred the certainty of knowing exactly what they were supposed to do," explained Vasilii Senatorov. For one 40-year-old employee, PTS offered his first chance to travel abroad. His outlook after joining the venture was "totally different" from before. He thought he might change jobs to look for an even greater opportunity in another organization.

Gringaut and Rodale were still discussing who would do the printing and when the magazine would be published while en route to the Moscow airport. A bus struck the van they were in, killing all of the occupants. After the accident, everyone working with PTS became dedicated to publishing the first issue. As a result, it was printed quickly, in January 1991. Because the sausage plant was not yet finished and Advertising Manager Tishin had sold only a few ads, Rodale Press agreed, given small print runs, to finance the printing of the first several issues.

■ **EXHIBIT 11.1B**

Rodale Press, Inc.
33 East Minor St.
Emmaus PA 18098
USA
215-967-5171
Fax: 215-965-5670

New Farmer
A joint publication of
Rodale Press &
Vneshtorgizdat, a major
Soviet publisher

Dear Prospect:

I'm happy to introduce you to NEW FARMER.

Just a word of explanation about circulation and advertising rates. As indicated in the media kit's circulation information, we expect circulation of NEW FARMER to be 205,000. But note that we plan to reach that circulation gradually during the first two years of publication and that the advertising rates for each issue will be adjusted to reflect circulation. Advertising rates for the first two issues (January/ February and March/April, 1991) can be found on the enclosed introductory rate card.

The circulation of the magazine (and therefore the advertising rates) will be determined by the rate of agricultural reform in the Soviet Union. Our marketing plan is to reach the economic decision-makers in the Soviet Union, the people who actually have the hard currency. These, of course, are the people you want to reach. As you might know, this audience is changing and growing almost daily. We want the circulation of the magazine to reflect this. Right now, hard currency and economic decisions in the agricultural area are still in the hands of relatively few government agencies (including state and collective farms). Accordingly, we have decided to set circulation for the first two issues at 50,000, a sufficient number to reach that audience. This will make NEW FARMER one of the largest farming magazines in the Soviet Union, even in its first few issues.

As agricultural and economic reform proceeds, as state and collective farms are broken up and economic decisions are increasingly decentralized (and actually made by "new farmers"), circulation will be increased accordingly. We now believe it is reasonable to expect circulation of NEW FARMER to each 205,000 by the end of 1992. But since Soviet President Mikhail Gorbachev has made agricultural reform his top priority, economic decentralization may occur much more swiftly and we may reach the 205,000 circulation figure much sooner than we now anticipate.

I (as well as our sales representatives) will regularly update you as our circulation grows and our advertising rates change. We expect NEW FARMER to be a very prominent advocate for economic and agricultural progress in the Soviet Union. Our magazine will be your access to the future leaders of Soviet agriculture.

Sincerely,

Tania Tishin

■ **EXHIBIT 11.1c**

**RODALE PRESS IN THE COMMONWEALTH
OF INDEPENDENT STATES
■ ADVERTISING RATES FOR *NEW FARMER***

Ad Size/Color	One–Time Rates			Three–Time Rates			Six–Time Rates		
	B&W	2-Color	4-Color	B&W	2-Color	4-Color	B&W	2-Color	4-Color
Full page	$2,505	$2,830	$3,250	$2,305	$2,575	$2,960	$2,255	$2,515	$2,895
2/3 page	1,775	2,010	2,310	1,640	1,825	2,100	1,600	1,785	2,055
1/2 page	1,375	1,555	1,790	1,270	1,415	1,625	1,240	1,385	1,590
1/3 page	950	1,075	1,430	875	980	1,300	855	955	1,275
1/4 page	800			740			720		
1/6 page	525			485			475		
1/12 page	300			275			270		
COVERS									
(4 color only)									
2nd & 3rd			3,510			3,195			3,125
4th			3,770			3,430			3,355

The partners decided on a press run of 50,000 copies of the first two issues, 75,000 for the next two issues, and 100,000 copies of issues 5 and 6 (see Exhibit 11.1D). Advertising was still a tough sell, and the team in Emmaus had received a letter in August stating that PTS was considering terminating the contract with the magazine's distributor. The sausage plant was still not on line, and Rodale Press was providing all of the venture's hard currency needs. Consequently, McCullagh reduced the press run of issue 5 to 75,000.

━━━━━━━━━━━━━━━━━━━━━━━━━━━━━ **DISTRIBUTION PROBLEMS**

After the first issue was printed in January 1991, Wessel and McCullagh went to Moscow. McCullagh went in early March to attend a celebration of *Novii Fermer's* successful launch. In late May, Wessel visited Moscow but spent most of his time on legal matters and on the award to PTS of 30 acres outside the city for the creation of an R&D station similar to the Rodale Institute. The men returned to Moscow together in September 1991 to check on the venture's progress. They discovered that distribution problems were much more serious than Rodale employees in Emmaus had known. McCullagh and Wessel tried unsuccessfully to reduce the print run of issue 5 below even the 75,000 level, and they postponed issue 6 altogether.

Private Russian farmers numbered only about 12,000 at the time. Thus, PTS had considered direct mail for distribution but found it to be a costly proposition (1.5 to 2 rubles per piece) with uncertain delivery. The services of state-owned magazine distributors were also expensive. Senatorov, however, contracted with an independent book distributor, Blagovest, to distribute the magazine to large farm cooperatives, on kiosks, and eventually through subscription.

When Rodale managers asked PTS whether all copies had been sold, PTS responded that they had been. PTS had received some revenue and could claim that it had sold all of the copies of *Novii Fermer* to the distributor, but Blagovest had not distributed them; they were sitting in the Blagovest warehouse. "PTS's response was a reflection of our different views of the world," said Wessel. "Once Blagovest had bought the magazines, PTS figured it was their problem."

Wessel explained what went through his mind at that time:

> When we heard this, we couldn't believe it. We were paying real money—U.S. dollars—to print the magazine. It was costing us at least $0.60 a copy. And we have no hard currency revenues, so the entire production cost represents a subsidy from Rodale Press.
>
> On the ruble side, the magazine sells on the newsstand for 4 rubles, but after the distributor takes a share, PTS gets only about 1.5 rubles, which is worth about $0.06 if we could convert the rubles. Now, everyone, both the Russians and the Americans, knew that we were losing money on the deal. But we were willing to accept that as long as the magazine was getting out to the readers, as long as we were spreading our message, helping people, and building a business for the future.

■ EXHIBIT 11.1D

RODALE PRESS IN THE COMMONWEALTH OF INDEPENDENT STATES
■ EXPECTED CIRCULATION FOR *NEW FARMER*

The 6 republics chosen for the circulation of *New Farmer*—Russia, Ukraine, Byelorussia, Lithuania, Latvia and Estonia—represent a majority of agricultural activity in the Soviet Union:

85.1% of all collective farms, 72.5% of all state farms, and more than 80% of all individual peasant farms are located in these areas.

Republics

Farms	Byelorussia	Ukraine	Russia	Lithuania	Latvia	Estonia	Total
Collective	1,614	7,885	12,200	749	327	173	22,948
State	893	2,557	12,832	311	251	136	16,980
Peasant	226	167	1,273	1,162	3,931	858	7,617
Totals	2,733	10,609	26,305	2,222	4,509	1,167	47,545

State, collective, and peasant farms: 50,000 copies

Libraries in target republics (75% of 32,000 libraries): 24,000 copies

Farm social clubs (25% of the 85,000 clubs): 21,000 copies

Special agricultural schools with libraries in the target regions: 500 copies

Weekend farmers and other individual subscribers: 25,000 copies

Distribution through kiosks: 74,500 copies

Samples and complimentary copies: 10,000 copies

Estimated first-year total circulation: 205,000 copies

What the Russians could not see was that magazines gathering dust in a warehouse were not achieving any of our goals. They were not being read; they were not doing any good for Russian farmers; they were not building up our brand name for the future. To add insult to injury, we were losing a lot of money. The Russians accepted this situation because they weren't paying the dollars and they were getting the benefit of the ruble revenue, small as it was. So I told them, if they really need the rubles, I'll just give them $0.06 for every copy that we don't print and save myself $0.54 a copy.

PTS talked to several distributors, but McCullagh and Wessel needed an iron-clad plan before they would approve it. A representative from a particular distributor had numerous ideas. McCullagh asked him, "How are we going to get the copies from our printer to the people?" He just did not respond. McCullagh even tried talking to him in Russian. "Which towns are you going to, and where are the newsstands?" he asked. The distributor could not answer because he did not have plans, just good intentions.

EDITORIAL PROBLEMS

The articles in the issues themselves were another problem. Some articles were acceptable; others were way off target for the intended Russian readers. Most U.S. farming is so advanced that it seems almost fantastical to Soviet readers. For articles, Rodale supplied PTS with back issues of *Organic Gardening* and *The New Farm* magazine, as well as copies of Rodale books and other U.S. agricultural magazines not published by Rodale. If PTS selected an article from one of these other magazines, Rodale would obtain permission for *Novii Fermer* to print the article. Rodale suggested that *Novii Fermer* limit the editorial scope of the publication and restrict itself to material of practical use to Russian farmers.

Many of the articles selected by the Russian editor, Yuri Naumov, violated all notions of serving a target audience, however. At first the Rodale people thought that perhaps they were not making themselves clear. They finally realized, however, that Naumov thought he had complete control over the contents of the magazine. He was simply ignoring input provided by DeVault, *Novii Fermer's* U.S. editor. As time went on, Wessel concluded:

> Either he does not want to follow our direction or he just cannot understand what we are trying to tell him; that is, he's either insubordinate or incompetent. I don't think he understands the concept of the magazine. For instance, in one issue, he ran an article directly from our *Organic Gardening* magazine which reviews riding lawn mowers— an entire article, along with specifications, devoted to things Russians not only couldn't dream of buying but never knew existed. Another article he ran looks like something out of a coffee-table book—just pretty pictures showing how nice it is in America, nothing of practical value to Russian farmers.

Following publication of those issues, DeVault tried to assert more authority in the approval of articles to be included in the magazine. Naumov accepted DeVault's advice but still wanted to make the decisions. He did not recognize DeVault as having any authority. In March 1991, Rodale started advising Senatorov to fire Naumov. In the ensuing months, that advice grew stronger. In September, McCullagh finally told Senatorov to fire Naumov because Senatorov had not yet done so.

THE SAUSAGE FACTORY

The sausage factory presented another problem. In April 1990, Nikolai Goliti, the Kudinova farm director, told Rodale that the sausage equipment could be installed in the plant by the end of the following month. U.S. suppliers of the equipment prepared it for shipment. By the end of May, however, the plant was nowhere near completion, so Rodale put the equipment into storage in the United States. Wessel traveled to Moscow four times in the summer of 1990. Each time he was assured that the plant would be completed in six weeks, so six weeks later he would return. After storing the equipment for almost a year, upon assurances of the plant's completion, Rodale finally sent the equipment to Russia and stored it in Kudinova. When Wessel visited the farm at the beginning of September 1991, the equipment was sitting idle in a storage shed on the property. Goliti had told him then that the plant would be finished in two months, in time for Wessel and McCullagh's November visit.

Wessel attempted to identify why the factory had suffered such delays. One reason had to do with materials procurement. Bricks, for instance, were available domestically but were often in short supply, especially for those businesses, such as PTS, that operated outside the centrally planned economy. Most bricks were produced by government-operated factories, and most of that production went to fill government orders. PTS could purchase bricks only if extra bricks had been produced. In addition, at the time, the government was trying to fill production with government orders to stabilize the economy, which meant that bricks were even harder to come by than usual.

Sometimes PTS would turn to the black market for bricks, where prices were often 10 times the government rate. Moreover, when the company was successful in locating bricks, it had to purchase them immediately and find a truck to transport them. Once the bricks arrived at the factory, PTS encountered another problem, a shortage of skilled labor for construction. Goliti was not particularly helpful because he was involved in 11 other projects.

At first, Wessel could not understand why PTS had not informed Rodale of the extent of the delays or, at least, been more realistic about timing. After a while, however, he learned an important lesson. As he explained:

> The Russians do not like to share bad news with you, so they bend the truth a bit. They will find a way to put the best possible light on a situation, then, and after the fact, come up with excuses. Nobody wants to take responsibility. We still do not have a factory, and I just got a letter saying it will be completed during the first quarter of 1992. It's beginning to look as if it will never get done.

By November 1991, Wessel was wondering whether Rodale could get out of the sausage factory altogether. The company's expertise was not in the manufacture of sausage; even if the plant were up and running, Rodale would not know how to manage it. The original magazine concept required hard currency because it did not include advertising. If *Novii Fermer* could earn hard currency advertising revenues, it might be a self-sustaining proposition. Rodale's challenge was to convince the farm director that he needed a partner who, unlike Rodale, knew and cared about the manufacture of sausage. Rodale's investment in the sausage plant was the equipment, which was still in storage at Kudinova. Wessel believed that Rodale could recover its investment one of three ways: convince the farm to buy the equipment, find another partner for the farm, or repossess the equipment and to sell it.

THE MEETING IN NOVEMBER

Wessel leaned forward at this point and reflected on the overall progress of the venture:

> The Russians feel that the Americans have no business telling them what to do. Our ownership of PTS is 50 percent. Vneshtorgizdat has 25 percent; and the State Farm has 25 percent. I have tried to explain to them the golden rule: We've got the gold, so we'll make the rules. They don't like it. The PTS managers act as if they are our partners, rather than our employees.

Wessel also was frustrated by PTS workers' perception that they should be given shares in the company but that the managers of the venture were responsible for profitability, with no participation required on the workers' part. They seemed less concerned with whether the enterprise succeeded than with whether the individuals could come together, feel a sense of belonging, and commiserate about their sad lots in life. Wessel sensed an almost mystical feeling of the family and union in a collective venture. Undoubtedly, these differing views of the business had clouded communications on many occasions.

Wessel also believed that the PTS employees did not seem to benefit from contact with the Rodale managers. He wondered whether he and McCullagh had sufficiently impressed upon the PTS workers the fact that "business is about doing things." For example, PTS still had no sausage and no marketing plan for selling the sausage, yet several employees wanted to open a restaurant where they could serve the sausage. At the same time, he realized that part of the problem might be that Rodale had not done enough to understand the Russian people:

> We have been told that the Europeans make a greater effort than we do to understand the problems of the Soviet Union. Europeans seem to devote more time to understanding the nature and root cause of their problems. Americans, they say, just want you to do the job—they do not care how you get it done.

With these problems on his mind, Wessel looked ahead to the next Moscow visit that he and McCullagh had planned for mid-November, only a few days away. He knew that they would have to make several critical decisions. Should they refuse to participate in the venture unless the sausage factory were removed from the deal? Would it be fair or wise to fire the editor who had ignored their previous directives and did not seem to understand the purpose of *Novii Fermer?* How would they locate a new distributor for the magazine? If these issues could not be resolved, should he suggest that Rodale pull out of the deal altogether?

PART

INTERNATIONAL CAPITAL MARKETS

OVERVIEW OF GLOBAL CAPITAL MARKETS

12

CHAPTER

KEY CONCEPTS

THE FACTORS LEADING TO THE GLOBALIZATION OF CAPITAL MARKETS ▬

THE GLOBAL CAPITAL MARKETS WHERE FUNDS CAN BE RAISED AND HOW CAPITAL MARKETS CAN BE CLASSIFIED ▬

THE MOTIVATION FOR CORPORATIONS TO RAISE FUNDS OUTSIDE THEIR DOMESTIC MARKET ▬

THE TRADITIONAL PROCESS OF UNDERWRITING SECURITIES ▬

A BOUGHT DEAL ▬

SEC RULE 144A, WHICH ENCOURAGES NON–U.S. CORPORATIONS TO ISSUE SECURITIES IN THE U.S. PRIVATE PLACEMENT MARKET ▬

THE FINANCIAL INTERMEDIARIES IN THE UNDERWRITING PROCESS ▬

THE COMPOSITION OF THE GLOBAL EQUITY MARKET ▬

ELECTION BY CORPORATIONS TO HAVE THEIR STOCK TRADED ON STOCK EXCHANGES IN OTHER COUNTRIES AS WELL AS ON THE EXCHANGES IN THEIR OWN COUNTRY ▬

AMERICAN DEPOSITARY RECEIPTS AND INTERNATIONAL DEPOSITARY RECEIPTS ▬

EUROEQUITY ISSUES ▬

Because of the globalization of capital markets throughout the world, a corporation is not limited to raising funds in the capital market where it is domiciled. Globalization *means the integration of capital markets throughout the world into a global capital market.*

In this chapter, we present an overview of the global capital markets where funds can be raised. The motivation for corporations to raise funds outside their market is discussed. To understand the fund-raising process in capital markets, we explain the underwriting process and the financial entities that are permitted to partake in underwriting activities. We then look at how corporations can raise common stock (equity) outside their local capital market. In the next two chapters, we look at the various debt markets where corporations can raise funds outside their local market. Capital market instruments that have been developed to control the risks associated with raising funds in the global capital market are explained in Chapter 15.

INTEGRATED VERSUS SEGMENTED WORLD CAPITAL MARKETS

A corporation may seek to raise funds outside its local capital market with the expectation of doing so at a cost lower than that in its local capital market. Whether this is possible depends on the degree of integration of capital markets.

At the two extremes, the world capital markets can be classified as either *completely segmented* or *completely integrated.* In the former case, investors in one country are not permitted to invest in the securities issued by an entity in another country. As a result, in a completely segmented market, the required return of securities of comparable risk that are traded in different capital markets throughout the world is different even after adjusting for taxes and foreign exchange rates. An implication is that if a corporation raises funds in the capital market of another country, it may be able to do so at a cost that is lower than raising them in its local capital market.

At the other extreme is a completely integrated capital market in which no restrictions prevent investors from investing in securities issued in any capital market throughout the world. In such an ideal world capital market, the required return on securities of comparable risk will be the same in all capital markets after adjusting for taxes and foreign exchange rates. An implication is that the cost of funds will be the same regardless of where in the capital markets throughout the world a corporation elects to raise those funds.

Real-world capital markets are neither completely segmented nor completely integrated. Rather they fall somewhere in between. Such markets can be referred to as *mildly segmented* or *mildly integrated.* An implication for corporate fund-raising is that in a world capital market that can be characterized in this way, there are opportunities to raise funds at a lower cost in some capital markets outside the local capital market.

It is important to emphasize that we are talking about capital markets in general. There are markets for different instruments. More specifically, there are equity (common stock) markets and debt markets. The degree of integration can be different for these two markets. Later in this chapter we will discuss the evidence on the degree of integration of equity markets.

FACTORS LEADING TO THE BETTER INTEGRATION OF CAPITAL MARKETS

In recent years, several factors have led to the better integration of capital markets throughout the world. We can classify these factors as follows: (1) deregulation or liberalization of capital markets and activities of market participants in key financial centers of the world; (2) technological advances for monitoring world markets, executing orders, and analyzing financial opportunities; and (3) increased institutionalization of capital markets. These factors are not mutually exclusive. We discuss each factor below.

DEREGULATION

Global competition has forced governments to deregulate or liberalize various aspects of their capital markets so that their financial-oriented entities could compete effectively in global capital markets. Two types of deregulation have led to a greater integration of global capital markets: (1) *market deregulation* and (2) *institutional deregulation*.[1]

The first type of deregulation refers to deregulation of the basic structure of the market. Within major national capital markets, this has taken the form of eliminating interest rate ceilings and fixed commissions on security transactions. The following are other deregulation measures to open a country's capital market to global participants:

- Eliminating foreign exchange controls.
- Relaxing restrictions on the purchase of domestic securities by foreign investors.
- Relaxing various restrictions on the issuance of bonds by foreign borrowers.
- Allowing foreign commercial banks to more actively participate in the local loan market.
- Allowing foreign securities firms and commercial banks to be involved in underwriting bonds sold in the domestic market.
- Allowing foreign financial institutions to be active participants in that country's government bond market.
- Reducing or eliminating withholding taxes or transfer taxes imposed on foreign investors.

---

[1] William A. Schreyer, "The Globalization of Financial Markets," ch. 2 in *Investing and Risk Management*, vol. I, ed. Robert Lawrence Kuhn (Homewood, Ill.: Dow Jones–Irwin, 1990), p. 31.

The second type of deregulation is institutional deregulation. This involves the liberalization or elimination of restrictions on the financial activities of financial institutions. Examples include restrictions on the activities that commercial banks and securities firms can undertake and restrictions on the types of investments in which regulated financial institutions may invest.

TECHNOLOGICAL ADVANCES

Technological advances have increased the integration and efficiency of the global capital market. Advances in telecommunication systems link security dealers throughout the world so that orders can be executed within seconds. Advances in computer technology, coupled with advanced telecommunication systems, allow the transmission of real-time information on security prices and other key financial information, allowing market participants to monitor global markets and simultaneously assess how this information will impact the risk/return profile of their portfolios. Significantly improved computing power allows the instant manipulation of real-time market information so that arbitrage opportunities can be identified. Once identified, telecommunication systems permit the rapid execution of orders to capture the opportunities identified.

INSTITUTIONALIZATION OF CAPITAL MARKETS

Participants in the U.S. capital markets have shifted from a market dominated by retail (i.e., household) investors to one dominated by financial institutions, particularly pension funds, insurance companies, and mutual funds. This phenomenon is referred to as the *institutionalization of capital markets.* The same thing is occurring in other industrialized countries. Unlike a retail-investor dominated market, financial institutions have been more willing to transfer funds across national borders to improve portfolio diversification and/or exploit perceived mispricing of securities in foreign countries.

The potential portfolio diversification benefits associated with global investing have been documented in numerous studies.[2] These studies have heightened the awareness of investors about the virtues of global investing. Specifically, because international capital markets are less than perfectly positively correlated (i.e., they do not move exactly together), by including securities from other countries, the expected return can be increased without increasing risk.

CLASSIFICATION OF CAPITAL MARKETS

There is no uniform system for classifying the global capital markets, but we believe that the following is appropriate. From the perspective of a given country, capital markets can be classified into two markets, an *internal market* and an *exter-*

---

[2] See Bruno Solnik, *International Investments* (Reading, Mass.: Addison-Wesley, 1988), Ch. 2.

nal market. The internal market is also called the *national market.* It can be decomposed into two parts, the *domestic market* and the *foreign market.* The domestic market is where issuers domiciled in the country issue securities and where those securities are subsequently traded.

The foreign market of a country is where issuers not domiciled in the country issue securities and where those securities are subsequently traded. The rules governing the issuance of foreign securities are imposed by regulatory authorities where the security is issued. For example, securities issued by non–U.S. corporations in the United States must comply with the regulations set forth in U.S. securities law and other requirements imposed by the Securities and Exchange Commission. A non–Japanese corporation that seeks to offer securities in Japan must comply with Japanese securities law and regulations imposed by the Japanese Ministry of Finance.

The *external market,* also called the *international market,* includes securities with the following distinguishing features: (1) they are underwritten by an international syndicate, (2) they are offered at issuance simultaneously to investors in a number of countries, and (3) they are issued outside the jurisdiction of any single country. The external market is commonly referred to as the *offshore market* or, more popularly, the *Euromarket.*

The classification we use is by no means universally accepted. Some market observers and compilers of statistical data on market activity refer to the external market as consisting of the foreign market and the Euromarket.

We refer to the collection of all of these markets—the domestic market, the foreign market, and the Euromarket—as the global capital market. Figure 12.1 summarizes the classification. The global capital market can be further divided based on the type of financial claim, equity or debt.

■ FIGURE 12.1

CLASSIFICATION OF GLOBAL FINANCIAL MARKETS

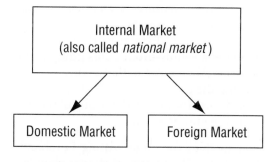

THE ISSUANCE OF SECURITIES

Corporations that seek to raise funds use the services of an investment banker. Basically, investment bankers perform two general functions. They assist corporations in obtaining those funds. Investment banking firms act as brokers or dealers for investors who wish to invest funds.

UNDERWRITING PROCESS

The traditional role associated with investment banking is the underwriting of securities. The typical underwriting process involves three functions: (1) advising the issuer on the terms and the timing of the offering, (2) buying the securities from the issuer, and (3) distributing the issue to the public. The adviser role may require investment bankers to design a security structure that is more palatable to investors so as to reduce the cost of funds for its client.

The underwriting process need not involve the second function—buying the securities from the issuer. When the investment banking firm agrees to buy the securities from the issuer at a set price, the underwriting arrangement is referred to as a *firm commitment*. The risk that the investment banking firm accepts in a firm commitment underwriting arrangement is that the price it pays to purchase the securities from the issuer will be less than the price it receives when it reoffers the securities to the public. In contrast, in a *best efforts* underwriting arrangement, the investment banking firm agrees only to use its expertise to sell the securities; it does not buy the entire issue from the issuer. The fee earned from underwriting a security is the difference between the price paid to the issuer and the price at which the investment bank reoffers the security to the public, called the *gross spread*.

The typical underwritten transaction involves so much risk of capital loss that for a single investment banking firm undertaking it alone would expose it to the danger of losing a significant portion of its capital. To share this risk, an investment banking firm forms a syndicate of firms to underwrite the issue. The gross spread is then divided among the lead underwriter(s) and the other firms in the underwriting syndicate. The lead underwriter manages the deal (*runs the books* for it). In many cases, there may be more than one lead underwriter, in which case the lead underwriters are said to *colead* or *comanage* the deal.

To realize the gross spread, the entire securities issue must be sold to the public at the planned reoffering price. This usually requires a great deal of marketing muscle. Investment banking firms have an investor client base (retail and institutional) to which they attempt to sell the securities. To increase the potential investor base, the lead underwriter puts together a selling group. This group includes the underwriting syndicate plus other firms that are not in the syndicate.

Not all deals are underwritten using the traditional syndicate process we have described. Variations include the *bought deal* for the underwriting of bonds and the standby arrangement for underwriting common stock.

BOUGHT DEAL. The most popular method for underwriting Eurobonds is the *bought deal*. Eurobonds are bonds issued in the Euromarket; these bonds are discussed in the next chapter. The bought deal was introduced in the Eurobond market in 1981 when Credit Suisse First Boston purchased a $100 million issue from General Motors Acceptance Corporation without lining up an underwriting syndicate prior to the purchase. Thus, Credit Suisse First Boston did not use the traditional syndication process to diversify the capital risk exposure associated with an underwriting that we described earlier.[3]

The mechanics of a bought deal are as follows. The lead manager or a group of managers offers a potential issuer of debt securities a firm bid to purchase a specified amount of the securities with a certain interest (coupon) rate and maturity. The issuer is given a day or so (or perhaps just even be a few hours) to accept or reject the bid. If the bid is accepted, the investment banking firm has bought the deal. It can, in turn, sell the securities to other investment banking firms for distribution to their clients and/or distribute the securities to its clients. Typically, the investment banking firm that buys the deal has presold most of the issue to its institutional clients.

The reason for the rise in bought deals is as follows. Corporations that sought financing wanted to act quickly to take advantage of perceived opportunities elsewhere in the world for raising funds. Because of increased volatility of interest rates and foreign exchange rates in the 1980s, attractive financing opportunities could disappear quickly during the time when the investment banker was lining up the traditional underwriting syndicate. This required that investment banking firms be prepared to respond on short notice to commit funds to a deal if requested by its corporate client. This meant that the investment banking firm had very little time to line up a syndicate, favoring the bought deal.

This is true not only in global markets but also in the domestic market. For example, in the United States prior to 1982, the ability of corporations to take advantage of favorable interest rates by issuing bonds was limited because of the lengthy period it took to obtain approval to issue securities by the Securities and Exchange Commission (SEC). In 1982 the SEC approved Rule 415, popularly referred to as the *shelf registration rule,* which permits certain issuers to issue securities on very short notice. Investment bankers had to respond to this flexibility granted to issuers by committing to deals prior to lining up the traditional syndicate.

The risk of capital loss in a bought deal may not be as great as it may first appear. Some deals are so straightforward that a large investment banking firm may have enough institutional investor interest that the risks of distributing the issue at the reoffering price are small. Moreover, in the case of bonds, there are hedging strategies using various interest rate risk control tools that reduce the risk of realizing a loss of selling the bonds at a price below the reoffering price.

STANDBY UNDERWRITING ARRANGEMENTS. A corporation can issue new common stock directly to existing shareholders via a preemptive rights offering. A preemptive right grants existing shareholders the right to buy some proportion of the new shares issued at a price below market value. This ensures that they may

---

[3] The bought deal found its way into the United States in mid-1985 when Merrill Lynch bought a $50 million bond issue from Norwest Financial.

maintain their proportionate equity interest in the corporation. For the shares sold via a preemptive rights offering, the underwriting services of an investment banker are not needed. However, the issuing corporation uses the services of an investment banker to distribute common stock that is not subscribed to. A *standby underwriting arrangement* is used in such instances. This arrangement calls for the underwriter to buy the unsubscribed shares. The issuing corporation pays a standby fee to the investment banking firm.

In the United States, the practice of issuing common stock via a preemptive rights offering is uncommon. In other countries, it is much more common; in some countries, it is the only means by which a new offering of common stock may be sold.

PUBLIC OFFERINGS VERSUS PRIVATE PLACEMENTS

In addition to underwriting securities for distribution to the public, investment banking firms place securities with a limited number of institutional investors such as insurance companies, investment companies, and pension funds. Typically, public and private offerings of securities differ in terms of the regulatory requirements that must be satisfied by the issuer. For example, in the United States, the Securities Act of 1933 and the Securities Exchange Act of 1934 require that all securities offered to the general public must be registered with the SEC, unless there is a specific exemption. Specifically, Section 4(2) of the 1933 Act exempts from registration "transactions by an issuer not involving any public offering."

The investment bankers may be involved with lining up the investors as well as designing the issue. Or, if the issuer has already identified the investors, the investment banker may serve only in an advisory capacity. Work as an adviser generates fee income, as does arranging the placement with investors. An investment banker can also participate in the transaction on a best efforts underwriting arrangement.

Securities for risky emerging companies are placed in the private placement market. Investment banking firms work with these clients in developing a business plan and advise them how to raise funds. They also negotiate on behalf of their clients with venture capital firms—that is, firms that specialize in acquiring equity interest in risky emerging companies.

In the United States, one restriction imposed on privately placed securities is that they may not be resold for two years after acquisition. Thus, there is no liquidity in the market for that time period. Buyers of privately placed securities must be compensated for the lack of liquidity, which raises the cost to the issuer of the securities.

In April 1990, however, SEC Rule 144A became effective. This rule eliminates the two-year holding period by permitting large institutions to trade securities acquired in private placement among themselves without having to register these securities with the SEC. Under Rule 144A, a large institution is defined as one holding at least $100 million worth of the security.

Rule 144A will encourage non–U.S. corporations to issue securities in the U.S. private placement market for two reasons. First, it will attract new large institutional investors into the market who were unwilling previously to buy private placements because of the requirement to hold the securities for two years. Such an increase in the number of institutional investors may encourage non–U.S. entities to issue securities. Second, foreign entities have been unwilling to raise funds in the United States prior to establishment of Rule 144A because they had to register their securities and furnish the necessary disclosure set forth by U.S. securities laws. Private placement requires less disclosure. Rule 144A also improves liquidity, reducing the cost of raising funds.

COMMERCIAL BANKS VERSUS SECURITIES FIRMS

Thus far, we have focused on what underwriters do and the risks that they take. Now we look at which financial entities may be underwriters. Those who may perform underwriting activities vary from country to country.

Financial intermediaries that may be involved in the underwriting process can be classified as securities firms and commercial banks. In the United States, the activities of underwriting securities are associated with securities firms. However, not all securities firms underwrite securities.

Commercial banks are financial intermediaries that accept deposits. With the funds raised through deposits and other funding sources, commercial banks make direct loans to various entities and invest in securities. They are highly regulated because of the important role that they play in a country's financial system. Demand deposit accounts are the principal means that individuals and business entities use for making payments, and government monetary policy is implemented through the banking system.

Commercial banks provide numerous services in our financial system. The services can be broadly classified as (1) individual banking, (2) institutional banking, and (3) global banking. *Individual banking* encompasses consumer lending, residential mortgage lending, consumer installment loans, and credit card financing. Loans to corporations and government entities fall into the category of *institutional banking.* It is in the area of global banking that banks have begun to compete head-to-head with securities firms that are engaged in investment banking activities. *Global banking* covers a broad range of activities involving corporate financing and capital market and foreign exchange products and services.

Corporate financing involves procuring funds for a bank's customers. This can go beyond traditional bank loans to involve the underwriting of securities. Regulations imposed may limit bank activities in this area. In assisting its customers in obtaining funds, banks can provide guarantees or commitments. Guarantees include standby letters of credit a bank guarantees to a third party (the holder of the debt of its customer) to make payments should its customer fail to do so. A bank can provide commitments to provide a client with credit at some specified time in the future. Examples of this include note issuance facilities and variants that we will describe in Chapter 14. These commitments have in fact blurred the distinction between capital market instruments (bonds and equity securities) and loans. As a result, commitments made by commercial banks can be viewed as an underwriting of a security.

Restrictions on underwriting activities vary from country to country. In the United States, for example, the Banking Act of 1933 included provisions that restricted banks from underwriting corporate securities. These provisions, more popularly referred to as the *Glass-Steagall Act,* were imposed on activities of commercial banks in the United States, not those overseas. U.S. commercial banks are not barred from underwriting or dealing in corporate bonds outside the United States, nor are they restricted from aiding in the private placement of corporate securities. Subsequent legislation, court rulings, and regulatory decisions have whittled away at the barriers against commercial banks engaging in investment banking activities, and it is anticipated that subsequent action will weaken the distinction between commercial banks and securities firms.

The architects of the Japanese financial system have followed the policy of separating commercial banking and investment banking activities. Japan's securities and exchange law prohibits nonsecurities companies from dealing in any securities except government or government-related bonds. As in the United States, reforms are under consideration to blur the distinction between commercial banks and securities firms.

In contrast to the U.S. and Japanese systems, and those of probably any other country with a well-developed capital market, the German capital market is more interdependent with its banking system because most intermediation of funds is via banks. Consequently, in the German capital markets, banks are the largest group of investors. Germany has two types of banks: universal banks and "special" banks. The activities of universal banks include the usual commercial banking business and any kind of securities business. The latter activity includes the underwriting, trading, and investing in securities. Thus, there is no separation of the banking and securities businesses in Germany. As a result the secondary market for both stocks and bonds is mainly an interbank market. The special banks provide financing for specific needs such as mortgage financing and consumer financing.

In the Euromarket, commercial banks and securities firms can compete with each other without the interference of domestic restrictions. Table 12.1 shows, as of mid-1994, the 50 largest banks in the world measured in U.S. dollars and ranked in terms of total assets. The top ten banks are Japanese. The only two U.S. commercial banks in the top 50 are Citibank (34th) and Bank of America (46th). The list in Table 12.1, however, is misleading because regulations differ across countries. Specifically, U.S. regulations prevent greater degrees of leverage for large banks; Japanese regulations do not apply this brake.

GLOBAL EQUITY MARKET

Table 12.2 provides a comparative analysis of the size, measured in U.S. dollars, of the equity markets of the world. The stock markets of the United States and Japan are the largest in the world. Because the markets are measured in U.S. dollars, the relative size of the U.S. and Japanese markets varies as the value of the yen changes relative to the dollar, with the U.S. market increasing when the yen depreciates and decreasing when the yen appreciates. The third largest market, which trails considerably behind that of the United States and Japan, is the U.K. market.

■ TABLE 12.1

THE 50 LARGEST BANKS IN THE WORLD RANKED BY
TOTAL ASSETS AS OF MID-1994

Rank	Bank Name	Country	Total Assets in Millions of U.S. Dollars
1	Dai-Ichi Kangyo Bank	Japan	502,669
2	Fuji Bank	Japan	501,729
3	Sumitomo Bank Ltd	Japan	493,473
4	Sakura Bank Ltd	Japan	491,952
5	Sanwa Bank	Japan	489,878
6	Mitsubishi Bank	Japan	455,895
7	Norinchukin Bank	Japan	428,240
8	Mitsubishi Trust & Banking	Japan	385,846
9	Industrial Bank of Japan	Japan	384,063
10	Mitsui Trust & Banking Company	Japan	370,003
11	Sumitomo Trust & Banking Ltd	Japan	369,073
12	Credit Lyonnais	France	338,906
13	Industrial & Comm Bank of China	China–People's Rep.	337,487
14	Deutsche Bank Ag	Germany	319,252
15	Tokai Bank Ltd	Japan	308,433
16	Long-Term Credit Bank of Japan	Japan	298,946
17	Credit Agricole	France	282,915
18	Bank of China	China–People's Rep.	273,647
19	Yasuda Trust & Banking	Japan	271,078
20	Daiwa Bank	Japan	269,101
21	Societe Generale	France	259,838
22	Asahi Bank	Japan	259,702
23	ABN Amro Holding N.V.	Netherlands	252,984
24	Banque Nationale de Paris	France	250,486
25	Barclays Bank PLC	United Kingdom	245,891
26	Bank of Tokyo	Japan	239,924
27	Toyo Trust & Banking	Japan	231,106
28	National Westminster Bank PLC	United Kingdom	226,419
29	Dresdner Bank	Germany	219,754
30	Union Bank of Switzerland	Switzerland	210,191
31	Westdeutsche Landesbank Girozen	Germany	191,399
32	People's Construction Bank of China	China–People's Rep.	183,584
33	Agricultural Bank of China	China–People's Rep.	181,968
34	Citibank, N.A.	USA	175,712
35	Banque Paribas	France	167,707
36	Bayerische Vereinsbank	Germany	165,660
37	Commerzbank Ag	Germany	163,796
38	Nippon Credit Bank	Japan	163,325
39	Cep Caisses D'Epargne et Prevoy	France	157,669
40	Shoko Chukin Bank	Japan	157,366
41	Credit Suisse	Switzerland	156,938
42	Bayerische Hypotheken Und Wechs	Germany	151,934
43	Bayerische Landesbank Girozentr	Germany	149,061
44	Hong Kong and Shanghai Bank Cor	Hong Kong	146,504
45	Swiss Bank Corporation	Switzerland	139,890
46	Bank of America NT&SA	USA	136,693
47	Zenshinren Bank	Japan	135,989
48	Chuo Trust & Banking	Japan	135,292
49	Rabobank Nederland	Netherlands	130,470
50	Deutsche Genossenschaftsbank	Germany	127,196

SOURCE: Data as provided by EURABANK^R database of Sleigh Corporation, Franklin Lakes, New Jersey.

■ TABLE 12.2

ESTIMATED TOTAL MARKET VALUE OF NATIONAL STOCK MARKETS INCLUDED IN MORGAN STANLEY CAPITAL INTERNATIONAL INDICES AS OF DECEMBER 31, 1994 (IN BILLIONS OF U.S. DOLLARS

Area and Country		Estimated Market Value
United States		$ 4,626.3
Canada		288.0
Europe		3,275.0
Austria	$ 30.7	
Belgium	84.0	
Denmark	46.6	
Finland	36.8	
France	444.3	
Germany	476.9	
Ireland	19.5	
Italy	177.1	
Netherlands	224.4	
Norway	36.1	
Spain	151.3	
Sweden	118.3	
Switzerland	284.0	
United Kingdom	1,145.0	
Asia and Far East		4,425.9
Australia	212.4	
Hong Kong	241.2	
Japan	3,624.5	
Malaysia	182.0	
New Zealand	26.4	
Singapore	139.4	
South African gold mines		24.6
"World"		$12,639.8

SOURCE: *Morgan Stanley Capital International Perspective,* January 1995, p. 5 (Adapted by the authors).

MULTIPLE LISTINGS ON NATIONAL EXCHANGES

Stocks of some firms are listed for trading on stock exchanges in other countries as well as on the exchanges in their own country. Some stocks of very large firms are listed on stock exchanges in several countries. Table 12.3 shows the number of stocks of firms from foreign countries that are listed on national exchanges and clearly indicates that multiple listing of stocks is a relatively common phenomenon.

The readiness of an exchange to list and trade the shares of a foreign country varies across countries and exchanges. In the United States, for example, actual shares of foreign companies are not traded; rather, the trading involves the rights to a number of shares that are held in trust. Called *American depositary receipts,* or ADRs, these rights are to ownership of shares in a relatively small set of companies that have SEC approval for an ADR-type of listing. (More detail on ADRs is available in a subsequent section of this chapter.) Thus, foreign firms that seek listing for their shares on U.S. exchanges face some costs. In other countries, regulations on the listing and trading of stock of a foreign company are not particularly stringent or costly. In the United Kingdom, for example, the rules on the issuance and trading of foreign companies' shares are basically the same as those for issuing domestic firms' stock.[4]

Does listing a stock on a foreign stock market increase the wealth of shareholders? That is, are there positive stock price effects from listing on a foreign stock market? Two studies investigated this issue, one looking at U.S. firms that listed on non–U.S. exchanges[5] and one examining foreign firms that listed on U.S. exchanges.[6] Neither study found any benefits to shareholders from listing outside the domestic market. Other reasons, however, have been suggested as to the reason that corporations list shares on several markets throughout the world. These will be discussed later in this chapter.

Research suggests that firms whose shares are listed on exchanges in different countries tend to be quite large, in terms of assets, and to have a relatively substantial amount of foreign sales revenue.[7]

■ **TABLE 12.3**

LISTINGS OF FOREIGN STOCKS ON NATIONAL EXCHANGES

Stock Exchange	Total Number of Stocks	Number of Foreign Stocks
Australian Stock Exchange	1,185	33
Vienna Stock Exchange (Austria)	142	45
Rio de Janeiro Stock Exchange (Brazil)	812	0
Montreal Stock exchange (Canada)	667	21
Toronto Stock Exchange (Canada)	1,193	54
Paris Bourse (France)	1,105	231
Frankfurt Stock Exchange (Germany)	743	354
Stock Exchange of Hong Kong	299	15
Bombay Stock Exchange (India)	2,447	0
Tokyo Stock Exchange (Japan)	1,752	125
Istanbul Stock Exchange (Turkey)	110	0
International Stock Exchange (United Kingdom)	2,559	563
American Stock Exchange (United States)	859	70
NASDAQ Stock Market (United States)	4,132	256
New York Stock Exchange (United States)	1,769	96

SOURCE: *Institutional Investor*, international ed. (April 1991), pp. 195–202.

---

[4] Harriet Creamer, "Issuing Securities in the United Kingdom," *International Financial Law Review*, special supplement, July 1990, pp. 54–61.

[5] John S. Howe and Kathryn Kelm, "The Stock Price Impacts of Overseas Listings," *Financial Management*, Autumn 1987, pp. 51–56.

[6] Gordon J. Alexander, Cheol S. Eun, and S. Janakiramanan, "International Listings and Stock Returns: Some Empirical Evidence," *Journal of Financial and Quantitative Analysis*, June 1988, pp. 135–151.

[7] Shahrokh M. Saudagaran, "An Empirical Study of Selected Factors Influencing the Decision to List on Foreign Stock Exchanges," *Journal of International Business Studies*, Spring 1988, pp. 101–127.

EUROEQUITY ISSUES

Euroequity issues are issued simultaneously in several national markets by an international syndicate. Bell Canada offered the first modern Euroequity offering in 1983. The offering, $43 million, was managed by the United Bank of Switzerland. By 1986, issuance of Euroequities totaled between $8 and $10 billion.[8] This growth was fueled by rising stock prices throughout the world, by the desire of investors to diversify their portfolios internationally and of corporations to expand their sources of equity funding, and by governments who sought international investors for the entities that they privatized. However, the market crash of October 1987 slowed the growth of this market. In 1987 issuance of Euroequities was about $15 to $18 billion (privatization offerings representing about half of this amount), but it declined to about $8 billion in 1988 (with only a small amount resulting from privatization offerings).

An increasing number of U.S. firms had equity offerings that included a Euroequity tranche. (In the financial vocabulary, the word *tranche*, which is French for slice or segment or cut, means a distinctive portion of the issue of a financial security. In this context, the word means that some of the newly issued equity shares were reserved for sale in Euromarkets.) Similarly, more European firms are offering equity securities with a U.S. tranche. For example, in 1990, 84 issues were offered by European firms with U.S. tranches having a market value of $3.85 billion compared to the first three quarters of 1991 in which 154 equity offerings with a total market value of $7.09 billion were made.[9]

Corporations have not limited their equity offerings to just their domestic equity market and a foreign market of another country. Instead, the offerings have been more global in nature. For example, the initial public offering (IPO) of British Telecommunications (the United Kingdom's government-owned telephone company) in 1984 was offered simultaneously in the United Kingdom, the United States, Japan, and Canada. The Dutch Aircraft manufacturer Fokker raised Dfls 500 million in equity the first half of 1992. There were seven tranches: the United States, the United Kingdom, Germany, Switzerland, Canada, Benelux, and the rest of the world.

The innovation in the Euroequities markets is not in terms of new equity structures. Rather, it is in the development of an efficient international channel for distributing equities. This development can probably be traced back to 1984 and 1985 when issues of three non–U.S. corporations, Nestlé, British Telecom, and Eselte, utilized the Euroequities market to raise equity. The depth and breadth of the market can be illustrated by Nestlé, which was able to use the international market to raise more than $400 million in equity funds three separate times in 1985.[10]

The size of the Euroequities market, however, is still considerably smaller than that of the Eurobond market discussed in the next chapter.

[8] P. L Gilibert, B. Lygum, and F. Wurtz, "The International Capital Market in 1986," *Cahiers BEI/EIB Papers* (Luxembourg: European Investment Bank, March 1987).

[9] As reported in Janine Schultz, "International Equity Tranches to Shed Weak Sister Image," *Corporate Financing Week* special supplement, November 25, 1991, pp. 1 and 8.

[10] Julian Walmsley, *The New Financial Instruments* (New York: John Wiley, 1988), p. 328.

INTERNATIONAL DEPOSITARY RECEIPTS

When a corporation issues equity outside its domestic market and the equity issue is subsequently traded in the foreign market, it is typically in the form of an *international depositary receipt* (IDR). Banks issue IDRs as evidence of ownership of the underlying stock of a foreign corporation that the bank holds in trust. Each IDR may represent ownership of one or more shares of common stock of a corporation. The advantage of the IDR structure is that the corporation does not have to comply with all the regulatory issuing requirements of the foreign country where the stock is to be traded. IDRs are typically sponsored by the issuing corporation. That is, the issuing corporation works with a bank to offer its common stock in a foreign country via the sale of IDRs.

As an example, consider the U.S. version of the IDR, the American depositary receipt (ADR), mentioned earlier. The success of the ADR structure in fact resulted in the rise of IDRs throughout the world. ADRs are denominated in U.S. dollars and pay dividends in them. The holder of an ADR does not have voting or pre-emptive rights.

ADRs can arise in one of two ways. First, one or more banks or security firms can assemble a large block of the shares of a foreign corporation and issue ADRs without the participation of that foreign corporation. More typically, the foreign corporation that seeks to have its stock traded in the United States sponsors the ADRs. In these instances, only one depositary bank issues them. A sponsored ADR is commonly referred to as an *American depositary share* (ADS). Periodic financial reports are provided in English to the holder of an ADS. ADSs can be traded either on one of the two major organized exchanges (the New York Stock Exchange and the American Stock Exchange), traded in the over-the-counter market, or privately placed with institutional investors. The nonsponsored ADR is typically traded in the over-the-counter market.

In the British Telecom IPO we cited earlier, the offering in the United States was an ADS (since it was sponsored by British Telecom) and listed on the New York Stock Exchange. Each ADS represented 10 shares of British Telecom.

The following are two more recent examples. In 1991, Orbital Engine Corporation, an Australian corporation, made an IPO in the United States via an ADS to raise U.S. $87 million. The offering was underwritten by a syndicate led by Merrill Lynch, SG Warburg, and Kidder Peabody. Orbital Engine's ADS is listed on the New York Stock Exchange.[11] The ADSs of Kia Motors, Korea's second largest automobile manufacturer, issued in the United States in November 1991 were privately placed rather than publicly offered. These are only two examples of the offerings in 1991, a year in which ADSs issued in the United States increased substantially. In 1990, only $104 million of ADSs were issued in the United States. In contrast, for the first 11 months of 1991, the amount of ADSs issued was $3.47 billion.[12]

---

[11] *International Financial Review,* November 2, 1991, p. 36.

[12] *Corporate Financing Week,* special supplement, December 23, 1991, p. 6.

IMPLICATIONS FOR MANAGERS

A multinational corporation seeking funds now has many choices as to the market in which it can raise funds. No longer constrained to fund-raising in its domestic market, the corporate treasurer can raise funds in the foreign market of other countries or in the Euromarket. The ability to raise funds at a lower cost can occur only if markets are not completely integrated. However, the motivation for raising funds may go beyond that of obtaining funds at a lower cost.

A corporation may seek to raise funds outside of its domestic market for several reasons. First, in some countries, large corporations seeking to raise a substantial amount of funds may have no other choice but to obtain financing in either the foreign market sector of another country or the Euromarket. This occurs because the fund-raising corporation's domestic market is not fully developed to be able to satisfy its demand for funds on globally competitive terms. Governments of developing countries have used these markets in seeking funds for government-owned corporations that they are privatizing.

The second reason is that there may be opportunities in the foreign market for obtaining a reduced cost of funding (considering issuing costs) that are not available in the domestic market. In the case of debt, its cost reflects two components: (1) the risk-free rate, which is accepted as the interest rate on U.S. Treasury security with the same maturity (called the base rate), and (2) a spread *to reflect the higher risks that investors perceive are associated with the issue or issuer. A corporate borrower who seeks reduced funding is attempting to reduce the spread. With the integration of capital markets throughout the world, such opportunities have diminished. Nevertheless, capital markets throughout the world have imperfections that prevent complete integration and thereby may permit a reduced cost of funds. These imperfections or market frictions occur because of differences in (1) security regulations in countries, (2) tax structures, (3) restrictions imposed on regulated institutional investors, and (4) the credit risk perception of the issuer. In the case of equity, a corporation is seeking to receive a higher value for its stock and to reduce the market impact cost of floating a large offering.*

The third reason is a desire by corporate treasurers to diversify their source of funding to reduce reliance on domestic investors. In the case of equities, diversifying funding sources may allow foreign investors who have very different perspectives of the future performance of the corporation. Raising equity funds also has two other advantages from the perspective of U.S. corporations: (1) some market observers believe that certain foreign investors are more loyal to corporations and look at long-term performance rather than short-term performance as do investors in the United States,[13] and (2) diversifying the investor base reduces the dominance of U.S. institutional holdings and its impact on corporate governance.

Finally, a corporation may issue a security denominated in a foreign currency as part of its overall foreign currency management. For example, consider a U.S. corporation that plans to build a factory in a foreign country and for which the construction costs will be denominated in the foreign currency. Also assume that the corporation plans to sell the

[13] "U.S. Firms Woo Investors in Europe and Japan," *Euromoney Corporate Finance*, March 1985, p. 45; and Peter O'Brien, "Underwriting International Corporate Equities," in *Capital Raising and Financial Structure*, ed. Robert L. Kuhn, vol. II (Homewood, Ill.: Dow Jones–Irwin, 1990), p. 120.

output of the factory in the same foreign country. Therefore, the revenue will be denominated in the foreign currency. The corporation then faces exchange rate risk: (1) the construction costs are uncertain in U.S. dollars because during the construction period, the U.S. dollar may depreciate relative to the foreign currency and (2) the projected revenue is uncertain in U.S. dollars because the foreign currency may depreciate relative to the U.S. dollar. Suppose that the corporation arranges debt financing for the plant in which it receives the proceeds in the foreign currency and the liabilities are denominated in the foreign currency. This financing arrangement can reduce exchange rate risk: (1) the proceeds received will be in the foreign currency and will be used to pay the construction costs and (2) the projected revenue can be applied to service the debt obligation.

Corporate Financing Week asked the corporate treasurers of several multinational corporations why they used nondomestic markets to raise funds.[14] Their responses reflected one or more of the reasons cited above. For example, the director of corporate finance of General Motors said that the company uses the Eurobond market with the objective of "diversifying funding sources, attract new investors and achieving comparable, if not cheaper, financing." A managing director of Sears Roebuck stated that the company "has a long-standing policy of diversifying geographical [funding] sources and instruments to avoid reliance on any specific market, even if the cost is higher." He further stated that "Sears cultivates a presence in the international market by issuing every three years or so."

Euromoney surveyed several firms that either listed stock on a foreign stock exchange or had a stock offering in a foreign market to find out why they did so.[15] One corporation surveyed was Scott Paper, a U.S. corporation, which listed its stock on the London Stock Exchange in November 1984. The stock had already been listed on the NYSE and a regional stock exchange, the Philadelphia Stock Exchange. The following reason for listing was given by an official in the company's public relations department:

> We had no immediate need for extra equity, but may well do so at some time in the future. We would like a broader stockholder base, and felt there would be some interest in the company overseas. The London Stock Exchange has high visibility, so it best served the purpose of getting the company's name known.[16]

A second firm surveyed was Saatchi & Saatchi, a U.K. corporation that raised equity in the United States via an ADR offering traded in the over-the-counter market. Several reasons were given for Saatchi & Saatchi's raising of equity in the United States. The firm had considerable U.S. activities and therefore felt it necessary to establish a presence in the U.S. equity market and a higher profile in the United States in general. Also, the firm wanted to offer stock options to its U.S. employees and apparently felt that having stocks traded in the U.S. equity market would make the options more attractive to employees.

Yet another set of reasons discussed earlier was given by a third firm in the Euromoney survey, Norsk Data, a Norwegian firm. It is in the high-technology industry

---

[14] Victoria Keefe, "Companies Issue Overseas for Diverse Reasons," Corporate Financing Week, special supplement, November 25, 1991, pp. 1 and 9.

[15] "Why Corporations Gain from Foreign Equity Listings," Euromoney Corporate Finance, March 1985, pp. 39–40.

[16] Ibid., p. 39.

and, before it sought foreign listing, had a history of earning per share growth of 60 percent. In 1981, the firm listed its stock on the London Stock Exchange and followed this several months later with an offering of new shares in London. In 1983 the firm raised funds in the U.S. equity market with the stock traded in the U.S. over-the-counter market. The chief executive officer of the firm gave the following reasons for listing:

> For major computer companies, the U.S. market is a very important source of funds, since it is alive to the possibility of high technology. However, we went to London first, since we felt a leap straight from Oslo to New York would be too great. Our major customers are in Germany, the UK and to a lesser extent, the U.S.[17]

In 1984, Norsk Data raised equity funds in a simultaneous U.S. and European offering. With respect to its various equity offerings, the chief executive officer stated:

> We have now brought equity up to the level of our competitors, and we have a natural balance sheet for a high growth, high technology company. That would have been very difficult if we had been limited to the Oslo stock market.[18] [Emphasis added.]

In addition, after these equity offerings on foreign markets, the firm was 60 percent owned by foreign investors, most of whom held nonvoting common stock. Thus, corporate control was not sacrificed.

In a survey conducted by the Economic Council of Canada of Canadian borrowers who raised funds outside Canada, 85 percent cited that the primary reason was the lower cost of funding.[19] The other reasons cited by the participants in the survey were diversification of the investor base (50 percent), ease of borrowing funds (37 percent), the presence of a subsidiary, parent, or affiliate in the country of borrowing (43 percent), the ability to attract new investors (30 percent), and publicity for the corporation's name (30 percent).

A survey of corporate managers investigating why U.S. corporations list on the London, Frankfurt, and Tokyo stock exchanges found the following four major motives:[20]

1. Increase visibility (awareness, name recognition, or exposure).

2. Broaden shareholder base (diversify ownership).

3. Increase access to financial markets.

4. Provide future market for products.

The most popular motive was the first one.

---

[17] Ibid., p. 40.

[18] Ibid., p. 40.

[19] A. Nigam, "Canadian Corporations and Governments, Financial Innovation and International Capital Markets," a paper prepared for the Economic Council of Canada, 1989.

[20] H. Kent Baker, "Why U.S. Companies List on the London, Frankfurt and Tokyo Stock Exchanges," *The Journal of International Securities Markets*, Autumn 1992, pp. 219–227.

QUESTIONS AND EXERCISES

12-1. What is meant by a completely segmented world capital market and what are the implications of such a market for raising funds?

12-2. What is meant by a completely integrated world capital market and what are the implications of such a market for raising funds?

12-3. How can world capital markets best be described?

12-4. What are the factors that lead to the better integration of the capital markets throughout the world?

12-5. What are the differences between a country's internal market and external market?

12-6. Distinguish between a country's domestic market and a foreign market.

12-7. What is the difference between a firm commitment underwriting and a best efforts distribution of a security?

12-8. How does a bought deal underwriting of a bond differ from a traditional underwriting?

12-9. What types of firms are involved in underwriting securities?

12-10. Some stocks are listed on several exchanges around the world. What are three reasons that a firm might want its stock to be listed on an exchange in the firm's home country as well as on exchanges in other countries?

12-11. What is the key feature of a so-called Euroequity issue?

12-12. What is the most important innovation that Euroequities have achieved?

12-13. What does it mean that a U.S. firm's new stock offering might contain a Euroequity tranche?

12-14. a. What is an IDR?

b. How does an IDR avoid the often cumbersome and usually costly regulations about the issuance of a domestic firm's securities in a foreign country?

12-15. What is the major difference between an American depositary receipt and an American depositary share?

REFERENCES

Baker, H. Kent. "Why U.S. Companies List on the London, Frankfurt and Tokyo Stock Exchanges." *The Journal of International Securities Markets*, Autumn 1992, pp. 219–227.

Creamer, Harriet. "Issuing Securities in the United Kingdom." *International Financial Law Review*, special supplement, July 1990, pp. 54–61.

Howe, John S., and Kathryn Kelm. "The Stock Price Impacts of Overseas Listing." *Financial Management*, Autumn 1987, pp. 51–56.

Keefe, Victoria. "Companies Issue Overseas for Diverse Reasons." *Corporate Financing Week,* special supplement, November 25, 1991, pp. 1 and 9.

Nigam, A. "Canadian Corporations and Governments, Financial Innovation and International Capital Markets," a paper prepared for the Economic Council of Canada, 1989.

O'Brien, Peter. "Underwriting International Corporate Entities." *Capital Raising and Financial Structure,* ed. Robert L. Kuhn, vol. II, *The Library of Investment Banking.* Homewood, Ill.: Dow Jones-Irwin, 1990, p. 120.

Saudagran, Shahrokh M. "An Empirical Study of Selected Factors Influencing the Decision to List on Foreign Stock Exchanges." *Journal of International Business Studies,* Spring 1988, pp. 101–127.

Solnik, Bruno. *International Investments.* Reading, Mass.: Addison-Wesley, 1988.

Walmsley, Julian. *The New Financial Instruments.* New York: John Wiley & Sons, 1988, p. 328.

"Why Corporations Gain from Foreign Equity Listings." *Euromoney Corporate Finance,* March 1985, pp. 39–40.

CASE 12.1
BRITISH TELECOMMUNICATIONS, PLC

Just after the market's close on December 3, 1984, Kathy Ellis, a vice president of Morgan Stanley, was awaiting a call from Richard Merley of Kleinwort, Benson, Limited, a British merchant bank. Since May, Kathy had been working with Richard on a multi-market initial public offering of equity for British Telecommunications, the United Kingdom's government-owned telephone monopoly. The U.K. government had decided to denationalize British Telecommunications (BT) in a public offering of 3,012,000,000 common shares, representing 50.2% of BT's total equity. The BT offering had been brought to market earlier on December 3, and trading in BT shares had commenced at the opening of the New York Stock Exchange that morning.

Because the British Telecommunications issue represented the largest initial public offering ever undertaken, a number of unusual measures had been taken to ensure adequate demand for BT shares. In order to provide credit to investors in BT, the offering had been structured as an installment sale. Payment for the shares was to be made in a series of three installments over a period extending 17 months beyond the initial offering date. In addition, the British government had sponsored a £10 million publicity campaign to promote the offering in the U.K. and had designed special incentives to encourage British individuals to participate in the stock sale, including the payment of bonus shares to purchasers of small blocks of BT stock. Finally, BT had decided to tap international demand for its shares by conducting the initial public offering simultaneously in four markets: London, New York, Tokyo, and Toronto. Kleinwort, Benson had represented the U.K. government in the transaction, and Morgan Stanley had served as lead manager of the U.S. offering.

The purpose of Kathy's phone call on the afternoon of December 3 was to discuss the extraordinary results of the first day of trading in BT shares. The price of partly-paid BT shares had risen to an 85% premium over the offering price in extremely active trading, and there was evidence that many of the 180 million shares placed in the U.S. had already flowed back to the U.K. Kathy knew that these results would raise questions about the viability of multi-market offerings, and was anxious to hear Kleinwort, Benson's reaction to the day's events.

THE INTERNATIONALIZATION OF EQUITY MARKETS

Although the British Telecommunications initial public offering was unique in terms of its size and complexity, cross-border equity offerings by large corporate issuers were not uncommon in the early 1980s. Corporations tapped foreign equity markets to achieve a variety of financial and strategic goals, including reducing capital costs, broadening their base of investors, increasing corporate exposure in foreign product markets, and facilitating the acquisition of foreign firms. By 1984 some 500 companies had acquired listings on stock exchanges outside their home countries.

In the U.S., most foreign stocks traded in the form of American Depository Receipts (ADRs). ADRs were negotiable receipts evidencing ownership of one or more shares of a foreign company. The ADR structure was developed by the Guaranty Trust Company (a predecessor of Morgan Guaranty Trust) in 1927 to facilitate trading and investment in foreign securities. Prior to the introduction of ADRs, individuals and institutions had been effectively barred from international equity diversification by practical barriers to the direct acquisition of shares in foreign markets. Because most foreign equities were bearer instruments, investors were reliant on financial publications, often published in foreign languages, for news regarding earnings, dividends, and annual meetings. Investors were usually required to ship stock certificates back to their country of origin in order to collect dividends or liquidate holdings, and, upon receipt of such payments, had to arrange special foreign exchange transactions to convert them into U.S. dollars.

ADRs provided U.S. investors with a convenient mechanism for investing in foreign securities. Guaranty Trust created ADRs by purchasing foreign shares in their country of origin, depositing the shares in that country's Guaranty Trust branch, and issuing dollar-denominated ADRs in the U.S. As transfer agent, the depository bank translated cash distributions on the underlying shares into U.S. dollars, distributed English language financial reports, and notified ADR holders of pending exchange offers, recapitalization plans, or shareholder meetings. For these services, the depository received a fee from the party requesting that the ADR facility be established. Although ADRs were sometimes sponsored directly by a foreign issuer, they were more commonly created at the request of U.S. market makers aware of investor demand for a specific foreign security. As U.S. registered securities, ADRs were subject to the Securities and Exchange Commission's disclosure and reporting regulations.

A typical ADR represented ownership of a single share of stock, although receipts were issued in units representing a fraction or multiple of a share if the price of a foreign stock was particularly high or low relative to U.S. norms. ADRs could be presented to the depository for conversion into the shares underlying them (and vice versa) at any time for a small service charge. The opportunities for international arbitrage afforded by this convertibility feature ensured that ADR prices did not diverge substantially from the exchange rate-adjusted value of the shares underlying them.

ADR volume grew rapidly after 1974, when the elimination of interest equalization taxes[1] and the lifting of the Federal Reserve's "voluntary guidelines" on foreign stock purchases freed institutional fund managers to diversify their port-

---

[1] The interest equalization tax was a surcharge imposed on the price of foreign securities purchased by Americans.

folios internationally. By 1984, approximately 550 ADRs were traded on exchanges or over-the-counter in the U.S. (see Exhibit 12.1A). Because the markets in which ADRs traded were often more liquid than foreign equity markets, ADRs were bought and sold by foreign as well as U.S. investors.

The success of the ADR structure in the U.S. market prompted depositary banks to offer similar facilities (known as International Depositary Receipts (IDRs)) in countries throughout the world. Dividends on IDRs were payable in the currency of the registered holder's choice.

Despite rapid increases in cross-border flows of equity capital, a variety of institutional and regulatory barriers to the "globalization" of equity trading and issuance remained in 1984. In some countries, such as Japan, governments placed explicit restrictions on equity flows, limiting foreign investors' holdings of stock in domestic companies and placing ceilings on domestic institutions' investments in foreign securities. In others, differences in accounting standards, disclosure requirements, and business practices inhibited the accurate valuation of foreign equities. However, an integrated international equity market was expected to evolve as the world's principal stock exchanges (New York, Tokyo, and London) yielded to pressures to standardize and coordinate their trading and underwriting practices. Many market observers predicted that a system of global 24-hour trading would emerge by the late 1980s, with international securities firms trading major corporations' shares continuously in one market after another as each day progressed.

THE TOKYO STOCK EXCHANGE

The Tokyo Stock Exchange (TSE) was the second largest in the world, with a market capitalization of $538 billion in October 1984. Trading in Japanese equities was transacted on the floor of the Tokyo Stock Exchange by some 83 regular exchange members[2] who bought and sold securities on behalf of customers and for their own accounts. In addition, 18 saitori members, whose role was similar to that of a specialist on the New York Stock Exchange, acted as intermediaries between the regular members. Unlike the NYSE, the Tokyo exchange operated under a system of fixed commissions and barred foreign securities firms from purchasing exchange memberships. It was estimated that commissions on institutional orders in Tokyo were three times those charged on the New York Stock Exchange.

The system of financial intermediation in Japan, including underwriting practices and disclosure regulations, closely paralleled the U.S. system. Glass-Steagall type restrictions separated the activities of commercial banks and securities firms. A Securities and Exchange Law, administered by the Ministry of Finance, regulated the issuance of securities and the operations of securities companies.

Commercial banks, which were the principal source of corporate credit and capital in Japan, were among the country's largest equity investors. Because

---

[2] In Tokyo, members joined the exchange as corporations and were allowed to send as many staff as they chose to the floor to trade. In contrast, London and New York exchange members joined as individuals.

Japanese banks held long-term equity positions in many of the public companies to which they loaned funds, the number of shares actively traded on the TSE was far fewer than the total listed on the exchange.

In contrast to the New York Stock Exchange, trading on the TSE was dominated by individuals (see Exhibit 12.1i). The predominant securities firm in Japan was Nomura Securities, whose $3 billion in shareholders' equity exceeded the capitalization of such American firms as Salomon Brothers and Merrill Lynch. Nomura was famed for its powerful retail sales force, which included a staff of 2,300 women who sold bonds and mutual funds door-to-door "the way Tupperware was sold in the United States."[3] As evidence of Nomura's clout with Japanese investors, market observers noted that Nomura's research recommendations had on occasion moved whole sectors of the Tokyo market.

With a domestic savings rate of 17.5%, Japan had become the world's largest creditor nation, exerting a significant influence on international capital markets. In 1984, in response to large U.S.-Japanese interest rate differentials, Japan's net purchases of $-denominated securities rose to $20 billion. Although 80% of these funds were invested in fixed income instruments, it was anticipated that the Japanese would soon become significant purchasers of U.S. and European equities.

Despite their size and growing international importance, Japanese financial markets remained heavily regulated throughout the early 1980s. The government fixed domestic interest rates at artificially low levels, regulated foreign exchange transactions, and restricted the participation of foreign financial institutions in Japanese markets. By the spring of 1984 Japan had begun to implement a variety of deregulatory measures aimed at internationalizing the yen and allowing greater foreign participation in the Japanese capital markets. Among these measures was a decision to allow foreign securities firms to purchase Tokyo Stock Exchange seats.

In 1984 the Ministry of Finance was considering a broad range of additional deregulatory proposals, including the elimination of fixed commissions on the TSE, an increase in the number of exchange seats, the introduction of futures trading on the Tokyo exchange, and provisions allowing nonexchange member firms to underwrite and trade bonds. In addition, Japanese insurance companies, trust banks and pension funds were pressuring the government to ease regulations limiting their investments in foreign securities to 10% of their assets.

THE LONDON STOCK EXCHANGE

Deregulatory pressures posed greater challenges in the British equity market than they did in Japan. Unlike the New York and Tokyo exchanges, where investment banks simultaneously underwrote, traded, and sold securities, the London exchange operated under a "single-capacity" system which separated the functions of principal and agent. Of the LSE's 4,000 members, 3,540 were "brokers" who acted as agents on behalf of their clients in the purchase and sale of securities on

---

[3] Mighty Nomura Tries to Muscle in on Wall Street," *Business Week*, December 16, 1985, pp. 76–77.

the exchange floor. Brokers were paid fixed commissions for executing transactions. The remaining 460 exchange members were "jobbers," who acted as intermediaries between buying and selling brokers. Jobbers traded securities for their own accounts, standing ready to buy or sell securities in which they made markets at all times. Jobbers earned profits in the form of a spread between the bid and offer prices they quoted.

The primary market for U.K. equities also differed from those of the U.S. and Japan. In contrast to the NYSE/TSE systems of offering new issues of stock to the public at prevailing market prices, exchange-listed companies in the U.K. were legally required to offer new issues of common shares to existing shareholders in amounts proportional to their original holdings of the issuer's stock. Such "rights offerings" were designed to protect shareholders from involuntary dilution of their ownership. Because underwriters were at risk for as long as three weeks in a typical rights offering, new issues were typically priced at substantial (15–20%) discounts to market prices.

Although no SEC-style regulatory agency existed in the United Kingdom, publicly-listed companies in the U.K. were controlled by the self-regulating activities of the London Stock Exchange. The LSE's rules delineated listing and disclosure requirements for listed companies, regulated the commissions charged on exchange trades, and established dealing procedures and codes of ethical conduct for exchange members.

In the early 1980s a variety of legal and competitive pressures forced the London exchange to begin the process of deregulation. The U.K.'s jobbing system, which had originally been instituted as a system of investor protection in a market dominated by individual investors, had grown inefficient. In theory, competition among jobbers was to have maintained a continuous market in all quoted shares, minimizing spread between bid and offer quotes. However, concentration among jobbers had increased dramatically by 1984, with five jobbing firms handling 90% of all LSE volume. As a result, fewer than 10% of all stocks traded in smooth, continuous markets with low bid/offer spreads. The increasing inefficiency of pricing under the jobbing system, the inability of inadequately capitalized jobbers to handle large trades, and dissatisfaction with high fixed commissions caused U.K. institutions to move volume off the London exchange, relying on brokers to arrange trades directly with other institutions or trading shares in ADR form on the New York exchange.

At the same time, U.K. issuers found several ways to circumvent legislation requiring that new equity be raised in rights offerings. Because stockholder approval was not required for issues of shares used to effect mergers or acquisitions, several companies had purchased unit investment trusts with their common shares, immediately liquidating the trusts' assets for cash. Others had issued low-premium convertible bonds in the Eurobond market, forcing conversion shortly after issuance.

These challenges to the LSE's regulatory control, combined with governmental charges that the exchange's fixed commission structure represented a restraint of trade, prompted the London exchange to agree to an aggressive plan of deregulation in 1983. By late 1985 the exchange was to abolish fixed commissions, abandon its single-capacity trading system, and admit foreign securities firms to membership. At the same time, the U.K. government was to establish a central securities regulatory commission. Like May Day in 1975, when the New York Stock Exchange moved to a system of negotiated commissions, the "Big Bang" in London was expected to spark a period of consolidation among intermediaries in the London market.

BRITAIN'S DENATIONALIZATION PROGRAM

Even before it introduced competition to the London securities markets, the Thatcher government had begun to attack inefficiency in other sectors of the British economy by denationalizing state-owned enterprises. In 1979, when the denationalization program was initiated, Britain's public corporations accounted for 10% of the country's GDP and 15% of total investment, and spanned industries as diverse as telecommunications, oil and gas, automobiles, airlines, and aerospace. The Conservative government believed that returning these companies to private ownership would revitalize Britain's economy by promoting competition and increasing individuals' participation in the British capital markets. Early in October 1984 John Moore, Financial Secretary to Britain's Treasury, declared that

> Our aim is to build upon our property-owning democracy and to establish a people's capital market, to bring capitalism to the place of work, ...and even to the home.[4]

In addition to fostering capitalist incentives among Britain's work force, the government hoped that broad individual ownership of the shares of denationalized companies would make it politically infeasible for the Labour Party ever to renationalize the companies privatized under the Thatcher program. The government planned to complete 12 sales of state-owned companies by the end of 1984, netting proceeds estimated at £7 billion.

The development of a retail equity market in the U.K. was considered essential to the successful placement of the billions of shares in public corporations scheduled to be offered on the London exchange from 1984 through 1987 (see Exhibit 12.1H). However, the government's efforts to create "capitalists out of commoners" ran counter to a trend toward institutional domination of equity markets throughout the world (see Exhibit 12.1I). Individual share ownership was particularly rare in Britain, where only 2% of the population owned equity securities in 1984. Since the 1960s, capital had been channeled to the U.K. equity market principally through tax-advantaged institutions, including pension funds, banks, unit trusts, and insurance companies. As a result, the percentage of United Kingdom equity held by individuals had declined from a level of 54% in 1960 to 25% in 1984.

THE BRITISH TELECOMMUNICATIONS IPO

The British Telecommunications IPO was the largest offering of equity ever brought to market in London, with proceeds exceeding the total value of all pre-

---

[4] "Privatization: Everybody's Doing It, Differently," *The Economist*, December 21, 1985, p. 85.

vious sales of public assets under the government's denationalization program. Because the market value of the BT offering represented 20% of the total 1984 investment budgets of London institutions, a number of unusual measures were taken to generate retail demand for BT shares.

The offering was structured as an installment sale to provide free financing to investors in BT and to prevent major disruptions in capital flows on the offering date, when institutions were expected to liquidate existing shareholdings and individuals to withdraw savings deposits in order to invest in BT. Because the offering totaled twice the £2 billion average annual new issue volume on the London exchange, installment dates spanning three calendar years were chosen: December 3, 1984, June 21, 1985, and April 8, 1986.

Prior to the British Telecommunications offering, little effort had been made to market public equity issues to retail investors in the U.K. On the announcement date for a typical British offering, the issuer disclosed the price at which a specific number of shares were offered for sale and published a prospectus describing the offering in at least two London newspapers. The offer for sale was then held open for a period of three to seven days, during which investors mailed applications for shares to the underwriters of the issue. Because no selling commissions were paid on primary equity issues, there was little direct selling by stockbrokers to retail investors.

In contrast to this relatively passive distribution process, the government embarked on a £10 million publicity campaign in June 1984 to generate retail interest in the British Telecommunications offering. Publicity for the offering included extensive television and newspaper coverage, direct mailings to 1.3 million potential investors, and two nationwide road shows conducted from specially-chartered trains.

In order to compensate for the lack of a national retail brokerage system, Kleinwort, Benson divided the U.K. into eighteen territories and appointed the strongest local broker in each region to market the offering. Selling commissions of approximately 2% were paid to brokers and banks handling individuals' applications for shares. An opinion polling firm was used to develop rough estimates of retail demand for BT shares in advance of the offering.

In addition to this marketing program, the government designed special incentives to enhance returns to individual investors in BT stock. Investors were offered a loyalty bonus of one share for every ten shares held continuously through November 30, 1987 (up to a maximum of 400 bonus shares) or, alternatively, bill vouchers against future BT telephone bills valued at £18 each (up to a maximum of 12 vouchers per investor). Each BT employee and pensioner was offered 54 ordinary shares free of charge, as well as discounts on additional purchases of BT shares.

Despite these measures, the London investment community was skeptical that the entire offering could be place in the U.K. As a result, the British underwriters advised the government to lay the groundwork for a simultaneous offering of shares in several foreign markets. Kleinwort, Benson initially estimated distribution of the offering as follows: U.K. institutions, 45%; U.K. individuals, 30%; BT employees, 5%; U.S., 9%; Japan, 9%; Canada, 2%. The U.S. and Canadian allotments were to be sold in the form of ADRs, each evidencing ownership of ten BT shares. BT ordinary shares were to be listed on the London exchange, and BT ADRs were to be listed on the New York and Toronto exchanges.

COORDINATING A MULTIMARKET OFFERING

Although the vast majority of the BT shares were to be placed in the U.K., flotation of a multi-market offering required that the terms of the offering conform to the underwriting conventions and regulatory restrictions of the U.S., Japan, and Canada. Morgan Stanley had begun working with Kleinwort, Benson as early as May to determine how best to reconcile the substantial differences in U.S. and U.K. underwriting practices.

Public issues of equity on the London market were usually structured as fixed price offerings. Because the LSE's single-capacity system separated underwriters from brokers and jobbers, new issues were priced with little prior knowledge of demand for an offering. Underwriters typically limited their risk by arranging through stockbrokers to have the majority of an issue sub-underwritten by institutional investors who were natural holders of the shares being issued. In return for agreeing to sub-underwrite shares at the fixed offering price, institutions were compensated with a portion of the underwriting spread.

Because the press was allowed to comment on an offering during the application period, a consensus of opinion regarding the pricing of an offering was usually formed before the close of applications. Because the tone of the publicity surrounding an offering had a significant influence on investor demand, most fixed price offerings were substantially over- or under-subscribed. In the event of an over-subscription, the issuer was responsible for allocating shares among competing applications.

The fixed price offering structure contrasted sharply with U.S. underwriting practices. In the U.S., an issuer first filed a preliminary prospectus (or "red herring") describing the offering and indicating a preliminary pricing range with the Securities and Exchange Commission (SEC). Over the subsequent 4-6 weeks, the SEC reviewed and commented on the prospectus while the underwriters circulated the red herring and marketed the offering to institutions and brokers via a "road show." SEC regulations strictly prohibited any additional pre-offering publicity. During this marketing period the underwriters solicited indications of interest (nonbinding commitments to purchase shares at a price) from investors. Based on this "book" of indications, the issue was priced after the market's close on the business day preceding the offering date. The following morning the underwriting agreements were signed, the prospectus was declared "effective" by the SEC, and the offering was made to the public. Trading in the shares commenced immediately.

It should be noted that U.K. issuers had the option of issuing shares in a minimum bid tender offer, which closely resembled a U.S. underwriting. In a tender offer, applicants for shares indicated a bid price as well as the number of shares they wished to purchase on their applications. The entire offering was underwritten at the minimum bid price. At the close of the application period, the offering price was fixed at the level necessary to fully subscribe the issue.

Although a minimum bid tender offer would have ensured efficient pricing of the BT shares, Kleinwort, Benson had advised the government that such a structure would discourage retail interest. It was expected that retail investors inexperienced with equity investments would feel uncomfortable valuing the stock, and that the reduced probability of an immediate price rise in the aftermarket would discourage applications from "stags," or speculators. Because a strong aftermarket performance of the BT shares was critical to the success of future offerings of state-owned assets, it was decided to offer BT shares at a fixed price.

Such British practices as pricing shares before soliciting bids from investors, providing investors with profit forecasts in offering prospectuses, and advertising issues during the application period conflicted with U.S. and Japanese underwriting practices and securities regulations. In order to overcome these differences, the several underwriters agreed to prepare preliminary "pathfinder" prospectuses to be circulated in all four markets before final pricing of the issue on November 16. The U.S. road show was shortened to ten days to match the more abbreviated U.K. offering schedule (see Exhibit 12.1j). The U.S. Securities and Exchange Commission and the Japanese Ministry of Finance agreed to allow profit forecasts to be included in the BT prospectuses, so that nearly identical documents could be circulated in all four markets. Finally, special care was taken to restrict pre-offering publicity to the U.K. market. For example, Kleinwort, Benson agreed not to place ads for the offering in the Frankfort edition of the *Financial Times,* which was widely read in the United States.

The British underwriters arranged for the entire U.K. offering to be sub-underwritten by British institutions. Unlike most sub-underwriting agreements, the BT agreement guaranteed that the sub-underwriters would be allotted 55% of the shares they underwrote.[5] Trading in BT shares was scheduled to commence at the opening of the New York exchange on December 3. Upon issuance, BT was to be included in the Financial Times Actuaries All-Share index, a market capitalization-weighted index of LSE stocks which served as the standard of investment performance in the U.K. At the offering price, BT represented 4.5% of the value of the FT index.

The terms of the underwriting agreements between the overseas underwriters and the U.K. government provided for the overseas allotment to be underwritten by the Bank of England from November 16 (Impact Day), when the offering was priced, until December 2 (Allotment Day), when the final allotment of shares among applicants was to be announced. This process deferred the determination of the size of the overseas allotment until after U.K. applications for shares had been received. It was hoped that uncertainty about the size of applicants' allotments would limit unauthorized "grey market" trading in BT shares during the application period.

---

[5] Sub-underwriters interested in purchasing shares in a public offering typically applied for shares alongside other investors during the application period. If the offering proved unsuccessful, the sub-underwriters would reduce (or withdraw) their applications, since a portion of the shares they had underwritten would be left unsold.

As she waited for Richard Merley to return her call, Kathy Ellis recalled the numerous structuring decisions the underwriters had considered over the past seven months. Among the questions which had arisen was how to allocate the offering price among the three installment payments. Because the U.K. government was less concerned with the timing of its receipt of proceeds than with maximizing demand for the offering, government officials had suggested that the payments be back-end loaded to provide maximal credit to investors. In response, the underwriters had noted that although investors in BT were legally obligated to pay the 1985 and 1986 installments, enforcement of this obligation would be impossible given the number and geographic dispersion of BT's shareholders. Thus, for practical purposes it had to be assumed that investors could default on future installment payments. After considering the risk of default under alternative structures, it was agreed that the offering price would be distributed among the three installments in the proportions 40%, 30%, and 30%.

This installment structure presented regulatory problems in the U.S., where the Federal Reserve's margin regulation ("Reg T") limited leverage on stock purchases to 50% of a stock's price. Morgan Stanley had applied for and received a special exemption from the Federal Reserve Board to allow for an installment sale of BT ADRs in the U.S. market. The Fed and SEC had ruled that U.S. investors in BT would be allowed to margin each of the BT installment payments up to 50%.

Another issue of concern to the U.S. underwriters was overseas investors' foreign exchange exposure on the BT installment payments.

Although the total offering price was to be fixed in British pence on November 16, the overseas installments were to be priced at the exchange rates prevailing on each of the three installment payment dates. As a result, overseas investors would be exposed to fluctuations in the value of their home currency relative to the £-Sterling over the 17-month installment payment period. While large institutional investors in the U.S. would have access to forward and futures markets to hedge this exchange risk, retail investors were likely to invest in amounts smaller than the £25,000 minimum denomination of a £-Sterling futures contract. Kathy had been responsible for devising a hedging mechanism to be offered to small investors unable to access the forward/futures markets.

In October, Richard had informed Kathy that British Telecom intended to pay an annual dividend of 9.3 pence per share, to be paid 40% in February, 60% in September each year. A single dividend of 5.6 pence was to be paid in August 1985. Because holders of partly-paid BT shares were to receive full voting and dividend rights during the installment period, the yield on BT shares was to be particularly rich during the first fifteen months of trading (see Exhibit 12.1M). Kleinwort, Benson and Morgan Stanley had analyzed the effect this dividend policy was likely to have on the pricing of BT shares.

The most significant disagreement among the underwriters arose during discussions of the pricing of the BT issue. In a preliminary pricing meeting in October, Kleinwort, Benson had argued that BT should be priced relative to dividend yields and price-earnings ratios of comparable U.K. companies.

BT's principal business was the provision of local, national, and international telecommunications services in the United Kingdom. BT was a major supplier of telephone apparatus for rent or purchase, and provided a range of other services, including telex, radiophone, data communications, and information services. BT enjoyed a monopoly on local telephone service and a near monopoly on its long distance service. In addition, the terms of BT's government license (effective 8/6/84 through 7/31/89) severely restricted competition in the U.K. long distance market through the end of the decade. However, BT was to be subject to price controls on local telephone services. Price increases on BT's services were to be limited to a rate equal to the British Retail Price Index (RPI) less 3%. Unlike the rate-of-return ceilings imposed on comparable U.S. utilities, the RPI-3 price controls would allow BT to pass cost savings through to its shareholders. Analysts at de Zoete & Bevan, a London brokerage firm, expected BT's pre-tax earnings to grow at an annual rate of 11% through 1989.

Disagreement over the pricing of the multi-market BT offering stemmed, in part, from differences in investors' perceptions of BT's business prospects. While BT was being touted as a high-tech telecommunications company with growth potential in the U.K., Morgan Stanley believed U.S. investors would value BT as a regulated utility. Kleinwort, Benson proposed a pricing range of 120-140 pence per share, implying a range of multiples of 10.2-11.9x BT's estimated fiscal 1985 (U.S. GAAP) earnings of 11.8 pence per share. Richard Merley argued persuasively for a price at the high end of the range, noting that Cable and Wireless, a recently denationalized British telecommunications company, was trading at a P/E of 14.5x in early October.

Since Morgan Stanley was to market the BT offering in the U.S., Kathy Ellis had analyzed the yields and P/Es of comparable U.S. telecommunications companies (see Exhibit 12.1L). Telecommunications monopolies, such as the post-divestiture regional holding companies of AT&T, were trading at multiples of 8-10x, and carried yields of approximately 8% as of September 1984.

Given the small size of the overseas allotment, Kleinwort, Benson had little patience for Morgan Stanley's attempts to influence the pricing of the offering. Richard had informed Kathy that Nomura Securities, which was underwriting the Japanese offering, had expressed confidence that it could underwrite up to 10% of the offering at any price Kleinwort, Benson considered appropriate. At the time, Kathy had wondered how Nomura could be so confident in its ability to place the BT shares.

On November 16 the BT offering was priced at 130 pence per share. As a result of a slight decline in interest rates during the application period and greater than anticipated retail interest in BT, the U.K. offering was five times oversubscribed. The government responded to the excess of U.K. applications by reducing the overseas allotment to 14% of the offering (from an original level of 20%) and selecting a share allocation rule in the U.K. which severely prejudiced large applications:

Size of Application	Number of Shares Allotted
200-400 shares	100% of application
800	500 shares
1,200	600
1,600-100,000	800
>100,000	0

Kathy Ellis was aware that reactions to the oversubscription varied widely. While the British government had called the offering a "roaring success," the Labour Party opposition was accusing the government of "presiding over the biggest giveaway in British commercial history."[6] In light of this controversy, Kathy was anxious to discuss the offering, and its implications for future multi-market offerings, with her colleagues at Kleinwort, Benson.

---

[6] "BT Stock Sale an Overwhelming Success," *Telephony,* December 24, 1984, p. 20

■ EXHIBIT 12.1A

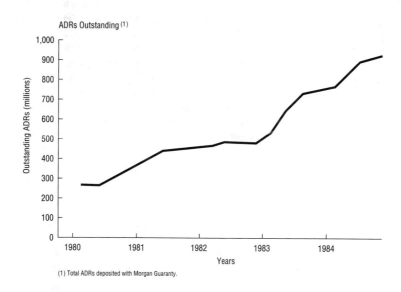

ADRs Outstanding (1)

(1) Total ADRs deposited with Morgan Guaranty.

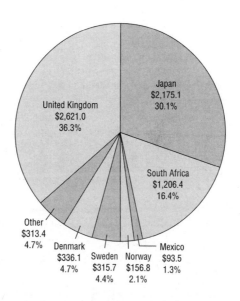

SOURCE: Morgan Stanley International.

EXHIBIT 12.1B

BRITISH TELECOMMUNICATIONS
TRADING/ISSUANCE OF FOREIGN EQUITIES IN THE U.S.: 1/1/80–6/1/84
($ MILLIONS)

	1980	1981	1982	1983	6 Months 1984
U.S. Investor Trades in Foreign Stocks[a]	$18,000	$19,000	$16,000	$30,500	$14,750
U.S. Equity Offerings by Foreign Issuers[a]	670	510	270	1,200	500

[a] Includes trades/offerings of ADRs.

SOURCES: *Wall Street Journal* and *Business Week*.

EXHIBIT 12.1C

BRITISH TELECOMMUNICATIONS
COMPARISON OF INTERNATIONAL EQUITY MARKETS
(OCTOBER 1, 1984)

Market	Total Market Capitalization ($ billions)	Annual Trading Volume ($ billions)	Average	
			P/E	Dividend Yield
United States (NYSE)	$1,588	$ 756	10.0x	4.7%
Japan (TSE)	538	267	24.8	1.2
United Kingdom (LSE)	208	48	10.5	4.8
Canada (All Exchanges)	122	25	19.7	3.5
MEMO: World Total (All Major Stock Exchanges)	$2,868	$1,188	11.8x	3.9%

SOURCE: Capital International Perspective.

■ EXHIBIT 12.1D

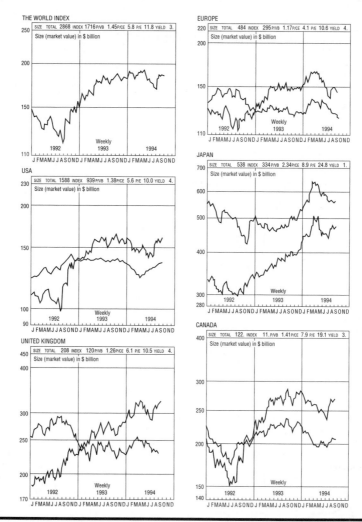

KEY:
/\/\/\ Bars represent weekly high, low, and close of index values.
—— Curve represents index relative to World Index, adjusted for exchange gains or losses relative to the U.S. dollar. Whenever the "relative to the world" curve moves upward, the national index is outperforming the World Index.
P/BV: Ratio of average price to book value.
P/E: Ratio of average price to earnings.
P/CE: Ratio of average price to cash flow.
Yield: Average dividend yield.

[1] The World and Europe Indices take into account foreign exchange fluctuations of the relevant currencies relative to the U.S. dollar.

SOURCE: Capital International Perspective.

■ **EXHIBIT 12.1E**

YEN/DOLLAR
SPOT EXCHANGE RATE

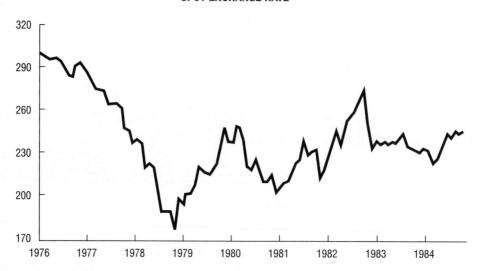

STERLING/DOLLAR
SPOT EXCHANGE RATE

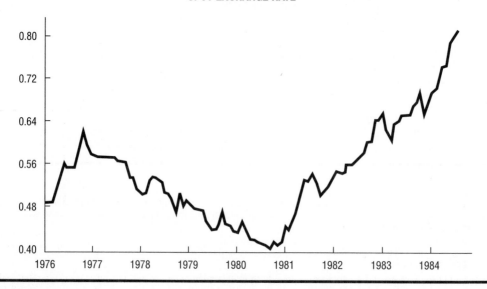

SOURCE: Alan Greenhorn, ed., *Financial Times Foreign Exchange Yearbook*, Financial Times Business Information Ltd., London, 1985, pp. 18–19.

■ CHANGES IN STOCK MARKET INDICES AND EXCHANGE RATES

BRITISH TELECOMMUNICATIONS
1982–1983

The following charts measure annual changes in the values of stock market indices and currencies. National stock market performance is measured in local currency and is based on the country's Capital International stock market index.

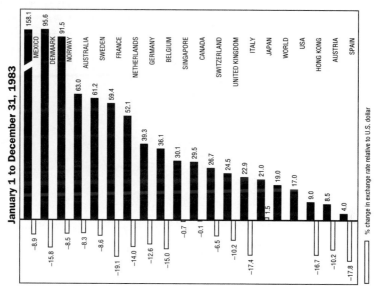

January 1 to December 31, 1983

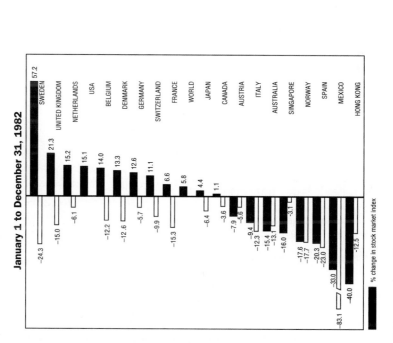

January 1 to December 31, 1982

[a] The World Index is an arithmetic weighted average of the performances of some 1,100 securities listed on the stock exchanges of the above 19 countries and expressed in U.S. dollars.

SOURCE: Capital International Perspective.

■ EXHIBIT 12.1G

BRITISH TELECOMMUNICATIONS
■ **INTEREST RATES AND EQUITY YIELDS**
(1978–1984)

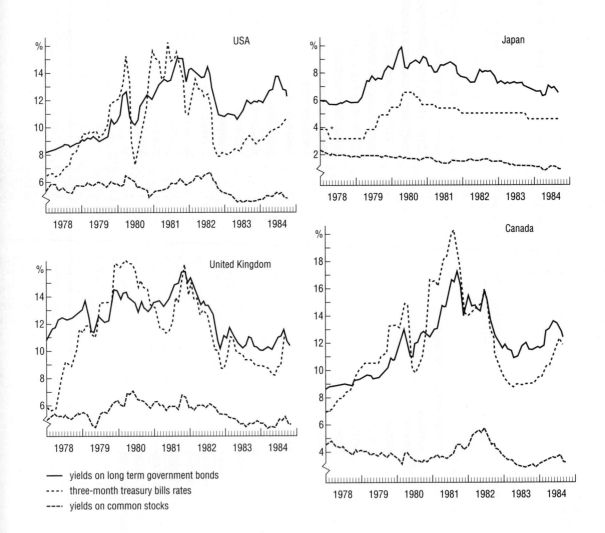

——— yields on long term government bonds
- - - - three-month treasury bills rates
— - — yields on common stocks

*Three-month treasury bill rates not available for Japan. Figures shown are two-month government securities yields.

Note: Yields on common stocks are based on the companies included in the Capital International stock market indices. Sources for government bonds and treasury bill rates are national sources, usually statistical bulletins of national banks.

SOURCE: Capital International Perspective.

■ **EXHIBIT 12.1H**

BRITISH TELECOMMUNICATIONS
■ PRIVATIZATION IN BRITAIN: 1981–1987

Completed Sales (1981–1984):

Company	Business	Date of Sale	Means of Sale	Net Proceeds (£ millions)
British Aerospace	Aerospace	2/81	Offer 51.6%	£ 43
Cable & Wireless	Telecommunications	10/81	Offer 49.4%	182
		12/83	Tender 27.9%	263
Amersham International	Radio Chemicals	2/82	Offer 100%	64
National Freight Co.	Road Haulage	2/82	Management buyout	5
Britoil	Oil	11/82	Tender 51%	627
Associated British Ports	Seaports	2/83	Offer 51.5%	46
		4/84	Tender 48.5%	51
International Aeradio	Aviation Communications	3/83	Private Sale	60
BR Hotels	Hotels	3/83	Private Sale	51
British Gas Onshore Oil	Oil	5/84	Private Sale	82
Enterprise Oil	Oil	6/84	Tender 100%	380
Sealink	Ferries	7/84	Private Sale	66
Jaguar	Cars	7/84	Offer 100%	297
British Technology Group and Others	Miscellaneous	—	Private Sales and Placings	716
Total				£3,044

Planned (1984–1987):

Company		Estimated Proceeds (£ millions)
British Telecommunications		£ 3,000–4,000
British Aerospace (remaining 48.4%)	⎫	346
Britoil (remaining 48.9%)	⎬ 1985	425
Cable & Wireless (remaining 22.7%)	⎭	640
British Airways	⎫	800–1,000
Royal Ordinance		200
National Bus	⎬ 1986	200
British Airports		350–500
British Gas	⎭	6,000–8,000
Rolls-Royce Aero Engines	⎫	300
Short Brothers	⎬ 1987	100
Thames Water		500
Other Water Authorities	⎭	500
Total		£13,361–16,711

SOURCE: *The Economist*, November 16, 1985, p. 102, and December 21, 1985, p. 86.

■ EXHIBIT 12.1I

BRITISH TELECOMMUNICATIONS
■ PARTICIPATION OF INDIVIDUAL INVESTORS IN
MAJOR EQUITY MARKETS, 1984

Country	Individual Shareholders		Individual Holdings as % of Total MV	Individual Trades as % of Total Volume
	Number	% of Population		
United States	41.0 million	20%	60%	12%
Japan	19.6 million	17	30	60
United Kingdom	1.4 million	2	25	NA

SOURCES: *The Economist* and *Barron's*.

■ EXHIBIT 12.1J

BRITISH TELECOMMUNICATIONS
■ SUMMARY TIME SCHEDULE FOR THE BRITISH
TELECOMMUNICATIONS OFFERING

Date	Event
Monday, October 26, 1984	Filing of preliminary prospectuses.
Monday, November 5– Tuesday, November 13	U.S. Road Show: Institutional and dealer meetings in selected cities across the U.S.
Friday, November 16	Announcement of initial public offering price per Ordinary Share in the U.K. offering and the commencement of the U.K. application period.
Week of November 26	U.S. underwriters make firm commitment as to the number of shares they will underwrite.
Wednesday, November 28	Last day applications are accepted in the U.K. offering.
Saturday, December 1	Announcement of the basis of share allotments in the U.K. offering.
Monday, December 3	Announcement of the U.S. dollar price of the initial installment of the ADRs and the commencement of trading in the U.S. and the U.K.
Monday, December 10	Closing. Payment for the initial installment and delivery of the ADRs in interim form.
Friday, June 21, 1985	Payment due on the second ADR installment.
Tuesday, April 8, 1986	Payment due on the final ADR installment.

SOURCE: Morgan Stanley & Co.

BRITISH TELECOMMUNICATIONS
■ SELECTED FINANCIAL DATA

The financial statements for the three months ended June 30, 1983 and 1984 are unaudited. In the opinion of the Board, they have been prepared on a basis consistent with annual reporting principles and contain all adjustments (consisting of only normally recurring adjustments) necessary to present fairly the financial position as of such dates, and the results of operations for such periods, of British Telecom.

Pro Forma Information (a)
(in millions, except per share amounts)

	Year ended March 31		Three months ended June 30	
	1984	1984(b)	1984	1984(b)
Income Statement Data			(unaudited)	
Amounts in accordance with UK GAAP:				
Net operating income	£ 1,534	$ 1,841	£ 453	$ 543
Income before taxes	1,151	1,381	358	430
Taxes on income	—	—	129	155
Net income	1,151	1,381	229	275
Net income attributable to Ordinary Shareholders	1,088	1,305	213	256
Earnings per Ordinary Share(a)	18.1p	$ 0.22	3.6p	$ 0.04
Earnings per ADS(a)	181.3p	$ 2.18	35.5p	$ 0.43
Amounts in accordance with US and Canadian GAAP(c):				
Net operating income	£ 1,529	$ 1,835	£ 450	$ 540
Income before taxes	1,237	1,484	379	455
Deferred taxes	579	694	183	220
Net income	658	790	196	235
Net income attributable to Ordinary Shareholders	595	714	180	216
Earnings per Ordinary Share(a)	9.9p	$ 0.12	3.0p	$ 0.04
Earnings per ADS(a)	99.2p	$ 1.19	30.0p	$ 0.36

	At March 31		At June 30	
	1984	1984(b)	1984	1984(b)
Balance Sheet Data			(unaudited)	
Amounts in accordance with UK GAAP:				
Property plant and equipment, net	£ 8,725	$10,470	£ 8,922	$10,706
Total assets	11,300	13,560	11,725	14,070
Total long-term liabilities(a)	3,167	3,800	3,153	3,784
Preference Shares	750	900	750	900
Retained earnings(a)	3,740	4,488	3,944	4,733
Ordinary Shareholders' equity (d)	5,240	6,288	5,444	6,533
Amounts in accordance with US and Canadian GAAP (c):				
Retained earnings(a)	£ 856	$ 1,027	£ 1,033	$ 1,240
Ordinary Shareholders' equity(d)	2,356	2,827	2,533	3,040

See accompanying footnotes.

continued on next page

■ **EXHIBIT 12.1K**

(CONTINUED)

Historical Information
(in millions, except per share amounts)

Income Statement Data	Year ended March 31						Three months ended June 30		
	1980	1981	1982	1983	1984	1984(b)	1983	1984	1984(b)
Amounts in accordance with UK GAAP:						(unaudited)			
Operating revenues									
Rentals	£ 1,129	£ 1,531	£ 1,993	£ 2,276	£ 2,334	£ 2,801	£ 585	£ 613	$ 736
Calls: telephone	2,192	2,691	3,301	3,433	3,697	4,436	880	976	1,171
telex and other	200	233	276	299	292	350	61	81	97
Sales and other operating revenues	80	115	193	406	553	664	109	142	170
Total operating revenues	3,601	4,570	5,763	6,414	6,876	8,251	1,635	1,812	2,174
Operating expenses									
Payroll costs	1,609	2,110	2,394	2,571	2,715	3,258	660	678	813
Depreciation	410	475	647	765	907	1,088	217	214	257
Other operating expenses	928	1,154	1,538	1,826	2,036	2,443	485	538	646
Less: own work capitalized	(200)	(283)	(308)	(328)	(316)	(379)	(82)	(71)	(85)
Total operating expenses	2,747	3,456	4,271	4,834	5,342	6,410	1,280	1,359	1,631
Net operating income	854	1,114	1,492	1,580	1,534	1,841	355	453	543
Net interest expense	537	544	556	549	544	653	138	134	161
Income before taxes and extraordinary items	317	570	936	1,031	990	1,188	217	319	382
Taxes on income	—	—	—	—	—	—	—	115	138
Extraordinary items	107	—	—	—	—	—	—	—	—
Net income (operating income after interest, taxation and extraordinary items)	£ 424	£ 570	£ 936	£ 1,031	£ 990	$ 1,188	£ 217	£ 204	$ 244
Amounts in accordance with US and Canadian GAAP(c):									
Income before taxes and extraordinary items	£ 317	£ 622	£ 1,010	£ 1,118	£ 1,076	$ 1,291	£ 239	£ 340	$ 407
Deferred taxes	133	325	499	576	495	594	110	163	195
Net income (operating income after interest, taxation and extraordinary items)(f)	281	297	511	542	581	697	129	177	212

Balance Sheet Data	At March 31				At June 30		
	1982	1983	1984	1984(b)	1983	1984	1984(b)
Amounts in accordance with UK GAAP:						(unaudited)	
Property, plant and equipment, net	£ 7,367	£ 8,119	£ 8,725	$10,470	£ 8,290	£ 8,922	$10,706
Total assets	9,016	10,248	11,300	13,560	10,567	11,725	14,070
Total long-term liabilities(e)	3,478	3,412	3,251	3,901	3,398	3,237	3,885
Retained earnings	2,679	3,710	4,700	5,640	3,927	4,904	5,885
Amounts in accordance with US and Canadian GAAP(c):							
Retained earnings	£ 693	£ 1,235	£ 1,816	$ 2,179	£ 1,364	£ 1,993	$ 2,392

(a) As a statutory corporation, the company's predecessor corporation was not financed by share capital. Pro forma earnings per share for the year ended March 31, 1984 have been calculated by reference to the share capital of the company and to net income for the year ended March 31, 1984, assuming that the adjusted capital structure of the company following the Combined Offering had been in effect throughout that year. Pro forma earnings per share for the three months ended June 30, 1984 have been calculated by reference to the share capital of the company and to net income for the three months ended June 30, 1984 assuming that the adjusted capital structure of the company following the Combined Offering had been in effect from April 1, 1984. Adjustments made comprise, in respect of the income statement, adjustments to the interest expense and preference dividend and, in respect of the balance sheet, adjustments to the long-term and current liabilities, share capital and retained earnings. These adjustments have been made to illustrate the impact of the issue of share capital.

(b) Translated at $1.20 to £1.00, the Noon Buying Rate on October 16, 1984.

(c) The principal difference between amounts shown in accordance with UK GAAP and those shown in accordance with U.S. and Canadian GAAP arises from the calculation of deferred income taxes. In the United Kingdom provision is made only for deferred taxation which is considered likely to become payable within the foreseeable future, whereas, under U.S. and Canadian GAAP, full provision for deferred taxation is required. No charge for deferred taxation was required in the five years ended March 31, 1984 under the application of U.K. GAAP, but a charge for deferred taxes of £115 million was required in the three months ended June 30, 1984.

(d) Ordinary Shareholders' equity represents the sum of Ordinary Shares and retained earnings.

(e) A liability of the company's predecessor corporation at March 31, 1984 under a deed of covenant to pension fund trustees was not transferred to the company and is not included in the total of liabilities for the purposes of this summary.

(f) Net income under U.S. and Canadian GAAP for the year ended March 31, 1980 includes extraordinary items of £97 million (after deducting deferred taxes of £10 million).

▪ EXHIBIT 12.1L

	Post-Divestiture AT&T[a]	BellSouth	Bell Atlantic	Ameritech	NYNEX	GTE
Market Valuation[f,g]	$ 19,381	$ 9,455	$ 7,458	$ 7,210	$ 7,018	$ 7,986
P/E: 1984-High	14.0x	8.3x	7.9x	6.9x	7.4	8.8
1984-Low	7.7	7.2	6.6	5.9	6.2	7.0
1984-Close[f,g]	13.7	8.3	7.9	6.9	7.4	7.7
Yield: 1984-High	7.7%	9.5%	9.8%	9.5%	10.2%	8.4%
1984-Low	6.1	8.0	8.4	8.1	8.5	6.9
1984-Close[f,g]	6.3	8.1	8.4	8.1	8.5	7.6
Market Value as a % of Book Value[f,g,h]	147.5	105.6	102.9	103.8	93.8	104.5
Operating Results[j]						
Revenues[k]	$33,533.2	$10,035.1	$7,962.2	$8,736.9	$9,834.2	$13,927.9
Five Year-CGR[l]	NA	11.3%	10.2%	9.2%	10.0%	7.4%
Net Income[k]	$ 1,364.8	$ 1,232.3	$ 964.2	$1,055.8	$ 938.0	$ 992.4
Five-Year-CGR[l]	NM	11.1%	7.4%	7.9%	7.0%	12.0%
Earnings Per Share	$ 1.40	$ 3.90	$ 9.94	$ 10.76	$ 9.52	$ 4.82
Projected EPS Growth[m]	NA	5.4%	5.1%	4.4%	4.0%	10.4%
Net Margin[k]	4.1%	12.3%	12.1%	12.1%	9.5%	7.1%
Cash Flow[k]	NM	NM	NM	NM	NM	3,142.7
Five Year-CGR	NM	NM	NM	NM	NM	9.6%
Dividend Payout:						
1981	NM	NM	NM	NM	NM	64.4
1982	NM	NM	NM	NM	NM	61.3
1983	NM	NM	NM	NM	NM	57.6
1984[n]	85.7%	66.7%	64.4%	55.8%	63.0%	62.2%
Dividend Growth (Five-Year CGR)	NM	NA	NA	NA	NA	3.2%
Credit Statistics[o]						
Long-term Debt/Book Capitalization[p]	40.4%	42.0%	39.4%	41.0%	42.1%	55.4%
Total Debt/Adjusted Book Capitalization[p]	45.5	43.9	40.6	42.0	44.1	57.6
Cash Flow/Long-term Debt[q]	NA	54.7%	56.6%	54.6%	48.7%	35.7%
Cash Flow/Total Debt[q]	NA	51.2	51.2	52.7	40.5	32.6
Pretax Fixed Charge Coverage	8.3x	4.3x	4.5x	4.7x	3.5x	3.9x
Pretax Return on Average Total Assets	NA	13.3%	12.4%	12.9%	11.9%	10.4%
Return on Average Shareholders' Equity	15.9[s]	13.4	12.4	13.2	12.2	15.0
Internal Cash Flow/Capital Expenditures[q]	NA	104.0	91.9	105.4	88.2	93.9
Senior Debt Rating (Moody's/S&P)	Aa1/AA	A1/AA+[t]	A3/AA−[t]	A3/AA[t]	AA3/AA[u]	Baa2/A−[t]

Notes:

[a] Financial information for post-divesture AT&T is for the 1984 year as projected in the AT&T Information Statement and Prospectus of November 8, 1983 (unless where noted).

[b] All reported figures translated to U.S.$ at $1.24 Canadian/U.S. dollar, the official Federal Reserve exchange rate on December 30, 1983 (unless where noted)

[c] Based on year ended March 31, 1984.

[d] All financial information based on year-end figures as of March 31, 1984 (no annualized latest 12-month figures available; thus, footnotes pertaining to latest 12-month data are not relevant to British Telecom).

[e] All British Telecom financials are translated into U.S. dollars using the Federal Noon Buying Rate as published by the Federal Reserve Bank of New York for October 15, 1984 at £1 = $1.2095.

[f] Based on closing prices as of September 14, 1984.

[g] Shares data as reported in the 10-Q for period ending June 30, 1984.

[h] Book value as reported in the 10-Q for period ending June 30, 1984.

[i] All figures reported in the 10-Q for the period ending June 30, 1984 are translated to U.S.$ at $1.31 Canadian/U.S. dollar, the official Federal Reserve exchange rate on August 3, 1984.

BRITISH TELECOMMUNICATIONS
■ **SUMMARY COMPARISON OF SELECTED TELECOMMUNICATIONS COMPANIES AS OF SEPTEMBER 14, 1984 ($ IN MILLIONS)**

Bell Canada[b]	MCI Communications[c]	United Telecommunications	Continental Telecom	Southern New England Telephone	Pacific Telecom Inc.	Cincinnati Bell	British Telecom[n,r]
$4,816	$1,771	$1,723	$1,422	$ 999	$ 468	$ 307	NA
9.7x	43.3x	9.9x	9.1	8.7x	15.2x	7.4x	NA
7.9	16.0x	7.5	7.1	6.7	7.5	6.2	NA
8.7[i]	20.3	8.9	7.9x	8.2	9.1	6.5	NA
7.4%	0.0%	10.5%	9.4%	9.4%	7.6%	8.3%	NA
6.1	0.0	8.3	7.2	7.3	3.6	7.0	NA
6.7[i]	0.0	9.9	8.5	7.8	6.4	7.9	NA
114.51	151.1	103.2	114.8	114.6	116.1	86.0	NA
$7.005.9[i]	$1,929.1	$2.702.9	$2,186.2	$1,229.4	$ 393.1	$ 437.2	$8,316.5
13.0%	86.5%	9.3%	17.3%	12.9%	18.0%	9.7%	17.7%
$ 610.2[i]	$ 86.8	$ 197.0	$ 184.5	$ 121.4	$ 49.9	$ 49.5	$ 702.7
15.8%	143.9%	6.6%	10.8%	13.2%	27.4%	4.5%	22.8%
$ 2.85	$ 0.36	$ 2.17	$ 2.55	$ 4.14	$ 1.33	$ 5.64	NA
0.0%	4.7%	11.6%	12.1%	6.0%	14.1%	8.5%	NA
0.7%	4.5%	7.3%	8.4%	9.9%	12.7%	11.3%	8.5%
579.8	$ 424.2	$ 691.7	$ 596.5	$ 297.4	$ 137.7	$ 128.7	$2,495.2
11.4%	115.1%	7.7%	12.4%	9.2%	46.9%	7.4%	NA
61.4	0.0	60.3	62.8	54.7	35.8	63.6	NM
63.6	0.0	69.1	67.2	76.5	34.0	63.7	NM
61.4	0.0	66.2	66.4	64.4	37.5	53.1	NM
57.9	0.0	84.8	65.1	63.0	55.6	51.8	NM
6.5	0.0	5.0	5.3	9.7	17.2	3.9	NM
45.9%	59.5%	52.1%	55.4%	39.9%	36.6%	37.5%	32.4%
48.7	60.2	52.8	57.6	40.7	42.2	39.6	34.6
42.0%	25.5%	38.8%	34.7	50.3	60.2	60.6	68.3
38.4	24.8	36.4	31.7	50.3	51.2	60.4	62.0
4.1x	2.1x	4.5x	3.3x	6.6x	6.7x	4.6x	3.4x
13.3%	13.6%	14.8%	10.8%	18.7%	17.1%	12.7%	13.5%
13.7	16.4	14.1	15.0	15.0	19.9	13.3	26.2
87.8	49.3	96.5	91.0	149.4	118.0	207.6	132.6
Aa2/AA	Baa3/BB+	Baa2/BBB+	Baa2/A−	Aa2/AA	NR	Aa2/AAA	NR

[j] Operating results based on latest 12-month calculated from June 30, 1984 10-Q.
[k] Annualized figures from latest 10-Q for period ending June 30, 1984.[l]Incorporates any historical restatement of revenues or earnings.
[m] Compound growth rate from 1983 to 1985 based on Institutional Brokers Estimate Service mean EPS estimates as of March 15, 1984.
[n] Dividend payout for 1984 based on 10-Q report EPS and dividends per share for period ending June 30, 1984.
[o] Credit statistics based on year ended December 31, 1983 (unless where noted).
[p] These statistics are calculated from the June 30, 1984 10-Q.
[q] Cash flow excludes AFDC, which is minimal in every case.
[r] Pretax interest coverage before federal taxes and after state and local taxes; does not include other fixed charges.
[s] Based on pro-forma shareholders' equity as of June 30, 1983.
[t] Has not been formally rated; the ratings shown here are hte lowest given to any former Bell Operating Company within the RMC.
[u] S&P rating is an actual preliminary rating though to date no issue has been offered.

CGR = Compound growth rate computed using the log-linear least squares method.

NA = Not available.   NM = Not meaningful.   NR = Not rated.

■ EXHIBIT 12.1M

BRITISH TELECOMMUNICATIONS
■ ANALYSIS OF INVESTOR RETURN BASED ON HYPOTHETICAL
7.0% YIELD AND A FLAT STOCK PRICE [a,b]

1984	Cash Flow
December	$(6.36)
1985	
January	0
February	0
March	0
April	0
May	0
June	$(4.77)
July	0
August	$ 0.67
September	0
October	0
November	0
December	0
1986	
January	0
February	$ 0.45
March	0
April	$(4.77)

Annual Yield Based on Holding Period from December 1984 to:	
August 1985:	13.67% plus
February 1986:	10.90% plus

[a] Assumes an ADS price of approximately $15.90, ($1.11 annual dividend per ADS and a 7.0% yield), implying initial, second and final installment prices of $6.36, $4.44, and $4.44 respectively.

[b] Dividend computed as follows: dividend as indicated in "Dividend Policy" section of the Preliminary Prospectus of 92.857 pence per ADS times the Noon Buying Rate on October 24, 1984 of $1.20 to £1.00.

SOURCE: Morgan Stanley & Co.

■ EXHIBIT 12.1N

BRITISH TELECOMMUNICATIONS
■ MONTHLY AVERAGE SPOT EXCHANGE RATES
(1980–1984)

DOLLAR/STERLING
MONTHLY AVERAGE SPOT EXCHANGE RATE

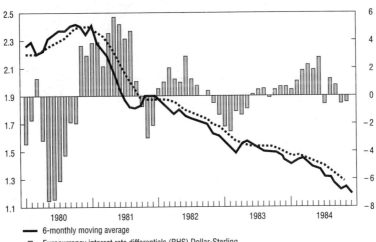

— 6-monthly moving average
▫ Eurocurrency interest rate differentials (RHS) Dollar-Sterling

YEN/STERLING
MONTHLY AVERAGE SPOT EXCHANGE RATE

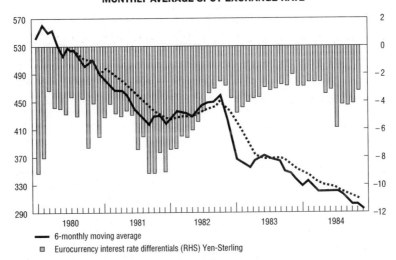

— 6-monthly moving average
▫ Eurocurrency interest rate differentials (RHS) Yen-Sterling

SOURCE: Alan Greenhorn, ed., *Financial Times Foreign Exchange Yearbook*. Financial Times Business Information Ltd., London, 1985, pp. 21-22.

■ EXHIBIT 12.10

BRITISH TELECOMMUNICATIONS
■ SELECTED SHORT-TERM INTEREST RATES
(OCTOBER 16, 1984)

	Yield		
Instrument	**3-Month**	**6-Month**	**One Year**
U.S. Domestic Certificates of Deposit	10.60%	10.80%	11.25%
Sterling Certificates of Deposit	10.50	10.38	10.38

SOURCES: *Financial Times* and *Wall Street Journal.*

13

KEY CONCEPTS

THE DIFFERENT SECTORS OF THE GLOBAL DEBT MARKET ▬

THE NATIONAL BOND MARKETS OF A COUNTRY ▬

THE EUROBOND MARKET ▬

THE DIFFERENT TYPES OF STRUCTURES IN THE
EUROBOND MARKET ▬

THE ALL-IN-COST OF FUNDS OF AN ISSUE, ITS
COMPUTATION, AND A COMPARISON WITH
ITS COST IN THE DOMESTIC AND
EUROBOND MARKETS ▬

EMBEDDED OPTIONS THAT MAY BE INCLUDED IN A
DEBT ISSUE ▬

VALUATION ISSUES WHEN A CORPORATION CONSIDERS
THE ISSUANCE OF A DEBT OBLIGATION
WITH EMBEDDED OPTIONS ▬

THE GENERAL FRAMEWORK FOR VALUING EUROBONDS ▬

INTRODUCTION

In the previous chapter, we explained the reasons that corporations raise funds outside their domestic market and focused on the global equity market. The global debt market can be divided into five sectors: (1) bond market, (2) medium-term note market, (3) commercial paper market, (4) note issuance facilities market, and (5) bank loan market.

Our focus in this chapter is on the global bond market and, in particular, the Eurobond sector of the global bond market. We review the various types of Eurobond structures; the complex bond structures available have features that grant either the issuer or bondholder, or both, some type of option. The general principles about assessing these options are discussed.

The Euromarket sector of the other four sectors of the global debt market is discussed in the next chapter. We begin this chapter with a review of the global bond market.

GLOBAL BOND MARKET

The global bond market consists of the various national bond markets (domestic bond markets and foreign bond markets throughout the world) and the *offshore bond*, or *Eurobond, market*.

FOREIGN BOND MARKET

The national bond market of a country consists of the domestic bond market and the foreign bond market. The largest national bond market in the world is the U.S. national bond market, followed by the Japanese national bond market.

The domestic market is where issuers domiciled in a country issue bonds and where those bonds are subsequently traded. A country's foreign bond market is where bonds of issuers not domiciled in the country are issued and subsequently traded. For example, in the United States, bonds are issued by non–U.S. entities and then subsequently traded on the U.S. foreign bond market. Bonds traded in the U.S. foreign bond market are called *Yankee bonds*.

In Japan, a yen-denominated bond issued by a British corporation and subsequently traded in Japan's bond market is part of the Japanese foreign bond market. Yen-denominated bonds issued by non–Japanese entities are called *Samurai bonds;* foreign bonds in the United Kingdom are known as *bulldog bonds;* in the Netherlands, *Rembrandt bonds;* and in Spain, *matador bonds*.

The rules governing the issuance of foreign bonds are imposed by regulatory authorities where the bond is issued. The regulations may impose (1) restrictions on the bond structures that may be issued (e.g., unsecured debt, zero-coupon bonds, convertible bonds), (2) restrictions on the minimum or maximum size of an issue and/or the frequency with which an issuer may come to market, (3) restrictions as to how long an issuer must wait to bring the issue to market (to avoid an oversupply of issues), (4) a minimum quality standard (credit rating) for the issue or issuer, (5) disclosure and periodic reporting requirements, and (6) restrictions on the types of financial institutions permitted to underwrite issues. The 1980s have been characterized by measures taken by governments to relax or abolish these restrictions so as to open up their bond market to issuers.

EUROBOND MARKET

In the previous chapter we described the Euromarket. The distinguishing features of the securities in this market are that (1) they are underwritten by an international syndicate, (2) at issuance they are offered simultaneously to investors in a number of countries, (3) they are issued outside the jurisdiction of any single country, and (4) they are in unregistered form.[1] The sector of the Euromarket in which bonds are traded is called the *Eurobond market*.

---

[1] In recent years, it has become increasingly difficult to classify a bond issue as a foreign bond or Eurobond. First, the most important characteristic of a Eurobond offering is the composition of the underwriting syndicate. However, when there is only one underwriter, the underwriting is referred to as

■ TABLE 13.1

**EUROBOND ISSUES BY CURRENCY AS OF YEAR-END 1992
(U.S. DOLLAR MILLION EQUIVALENT)**

	Volume	Percentage of market
U.S. dollar	128,484	37.4
Deutsche mark	35,077	10.2
Composite/dual	22,950	6.7
Australian dollar	5,017	1.5
Canadian dollar	15,865	4.6
U.K. pound sterling	23,858	6.9
Japanese yen	43,209	12.6
Other currencies	69,157	20.1
Total	343,617	100.0

SOURCE: Hung Q. Tran and Patrick Paradiso, "Eurocapital Markets," *The Handbook of Fixed Income Securities*, ed. Frank J. Fabozzi and T. Dessa Fabozzi (Burr Ridge, Ill.: BusinessOne-Irwin, 1994), p. 335.

Eurobonds can be denominated in several major currencies. Eurobonds are referred to by the currency in which the issuer agrees to denominate the payments. For example, U.S. dollar-denominated bonds are called *Eurodollar bonds* and Japanese yen-denominated bonds are called *Euroyen bonds*. Table 13.1 shows the size and market share of the Eurobond market by currency as of year-end 1992. The largest share of the Eurobond market is the Eurodollar bond, followed by Euroyen bonds and Eurodeutsche mark bonds.

Although Eurobonds are typically registered on a national stock exchange, the most common being the Luxembourg, London, or Zurich exchanges, the bulk of all trading is in the over-the-counter market. Listing is purely to circumvent restrictions imposed on some institutional investors who are prohibited from purchasing securities that are not listed on an exchange. Some of the stronger issuers have their issues privately placed with international institutional investors.

In September 1989 the first true "global bond" was issued. This was a 10-year, $1.5 billion offering by the World Bank. What made this issue a global bond is that it was offered simultaneously in the U.S. Yankee bond market and in the Eurobond

---

a bought deal and such types of underwritings are becoming increasingly common. A bond offering in which there is only one underwriter and in which the issue is primarily placed outside the national market of both the issuer and underwriter is not classified as a Eurobond offering by the traditional definition. Another characteristic of a Eurobond is that it is not regulated by the country in which the currency is denominated. In practice, only the United States and Canada do not place restrictions on U.S. dollar- or Canadian dollar-denominated issues sold outside these two countries. Regulators of other countries whose currencies are used in Eurobond issues have closely supervised such offerings. Their power to regulate Eurobond offerings comes from their ability to impose foreign exchange and/or capital restrictions. For a further discussion, see Michael Bowe, *Eurobonds* (United Kingdom: Square Mile Books, 1988), pp. 16–17.

market. This was the first attempt to surmount the fragmented market for U.S. dollar-denominated bonds. Since then, global bonds have accounted for three-quarters of the $3 to $4 billion raised by the World Bank.

A few corporations have since begun to issue global bonds. Since June 1990, Citicorp has had several global bond issues ranging from $1 to $1.5 billion; each issue was backed by credit card receivables and denominated in U.S. dollars. Two Canadian utility companies, Ontario-Hydro and Hydro-Quebec, have had several global bond offerings. The first global non–U.S. dollar issue was by Ontario-Hydro in December 1990, denominated in Canadian dollars. No global bond issues have been denominated in European currencies or Japanese yen.[2]

It is generally believed that three characteristics must be met for a corporation to issue global bonds.[3] First, the issuer must have a consistent demand for funds. Second, the amount of funds needed on a regular basis must be around $1 billion. Finally, the issuer must have a high credit rating. Since few corporations satisfy these conditions, the opportunity to raise funds via a global bond offering is limited.

TYPES OF EUROBOND STRUCTURES

Eurobonds can be classified by type of instrument as follows: (1) fixed-rate bonds, (2) floating-rate notes, and (3) equity-related bonds. Each structure is described below.

FIXED-RATE EUROBOND STRUCTURES

A fixed-rate bond is one in which the coupon rate remains the same over the life of the issue. More than half of Eurobonds have this feature. In the United States and Japan, coupon payments are made semiannually, but in the Eurobond market, coupon payments are made annually.

A fixed-rate bond can be callable or putable, or both. A *call* feature in a bond issue allows the issuer to redeem the issue prior to the maturity date at a specified price. The call feature is essentially a call option granted to the issuer by the bondholder allowing the issuer to redeem the issue before maturity should interest rates fall below the coupon rate on the issue. Once called, the issuer can issue new bonds at a lower interest rate. A call feature is common among U.S. corporate bonds, but it is less common in the Eurobond market. When a Eurobond is callable, the investor is typically offered greater protection against the issue being called than for callable

---

[2] The reason that yen-denominated issues have not been offered is that Japan's Ministry of Finance requires a fee to be paid to a bank to act as a commissioned agent. This is a fee in addition to the one that the issuer must pay to the underwriting group. The fee paid to Japanese banks raises the cost of funding so that a yen-denominated issue is too costly relative to global issues denominated in U.S. dollars.

[3] These three characteristics were suggested by Dan Roth, treasurer of the World Bank. (See Desmond Dodd, "New Currencies Seen as Next Test for Global Issues," *Corporate Financing Week*, special supplement, November 25, 1991, p. 9.)

U.S. corporate bonds. This is accomplished by making the price that the issuer must pay to redeem the issue greater than its par (or maturity) value. Issues may also have a mandatory call if changes in tax laws could adversely affect the tax status of the issue.[4]

A *putable bond* grants the bondholder the right to sell the bond back to the issuer at par value on designated dates. The advantage to the bondholder is that, if interest rates rise after the issue date, thereby reducing the value of the bond, the bondholder can force the issuer to repurchase the bond at par value. This ensures that the bond's price will stay close to par value.

DUAL CURRENCY BONDS. Some fixed-rate coupon issues that pay coupon interest in one currency pay the principal in a different currency. Such issues are called *dual currency bonds.* For example, the coupon payments can be made annually in Swiss francs while the principal can be paid at maturity in U.S. dollars. There are three types of dual currency bonds.

The first type of dual currency bond is one in which the exchange rate at which the principal and coupon are repaid is fixed at the time of issue. The second type differs from the first in that the exchange rate is the rate that prevails at the time a cash flow is made (i.e., at the spot exchange rate at the time a payment is made).

The third type offers either the investor *or* the issuer the choice of currency in which a cash flow can be denominated at the time the payment is made. These bonds are commonly referred to as *currency option bonds.* A specific example is the index currency option note (ICON) introduced by the Long-Term Credit Bank of Japan in 1985. Effectively, this third type of dual currency bond grants either the issuer or the bondholder an option to take advantage of a favorable exchange rate movement.

BONDS WITH NONEQUITY WARRANTS. Warrants are issued as part of a bond offering. A warrant grants its owner the right to enter into another financial transaction with the issuer. Most warrants are detachable from the host bond; that is, the bondholder may detach the warrant from the bond and sell it.

Several types of warrants have been issued as part of a Eurobond offering: equity warrants, debt warrants, currency warrants, and commodity warrants. Equity warrants will be discussed later. A *debt warrant* entitles the warrant owner to buy additional bonds from the issuer at the same price and yield as the host bond. The debt warrant owner will benefit if interest rates decline because a bond with a higher coupon can be purchased from the same issuer.

A *currency warrant* permits the warrant owner to exchange one currency for another at a set price (i.e., a fixed exchange rate). This feature protects the bondholder against a depreciation of the currency in which the bond's cash flows are denominated.

A *commodity warrant* permits the warrant owner to buy a certain amount of some specific commodity at a fixed price. The typical commodities that have been used in the Eurobond market are gold and oil.

---

[4] Another mechanism for the retirement of a corporate bond issue before maturity is a mandatory sinking fund requirement. Eurobonds with a sinking fund requirement are rare.

OTHER FIXED-RATE STRUCTURES. With a Eurostraight bond (i.e., a Eurobond with no embedded options), the same coupon interest is paid each year. Other types of fixed-rate coupon bonds do not pay the same amount of interest income periodically; the two most common examples are zero-coupon bonds and deferred coupon bonds.

A zero coupon bond does not pay any periodic coupon interest; instead, it is issued at a discount from par value. The bondholder realizes interest income when the bond matures; interest is the difference between the par value and the purchase price of the bond.[5] As an example, suppose that a corporation issues a five-year Eurodollar zero-coupon bond with a maturity value of $40 million and a yield of 7 percent. The issuer sells the bond for $28,519,447.[6] The difference between the $40 million maturity value and the price at which the bonds are issued represents the accrued interest that the investor receives if the bond is held five years to the maturity date. It is $11,480,553 in our example.

An advantage of a zero-coupon bond to issuers is that interest may be deducted annually even though the issuer does not make a cash payment to bondholders. Using our hypothetical zero-coupon Eurodollar bond, the annual accrued interest is calculated as follows:

Year	Accrued Liability	Accrued Interst
1	$30,515,808	$1,996,361
2	32,651,915	2,136,107
3	34,937,549	2,285,634
4	37,383,178	2,445,628
5	40,000,000	2,616,822

The accrued liability of the issuer is equal to the accrued liability at the beginning of the year times 1.07. The difference between the accrued liability between two years is the accrued interest that may be deducted by the issuer even though it is not paid.

Investors find zero-coupon bonds attractive during periods of declining interest rates because a zero-coupon issue locks in a yield for the investor. Also, investors in some countries are granted favorable tax treatment for realized capital gains. The favorable tax treatment means a lower tax rate than that applied to other income and, in some instances, may mean no tax at all on the capital gain. This favorable tax treatment is sometimes applied to the capital gain realized by buying a zero-coupon bond and holding it until maturity. So an investor who holds our hypothetical zero-coupon Eurobond until it matures will be treated as realizing a capital gain of $11,480,653, not interest income of that amount. It should be noted that in the United States, the accrued interest is taxed annually.

---

[5] In the United States, the first public offering of zero-coupon corporate bonds was by J.C. Penney Company, Inc., in April 1982.

[6] The price is simply the present value of $40 million five years from now discounted at 7 percent, that is, $40,000,000/(1.07)^5$.

Deferred coupon bonds postpone the payment of interest to some date prior to maturity. For example, a Eurodollar $40 million, five-year deferred coupon bond with a coupon rate of 7 percent may have the following structure. Rather than paying coupon interest of $2.8 million per year for five years as with a Eurostraight bond, the coupon payments can be structured as follows: no coupon payments for years 1, 2, and 3; $11.2 million ($2.8 million times 4) in year 4; and $2.8 million in year 5. The deferred coupon structure is tax motivated. Investors in some countries can purchase this bond and sell it before the first coupon payout, year 4 in our example. The market price just before the payout in year 4 will reflect the accrued interest. The capital gain realized by selling the issue prior to maturity is granted favorable tax treatment despite the fact that the capital gain represents accrued interest. Because of this tax advantage to the investor, an issuer can benefit through a lower coupon rate on the issue compared to a Eurostraight issue.

Finally, for some bond structures, the issuer pays a fixed-coupon payment, but two tranches are created so that the principal payment at maturity is indexed to some financial or commodity benchmark. Examples are Euroyen bonds called *bull* and *bear bonds.* With these bonds, one bond tranche, called the *bull tranche,* has a maturity value that rises in value if the Nikkei Dow Index of stocks in Japan rises. The *bear tranche* has a maturity value that declines in value if the same index declines. The issuer of this type of bond is hedged against the movement of the index since the change in maturity value of one tranche has the exact change for the other tranche.

FLOATING-RATE EUROBONDS

There is a wide variety of floating-rate Eurobonds. In the Eurobond market, almost all floating-rate issues are denominated in U.S. dollars with non–U.S. banks being the major issuers. The coupon rate on a Eurodollar floating-rate note is some stated spread over the London Interbank Offered Rate (LIBOR), the bid on LIBOR (referred to as *LIBID*), or the arithmetic average LIBOR and LIBID (referred to as *LIMEAN*). The size of the spread reflects the perceived credit risk of the issuer, spreads available in the syndicated loan market (discussed in the next chapter), and the liquidity of the issue. Typical reset periods for the coupon rate are either every six months or every quarter, with the rate tied to a six-month or three-month LIBOR, respectively. That is, the length of the reset period and the maturity of the index used to establish the rate for the period are matched.

Many issues have either a minimum coupon rate (or *floor*) that the coupon rate cannot fall below and a maximum coupon rate (or *cap*) that the coupon rate cannot rise above. An issue that has both a floor and a cap is said to be *collared.* Some issues grant the borrower the right to convert the floating coupon rate into a fixed-coupon rate at some time. Some issues, referred to as *drop-lock bonds,* automatically change the floating coupon rate into a fixed coupon rate under certain circumstances.

A floating-rate issue either has a stated maturity date, or it may be a *perpetual,* also called an *undated,* issue (i.e., with no stated maturity date).[7] For floating-rate

---

[7] The perpetual issue was introduced into the Eurobond market in 1984.

issues that do mature, the term is usually more than 5 years, with the typical maturity being between 7 and 12 years. There are callable and putable floating-rate notes; some issues are both callable and putable.

The typical floating-rate note has a coupon rate that increases with LIBOR. The coupon rate of some issues moves in the reverse direction of LIBOR: if LIBOR increases (decreases) the coupon rate on the issue decreases (increases). Such floating-rate note structures are called *reverse floaters* and were first issued by Japanese corporations. For example, a reverse floater of Kawasaki Steel has a coupon rate that floats based on the following formula: $15.00\% - 1.6 \times$ six-month LIBOR. Thus, if six-month LIBOR at the reset date is 5 percent, the coupon rate is 7 percent ($15\% - 1.6 \times 5\%$). If six-month LIBOR is higher, say, 8 percent, the coupon rate is 2.2 percent ($15\% - 1.6 \times 8\%$). There is a floor on the coupon of zero. The risk that the issuer faces is that LIBOR will decline. The advantage to an investor is that the issue can be used as a hedge to stabilize the return on a portfolio when interest rates rise.

EQUITY-LINKED EUROBONDS

The two types of equity-linked bonds are bonds with equity warrants and convertible bonds. An *equity warrant* permits the warrant owner to buy the issuer's common stock at a specified price.

A *convertible bond* grants the bondholder the right to convert the bond to a predetermined number of shares of common stock of the issuer. A convertible bond is therefore a corporate bond with an option to buy the issuer's common stock. The number of shares of common stock that the bondholder receives from exercising the option of a convertible bond is called the *conversion ratio*. The conversion privilege may be permitted for all or only some portion of the bond's life, and the conversion ratio may decline over time. Convertible issues are callable by the issuer. This is a valuable feature for the issuer because an important reason for using convertibles is that a firm seeking to raise additional capital would prefer to raise equity funds but deems the current market price of its stock too undervalued so that selling stock would dilute the equity of current stockholders. So it issues a convertible, setting the conversion ratio on the basis of a price it regards as acceptable. Once the market price reaches the conversion point, the firm wants to see the conversion occur in view of the risk that the price may decline again. It has therefore an interest in forcing conversion, even though this is not in the interest of the owners of the security because its price is likely to be adversely affected by the call.

CALCULATING THE COST OF A EUROBOND ISSUE

To compare the cost of issuing bonds in the domestic and Eurobond market, the first step is to calculate the all-in-cost of funds of an issue. The all-in-cost of funds considers the interest cost and the costs associated with issuing a security. Once the all-in-cost of funds is calculated, adjustments must be made to consider differences in the frequency at which interest payments are made.

ALL-IN-COST OF FUNDS

The *all-in-cost of funds* of a bond issue is the interest rate that makes the present value of the cash flow that the issuer must make to bondholders equal to the net proceeds received by the issuer. For example, consider a U.S. corporation that plans to issue $50 million of 10-year bonds in the United States. Suppose further that its investment banker indicates that 9 percent coupon bonds can be issued and that the issuance costs will be (1) $300,000 in underwriter spread and (2) $184,683 in registration and legal fees. Thus, the net proceeds to the issuer would be $49,515,317.

The second column of Table 13.2 shows the cash flow for this corporate bond issue. Notice that the coupon payments are semiannual payments since this is the practice in the U.S. bond market. The all-in-cost of funds is the interest rate that will make the present value of the cash flow shown in the second column equal to the proceeds of $49,515,317. The last three columns of the table show the present value if semiannual interest rates of 4.550 percent, 4.565 percent, and 4.575 percent are used. Notice that when 4.575 percent is used, the present value of the cash flow is equal to the proceeds that the issuer receives. Thus, 4.575 percent is the *semiannual* all-in-cost of funds.

Two approaches can be used to annualize the semiannual rate. One is simply to double the semiannual rate. The other is to calculate the compounded annual rate. The convention that has been adopted in the U.S. bond market is just to double the semiannual rate. An annual rate calculated in this manner is referred to as a *bond equivalent basis*. In our illustration, the all-in-cost of funds calculated on a bond equivalent basis is 9.150 percent (2 × 4.575%).

Consider now the same corporation that can issue a 10-year $50 million Eurodollar bond; its investment banker indicates that 9.125 percent coupon bonds can be issued and that the issuance costs would be (1) $290,000 in underwriter spread and (2) $43,543 in registration and legal fees. Thus, the net proceeds to the issuer would be $49,666,457. Table 13.3 shows the cash flow for this Eurobond issue. Note that cash flows are annual, not semiannual as with the U.S. bond issue. Three interest rates are used in the table. An annual interest rate of 9.23 percent makes the present value of the cash flow equal to the proceeds, $49,666,457.

COMPARING ALL-IN-COSTS OF U.S. AND EUROBOND ISSUES

It would seem that for our two hypothetical bond issues, the all-in-cost of funds is lower for the U.S. bond issue (9.15 percent) than for the Eurodollar bond issue (9.23 percent) by eight basis points.[8] This is an incorrect conclusion because of the convention used in the United States to annualize a semiannual rate.

An adjustment is required to make a direct comparison between the all-in-cost on a U.S. bond issue and that on a Eurodollar bond issue. It should be clear that the ability to pay annually rather than semiannually effectively reduces the cost of funding for an issuer. Given the all-in-cost on a Eurodollar bond issue, its all-in-cost *(AIC)* on a bond-equivalent basis is computed as follows:

---

[8] A basis point equals 0.0001, or 0.01 percent. One percentage point is therefore equal to 100 basis points.

$$2[(1 + AIC \text{ on Eurodollar bond})^{1/2} - 1]$$

Using our hypothetical Eurodollar bond issue that has a 9.23 percent all-in-cost, the all-in-cost on a bond equivalent basis is

$$2[(1.0923)^{1/2} - 1] = 0.0903 = 9.03\%$$

■ TABLE 13.2

ILLUSTRATION OF ALL-IN-COST OF FUNDS CALCULATION FOR A U.S. CORPORATE BOND ISSUE

ISSUE TERMS:

Par	= $50,000,000
Maturity	= 10 years
Coupon rate	= 9.00%
Semiannual payments	
Net proceeds	= $49,515,537

Six-Month Period	Cash Flow	Present value at 9.10% (SA = 4.550%)	Present value at 9.13% (SA = 4.565%)	Present value at 9.15% (SA = 4.575%)
1	2,250,000	2,152,080	2,151,772	2,151,566
2	2,250,000	2,058,422	2,057,832	2,057,438
3	2,250,000	1,968,840	1,967,993	1,967,428
4	2,250,000	1,883,156	1,882,076	1,881,356
5	2,250,000	1,801,202	1,799,910	1,799,050
6	2,250,000	1,722,814	1,721,331	1,720,344
7	2,250,000	1,647,837	1,646,183	1,645,081
8	2,250,000	1,576,123	1,574,316	1,573,112
9	2,250,000	1,507,531	1,505,586	1,504,290
10	2,250,000	1,441,923	1,439,856	1,438,480
11	2,250,000	1,379,171	1,376,996	1,375,549
12	2,250,000	1,319,150	1,316,881	1,315,370
13	2,250,000	1,261,740	1,259,390	1,257,825
14	2,250,000	1,206,830	1,204,408	1,202,797
15	2,250,000	1,154,309	1,151,827	1,150,176
16	2,250,000	1,104,073	1,101,542	1,099,858
17	2,250,000	1,056,024	1,053,452	1,051,741
18	2,250,000	1,010,066	1,007,461	1,005,729
18	2,250,000	1,010,066	1,007,461	1,005,729
19	2,250,000	966,108	963,478	961,729
20	52,250,000	21,458,806	21,397,324	21,356,439
Total present value		49,676,206	49,579,613	49,515,357

Semiannual all-in-cost = 4.575%
Annual all-in-cost (on a bond equivalent yield basis) = 9.15%

■ TABLE 13.3

ILLUSTRATION OF ALL-IN-COST OF FUNDS CALCULATION
FOR A EURODOLLAR BOND ISSUE

ISSUE TERMS:

Par   = $50,000,000
Maturity   = 10 years
Coupon rate = 9.125%
Annual payments
Net proceeds = $49,666,457

Year	Cash Flow	Present value at 9.15%	Present value at 9.20%	Present value at 9.23%
1	4,562,500	4,180,027	4,178,114	4,176,966
2	4,562,500	3,829,617	3,826,111	3,824,010
3	4,562,500	3,508,582	3,503,765	3,500,879
4	4,562,500	3,214,459	3,208,576	3,205,052
5	4,562,500	2,944,992	2,938,256	2,934,224
6	4,562,500	2,698,115	2,690,711	2,686,280
7	4,562,500	2,471,933	2,464,021	2,459,288
8	4,562,500	2,264,712	2,256,430	2,251,476
9	4,562,500	2,074,862	2,066,327	2,061,225
10	54,562,500	22,733,006	22,629,131	22,567,057
Total present value		49,920,306	49,761,442	49,666,457
Annual all-in-cost = 9.23%				

Notice that the all-in-cost bond equivalent basis is always less than the Eurodollar bond's all-in-cost. Now comparing the all-in-cost of the two bond issues on a bond equivalent basis, it can be seen that the Eurobond issue is cheaper by 12 basis points (9.03 percent versus 9.15 percent).

Alternatively, to convert the all-in-cost on a bond-equivalent basis of a U.S. bond issue to an annual pay basis so that it can be compared to the all-in-cost of a Eurodollar bond, the following formula can be used:

$$AIC \text{ on an Annual Pay Basis} = \left[\left(1 + \frac{AIC \text{ on a bond-equivalent basis}}{2}\right)^2 - 1\right]$$

For example, the all-in-cost on a bond equivalent basis for the U.S. bond issue is 9.15 percent, so the all-in-cost on an annual pay basis would be

$$[(1 + 0915/2)^2 - 1] = 0.0936 = 9.36\%$$

The all-in-cost on an annual basis is always higher than the all-in-cost on a bond-equivalent basis. Our conclusion once again is that the all-in-cost is higher for the U.S. bond issue relative to the Eurodollar bond issue.

VALUATION ISSUES

When a corporation is considering the issuance of a Eurobond, or any type of debt, it must consider how the inclusion of a feature would affect the price that it can realize for the issue. Or, equivalently, the corporation looks at the affect on the all-in-cost of funds. A feature that is favorable to an investor means that the investor would be willing to pay a higher price, or equivalently, accept a lower yield.

OPTION FEATURES EMBEDDED IN A BOND ISSUE

Many of the features that we described earlier are effectively options granted to either the issuer or the bondholder. There are some obvious examples:

- A call feature in a bond issue is an option granted by the bondholder to the issuer to "purchase" the issue from the bondholder prior to the maturity date.
- A put feature in a bond issue is an option granted by the issuer to the bondholder to sell the issue to the issuer prior to the maturity date.
- A conversion feature in a bond issue is an option granted by the issuer to the bondholder to buy from the issuer the issuer's common stock.
- A currency selection feature included in a bond issue that allows the bondholder to select the currency denomination of the coupon payment at each coupon payment date is an option granted by the bondholder.[9]
- A currency selection feature included in a bond issue that gives the issuer the option to select the currency denomination of the coupon payment at the coupon date is an option granted by the bondholder to the issuer.[10]

There are some less obvious examples of options embedded in a bond issue. For example, in a floating-rate note issue that has an interest cap or ceiling, the bondholder has effectively granted the issuer an option at *each* reset date to pay no more than the cap rate. Similarly, a floor in a floating-rate note issue effectively grants the bondholder an option at *each* reset date to receive no less than the floor rate.

The option-type features embedded in bond issues are options on either an interest rate, equity price, exchange rate, or commodity price. The call, put, cap, floor, and debt warrants are options on an interest rate. A convertible bond and an equity warranty are options on the issuer's stock. The currency option bond and currency warrants are options on currencies. Finally, a commodity warrant is an option on a commodity price.

OPTION VALUATION AND ARBITRAGE OPPORTUNITIES FOR ISSUERS

Because of the option-type feature embedded in bonds, issuers have used option pricing theory to determine whether they are paying a fair price when they are

---

[9] Bond issues that include this feature are called *currency option bonds* and are a special type of dual currency bond.

[10] This bond is also called a *currency option bond*.

acquiring an option from the bondholder or receiving a fair price when they are selling an option to bondholders. Obviously, issuers seek to buy undervalued options and sell overpriced options. Portfolio managers also value the embedded options to ensure that they are not overpaying for an option they are granted in a bond issue or are not being adequately compensated for an option they granted to the issuer.

The valuation of options embedded in a bond issue is not as straightforward as the valuation of an option on an individual asset. The reason is that an issue often has multiple option features. For example, an issue may be callable, putable, and convertible. It may seem that these options can be valued separately and then added, but this is not technically correct. The reason is that the exercise of one option extinguishes the value of the remaining options. For example, if an issue is callable, putable, and convertible, a bondholder who exercises the put option if interest rates rise makes worthless both the call feature granted to the issuer and the conversion option purchased from the issuer.

Arbitrage opportunities arise when issuers can buy cheap options and sell expensive ones. When the mispricing of options does occur, there are ways that the issuer can reduce its all-in-cost of funds by buying cheap options or selling expensive ones. Here are two examples.

Suppose that a corporation wants to issue a six-year floating-rate note in the Eurobond market without a cap and could do so by paying three-month LIBOR plus 100 basis points reset quarterly. Suppose further that the corporation could sell a floating-rate note with an interest cap of 13 percent that pays three-month LIBOR plus 115 basis points. This means that if LIBOR plus 115 basis points rises above 13 percent at any reset date, the bondholder agrees to accept only 13 percent. Notice that the inclusion of the cap, a feature that obviously benefits the issuer, requires that a spread of 15 basis points higher must be paid each year. As explained in Chapter 15, there is a market for interest rate caps. This means that the issuer could sell a six-year cap at some price. Suppose that the market price of a 13 percent, six-year cap is 20 basis points per year. If the issuer sells the cap, it effectively is in the following position. It has issued an uncapped six-year floating-rate note—which it intended to do initially—at a cost of three-month LIBOR plus 95 basis points. The cost is five basis points less than issuing an uncapped floating-rate note. The cost savings represents the fact that the issuer bought a cap for 15 basis points and sold it for 20 basis points. A natural question to ask is why investors who effectively sold the cap to the issuer did not require a higher spread. This may occur because institutional investors may be prevented from selling interest rate caps as stand-alone instruments. Thus, they could not participate directly in the interest rate cap market.

As a second example, suppose that a corporation can issue a Eurobond with a currency warrant. In this case, the issuer is selling a warrant to bondholders. The advantage to the issuer arises if it can effectively hedge its currency position more cheaply than the price it receives from selling the currency warrant. This can occur because retail investors are reluctant to buy exchange-traded or over-the-counter options or institutional investors may be restricted from taking a direct position in a currency option.

FRAMEWORK FOR VALUING EUROBONDS

The price that an investor pays for a Eurobond (or equivalently, the price that an issuer receives) depends on market interest rates, the risks associated with a particular issue, and unique features of the particular issue. In general, the price that an investor pays can be expressed as follows (assuming identical maturity and coupon rate):

Price of a "comparable" U.S. Treasury bond

minus

Value of the risk premium for accepting the credit risk associated with the issue

minus

Value of any options the bondholder grants to the issuer

plus

Value of any options the issuer grants to the bondholder

minus

Value of the risk premium required for accepting foreign exchange risk

plus

Value of any tax advantage associated with the issue

minus

Value of the premium required for accepting marketability risk

The key for the corporate treasurer is determining the value of each of these components.

While we have set forth the basic valuation framework in terms of price, the framework can be recast in terms of yield as follows (assuming the same maturity and coupon rate):

Yield on a "comparable" U.S. Treasury bond

plus

Yield premium required for accepting the credit risk associated with the issue

plus

Yield premium required for any options the bondholder grants to the issuer

minus

Yield give-up for any options the issuer grants to the bondholder

plus

Yield premium required for accepting foreign exchange risk

minus

Yield give-up for any tax advantage associated with the issue

plus

Yield premium required for accepting marketability risk

Because an inverse relationship exists between price and yield, a feature of a particular bond issue that increases risk and/or makes the bond less attractive to investors decreases the price of the bond and thus increases its yield.

IMPLICATIONS FOR MANAGERS

A corporate treasurer seeking to raise funds via a bond offering outside of its domestic market has a choice of issuing securities in the foreign bond market of another country or in the Eurobond market. The corporate treasurer must be familiar with the structures that can be used and when they best meet funding objectives.

Adding features to a bond issue that grant the bondholder the right to take advantage of a favorable price, interest rate, or exchange rate movement generally reduces the issuer's cost of funds. However, the corporate treasurer must make sure that the firm is being adequately compensated for granting any options. Similarly, including features that benefit the issuer means that the issuer raises the cost of an issue. The corporate treasurer must make sure that the firm does not overpay for these features. Arbitrage opportunities that occur due to market imperfections can result in a lower cost to the corporation when it can buy a cheap option or sell an expensive one.

Consequently, the cost of a Eurobond issue must consider any embedded options. Moreover, at an even more basic level, a comparison of the costs of issuing bonds in the domestic market and the Eurobond market must consider issuing costs and the conventions used in markets with respect to payment frequency and annualizing rates.

QUESTIONS AND EXERCISES

13-1. What are the distinguishing features of securities in the Euromarket?

13-2. What is meant by a *global bond issue?*

13-3. This excerpt, which discusses dual currency bonds, is taken from the *International Capital Market* published in 1989 by the European Investment Bank:

The generic name of dual-currency bonds hides many different variations which are difficult to characterize in detail. These variations on the same basic concept have given birth to specific names like Index Currency Option notes (ICON), foreign interest payment bonds (FIPS), forex-linked bonds, heaven and hell bonds, to name but a few. Despite this diversity it is, however, possible to attempt a broad-brush classification of the various types of dual-currency bonds.

The first category covers bond issues denominated in one currency but for which coupon and repayment of the principal are made in another designated currency at an exchange rate fixed at the time of issue. A second category comprises dual-currency bonds in which coupon payments and redemption proceeds are made in a currency different from the currency of denomination at the spot exchange rate that will prevail at the time of payment.

Within this category, one finds the forex-linked bonds, foreign currency bonds and heaven and hell bonds. A final category includes bonds which offer to issuers or the holder the choice of the currency in which payments and/or redemptions are to be made at the future spot exchange rate. ICONs fall into this latter category because there is an implicit option due to the exchange rate revision formula. Usually, these bonds are referred to as option currency bonds.

Irrespective of the above-mentioned categories, all dual- currency bonds expose the issuers and the holders to some form of foreign exchange risk.... Pricing dual-currency bonds is therefore an application of option pricing, as the bonds can be looked at as a combination of a straight bond and a currency option. The value of the straight bond component is obtained according to traditional fixed-rate bond valuation models. The pricing of the option component is, ex post, equal to the difference between the dual currency bond price and its straight bond component....

> a. Why do all currency bonds "expose the issuers and the holders to some form of foreign exchange risk" regardless of the category of bond?
>
> b. Do you agree that the pricing of all dual-currency bonds is an application of option pricing?
>
> c. Why should the price of the option component be "equal to the difference between the dual currency bond price and its bond component"?

13-4. What is a warrant?

13-5. What are the different types of warrants that have been included in Eurobond offerings?

13-6. What is the major currency in which floating-rate Eurobonds are denominated?

13-7. What is a reverse floating-rate Eurobond?

13-8. a. What is meant by the *all-in-cost of funds*?

   b. How is the all-in-cost of funds of an issue calculated?

13-9. Why is the all-in-cost of funds for an 8.125 percent coupon, 10-year Eurobond issue with a par value of $100 million and in which the proceeds to the issuer is $98,187,562 equal to 8.4 percent?

13-10. A manager is considering issuing a bond in the United States or in the Eurobond market. The manager has calculated that the all-in-cost of funds for a bond issued in the United States is 8.25 percent and 8.35 percent in the Eurobond market. In which market would the manager realize a lower all-in-cost of funds?

13-11. What are the features in Eurobond issues that are effectively options?

13-12. What features in Eurobond issues grant the issuer an option?

13-13. Why does an option granted to the issuer increase the issuer's all-in-cost of funds?

13-14. How do arbitrage opportunities arise for a corporation seeking to raise funds so as to reduce its all-in-cost of funds?

REFERENCES

Bowe, Michael. *Eurobonds* (United Kingdom: Square Mile Books, 1988).

Dodd, Desmond. "New Currencies See as Next Test for Global Issues." *Corporate Financing Week,* special supplement, November 25, 1991, p. 9.

CASE 13.1

THE TRAVELERS CORPORATION

Anne Melissa Dowling glanced out the window of her 10th floor office at the morning traffic beginning on the streets below. She had arrived early to check what the foreign markets had done overnight and to review the data her analysts had gathered about expanding The Travelers' role in the international markets. Later that afternoon she would meet with her new boss, Ken Lynch, who was anxious to hear her recommendations for their upcoming presentation at the Securities Department's investment strategy meeting.

Anne Melissa was a member of the Public Bond Department of the Travelers Insurance Company, headquartered in Hartford, Connecticut. She had recently been hired by The Travelers, having worked previously at The Aetna Life and Casualty Company after graduating from Columbia Business School several years earlier. Her title was assistant investment officer in charge of international investments (nonequity), a newly created position in the department. The Travelers was interested in foreign bonds as an additional investment alternative for their portfolios, and Anne Melissa had been hired to research the possibilities and direct the investment efforts. The meeting next week would be her first major presentation to senior management.

THE TRAVELERS CORPORATION

The Travelers Corporation was one of the world's largest multiline insurance and health services institutions. Through its affiliated companies, it offered a wide range of products and services, including property and casualty insurance; life, accident and health insurance; health-care delivery systems; pension and investment management services; private placement loans; financial planning; mutual funds; trust services; cash management; residential and commercial mortgages; real estate development; IRAs; and Keogh plans. Financial highlights for The Travelers are shown in Exhibit 13.1A.

In 1985 the company instituted a corporate reorganization to reflect the widening role of The Travelers as a diversified financial services company. During the past decade, the financial services industry had experienced a rapid pace of change. The financial marketplace had become increasingly more complex as deregulation and competition offered investors more choices than ever before. Investment alternatives and emerging new investment tools were continually expanding, and financial services companies were constantly searching for innovative, creative approaches to new opportunities. Increasingly in the dynamic financial environment, firms were also expanding their expertise worldwide. Recognizing the changing environment and the increasing sophistication of its customers, The Travelers had organized its operations into five major groups: National Accounts, which served primarily large and medium-sized organizations; Agency Marketing, which concentrated on individual and small business owners; Business Diversification, which focused on the middle-income market; Finance, Communications, and Information Processing; and Investment.

■ EXHIBIT 13.1A

THE TRAVELERS CORPORATION
■ FINANCIAL HIGHLIGHTS
(MILLIONS OF DOLLARS)

	1985	1986
Revenue	$11,637.6	$12,837.3
Operating earnings	307.9	432.0
Net income	300.2	430.0
Assets	33,313.4	37,039.7
Shareholders' equity	3,161.8	3,764.6
Investment income		
Life business	2,474.1	2,625.4
Property-casualty	480.5	519.6
Consolidated, at year-end		
Long-term investments	25,206.1	28,136.8
Cash and short-term securities	1,163.8	1,278.2
Funds managed for others	9,833.7	12,104.6
Total funds managed	39,158.2	44,664.6

THE INVESTMENT GROUP

In 1986, the Investment Group managed nearly $52 billion for Travelers' shareholders, individual policyholders, individual investors, and corporate clients. The sources of these funds ranged from the pension plans of some of the largest U.S. corporations to mutual fund investments for individuals. The Investment Group was further divided into four departments: The Travelers Investment Management Company, the Real Estate Investment Department, the Keystone Group (which primarily provided mutual fund management), and the Securities Department. See Exhibit 13.1B for an organization chart.

THE SECURITIES DEPARTMENT

The Travelers Securities Department was responsible for portfolio management, credit analysis, trading, lending, new product development, and reporting and systems integration. The department managed $34.9 billion in assets of the Travelers Companies. Major asset holdings included public bonds, private placements, money market securities, and mortgage loans. Common stocks, convertible securities, real estate equity, and financial futures were all selectively used when appropriate. These funds were managed as 20 separate portfolios, segmented by line of business (see Exhibit 13.1C). Each portfolio was assigned to a manager whose efforts were concentrated on managing the particular needs and objectives of that portfolio. The portfolios were then coordinated to achieve consolidated corporate goals.

■ EXHIBIT 13.1B

THE TRAVELERS CORPORATION

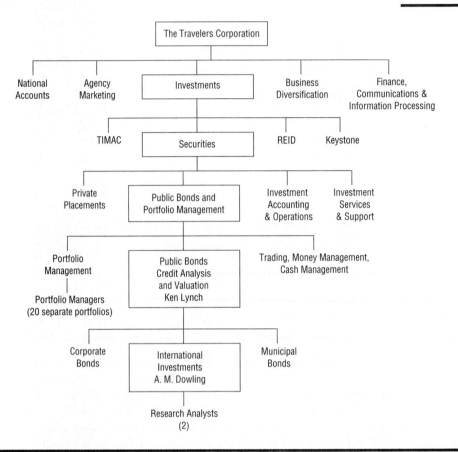

The Public Bond Research Department, headed by Ken Lynch, included cor-porate bonds, municipal bonds, and the recently added International Investments. Each group's asset manager and analysts were responsible for analyzing and valu-ing the various bonds in their particular area. Their job was to determine those bonds that they believed would provide superior returns and then to provide their "recommended buy" and "recommended sell" lists to each portfolio manager.

INVESTMENT PHILOSOPHY

The investment objective of the Securities Department was to achieve superior total returns for its portfolios, subject to liquidity, tax, and surplus constraints and in accordance with the risk tolerance of its clients. (The department's clients were primarily the various business units of The Travelers Companies.) In a collabora-

The Travelers Securities Department manages the following portfolios:

Life portfolios
Group (guaranteed income contracts)
Group pension
Life corporate
Global Life and Annuity Company
Annuity (deferred individual)
Group life
Individual life
Life health
Global Life Insurance Company (Annuities)
Universal life

Property/Casualty portfolios
PC Corporate
Agency Marketing—commercial lines
National Accounts—commercial lines
Agency Marketing—personal lines
PC Health
Special Liabilities Group—commercial lines
Business Diversification—commercial lines
Business Diversification—personal lines
Financial guarantees

Other
The Prospect Company—securities segment

tive effort with The Travelers business groups, the department actively managed the asset/liability relationship of each portfolio, setting explicit duration targets and diversification parameters for each account.

The portfolio managers were evaluated by comparing each group of assets in their portfolios to an appropriate standard or "bogey." Each "bogey" had been established by choosing an appropriate market index. Portfolio managers were evaluated quarterly but had monthly meetings to review performance.

The asset managers and their analysts were evaluated by comparing their "recommended buy" list with their "recommended sell" list. The hope was that their "buy" list would outperform their "sell" list and outperform the bogeys as well.

THE CASE FOR INTERNATIONAL INVESTMENT AT THE TRAVELERS

The Travelers was well known as a sophisticated investor, especially in evaluating investment opportunities within North America. Its international expertise, however, was limited. Although highly knowledgeable about Canadian investment, as well as private placements throughout the world, The Travelers was relying on Anne Melissa to create a department devoted fully to exploring foreign investment opportunities. Presently, The Travelers' international investments were below the insurance industry's maximum percentage of admitted assets that could be held in foreign investments. The insurance industry is highly regulated and had placed restrictions on life insurance companies such that 10 percent of admitted assets could be Canadian investments and 1 percent could be other foreign assets. The Property/Casualty portfolios were allowed 10 percent of admitted assets in gross foreign holdings. The Travelers was counting on Anne Melissa's expertise in foreign currency management, the Eurodollar bond market, the Yankee bond market, and the nondollar bond markets throughout the world to move the company ahead in the foreign investment arena.

The Travelers owned a Canadian subsidiary that wrote business in Canadian dollars. The net exposure in Canadian dollars was about $250 million each year. Before Anne Melissa's arrival, this Canadian currency exposure was 100 percent hedged with forward contracts on a rolling basis. However, Anne Melissa had two strong reasons for believing a more active approach to this exposure could be profitable. The first reason was the cost of hedging the Canadian dollar exposure. Because interest rates were higher in Canada than in the United States, and had been for some time, there was a carrying cost to selling the Canadian dollar forward or hedging. The second reason, or cost, Anne Melissa saw to fully hedging the Canadian dollars was an "opportunity cost"; that is, in being 100 percent hedged, Travelers eliminated any potential gain from a strengthening Canadian dollar.

Travelers had not been significantly involved in either the U.S. dollar-pay foreign bond market (including both the Eurodollar bond market and the Yankee bond market) or any other nondollar bond market. Anne Melissa realized opportunity existed in each of these markets, and her job was to see how well each would fit into The Travelers' overall portfolio.

Expanded investment in U.S.–pay foreign bonds represented obvious credit diversification. In 1986, the Eurodollar bond market contained almost 2,000 issues valued at $196 billion, and the Yankee bond market value was estimated at $41.9 billion (see Exhibit 13.1D). Although the international marketplace was highly fluid and intimately linked across countries, the credit risks facing different countries and companies based outside the United States were different from those facing the United States and many of the U.S.–based companies. The disclosure requirements for foreign companies were significantly less than those for domestic companies, which made credit analysis of these companies much more challenging than for domestic companies. Additionally, in the wake of the less developed country (LDC) debt crises and other global risks, internal credit limits for foreign countries and companies within those countries would need to be developed at The Travelers.

Anne Melissa believed an opportunity also existed for adding nondollar bonds to the firm's portfolios. The benefits of currency diversification and market diversification were appealing. The size of the market alone seemed to justify The Travelers' investment. At the end of 1986, the world market capitalization of pub-

■ **EXHIBIT 13.1**ᴅ

THE TRAVELERS CORPORATION
■ DOMESTIC AND INTERNATIONAL BONDS BY SECTOR

		Local Currency (billions)		U.S. Dollars (billions)	Percentage of Total
U.S. dollar	Teasury	$	771.9	$ 771.9	13.0
	Agency	$	629.4	$ 629.4	10.6
	State and local	$	593.9	$ 593.9	10.0
	Corporate	$	712.0	$ 712.0	12.0
	Yankee	$	41.9	$ 41.9	0.7
	Euro	$	196.3	$ 196.3	3.3
	FRNs	$	97.5	$ 97.5	1.6
Japanese yen	Government	Y	74,715	$ 373.2	6.3
	Gov't gtd.	Y	42,158	$ 210.6	3.5
	Municipal	Y	20,878	$ 104.3	1.8
	Bank debentures	Y	41,290	$ 206.2	3.5
	Other domestic	Y	13,574	$ 67.8	1.1
	Samurai	Y	5,122	$ 25.5	0.4
	Euro	Y	2,358	$ 11.8	0.2
Deutsche mark	Government	DM	244.3	$ 99.9	1.7
	State and local	DM	27.7	$ 11.3	0.2
	Bank bonds	DM	630.3	$ 259.6	4.4
	Schuldecheine	DM	827.9	$ 338.3	5.7
	Other domestic	DM	2.4	$ 1.0	0.0
	Euro	DM	106.7	$ 44.4	0.7
Italian lira	Government	Lira	331,726	$ 198.9	3.4
	Public enterprises	Lira	26,677	$ 14.2	0.2
	Other domestic	Lira	4,646	$ 56.8	1.0
	Euro	Lira	275	$ 0.1	0.0
U.K. sterling	Government	L	118.3	$ 170.9	2.9
	Domestic corporate	L	2.2	$ 3.2	0.1
	Bulldog	L	3.5	$ 5.1	0.1
	Euro	L	5.5	$ 8.0	0.1
French franc	Government	Ffr	365.6	$ 48.7	0.8
	Public sector	Ffr	601.5	$ 44.4	1.3
	Other domestic	Ffr	320.1	$ 18.1	0.7
	Euro	Ffr	9.2	$ 7.4	0.0
Canadian dollar	Government	C$	79.5	$ 56.8	1.0
	Provincial	C$	62.1	$ 44.4	0.7
	Corporate	C$	25.3	$ 18.1	0.3
	Euro	C$	10.3	$ 7.4	0.1
Belgian franc	Government	Bfr	2,285.7	$ 45.8	0.8
	State and local	Bfr	657.5	$ 13.1	0.2
	Public enterprises	Bfr	197.3	$ 3.9	0.1
	Other domestic	Bfr	1,647.6	$ 32.9	0.6
	Euro	Bfr	14.0	$ 0.3	0.0

continued on next page

(CONTINUED)

		Local Currency (billions)		U.S. Dollars (billions)	Percentage of Total
Swedish krona	Government	Skr	238.5	$ 31.5	0.5
	Other domestic	Skr	382.4	$ 50.5	0.9
Swiss franc	Government	Sfr	12.4	$ 6.0	0.1
	State and local	Sfr	8.1	$ 3.9	0.1
	Domestic corporate	Sfr	47.4	$ 23.0	0.4
	Foreign	Sfr	61.4	$ 29.8	0.5
Dutch guilder	Government	Dfl	112.5	$ 40.8	0.7
	Foreign	Dfl	15.3	$ 5.6	0.1
	Euro	Dfl	10.1	$ 3.8	0.1
Australian dollar	Government	A$	36.2	$ 24.7	0.4
	Other domestic	A$	15.0	$ 10.3	0.2
	Euro	A$	5.0	$ 3.4	0.1
Danish krone	Government	Dkr	293.4	$ 32.8	0.6
	Euro	Dkr	2.5	$ 3.4	0.0
ECU	Euro	ECU	16.6	$ 14.8	0.2
New Zealand dollar	Government	NZ$	10.8	$ 5.4	0.1
	Euro	NZ$	2.2	$ 1.1	0.0
				$5,938.0	100.0%

SOURCE: Merrill Lynch Special Report No. 14.

licly issued bonds was estimated by Salomon Brothers to be $7,776 billion. U.S. dollar bonds accounted for $3,660 billion, or only 47 percent of the world bond market, while yen bonds alone accounted for approximately 19.7 percent, or $1,530 billion. Bonds denominated in European currencies made up about 30.7 percent, or $2,386, of the total market. A comparison of the figures for 1984 and 1985 shows that the amount of publicly issued nondollar bonds had grown rapidly (see Exhibit 13.1E). However, even though investment in nondollar bonds appeared intuitively correct, Anne Melissa was not forgetting that the vast majority of The Travelers' liabilities were denominated in U.S. dollars and that all of its business was written based on the state of the U.S. economy, not the world economy.

Investment in nondollar bonds represented a completely uncharted territory for The Travelers. In exploring this opportunity, Anne Melissa and her analysts would need to understand the characteristics and risks of these markets and demonstrate that nondollar bonds could improve the risk-adjusted performance of the firm's portfolios. Classical diversification theory told Anne Melissa that the more diversified a portfolio, the less volatile its returns. Historical returns on foreign government securities in seven of the world's major currencies showed that returns on foreign bonds compared favorably with U.S. dollar returns (see Exhibit 13.1F). Even though Anne Melissa believed that nondollar bonds would, on a risk-adjusted basis, give superior returns in the long run, a number of issues needed to be addressed. As John Maynard Keynes had once said, "In the long run we are all dead." Had the dollar fallen so much recently that it was about to turn around and make all nondollar bonds poor investments? Were there opportunities for nondollar bonds in a rising U.S. dollar environment? What criteria would she use to choose nondollar bonds? Domestic players certainly had an advantage in these markets. Given Anne Melissa's present personnel resources (two foreign analysts), did she have the capability to analyze all of the foreign credits that could represent value? Would the foreign currency exposure need to be managed and, if so, using which risk management techniques? An even more compelling issue was the basic objective of investing in nondollar bonds. Did this investment represent a "bond market play" or rather a "currency play," or both?

Anne Melissa was well aware of the complexity of putting together the non-dollar investment strategy. How would the performance of nondollar bonds be evaluated? How would the optimal allocation of international assets be determined for both nondollar and U.S. dollar assets?

Before Anne Melissa was ready for the Investment Strategy meeting to discuss increasing The Travelers' involvement foreign investments, she decided to analyze each of the following issues separately and as part of the larger objective of The Travelers to become a force in international investment: (1) management of the Canadian dollar exposure, (2) larger investment in U.S.–pay foreign bonds, and (3) the purchase of nondollar foreign bonds. Her analysts had gathered the data in Exhibits 13.1F to 13.1H to help her. Clearly, the task ahead of her was a challenging one.

■ EXHIBIT 13.1E

THE TRAVELERS CORPORATION
■ CURRENCY OF DENOMINATION PUBLICLY ISSUED BONDS
OUTSTANDING 1984 TO 1986 (BILLIONS OF U.S. DOLLARS)

	1984		1985		1986	
U.S. dollar	$2,653	56.7%	$3,119	50.5%	$3,660	47.0%
Japanese yen	779	16.7	1,081	17.5	1,530	19.7
Deutsche mark	299	6.4	639	10.3	849	10.9
Lira	185	4.0	275	4.4	382	4.9
French franc	152	3.2	173	2.8	245	3.2
Sterling	122	2.6	211	3.4	232	3.0
Dutch guilder	111	2.4	123	2.0	161	2.1
Belgian franc	78	1.7	111	1.8	150	1.9
Canadian dollar	76	1.6	131	2.1	147	1.9
Danish krone	71	1.5	102	1.6	135	1.7
Swedish krona	56	1.2	101	1.6	126	1.6
Swiss franc	50	1.1	77	1.2	106	1.4
Australian dollar	48	1.0	50	0.8	55	0.7
	$4,680		$6,192		$7,776	

SOURCE: Salomon Brothers.

■ EXHIBIT 13.1F

THE TRAVELERS CORPORATION
■ ANNUAL RETURNS OF GOVERNMENT SECURITIES

	United States	Japan	Germany	France	Switzerland	Canada	United Kingdom
In Local Currency							
1975	8.92	18.69	19.11	19.94	23.13	4.18	34.26
1976	16.99	13.38	23.88	3.30	23.99	16.28	9.65
1977	−0.44	36.36	28.43	10.80	13.94	6.50	47.45
1978	−1.51	2.99	−6.88	20.80	14.49	3.02	−6.09
1979	−1.16	−14.67	−5.90	−9.28	−12.70	0.01	5.22
1980	0.39	8.82	−3.71	1.33	−1.37	3.68	19.55
1981	−7.31	13.52	4.64	1.90	−4.72	−0.33	0.29
1982	44.96	9.60	27.76	22.85	21.23	36.06	53.33
1983	0.15	13.22	3.28	25.02	0.30	9.80	16.86
1984	15.01	18.36	21.13	23.04	1.20	14.11	7.16
1985	30.45	12.87	13.80	23.46	9.53	21.74	9.36
1986	26.58	22.92	10.19	23.78	9.46	15.26	11.97
In U.S. Dollars							
1975	8.92	17.05	9.61	19.25	19.29	1.54	15.70
1976	16.99	18.16	37.60	−7.00	32.97	16.89	−8.84
1977	−0.44	66.31	44.27	16.85	39.73	−1.57	66.33
1978	−1.51	27.71	7.03	35.59	40.44	−4.93	−0.57
1979	−1.16	−31.18	−0.49	−5.46	−11.09	1.59	14.59
1980	0.39	28.67	−15.85	−10.03	−12.07	1.33	29.01
1981	−7.31	4.78	−7.68	−18.94	−4.72	0.39	−19.77
1982	44.96	2.63	20.23	4.02	8.02	31.30	29.89
1983	0.15	14.68	−9.94	0.92	−7.74	8.42	4.72
1984	15.01	8.92	4.70	6.16	−15.16	7.47	−14.34
1985	30.45	42.13	47.20	59.69	38.72	15.04	36.58
1986	26.58	55.40	39.75	45.05	39.59	16.69	14.64

■ EXHIBIT 13.1G

THE TRAVELERS CORPORATION
■ LONG-TERM BOND PERFORMANCE
(JANUARY 1975 TO DECEMBER 1986)

	Mean Total Return in Dollars (% per year)	Capial Gain (% per year)	Yield (% per year)
U.S. dollar	11.09	1.09	10.00
Japanese yen	21.27	5.24	7.77
Deutsche mark	14.70	3.42	7.89
French franc	12.18	1.40	12.51
Swiss franc	14.00	3.51	4.70
Canadian dollar	7.85	0.04	10.82
Pound sterling	14.08	4.87	12.55

■ EXHIBIT 13.1ʜ

THE TRAVELERS CORPORATION
■ BOND RETURN CORRELATION MATRIX BASED ON
MONTHLY RETURNS OF GOVERNMENT SECURITIES

	United States	Japan	Germany	France	Switzerland	Canada	United Kingdom
Unadjusted Returns (measured in domestic currency)—January 1975 to December 1986							
United States	1.00	—	—	—	—	—	—
Japan	0.36	1.00	—	—	—	—	—
Germany	0.40	0.49	1.00	—	—	—	—
France	0.25	0.23	0.27	1.00	—	—	—
Switzerland	0.38	0.27	0.38	0.25	1.00	—	—
Canada	0.76	0.31	0.41	0.22	0.36	1.00	—
United Kingdom	0.24	0.19	0.24	0.20	0.28	0.30	1.00
Dollar–Adjusted Returns—January 1975 to December 1986							
United States	1.00	—	—	—	—	—	—
Japan	0.19	1.00	—	—	—	—	—
Germany	0.19	0.53	1.00	—	—	—	—
France	0.05	0.37	0.56	1.00	—	—	—
Switzerland	0.14	0.53	0.73	0.59	1.00	—	—
Canada	0.61	0.16	0.25	0.10	0.19	1.00	—
United Kingdom	0.12	0.28	0.37	0.27	0.40	0.24	1.00

KEY CONCEPTS

MEDIUM-TERM NOTES AND WHAT DISTINGUISHES THEM FROM CORPORATE BONDS ▬

IMPORTANCE OF MEDIUM-TERM NOTES AS A FUNDING SOURCE ▬

STRUCTURED MEDIUM-TERM NOTES ▬

COMMERCIAL PAPER AND WHAT DISTINGUISHES U.S. AND EUROCOMMERCIAL PAPER ▬

NOTE ISSUANCE FACILITY AND ITS DIFFERENT TYPES ▬

VARIOUS SOURCES OF BANK BORROWING ▬

EUROCURRENCY LOANS ▬

SYNDICATED LOANS ▬

BANKER'S ACCEPTANCE AND ITS USE IN FINANCING INTERNATIONAL TRANSACTIONS ▬

SECURITIZATION OF CAPITAL MARKETS ▬

INTRODUCTION

As we explained in the previous chapter, the five sectors of the global debt market are the (1) bond market, (2) medium-term note market, (3) commercial paper market, (4) note issuance facilities market, and (5) bank loan market. In the previous chapter, we focused on the Eurobond sector of the bond market. In this chapter, we look at raising funds in the other four sectors. In addition, we discuss a form of borrowing called acceptance financing.

A *medium-term note* (MTN) is a corporate debt instrument with the unique characteristic that notes are offered continuously to investors by an agent of the issuer. Investors can select from several maturity ranges: 9 months to 1 year, more than 1 year to 18 months, more than 18 months to 2 years, and so on up to 30 years. Not all corporations can issue MTNs; the market is limited to corporations with an investment-grade credit rating.

The use of *medium-term note* to describe this corporate debt instrument is misleading. Traditionally, the term *note* or *medium-term* refers to debt issues with a maturity greater than 1 year but less than 15 years. Certainly this is not a characteristic of MTNs since they have been sold with maturities from nine months to 30 years, and even longer. For example, in July 1993, Walt Disney Corporation issued a security with a 100-year maturity off its medium-term note shelf registration.

EuroMTNs, as with any Euromarket security, are not subject to national regulations and therefore are not registered. In the United States, medium-term notes are registered with the Securities and Exchange Commission under Rule 415 (the shelf registration rule), which gives a corporation the maximum flexibility for issuing securities on a continuous basis. This procedure must be followed by non–U.S. corporations that want to issue MTNs in the United States and sell them via a public offering. This means that non–U.S. corporations must furnish periodic financial statements prepared in conformity with U.S. accounting standards. To avoid this cost, a foreign corporation can privately place its MTN issue under SEC Rule 144A, which was adopted in 1990.

General Motors Acceptance Corporation first used medium-term notes in 1972 to fund automobile loans with maturities of five years and less. The purpose of the MTN was to fill the funding gap between commercial paper and long-term bonds. For this reason, they are referred to as *medium-term*. The medium-term notes were issued directly to investors without the use of an agent. Only a few corporations issued MTNs in the 1970s and by 1981 only about $800 million of MTNs were outstanding. The market was hampered from developing for two reasons. First, because the issues must be registered with the SEC, registration costs made the issuance of MTNs expensive relative to other funding sources. This cost could be avoided by privately placing MTNs. However, private placements carry a higher interest cost. Second, there was no secondary market for MTNs.

The investment banking firm of Merrill Lynch pioneered the modern-day medium-term note in 1981. The first medium-term note issuer was Ford Motor Credit Company. By 1983, GMAC and Chrysler Financial used Merrill Lynch as an agent to issue medium-term notes. Merrill Lynch and other investment banking firms committed funds to make a secondary market for MTNs, thereby improving liquidity. In 1982, Rule 415 was adopted, making it easier for issuers to sell registered securities on a continuous basis. The EuroMTN was introduced in 1986.

Table 14.1 shows the amount of the worldwide MTN market as of year-end 1992.[1] A portion of the $47 billion of the $223 billion outstanding in the United

---

[1] Unless otherwise indicated, the data cited in this chapter were reported in Leland E. Crabbe, "The Anatomy of the Medium-Term Note Market," *Federal Reserve Bulletin,* August 1993, pp. 752–768.

SIZE OF THE WORLDWIDE MEDIUM-TERM NOTE MARKET
YEAR-END 1992 (BILLIONS OF DOLLARS)

Market Sector		Amount outstanding
U.S. market		$223
Public MTNs of U.S. corporations	$176	
Federal agency and others	16	
Private placements	31	
EuroMTNs		50
Non–U.S. foreign domestic markets		10
Total		$283

Based on information obtained from Merrill Lynch & Co., Websters Communications International, Federal Reserve Board.

SOURCE: Leland E. Crabbe, "The Anatomy of the Medium-Term Note Market," *Federal Reserve Bulletin*, August 1993, p. 752.

States represents obligations of foreign corporations. However, the use of the MTN market by foreign corporations to raise funds will increase as a result of Rule 144A. The growth of the EuroMTN has been phenomenal, increasing from $10 billion in early 1990 to $68 billion in May 1993.

Borrowers have flexibility in designing MTNs to satisfy their own needs. They can issue fixed- or floating-rate debt. The coupon payments can be denominated in U.S. dollars or in a foreign currency. In the previous chapter, we described the various security structures available to a corporate treasurer when contemplating the offering of a Eurobond. MTNs have been designed with the same features.

When the treasurer of a corporation contemplates the offering of either a EuroMTN or Eurobond, two factors should be considered. The most obvious is the all-in-cost of funds. The second is the flexibility afforded the issuer in structuring the offering. The tremendous growth in the EuroMTN market is evidence of the relative advantage of EuroMTNs with respect to cost and flexibility for some offerings. However, the fact that some corporations raise funds by issuing both Eurobonds and EuroMTNs is evidence that there is no absolute advantage in all instances and market environments.

DISTRIBUTION OF MTN OFFERINGS

Medium-term notes differ from corporate bonds in the manner in which they are distributed to investors when they are initially sold. Although some investment-grade corporate bond issues are sold on a best-efforts basis, they typically are underwritten by investment bankers. MTNs have been traditionally distributed on a best-efforts basis by either an investment banking firm or other broker/dealers acting as agents. Another difference between corporate bonds and MTNs when they are offered is that MTNs are usually sold in relatively small amounts on a continuous or an intermittent basis while corporate bonds are sold in large, discrete offerings.

The issuer posts MTN rates over a range of maturities, for example, 9 months to one year, one year to 18 months, 18 months to two years, and annually thereafter. The issuing corporation's agents then make the offering rate schedule available to their investor base interested in MTNs. An investor interested in the offering contacts the agent. In turn, the agent contacts the issuer to confirm the terms of the transaction. Because the maturity range in the offering rate schedule does not specify a specific maturity date, the investor can choose the final maturity subject to approval by the issuer. In the United States, the minimum size of an MTN offering that an investor can purchase typically ranges from $1 million to $25 million.

The offering rate schedule can be changed at any time by the issuer either in response to changing market conditions or because the issuer has raised the desired amount of funds at a given maturity. In the latter case, the issuer can either not post a rate for that maturity range or can lower the rate.

STRUCTURED MTNs

At one time the typical MTN was a fixed-rate debenture that was noncallable. Of the $283 billion outstanding, most have this characteristic.[2] It is common today for issuers of MTNs to couple their offerings with transactions in the derivative markets (options, futures/forwards, swaps, caps, and floors) to create debt obligations with more interesting risk/return features than are available in the corporate bond market. Specifically, an issue can be floating rate over all or part of the life of the security, and the coupon reset formula can be based on a benchmark interest rate, an equity index or individual stock price, a foreign exchange rate, or a commodity index. There are even MTNs with coupon reset formulas that vary inversely with a benchmark interest rate. That is, if the benchmark interest rate increases (decreases), the coupon rate decreases (increases). MTNs can have various embedded options included.

MTNs created when the issuer simultaneously transacts in the derivative markets are called *structured notes*. It is estimated today that the new issue volume of structured notes is 20 to 30 percent of new issuance volume in the United States. In the EuroMTN market, it is 50 to 60 percent.[3] The most common derivative instrument used in creating structured notes is a swap. We will discuss the swap market in Chapter 15 and illustrate how it can be used to create a structured note.

The use of the derivative markets in combination with an offering allows borrowers to create investment vehicles that are more customized for institutional investors who wish to satisfy their investment objectives but are forbidden from using swaps for hedging. Moreover, swaps allow institutional investors restricted to investing in investment-grade debt issues the opportunity to participate in other asset classes to make a market play. For example, an investor who buys an MTN

---

[2] Ibid.

[3] Ibid., p. 767.

whose coupon rate is tied to the performance of the S&P 500 is participating in the equity market without owning common stock. If the coupon rate is tied to a foreign stock index, the investor is participating in the equity market of a foreign country without owning foreign common stock. In exchange for creating a structured note product, borrowers can reduce their funding costs by as much as 10 to 15 basis points.[4]

COMMERCIAL PAPER MARKET

Commercial paper refers to short-term unsecured promissory notes issued in the open market as an obligation of the issuing entity. Corporations and sovereign entities are issuers of commercial paper. The original purpose of commercial paper was to provide short-term funds for seasonal and working capital needs, but it has been issued for other purposes in recent years, frequently for "bridge financing." For example, suppose that a corporation needs long-term funds to build a plant or acquire equipment. Rather than raising long-term funds immediately, the issuer may elect to postpone the offering until more favorable capital market conditions prevail. The funds raised by issuing commercial paper are used until longer-term securities are sold. Commercial paper has been used as bridge financing to finance corporate takeovers.[5]

ISSUERS OF COMMERCIAL PAPER

Corporate issuers of commercial paper can be divided into financial companies and nonfinancial companies. The three types of financial companies are captive finance companies, bank-related finance companies, and independent finance companies. *Captive finance companies* are subsidiaries of equipment-manufacturing companies. Their primary purpose is to secure financing for the customers of the parent company. The three major U.S. automobile manufacturers, for example, have captive finance companies: General Motors Acceptance Corporation (GMAC), Ford Motor Credit Company, and Chrysler Financial. GMAC is by far the largest issuer of commercial paper in the United States. *Bank-related finance companies* may have a finance company subsidiary that provides loans to individuals and businesses to acquire a wide range of products. *Independent finance companies* are those that are not subsidiaries of equipment-manufacturing firms or bank holding companies.

The typical issuers of commercial paper are those with high credit ratings, but smaller and less well-known companies with lower credit ratings have been able to issue paper in recent years. They have been able to do so by means of credit support from a firm with a high credit rating (such paper is called *credit-supported commercial*

---

[4] James Nevler, "A Crash Course in Structured Notes," *Global Finance*, October 1993, pp. 43–47.

[5] Commercial paper also has been used as an integral part of an interest rate swap transaction. We discuss interest rate swaps in Chapter 15.

paper) or by collateralizing the issue with high-quality assets (such paper is called *asset-backed commercial paper*). An example of credit-supported commercial paper is an issue supported by a letter of credit. The terms of such a letter of credit specify that the bank issuing the letter guarantees that it will pay off the paper when it comes due if the issuer fails to. Banks charge a fee for letters of credit. From the issuer's perspective, the fee enables it to enter the commercial paper market and obtain funding at a lower cost than bank borrowing. Paper issued with this credit enhancement is referred to as *LOC paper*. The credit enhancement may also take the form of a surety bond from an insurance company.[6]

DISTRIBUTION OF COMMERCIAL PAPER

Commercial paper is classified as either *direct paper* or *dealer paper*. Direct paper is sold by the issuing firm directly to investors without using a securities firm or bank as an agent. A large majority of the issuers of direct paper are financial companies. Because they require a continuous source of funds to provide loans to customers, they find it cost effective to establish a sales force to sell their commercial paper directly to investors. In the case of dealer-placed commercial paper, the issuer uses the services of an agent, either a securities firm or bank, to sell its paper. The agent, however, does not underwrite the issue. Instead, it sells the paper on a best-efforts basis.

In the United States, the dealer market historically has been dominated by large securities firms because commercial banks were prohibited from acting as agents in commercial paper issuance by the Glass-Steagall Act. In June 1987, however, the Federal Reserve Board granted subsidiaries of bank holding companies permission to sell commercial paper. Securities firms still dominate the dealer market, but commercial banks are making inroads. This seems natural because for the most part, the funds raised in the commercial paper market substitute for those previously raised via short-term bank loans. Banks obviously seek the income associated with commercial paper placement fees to recoup part of the lost interest income from borrowers who use the commercial paper market to replace short-term bank loans.

FOREIGN COMMERCIAL AND EUROCOMMERCIAL PAPER

Other countries have developed their own commercial paper market. For example, in November 1987, the Japanese Ministry of Finance (MOF) approved the issuance of commercial paper by Japanese corporations in the domestic market. A few months later, the MOF approved the issuance of yen-denominated commercial paper in Japan by non–Japanese entities. Such paper is referred to as *Samurai commercial paper.*

The Eurocommercial paper is issued and placed outside the jurisdiction of the currency of denomination. Several differences between U.S. commercial paper and

---

[6] A surety bond is a policy written by an insurance company to protect another party against loss or violation of a contract.

■ TABLE 14.2

ISSUANCE OF EUROCOMMERCIAL PAPER MARKET
(BILLIONS OF US$)

Year Ending	Issuance
1988	$57.1
1989	54.2
1990	48.3
1991	35.9
1992	28.9

SOURCE: Hung Q. Tran and Patrick Paradiso, "Eurocapital Markets," *The Handbook of Fixed Income Securities*, ed. Frank J. Fabozzi and T. Dessa Fabozzi (Burr Ridge, Ill.: Irwin Professional Publishing, 1994), p. 344.

Eurocommercial paper exist with respect to the characteristics of the paper and the market itself. First, commercial paper issued in the United States usually has a maturity of less than 270 days; the most common maturity range is 30 to 50 days or less.[7] The maturity of Eurocommercial paper can be considerably longer. Second, as a safeguard against an issuer being unable to issue new paper at maturity, commercial paper typically is backed by unused bank credit lines. An issuer must have unused bank credit lines in the United States, but it is possible to issue commercial paper without it in the Eurocommercial paper market. Third, U.S. commercial paper can be directly placed or dealer placed; the Eurocommercial paper is dealer placed. The fourth distinction is the greater diversity of dealers in the Eurocommercial paper market. In the United States, only a few dealers dominate the market. Finally, because of the longer maturity of Eurocommercial paper than U.S. commercial paper, there is more trading of Eurocommercial paper. In the United States, investors of commercial paper are typically buy and hold, thus making the market illiquid.

Table 14.2 shows the issuance of Eurocommercial paper from 1988 to 1992. Note the dramatic decline in the use of this vehicle for short-term financing. The reason for this has been the increased use of the EuroMTNs for short-term financing.

---

[7] *Money Market Instruments* (New York: Merrill Lynch Money Markets Inc., 1989), p. 16. There are reasons for this. First, the Securities Act of 1933 requires that securities be registered with the SEC. Special provisions in the 1933 act exempt commercial paper from registration so long as the maturity does not exceed 270 days. To avoid the costs associated with registering issues with the SEC, issuers rarely issue commercial paper with maturities exceeding 270 days. Another consideration in determining the maturity is whether the paper would be eligible collateral by a bank if it wanted to borrow from the Federal Reserve Bank's discount window. To be eligible, the maturity of the paper may not exceed 90 days. Since eligible paper trades at a lower cost than paper that is not eligible, issuers prefer to issue paper whose maturity does not exceed 90 days.

NOTE ISSUANCE FACILITIES

A corporation that seeks short-term funding can issue short-term securities. A corporation can use a commercial paper program to issue securities to investors using an agent. The risk that the corporation faces is that when the paper becomes due and the corporation requires additional short-term financing, market conditions may be such that the corporation cannot sell its paper.

To eliminate this risk, the note issuance facility was developed. A *note issuance facility* is a contract between a borrower and a group of banks (a syndicate) in which the banks assure the borrower that it can issue short-term notes (usually with a maturity of three to six months), called *Euronotes*, over a designated future time period. The bank syndicate assures the borrower that it can raise short-term funds by agreeing either to extend credit to the borrower or to buy the borrower-issued Euronotes that cannot be sold at a predetermined minimum price. The length of the agreement is typically five to seven years. The bank syndicate receives a fee for its commitment.

The bank syndicate is said to have underwritten the agreement because it has committed funds to the issuer should the issuer not be able to issue the Euronotes. Thus, note issuance facilities as just described are referred to as *underwritten* or *committed note issuance facilities*. In contrast, medium-term note and commercial paper programs are referred to as *uncommitted* or *nonunderwritten note issuance facilities* since the agent sells the securities only on a best-efforts basis and does not commit to provide funds to the issuer. Thus, the nomenclature sometimes used by market participants is to refer to note issuance facilities as both *underwritten* and *nonunderwritten programs*. In this chapter we use the term *note issuance facility* to mean the underwritten type.

The first note issuance facility was created in 1981. The market grew steadily to reach $34 billion by 1985. However, its use subsequently declined for two reasons. First, capital requirements have been imposed on banks that underwrite a note issuance facility. Second, those multinational corporations that had strong credit ratings felt that this back-up facility was unnecessary and just increased the cost of raising short-term funds because of the commitment fee that must be paid. Consequently, rather than using note issuance facilities, multinational corporations have more effectively used the Eurocommercial paper market to raise short-term funds.

There are variants of the note issuance facility. For example, a *transferable underwritten facility* allows the banks that have underwritten the facility to transfer their commitments to a counterparty. A *multiple component facility* allows the borrower to raise funds in a variety of forms other than issuing Euronotes. For example, the facility may allow the issuer to raise funds via banker's acceptances (discussed later in this chapter) rather than Euronotes.

BANK LOANS

As an alternative to the issuance of securities, a corporation can raise funds by borrowing from a bank. A corporation has five sourcing alternatives: (1) a domestic bank in the corporation's home country, (2) a subsidiary of a foreign bank that is established in the corporation's home country, (3) a foreign bank domiciled in a country where the corporation is doing business, (4) a subsidiary of a domestic bank that has been established in a country where the corporation is doing business, or (5) an offshore or Eurobank.

Loans made by offshore banks are referred to as *Eurocurrency loans*. A loan can be denominated in a variety of currencies. Loans denominated in U.S. dollars are called *Eurodollar loans*. Similarly, there are *Euroyen loans* and *Eurodeutsch mark loans* denominated in Japanese yen and German deutsch marks, respectively. Loans denominated in European currency units are called *EuroECU loans*.

A *syndicated bank loan* is one in which a group (i.e., syndicate) of banks provides the funds to the borrower. The need for a group of banks arises because the amount the borrower seeks may be too large for any one bank to be exposed to the credit of that borrower. Therefore, the syndicated bank loan market is used by borrowers who seek to raise large amounts of funds in the loan market rather than through the issuance of securities.

The interest rate on a syndicated bank loan floats based on some reference rate, typically LIBOR. The term of the loan is fixed. A syndicated loan is typically structured so that it is amortized according to a predetermined schedule, and repayment of principal begins after a specified number of years (typically not longer than five or six years). However, structures in which no repayment of the principal is made until the maturity date can be arranged. Such loan structures are referred to as *bullet loans*.

A syndicated loan is arranged by either a bank or a securities firm. The arranger then lines up the syndicate. Each bank in the syndicate provides the funds for which it has committed. The banks in the syndicate have the right to subsequently sell their loan to other banks.

The issuance of bonds, medium-term notes, commercial paper, and Euronotes are alternatives to bank loans. The issuance of securities in the foreign markets and the Euromarkets increased substantially, in stark contrast to syndicated bank loans. This phenomena whereby greater use is made of the wide range of securities rather than bank loans is referred to as the *securitization* of capital markets.[8]

BANKER'S ACCEPTANCES

Simply put, a *banker's acceptance* is a vehicle created to facilitate commercial trade transactions. The instrument is so titled because a bank accepts the ultimate responsibility to repay a loan to its holder. The use of banker's acceptances to finance a commercial transaction is referred to as *acceptance financing*.

The transactions in which banker's acceptances are created include (1) importing of goods into the United States, (2) exporting of goods from the United States to foreign entities, (3) storing and shipping goods between two foreign countries

---

[8] The term *securitization* is actually used in two ways. It is in the broadest sense that we use it here. In a more narrow sense, the term *securitization* more specifically, asset securitization, describes the process of pooling loans and issuing securities backed by these loans.

where neither the importer nor the exporter is a U.S. firm,[9] and (4) storing and shipping goods between two entities in the United States.

ILLUSTRATION OF THE CREATION OF A BANKER'S ACCEPTANCE

The best way to explain the creation of a banker's acceptance is by an illustration. Several entities are involved in our transaction:

- Car Imports Corporation of America (Car Imports), a firm in New Jersey that sells automobiles.
- Germany Fast Autos Inc. (GFA), a manufacturer of automobiles in Germany.
- First Hoboken Bank (Hoboken Bank), a commercial bank in Hoboken, New Jersey.
- Berlin National Bank (Berlin Bank), a bank in Germany.
- High-Caliber Money Market Fund, a mutual fund in the United States that invests in money market instruments.

Car Imports and GFA are considering a commercial transaction. Car Imports wants to import 15 cars manufactured by GFA. GFA is concerned with the ability of Car Imports to make payment on them when they are delivered.

Acceptance financing is suggested as a means to facilitate the transaction. Car Imports offers $300,000 for the 15 cars. The terms of the sale stipulate payment to be made to GFA 60 days after it ships the cars to Car Imports. GFA determines whether it is willing to accept the $300,000. In considering the offering price, GFA must calculate the present value of the $300,000 because it will not be receiving payment until 60 days after shipment. Suppose that GFA agrees to these terms.

Car Imports arranges with its bank, Hoboken Bank, to issue a letter of credit. The letter of credit indicates that Hoboken Bank will make good on the payment of $300,000 that Car Imports must make to GFA 60 days after shipment. Hoboken Bank sends the letter of credit, or time draft, to GFA's bank, Berlin Bank. Upon receipt of the letter of credit, Berlin Bank notifies GFA, which then ships the 15 cars. After the cars are shipped, GFA presents the shipping documents to Berlin Bank and receives the present value of $300,000. GFA is now out of the picture.

Berlin Bank presents the time draft and the shipping documents to Hoboken Bank. The latter then stamps "accepted" on the time draft. By doing so, Hoboken Bank has created a banker's acceptance. This means that Hoboken Bank agrees to pay the holder of the banker's acceptance $300,000 at the maturity date. Car Imports will receive the shipping documents so that it can procure the 15 cars once it signs a note or some other type of financing arrangement with Hoboken Bank.

At this point, the holder of the banker's acceptance is Berlin Bank. It has two choices: to continue to hold the banker's acceptance as an investment in its loan portfolio or to request that Hoboken Bank make a payment of the present value of $300,000. Let's assume that Berlin Bank requests payment of the present value of $300,000.

---

[9] Banker's acceptances created from these transactions are called *third-country acceptances*.

Now the holder of the banker's acceptance is Hoboken Bank. It has two choices: retain the banker's acceptance as an investment as part of its loan portfolio or sell it to an investor. Suppose that Hoboken Bank chooses the latter, and that High-Caliber Money Market Fund is seeking a high-quality investment with the same maturity as that of the banker's acceptance. Hoboken Bank sells the banker's acceptance to the money market fund at the present value of $300,000. Rather than sell the instrument directly to an investor, Hoboken Bank could sell it to a dealer who would then resell it to an investor such as a money market fund. In either case, at the maturity date, the money market fund presents the banker's acceptance to Hoboken Bank, receiving $300,000, which the bank in turn recovers from Car Imports.

RATES BANKS CHARGE ON ACCEPTANCES

To calculate the rate to charge the customer for issuing a banker's acceptance, the bank determines the rate for which it can sell its banker's acceptance in the open market. To this rate it adds a commission.

IMPLICATIONS FOR MANAGERS

A corporate treasurer has several choices when seeking to raise short-term and medium-term funds in the Euromarket. These include EuroMTNs, Eurocommercial paper, Euronotes, Euroloans, and acceptance financing. EuroMTNs actually offer the opportunity to obtain long-term financing as well as short-term and medium-term funds.

EuroMTNs offer flexibility in designing securities that are customized for institutional investors. This flexibility is due to the development of the swap market. As a result, corporations can use EuroMTNs as an alternative to Eurobonds. Moreover, this flexibility to provide customized securities makes EuroMTNs a more attractive short-term financing vehicle than Eurocommercial paper and Euronotes.

QUESTIONS AND EXERCISES

14-1. What is a Euro medium-term note?

14-2. What is the method by which Euro medium-term notes are distributed?

14-3. Why do Euro medium-term notes give borrowers flexibility in designing securities to satisfy their own needs?

14-4. What is a structured Euro medium-term note?

14-5. What is commercial paper?

14-6. How does the Eurocommercial paper differ from commercial paper issued in the United States?

14-7. How is Eurocommercial paper sold?

14-8. What is the risk that the issuer of commercial paper faces?

14-9. a. What is a note issuance facility?

    b. How is the note issuance facility a response to the risk discussed in part (a)?

14-10. What is a syndicated loan?

14-11. Who are the parties in a syndicated loan?

14-12. What is meant by the *securitization of capital markets?*

14-13. What is meant by *acceptance financing?*

14-14. What determines the rate that a bank charges in acceptance financing?

REFERENCES

Crabbe, Leland E. "The Anatomy of the Medium-Term Note Market." *Federal Reserve Bulletin,* August 1993, pp. 752–768.

Money Market Instruments. New York: Merrill Lynch Money Markets, Inc., 1989, p. 16.

Nevler, James. "A Crash Course in Structured Notes." *Global Finance,* October 1993, pp. 43–47.

Stigum, Marcia. *The Money Market.* Homewood, Ill.: Dow Jones–Irwin, 1990, p. 1007.

CASE 14.1

JAPANESE YEN SHORT-TERM NOTE

Lisa Johnson, assistant treasurer of Blake Industries, was trying to determine whether Blake should be interested in the latest short-term investment product to cross her desk. It was a Japanese yen interest rate/FX note that was being offered by the CS First Boston Structured Notes Group. As the individual responsible for cash management at Blake Industries, Lisa was always looking for ways to enhance the return on the short-term portion of the company's portfolio. At the same time, she needed to determine whether the trade-off between risk and reward was appropriate on any security she added to the portfolio.

BLAKE INDUSTRIES

Blake Industries was a diversified, family-owned business. Founded in 1868 by Thomas Blake, the company was initially a lumber mill. Over time, Blake expanded into forestry, paper and pulp manufacturing, and transportation. By the beginning of World War II, Blake was one of the 10 largest integrated paper companies in the United States and operated the third largest trucking company in the Southeast. During the war, Blake experienced an enormous growth in profitability, which funded a rapid diversification effort by Thomas Blake's great-grandson, Walter.

Anticipating the expanding role of communication in modern society, Walter invested aggressively in radio, newspapers, and television. The company eventually held two major daily newspapers, three regional magazines, several radio stations, and network-affiliated television stations in Memphis, Tennessee, Birmingham, Alabama, and Richmond, Virginia.

In 1984, the family established a proprietary finance group with offices in New York City. Lisa was affiliated with this group, which had a portfolio of securities, equities, and bonds with a market value of $1.2 billion. Decisions to allocate funds among different types of assets and maturities were made by an investment committee chaired by the corporate treasurer and of which Lisa was a member. The committee was bearish on U.S. securities and had almost 40 percent of the company's total assets in money market and short-term (less than two years) securities. Because yields were generally low on the short end of the curve (see Exhibit 14.1A), Lisa was even more interested than usual in getting a few extra basis points.

THE OFFERING

The note that CS First Boston was proposing was tied to both the value of the yen and the Japanese interest rate. The note would have a fixed-rate coupon of 10.5 percent but would repay a variable principal according to the following formula:

$$\text{Principal Redemption} = 100\% \times \left[3 - 2 \times \left(\frac{109.00}{JPY / USD} \right) \times \left(\frac{JPY\ LIBOR}{2.25\%} \right) \right]$$

The indicative term sheet for the proposed note is given in Exhibit 14.1B.

This case was written by Mark R. Eaker, professor of Business Administration. Copyright © 1994 by the University of Virginia Darden School Foundation, Charlottesville, Va. All rights reserved.

■ **EXHIBIT 14.1A**

JAPANESE YEN SHORT-TERM NOTE
■ **U.S. GOVERNMENT YIELD CURVE**

January 6, 1994

3 month	3.106
6 month	3.319
1 year	3.576
2 year	4.200
3 year	4.509
5 year	5.182
10 year	6.346

SOURCE: Bloomberg Business News Service, Princeton, NJ.

■ **EXHIBIT 14.1B**

JAPANESE YEN SHORT-TERM NOTE
■ **SHORT-TERM JAPANESE YEN INTEREST RATE/FX NOTE:**
INDICATIVE TERMS AND CONDITIONS

CS First Boston Structured Notes

Issuer	Acceptable highly rated issuer
Issue size	U.S.$20,000,000
Maturity	January 6, 1995
Issue price	100.00%
Denomination	All payments in U.S. dollars
Coupon payments	Semiannually
Day-count basis	30/360
Coupon rate	10.50%
Principal redemption	$100\% \times \left[3 - 2 \times \left(\dfrac{109.00}{JPY/USD} \right) \times \left(\dfrac{JPY\ LIBOR}{2.25\%} \right) \right]$
Maximum redemption	100.00%
Minimum redemption	0.00%
JPY/USD determination	For the purposes of calculating the principal redemption, *JPY/USD* shall be the bid-side Japanese yen per U.S. dollar exchange rate as determined by the Bank of Tokyo and published on Telerate page 35360 on 19 December 1994.
JPY LIBOR determination	For the purposes of calculating the principal redemption, *JPY LIBOR* shall be the 11:00 a.m. London time setting for the three-month *JPY LIBOR* rates as published by the British Bankers Association on Telerate page 3750 on 19 December 1994.
Current JPY/USD	109.00
Current JPY LIBOR	2.25000%
Implied principal redemption	100.00%

This indicative term sheet is neither an offer to sell securities nor a solicitation of an offer to buy securities. The offer is made only by the prospectus and the related prospectus supplements.

In order to see how the note might perform, Lisa produced charts (Exhibits 14.1c and 14.1d) for the JPY/USD and the yen LIBOR over the past three years. Although she was not an expert on Japan's economy or its markets, she believed that the historical data would be helpful in determining possible outcomes.

■ EXHIBIT 14.1c

JAPANESE YEN SHORT-TERM NOTE

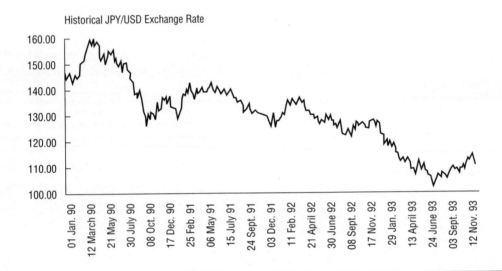

Historical JPY/USD Exchange Rate

JAPANESE YEN SHORT-TERM NOTE

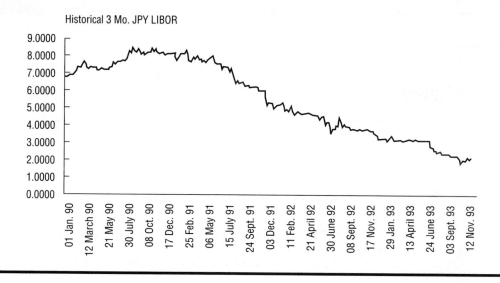

Historical 3 Mo. JPY LIBOR

KEY CONCEPTS

OVER-THE-COUNTER OPTIONS AND EXCHANGE-TRADED OPTIONS AND WHY THERE MAY BE A PREFERENCE FOR THE FORMER ▬

INTEREST RATE SWAP ▬

INTERPRETATION OF A POSITION IN AN INTEREST RATE SWAP ▬

CALCULATION OF THE SWAP RATE ▬

DETERMINATION OF THE VALUE OF A SWAP ▬

SWAPTIONS AND THEIR USE BY CORPORATE TREASURERS ▬

TYPES OF TRANSACTIONS IN THE SECONDARY MARKET FOR SWAPS ▬

RATE CAPS AND FLOORS AND THE CREATION OF AN INTEREST RATE COLLAR ▬

THE BASIC CURRENCY SWAP STRUCTURE AND THE MOTIVATION FOR USING CURRENCY SWAPS ▬

CREATION OF A STRUCTURED NOTE USING SWAPS ▬

INTRODUCTION

Corporate treasurers have a wide range of products to control interest rate risk and exchange rate risk. These include futures/forward contracts, options, swaps, and interest rate agreements. Futures/forward contracts and options have been discussed in other chapters. In this chapter we will explain how over-the-counter options, interest rate swaps, forward rate agreements, interest rate agreements, and currency swaps can be used to control interest rate and exchange rate risk for borrowers. We will also explain the role of swaps in the creation of structured notes that are offered in the Euro medium-term note market.

An option is a contract in which its writer grants its buyer the right, but not the obligation, to purchase from or sell to the writer something at a specified price within a specified period of time (or at a specified date). Options, like other financial instruments, may be traded either on an organized exchange or in the over-the-counter (OTC) market.

Exchange-traded options have three advantages. First, the exercise price and expiration date of the contract are standardized. Second, as in the case of futures contracts, the direct link between buyer and seller is severed after the order is executed because of the interchangeability of exchange-traded options. The clearinghouse, which is associated with the exchange where the option trades, performs the same function in the options market that it does in the futures market. Finally, the transaction costs are lower for exchange-traded options than for OTC options.

The higher cost of an OTC option reflects the cost of customizing the option for the many situations in which a borrower needs to have a tailor-made option because the standardized exchange-traded option does not satisfy its financing objectives. Commercial banks and securities firms act as principals as well as brokers in the OTC options market. While an OTC option is less liquid than an exchange-traded option this is typically not of concern to a borrower who uses the OTC option as part of a financing strategy and intends to hold it until the expiration date.

The following are two examples of how and why options can be customized. First, a corporate treasurer may want to buy an option to protect against an adverse movement not in the level of interest rates but in the amount of the credit spread. For example, suppose that a treasurer of a corporation believes that the level of U.S. Treasury rates will decline in the next three months when the corporation plans to issue $50 million in bonds with a maturity of ten years. However, the corporate treasurer believes that the credit spread to the U.S. Treasury rate that the firm will have to pay is currently satisfactory and is concerned that three months from now it may increase.[1] Suppose that the corporation is rated single A and that the credit spread is now 100 basis points. The corporate treasurer may be able to find a commercial bank or securities firm that is willing to sell an option structured so that if the credit spread on single A-rated corporate bonds is higher than 100 basis points three months from now, the counterparty will pay the corporation the present value difference between the credit spread three months from now and 100 basis points times $50 million for ten years. For example, if the credit spread three months from now is 130 basis points, the counterparty will pay the corporation the present value of 30 basis points (0.0030) times $50 million. That is, the counterparty will pay the present value of $150,000 a year for ten years. Such an option must be customized since no exchange-traded options are available to protect against changes in credit spreads.

As a second example, consider currency options. Only options on the major currencies are traded on exchanges. An option on any other currency must be

---

[1] Remember that the rate that a corporation must pay when it issues a bond is the base rate (that is, the rate on a comparable Treasury security) plus the credit spread.

purchased in the over-the-counter market. As another example, it is possible for a corporate treasurer to obtain an option that protects in one agreement against both interest rate risk and currency risk. For example, suppose that a corporation plans to issue yen-denominated bonds in the Japanese bond market 53 days from now and exchange those yen for Canadian dollars. The corporate treasurer can buy one option that expires 53 days from now that protects against both a decline in the Japanese yen relative to the Canadian dollar and a rise in the level of interest rates in Japan.

INTEREST RATE SWAPS

In an *interest rate swap*, two parties (called *counterparties*) agree to exchange periodic interest payments. The dollar amount of the interest payments exchanged is based on some predetermined dollar principal, which is called the *notional principal amount*. The dollar amount each counterparty pays to the other is the agreed-upon periodic interest rate times the notional principal amount. The only dollars that are exchanged between the parties are the interest payments, not the notional principal amount. In the most common type of swap, one party agrees to pay the other party fixed interest payments at designated dates for the life of the contract. This party is referred to as the *fixed-rate payer*. The other party, who agrees to make interest rate payments that float with some reference rate, is referred to as the *floating-rate payer*. The frequency with which the interest rate that the floating-rate payer must pay is called the *reset frequency*.

The reference rates that have been used for the floating rate in an interest rate swap are those on various money market instruments: Treasury bills, the London Interbank Offered Rate, commercial paper, banker's acceptances, certificates of deposit, the federal funds rate, and the prime rate. The most common is the London Interbank Offered Rate (LIBOR). LIBOR is the rate at which prime banks offer to pay on Eurodollar deposits available to other prime banks for a given maturity. Basically, it is viewed as the global cost of bank borrowing. There is not just one rate but a rate for different maturities. For example, there is a one-month LIBOR, three-month LIBOR, and six-month LIBOR.

To illustrate an interest rate swap, suppose that for the next five years, party X agrees to pay party Y 10 percent per year, while party Y agrees to pay party X six-month LIBOR (the reference rate). Party X is a fixed-rate payer/floating-rate receiver, while party Y is a floating-rate payer/fixed-rate receiver. Assume that the notional principal amount is $50 million and that payments are exchanged every six months for the next five years. This means that every six months, party X (the fixed-rate payer/floating-rate receiver) will pay party Y $2.5 million (10 percent × $50 million ÷ 2). The amount that party Y (the floating-rate payer/fixed-rate receiver) will pay party X will be six-month LIBOR times $50 million divided by 2. If six-month LIBOR is 7 percent, party Y will pay party X $1.75 million (7% × $50 million ÷ 2). Note that we divide by 2 because one-half year's interest is being paid.

As we shall illustrate later, corporate treasurers can use an interest rate swap to alter the cash flow character of liabilities from a fixed-rate basis to a floating-rate basis or vice versa.

ENTERING INTO A SWAP AND COUNTERPARTY RISK

Interest rate swaps are over-the-counter instruments. This means that they are not traded on an exchange. An institutional investor wishing to enter into a swap transaction can do so through either a securities firm or a commercial bank that transacts in swaps.[2] These entities can do one of the following. First, they can arrange or broker a swap between two parties that want to enter into an interest rate swap. In this case, the securities firm or commercial bank is acting in a brokerage capacity.

The second way in which a securities firm or commercial bank can get an institutional investor into a swap position is by taking the other side of the swap. This means that the securities firm or the commercial bank is a dealer rather than a broker in the transaction. Acting as a dealer, the securities firm or the commercial bank must hedge its swap position in the same way that it hedges its position in other securities that it holds. Also it means that the dealer (which we refer to as a *swap dealer*) is the counterparty to the transaction. Goldman Sachs, for example, is a swap dealer. If an institutional investor entered into a swap with Goldman Sachs, the institutional investor will look to Goldman Sachs to satisfy the obligations of the swap; similarly, Goldman Sachs looks to the institutional investor to fulfill its obligations as set forth in the swap. Today, most swaps are transacted using a swap dealer.

The risk that the two parties assume when they enter into a swap is that the other party will fail to fulfill its obligations as set forth in the swap agreement. That is, each party faces default risk. The default risk in a swap agreement is called *counterparty risk*. In fact, counterparty risk is more general than the default risk for only a swap agreement. In any agreement between two parties that must perform according to the terms of a contract, counterparty risk is the risk that the other party will default. With futures and exchange-traded options, the counterparty risk is the risk that the clearinghouse established to guarantee performance of the contracts will default. Market participants view this risk as small. In contrast, counterparty risk in a swap can be significant.

Because of counterparty risk, not all securities firms and commercial banks can be swap dealers. Several securities firms have actually established subsidiaries that are separately capitalized so that they have a high credit rating, which permits them to enter into swap transactions as a dealer.

Thus, it is imperative to keep in mind that any party entering into a swap is subject to counterparty risk.

INTERPRETING A SWAP POSITION

A swap position can be interpreted in two ways: (1) a package of forward/futures contracts and (2) a package of cash flows from buying and selling cash market instruments.

---

[2] Don't get confused here about the role of commercial banks. A bank can use a swap in its asset/liability management. Or a bank can transact (buy and sell) swaps to clients to generate fee income. It is in the latter sense that we are discussing the role of a commercial bank in the swap market here.

PACKAGE OF FORWARD CONTRACTS. Consider the hypothetical interest rate swap described earlier to illustrate a swap. Let's look at party X's position. Party X has agreed to pay 10 percent and receive six-month LIBOR. More specifically, assuming a $50 million notional principal amount, X has agreed to buy a commodity called "six-month LIBOR" for $2.5 million. This is effectively a six-month forward contract where X agrees to pay $2.5 million in exchange for delivery of six-month LIBOR. If interest rates increase to 11 percent, the price of that commodity (six-month LIBOR) is higher, resulting in a gain for the fixed-rate payer, who is effectively long a six-month forward contract on six-month LIBOR. The floating-rate payer is effectively short a six-month forward contract on six-month LIBOR. There is therefore an implicit forward contract corresponding to each exchange date.

Consequently, interest rate swaps can be viewed as a package of more basic interest rate control tools, such as forwards. The pricing of an interest rate swap then depends on the price of a package of forward contracts with the same settlement dates in which the underlying for the forward contract is the same reference rate.

While an interest rate swap may be nothing more than a package of forward contracts, it is not a redundant contract for several reasons. First, maturities for forward or futures contracts do not extend out as far as those of an interest rate swap; an interest rate swap with a term of 15 years or longer can be obtained. Second, an interest rate swap is a more transactionally efficient instrument. By this, we mean that in one transaction an entity can effectively establish a payoff equivalent to a package of forward contracts. The forward contracts would each have to be negotiated separately. Third, the interest rate swap market has grown in liquidity since its establishment in 1981; interest rate swaps now provide more liquidity than forward contracts, particularly long-dated (i.e., long-term) forward contracts.

PACKAGE OF CASH MARKET INSTRUMENTS. To understand why a swap can also be interpreted as a package of cash market instruments, consider an investor who enters into the transaction below:

- Buy a $50 million par of a five-year floating-rate bond that pays six-month LIBOR every six months.
- Finance the purchase by borrowing $50 million for five years on terms requiring a 10 percent annual interest rate paid every six months.

The cash flows for this transaction are set forth in Table 15.1. The second column of the table shows the cash flow from purchasing the five-year floating-rate bond. There is a $50 million cash outlay and then 10 cash inflows. The amount of the cash inflows is uncertain because they depend on future LIBOR. The next column shows the cash flow from borrowing $50 million on a fixed-rate basis. The last column shows the net cash flow from the entire transaction. As the last column indicates, there is no initial cash flow (no cash inflow or cash outlay). In all 10 six-month periods, the net position results in a cash inflow of LIBOR and a cash outlay of $2.5 million. This net position, however, is identical to the position of a fixed-rate payer/floating-rate receiver.

It can be seen from the net cash flow in Table 15.1 that a fixed-rate payer has a cash market position that is equivalent to a long position in a floating-rate bond and a short position in a fixed-rate bond—the short position being the equivalent of borrowing by issuing a fixed-rate bond.

What about the position of a floating-rate payer? It can be easily demonstrated that the position of a floating-rate payer is equivalent to purchasing a fixed-rate bond and financing that purchase at a floating-rate, where the floating rate is the reference rate for the swap. That is, the position of a floating-rate payer is equivalent to a long position in a fixed-rate bond and a short position in a floating-rate bond.

CONVENTION FOR QUOTING SWAP RATES

The convention that has evolved for quoting swaps rates is for a swap dealer (a commercial bank or securities firm) to set the floating rate equal to the reference rate and then quote the fixed rate that will apply. To illustrate this convention, consider the following 10-year swap terms available from a dealer:

Floating-rate payer

Pay floating rate of six-month LIBOR.

Receive fixed rate of 8.75 percent.

■ **TABLE 15.1**

CASH FLOW FOR THE PURCHASE OF A FIVE-YEAR FLOATING-RATE BOND FINANCED BY BORROWING ON A FIXED-RATE BASIS

Transaction: Purchase $50 million of a five-year floating-rate bond: floating rate = LIBOR, semiannual pay

Borrow $50 million for five years: fixed rate = 10%, semiannual payments

Cash Flow (in millions of dollars) from

Six-Month Period	Floating-Rate Bond (*)	Borrowing	Net
0	− $50	+$50.0	$0
1	+ $(LIBOR_1/2) \times 50$	− 2.5	+ $(LIBOR_1/2) \times 50 - 2.5$
2	+ $(LIBOR_2/2) \times 50$	− 2.5	+ $(LIBOR_2/2) \times 50 - 2.5$
3	+ $(LIBOR_3/2) \times 50$	− 2.5	+ $(LIBOR_3/2) \times 50 - 2.5$
4	+ $(LIBOR_4/2) \times 50$	− 2.5	+ $(LIBOR_4/2) \times 50 - 2.5$
5	+ $(LIBOR_5/2) \times 50$	− 2.5	+ $(LIBOR_5/2) \times 50 - 2.5$
6	+ $(LIBOR_6/2) \times 50$	− 2.5	+ $(LIBOR_6/2) \times 50 - 2.5$
7	+ $(LIBOR_7/2) \times 50$	− 2.5	+ $(LIBOR_7/2) \times 50 - 2.5$
8	+ $(LIBOR_8/2) \times 50$	− 2.5	+ $(LIBOR_8/2) \times 50 - 2.5$
9	+ $(LIBOR_9/2) \times 50$	− 2.5	+ $(LIBOR_9/2) \times 50 - 2.5$
10	+ $(LIBOR_{10}/2) \times 50 + 50$	− 52.5	+ $(LIBOR_{10}/2) \times 50 - 2.5$

Note: The subscript for LIBOR indicates the six-month LIBOR as per the terms of the floating-rate bond at time t.

Fixed-rate payer

Pay fixed rate of 8.85 percent.

Receive floating rate of six-month LIBOR.

The offer price that the dealer would quote the fixed-rate payer would be to pay 8.85 percent and receive LIBOR "flat." (The word *flat* means with no spread.) The bid price that the dealer would quote the floating-rate payer would be to pay LIBOR flat and receive 8.75 percent. The bid-offer spread is 10 basis points, which is the fee earned by the dealer.

The fixed rate is some spread above the U.S. Treasury yield curve with the same term to maturity as the swap. In our illustration, suppose that the 10-year Treasury yield is 8.35 percent. Then the offer that the dealer would quote to the fixed-rate payer is the 10-year Treasury rate plus 50 basis points versus receiving LIBOR flat. For the floating-rate payer, the bid quoted would be LIBOR flat versus the 10-year Treasury rate plus 40 basis points. The dealer would quote the swap above as "40-50," meaning that it is willing to enter into a swap to receive LIBOR and pay a fixed rate equal to the 10-year Treasury rate plus 40 basis points; it would be willing to enter into a swap to pay LIBOR and receive a fixed rate equal to the 10-year Treasury rate plus 50 basis points. The difference between the Treasury rate paid and received is the bid-offer spread.

DIGRESSION: THE EURODOLLAR CD FUTURES CONTRACT

To understand how to calculate the swap rate for a LIBOR-based swap and the value of a swap, it is necessary to understand the Eurodollar CD futures contract. This futures contract is one of the most heavily traded futures contracts in the world because it is frequently used to trade the short end of the yield curve, and many corporate treasurers have found this contract to be the best vehicle for a wide range of hedging situations.

Eurodollar certificates of deposit (CDs) are denominated in dollars but represent the liabilities of banks outside the United States. The contracts are traded on both the International Monetary Market of the Chicago Mercantile Exchange and the London International Financial Futures Exchange. The rate paid on Eurodollar CDs is LIBOR.

The three-month Eurodollar CD is the underlying instrument for the Eurodollar CD futures contract. The contract is for $1 million of face value and is traded on an index price basis. The index price basis in which the contract is quoted is equal to 100 minus the annualized futures LIBOR rate. For example, a Eurodollar CD futures price of 94.00 means a futures rate for three-month LIBOR of 6 percent.

The minimum price fluctuation (tick) for this contract is .01 (or .0001 in terms of LIBOR). This means that the price value of a basis point change in LIBOR for this contract is $25, found as follows. The simple interest on $1 million for 90 days is equal to

$$\$1,000,000 \times (\text{LIBOR} \times 90/360)$$

If LIBOR changes by one basis point (.0001), then

$$\$1,000,000 \times (.0001 \times 90/360) = \$25$$

The Eurodollar CD futures contract is a cash settlement contract. That is, the parties settle in cash for the value of a Eurodollar CD based on LIBOR at the settlement date. There are contracts for settlement for five years out.

CALCULATING THE SWAP RATE

At the initiation of an interest rate swap, the counterparties are agreeing to exchange future interest rate payments and no upfront payments by either party are made. This means that the swap terms must be such that the present value of the cash flows for the payments to be made by the counterparties must be equal. This is equivalent to saying that the present value of the cash flows of payments to be received by the counterparties must be equal. The equivalence of the cash flows is the principle in calculating the swap rate.

For the fixed-rate side, once a swap rate is determined, the payments of the fixed-rate payer are known. However, the floating rate payments are not known because they depend on the value of the reference rate at the reset dates. For a LIBOR-based swap, the Eurodollar CD futures contract can be used to establish the forward (or future) rate for three-month LIBOR. Given the cash flow based on the forward rate for three-month LIBOR, the swap rate is the interest rate that will make the present value of the payments on the fixed-rate side equal to the payments on the floating-rate side.

The next question is: What interest rate should be used to discount the payments? The appropriate rate to discount any cash flow is the theoretical spot rate. Each cash flow should be discounted at a unique discount rate. Where do we get the theoretical spot rates? Spot rates can be obtained from forward rates. They are the same three-month LIBOR forward rates derived from the Eurodollar CD futures contract that can be used to obtain the theoretical spot rates.

Let's illustrate the procedure with an example. Consider the following hypothetical swap:

Swap term: Three year swap.

Notional amount: $100 million.

Fixed receiver: Actual/360-day count basis and quarterly payments.

Floating receiver: Three-month LIBOR, actual/360-day count basis, quarterly payments, and quarterly reset.

Our worktable for calculating the swap rate is Table 15.2. The first column just lists the quarterly periods. A Eurodollar CD futures contract with a settlement date corresponds to each period. The second column shows the number of days between the period for each Eurodollar CD futures contract. The third column shows the futures price for each contract. We know that the future three-month LIBOR rate is found by subtracting the futures price from 100. This is shown in Column (4) representing the forward rate.[3]

---

[3] In practice, the forward rate is adjusted for the convexity of the Eurodollar CD futures contract.

■ TABLE 15.2

DETERMINING THE SWAP RATE

GOAL: DETERMINATION OF SWAP RATE
Three-year swap
Notional amount: $100 million

FIXED RECEIVER:
Actual/360-day count basis
Quarterly payments

FLOATING RECEIVER:
Three-month LIBOR
Actual/360-day count basis
Quarterly payments and reset

Swap rate is the rate that will produce a fixed cash flow whose present value will equal the present value of the floating cash flow: in the illustration the swap rate is equal to 4.987551%.

(1)	(2)	(3)	(4)	(5)	(6)	(7)	(8)	(9)
						Present Value		Present Value
Period	Day Count	Futures Price	Forward Rate	Discount Factor	Floating Cash Flow	of Floating CF	Fixed Cash Flow	of Fixed CF
1	91	—	4.05	1.00000	—	—	—	—
2	90	95.85	4.15	0.98998	1,012,500	1,002,351	1,246,888	1,234,390
3	91	95.45	4.55	0.97970	1,049,028	1,027,732	1,260,742	1,235,148
4	91	95.28	4.72	0.96856	1,150,139	1,113,978	1,260,742	1,221,104
5	91	95.10	4.90	0.95714	1,193,111	1,141,974	1,260,742	1,206,706
6	94	94.97	5.03	0.94505	1,279,444	1,209,137	1,302,305	1,230,741
7	91	94.85	5.15	0.93318	1,271,472	1,186,516	1,260,742	1,176,503
8	90	94.75	5.25	0.92132	1,287,500	1,186,201	1,246,888	1,148,784
9	91	94.60	5.40	0.90925	1,327,083	1,206,657	1,260,742	1,146,335
10	91	94.50	5.50	0.89701	1,365,000	1,224,419	1,260,742	1,130,899
11	91	94.35	5.65	0.88471	1,390,278	1,229,993	1,260,742	1,115,392
12	93	94.24	5.76	0.87198	1,459,583	1,272,732	1,288,451	1,123,507
13	91	94.10	5.79	0.85947	1,456,000	1,251,387	1,260,742	1,083,569
Total						14,053,077		14,053,078

Explanation of columns:
Column (2): Day count refers to the number of days in the period.
Column (3): The Eurodollar CD futures price.
Colunn (4): The forward rate for LIBOR found from the futures price of the Eurodollar CD futures contract as follows:
100.00 – Future Price
Column (5): The discount factor is found as follows:

$$\frac{\text{Discount Factor in the Previous Period}}{[1 + (\text{Forward Rate in Previous Period} \times \text{Number of Days in Period}/360)]}$$

Number of days in period is found in column (2).

Column (6): The floating cash flow is found by multiplying the forward rate and the notional amount, adjusted for the number of days in the payment period. That is:

$$\frac{\text{Forward Rate Previous Period} \times \text{Number of Days in Period}}{360} \times \text{Notional Amount}$$

Column (7): Present value of floating cash flow, found as follows:

$$\text{Column (5)} \times \text{Column (6)}$$

Column (8): This column is found by trial and error, based on a guess of the swap rate. To determine the fixed cash flow, the cash flow must be adjusted for the day count, as follows:

$$\frac{\text{Assumed Swap Rate} \times \text{Number of Days in Period}}{360} \times \text{Notional Amount}$$

Column (9): Present value of fixed cash flow, found as follows:

$$\text{Column (5)} \times \text{Column (7)}$$

The discount rates that will be used to discount the cash flows (payments) will be calculated from the forward rates. The discount factor (i.e., the present value of $1 based on the spot rate) is found as follows:[4]

$$\frac{\text{Discount Factor in the Previous Period}}{\left[1 + (\text{Foward Rate in Previous Period} \times \text{Number of Days in Period}/360)\right]}$$

The discount factors are shown in Column (5).

The floating cash flow is found by multiplying the forward rate and the notional amount. However, the forward rate must be adjusted for the number of days in the payment period. The formula to do so is

$$\frac{\text{Foward Rate Previous Period} \times \text{Number of Days in Period}}{360} \times \text{Notional Amount}$$

These values represent the payments by the floating-rate payer and the receipts of the fixed-rate receiver. The values are shown in Column (6). The present value of each of these cash flows is shown in Column (7) using the discount factor shown in Column (5). The present value of the floating cash flow is $14,053,077.

In order for no other payments to be exchanged between the counterparties other than the interest payments, the swap rate must be set such that the present value of the fixed cash flows is equal to the same value, $14,053,077. This can be

---

[4] The formulas presented below are taken from Chapter 6 of Ravi E. Dattatreya, Raj E.S. Venkatesh, and Vijaya E. Venkatesh, *Interest Rate & Currency Swaps* (Chicago: Probus Publishing, 1994).

found only by trial and error. For our hypothetical swap, when a swap rate of 4.987551 percent is tried, the cash flow is as shown in Column (8). In determining the fixed cash flows, each cash flow must be adjusted for the day count, as follows:

$$\frac{\text{Assumed Swap Rate} \times \text{Number of Days in Period}}{360} \times \text{Notional Amount}$$

Using the discount factors in Column (5), the present value of the fixed cash flows equals $14,053,078. Therefore, the swap rate is 4.987551 percent, since this is the rate that equates the present value of the floating and fixed cash flows.

The swap spread is the spread over the same maturity Treasury. Given the swap rate, the swap spread can be determined. For example, since this is a three-year swap, the three-year on-the-run Treasury rate would be used as the benchmark. If the yield on that issue is 4.587551 percent, the swap spread is then 40 basis points.

The calculation of the swap rate for all swaps follows the same principle: equating the present value of the cash flows.[5]

VALUING A SWAP

Once a swap transaction is completed, changes in market interest rates will change the cash flow of the floating rate side of the swap. The value of an interest rate swap is the difference between the present value of the cash flow of the two sides of the swap. The three-month LIBOR forward rates from the current Eurodollar CD futures contracts are used to (1) calculate the floating cash flows and (2) determine the discount factors at which to calculate the present value of the cash flows.

To illustrate this, consider the three-year swap used to demonstrate how to calculate the swap rate. Suppose that one year later, interest rates change such that Column (3) in Table 15.3 shows the prevailing futures price for the Eurodollar CD futures contract. Columns (4) and (5) then show the corresponding forward rates and discount factors. Column (6) shows the floating cash flow based on the forward rates in Column (4), and Column (7) shows the present value of the floating cash flow using the discount factors in Column (5). The present value of the floating cash flow is $11,485,949. This means that the floating-rate payer has agreed to make payments with a value of $11,485,949, and the fixed-rate payer will receive a cash flow with this value.

Now let's look at the fixed-rate side. The swap rate is fixed over the life of the swap. The fixed cash flow is given in Column (8), and the present value based on the discount factors in Column (5) is shown in Column (9). The present value of the fixed cash flows is $9,501,601. This means that the fixed-rate payer has agreed to make payments with a value of $9,501,603 and the floating-rate payer will receive a cash flow with this value.

From the fixed-rate payer's perspective, a floating cash flow with a present value of $11,485,949 is going to be received and a fixed cash flow with a present value of

---

[5] For a more detailed explanation of how this is done with more complicated swaps, see Chapter 6 of Dattatreya, Venkatesh, and Venkatesh, *Interest Rate & Currency Swaps*.

$9,501,603 is going to be paid out. The difference between these two present values, $1,984,346, is the value of the swap. It is a positive value for the fixed-rate payer because the present value of what is to be received exceeds the present value of what is to be paid out.

From the floating-rate payer's perspective, a floating cash flow with a present value of $11,485,949 is going to be paid out and a fixed cash flow with a present value of $9,501,603 is going to be received. Once again, the difference between these two present values, $1,984,346, is the value of the swap. It is a negative value for the floating-rate payer because the present value of what is to be received is less than the present value of what is to be paid out.

■ TABLE 15.3

DETERMINING THE VALUE OF A SWAP

GOAL: DETERMINATION OF SWAP VALUE AFTER ONE YEAR
Two-year swap
Notional amount: $100 million

FIXED RECEIVER:
Swap rate 4.987551 percent
Actual/360-day count basis
Quarterly payments

FLOATING RECEIVER:
Three-month LIBOR
Actual/360-day count basis
Quarterly payments and reset

(1)	(2)	(3)	(4)	(5)	(6)	(7)	(8)	(9)
						Present Value		Present Value
Period	Day Count	Futures Price	Forward Rate	Discount Factor	Floating Cash Flow	of Floating CF	Fixed Cash Flow	of Fixed CF
1	91	—	5.25	1.00000	—	—	—	—
2	94	94.27	5.73	0.987045	1,370,833	1,353,074	1,302,305	1,285,434
3	91	94.22	5.78	0.972953	1,448,417	1,409,241	1,260,742	1,226,642
4	90	94.00	6.00	0.958942	1,445,000	1,385,671	1,246,888	1,195,693
5	91	93.85	6.15	0.944615	1,516,667	1,432,667	1,260,742	1,190,916
6	91	93.75	6.25	0.929686	1,554,583	1,445,274	1,260,742	1,172,094
7	91	93.54	6.46	0.915227	1,579,861	1,445,931	1,260,742	1,153,865
8	93	93.25	6.75	0.900681	1,668,833	1,503,086	1,288,451	1,160,483
9	91	93.15	6.85	0.885571	1,706,250	1,511,005	1,260,742	1,116,476
						11,485,949		9,501,603

Present Value of floating cash flow $11,485,949
Present Value of fixed cash flow $ 9,501,603
Value of swap $ 1,984,346

APPLICATION

So far we have merely described an interest rate swap and looked at its character-istics. We still have not provided an explanation of how they can be used. In this section, we do so using a basic or generic swap.

Consider two U.S. entities, a triple-A-rated commercial bank and a triple-B-rated nonfinancial corporation that both want to raise $100 million now for 10 years. The bank wants to raise floating-rate funds, and the nonfinancial corpora-tion wants to raise fixed-rate funds. The interest rates available to the two entities in the U.S. bond market are as follows:

Bank: Floating rate = Six-month LIBOR + 30 basis points.

Nonfinancial corporation: Fixed-rate = 12 percent.

Suppose instead that both entities could issue securities in the Eurodollar bond market and that the following terms are available in the Eurodollar bond market for 10-year securities for these two entities:

Bank: Fixed rate = 10.5 percent.

Nonfinancial corporation: Floating rate = 6-month LIBOR + 80 basis points.

Notice that we have indicated the terms that the bank could obtain on fixed-rate financing and that the nonfinancial corporation could obtain on floating-rate secu-rities. You'll see why we did this shortly. First, let's summarize the situation for the two entities in the U.S. domestic and Eurodollar bond markets:

Floating-Rate Securities

Entity	Bond Market	Rate
Bank	U.S. domestic	6-mo. LIBOR + 30 bp
Nonfinancial corporation	Eurodollar	6-mo. LIBOR + 80 bp
		Credit spread = 50 bp

Fixed-Rate Securities

Entity	Bond Market	Rate
Bank	U.S. domestic	10.5%
Nonfinancial corporation	Eurodollar	12.0%
		Credit spread = 150 bp

Notice that the credit spread for the floating-rate securities (50 basis points) is narrower than the credit spread for fixed-rate securities (150 basis points). This pro-vides an opportunity for both entities to reduce the cost of raising funds. To see how, suppose that each entity issued securities in the Eurodollar bond market and then simultaneously entered into the following 10-year interest rate swap with a $100 million notional principal amount offered by an intermediary:

Bank
Pay floating rate of 6-month LIBOR
Receive fixed rate of 10.60%

Nonfinancial corporation
Pay fixed rate of 10.65%
Receive floating rate of 6-month LIBOR

The cost of the issue for the bank would then be as follows:

Interest paid	
On fixed-rate Eurodollar bonds issued	= 10.5%
On interest rate swap	= 6-mo. LIBOR
Total	= 10.50% + 6-month LIBOR
Interest received	
On interest rate swap	= 10.60%
Net cost	
Interest paid	= 10.50% + 6-month LIBOR
Interest received	= 10.60%
Total	= 6-month LIBOR − 10 bp

The cost of the issue for the nonfinancial corporation would then be as follows:

Interest paid	
On floating-rate Eurodollar bonds issued	= 6-month LIBOR + 80 bp
On floating rate swap	= 10.85%
Total	= 11.65% + 6-month LIBOR
Interest received	
On interest rate swap	= 6-month LIBOR
Net cost	
Interest paid	= 11.65% + 6-month LIBOR
Interest received	= 6-month LIBOR
Total	= 11.65%

The transactions are diagramed in Figure 15.1. By issuing securities in the Eurodollar bond market and using the interest rate swap, both entities were able to reduce their cost of issuing securities. The bank was able to issue floating-rate securities for six-month LIBOR minus 10 basis points rather than issuing floating-rate securities in the U.S. domestic bond market for six-month LIBOR plus 30 basis points, thereby saving 40 basis points. The nonfinancial corporation saved 35 basis points (11.65% versus 12%) by issuing floating-rate bonds in the Eurodollar bond market and using the interest rate swap.

The point of this illustration is that if differences in credit spreads exist in different sectors of the bond markets, borrowers can use the interest rate swap to arbitrage the inconsistency. Whether they do exist is another question that we address later.

Finally, let's look once again at the intermediary in this transaction. The intermediary pays a floating rate of six-month LIBOR to the nonfinancial corporation and receives six-month LIBOR, so there is no net gain or loss on the floating-rate payments. However, the intermediary pays a fixed rate of 10.60 percent to the bank but receives 10.65 percent from the nonfinancial corporation, realizing 5 basis points for its intermediary services.

INTEREST RATE SWAP

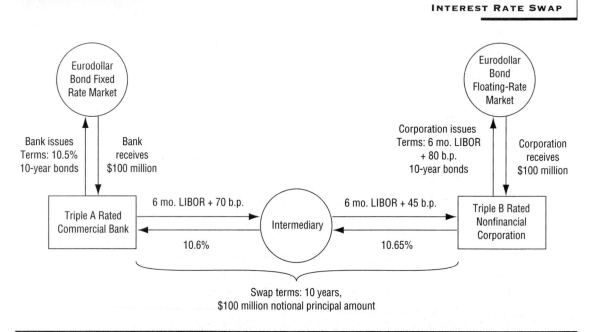

Swap terms: 10 years,
$100 million notional principal amount

DEVELOPMENT OF THE INTEREST RATE SWAP MARKET

The interest rate swap was first developed in late 1981. By 1987, it had grown to more than $500 billion (in terms of notional principal amount). What is behind this rapid growth? As our illustration demonstrated, corporate borrowers can use an interest rate swap to exploit any perceived capital market imperfection. Although not demonstrated here, an interest rate swap can also be used by institutional investors to change the nature of assets or liabilities to enhance returns in an imperfect capital market.

The initial motivation of the growth of the interest rate swap market was for borrowers to exploit what was perceived to be "credit arbitrage" opportunities due to differences between the credit spread between lower- and higher-rated credits in the U.S. and Eurodollar bond fixed-rate market and the same spread in these two floating-rate markets. For example, in our illustration, the credit spread was assumed to be 50 basis points in the floating-rate markets and 150 basis points in the fixed-rate markets. Publications by dealer firms[6] and academic research suggested this motivation.[7] Basically, the argument for swaps was based on a well-known

---

[6] See, for example, T. Lipsky and S. Elhalaski, *Swap-Driven Primary Issuance in the International Bond Market* (Salomon Brothers Inc., 1986).

[7] See, for example, James Bicksler and Andrew Chen, "An Economic Analysis of Interest Rate Swaps," *Journal of Finance*, July 1986, pp. 645–655.

economic principle of comparative advantage in international economics. The argument in the case of swaps is that even though a high credit-rated issuer could borrow at a lower cost in both the fixed-rate and floating-rate markets (that is, an absolute advantage in both), it will have a *comparative* advantage relative to a lower credit-rated issuer in one of the markets (and a comparative disadvantage in the other). Under these conditions, each borrower could benefit from issuing securities in the market in which it has a comparative advantage and then swap obligations to the desired type of financing required. The swap market was the vehicle for swapping obligations.

Several observers challenged the notion that there existed a "credit arbitrage." It should be evident that the comparative advantage argument, while based on arbitrage, is not based on the existence of an irrational mispricing but on equilibria in segmented markets. If two completely segmented markets are each a perfectly competitive market and have different prices for risk, a transactor in both markets simultaneously sees an imperfectly competitive market and can make money. Those who challenge the credit arbitrage notion argue that the differences in credit spreads in the fixed-rate and floating-rate markets represent differences in the risk faced by lenders in these two markets. For example, the interest rate for a floating-rate note effectively represents a short-term interest rate. The credit spread on floating-rate notes therefore represents a spread in the short-term market. In contrast, the credit spread on fixed-rate medium and long-term notes represents the spread in that maturity sector. There is no reason that the credit spreads have to be the same.[8]

Despite the arguments that credit arbitrage opportunities were rare in reasonably efficient global financial markets and that, even if they did exist, they would be quickly eliminated by arbitrage, the number of interest rate swap transactions increased substantially. Other reasons were offered for the continued growth of the market. One explanation was suggested in a May 1984 article, sponsored by Citicorp, that appeared in *Euromoney*:

> The nature of swaps is that they arbitrage market imperfections. As with any arbitrage opportunity, the more it is exploited, the smaller it becomes ....
>
> But some of the causes of market imperfections are unlikely to disappear quickly. For example, insurance companies in many countries are constrained to invest mainly in instruments that are domestic in that country. That requirement will tend to favour domestic issuers artificially, and is unlikely to be changed overnight. And even in the world's most liquid markets there are arbitrage opportunities. They are small and exist only briefly. But they exist nevertheless.[9]

As this quote demonstrates, as early as 1984 it was argued that the difference in credit spreads in the two markets may be due to differences in regulations in two

---

[8] Cooper and Mello, for example, demonstrate that differences in quality spreads between the fixed-rate and floating-rate markets are consistent with option pricing theory. See Ian Cooper and Antonio Mello, "Default Spreads in the Fixed and Floating Rate Markets: A Contingent Claims Approach," *Advances in Futures and Options Research* 3, 1988, pp. 269–290.

[9] "Swap Financing Techniques: A Citicorp Guide," special sponsored section, *Euromoney*, May 1984, pp. S1–S7.

countries. Similarly, differences in tax treatment across countries also create market imperfections that can be exploited using swaps.[10] Thus, swaps can be used for regulatory or tax arbitrage.

Rather than relying on any arbitrage argument, one study suggests that the market grew because it allowed borrowers to raise the type of financing that was not possible prior to the introduction of interest rate swaps.[11] That is, swaps help complete the markets. To understand this argument, let's look at the instruments available to borrowers prior to the introduction of interest rate swaps. They include (1) long-term fixed-rate instruments, (2) long-term floating-rate instruments, and (3) short-term debt. The interest rate for a borrower is composed of the risk-free rate for the relevant maturity plus a credit spread. Consider borrowers with the following expectations:

- Borrower A believes that the risk-free rate will rise in the future and its credit will weaken. This borrower will want to borrow long-term with a fixed rate to lock in the prevailing risk-free rate and credit spread.

- Borrower B believes that the risk-free rate will fall in the future but that its credit will weaken. In this case, the borrower will prefer to issue a long-term floating-rate instrument to lock in the credit spread but at the same time to take advantage of an anticipated decline in the risk-free rate.

- Borrower C believes that the risk-free rate will fall in the future but that its credit will strengthen in the future. The instrument of choice for this borrower is short-term floating debt because its cost of funds in the future will be lower due to the expected decline in the risk-free rate and the lower credit spread that will be imposed by the market.

- Borrower D believes that the risk-free rate will rise in the future and that its credit will strengthen in the future. This borrower would want to fix the risk-free rate but would want the credit spread to float. Which instrument will this borrower prefer to issue? D cannot use the three instruments listed above to take advantage of its expectations.

D can use an interest rate swap, however, to fix the risk-free rate for the term of the swap while allowing the credit spread to float. In essence, this particular reason for the growth of the interest rate swap market is based on asymmetric information. That is, the borrower possesses information (belief, at least) that the market does not possess, namely that the borrower's credit will improve.

Finally, another argument suggested for the growth of the interest rate swap market is the increased volatility of interest rates that has led borrowers and lenders to hedge or manage their exposure. However, as we pointed out earlier in

---

[10] This applies even more so to currency swaps that we discuss later in this chapter. Several examples of how swaps can be used to exploit differences in taxes are given in Clifford W. Smith, Charles W. Smithson, and Lee MacDonald Wakeman, "The Evolving Market for Swaps," *Midland Corporate Finance Journal*, Winter 1986, pp. 20–32.

[11] Marcelle Arak, Arturo Estrella, Laurie Goodman, and Andrew Silver, "Interest Rate Swaps: An Alternative Explanation," *Financial Management*, Summer 1988, pp. 12–18.

this chapter, the risk-return characteristics can be replicated by a package of forward contracts. Yet the liquidity of interest rate forward contracts is not as good as that of interest rate swaps. The ease with which swap transactions can be entered into or liquidated was facilitated by the standardization of documentation published by the International Swap Dealers Association in early 1987. Moreover, the cost of a swap to hedge or manage a position is less than that of a package of interest rate forward contracts.

ROLE OF THE INTERMEDIARY. To understand how the market evolved, we must look at the role of the intermediary in an interest rate swap. The intermediaries in the transactions were commercial banks and securities firms. In the early stages of the market, these intermediaries sought out end users of swaps. That is, they sought from their client base those entities that needed the swap to accomplish a funding or investing objective. The two entities would then be matched by the intermediary. In essence, the intermediary in this type of transaction performed the functions of a broker.

The only time that the intermediary would take the opposite side of a swap (that is, would act as a principal) was to balance out the transaction. For example, if an intermediary had two clients that were willing to do a swap but one wanted the notional principal amount to be $100 million and the other wanted it to be $85 million, the intermediary might become the counterparty to the extent of $15 million. That is, the intermediary would warehouse or take a position in the transaction as a principal to the extent of $15 million. To protect itself against an adverse interest rate movement, the intermediary would hedge its position.

We have yet to address another problem in an interest rate swap. In our two illustrations, the parties to the swap had to be concerned that the other party would default on its obligation. A default did not mean that any principal was lost since the notional principal amount was not exchanged, but it did mean that the objective for which the swap was entered into would be impaired. Since the early transactions involved a higher and lower credit-rated entity, the former was concerned with the potential for default of the latter. To reduce the risk of default, many of the transactions required that the lower credit-rated entity obtain a guarantee from a highly rated commercial bank. As the number and size of the transactions increased, many intermediaries became comfortable with the transactions and, instead of acting as brokers, became principals. As long as an intermediary had one entity willing to do a swap, the intermediary was willing to be the counterparty to the swap. Consequently, interest rate swaps became part of an intermediary's inventory of product positions. Advances in quantitative techniques and futures products for hedging complex positions such as swaps made the protection of large inventory positions feasible.

Another factor forced intermediaries to become principals rather than brokers in swaps. As more intermediaries entered the swap market, bid-ask spreads on swaps declined sharply. To make money in the swaps market, intermediaries had to do a sufficient volume of business. This could be done only if an intermediary had (1) an extensive client base willing to use swaps and (2) a large inventory of swaps, necessitating intermediaries to act as principals. For example, in a survey by *Euromoney*,[12] 150 multinationals and supranationals were asked to identify the characteristics that make a swap house efficient. The results of the survey indicated that the speed at which a swap could be arranged for a client was the most important criterion. That speed depends on the two factors just cited. The same survey also found that clients are less interested in brokered deals than transactions in which the intermediary is a principal.

Consequently, we can describe the development of the swap market as one that began to exploit real or perceived imperfections in the capital market but evolved into a transactionally efficient market for accomplishing asset/liability objectives.

SECONDARY MARKET FOR SWAPS

The three general types of transactions in the secondary market for swaps are (1) a swap reversal, (2) a swap sale (or assignment), and (3) a swap buy-back (or closeout or cancellation).

In a *swap reversal*, the party that wants out of the transaction arranges for a swap in which (1) the maturity on the new swap is equal to the time remaining of the original swap, (2) the reference rate is the same, and (3) the notional principal amount is the same. For example, suppose that entity X entered into a five-year swap with a notional principal amount of $50 million in which it pays 10 percent and receives LIBOR, but that two years later, X wants out of the swap. In a swap reversal, X would enter into a three-year interest rate swap with a counterparty different from the original counterparty, say Z, in which the notional principal amount is $50 million and X pays LIBOR and receives a fixed rate. The fixed rate that X receives from Z depends on prevailing swap terms for floating-rate receivers at the initiation of the three-year swap.

The major drawback of this approach is that the entity is still liable to the original counterparty, say Y, as well as to the new counterparty, Z. That is, the entity now has two offsetting interest rate swaps on its books instead of one and, as a result, has increased its default risk exposure.

The *swap sale* or *swap assignment* overcomes this drawback. In this secondary market transaction, the party that wishes to close out the original swap finds another party that is willing to accept its obligations under the swap. In our illustration, this means that X finds another party, say, A, that will agree to pay 10 percent to Y and receive LIBOR from Y for the next three years. A will have to be compensated to accept the position of X, or A will have to be willing to compensate X. The compensation depends on the value of the swap. If from X's perspective the swap has a positive value, that is the value A must pay to X. If, on the other hand, the value of the swap from X's perspective is negative, X must compensate A.

Once the transaction is completed, A, not X, is obligated to perform under the swap terms. (An intermediary could act as principal and become party A to help its client X.)

---

[12] *Euromoney*, special supplement on swaps, July 1987, p. 14.

To accomplish a swap sale, the original counterparty, Y in our example, must agree to the sale. A key factor in whether Y will agree is whether it is willing to accept A's credit. For example, if A's credit rating is triple-B but X's is double-A, Y would be unlikely to accept A as a counterparty.

A *buyback* or *close-out sale* (or *cancellation*) involves the sale of the swap to the original counterparty. As in the case of a swap sale, one party might have to compensate the other, depending on how interest rates and credit spreads have changed since the inception of the swap.

BEYOND THE GENERIC SWAP

Thus far, we have described the plain vanilla or generic interest rate swap. Nongeneric swaps have evolved as a result of the asset/liability needs of borrowers and lenders. Examples of nongeneric swaps are described below. A complete explanation for the asset/liability motivation for such swaps is beyond the scope of this chapter.

In a generic swap, the notional principal amount does not vary over the life of the swap. Thus, it is sometimes referred to as a *bullet swap*. In a *basis rate swap*, both parties exchange floating-rate payments based off different reference rates. For example, one party might exchange DM LIBOR for U.S. LIBOR.

A *forward swap* is simply a forward contract on an interest rate swap. The terms of the swap are set today, but the parties agree that the starting date of the swap will begin at a specified date in the future.

The second generation of products in the interest rate swap market is an option on a swap, commonly referred to as a *swaption*. A swaption effectively allows an entity to reverse the terms of an existing swap so that it can terminate a swap agreement. A swaption that can be exercised at any time prior to the expiration date (i.e., American type) or only at the expiration date (i.e., European type) may be purchased.

FORWARD RATE AGREEMENT

A forward rate agreement (FRA) is a customized agreement between two parties (one of whom is a dealer firm—a commercial bank or securities firm) by which the two parties agree at a specified future date to exchange an amount of money based on a reference rate and a notional principal amount. FRAs are available in many developed countries.

To illustrate an FRA, suppose that Industrial Products Company and a commercial bank enter into the following three-month FRA whose notional principal amount is $10 million: if one-year LIBOR three months from now exceeds 9 percent, the commercial bank must pay the Industrial Products Company an amount determined by the following formula:

$$(\text{1-year LIBOR 3 months from now} - 0.09) \times \$10,000,000$$

For example, if one-year LIBOR three months from now is 12 percent, Industrial Products Company receives

$$(0.12 - 0.09) \times \$10,000,000 = \$300,000$$

If one-year LIBOR three months from now is less than 9 percent, Industrial Products Company must pay the commercial bank an amount based on the same formula.

Borrowers and investors can use FRAs to hedge against adverse interest rate risk by locking in a rate. To see how a borrower can use an FRA, consider the preceding hypothetical FRA. Suppose that the management of Industrial Products Company plans three months from now to borrow $10 million for one year. The firm can borrow funds at some spread over one-year LIBOR, which is currently 9 percent. The risk that the firm faces is that three months from now one-year LIBOR will be higher than 9 percent. Suppose further that management wishes to eliminate the risk of a rise in one-year LIBOR by locking in a rate of 9 percent. By entering into the hypothetical FRA, Industrial Products Company management has eliminated it. Should one-year LIBOR rise above 9 percent three months from now, under the terms of the FRA, the commercial bank is obligated to make up the difference. If one-year LIBOR three months from now is below 9 percent, the Industrial Products Company does not benefit from the lower rate because it must pay the commercial bank an amount such that the effective cost of borrowing is 9 percent.

Effectively, an FRA is nothing more than an interest rate swap in which the maturity of the swap is one period. Or one can think of an interest rate swap as a package of FRAs with serial maturities.

INTEREST RATE AGREEMENT

An interest rate agreement is an agreement between two parties whereby one party, for an up-front premium, agrees to compensate the other if a designated interest rate, called the *reference rate,* is different from a predetermined level. When one party agrees to pay the other when the reference rate exceeds a predetermined level, the agreement is referred to as an *interest rate cap* or *ceiling.* The agreement is referred to as an *interest rate floor* when one party agrees to pay the other when the reference rate falls below a predetermined level. The predetermined interest rate level is called the *strike rate.*

The terms of an interest rate agreement include the following:

1. The reference rate.
2. The strike rate that sets the ceiling or floor.
3. The length of the agreement.
4. The frequency of settlement.
5. The notional principal amount.

For example, suppose that C buys an interest rate cap from D with terms as follows:

1. The reference rate is six-month LIBOR.

2. The strike rate is 8 percent.

3. The agreement is for seven years.

4. Settlement is every six months.

5. The notional principal amount is $20 million.

Under this agreement, every six months for the next seven years, D will pay C when six-month LIBOR exceeds 8 percent. The payment will equal the dollar value of the difference between six-month LIBOR and 8 percent times the notional principal amount divided by 2. For example, if six months from now six-month LIBOR is 11 percent, then D will pay C 3 percent (11 percent – 8 percent) times $20 million divided by 2, or $300,000. If six-month LIBOR is 8 percent or less, D does not have to pay anything to C.

As an example of an interest rate floor, assume the same terms as the interest rate cap we just illustrated. In this case, if six-month LIBOR is 11 percent, C receives nothing from D, but if six-month LIBOR is less than 8 percent, D compensates C for the difference. For example, if six-month LIBOR is 7 percent, D will pay C $100,000 [(8% – 7%) × $20 million ÷ 2].

Interest rate caps and floors can be combined to create an *interest rate collar*. This is done by buying an interest rate cap and selling an interest rate floor.

In an interest rate agreement, the buyer pays an up-front fee, which represents the maximum amount that the buyer can lose and the maximum amount that the writer of the agreement can gain. The only party required to perform is the writer of the interest rate agreement. The buyer of an interest rate cap benefits if the underlying interest rate rises above the strike rate because the seller (writer) must compensate the buyer. The buyer of an interest rate floor benefits if the interest rate falls below the strike rate, because the seller (writer) must compensate the buyer.

In essence, these contracts are equivalent to a package of interest rate options. Once again, a complex contract can be seen to be a package of basic contracts, options in the case of interest rate agreements.

CURRENCY SWAPS

In an interest rate swap, the two counterparties agree to exchange interest payments with no exchange of principal. A currency swap involves an exchange of both interest and principal. The best way to explain a currency swap is with an illustration.

Assume that two companies, a U.S. company and a Swiss company, seek to borrow for 10 years in the domestic currency; that is, the U.S. company seeks $100 million in U.S. dollar-denominated debt, and the Swiss company seeks 127 million Swiss franc-denominated debt. For reasons that we will explore later, let's suppose that both want to issue 10-year bonds in the bond market of the other country, denominated in the other country's currency. That is, the U.S. company wants to issue the Swiss franc equivalent of $100 million in Switzerland, and the Swiss company wants to issue the U.S. dollar equivalent of FR 127 million in the United States.

Let's assume the following:

1. At the time that both companies want to issue their 10-year bonds, the spot exchange rate between U.S. dollars and Swiss francs is 1.0 U.S. dollar for 1.27 Swiss francs.

2. The coupon rate that the U.S. company would have to pay on the 10-year Swiss franc-denominated bonds issued in Switzerland is 6 percent.

3. The coupon rate that the Swiss company would have to pay on the 10-year U.S. dollar-denominated bonds issued in the United States is 11 percent.

By the first assumption, if the U.S. company issues the bonds in Switzerland, it can exchange the FR 127 million for $100 million. By issuing $100 million of bonds in the United States, the Swiss company can exchange the proceeds for FR 127 million. Therefore, both get the amount of financing they seek.

Assuming that the coupon rates given by the last two assumptions and assuming for purposes of this illustration that coupon payments will be made annually,[13] the cash outlays that the companies must make for the next 10 years are summarized:

Year	U.S. Company	Swiss Company
1–10	FR 7,620,000	$ 11,000,000
10	127,000,000	100,000,000

Each issuer faces the risk that each time a liability payment must be made, its domestic currency will have depreciated relative to the other currency, requiring more of the domestic currency to satisfy the liability. That is, both are exposed to foreign exchange risk.

In a currency swap, the two companies issue bonds in the other's bond market. The currency swap agreement requires the following:

1. The two parties exchange the proceeds received from the sale of the bonds.

2. The two parties make the coupon payments to service the debt of the other party.

3. At the termination date of the currency swap (which coincides with the maturity of the bonds), both parties agree to exchange the par value of the bonds.

In our illustration, this involves the following:

1. The U.S. company issues 10-year, 6 percent coupon bonds with a par value of FR 127 million in Switzerland and gives the proceeds to the Swiss company. At the same time, the Swiss company issues 10-year, 11 percent bonds with a par value of $100 million in the United States and gives the proceeds to the U.S. company.

---

[13] In practice, U.S. coupon payments are made semiannually. The practice for bonds issued in the Eurobond market is to pay coupon interest once per year.

2. The U.S. company agrees to service the interest payments of the Swiss company by paying $11,000,000 per year for the next 10 years to the Swiss company; the Swiss company agrees to service the interest payments of the U.S. company by paying FR 7,620,000 for the next 10 years to the U.S. company.

3. At the end of 10 years (this would be the termination date of this currency swap because it coincides with the maturity of the two bond issues), the U.S. company agrees to pay $100 million to the Swiss company, and the Swiss company agrees to pay FR 127 million to the U.S. company.

This is illustrated in Figure 15.2.

Now let's assess what this transaction has done. Each party received the amount of financing it sought. The U.S. company's interest payments are in dollars, not Swiss francs; the Swiss company's interest payments are in Swiss francs, not U.S. dollars. At the termination date, both parties will receive an amount sufficient in their local currency to pay off the holders of their bonds. With the interest payments and the principal repayment in their local currency, neither party faces foreign exchange risk.

■ **FIGURE 15.2**

CURRENCY SWAP

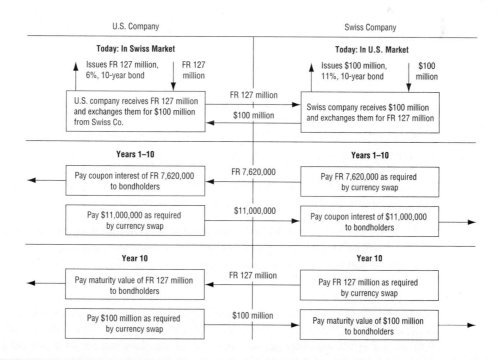

In practice, the two companies would not deal directly with each other. Instead, either a commercial bank or a securities firm would be involved as an intermediary in the transaction as either a broker or a dealer. As a broker, the intermediary simply brings the two parties together, receiving a fee for the service. If instead the intermediary serves as a dealer, it not only brings the two parties together but also guarantees payment to both of them. Thus, if one party defaults, the counterparty will continue to receive its payments from the dealer. Of course, in this arrangement, both parties are concerned with the dealer's credit risk. When the currency swap market started, transactions were typically brokered. The more prevalent arrangement today is that the intermediary acts as a dealer.

As we explained earlier in this chapter, an interest rate swap is nothing more than a package of forward contracts. The same is true for a currency swap; it is simply a package of currency forward contracts.

Earlier we described the principles of valuing an interest rate swap. The same principle applies to a currency swap. Information in the forward market for foreign currency and Eurodollar CD market is used to determine the present value of the two sides of the currency swap. The difference between the two present values is the swap value.

MOTIVATION FOR CURRENCY SWAPS

Now consider why both companies may find a currency swap beneficial. In a global capital market where there are no market imperfections because of regulations, taxes, and transactions costs, the cost of borrowing should be the same whether the issuer raises funds domestically or in any foreign capital market. In a world with market imperfections, it may be possible for an issuer to reduce its borrowing cost by borrowing funds denominated in a foreign currency and hedging the associated exchange rate risk. This is what is meant by an *arbitrage opportunity*. The currency swap allows borrowers to capitalize on any such arbitrage opportunities.

Prior to the establishment of the currency swap market, capitalizing on such arbitrage opportunities required the use of the currency forward market. The market for long-dated forward exchange rate contracts is thin, however, which increases the cost of eliminating foreign exchange risk. Eliminating foreign exchange risk in our U.S.–Swiss illustration would have required each issuer to enter 10 currency forward contracts (one for each cash payment that the issuer was committed to make in the foreign currency). The currency swap provides a more transactionally efficient means to protect against foreign exchange risk when an issuer (or its investment banker) has identified an arbitrage opportunity and seeks to benefit from it.

As the currency swap market has developed, arbitrage opportunities for reducing funding costs available in the early days of the swap market have become less common. In fact, it was the development of the swap market that reduced arbitrage opportunities. When these opportunities do arise, they last for only a short period of time.

There is another motivation for currency swaps. Some companies seek to raise funds in foreign countries to increase their recognition by foreign investors, despite the fact that the cost of funding is the same as in the United States. The U.S. company in our illustration might have been seeking to expand its potential sources of future funding by issuing bonds today in Switzerland.

CURRENCY/INTEREST RATE SWAPS

In our illustration, we assumed that both parties made fixed cash-flow payments. Suppose instead that one of the parties sought floating-rate rather than fixed-rate financing. Returning to the same illustration, assume that instead of fixed-rate financing, the Swiss company wanted LIBOR–based financing. In this case, the U.S. company would issue floating-rate bonds in Switzerland. Suppose that it could do so at a rate of LIBOR plus 50 basis points. Because the currency swap would call for the Swiss company to service the interest payments of the U.S. company, the Swiss company will make annual payments of LIBOR plus 50 basis points. The U.S. company will still make fixed-rate payments in U.S. dollars to service the debt obligation of the Swiss company in the United States. Now, however, the Swiss company will make floating-rate payments (LIBOR plus 50 basis points) in Swiss francs to service the debt obligation of the U.S. company in Switzerland.

SWAPTIONS

It is not difficult to see why swaptions would be attractive in the case of currency swaps. Suppose that the 10-year bonds of either issuer are callable and that interest rates decline sufficiently in the United States so that the Swiss company will find it economic to call the bonds. The Swiss company will still be responsible for making the payments as specified in the currency swap. An option to exit the currency swap would be needed to offset these obligations.

SWAPS AND THE CREATION OF STRUCTURED EUROMTNS

As explained in Chapter 14, corporations can customize EuroMTNs for institutional investors who want to make a market play on interest rate, currency, and/or stock market movements. That is, the coupon rate on the issue will be based on the movements of these financial variables. A corporation can do so in such a way that it can still synthetically fix the coupon rate. This can be accomplished by simultaneously issuing a EuroMTN and entering into a swap. EuroMTNs created in this way are called *structured MTNs*. As noted in Chapter 14, about 50 to 60 percent of EuroMTNs are structured MTNs.

Interest rate swaps, currency swaps, and equity swaps are used in the creation of structured notes. It is not necessary to go into detail in discussing equity swaps. Basically, they involve swapping a fixed or a floating interest rate for the return on some stock market index. For example, an equity swap can involve a swap of LIBOR plus 300 basis points for the return on the S&P 500, or an equity swap can call for the swap of a fixed interest rate, say, 7 percent, for the return on the German stock market index, the DAX.

The following illustrations demonstrate how swaps can be used to create a structured note.

CREATION OF AN INVERSE FLOATING-RATE MTN

MTNs have been issued in which the coupon rate changes in the opposite direction of the change in some reference interest rate such as LIBOR. To see how this can be done using an interest rate swap, let's assume the following. The Inverto Corporation wants to issue $100 million of a five-year fixed-rate EuroMTN. The firm's banker indicates that the yield it would have to offer is 6.10 percent. However, it recommends that the corporation issue an inverse floating rate EuroMTN and proposes the following two transactions:

Transaction 1: Issue a five-year inverse floating-rate EuroMTN with a coupon rate that resets every six months based on the following formula (13% – LIBOR).

Transaction 2: Enter into a five-year interest rate swap with its banker with a notional principal amount of $100 million in which semiannual payments are exchanged as follows:

Inverto Corporation pays LIBOR.

Inverto Corporation receives 7 percent.

Notice that Inverto Corporation's EuroMTN is an inverse floating rate note because as LIBOR increases, the coupon rate decreases. However, while the EuroMTN may have an inverse floating rate, the combination of the two transactions results in a fixed-rate financing for Inverto Corporation, as follows:

Inverto Corporation receives	
From its banker for swap	7%
Inverto Corporation pays	
To EuroMTN holders	13% – LIBOR
To its banker for swap	LIBOR
Net payments	[(13% – LIBOR) + LIBOR] – 7% = 6%

The advantage of this structured MTN is that the issuer was able to obtain a funding cost of 6 percent rather than 6.1 percent if it issued a fixed-rate MTN.

An inverse floater whose payments are denominated in a currency other than U.S. dollars can also be created by using a currency swap.

CREATION OF A EuroMTN WITH A FLOATING RATE BASED ON THE S&P 500

There are MTNs in which the coupon rate is based on the return on some stock market index. This can be accomplished using an equity swap. To see how, let's assume the following. Beeper Corporation wants to issue $80 million of a four-year fixed rate EuroMTN. The firm's banker indicates that the yield it would have to offer is 5.9 percent. However, it recommends that the corporation issue a EuroMTN whose coupon rate is based on the S&P 500 and proposes the following two transactions

Transaction 1: Issue a four-year floating-rate EuroMTN that has a coupon rate that resets every six months based on the return on the S&P 500.

Transaction 2: Enter into a four-year equity swap with its banker with a notional principal amount of $80 million in which semiannual payments are exchanged as follows:

Beeper Corporation pays 5.75 percent.

Beeper Corporation receives the return on the S&P 500 with a minimum rate of 0 percent.

Although the EuroMTN may have a floating rate based on the performance of the S&P 500, the combination of the two transactions results in a fixed-rate financing for Beeper Corporation as demonstrated below:

Beeper Corporation receives	
From its banker for swap	S&P 500 return
Beeper Corporation pays	
To EuroMTN holders	S&P 500 return
To its banker for swap	5.75%
Net payments: [S&P 500 return − (S&P 500 return − 5.75%)] = 5.75%	

The advantage of this structured MTN is that the issuer was able to obtain a funding cost of 5.75 percent rather than 5.9 percent if it issued a fixed-rate MTN.

Although the coupon rate on this EuroMTN is based on the return on the S&P 500, another major stock market index outside the United States could be used.

IMPLICATIONS FOR MANAGERS

With the advent of customized risk control products, a corporate treasurer has the opportunity to more effectively control the risks associated with global debt financing. A corporation may use the global debt market to exploit market imperfections so as to reduce its cost of funding. While today opportunities are rare to exploit simple credit arbitrage that we illustrated in this chapter, more complex arbitrages are possible.

One such arbitrage was described in Chapter 13, where we explained how a corporation can issue a Eurobond that has an embedded option and effectively strip off that option. Our example in that chapter was the effective buying of an interest rate cap by issuing a floating-rate note and selling it in the interest rate cap market that we described in this chapter. Consequently, a corporate treasurer must recognize not only the different structures in the Eurobond market but also the customized risk control products market so that arbitrage opportunities can be identified and then exploited. Moreover, it may be possible for a corporation to issue a structured note in the EuroMTN market using a swap.

Even a corporate treasurer who is not as aggressive in pursuing such opportunities must be comfortable with these markets. We cited evidence in Chapter 12 that some corporations will issue bonds in the Eurobond market or foreign bond market sector of other countries just to diversify funding sources. When the bonds issued in such circumstances are not denominated in the issuer's home currency, it may be necessary to hedge the currency risk. A currency swap is a more transactionally efficient vehicle for doing so than a package of exchange rate forward contracts.

QUESTIONS AND EXERCISES

15-1. What is an over-the-counter option?

15-2. Why would a corporate treasurer prefer to buy an over-the-counter option rather than an exchange-traded option?

15-3. What is the counterparty risk faced by a corporation that purchases an over-the-counter option?

15-4. If the Eurodollar CD futures contract is quoted at 91.75, what is the annualized futures three-month LIBOR rate?

15-5. Consider an interest rate swap with these features: maturity is five years, notional principal amount is $100 million, payments occur every six months, the fixed-rate payer pays a rate of 9.05 percent and receives LIBOR, and the floating-rate payer pays LIBOR and receives 9 percent. Now suppose that at a payment date, LIBOR is at 6.5 percent. What is each party's payment and receipt at that date?

15-6. Suppose that a dealer quotes these terms on a five-year swap: fixed-rate payer to pay 9.5 percent for LIBOR and floating- rate payer to pay LIBOR for 9.3 percent.
   a. What is the dealer's bid-asked spread?
   b. How would the dealer quote the terms by reference to the yield on five-year Treasury notes?

15-7. Give two interpretations of an interest rate swap.

15-8. How is the cash flow for the floating-rate side of a LIBOR swap determined?

15-9. How is the swap rate calculated?

15-10. How is the value of a swap determined?

15-11. Describe the role of an intermediary in a swap.

15-12. What types of transactions occur in the secondary market for an interest rate swap?

15-13. Consider the three-year swap shown in Table 15.3. Suppose that one year later the Eurodollar CD futures prices are as follows:

Period	Day Count	Future Prices
1	91	
2	94	96.70
3	91	96.70
4	90	96.66
5	91	96.60
6	91	96.55
7	91	96.52
8	93	96.47
9	91	96.40

What is the value of the swap?

15-14. The following table shows information for a three-year swap.

(1) Period	(2) Day Count	(3) Futures Price	(4) Forward Rate	(5) Discount Factor	(6) Floating Cash Flow
1	90	—	5.65	1.00000	—
2	91	94.25	5.75	0.98592	1,428,194
3	90	94.15	5.85	0.97195	1,437,500
4	90	94.05	5.95	0.95794	1,462,500
5	91	93.88	6.12	0.94374	1,504,028
6	90	93.80	6.20	0.92952	1,530,000
7	91	93.74	6.26	0.91518	1,567,222
8	90	93.65	6.35	0.90108	1,565,000
9	91	93.50	6.50	0.88684	1,605,139
10	91	93.45	6.55	0.87251	1,643,056
11	91	93.38	6.62	0.85830	1,655,694
12	90	93.28	6.72	0.84432	1,655,000
13	91	93.20	6.80	0.83022	1,698,667

Demonstrate that the swap rate is 6.1922 percent.

15-15. Suppose the Hieber Machinery Corporation buys an interest rate cap that has these terms: the reference rate is three-month LIBOR, the cap will last for five years, payment is quarterly, the strike rate is 5.5 percent, and the notional principal amount is $10 million. Suppose further that at the end of some three-month period, three-month LIBOR is 6.1 percent.

a. What is the amount of the payment that Hieber Machinery Corporation will receive?

b. What would the writer of this cap pay if three-month LIBOR is 5.45 percent instead of 6.1 percent?

15-16. What is the relationship between an interest rate agreement and an option on an interest rate?

15-17. How can an interest rate collar be created?

15-18. What is the drawback to using currency forward contracts for hedging long-dated positions?

15-19. Consider this quotation from *Euromoney* of September 1989:

> Enterprise Oil itself recently purchased what it claims to be the biggest currency option obtained by a corporate client. In March it spent over $15 million as the premium on a 90-day currency option. . . .
> The Chemical [Bank]-arranged option was used to lock in exchange rate protection on $1.03 billion of a $1.45 billion liability incurred in the acquisition of US-based gas transmission company, Texas Eastern. . . .
> The need for the option arose since Enterprise Oil was paying for a dollar liability by raising sterling-denominated equity. The option is a dollar-call option which gives the company the right to buy dollars at a dollar/sterling exchange rate of $1.70 for a 90-day period.
> Enterprise bought the option out-of-the-money on March 1 with dollar/sterling exchange rates at $1.73. It reduced its premium on currency options by taking the option a long way out-of-the-money.

Discuss Enterprise Oil's financing strategy and rationale for the purchase of the currency options.

15-20. The quotation following is from a 1991 issue of *Corporate Financing Week*:

> To purchase additional aircraft, a major international carrier needed to borrow $105 million and then convert its dollar liability to a currency matching its passenger revenues. . . .
>
> SBCM [Sumitomo Bank Capital Markets] executed an amortizing cross-currency swap in which the carrier pays a monthly yen amount in return for a semi-annual U.S. dollar Libor-based payment. The fixed-yen payments on the swap represent interest plus amortization of principal on the yen equivalent of the U.S. dollar borrowing, and the floating Libor payments represent semi-annual interest plus amortization of the U.S. dollar principal amount.

   a. Discuss the rationale for this currency swap transaction.

   b. What alternative hedging techniques might have been used to achieve the same end?

15-21. What are the reasons that a corporation would use a currency swap?

15-22. a. What is a swaption?

   b. Explain why a corporation treasurer might want to buy a swaption.

15-23. The chief executive officer of a multinational corporation met with the firm's chief financial officer. The CEO questioned the rationale of the firm's issuance of a 10-year medium-term note whose coupon rate depended on the return on the German stock market index (DAX). The CEO felt that the firm was speculating on the performance of that index. The CFO explained that the issuance of the medium-term note in question did not expose the firm to the movement of the German stock market.

   a. How is it possible for the firm not to be exposed to the movement of the German stock market?

   b. To what type of risk is the firm exposed?

REFERENCES

Arak, Marcelle, Arturo Estrella, Laurie Goodman, and Andrew Silver. "Interest Rate Swaps: An Alternative Explanation." *Financial Management*, Summer 1988, pp. 12–18.

Bicksler, James, and Andrew Chen. "An Economic Analysis of Interest Rate Swaps." *Journal of Finance*, July 1986, pp. 645–655.

Cooper, Ian, and Antonio Mello. "Default Spreads in the Fixed and in the Floating Rate Markets: A Contingent Claims Approach." *Advances in Futures and Options Research* 3, 1988, pp. 269–290.

Dattatreya, Ravi E., Raj E.S. Venkatesh, and Vijaya E. Venkatesh. *Interest Rate & Currency Swaps*. Chicago: Probus Publishing, 1994.

Special supplement on swaps. *Euromoney*, July 1987, p. 14.

Lipsky, T., and S. Elhalaski. *Swap-Driven Primary Issuance in the International Bond Market.* Salomon Brothers, Inc., 1986.

Smith, Clifford W., Charles W. Smithson, and Lee MacDonald Wakeman. "The Evolving Market for Swaps." *Midland Corporate Finance Journal,* Winter 1986, pp. 20–32.

CASE 15.1

SALLIE MAE:
REVERSE YEN PERLS^{SM} ISSUE

On December 8, 1988, Bob Levine, treasurer and assistant vice president of Corporate Finance at the Student Loan Marketing Association (Sallie Mae) received an interesting phone call from Debbie DeCotis, a principal in Morgan Stanley's Capital Markets Group. Debbie informed Bob that current market conditions seemed favorable for the possible issuance of $50 million in 5-year, 11 7/8 percent Reverse Yen Principal Exchange Rate Linked Securities^{SM} (Reverse PERLS)^{SM} and that there was an opportunity in the marketplace for Sallie Mae to acquire attractively priced, fully hedged, fixed-rate debt. The all-in-cost of these funds to Sallie Mae, 20 basis points above comparable five-year Treasury notes, would be well below the spreads Sallie Mae usually obtained through straight debt issues of comparable maturity.

Morgan Stanley often approached Sallie Mae when it saw such opportunities, because Sallie Mae was generally receptive to adding to its cash reserve position when attractively priced debt became available. Also Sallie Mae was one of the few triple-A-rated corporations that could successfully issue such securities. Bob realized that in the current environment of volatility in interest rates, foreign exchange, and forward rates, a quick response to Debbie's proposal was crucial if Sallie Mae wanted to take advantage of this opportunity.

The $50 million Reverse Yen PERLS issue raised a host of considerations that Bob would have to address, including the implications of this issue for Sallie Mae's current cash position, its need for inexpensively priced debt, and its risk-averse policy toward interest rate and currency-exchange rate risk. Furthermore, he would have to take the proposal to Mitch Johnson, senior vice president of Corporate Finance at Sallie Mae, for his consideration before responding to the Morgan Stanley proposal. Mitch would make a final decision based largely on Bob's analysis and suggestions.

THE FEDERALLY SPONSORED CREDIT AGENCIES

Sallie Mae was one of five financial intermediaries in the capital markets established by the federal government to assist in developing sectors of the economy that the government deemed worthy of special support. The other agencies were the Federal Home Loan Banks (FHLB), the Federal Home Loan Mortgage Corporation (Freddie Mac), the Federal National Mortgage Association (Fannie Mae), and the Farm Credit Banks (FCBs). The government-sponsored enterprises worked in tandem with private institutions such as commercial banks, thrifts, and other lending organizations to channel funds to specific areas.

By issuing their own debt in the money and capital markets or selling their own pass-through securities, the agencies provided funds to retail institutions

This case was prepared by Troy A. Muniz under the supervision of Mark Eaker, professor of Business Administration. Copyright © 1989 by the Darden Graduate Business School Foundation, Charlottesville, Va. Rev. 9/90.

through loan agreements or by outright purchase of the loan assets of institutions. The lending organizations could thus provide more loans to qualifying individuals or institutions than would otherwise be possible and could take fees for originating and servicing assets sold to the federal agencies. The first three intermediaries (FHLB, Freddie Mac, and Fannie Mae) provided liquidity to the flow of funds from the private sector to the mortgage and housing market. The FCBs assisted in the flow of funds to support agriculture, and Sallie Mae supported the education sector of the economy by providing liquidity to financial institutions that made student loans through a variety of federally sponsored programs.

Many organizations within the national government served an intermediary role in the transfer of funds to individuals and organizations, but two factors set these agencies distinctly apart from other government organizations. The first was that these agencies were wholly owned by the private sector. Although they had special ties with the federal government (such as the appointment of board members by the president, the availability of substantial credit facilities from the Treasury, and several other tax and regulatory relationships), these agencies operated as privately held corporations. They were subject to the competitive environment in raising funds and managing their operations, and their stockholders and lenders ultimately bore the risk of the companies' activities.

The second factor that distinguished the federally sponsored agencies was the manner in which they raised their funds. Whereas most other government agencies obtained funds directly from the federal government, these agencies borrowed directly in the financial markets. Thus they were not subject to the vagaries of the federal budgeting and appropriations process.

The securities of these agencies were not technically guaranteed by the U.S. government, but several factors diminished the perceived credit risk of the government agencies in the minds of investors. First, although they financed all of their programs in the private sector, many of the agencies had lines of credit still available to them through previous arrangements with the federal government. Second, federal agency assets were of high quality and were generally insured or otherwise backed by the full faith and credit of the U.S. government. Third, because of the close relationship they maintained with the federal government, these agencies pursued conservative credit policies in funding their operations. Finally, the general perception in the markets was that the federal government, while not guaranteeing solvency, would intervene before allowing any of these agencies to default on their obligations.

The federally sponsored agencies were some of the largest participants in the U.S. financial sector. The FHLB, Fannie Mae, and FCBs each had more assets than the largest thrift institutions and would be among the 10 largest commercial banks in the country:

> The federally sponsored credit agencies were created to alter the flow of funds in cases in which the allocation of resources achieved through market forces was believed to be suboptimal. However, as the U.S. financial system becomes less regulated, the ability and the need of the sponsored agencies to influence the allocation of resources by serving as intermediaries may be lessened... [but] for the time being, the sponsored agencies are important participants in the money and capital markets. Their financial

resources are substantial, they have developed expertise in their areas, and they are well established among the borrowers and lenders in the credit markets that they serve. Their activities enhance the liquidity in these markets and foster the integration of the various components of the financial system.[1]

HISTORY OF SALLIE MAE

The stockholder-owned Student Loan Marketing Association was chartered by an act of Congress in 1972, but its origin and its role in the creation of a secondary market for student loans arose earlier.

Prior to World War II, fewer than 1 in 17 Americans sought a college education. By the 1950s and early 1960s, however, the number of individuals seeking higher education had increased to 1 in 5, yet this period was a difficult one for students to obtain financing to go to college. Not until the launch of Sputnik by the Soviet Union in 1957 and the subsequent fear that the United States was falling behind educationally did national consensus prompt the U.S. government to reassess its position of noninvolvement in education financing.

The economic, political, and educational climate of the 1960s made obtaining education credit difficult for several reasons. First, an increase in the college age population and declining employment opportunities for minorities increased the demand for higher education. The 1960s were also marked by rising inflation, tight monetary credit, and budget constraints because of U.S. involvement in Vietnam. Students found that the expenses of a college education ever increasing. The biggest barrier to obtaining education financing for students was, however, the reluctance of lenders to make low-cost loans to students because these loans generally carried a higher default risk and lower return than other loans. Even when banks, savings and loans, and other credit institutions were willing to make student loans, they were willing to include only a limited number of such loans in their total portfolio. Once made, the lender had no choice but to hold the loans until maturity. With the loans' higher default risks, and in light of high inflation and volatile interest rates, and their large market risk, many prudent lenders were unwilling to participate in student loans solely for "socially responsible" reasons.

On November 8, 1965, the U.S. Congress and President Lyndon B. Johnson, long a proponent of higher education assistance, joined together to enact the Higher Education Act of 1965, which established the Guaranteed Student Loan Program (GSLP). This program did not provide for direct federal aid to students; it was designed to facilitate the granting of education credit to individuals by making student loans more attractive to both lenders and individuals. By insuring interest and principal repayments against default through the backing of the full faith and credit of the U.S. government, and by paying a fixed "special allowance" over the interest rate paid by GSLP loans, the federal government hoped to reduce interest rates and default risks to lenders.

---

[1] Michael J. Moran, "The Federally Sponsored Credit Agencies," *Instruments of the Money Market*, Federal Reserve Bank of Richmond, 1986, pp. 156–157.

Several problems existed with the GSLP, which gave rise to numerous changes in the program in ensuing years. By far the biggest problems arose in the period of volatile interest rate fluctuations, during the early 1970s when financial institutions were unable to sell their unprofitable student loan portfolios and thus were unwilling to increase their student loan holdings. Education financing was again at a standstill.

Dr. James J. O'Leary, an insurance industry economist, is credited with conceiving the idea for Sallie Mae. His concept was improved upon by a talented and innovative management team headed by Sallie Mae's president and chief executive officer, Edward J. Fox. Sallie Mae's function, modeled primarily after existing federally sponsored agencies, was essentially (1) to borrow inexpensively from the Federal Financing Bank (FFB), and later in the capital markets, at rates slightly above U.S. Treasury rates, and (2) to purchase GLSP loans and make secured advances to qualified lenders for those loans with the proceeds. The return on GSLP student loans, at 3.5 percent above the three-month Treasury bill note, provided Sallie Mae a gross spread on its assets of around 3.0 percent. The attraction to the lending institutions was that Sallie Mae could either purchase the loans and service them itself or, if Sallie Mae bought the loans but chose not to take physical possession of them, the originating lender could make fees for servicing the loans. In either case, lenders had a liquid market in which to sell their student loans and were consequently less averse to making more loans. The result was that Sallie Mae created a more efficient and liquid market for lenders who wished to provide education credit and for students who wanted to obtain it. Exhibit 15.1A illustrates Sallie Mae's role as an intermediary in the educational financing market.

▪ EXHIBIT 15.1A

SALLIE MAE
▪ INTERMEDIARY FUNCTION OF SALLIE MAE

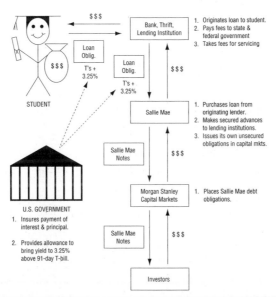

Sallie Mae's management team had made it one of the most competitive and profitable financial institutions in the United States and a Fortune 100 company. As data in Exhibit 15.1B indicate, by December 31, 1987, total assets had grown to $22.9 billion (from almost half that figure three years earlier) with total net income of $181 million (an increase of 25 percent over the previous year). In 1987, Sallie Mae earned an impressive after-tax return on equity of 26.5 percent.

■ EXHIBIT 15.1B

SALLIE MAE

■ SELECTED FINANCIAL STATEMENTS AS OF MARCH 31, 1988
(IN MILLIONS EXCEPT PER SHARE DATA)

A. *Income Statements*

	Years Ended December 31			Three Months Ended March 31, (unaudited)	
	1985	1986	1987	1987	1988
Interest income on loans					
Insured student loans purchased	$ 706.47	$ 735.49	$ 864.48	$190.57	$241.99
Deferred income	(15.58)	(14.31)	(10.41)	(2.62)	(2.57)
Servicing costs	(51.70)	(62.79)	(75.39)	(17.37)	(20.25)
Insured student loans purchased, net	$ 639.18	$ 658.40	$ 778.68	$170.58	$219.17
Warehousing advances	426.16	446.24	545.09	112.93	151.63
Total interest income	$1,065.34	$1,104.64	$1,323.77	$283.51	$370.80
Income from investments, principally interest	150.55	195.05	258.54	49.23	76.63
Total interest income, net	$1,215.90	$1,299.69	$1,582.31	$332.74	$447.43
Interest expense	978.09	1,035.54	1,269.45	259.96	359.49
Net interest income	$ 237.80	$ 264.15	$ 312.87	$ 72.77	$ 87.94
Operating expenses					
Salaries and benefits	21.61	25.33	29.37	6.33	7.59
Other	14.40	16.56	21.04	4.06	4.71
Total operating expenses	$ 36.01	$ 41.90	$ 50.41	$ 10.39	$ 12.31
Income before income taxes	$ 201.80	$ 222.26	$ 262.46	$ 62.38	$ 75.63
Federal income taxes					
Current	$ 51.10	$ 25.88	$ 55.63	$ 15.27	$ 21.76
Deferred	27.37	51.82	25.81	4.67	0.19
Total federal income taxes	$ 78.47	$ 77.70	$ 81.44	$ 19.93	$ 21.95
Net income	$ 123.33	$ 144.56	$ 181.02	$ 42.45	$ 53.69
Earnings per common share	$ 2.45	$ 3.08	$ 4.14	$ 0.95	$ 1.26

From the beginning, Sallie Mae's board of directors and CEO Fox had attempted to manage Sallie Mae as if it were a traditional corporation to compensate shareholders, lenders, educational institutions, and students alike with the rewards of improved intermediation in the educational finance market. Following

■ EXHIBIT 15.1B

B. Consolidated Balance Sheets

	December 31, 1986	December 31, 1987	March 31, 1988 (unaudited)
ASSETS			
Loans:			
Insured student loans purchased	$ 8,258	$10,141	$10,792
Deferred income	(83)	(98)	(100)
Insured student loans purchased, net	$ 8,175	$10,043	$10,691
Warehousing advances	6,527	8,357	8,061
Total loans	$14,702	$18,400	$18,752
Cash and investments	3,122	3,836	5,240
Other assets, principally accrued interest payable	409	627	555
Total assets	$18,232	$22,864	$24,547
LIABILITIES AND STOCKHOLDERS' EQUITY			
Liabilities:			
Short-term borrowings	$ 4,517	$ 6,571	$ 8,513
Long-term borrowings	12,424	14,672	14,498
Other liabilities, principally accrued interest payable	436	737	613
Convertible sub. debentures	200	200	200
Total liabilities	$17,577	$22,179	$23,824
Stockholders' equity:			
Preferred stock (par value $50,00 5mm sh. auth., 4.5 outstd.)	244	225	225
Voting common stock (par value $.50, 50mm sh. auth., 11.6 outstd.)	7	6	6
Nonvoting common stock (par value $.50, 50mm sh. auth., 30.3 outstd.)	13	15	15
Additional paid-in capital	130	133	134
Retained earnings	421	575	621
Equity before treasury stock	$ 816	$ 954	$ 1,001
Treasury stock, at cost	161	270	278
Total stockholders' equity	$ 655	$ 684	$ 723
Total liabilities and equity	$18,232	$22,864	$24,547

(continued on next page)

(CONTINUED)

C. Selected Financial Data

	1980	1981	1982	1983	1984	1985	1986	1987
At December 31								
Student loans	$1,217.1	$2,071.5	$3,222.0	$4,581.4	$ 5,572.9	$ 6,798.5	$ 8,174.7	$10,043.1
Warehousing advances	1,421.6	2,754.9	3,191.1	3,285.3	4,230.1	5,480.8	6,526.9	8,357.1
Total assets	2,782.1	5,171.3	7,506.8	9,118.6	11,620.2	14,450.1	18,232.1	22,863.5
Stockholders' equity	51.2	67.7	103.3	502.6	576.6	675.6	654.8	684.2
For year ended December 31								
Net interest income	27.0	50.2	90.1	146.3	198.0	237.8	264.2	312.9
Net income	9.4	18.0	37.8	66.6	99.3	123.3	144.6	181.0
Earnings per common share	0.27	0.52	1.08	1.37	1.91	2.45	3.08	4.14
Dividends per common share	0.04	0.04	0.06	0.08	0.12	0.18	0.27	0.41
Return on common equity %	20.22%	30.63%	44.82%	33.82%	27.45%	28.42%	31.08%	38.94%
Return on earning assets	0.45	0.45	0.62	0.83	1.00	0.97	0.90	0.90
Average 91-day T-bill rate	12.08	14.75	11.13	8.96	9.96	7.73	6.15	6.00

SOURCE: Sallie Mae Annual Report, 1987.

this basic philosophy, Sallie Mae became one of several financial institutions that could give the bonds it backed a triple-A rating through its irrevocable letters of credit, which rating translated, of course, into lower interest expense on its debt obligations.

Sallie Mae, listed on the New York Stock Exchange was well known within the investment banking community as an active and innovative participant in the capital markets. Sallie Mae was receptive to unconventional and unique debt instruments in its search for inexpensive debt:

> Sallie Mae's ability to get a deal done quickly and its willingness to test financing ideas that Wall Street spends long hours fashioning has made the issuer a favorite client of investment banking firms. For this reason, Sallie Mae is one of the first issuers Wall Street firms go to when they have a new security.[2]

Sallie Mae's unique position as a triple-A borrower of funds and its penchant for issuing new and untested financial instruments in a period of market volatility allowed it successful participation in many new debt-instrument issues in the 1980s. It was among the first companies in the United States to use interest rate swaps and variable rate notes in its efforts to match-fund its portfolio of assets and liabilities. Sallie Mae was the first U.S. issuer of indexed currency-option notes (in 1985) and of yield curve notes (1986), and in March of 1987, Sallie Mae issued the first PERLS through Morgan Stanley & Co. According to Albert Lord, executive vice president and chief financial officer of Sallie Mae,

> On average, Sallie Mae saves about 25 basis points on these kinds of deals compared with what it would pay if it issued regularly through the agency market where agency borrowers issue securities at intervals established with the U.S. Treasury. I would guess that through the agency market we would be borrowing at about 30 or 40 basis points over treasuries....The savings Sallie Mae realizes by relying on innovative financings has been a key contributor to the agency's strong financial position.[3]

PRODUCTS AND SERVICES[4]

Sallie Mae's clients were financial institutions, educational institutions, and certain state agencies. It provided financial services related to education credit primarily through (1) loan purchases—making a secondary market for student loans; (2) warehousing advances to commercial lenders, educational institutions, and public sector organizations involved in those loan programs; (3) dealing in obligations related to insured education loans and education facilities, including the direct financing of education facilities; and (4) other services that supported the credit needs of students.

---

[2] Marci Baker, "Sallie Mae Tests Markets," *Pensions and Investment Age,* May 12, 1986, p. 63.

[3] Ibid.

[4] The information provided in the following sections was obtained in large part from "Sallie Mae Offering Circular" issued June 27, 1988, by Morgan Stanley & Co.

LOAN PURCHASES

Sallie Mae purchased GSLP, PLUS, SLS, and HEAL loans from eligible lenders—commercial banks, savings and loan associations, mutual savings banks, credit unions, certain pension funds and insurance companies, educational institutions, and state and private nonprofit direct lending and secondary market agencies. Sallie Mae purchased most of its loan assets just prior to their conversion to repayment after borrowers graduated or left school. It generally purchased loans at a price of par or greater, and Sallie Mae or one of its servicing agents assumed responsibility for servicing the loans after purchase. Student loans were insured or reinsured by the federal government if certain program requirements were met. Repayment periods on the loans were between 5 and 10 years, during which time the loans continued to earn interest rates of 7 percent to 9 percent. In addition to the stated interest rate, a "special allowance" was paid by the secretary of education in amounts that, together with the stated interest rate, increased the loan yields to approximately 3.5 percent over the average bond equivalent rate of all 91-day Treasury bill auctions conducted each calendar quarter (3.25 percent for loans originated after November 16, 1986). These features, as well as Sallie Mae's stringent purchase criteria and servicing procedures, minimized the risk of losses on its insured student loan assets. Furthermore, the principal portion of the loan was risk free because the U.S. government would repay principal to the lender in the event of default.

There were several direct sources for repayment of the loans: (1) the borrower, (2) the federal government or the state or nonprofit agency that insured or guaranteed the loan, (3) the selling institution, and in some circumstances, (4) the servicing agent. However, it was primarily the guarantee of the U.S. government to stand behind the loans that made them (and consequently Sallie Mae's balance sheet) of such high quality.

The structure and characteristics of federally guaranteed student loans were changed considerably over the years to enhance the liquidity and desirability of these assets to lenders. The floating "allowance" over the fixed interest rate of the loans was ordinarily the primary feature that made student loans attractive to lenders and profitable to Sallie Mae, but because of competing uses for their available funds and fees for originating and servicing these loans, by 1987 many lenders preferred selling these assets to Sallie Mae and obtaining funds to make new loans. With virtually risk-free assets paying a guaranteed rate of 3.25 to 3.5 percent above the 91 day T-bill rate and Sallie Mae's ability to raise debt at very competitive rates, Sallie Mae manages to achieve a spread with which to manage operations, cover noninterest expenses, and compensate shareholders.

WAREHOUSING ADVANCES

These advances were secured loans made by Sallie Mae to financial and educational institutions to fund GSLP loans and other forms of education-related credit. These loans were at least 100 percent collateralized by existing insured loan portfolios or certain types of marketable obligations issued or guaranteed by the U. S.

government. Sallie Mae performed credit analyses of the borrowing institutions, and the interest rate on the advance was a function of both credit and the term of the loan. Most advances were made at a floating interest rate at a specified spread to the bond-equivalent yield of the 91-day U.S. Treasury bill rate established at the most recent weekly auction of such instruments. Advances were also made at rates that varied with the London Interbank Lending Rate (LIBOR) and at fixed rates. As of March 31, 1988, the average term to maturity of outstanding warehousing advances was approximately 4 years and constituted approximately 43 percent of Sallie Mae's total loan portfolio of $18.8 billion.

ADDITIONAL PRODUCTS AND SERVICES

Sallie Mae also provided education-related financial services such as issuing letters of credit to state student loan revenue bonds, direct lending for privately insured education loans to students pursuing professional graduate degrees in business, engineering, the health professions, and law, and the financing and refinancing of educational training facilities and student and faculty housing. According to its charter, Sallie Mae could also engage in other activities that its board of directors deemed to be in support of the credit needs of students.

SALLIE MAE FINANCING

Sallie Mae obtained funds for its operations and the financing of its asset purchases from the sale of debt securities in the money and capital markets. Originally, its financing came from the FFB, which, in turn, received its financing from the U.S. Treasury. In May 1981, Sallie Mae began to issue nonguaranteed short-term discount notes, and in January 1982 voluntarily ceased all borrowings from the FFB under an agreement to end federal financing of the corporation. Outstanding Sallie Mae borrowings from the FFB on March 31, 1988, totaled $4.9 billion at a variable interest rate of .125 percent above the 91-day Treasury bill rate and had an original term to maturity of 15 years. From 1982 through March 31, 1988, however, Sallie Mae issued, both publicly and through private placements, $18.6 billion of debt with original terms to maturity of six months to 38 years, through a variety of variable and fixed-rate, short-, and long-term debt instruments.

Sallie Mae used interest rate and currency swap agreements, purchases of U.S. Treasury securities, other high-quality fixed-rate assets, and other hedging techniques to reduce as much as possible its exposure to interest rate and currency fluctuations arising out of its financing activities.

By maintaining a match-funded portfolio of assets and liabilities, Sallie Mae attempted to minimize its interest rate sensitivity (the effect of fluctuating interest rates on the yields of assets, the costs of liabilities, and consequently, net interest income). Sallie Mae funded its variable rate assets with variable rate debt and long-term, fixed-rate debt converted to variable rate debt through the use of interest exchange (swap) agreements. Exhibit 15.1c reflects Sallie Mae's sensitivity to interest rate changes as of March 31, 1988.

■ EXHIBIT 15.1c

SALLIE MAE
■ INTEREST RATE SENSITIVITY
MARCH 31, 1988 (IN MILLIONS)

	Sensitivity Period					
	3 Months or Less	3 to 6 Months	6 Months to 1 Year	1 to 2 Years	2 to 5 Years	Over 5 Years
Assets						
Student loans	$10,370	$ 20	$ 44	$ 92	$ 16	$ 149
Warehousing advances	5,510	355	248	635	940	373
Cash and investments	2,777	27	11	254	1,228	943
Other assets	466	0	0	0	0	89
Total	$19,123	$402	$303	$ 981	$2,184	$1,554
Liabilities and equity						
Short-term borrowings	$ 7,220	$812	$481	0	0	0
Long-term notes	5,937	0	0	$1,501	$4,037	$3,023
Swap agreements	5,271	(91)	(81)	(760)	(2,230)	(2,109)
Other liabilities	239	168	0	0	0	206
Conv. sub. debentures	0	0	0	0	0	200
Stockholders' equity	225	0	0	0	0	498
Total	$18,892	889	$400	$ 741	$1,807	$1,818
Period gap	$ 231	($487)	($ 97)	$ 240	$ 377	($ 264)
Cumulative gap	$ 231	($256)	($353)	($ 113)	$ 264	$ 0

SOURCE: Student Loan Marketing Association Prospectus, June 27, 1988.

CORPORATE PHILOSOPHY ■

As outlined in Sallie Mae's 1987 *Annual Report,* it had always adhered to certain management principles and a consistent corporate philosophy in maximizing shareholder value and serving the needs of the educational finance market:

1. *Attainment of service leadership.* Sallie Mae strived to provide the highest-quality service to all segments of the lenders, schools, guarantors, and students and their parents.

2. *Maximization of return on equity.* Sallie Mae sought to provide investors with the greatest possible return on their investment over the long term, primarily by achieving consistently strong growth of quality earnings and maintenance of balance sheet quality.

3. *Management of credit risk.* Sallie Mae acquired loan assets that were either fully insured by the federal government—primarily guaranteed student loans—or collateralized by federally related securities or other acceptable collateral. Credit risk on loans made to student and parent borrowers under 1987 pilot education loan plans was covered by private insurance.

4. *Management of interest rate risk.* Sallie Mae avoided exposure to all interest rate risk by matching the interest rate sensitivities of virtually all of its assets and liabilities.

5. *Attainment of low-cost funding.* Sallie Mae tried to achieve the lowest cost of funds by tapping domestic and international capital markets within its credit and interest rate risk policies.

6. *Containment of servicing costs.* Approximately 45 percent of Sallie Mae's loan portfolio was serviced internally at the association's own Loan Servicing Centers. The rest of the portfolio was serviced by 12 servicing agents. Sallie Mae worked continuously on increasing the efficiency and quality of student-loan servicing while containing the cost of servicing, its largest operational expense.

7. *Control of operating expenses.* Sallie Mae controlled operating expenses by minimizing the size of the infrastructure used to manage its operations.[5]

PRINCIPAL EXCHANGE RATE LINKED SECURITIES

In March 1987, Morgan Stanley & Co. approached Sallie Mae with a new and innovative product to the capital markets called PERLS. Sallie Mae was to be the first corporation to issue the new notes, a product that, properly hedged, would provide Sallie Mae with funds at rates well below the spreads it had previously enjoyed over U.S. Treasury securities of comparable maturity.

Morgan Stanley had created this product in an atmosphere of intense global competition for funds and volatility in interest and currency rate movements, and in foreign debt markets, to appeal to investors who might otherwise be restricted from investing in foreign instruments either by law or charter. Capital market participants such as insurance companies, pension fund managers, mutual funds, and thrifts were generally restricted from global investments. PERLS, however, would let many individuals and organizations take advantage of favorable currency movements through top-credit U.S. corporations, without actual investment abroad.

The structure of PERLS notes was simple. The notes functioned as typical notes in every respect except in the final principal repayment. The face value of the instrument was U.S.–dollar denominated, with a semiannual coupon payment paid in U.S. dollars. The final principal payment, while paid in U.S. dollars, depended entirely on the foreign currency exchange rate formula stipulated in the note agreement. For example, Sallie Mae's first issue of PERLS were three-year, $100 million PERLS with a coupon of 12.125 percent and a final principal repayment based on the U.S.–dollar equivalent of 142.5 million Australian dollars at maturity. Thus, the investor would invest U.S. $1,000, receive semiannual coupon payments of 6.0625 percent on U.S. $1,000 from a triple-A rated borrower, and receive a U.S.–dollar-denominated final principal payment equal to the spot rate of

---

[5] *Sallie Mae Annual Report,* 1987, p. 2.

A.$1,425 at maturity. The actual amount of the U.S.–dollar principal payment was determined by the exchange rate for Australian dollars at maturity. Depending on the exchange rate in three years for Australian dollars, investors would earn more than the coupon rate, precisely the coupon rate, or less than the coupon rate. If the A.$/U.S.$ exchange rate in three years was 1.425, the final principal repayment would be $1,000, and the eventual yield to maturity would be 12.125 percent. If the A.$/U.S.$ strengthened in value to A.$/U.S.$ = 1.3, however, the final principal repayment would increase to $1,096, and the security would yield 14.78 percent. On a standard PERLS issue, the investor was betting that the dollar would fall against the indexed currency prior to the maturity date. Consequently, PERLS were generally issued when investors believed that the dollar had topped out and was likely to drop.

PERLS allowed investors to earn a high dollar coupon and benefit even further by attractive currency movements. Also, with only the final principal payments linked to a particular currency, the investor faced foreign-currency risk on only the final principal payment, not on each of the interest payments, and at one specific time rather than semiannually or annually throughout the life of the note. The investor could enter the options or forward currency market at any time and lock into the exchange rate at maturity, which reduced or eliminated the exchange risk.

Because the final principal payment was linked to a particular exchange rate vis-à-vis the U.S. dollar, the movement in the rate could change the final rate of return to the investor or the corresponding cost of funds to the issuing company.

By December 8, 1988, Sallie Mae had several outstanding PERLS, and both Morgan Stanley and Sallie Mae had become enormously successful in placing these issues:

> For Sallie Mae, long an innovative "commodity user" of money, the [Australian] PERLS were a cheap way to borrow. And by swapping out of them. . . immediately, the agency avoided the currency risk. Soon after the initial Sallie Mae issue, Morgan Stanley tried a repeat performance with a lesser rated borrower—Associates Corp. of America—and found the market less than receptive to the single-A rated finance company."[6]

THE REVERSE YEN PERLS ISSUE

PROPOSAL FOR NOTE ISSUANCE

Debbie DeCotis had approached Bob Levine with a note issuance opportunity that was a slight variation on the standard PERLS issues with which he had worked. Debbie proposed the issuance of $50 million par value, five-year, 11 7/8 percent Reverse Yen PERLS, due December 19, 1993. The notes operated as normal coupon notes, paying semiannual interest payments of 5.9375 percent in U.S. dollars. The principal on the notes would be repayable at maturity in dollars at an amount equal

---

[6] Richard Karp, "A $100 Million Set of PERLS for Sallie Mae," *Institutional Investor*, May 1987, pp. 30–31.

to U.S.$100 million less the U.S.–dollar equivalent of 6,177.5 million yen. Thus, the formula for the final principal repayment was U.S.$100,000,000 – (yen 6,177,500,000/yen @ spot) on December 19, 1993. Sallie Mae would receive $50,000,000 less any fees at issue. Morgan Stanley would take a fee of .625 percent of the par amount for its services in placing the issue, and Sallie Mae would pay a .315 percent fee on the net proceeds for a stamp tax on the notes. The notes would represent unsecured obligations of Sallie Mae and would not be guaranteed by the United States or any government agency other than Sallie Mae.

After Bob finished talking to Debbie, he went to his Reuters screen. The current spot rate of exchange for Japanese yen was yen123.55/U.S.$1. Exhibit 15.1D indicates that the yen had been steadily increasing since a low of yen260.48/U.S.$1 in February 1985 and had reversed slightly in relation to the U.S. dollar only once since that time. If investors expected the dollar to bottom out, this moment was the most favorable for placing Reverse PERLS. If the yen remained unchanged against the dollar, however, at yen123.55/U.S.$1, Sallie Mae would eventually have to pay the face value of the notes at maturity and the return to the investor would equal the coupon (11.875 percent). If the value of the dollar increased by the date of maturity, Sallie Mae would have to pay a premium to the investor based on the redemption formula, which would considerably increase the return to the investor.

As was typical with all Morgan Stanley proposals Debbie brought to Bob, this one included provisions for fully hedging the notes' inherent risks to Sallie Mae. The proposal included an all in cost of funds of 9.16 percent, or roughly 20 basis points above comparable five-year Treasuries, a spread well below the benchmark

■ EXHIBIT 15.1D

SALLIE MAE

■ HISTORIC YEN/U.S. DOLLAR EXCHANGE RATES
(MONTHLY AVERAGE)

	1984	1985	1986	1987	1988
January	233.80	254.18	199.89	154.83	127.69
February	233.60	260.48	184.85	153.41	129.17
March	225.27	257.92	178.69	151.43	127.11
April	225.20	251.84	175.09	143.00	124.90
May	230.48	251.73	167.03	140.48	124.79
June	233.57	248.84	167.54	144.55	127.47
July	243.07	241.14	158.61	150.29	133.02
August	242.26	237.46	154.18	147.33	133.77
September	245.46	236.53	154.73	143.29	134.32
October	246.75	214.68	156.47	143.32	128.68
November	243.63	204.07	162.85	135.40	123.20
December	247.96	202.79	162.05	128.24	

SOURCE: *Federal Reserve Bulletin*, "Foreign Exchange Rates" table, and Federal Reserve Board G.5 (405) release.

SALLIE MAE
■ FOREIGN-CURRENCY EXCHANGE RATES
(DECEMBER 8, 1988)

	DM/U.S.$	U.S.$/U.K.	C.$/U.S.$	FFr/U.S.$	SFr/U.S.$	YEN/U.S.$
Spot	1.7365	1.8555	1.1932	5.9325	1.4635	123.55
1 Month	1.7302	1.8502	1.1944	5.9246	1.4581	123.08
2 Months	1.7242	1.8440	1.1962	5.9210	1.4527	122.62
3 Months	1.7191	1.8385	1.1983	5.9167	1.4479	122.17
6 Months	1.7025	1.8222	1.2038	5.9057	1.4317	120.80
12 Months	1.6700	1.7971	1.2128	5.8838	1.3990	117.98

SOURCE: First Wachovia, "Foreign Exchange Review," December 1988.

35–40 basis points above five-year Treasuries at which Sallie Mae would be able to borrow through traditional "vanilla" note issuances. Sallie Mae reported its typical spreads over shortterm Treasuries, using discount notes, as:

	October 3, 1988 Spread
1 Month	N/A
3 Months	0.78%
6 Months	0.60
12 Months	0.52

Before going to Mitch with his opinions, Bob decided to analyze the market rates and the Morgan Stanley proposal. Exhibit 15.1E shows selected foreign exchange rates. Interbank Eurocurrency rates for the yen as of December 8, 1989, were as follows:

INTERBANK EUROCURRENCY RATES

Average of Bid and Offer Rates

	EuroYen	EuroDollar
1 Month	4 5/8%	9 1/2 %
3 Months	4 1/2	9 5/16
6 Months	4 1/2	9 5/16
1 Year	4 1/2	9 7/16
2 Years	4 3/8	9 3/8
3 Years	4 3/8	9 1/4
4 Years	4 1/4	9 1/8
5 Years	4 1/8	9 1/16

and selected Treasury security yields on December 7 were:[7]

_____

[7] *Wall Street Journal*, December 8, 1988.

	Bond-Equivalent Yield
3 Months	8.24%
6 Months	8.64
1 Year	8.84
2 Years	8.92
3 Years	8.95
4 Years	8.95
5 Years	8.96

How did Morgan Stanley propose hedging this transaction and achieving such a favorable cost of funds for Sallie Mae? What were the markets saying about the forward rate for yen versus U.S. dollars, and how did this intelligence affect Bob's decision to go with the Morgan Stanley deal? What other alternative means of hedging could Morgan Stanley have used to hedge this transaction? Was Morgan Stanley's proposed cost of funds consistent with market rates?

Also at issue were Sallie Mae's cash position and the way this $50 million of fixed-rate debt might alter it. Bob asked Doug Morrison, who managed Sallie Mae's daily cash position, how important having access to these funds was to the company if they were indeed as attractively priced as Morgan Stanley maintained. Bob learned that, although Sallie Mae had over $1 billion in liquid funds, additional funds would be necessary for GSLP loan purchases in the following month. These loans would earn the standard variable return of 3.25% above 91-day T-bills.

With variable rate program purchases planned for the following month, how could Bob justify more fixed-rate debt, no matter how cheap it was? Could he take advantage of Sallie Mae's cheap access to fixed-rate debt today for its purchase of variable-rate assets next month? What risks still faced Sallie Mae once it obtained the proceeds from the reverse PERLS issuance? What exposure did Sallie Mae face until next month's purchase of GSLP assets and afterward? These were all questions Mitch Johnson might ask when Bob came to him with his final recommendation.

GLOSSARY

Absolute purchasing power parity exists when a good sells for the same effective price (i.e., adjusted for the exchange rate) in two different currencies.

Adjustable fixed exchange rate is a currency price that does not vary day-to-day, but which may be changed occasionally when economic or political changes dictate.

Aggregate demand is the total demand for goods and services in an economy.

Appreciate. A currency that appreciates increases in value relative to another currency.

Arbitrage involves the simultaneous purchase and sale of an asset, such as a currency, at different prices. It produces a risk-free, instantaneous profit.

An *ask price* is the price at which someone is willing to sell an asset.

Balance of payments refers to the record of international transactions.

Balance of trade refers to the net of exports and imports of goods.

Barter is the exchange of real goods without the use of currency.

A *bid price* is the price at which someone is willing to buy an asset.

The *bid-ask spread* is the difference between the lowest available ask price and the highest available bid price. It measures the cost of simultaneously buying at the ask and selling at the bid. This is a measure of the components of the cost of trading.

Bilateral relationships involve two principals.

A *call option* is an asset that gives the owner the right, but not the obligation, to buy an asset at a fixed price for a fixed period of time. If the option can be exercised at any time before it expires, it is an American call option. If it can be exercised only at expiration, it is a European call option.

Capital budgeting is the comparison of the cost and benefit of investment alternatives.

Capital Account balance is a country's net of private and long-term government transactions in real and financial assets.

Chicago Mercantile Exchange in Chicago maintains active futures and options markets in a small number of foreign currencies.

The *closing (settle) price* is the price of the last trade of the day in a given market.

A *cross rate* is the exchange rate between the currencies of countries A and B that is implied by their respective exchange rates with a third country, e.g., country C. See triangular arbitrage.

Current Account balance is a country's net position from trade in goods, service transactions and unilateral transfers.

A *delivery date* is the agreed upon date for the delivery of an asset contracted for in a forward or futures market.

Derivative securities take (derive) their value from some other asset, usually referred to as the underlying asset.

Devaluation refers to the depreciation, usually abrupt, of a currency.

A *direct quote* identifies the price of a foreign currency in terms of a home currency.

Discrepancies are the differences between the total credits and the total debits in the balance of payments.

Economic risk is risk created by changes in the economy.

Effective yield is the rate of return that equates the present value of costs to the present value of benefits.

Equilibrium price equates the quantity supplied of an asset to the quantity demanded.

Eurocurrencies are currencies traded in Europe, regardless of their country of origin.

Exchange rate risk is the risk of a loss of value associated with a change in the price of a currency.

Exchange Rate Mechanism is the rules governing the price relationships among a group of European currencies.

Exercise price—see call option.

Expenditure-reducing policies are government policies that reduce aggregate demand for goods and services in a country.

Exports are goods shipped out of one country to another country.

Expropriation refers to the use of government power to acquire assets. The government may or may not compensate the owners of the assets.

External corrections are economic adjustments accomplished by changes in economic relationships with foreign countries.

Fixed exchange rates are currency prices maintained at a constant value. This often requires government intervention to absorb temporary imbalances in supply and demand at the fixed exchange rate value.

Floating exchange rates vary continuously according to fluctuations in supply and demand in the currency market.

Foreign direct investment (FDI) is the acquisition or creation of businesses controlled by foreigners.

Foreign exchange reserves are foreign financial assets owned by central banks.

Forwards and futures contracts involve asset transactions with a price agreed upon at the time of transaction but delivery at a later date. See Table 4.3 for a description of the differences between forwards and futures.

The *G-7* countries are 7 countries with large economies that attempt to coordinate economic policies: Canada, France, Germany, Italy, Japan, the United Kingdom, and the United States.

The *GNP deflator* is an index that accounts for inflation in the economy.

The *gold standard* is a system of exchange rates fixed in terms of gold.

Gold points establish the prices of a currency, in terms of gold, at which there is a profit from buying or selling a currency at the market price and simultaneously selling or buying it at the official gold standard exchange rate.

The *Goods and Services balance* is a country's net transactions in goods and services.

Gross domestic product (GDP) is the sum of all goods and services produced in a country.

Gross national product (GNP) is equal to Gross Domestic Product (GDP) adjusted for net factor payments to foreigners. For example, a German firm may earn income in Brazil. That income is included as part of Brazil's GDP when calculating its GNP and are added to Germany's GDP when calculating its GNP.

Imports are goods shipped into one country from another country.

An *indirect quote* is the price of the home currency in terms of the foreign currency.

The *interbank market* for exchange rates is a dealer market involving large transactions, typically of $1,000,000 value or more.

Interest rate parity (IRP) refers to the relationship among interest rates of equal maturity in two countries and the forward rate for the same maturity and the spot rate.

Internal corrections are economic adjustments accomplished by changing economic relationships within a country.

The *International Monetary Fund (IMF)* is an international organization formed after World War II. It facilitates international currency relationships.

International transfer payments are gifts flowing from one country to another.

The *International Monetary Market (IMM)*, part of the Chicago Mercantile Exchange, is an organized market trading currency futures contracts.

The *law of one price* states that identical goods must sell at identical effective prices.

Maturity is the time at which a contract ends.

Merchandise trade is the export of goods.

A *multinational corporation (MNC)* operates in at least several countries.

The *nominal rate of interest* is the interest rate that includes any expectation of inflation.

Open interest is the number of contracts outstanding.

Option—see call option.

An *over-the-counter market* is a market in which traders are linked electronically not physically.

Political risk is the uncertainty about future values created by political factors.

PPP equilibrium refers to adjustments that are consistent with purchasing power parity, i.e., adjustments where inflation differences are exactly offset by changes in exchange rates.

The *Producer Price Index* adjusts for inflation in goods produced in an economy.

A *put option* is the right to sell. See *call option*.

The *real exchange rate* adjusts for inflation differences between two countries.

Relative purchasing power parity holds if the exchange rate adjusts to exactly offset inflation differences between two countries.

Services are transactions in non-tangibles such as consulting, interest and dividends, and royalties.

The *Smithsonian Agreement* governed international monetary relationships.

Special Drawing Rights are purchasing power (money) created by the International Monetary Funds.

The *spot market* is the market for immediate delivery of currencies.

Strike price—see call option.

A *trade-weighted index of exchange rates* reflects changes in the values of trading partners relative to the home currency. The changes are weighted to reflect the volume of trade between the home country and each of its partners.

Triangular arbitrage is the simultaneous transaction in the currencies of three countries such that the trader makes money although the trades offset each other.

Unilateral transfers. See *international transfer payments*.

INDEX

A

B

F

G

S

T